Second Edition

Personnel Management

MODERN CONCEPTS & TECHNIQUES

WILL MOTIVATION AND
PERFORMANCE TAKE PLACE?

A MODEL OF MOTIVATION

Could the employee do the job if he or she wanted to?

Ch. 2   *Equal Opportunity and the Law*

Ch. 3   *Job Analysis*
           Adequate organization and job
           descriptions? What skills and
           abilities are required to perform
           the job?

Chs. 4–6 *Selection*
           Do applicants have the aptitude
           and potential to do the job?

Ch. 7   *Orientation and Technical Training*
           Provide employees with basic skills

Take Corrective Action

Is he or she motivated to perform?

Ch. 8   *Fundamentals of Motivation*

Ch. 9   *Establishing Pay Plans*

Ch. 10   *Financial Incentives*

Ch. 11   *Benefits*

Ch. 12   *Nonfinancial Motivators*
           Job enrichment, etc.

Take Corrective Action

Ch. 13   *Appraise Performance*
           Did motivation take place?

Chs. 14, 15 *Identify Problem*
           Reorganize jobs?
           Change selection standards?
           Training called for?
           New incentives needed?
           Counseling needed?
           Employee and management
           development needed?

NO   YES → REWARDS

THE ENVIRONMENT OF PERSONNEL MANAGEMENT

Ch. 16   *Labor Relations and Grievances*

Ch. 17   *Employee Safety and Health*

Ch. 18   *Personnel Management and the
           Quality of Work Life*

Second Edition

Personnel Management

MODERN CONCEPTS & TECHNIQUES

Gary Dessler
PROFESSOR OF MANAGEMENT
FLORIDA INTERNATIONAL UNIVERSITY

RESTON PUBLISHING COMPANY, INC.
A PRENTICE-HALL COMPANY
RESTON, VIRGINIA

Library of Congress Cataloging in Publication Data

Dessler, Gary.
    Personnel management.

    Bibliography: p.
    Includes index.
    1. Personnel management. I. Title.
HF5549.D4379 1981   658.3   80-29642
ISBN 0-8359-5518-4

© 1981 by Reston Publishing Company, Inc.
A Prentice-Hall Company
Reston, Virginia 22090

3 5 7 9 10 8 6 4 2

PRINTED IN THE UNITED STATES OF AMERICA

to my Parents

TABLE OF CONTENTS

PREFACE

This second edition of **Personnel Management** again provides students in Human Resource Management or Personnel Management courses with a complete, comprehensive review of essential Personnel Management concepts and techniques in a highly readable and understandable form.

The book has several distinguishing characteristics. While it again focuses almost entirely on essential Personnel Management material such as job analysis, testing, compensation, and appraisal, *maintaining performance* and *developing a personnel management philosophy* are used as integrating themes. Practical applications—such as how to appraise performance, how to establish pay plans, and how to handle grievances—are again used throughout to provide students with important personnel management skills. All managers have personnel-related responsibilities, and so **Personnel Management** is aimed at all students of management, not just those who will someday carry the title of Personnel Manager. The legal environment of Personnel Management—equal employment, labor relations, and occupational safety—is covered fully. Experiential exercises and case incidents are provided at the end of most chapters; these give students an opportunity to meet in small groups and apply the concepts and techniques found in each chapter. A completely revised and very complete instructor's manual is available.

I had the benefit of receiving extremely useful comments and reviews on the first edition from a wide range of adopters. In response to their comments, and in response to the changes that have taken place since the first edition was published, several significant changes have been made in this second edition. First, all chapters in the book have been thoroughly updated and many new topics added. Updated and/or new material includes, for example, discussions of: the impact of inflation on pension planning; techniques for training performance appraisers; recent "reverse discrimination" decisions; union influences on compensation decisions; stock purchase plans; quality circles; and changes in OSHA, and the use of behavior modification to improve safe behavior at work. Second, discussions of legal considerations in **Personnel Management** have been beefed up in virtually all chapters. New material here includes, for example, discussions of: fair employment and performance appraisal; privacy in testing; reverse discrimination; the pregnancy discrimination act; the legal impact of job analysis; the Labor Law Reform Bill of 1978 (which, while not law, still may indicate the trend of Labor Law reform); and the role of decertification elections in labor-management relations. Third, several chapters (or parts thereof) have been substantially rewritten to provide more focus and to include new topics. In particular, Chapters 7 (*Orientation and Technical Training*), 15 (*Employee and Management Development*), and 14 (*Face to Face Communicating*) have been rewritten, and new topics added to Chapters 8 (*Fundamentals of Motivation*), 9 (*Establishing Pay Plans*), 10 (*Financial Incentives*), and 12 (*Non-financial Methods for Improving Performance at Work*).

Finally, other, more general changes in this edition include: more emphasis on using personnel management concepts and techniques to improve performance and productivity at work; a greater emphasis on the line superviser's role in personnel, including the superviser's role in training, job analysis, job evaluation, and labor relations, for instance; a reduction in the use of long lists and checklists; a new chapter on career planning and development; a slight reorganization of material, with the equal-employment chapter now moved to Chapter 2 (from Chapter 15); case incidents added to each chapter; a transfer of the discussions on weighted application blanks, and the factor comparison evaluation method to appendices in their respective chapters; and more emphasis on the actual implementation of personnel programs, including how to implement a good faith effort affirmative action strategy, and how to implement a job evaluation program.

While I am solely responsible for the final product I want to thank several people for their assistance. My colleague Enzo Valenzi made extremely useful suggestions, as did Professors Douglas R. Sherk, R. W. Griffeth, Ralph Bergmann, Charlotte Erb, Jerry Galen, Howard W. Oden, David G. Haines, Thomas S. Melly, L. G. Wilson, and Stuart A. Youngblood.

At Reston Publishing Company, Fred Easter, Executive Editor, and Patricia Rayner, Editor, effectively managed the publication, and design and production of the book. My son Derek was a source of encouragement and assisted me with the typing of the manuscript, and my wife Claudia assisted me with the index and by reviewing portions of the manuscript.

*   *   *

ACKNOWLEDGEMENTS: The following publishers or individuals, in addition to those cited in the text, allowed us to reproduce exhibits or other materials. Dale Yoder, *Personnel Management and Industrial Relations* (Englewood Cliffs, N.J., Prentice-Hall, Inc.; 1970) pp. 223, 324, 480: "Job Questionnaires" case for Chapter 3; "Vice President for discouragement" case for Chapter 5, "Use of references" case for Chapter 6; and "France Rivet Company" case for Chapter 16. In Chapter 8, the experiential exercise is based on George H. Litwin and Robert A. Stringer, Jr., *Motivation and Organizational Climate* (Boston: Division of Research, Graduate School of Business, Harvard University, 1968) pp. 173–76. In Chapter 10, experiential exercise from John Ivancevich, Andrew Szilagyi, Jr. and Marc Wallace, Jr., *Organizational Behavior and Performance* (Santa Monica: Goodyear Publishing, 1977) pp. 470–71. Case for Chapter 12, "The Tarnished Company Image" from Andrew DuBrin, *Human Relations, a Job Oriented Approach* (Reston, Va.: Reston Publishing, 1978). Experiential exercise for Chapter 15 from Norman R.F. Maier, *Psychology in Industrial Organizations*, 4th ed., (Boston: Houghton Mifflin Co., 1973) pp. 295–99.

GARY DESSLER

Second Edition

Personnel Management

MODERN CONCEPTS & TECHNIQUES

When you finish studying

1 Introduction to Personnel Management: Philosophy and Plan

You should be able to:

1. Explain what personnel management is and the role it plays in the "management process."
2. Give several examples of how personnel management concepts and techniques can be of use to all managers.
3. Compare and contrast line and staff authority.
4. Cite the personnel management responsibilities of line managers, and staff (personnel) managers.
5. Discuss the factors that influence one's personnel management philosophy.
6. Compare and contrast "Theory X" and "Theory Y" management assumptions.
7. Present and explain the rationale for our Motivation Model.

OVERVIEW

The purpose of this chapter is to explain what personnel management is and the plan of this book. We explain that personnel management—activities like recruiting, hiring, training, appraising and paying employees—is both a part of every manager's job, as well as a separate "staff function," one through which the personnel director assists all managers in important ways. Also explained are some factors that affect a manager's philosophy of personnel management, including the fact that personnel activities can affect productivity and performance at work. Finally, the performance Motivation Model that is used to tie the chapters in this book together, and to relate each chapter to improving performance is outlined.

THE MANAGER'S "PERSONNEL MANAGEMENT" JOBS

The Management Process [1]

There are five basic functions managers perform. These are planning, organizing, staffing, leading, and controlling, and, in total, they represent what is often called the "Management Process." [2]

2   Some of the specific activities involved in each function include:

Planning: Establishing goals and standards; developing rules and procedures; developing plans and forecasting—predicting or projecting some future occurrence.

Organizing: Giving each subordinate a separate task; establishing departments; delegating authority to subordinates; establishing channels of authority and communication; coordinating the work of subordinates.

Staffing: Deciding what type of people should be hired; recruiting prospective employees; selecting employees; setting performance standards; compensating employees; evaluating performance; counseling employees; training and developing employees.

Leading: Getting others to get the job done; maintaining morale; motivating subordinates.

Controlling: Setting standards—such as sales quotas, quality standards, or production levels; checking to see how actual performance compares with these standards; taking corrective action as needed.

A Focus On "Staffing"—Personnel Management

Exhibit 1.1   The "Personnel Management" Aspect of the Manager's Job

"Staffing" — recruiting, selecting, compensating, appraising, training, etc. — is one of the basic functions all managers perform, and the one we'll focus on in this book.

As illustrated in Exhibit 1.1, we are going to focus on one of these functions in this book—the "staffing" or *personnel management* function. The topics discussed are aimed at supplying the concepts and techniques needed to carry out the "people" or personnel aspects of a manager's job. These include:

Job analysis (determining the nature of each employee's job)

Planning manpower needs and *recruiting* job candidates

Interviewing job candidates

Selecting job candidates

Orienting and *training* new employees

Wage and salary management (how to *compensate* employees)

Providing *incentives* and *benefits*

Appraising performance

Face-to-face *communicating* (providing feedback; counseling, disciplining)

Developing managers

And what a manager should know about:

Equal opportunity and affirmative action

Employee health and safety

Handling grievances and labor relations

Why Is "Personnel Management" Important to All Managers?

Why are these concepts and techniques important to all managers? Perhaps it is easier to answer this by listing some of the "personnel" mistakes a manager typically wants to avoid, such as:

Hiring the wrong person for the job

High turnover

Employees not doing their best

Wasting time with useless interviews

Having your company taken to court because of your "discriminatory" actions

Being cited under federal "OSHA" laws for unsafe practices

Having some employees think their salaries are grossly unfair and inequitable relative to others in the organization

A lack of training undermining the department's effectiveness

Committing an "unfair" labor practice

Carefully studying this book can help you avoid mistakes like these. And, more importantly, it can help ensure that you get results—through others. Remember that a manager could do everything else "right"—like lay brilliant plans, draw clear organization charts, set up modern assembly lines, and use

4   modern accounting controls—and yet still fail as a manager (by hiring the wrong people, or by not motivating subordinates, for instance). On the other hand, many managers—whether presidents, generals, governors, or foremen—have been successful even with inadequate plans, organization, or controls. They were successful because they had the knack of hiring the right people for the right jobs and motivating, appraising, and developing them. Remember as you read this book that *getting results* is the bottom line of managing, and that as a manager you will have to get these results through people. As one company president summed up:

> For many years it has been said that capital is the bottleneck for a developing industry. I don't think this any longer holds true. I think it's the work force and the company's inability to recruit and maintain a good work force that does constitute the bottleneck for production. I don't know of any major project backed by good ideas, vigor, and enthusiasm that has been stopped by a shortage of cash. I do know of industries whose growth has been partly stopped or hampered because they can't maintain an efficient and enthusiastic labor force, and I think this will hold true even more in the future. . . . [3]

LINE AND STAFF ASPECTS OF PERSONNEL MANAGEMENT

All managers are, in a sense, "personnel managers," since they all get involved in tasks like recruiting, interviewing, selecting, and training. Yet most firms also have a Personnel Department with its own Personnel Manager. How do the duties of this Personnel Manager and his or her "staff" relate to the personnel management duties of the other "line" managers in the firm?

Before answering this question, we should distinguish between *line* and *staff* managers. Both types of managers are similar in that as managers they are both authorized to direct the work of others—to be someone's boss. They differ, however, in that line managers are charged with managing traditionally "basic" departments like production and sales. Staff managers, on the other hand, are authorized to *assist and advise* line managers in accomplishing these basic goals. These ideas are illustrated in Exhibit 1.2. Here (as is usually the case) the personnel manager is a *staff* manager. He or she is responsible for advising line managers (like those for production and marketing) in areas like recruiting, hiring, and compensation. The managers for production and marketing are *line* managers. They have direct responsibility for accomplishing the basic goals of the organization.

Line Manager's Personnel Management Responsibilities

What are the specific personnel management responsibilities of line managers? [4] According to one expert, "The direct handling of people is, and always

Exhibit 1.2 Line and Staff Authority

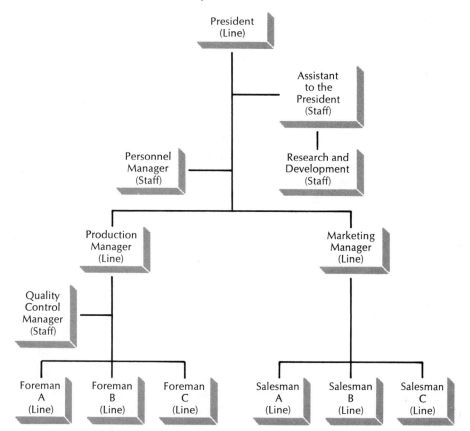

Source: Dessler, *Management Fundamentals,* p. 111.

has been, an integral part of every line manager's responsibility, from president down to the lowest level supervisor." **5**

For example, one major company outlines their *line supervisor's responsibilities for effective personnel management* under the following general headings:

1. *Placing* the right person on the right job
2. *Starting* new employees in the organization (*orientation*)
3. *Training* employees for jobs that are new to them
4. *Improving job performance* of each person
5. *Gaining creative cooperation* and developing smooth working relationships
6. *Interpreting* the company policies and procedures
7. *Controlling labor costs*
8. *Developing* potential abilities of each person
9. *Creating* and maintaining a high level of departmental *morale*
10. *Protecting* health and physical conditions of employees

6

In small organizations, line managers may carry out all these personnel management duties unassisted. But as the organization grows they need the assistance, specialized knowledge, and advice of a separate personnel staff. [6]

The Personnel Department Staff's Personnel Management Responsibilities

The personnel department provides this specialized assistance. [7] In doing so, the personnel director carries out three distinct functions, as follows:

1. A *"line" function.* First, the personnel director performs a "line" function by directing the activities of the people in his or her own department and in service areas (like the plant cafeteria). In other words, he or she exerts *line authority* within the personnel department.

    Personnel managers are also likely to exert *implied authority.* This is because line managers know the personnel director often has access to top management in personnel areas like testing, and affirmative action. As a result personnel directors' "suggestions" are often viewed as "orders from topside." And this implied authority often carries even more weight with supervisors troubled with human resources or "personnel" problems.

2. A *coordinative function.* Personnel directors also function as coordinators of personnel activities, a duty often referred to as "functional control." Here the personnel director and department act as ". . . the right arm of the top executive to assure him that personnel objectives, policies, and procedures (concerning, for example, occupational safety and health) which have been approved and adopted are being consistently carried out by line managers." [8]

3. *Staff (service) functions.* Service to line management is the "bread and butter" of the personnel director's job. For example, personnel *assists* in the hiring, training, evaluating, rewarding, counseling, promoting, and firing of employees at all levels. It also *administers* the various benefit programs (health and accident insurance, retirement, vacation, etc.). It *assists* line managers in their attempts to comply with equal employment and occupational safety laws. And, it has an important role with respect to grievances and labor relations. [9]

    As part of these service activities, the personnel director (and department) also carry out an "innovator" role. They do this by providing "up to date information on current trends and new methods of solving problems." [10] For example, there is currently much interest in improving the quality of work life and in providing career planning for employees. Personnel directors stay "on top" of such trends, and help their organizations implement the necessary programs.

Cooperative Line and Staff Personnel Management: An Example

Exactly what personnel management activities are carried out by line managers and staff managers? Actually, there is no single division of line and staff responsibility that is applied across the board in all organizations. But to illustrate what such a division might look like, an example is presented in Exhibit 1.3. [11] This shows some possible personnel-related responsibilities of line managers and staff managers in four areas: *employment* (recruiting, hiring, etc.); *safety; training;* and *labor relations.*

For example, in the area of *employment* it is the line manager's responsibility to specify the qualifications of employees needed to fill specific positions. Then the personnel department takes over. They develop sources of qualified applicants and conduct initial screening interviews. They administer the appropriate tests. Then, they refer the best candidates to the supervisor (line manager) who interviews and selects the ones he or she wants. A similar division of duties between line and staff is presented (in Exhibit 1.3) for the *safety, training,* and *labor relations* areas.

In summary, personnel management (as discussed in this book) is an integral part of *every* manager's job. Whether you are a first line supervisor, a middle manager, or president; or whether you're a production manager, sales manager, office manager, hospital administrator, county manager (or a personnel manager), getting results through people is the "name of the game." And to do this a good working knowledge of the personnel management concepts and techniques discussed in this book is vital.

DEVELOPING YOUR PERSONNEL MANAGEMENT PHILOSOPHY

People's actions are always based in part on the basic assumptions they make and this is especially true in regard to personnel management. The basic assumptions you make about people—such as, Can they be trusted? Do they dislike work? Can they be creative, Why do they act as they do? and, How should they be treated?—together comprise your philosophy of personnel management. And every personnel decision you make—the people hired, the training provided, and the benefits offered, etc.—reflects (for better or worse) this basic philosophy.

How does one go about developing such a philosophy? To some extent it is preordained. There is no doubt that a person brings to a job an initial philosophy based on his or her experiences, education, and background. But this philosophy doesn't have to be "set in stone." It should and will continually evolve as the person accumulates new knowledge and experiences. Some of the factors that will influence this evolving philosophy are summarized in Exhibit 1.4 and discussed on the following pages: They include top management's personnel philosophy and the need to improve productivity at work.

Influence of Top Management's Philosophy

One of the things molding a manager's personnel philosophy is that of the organization's top management. While top management's philosophy may or

8   **Exhibit 1.3**   Division of Responsibility Between Staff and Line in Personnel
Management

A. EMPLOYMENT

Personnel—employment specialist (staff)

1 *Develop* sources of qualified applicants from local labor market. This requires carefully planned community relations, speeches, advertisements, and active high school, college, and technical school recruiting. [Second step.]

2 Conduct *skilled* interviews, give *scientific* tests, and make thorough reference checks, etc., using requisition and job description as guides. Screening must meet company standards and conform with *employment laws*. [Third step.]

3 Refer best candidates to supervisor, after physical examinations and qualifications for the positions available have been carefully *evaluated*. [Fourth step.]

4 Give new employees preliminary *indoctrination* about the company, benefit plans, general safety, first aid, shift hours, etc. [Sixth step.]

5 Keep *complete record* of current performance and future potential of each employee. [Tenth step.]

6 *Diagnose* information given in separation interviews, determine causes, and take positive steps to correct. [Twelfth step.]

Department supervision (line)

1 Prepare *requisition* outlining specific qualifications of employees needed to fill specific positions. Help create reputation that will attract applicants. [First step.]

2 *Interview* and *select* from candidates screened by Personnel. Make specific *job assignments* that will utilize new employees' highest skills to promote maximum production. [Fifth step.]

3 *Indoctrinate* employees with specific details regarding the sections and jobs where they are to be assigned—safety rules, pay, hours, "our customs." [Seventh step.]

4 *Instruct* and *train* on the job according to planned training program already worked out with Personnel. [Eighth step.]

5 *Follow up, develop,* and *rate* employee job performance; *decide on* promotion, transfer, layoff, or discharge. [Ninth step.]

6 Hold separation *interview* when employees leave—determine causes. Make internal department *adjustments* to minimize turnover. [Eleventh step.]

B. SAFETY

Personnel—safety specialist (staff)

1 Have periodic *inspections* by trained engineer in order to *promote* safe working conditions, use of protective equipment, etc. Make *recommendations* for accident prevention.

2 *Analyze* jobs to develop safe practice rules. Utilize communications skills to get rules understood and accepted. Promote safety education.

3 Function as engineering *consultant* regarding the *design* of new machinery, guards, and safety devices; proper floor maintenance; and procedures for safe operation of machinery.

4 *Investigate* accidents; *analyze* causes, safety reports; *interpret* statistics; submit *recommendations* for accident prevention based on broad know-how.

5 Work with insurance carrier on workmen's compensation cases through courts; should have *technical knowledge of law.*

6 *Prepare* material for safety meetings—statistics on accident causes, progress reports, educational material.

Department supervision (line)

1 Assist in *working out* practical safety applications; *decide on* appropriations to cover costs of installations (guards, lighting, materials handling, etc.) consistent with production and budget standards.

2 *Direct employees* in the consistent application of safe work habits; give *recognition* to careful workers and to safety suggestions submitted.

3 Set up adequate *controls* to assure that guards and devices are used; *develop* employee sense of responsibility and supervisory follow-up.

4 *Enforce* good housekeeping standards; set a good *example* in safety; maintain consistent *discipline* in administration of safety rules.

5 Prepare *reports of accidents* promptly and accurately; *consistently apply* practical preventive measures recommended by safety specialists.

6 *Work with* the safety committee to *apply* safety measures developed with it. Demonstrate interest in daily behavior.

(Continued)

C. TRAINING

Personnel—training specialist (staff)

1 *Research* to develop over-all plans, objectives, responsibility, and needs; develop outside contacts and information.
2 *Help* president develop over-all *approach* and *plan* for supervisory and executive development to meet organization needs. Administer and coordinate program.
3 Give *advice* and *assistance* to *spark-plug* company units in planning, organizing, conducting employee and supervisory training and educational programs.
4 *Prepare* training outlines and visual aids in accordance with latest research in education in order to accelerate learning.
5 *Train* department supervisors to develop teaching skills in order to conduct their own training most effectively.
6 Provide conference leadership in certain types of training; *evaluate* results.

Department supervision (line)

1 Recognize and *decide on* department training *needs*; advise Personnel on focus needed and specific application.
2 Sincerely and *actively implement* executive development according to over-all plans. Share *information*, provide challenging assignments, and *coach*.
3 *Utilize* Personnel training specialists to help decide on tailor-made programs to meet department needs for job, apprentice, and supervisory training.
4 Give daily *coaching* and individual *training* to subordinates to meet job standards; judge their progress and suggest areas for improvement.
5 *Assume* responsibility, in some areas, for running department training to develop potentials of people.
6 *Decide on* future training as result of evaluations of past training activities.

D. LABOR RELATIONS

Personnel—labor relations specialist (staff)

1 *Diagnose underlying causes* of labor difficulties, *anticipate* disruptions, work with line management on preventive measures to *stabilize* and *build trust in* relationships.
2 Carry on skilled *research* in preparation of labor contract—objectives, terms, wordings. *Integrate* external data and internal needs.
3 Act as management *spokesman* or *adviser* to company negotiators in bargaining with union, or as *liaison* with company lawyer on technical matters.
4 *Train* all levels of management in *contract interpretation* and administration; handle legal and nonlegal interpretation questions; maintain and administer seniority lists accurately.
5 *Advise* supervision and *find out the facts* on grievances; interpret contracts, policies, precedents, when requested; be company *adviser* or *spokesman* on third-stage grievances and in arbitration.
6 Maintain continued direct contacts with top union officials, local and international; keep an open *channel of communication* on major issues.

Department supervision (line)

1 *Establish day-to-day relationship* of mutual respect and trust with union officials; apply labor laws and labor contract consistently, firmly, fairly.
2 *Advise* company negotiators of contract changes needed to *promote* smooth, efficient department production.
3 *Assist* in bargaining sessions where department issues are involved; explain special problems and give technical advice.
4 *Consistently* apply labor contract terms, after training or advice by Personnel staff; apply seniority principles in promotion, transfer, lay-off, and so forth.
5 Make final *decisions* on grievances after careful investigation and consideration of advice from Personnel. Gather background data requested by Personnel.
6 Maintain on-the-job *direct contacts* with department union stewards and employees in order to build sound relationships.

Exhibit 1.4   Some Factors Influencing Your Personnel Management Philosophy

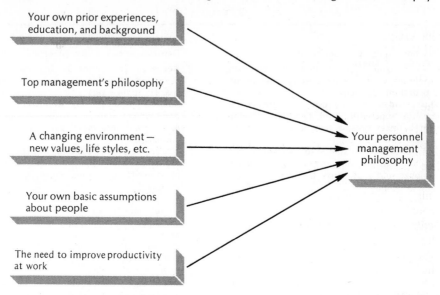

may not be stated, it will usually be communicated by their actions and permeate every level and department in the organization. For example, here is part of the personnel philosophy of Dr. Edwin Land, Chief Executive Officer of the Polaroid Corporation:

> . . . to give everyone working for the company a personal opportunity within the company for full exercise of his talents—to express his opinions, to share in the progress in the company as far as his capacity permits, and to earn enough money so that the need for earning more will not always be the first thing on his mind. The opportunity, in short, to make his work here a fully rewarding and important part of his life. [12]

What sort of effect does a philosophy like this have? For one thing, all personnel policies and actions at Polaroid flow directly or indirectly from Land's basic aims. For example, there is a top-level personnel policy committee. This consists of top corporate officers and is chaired by a senior vice president, and members of the personnel department serve as staff, providing advice to the committee. The existence of this high-powered committee reflects the company's commitment to Land's personnel philosophy. And, its existence helps ensure that all Polaroid's personnel policies and practices—such as in the areas of training, promotions, and layoffs—also reflect this basic philosophy.

Influence of One's Own Basic Assumptions About People

Your personnel management philosophy will also be influenced by the basic assumptions you make about people. For example, Douglas McGregor distinguishes between two sets of assumptions that he classified as "Theory X" and "Theory Y." He says that the Theory X assumptions hold that:

1. The average human being has an inherent dislike of work and will avoid it if he can.
2. Because of their human characteristic of dislike of work, most people must be coerced, controlled, directed, and threatened with punishment to get them to put forth adequate effort.
3. The average human being prefers to be directed, wishes to avoid responsibility.

At the other extreme, some managers' actions reflect a set of "Theory Y" assumptions. These hold that:

1. The average human being does not inherently dislike work.
2. External control and the threat of punishment are not the only means for bringing about effort toward organizational objectives.
3. People are motivated best by satisfying their "higher order" needs for achievement, esteem, and self-actualization.
4. The average human being learns, under proper conditions, not only to accept but also to seek responsibilities.
5. The capacity to exercise a relatively high degree of imagination, ingenuity, and creativity in the solution of organizational problems is widely, not narrowly, distributed in the population. [13]

Likert's System IV. Rensis Likert says that assumptions like these manifest themselves in two basic types or systems of organizations, which he calls System I and System IV. In System I organizations, he says:

1. Management is seen as having no confidence or trust in subordinates.
2. The bulk of decisions and the goal-setting of the organization are made at the top.
3. Subordinates are forced to work with fear, threats, and punishment.
4. Control is highly concentrated in top management.

In their place, Likert proposes System IV, an organization built on Theory Y-type assumptions. In System IV organizations:

1. Management is seen as having complete confidence and trust in subordinates.
2. Decision making is widely dispersed and decentralized.
3. Workers are motivated by participation and involvement in decision making.
4. There is extensive, friendly superior-subordinate interaction.
5. There is widespread responsibility for control with the lower echelon fully involved. [14]

Influence of a Changing Environment

Fundamental changes now occurring will also influence your personnel management philosophy. [15]

Dissatisfaction and a New Work Force. For example, there is little doubt that many workers are dissatisfied and that this is becoming an increasing concern of many managers. [16] Given the changes taking place in our work force, these problems can only become more important over time. For example (according to the Bureau of Labor Statistics), only 20% of the jobs in the United States require more than a high school education. Yet an increasing number of workers have college degrees, and it is estimated that in 1980 one out of every four entering the labor force had one. [17] As the supply of college graduates slowly outstrips demand, more graduates will find themselves in jobs for which they are "overqualified." Dealing with the dissatisfaction caused by this situation and learning how to motivate a better educated work force will therefore become critical issues in the future.

New Lifestyles. Men and women of all ages (but particularly the young) seem more interested in choosing a lifestyle and career than just a job. Therefore career development and adapting work to the lifestyles and changing interests of workers will become increasingly important.

New Laws. A variety of new laws have been passed that drastically alter the actions managers can take. For example, equal employment opportunity laws bar discrimination on the basis of race, age, religion, sex, and national origin. As a result, managers are now legally bound to ferret out and correct instances of discrimination. And they must be able to prove in court that their actions (in hiring, evaluating, promoting, etc.) were not discriminatory. Other laws—for example, covering occupational safety and health, and labor relations —are among the other new personnel-related constraints managers will have to deal with.

Changes in Values. Some also feel that basic work values are changing. Years ago it was assumed that a "work ethic" motivated workers to work hard and do their best. Today, some feel, this commitment to work is on the decline. If so, then motivating employees may become a more difficult task. [18]

The Need to Improve Performance and Productivity at Work

There is also another factor that will influence a manager's personnel philosophy: In the 1980s personnel managers and line managers (through their personnel roles) will have to become key persons in using personnel management concepts and techniques to improve productivity and performance at work.

The Problems. Today employers are faced with a productivity problem of alarming proportions. [19] In 1978 the U.S. ranked 6th among the world's 7 leading industrial nations in productivity gains, posting a productivity increase of only 2.5% in that year compared with Japan's 8.3%, France's 4.9%, Canada's 4.2%, West Germany's 3.7%, and Italy's 2.9%. Only Great Britain, with a 1.6% increase, registered a productivity gain smaller than that of the United

States. In 1979 the productivity rate of American businesses and workers as measured by economic output in relation to paid hours spent on the job actually fell 0.9%, only the second time since 1947 that the rate has declined for a full year. A recent government report entitled *Work in America* notes that worker productivity is low, and goes on to cite problems like absenteeism, turnover, wildcat strikes, sabotage, poor quality products, and reluctance by workers to commit themselves to their work tasks as some of the reasons. [20] A recent gallup poll suggests that 50% of all wage earners could accomplish more each day if they tried; 30% of the wage earners said those increases could be 20% or more. [21] As a share of the Gross National Product, after tax profits in the 25-year period from 1950 to 1975 declined from 9% to less than 5%. [22] In a 1975 survey of 6,000 business managers, the American Management Association found serious worry over productivity, but two-thirds of the respondents in the survey reported that companies were making no special efforts to evaluate executive productivity. [23] If the present trends continue, then by the year 2000, 140 million Japanese may be producing the same amount of goods and services as 220 million Americans.

Undoubtedly many factors are contributing to this problem. One problem is demography. [24] Since the mid-1960s a growing proportion of the labor force has been comprised of young and inexperienced workers. Although better educated than their parents, their output has been lower, and this accounts for about one-tenth of the slowdown in nonagricultural productivity. In addition, many believe the work ethic that once drove people to do their best has all but disappeared, and that this may itself be related to the decrease in craftsmanlike jobs in today's automated society. Capital improvements have also not kept pace with those made by industry in other industrialized nations, and in Japan government expenditures on productivity improvement are over six times the amount spent by the U.S. government, whose federal budget is five times larger than Japan's. [25] There has also been a decline in research and development expenditures: despite rapid growth over the 1955–1969 period, R&D spending has declined in real terms since 1970. Others argue that forced expenditures on pollution abatement, and on occupational safety and health equipment divert investible resources from productive capital equipment to nonproductive equipment. The result is a smaller and/or older stock of capital goods than would otherwise be the case and a subsequent decline in labor productivity growth. [26] (For instance, American industries devoted more than 5% of their total capital spending in 1976–78 just to reducing pollution.) Free market economists like Milton Friedman contend that the private sector has been subjected to increasing intervention and control by the public sector and that this has also reduced productivity. The development and enforcement of laws governing labor relations, equal employment opportunity, and health and safety require federal, state, and municipal enforcement agencies. This leads to increased tax rates and, perhaps, to a corresponding reduction in the incentive to work. [27] Undoubtedly, such factors have all contributed to the current productivity crisis in America

14   (and in much of the rest of the industrialized world), but, whatever the causes, many executives today conclude that productivity improvement has become urgent, not just desirable. [28]

Some Solutions.   There are many things that can be done to improve this grim productivity picture. For example, there are (as we saw) many legislative factors that may inhibit productivity (for example, pollution control equipment and occupational safety equipment). Yet, many believe that reducing or eliminating current legislative controls would actually have a predominantly adverse affect on society. And, in any case, this is not an issue that any individual manager usually has much control over. Worker productivity could also be increased by investing more heavily in more modern equipment—whether this involves steel mills or new computerized typewriters for secretaries. While useful, however, this is only part of the solution since, ultimately, virtually all service and manufacturing activities (no matter how automated) rely heavily on human beings. Even in the most highly automated auto assembly plants, for example, poor employee attendance, a resistant attitude on the part of workers, and worker sabotage can drastically curtail productivity. And, in relatively non-automated industries this is especially the case.

Another way to improve productivity and performance (and the one focussed on in this book) is to improve human behavior at work through the application of modern personnel management concepts and techniques. There are, in other words, personnel management concepts and techniques that are being used today in organizations that have been shown to be effective for improving the productivity and performance of employees, and explaining how to use these techniques is one purpose of this book. We explain, for example, how to use interviewing and other selection techniques to hire high-performers, how to train and motivate employees, and how to use incentives, benefits, and positive reinforcement to improve performance at work. In summary, the need to improve productivity and performance at work will have an important influence on managers' personnel management philosophies over the next few years, and explaining how to improve performance through modern personnel management techniques will therefore be one purpose of this book.

Productivity and Personnel Management.   Can personnel management techniques really have an impact on an organization's "bottom line?" Many contend that the answer is "no." For example, one writer argues that one reason line managers often do not listen to their personnel departments is because "personnel" has been traditionally viewed as mostly a clerical job, one which involves being the "keeper of records and the holder of application forms." Another, perhaps more serious criticism of the personnel role, according to this writer, is its traditional "lack of focus on performance." He says that as an advisory function, the human resources department does not have a clear, direct link to the generation of profit. Sales managers can track sales, which link directly to profits, he says. Similarly, production managers can track production costs and volume, both of which relate directly to profits. Traditionally, however, the personnel department has not been able to point to any "bottom line" results like these, nor, in many cases have they tried. As a result, "personnel management" has not, in general, been closely associated with the idea of productivity and performance improvement. [29]

Yet this situation is changing, and it is changing very quickly. As one writer says, "productivity is the problem—and personnel is definitely part of the solution." [30] He says that personnel management techniques as applied both by personnel management departments and by line managers in their "personnel" roles have already been shown to have a real impact on productivity and performance. In the U.S. government, for example, researchers found that using a personnel screening test to choose high-potential computer programmers could result in savings of millions of dollars per year. As another example, R.J. Reynolds invested $2½ million in a company-sponsored "health maintenance organization" (HMO). (An HMO is an alternative to a traditional health care insurance plan, and is one in which the company contracts with a group of doctors and health professionals to service all the firm's employees, usually at company expense.) At Reynolds, they found that under the HMO, employee hospitalization has declined 52%. Savings for 30,000 employees, as compared with their conventional plan, will permit payback of the investment in 24 months, plus the gains enjoyed from increased productivity. [31] Many other examples could be cited. Productivity incentives like "Scanlon Plans" can have a marked effect on performance, for instance. Occupational safety and health programs can reduce costs for lost-time accidents and illnesses. Methods-improvement training can improve the efficiency of employees. Even in relatively "hard-nosed" industries like Steel, managers are beginning to find that personnel-related techniques like "quality circles" in which employees are asked to identify performance bottlenecks and suggest solutions are now being used to boost performance. [32] The fact is that virtually every topic discussed in this book—job analysis, interviewing, testing, training, incentives, and appraisal, for instance—can and will have a measurable impact on productivity and performance. And, as a result, the subject of personnel management has taken on a new and more crucial importance in the "low productivity" 1980s.

Personnel Management Performance/Motivation Model. How does each of the topics (chapters) discussed impact performance? The personnel management performance/motivation model presented in Exhibit 1.5 will help answer this. This model is based on the assumption that an employee's performance depends on two things—on that person's *ability* to do the job and on his or her *motivation* to do so. One without the other will not suffice: telling someone a promotion to sales manager will occur if monthly sales hit $1 million probably will not result in $1 million sales (even if the person *wants* to be sales manager) unless the person *also* has the ability to sell $1 million worth of goods; both *desire* (motivation) and *ability* are required. This is the essence of improving human productivity and performance. And it is an idea that has important implications for all of a manager's "personnel management" activities. We can illustrate how by working through Exhibit 1.5.

Exhibit 1.5 A Performance Motivation Model

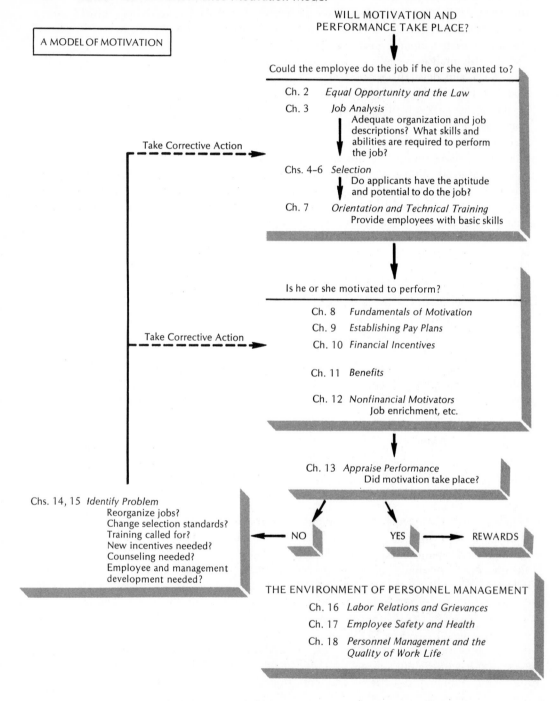

WILL MOTIVATION AND
PERFORMANCE TAKE PLACE?

A MODEL OF MOTIVATION

Could the employee do the job if he or she wanted to?

Ch. 2   *Equal Opportunity and the Law*

Ch. 3   *Job Analysis*
Adequate organization and job descriptions? What skills and abilities are required to perform the job?

Take Corrective Action

Chs. 4–6 *Selection*
Do applicants have the aptitude and potential to do the job?

Ch. 7   *Orientation and Technical Training*
Provide employees with basic skills

Is he or she motivated to perform?

Ch. 8   *Fundamentals of Motivation*

Ch. 9   *Establishing Pay Plans*

Ch. 10   *Financial Incentives*

Take Corrective Action

Ch. 11   *Benefits*

Ch. 12   *Nonfinancial Motivators*
Job enrichment, etc.

Ch. 13   *Appraise Performance*
Did motivation take place?

Chs. 14, 15 *Identify Problem*
Reorganize jobs?
Change selection standards?
Training called for?
New incentives needed?
Counseling needed?
Employee and management
development needed?

NO   YES   REWARDS

THE ENVIRONMENT OF PERSONNEL MANAGEMENT

Ch. 16   *Labor Relations and Grievances*

Ch. 17   *Employee Safety and Health*

Ch. 18   *Personnel Management and the
Quality of Work Life*

The model shows how each personnel management activity contributes to an employee's performance. For example the first step is to answer the question, "Could the employee do the job if he or she wanted to?": and there are several "personnel management" things one can do to help ensure that the answer is "yes." First, analyze the job: here carefully determine the "human requirements" of the job and develop an organization structure and job descriptions. Next is selection: here ensure that persons are hired with the aptitude and potential to do the job. Third, orient and train these people: here provide them with the basic skills they need to carry out their jobs. Thus, if everything is done right to this point one can at least be fairly sure that subordinates *are capable* of *accomplishing their tasks*—that they have the *ability* to do so.

Next ask "Is the reward important to the employees—are they motivated (do they have the *desire*) to do the job?" This involves some of the most important personnel management activities. For example, it helps determine the *wages* and *salaries* paid employees, their *financial incentives*, and *the nonfinancial incentives* needed to get their jobs done.

Now (assuming both ability and motivation are present) the employees should be motivated and performance should be high. The next step is to Appraise Performance. Here, then ask, "Did motivation and performance take place?" And, "If not, why not?" If the answer is "no," identify the problem. Should you reorganize? Change selection standards? Provide more training? Develop new incentives? Provide counseling? In other words, *identify the problem* (if any) and *take corrective action.*

The personnel management "performance motivation model" (Exhibit 1.5) will be used throughout this book. It helps show how the chapters relate to one another. And *it helps illustrate how each personnel management activity contributes directly to employee motivation and performance.*

Personnel Management: A Systems View. You can also use the model to help take a systems, "tying it all together," view of the personnel management activities. As can be seen in Exhibit 1.5, each personnel action has an influence on all the others. For example, the people hired will help determine the training that is reqired, the appropriate incentive system, and the best package of benefits.

Or take another example. Many managers are surprised when they don't get high performance from their subordinates, even after applying the sorts of "motivation" techniques discussed in chapters 8–12. The reason, of course, is that *all* the personnel activities—the people hired, the training provided, how performance is appraised, etc.—affect performance. Thus, good performance really begins with hiring decisions—with finding the right person for the right job. And it is further affected by the training provided, the incentive plan, and how performance is appraised. It is this *interrelatedness* among the personnel activities that the model also helps to illustrate.

THE PLAN OF THIS BOOK

This book is built around two basic themes. First, it is assumed that "personnel management" is *every* manager's responsibility—not just those in the personnel department. So throughout this book there is an emphasis on practical material that any manager will need in carrying out day-to-day management responsibilities. The second theme is that motivating employees and improving productivity and performance at work is a basic cornerstone of a sound personnel management philosophy. Therefore the performance/motivation model is used to structure the presentation of materials in this book as follows:

Section I   Recruitment and Placement

This section is aimed at ensuring that people are hired who are capable—who have the *ability*—to get their jobs done. In terms of performance (as you can see from our model), it is aimed at ensuring that the first requirement for performance—*that each employee can successfully "do the job"*—is met. This first section contains the following chapters:

Chapter 2 *Equal Employment Opportunity and the Law* (What a manager should know about equal opportunity laws as they relate to personnel management activities like interviewing, selecting employees, and performance appraisal)

Chapter 3 *Organizing and Analyzing Jobs* (How to organize; how to analyze a job; how to determine the "human" requirements of the job)

Chapter 4 *Personnel Planning and Recruiting* (Determining what sorts of people need to be hired; recruiting them)

Chapter 5 *Interviewing Job Candidates* (How to interview candidates to help ensure that the right person is hired for the right job)

Chapter 6 *Other Selection Techniques* (Some other techniques—like testing—that are used to ensure that the right people are being hired)

Chapter 7 *Orientation and Technical Training* (Providing the training necessary to ensure that employees have the knowledge and skills necessary to accomplish their tasks)

Section II   Compensation and Motivation

This section is aimed at explaining the second big requirement for employee performance—*ensuring that the rewards are important ones to the employees*—that they have the *desire* to do their jobs. The following are explained:

Chapter 8 *Fundamentals of Motivation* (A detailed look at what motivation is and how to motivate employees)

Chapter 9   *Establishing Pay Plans* (How to develop equitable, practical pay plans for employees)

Chapter 10   *Financial Incentives* and *Benefits and Services* (How to pro-
      & 11   vide special financial incentives and benefits for motivating employees)

Chapter 12   *Nonfinancial Motivation Techniques* (How to use techniques like "management by objectives" to motivate employees)

Section III   *Appraisal and Development*

Section III turns to the concepts and techniques needed for appraising employees' performance and making any necessary changes. Three topics are discussed:

Chapter 13   *Performance Appraisal* (Techniques for appraising performance)

Chapter 14   *Face-to-Face Communicating* (How to communicate with employees—providing feedback, counseling, and disciplining)

Chapter 15   *Employee and Management Development* (Concepts and techniques for developing more capable employees, managers, and organizations)

Section IV   *The Environment of Personnel Management*

Finally, some critical personnel-related legislation and concepts are discussed, with an emphasis on the practical knowledge needed to carry out day-to-day management responsibilities. Covered are:

Chapter 16   *Labor Relations and Grievances* (Important labor laws, how to avoid "unfair labor practices," and how to handle grievances are reviewed)

Chapter 17   *Employee Safety and Health* (The causes of accidents, how to make the work place safe, and laws governing the employer's responsibilities in regard to employee safety and health)

Chapter 18   *Conclusion: Career Planning, Personnel Management and the Quality of Work Life* (This final chapter sums up and ties together the material in this book, further defines a "personnel management philosophy," and ties the latter to career planning and the "quality of work life")

SUMMARY

1. There are certain basic functions all managers perform: planning, organizing, "staffing," leading, and controlling. These represent what is often called the "Management Process."

2. Staffing—or personnel management—is the function focussed on in this book. It includes activities like recruiting, selecting, training, compensating, appraising, and developing.

3. A knowledge of personnel management concepts and techniques is important because managers get things done through others. You could be a brilliant planner and organizer, for example, but if you hire the wrong people and can't motivate them you will still fail as a manager.

4. All managers are authorized to direct the work of subordinates—they are always someone's boss. Line managers also have direct responsibility for accomplishing the basic goals of the organization. Staff managers are authorized to assist and advise line managers in accomplishing these basic goals.

5. Personnel management is very much a part of *every* line manager's responsibility. These personnel management responsibilities include placing the right person on the right job, orienting, training, and working to improve his or her job performance.

6. The personnel director (and his or her department) carry out three main functions. First, he or she exerts *line authority* in his own unit and implied authority elsewhere in the organization. He or she exerts a *coordinative function* to ensure that the personnel objectives and policies of the organization are coordinated and carried out. And he or she provides various *staff services* to line management: for example, personnel assists in the hiring, training, evaluating, rewarding, promoting, and disciplining of employees at all levels.

7. Peoples' actions are always based in part on the basic assumptions they make, and this is why it is important to develop an overall guiding philosophy of personnel management. Five factors that will influence your own personnel management philosophy include prior experiences, education, and background; top management's philosophy; a changing environment (new values, lifestyles, etc.); basic assumptions about people; and the need to motivate subordinates, and improve performance and productivity at work.

8. Because performance is so important, this book is organized around the performance/motivation model as a framework. The material in Section I is aimed at ensuring that the first major requirement for performance—that each employee is capable of accomplishing the task, and obtaining the reward—is met. Section II is aimed at explaining how to motivate employees. Section III turns to the concepts and techniques needed for appraising employee's performance and making any necessary changes. Finally, in Section IV some critical personnel-related legislation and concepts are discussed.

9. The remainder of this book is aimed at providing *all* managers (not just future "personnel directors") with the practical concepts and techniques needed to carry out the "personnel management" aspects of their jobs. But while studying these chapters also make sure to understand (by following our framework) how each chapter's material relates to motivating employees, and to performance.

Jack Nelson's Problem*

As a new man on the Board of Directors for a local savings and loan association, Jack Nelson was being introduced to all the employees in the home office. When he was introduced to Ruth, he was curious about her work and asked her what her machine did. Ruth replied that she really did not know what the machine was called or what it did. She explained that she had only been working there for two months. She did, however, know precisely how to operate the machine and according to her supervisor, she was an excellent employee.

At one of the branch offices, the supervisor in charge spoke to Mr. Nelson quite confidentially, telling him that "something was wrong" but she didn't know what. For one thing, she explained, employee turnover was too high and no sooner had one girl been put on a job, when another one resigned. With customers to see and loans to be made, she explained that she had little time to work with the new employees as they came and went.

Each branch supervisor hired her own employees with no communications with the home office or other branches. When an opening developed, she did the best she could to find a suitable employee to replace the worker who quit.

After touring the twenty-two branches and finding similar problems in many of them, Mr. Nelson wondered what the home office should do or what action he should take. The savings and loan firm was generally regarded as a well-run institution that had grown from 27 to 191 employees during the past eight years. The more he thought about the matter the more puzzled Mr. Nelson became. He couldn't quite put his finger on the problem, and he didn't know whether or not to report his findings to the president.

1. What do you think was causing some of the problems in the savings and loan home office and branches?
2. Do you think setting up a personnel unit in the main office would help?
3. What functions should it carry out, specifically? What personnel functions would then be carried out by supervisors and other line managers?

---

* Claude S. George, Jr., *Supervision in Action* (Reston, Virginia: Reston Publishing Company, Inc., 1977) pp. 126–127.

22 **DISCUSSION QUESTIONS**

1. Explain what personnel management is and how it relates to the management process.
2. Give several examples of how personnel management concepts and techniques can be of use to all managers.
3. Compare and contrast the work of line and staff managers; give examples of each.
4. What do we mean by a "personnel management philosophy"? What factors influence it? Why is it important?
5. Compare and contrast Theory X and Theory Y management assumptions.
6. Present and explain the rationale for our personnel performance motivation model.

NOTES

1. Gary Dessler, *Management Fundamentals* (Reston, Va.: Reston Publishing, 1977), p. 2; William Berliner and William McClarney, *Management Practice and Training* (Homewood, Ill.: Irwin, 1974), p. 11.

2. Based on Dessler, *Management Fundamentals*, pp. 3–4.

3. Quoted in Fred K. Foulkes, "The Expanding Role of the Personnel Function," *Harvard Business Review* (March–April 1975), pp. 71–84.

4. The remainder of this section is based largely on Robert Saltonstall, "Who's Who in Personnel Administration," *Harvard Business Review*, Vol. 33 (July–August 1955), pp. 75–83; reprinted in Paul Pigors, Charles Meyers, and F. P. Malm, *Management of Human Resources* (New York: McGraw-Hill, 1969), pp. 61–73.

5. Saltonstall, "Who's Who in Personnel Administration," p. 63.

6. *Ibid.*, p. 64.

7. For a detailed discussion of the responsibilities and duties of the personnel department, see Mary Zippo, "Personal activities: where the dollars went in 1979," *Personnel*, 1980, pp. 61–67.

8. Saltonstall, p. 65.

9. Fred K. Foulkes and Henry Morgan, "Organizing and Staffing the Personnel Function," *Harvard Business Review* (May–June 1977), p. 146.

10. *Ibid.*, p. 149.

11. Saltonstall, pp. 68–69.

12. Quoted in Foulkes and Morgan, "Organizing and Staffing the Personnel Function," p. 144.

13. Douglas McGregor, *The Human Side of Enterprise* (New York: McGraw-Hill, 1960), pp. 16–18; quoted in Daniel Wren, *The Evolution of Management Thought* (New York: Ronald Press, 1972), pp. 449–450.

14. Based on Paul Hersey and Kenneth Blanchard, *Management of Organizational Behavior* (Englewood Cliffs, N.J.: Prentice-Hall, 1969), pp. 52–56.

15. See, for example, Jack English, "The Road Ahead for the Human Resources Function," *Personnel*, 1980, pp. 35–39. D. Quinn Mills, "Human Resources in the 1980's," *Harvard Business Review* (July–August 1979), pp. 154–163.

16. See *Work in America*, Report of a Special Task Force to the Secretary of Health, Education, and Welfare (Cambridge, Mass.: The MIT Press, 1973).

17. Foulkes, "The Expanding Role of the Personnel Function," p. 72: Max Carey, "Revised Occupational Projections for 1985," *Monthly Labor Review* (November 1976), pp. 10–22.

18. Lawrence Wangler, "The Intensification of the Personnel Role," *Personnel Journal* (February 1979), pp. 111–119.

19. Campbell McConnell, "Why is U.S. Productivity Slowing Down?", *Harvard Business Review*, Vol. 57, (March–April 1979), pp. 36–61.

20. Work in America: Report of the Special Task Force of the Secretary of Health, Education, and Welfare (Cambridge, Mass.: MIT Press, 1973).

21. Quoted in Thomas Connelan, *How to Improve Human Performance* (New York: Harper and Row, 1978), p. 4.

22. Connelan, *Human Performance*, p. 7.

23. Mildred Katezell, *Productivity: The Measure and the Myth* (New York: Amacom, 1975) quoted in Joel Ross, *Managing Productivity* (Reston, Va.: Reston Publishing, 1977), p. 3.

24. "America the Sluggish," *The Economist* (July 26, 1980), pp. 14–17.

25. Joel Ross, *Managing Productivtiy* (Reston, VA: Reston Publishing Co., 1977), p. 3.

26. McConnell, p. 48.

27. McConnell, p. 48.

28. "How to Promote Productivity," *Business Week*, July 24, 1978.

29. T. F. Cawsey, "Why Line Managers Don't Listen to their Personnel Departments," *Personnel* (January–February 1980), pp. 11–20.

30. Lawrence Baytos, "Nine Strategies for Productivity Improvement," *Personnel Journal* (July 1979), pp. 446–449.

31. *Ibid.*, p. 454.

32. "Steel Seeks Higher Output via Workplace Reform," *Business Week* (August 18, 1980), p. 98.

Part One

Recruitment and Placement

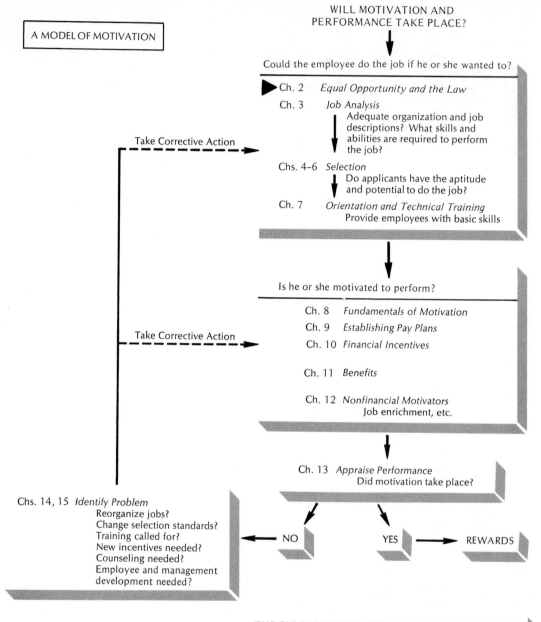

A MODEL OF MOTIVATION

WILL MOTIVATION AND
PERFORMANCE TAKE PLACE?

Could the employee do the job if he or she wanted to?

Ch. 2   *Equal Opportunity and the Law*

Ch. 3   *Job Analysis*
Adequate organization and job
descriptions? What skills and
abilities are required to perform
the job?

Chs. 4–6 *Selection*
Do applicants have the aptitude
and potential to do the job?

Ch. 7   *Orientation and Technical Training*
Provide employees with basic skills

Take Corrective Action

Is he or she motivated to perform?

Ch. 8   *Fundamentals of Motivation*
Ch. 9   *Establishing Pay Plans*
Ch. 10   *Financial Incentives*

Ch. 11   *Benefits*

Ch. 12   *Nonfinancial Motivators*
Job enrichment, etc.

Take Corrective Action

Ch. 13   *Appraise Performance*
Did motivation take place?

Chs. 14, 15 *Identify Problem*
Reorganize jobs?
Change selection standards?
Training called for?
New incentives needed?
Counseling needed?
Employee and management
development needed?

NO   YES   REWARDS

THE ENVIRONMENT OF PERSONNEL MANAGEMENT

Ch. 16   *Labor Relations and Grievances*
Ch. 17   *Employee Safety and Health*
Ch. 18   *Personnel Management and the
Quality of Work Life*

2 Equal Opportunity and the Law

You should be able to:

1. *Avoid some important employment discrimination problems.*
2. *Cite the main features of at least five recent employment discrimination laws.*
3. *Define "adverse impact" and explain how it is proved, and what its significance is.*
4. *Cite specific discriminatory personnel management practices in: recruitment, selection and promotion, transfer, layoffs, and benefits.*
5. *Explain two defenses an employer can use in the event of discriminatory practice allegations.*
6. *Explain how an employer would go about setting up an affirmative action program.*

OVERVIEW

This chapter begins a new section of the book, the section on recruitment and placement. In terms of our model, this material is important because it is through recruitment and placement that a manager ensures that he or she hires employees who have the ability to perform effectively. The main purpose of this chapter is to provide the knowledge needed to deal effectively with Equal Employment Opportunity questions on the job, especially as they relate to recruitment and placement. First reviewed are some employment discrimination laws (including Title VII of the 1964 Civil Rights Act and "EEOC" guidelines): We describe in broad terms the main features of this legislation. Next there is a discussion of some specific discriminatory personnel management practices—in recruitment, selection, promotion, transfers, layoffs, and benefits.

Also explained are the two basic defenses an employer can use in the event of a discriminatory practice allegation: "business necessity" and "bona fide occupational qualification." Finally, "affirmative action" and each of the eight steps in an affirmative action program are discussed.

INTRODUCTION: SOME BACKGROUND

Legislation barring discrimination against members of minority groups in the United States is certainly nothing new. The Fifth Amendment of the U.S.

28   Constitution, for example (which was ratified in 1791) states that "No person shall . . . be deprived of life, liberty, or property, without due process of law . . ." The Thirteenth Amendment (ratified in 1865) specifically outlawed slavery and has been held by the courts to bar racial discrimination. The Fourteenth Amendment (ratified in 1868) makes it illegal for any state to ". . . make or enforce any law which shall abridge the privileges and immunities of citizens of the United States. . . ." (The courts have generally viewed this law as barring discrimination on the basis of sex or national origin, as well as race.) Other legislation, as well as a number of court decisions, substantiate the fact that discrimination against minorities was—in theory at least—illegal as early as the turn of the century. [1]

As a practical matter, though, Congress and various presidents were reluctant to initiate dramatic action on equal employment issues until the early 1960s. At that point "they were finally prompted to act primarily as a result of civil unrest among the minorities and women" who eventually became protected by the new legislation discussed in this chapter. [2]

But before proceeding it is important to emphasize how crucial a complete understanding of these laws is. Today no manager from first-line foreman to president can get through a workday without facing discrimination-related problems. Today, every time employers advertise job openings, recruit, interview, test, or select candidates or appraise employees, it is necessary to take into account these equal rights laws. And that is only the beginning—a variety of other personnel management-related activities including promotion, transfer, layoffs, and benefits are also impacted by this legislation. And, as a manager, a complete understanding of these laws is necessary not only for your own protection but to protect the interests of your employer as well.

RECENT EMPLOYMENT DISCRIMINATION LEGISLATION

Title VII of the 1964 Civil Rights Act

What the Law Says. Title VII (as amended by the 1972 Equal Employment Opportunity Act) says that an employer cannot discriminate on the basis of race, color, religion, sex, or national origin. It states that it shall be an unlawful employment practice for an employer: [3]

(1) *To fail or refuse to hire or to discharge an individual* or otherwise to discriminate against any individual with respect to his compensation, terms, conditions, or privileges of employment, because of such individual's race, color, religion, sex, or national origin;

(2) *To limit, segregate, or classify his employees or applicants for employment* in any way that would deprive or tend to deprive any individual of employment opportunities or otherwise *adversely affect* his status as an employee, because of such individual's race, color, religion, sex, or national origin.

Who Does Title VII Cover? Title VII of the Civil Rights Act bars discrimination on the part of all public and private employers of fifteen or more persons. In addition, it covers all private and public educational institutions, and state and local governments. Public and private employment agencies are similarly barred from failing or refusing to refer for employment any individual because of race, color, religion, sex, or national origin. Labor unions with fifteen or more members are barred from excluding, expelling, or classifying its membership because of race, color, religion, sex, or national origin. Joint labor-management committees established for selecting workers for apprenticeship and training similarly cannot discriminate against individuals.

The EEOC. EEOC stands for Equal Employment Opportunity Commission, which was instituted by Title VII. The EEOC consists of five members who are appointed by the President with the advice and consent of the Senate; each member serves a term of five years.

The establishment of the EEOC greatly enhanced the federal government's ability to enforce employment antidiscrimination laws. The EEOC receives and investigates job discrimination complaints: when it finds reasonable cause that the charges are justified, attempts are made (through conciliation) to reach an agreement eliminating all aspects of the discrimination. If this conciliation fails, the EEOC has the power to go directly to court to enforce the law. Under the Equal Employment Opportunity Act of 1972, discrimination charges may be filed by the EEOC on *behalf* of a grieved individual, as well as by the individuals themselves. As the Commission points out, "With these new powers, EEOC legal actions against employers violating the law will increase rapidly and significantly." [4]

Executive Orders

Former President Johnson issued executive orders 11246 and 11375 to widen the impact of employment antidiscrimination laws, and the effects of these orders have been three-fold. First, they prohibit employment discrimination by employers with federal contracts of more than $10,000 (and their subcontractors), and by contractors and subcontractors in federally assisted construction projects.

Second, they established the Office of Federal Contract Compliance (OFCC) in the U.S. Department of Labor. This office is responsible for implementing the executive orders.

The executive orders also require "affirmative action" programs (discussed below) by all federal contractors and subcontractors. All firms with contracts over $50,000 and 50 or more employees must develop and implement such programs, which are then monitored by the assigned federal compliance agency.

Uniform Guidelines on Employee Selection Procedures

Detailed guidelines to be used by employers were approved on August 25, 1978, by the EEOC, Civil Service Commission, Department of Labor, and

30   Department of Justice. [5] These guidelines, which supersede earlier guidelines developed by the EEOC in 1970, explain "highly recommended":

selection procedures	pre-employment inquiries, and
records and reports	overall affirmative action programs
procedural regulations	

For example, the guidelines on employee selection procedures explain that any employment selection devices (including but not limited to written tests) that have the effect of screening out disproportionate numbers of women or minorities should be "validated." And, the guidelines explain in detail how an employer can validate a selection device. (We explain this validation process below.)

Other guidelines address sex discrimination. They state, for example, that fringe benefits must be equal for both sexes, and that disabilities due to pregnancy and childbirth must be treated by an employer like any other temporary disability. [6]

Court Decisions: Griggs v. The Duke Power Company
Albemarle v. Moody

Hundreds of court cases involving employment discrimination laws have been heard in recent years. [7] It is not possible to even touch on all of them in this book, but we should discuss what were probably the two most important. Griggs v. Duke Power and Albemarle Paper Co. v. Moody.

The Griggs case.   In the Griggs case, a suit was brought against the Duke Power Company on behalf of Griggs, an applicant for a job as a coal handler. At the time the Company required its coal handlers to be high school graduates. The plaintiff (Willie Griggs) claimed that this requirement was *unfairly* discriminatory in that it wasn't related to success on the job (wasn't *valid*) and resulted in a disproportionate number of blacks being disqualified.

Duke Power Company lost the case. The decision of the Supreme Court was unanimous, and in his opinion Chief Justice Burger laid out several crucial rulings: (1) *Discrimination need not be overt*, and (2) *the employment practice must be shown to be related to job performance*. First, the court established the fact that discrimination on the part of the employer need not be overt: the employer does not have to be shown to have intentionally discriminated against any individual. Second, the practice (in this case requiring the high school certificate) must be shown to be job-related. In the words of Chief Justice Burger:

> The act proscribes not only overt discrimination but also practices that are fair in form, but discriminatory in operation. The touchstone is *business necessity. If an employment practice which operates to exclude Negroes cannot be shown to be related to job performance*, (valid) the practice is prohibited. [8] (Italics added.)

Chief Justice Burger's opinion also (3) *clearly placed the burden of proof on the employer to show that the hiring standard is job-related.* In his words ". . . Congress has placed upon the employer the burden of showing that any given requirement must have a manifest relationship to the employment in question."

Albemarle Paper v. Moody.   In the *Griggs* case, the supreme court decided that a screening tool (like a test) had to be "job-related," (or "valid") in that performance on the test must be related to performance on the job. And, the court held that the burden of proof was on the *employer* to show that the screening tool was in fact related to job performance. The *Albemarle* case is important because in this case the court provided additional details regarding exactly how an employer should go about validating a screening tool—go about proving, in other words, that the test or other screening tool is in fact related to ("predicts") performance on the job. In the *Albemarle* case, for example, the court emphasized that if a test is to be used to screen candidates for a job, then the nature of that job—its specific duties and responsibilities—must first be carefully analyzed and documented. Similarly, the court held that the performance standards for employees on the job in question should be as clear and unambiguous as possible.

In arriving at its decision, the court cited the EEOC guidelines concerning "acceptable" selection procedures, and thereby made these guidelines the "law of the land." [9] After *Albemarle* it was clear that any tests or screening tools that had the effect of screening out a disproportionate number of minorities or women had to be *validated*. That is, the court ruled that screening procedures must be related to actual performance on the job: in other words, must be shown to validly predict performance. It was further ruled that the EEOC guidelines provided procedures for doing so. [10]

The Equal Pay Act of 1963

This Act requires most employers to provide equal pay for men and women performing similar work. In 1972, coverage of this act was extended to an estimated 15 million administrative, professional, and sales people.

The Age Discrimination in Employment Act of 1967

This act applies to employers of 25 or more persons. It prohibits them from discriminating against a person 40 to 65 in any area of employment because of age.

State and Local Laws

In addition to the federal laws, many state and local governments also prohibit employment discrimination: In many cases the state and local laws cover employers (like those with fewer than 15 employees) not covered by federal legislation. [11]

When EEOC receives a discrimination charge, it defers it (for a limited time) to the state and local agencies that have comparable jurisdiction (e.g., a state fair employment commission). The procedures these agencies use in handling the complaints and the requirements for affirmative action vary. However, if satisfactory remedies are not expeditiously achieved, the charges are referred to EEOC for resolution. [12]

This legislation (Title VII, state laws, etc.) is summarized in Exhibit 2.1.

Exhibit 2.1 Summary of Important Recent Equal Employment Legislation

Legislation	What It Does
Title VII of 1964 Civil Rights Act, as amended	Bars discrimination because of race, color, religion, sex, or national origin; and instituted EEOC
Executive Orders	Prohibit employment discrimination by employers with federal contracts of more than $10,000 (and their subcontractors); establish office of federal compliance; require affirmative action programs
Federal agency guidelines	Guidelines covering discrimination based on sex, national origin, and religion, as well as employee selection procedures; for example, require validation of tests
Court decisions: *Griggs* v. *Duke Power Co., Albemarle* v. *Moody*	The court ruled that: job requirements must be related to job success; discrimination need not be overt; the burden of proof is on the *defendant* to prove the qualification is valid.
Equal Pay Act of 1963	Equal pay for men and women must be provided for performing similar work
Age Discrimination in Employment Act of 1967	Prohibits discriminating against a person 40-65 in any area of employment because of age
State and legal laws	Often cover organizations too small to be covered by federal laws

What Is "Adverse Impact"?

To pursue a discrimination case, the plaintiff (the one allegedly discriminated against) has only to establish a "prima facie case" of discrimination: to do this, he or she has to show that the employer's selection procedures have an "adverse impact" on a protected minority group. Adverse impact "refers to the total employment process that results *in a significantly higher percentage of a protected group in the candidate population being rejected* for employment, placement, or promotion." [13]

What does this mean? If a minority (protected group) applicant for a job feels discriminated against, he need only show that the selection procedures result in an "adverse impact" on his minority group. (For example, if 80% of the white applicants pass the test, but only 20% of the black applicants pass, a black applicant has a prima facie case proving adverse impact.) *Then, once he has proved his point, the burden of proof shifts to the employer.* It becomes the employer's task to prove that the test, application blank, interview, etc., is a valid predictor of performance on the job (and that it is applied fairly and equitably to both minorities and nonminorities).

How Can "Adverse Impact" Be Proved?   Actually, it is not too difficult for an applicant to show that some personnel procedure (such as a test used for selection) has an adverse impact on a protected group. There are four basic approaches that can be used: [14]

1. *Disparate rejection rates.* This is a comparison of the rejection rates between a minority group and another group (usually the remaining nonminority applicants). For example, ask, "Is there a disparity between the percentage of blacks among those *applying* for a particular position and the percentage of blacks among those *hired* for the position?"; or, "Do proportionately more blacks than whites fail the written examination given to all applicants?" If the answer to either question is "yes," the employer could be faced with a lawsuit. Specifically, Federal agencies have adopted as a rule of thumb the following: "a selection rate for any racial, ethnic or sex group which is less than four-fifths (4/5) (or eighty percent) of the rate for the group with the highest rate will generally be regarded as evidence of adverse impact, while a greater than four-fifths rate will generally not be regarded as evidence of adverse impact. For example, suppose 90% of male applicants are hired, but only 60% of females are hired. Then, since 60% is less than 4/5 of 90%, adverse impact exists. [15]

2. *Restricted policy.* This is a demonstration that the employer has been using a hiring policy (either intentionally or not) to exclude members of a minority group. Here the problem is fairly straightforward. For example, policies have been unearthed against hiring women as barmaids and against hiring unwed mothers. Evidence of restricted policies like these is enough to prove adverse impact and leave one open to litigation.

3. *Population comparisons.* Here a comparison is made of the percentage of a firm's minority group employees and the percentage of that minority in the general population in the surrounding community. [16]

4. *McDonnell–Douglas test.* This test involves showing that the applicant was qualified, but was rejected by the employer who is still seeking applicants for the position. Here the rejected minority candidate uses the following guidelines as given by the U.S. Supreme Court: (a) that he or she belongs to a racial minority; (b) that he applied and was qualified for a job in which the employer was seeking applicants; (c) that, despite his qualifications, he was rejected; and (d) that, after his rejection, the position remained open and the employer continued to seek applicants from persons of complainant's qualifications. If all these conditions are met, then adverse impact is established.

Adverse Impact: A Summary.   Assume a member of a protected or minority group is turned down for a job, based on a test score (although it could have been interview questions, application blank responses, etc.). Further assume that this person feels that he or she was discriminated against due to being in a minority, and decides to sue the employer.

Basically, all he need do is show that the employer's personnel procedures (such as the selection test) has an *adverse impact* on members of his minority group, and there are four criteria he can apply here: disparate rejection rates, restricted policy, population comparisons, and the McDonnell–Douglas test.

34   Once he has shown adverse impact to the satisfaction of the court, *the burden of proof shifts to the employer.*

But note that there is *nothing* in the law that says that because some procedure has an adverse impact on a protected minority group the procedure is unusable. In fact it could (and does) happen that some tests screen out disproportionately higher numbers of blacks than whites, for instance. What the law *does* say is that once the applicant has made his or her case (showing adverse impact) the burden of proof shifts to the employer. The latter must then prove that the selection procedure (or promotion criteria, etc.) is a valid predictor of job performance, and that the procedure is applied fairly to both minorities and nonminorities.

DEFENSES (AND EXCEPTIONS) TO DISCRIMINATORY PRACTICE ALLEGATIONS[17]

Once adverse impact has been shown to exist, there are basically two defenses an employer can use, both of which relate to job performance: "business necessity" and "bona fide occupational qualification" (BFOQ). In other words, suppose an applicant or employee brings suit against the company. He shows that a personnel practice—an application blank, a test, etc.—has an *adverse impact* on his minority group (for example, a disproportionately higher number of them fail the test).

The employer will likely want to defend himself, and there are two basic approaches he can take. One is to prove that the practice in question (like the test) is justified due to "business necessity"; the other is to justify the personnel practice based on a "bona fide occupational qualification (BFOQ)." Both are generally difficult to uphold. The more usual defense is to demonstrate the validity and fairness of the allegedly discriminatory practice, a procedure that is viewed here as a special case of the "business necessity" defense.

Bona Fide Occupational Qualification (BFOQ)

Title VII provides that "it shall not be an unlawful employment practice for an employer to hire an employee . . . on the basis of religion, sex, or national origin *in those certain instances where religion, sex, or national origin is a bona fide occupational qualification* reasonably necessary to a normal operation of that particular business or enterprise." The BFOQ defense is most frequently used with respect to sex discrimination: it can *only* be used as a defense against charges of discrimination based on religion, sex, or national origin (not race). The BFOQ exception is usually interpreted narrowly by the courts. For example:

1. *Religion* is a BFOQ in the case of religious organizations or societies that require employees to share a particular religion.
2. *National origin* is a BFOQ in the case of organizations promoting the interests or exemplifying the culture of a particular national group.

3. *Sex* is a BFOQ for positions requiring specific physical characteristics necessarily possessed by only one sex. This includes positions such as actors, models, and restroom attendants.
4. The courts have *not* accepted sex as a BFOQ for positions just because they require overtime or the lifting of heavy weights.
5. *Sex* was not a BFOQ for parole and probation officers.
6. The courts held that it was illegal to apply a "no marriage" rule solely to stewardesses (and not to male employees), and that this regulation could not be justified as BFOQ because of customer preference.
7. The courts have held that a company could not exclude women with pre-school children from employment opportunities unless they also excluded men with pre-school children.

Business Necessity

"Business necessity" is a defense created by the courts, and if the discriminatory item cannot be defended as a BFOQ, it generally must be defended as a "business necessity," usually by *validating* the item. "Business necessity" can be used to justify an otherwise discriminatory employment practice (for example one that has an adverse impact on a protected minority group). In *Robinson* v. *Lorillard Corporation*, the court defined the "business necessity" defense as follows: [18]

> The applicable test is not merely whether there exists a business purpose for adhering to a challenged practice. The test is whether there exists an *overriding legitimate business purpose* such that the practice is necessary to the safe and efficient operation of the business; thus, the business purpose must be sufficiently compelling to override any racial impact; and the challenged practice must effectively carry out the business purpose it is alleged to serve . . .

It is not easy to prove that a practice is required for "business necessity." For example, in one case the courts held that saving a small amount of money (by discharging persons who had been garnisheed because it costs money to process garnishments) did not raise the practice to a level of a business necessity. In another case, the company's seniority system was not justified by "business necessity" *unless* there was no reasonable available alternative to serve the legitimate ends of safety and efficiency. On the other hand, in *Spurlock* v. *United Airlines*, a minority candidate sued United Airlines, stating that its requirements that pilot candidates have 500 hours flight time and college degrees were unfairly discriminatory. The court held that in light of the cost of the training program and the tremendous human and economic risks involved in hiring "unqualified" candidates the selection standards were required by "business necessity," and were job related.

Attempts by employers to show that their tests (or other selection standards) are valid represent one example of the "business necessity" defense. Here (as discussed) the employer is required to *prove* that the standard or test is a

36   valid predictor of performance on the job. Where validity *can* be established the courts have generally supported the use of the standard or test as a "business necessity."

Good Intentions Alone Are No Defense [19]

Keep in mind that a personnel practice may be unfairly discriminatory even though the employer didn't intend it to be and was not motivated by bad faith. In the *Griggs* case, for example, the court commended some of the employer's efforts to "help the undereducated employees through company financing of two-thirds the cost of tuition for high school training." Yet the court *still* struck down the company's education and testing standards saying:

> Good intent or absence of discriminatory intent does not redeem procedures or testing mechanisms that operate as "built in headwinds" for minority groups and are unrelated to measuring job capability.

Similarly, making a "good faith" effort to design an unbiased test or to validate procedures is irrelevant if the device ends up producing an adverse impact and cannot be shown to be job-related.

A Collective Bargaining Agreement Is No Defense [20]

The courts have consistently held that a company cannot use its collective bargaining agreement as a defense in explaining why they discriminated against minority individuals. In one case, for example, the court held that the company and union were *both* liable for a seniority system that discriminated against blacks. This was the case even though the company thought it was obliged to adhere to the system because of its collective bargaining agreement.

The courts have also held that antidiscrimination laws must be regarded as more important than rights embodied in a labor contract. For example, the courts have held that a union had no valid claim against the employer who violated seniority system provisions (in its collective bargaining agreement) in order to eliminate the effects of past discrimination and comply with the affirmative action requirements of its government contract.

DISCRIMINATORY PERSONNEL MANAGEMENT PRACTICES

Some practical implications of this employment discriminatory legislation can be illustrated with the following listing of potentially discriminatory personnel management practices that should *generally* be avoided. [21]

Recruitment

Word of Mouth. An employer generally cannot rely on word-of-mouth dissemination of information about work opportunities where the work force is all or substantially all white.

Misleading Information. It is unlawful to give false or misleading information to members of any group or to fail or refuse to inform them of work opportunities and the procedures for obtaining them.

Help Wanted Ads. "Help wanted—male" and "Help wanted—female" advertising classifications are violations of laws forbidding sex discrimination in employment unless sex is a BFOQ. Also one generally should not advertise in any way that suggests that applicants 40–65 years of age are being discriminated against. For example, one cannot advertise for a "young" man or woman.

Selection Standards and Pre-employment Inquiries

There are a number of management practices here that have the potential for being unfairly discriminatory and that managers would therefore do well to avoid. [22] Keep in mind, however that "with the exception of personnel policies calling for outright discrimination against the members of some protected group, it is not really the intrinsic nature of an employer's personnel policies or practices that the courts object to. Instead, it is the *results* of applying a policy or practice in a particular way or in a particular context that leads to an adverse impact on some protected group." [23] The following pre-employment inquiries (concerning marital status, hair color, and so on) should thus be viewed not as illegal per se but as problem questions that may be potentially illegal. They are *problem* questions because they tend to identify an applicant as a member of a protected group or to disfavor members of a protected group. However, they become *illegal* questions if it can be shown that the questions as used do screen out disproportionately more of a protected group's applicants, *and* that the employer cannot prove the question is required as a "business necessity" (usually, that it is a valid predictor of on-the-job performance). Thus, if an employer is sure that its hiring practices are not unfairly discriminatory— that, for example they hire as many female applicants as male—then the employer may choose to continue asking these "problem questions." On the other hand, these questions tend to be "red flags" to the EEOC and it is probably safe to say that employers would do best to eliminate them, or at least to delay asking them until after the applicant has been hired, when such questions might be useful for, say, insurance purposes. [24]

Marital Status (including husband's name). The EEOC treats these questions with suspicion because of the possibility that an employer could use them to discriminate against women on the basis of their marital status. [25] Furthermore, it would be difficult to show the relevancy of this inquiry to a person's qualifications for a job.

Hair and Eye Color. Questions concerning hair and eye color may suggest an applicant's race and are difficult or impossible to justify as job-related.

Childcare (including ages of the children, questions about what arrangements have been made for childcare, etc.). These questions have been used to exclude women with preschool-age children or young children in general. Further, they tend to disproportionately screen out protected groups who have more children on the average. If such questions must be asked, the application form should emphasize that answers are required of both male and female applicants.

Age. Most applicants still ask an applicant's age, although this can be an obvious red flag to someone looking for age discrimination. Recall that the age discrimination in employment act protects those between the ages of 40 and 65; refusal to hire those younger or older is not prohibited.

Educational Requirements. An educational requirement may be held illegal where (1) it can be shown that minority groups are less likely to possess the educational qualifications (such as a high school diploma), and (2) such qualifications are also not job-related (or validated). For example, in the *Griggs* v. *Duke Power* case, a high school diploma was found *both* unnecessary for job performance, as well as discriminatory against blacks. In other cases, a public school board was found to have unlawfully discriminated against blacks by requiring a master's degree (and specific scores on Graduate Record Examinations) *that had not been validated* as predictors of job performance. A requirement for a college degree for management trainee positions was found to be unfairly discriminatory against blacks in another case.

Tests. According to Chief Justice Burger:

Nothing in the [Title VII] act precludes the use of testing or measuring procedures; obviously they are useful. What Congress has forbidden is giving these devices and mechanisms controlling force *unless they are demonstrating a reasonable measure of job performance.*

Tests which disproportionately screen out minorities or women *and* which are not job-related are deemed unlawful by the courts. However, one point is worth repeating: the fact that a test (or other selection standard) screens out a disproportionate number of minorities or women is not *by itself* sufficient to prove that the test *unfairly* discriminates. To do this, it must also be shown that the tests (or other screening devices) are not job-related. Job-relatedness is usually proven through a validation study.

Relative's Preference. An employer should not give preference to relatives of current employees with respect to employment opportunities if the current employees are substantially nonminority.

Height, Weight, and Physical Characteristics. Physical characteristics (such as height and weight) that can have an adverse impact upon certain ethnic groups or women are problem questions unless they can be shown to be job-related. For example, one company required that a person weigh a minimum of 150 pounds for positions on its assembly lines. This requirement was held to discriminate unfairly against women.

Arrest Records. An applicant's arrest record cannot be used to disqualify the person automatically for a position because there is always a presumption of innocence until proven guilty. In addition, (1) arrest records in general have not been shown valid for predicting job performance and (2) historically, a higher proportion of blacks than whites has been arrested. Thus, disqualifying applicants based on arrest records automatically has an adverse impact on blacks. Therefore, unless security clearance is necessary, an applicant generally should not be asked whether he or she has ever been arrested or spent time in jail.

Discharge Due to Garnishment. A disproportionately higher number of minorities are subjected to garnishment procedures. (Here creditors make a claim to a portion of the person's weekly wages.) Therefore, firing—or failing to hire—a minority whose salary has been garnisheed is illegal, unless the employer can show some overriding "business necessity."

Other Hiring Standards. A number of other selection standards or tools have been held unlawful because as they were used in the specific instances some or all of their elements adversely affected minorities *and* were not shown to be job-related. These include certain interview questions, background investigations, medical exams, psychological exams, and polygraph tests. Again, an employer *can* use these devices, but may be asked to prove they are job-related.

Summary of Selection Guidelines. Exhibit 2.2 summarizes some suggested pre-employment guidelines. With respect to "age," for example, it is alright to ask the person's age once hired, or whether "you are over 18." On the other hand, it is recommended that the question, "how old are you?" be avoided or that the interviewer write down the applicant's estimated age before hiring.

Promotion, Transfer, Layoff Benefits

Seniority Systems. Certain seniority systems (in which people are promoted based on how long they have been with the company) may have the effect of perpetuating past discriminatory promotion and transfer practices, and may therefore be illegal. For example, prior to the passing of EEO legislation, minorities and women were often assigned only to "hot, dirty, low-paying" departments. [26] Similarly, rules sanctified by collective bargaining agreements prohibited transfers from one department to another unless the worker forfeited job seniority. As a result the person making the transfer often lost some or all accrued seniority, since his seniority applied only to his job (not all those in the plant). Furthermore, the entry-level job in the new department often paid less than the job the long-term minority or female employee currently held in the "hot, dirty, low-paying" department. The overall effect was to "freeze" minorities and women into less favorable departments.

Subject	Can Do or Ask	Best not to Do or Ask
Sex	Notice appearance.	Make comments or notes unless sex is a BFOQ.
Marital status	Status after hiring, for insurance purposes.	Are you married? Single? Divorced? Engaged?
		Living with anyone? Do you see your ex-spouse?
Children	Numbers and ages of children after hiring, for insurance purposes.	Do you have children at home? How old? Who cares for them? Do you plan more children?
Physical data	Explain manual labor, lifting, other requirements of the job. Show how it is performed. Require physical exam.	How tall are you? How heavy?
Criminal record	If security clearance is necessary, can be done prior to employment.	Have you ever been arrested, convicted or spent time in jail?
Military status	Are you a veteran? Why not? Any job-related experience?	What type of discharge do you have? What branch did you serve in?
Age	Age after hiring. "Are you over 18?"	How old are you? Estimate age.
Housing	If you have no phone, how can we reach you?	Do you own your home? Do you rent? Do you live in an apartment or a house?

Source: Reprinted from the May 26, 1975 issue of *Business Week* by special permission. Copyright 1975 by McGraw-Hill, Inc. Reprinted in Robert Mathis and John Jackson, *Personnel* (St. Paul: West Publishing Co., 1976), p. 104. See also Clifford Koen, Jr., "The Pre-Employment Inquiry Guide," *Personnel Journal*, October, 1980, 825–829.

Courts have generally found such seniority systems illegal. And they have ordered modification of collective bargaining agreements to provide that "plant-wide seniority" (rather than "job seniority") become the basis for competition for promotion, transfer, and resistance to layoffs.

However in May 1977, the U.S. Supreme Court (in *T.I.M.E.–D.C. Inc.* v. *United States*) held that a seniority system does *not* become illegal simply because it allows employees with vested seniority rights to continue to exercise those rights at the expense of persons discriminated against before the law (Title VII) became effective. The ruling will probably have the effect (according to *Time Magazine*) of reducing or eliminating seniority systems as "whipping boys for job bias activists." **27**

Collective Bargaining Agreements. In the past, some collective bargaining agreements excluded minorities and women from employment, sometimes by stating that only "experienced" persons could obtain the better jobs. (The minorities and women were often unable to obtain the experience necessary for more advanced jobs.) Where this has been the case, the courts have held that requirements such as "previous experience" for promotion or transfer are discriminatory and illegal.

AFFIRMATIVE ACTION PROGRAMS[28]

Equal Employment Opportunity Versus Affirmative Action [29]

Equal employment opportunity has as its goal ensuring that anyone regardless of race, color, sex, religion, national origin, or age has an equal chance for a job based on their qualifications.

Affirmative action goes beyond equal employment opportunity. It requires the employer to make *an extra effort* to hire and promote those in the protected minority. According to one writer, the implication is sometimes that the most important qualification is membership in the protected minority. [30]

Specifically, affirmative action includes those specific actions (in recruitment, hiring, upgrading jobs, etc.) that are designed and taken for the purpose of eliminating the present effects of past discrimination. According to the EEOC, the most important measure of an affirmative action program is its *results*. The program should result in "measurable, yearly improvement in hiring, training, and promotion of minorities and females in all parts of your organization."

Affirmative Action and the Supervisor

Affirmative action is not something that just needs to be understood by the company's president or personnel managers. Instead, managers at any level find themselves almost daily in need of a good understanding of affirmative action and how it works. As the EEOC writes:

> All company officials and managers should clearly understand their own responsibilities for carrying out equal employment opportunity and affirmative action as a basic part of their jobs. . . .

The Steps in an Affirmative Action Program

According to the EEOC, an "ideal" affirmative action program consists of eight steps as follows:

1. Issue a written equal employment *policy* and affirmative action commitment statement.
2. Appoint a *top official* with responsibility and authority to direct and implement the program.
3. *Publicize* the policy and affirmative action commitment.
4. *Survey* present minority and female employment by department and job classification.
5. *Develop goals* and timetables to improve utilization of minorities, males and females, in each area where underutilization has been identified.
6. Develop and implement *specific programs* to achieve goals: This is the heart of the program. Review the entire personnel management system to identify barriers to equal employment opportunity and make needed changes.
7. Establish an *internal audit* and reporting system to monitor and evaluate progress in each aspect of the program.

42   8. Develop *support* of in-house and community programs.

Each step (as suggested by the EEOC) will be discussed in turn, with special emphasis on steps 4, 5, and 6—the "heart" of the affirmative action program.

Step 1: Issue Written Equal Employment Policy Statement and Affirmative Action Commitment

According to the EEOC, the first step is for the employer's chief executive to issue a statement of personal commitment, also covering legal obligations and the importance of EEO as a business goal. He or she should assign specific responsibility and accountability to every executive and manager. The statement should include, but not necessarily be limited to, such things as:

1. Equal employment opportunity for all persons, regardless of race, creed, color, sex, national origin, or age, is fundamental company policy. EEO is a legal, social, and economic necessity for the company.
2. The Equal Employment Policy will require special affirmative action throughout the company to overcome effects of past discrimination. It cannot be a "neutral" policy but requires new goal-setting and evaluation procedures.
3. The affirmative action program will affect all personnel practices. These will include (but not be limited to) recruiting, hiring, transfer, promotions, training, compensation, benefits, layoffs, and terminations.
4. Responsibility for the affirmative action program is assigned to a major company executive. However, all management personnel share in this responsibility and will be assigned specific tasks. Management performance on this program will be evaluated as is performance on other company goals.
5. Successful performance on affirmative action goals will provide positive benefits to the company. It will do this through fuller utilization and development of previously underutilized human resources.

Step 2: Appoint a Top Official with Responsibility and Authority to Implement the Program

According to the EEOC, the importance the employer places on its affirmative action program is indicated by the person that is placed in charge of it, and the authority he or she has to implement it. According to the EEOC, the best person for the job is a top management official. He or she should be named *director* or *manager* of the organization's affirmative action program, and should be directly responsible to the chief executive. The job will require a major time commitment, and "cannot be added on to an existing full-time job."

Affirmative Action Director's Responsibilities.   Some typical duties for this person include:

Developing the equal employment policy statement and a written affirmative action program.

Assisting line managers in collecting and analyzing employment data and
identifying problem areas.

Design, implement, and monitor the company's internal EEO audit and
reporting systems.

This person should also report (at least quarterly) to the chief executive on
the company's progress and serve as a liaison between the company, government agencies, and minority and women's organizations. He or she
should also see to it that the current affirmative action legal information is
disseminated to responsible officials.

Step 3: Publicize the Affirmative Action Program

First, provide publicity *internally*. This starts with the chief executive's
overall policy statement and also includes informing all managers and supervisors
that their performance on affirmative action will be graded as part of their normal performance evaluation. Educational materials, meetings, and training sessions should be held regularly to communicate legal requirements to managers
and supervisors. [31]

In addition, all employees need to be informed of company EEO and affirmative action policies. EEO posters should be placed on bulletin boards, notices
should be placed in company newsletters and pay envelopes, and the company's
policy included in its employee handbook. Meetings should be held with minority and female employees to request their suggestions in developing the affirmative action program. Union officials should be invited to cooperate in developing
and implementing the program from the start.

Second, provide *external* publicity. For example, the employer should provide annual, personal letters to all regular recruitment sources. These should
include a copy of the equal employment policy, and state the employer's interest
in interviewing and hiring previously underrepresented groups for all positions.

In addition, inform the media that help-wanted ads cannot be placed in
sex-segregated ("male-female") columns. Include a statement that you are an
"equal opportunity employer" in all advertising. Contact new recruiting sources
who have special contact with women and minority groups. Notify all subcontractors, vendors, and suppliers in writing of your equal employment policy.

Step 4: Survey and Analyze Minority and Female Employment by Department and Job Classification

This is the first step toward defining specific affirmative action goals. And,
this is also the first of three steps that comprise the "heart" of the EEO's recommended affirmative action program.

Determine Current Status of Minority Employment.   First, as illustrated
in Exhibit 2.3, the employer should determine the status of minorities and
women in the company by geographical location, department, and job descrip-

Exhibit 2.3 Affirmative Action Program/Quarterly Statistical Report

Form T

Organizational Unit _____
Location _____
Time Period _____

Job Categories	All Employees			Male				Female			
	Total	Male	Female	Negro	Oriental	American Indian	Spanish Surnamed American	Negro	Oriental	American Indian	Spanish Surnamed American
	(1)	(2)	(3)	(4)	(5)	(6)	(7)	(8)	(9)	(10)	(11)
Officials & Managers											
Professionals											
Technicians											
Sales Workers											
Office & Clerical											
TOTAL Lines 1-5											
Craftsmen (Skilled)											
Operatives (Semi-Skilled)											
Laborers (Unskilled)											
Service											
Total Lines 7-10											
TOTAL All Lines											

In columns 1, 2, and 3, include all employees in the establishment including those in min. groups. (The data below shall be included in the figures for the appropriate occupation categories above.)

On-the-job trainees											
Apprentices											
Production											
White Collar											

(Report only employees enrolled in formal on-the-job training programs.)

Date of Survey _____   Person Preparing Report _____   Signature _____
                                                                        Name (Typed)

Source: "Affirmative Action and Equal Employment," U.S. Equal Employment Opportunity Commission, January 1974.

tion. This will help identify jobs, departments, or units in which there may be significant "underutilization" or "concentration" of minorities and/or females and males. *Underutilization* has been defined as having fewer minorities or women in a particular job category than would reasonably be expected by their presence in the "relevant job market." Most companies find that defining "underutilization" in their own case is no easy matter. For example, for high level managers and highly trained professionals, the "market" may be national; for laborers and some white-collar workers, the market may be local. (Furthermore, some of the statistics that firms are supposed to take into account—for instance, concerning the number of black engineers—are often not available.) [32]

Identify Areas of Underutilization and Concentration. Based on the employee survey, it may turn out that certain groups are underutilized in certain areas or jobs in the company. For example, women and minority males are often underutilized in jobs such as: managers, professionals, technicians, and salesworkers. Once it has been determined that the firm is underutilizing women or minorities, it should determine the *extent* of such underutilization. To do this, survey the labor area (the area in which one can reasonably expect to recruit). One goal here is to compare the number of women and minorities in each job with the percentage of women and minorities in the labor area. Based on this comparison, one can determine the extent of underutilization. A second goal here is to determine the *availability* of promotable and transferable females and minorities in the organization.

Step 5: Develop Goals and Timetables

This is basically a three-step process:

1. First, *set long-range goals*. Here the employer sets the long-range goals and timetables needed to eliminate employment discrimination and the effects of past discrimination. The survey of present employment and analysis of underutilization will provide the basic data needed for formulating these goals.
2. Next, *set annual intermediate targets*. Once long-range goals are set, specific numerical annual targets should be developed (contends the EEOC) for hiring, training, transferring, and promoting women and minorities to reach each long-term goal.
3. Then, *identify the causes of underutilization*. According to the EEOC, achieving long-range goals and intermediate targets begins with identifying present discriminatory barriers in the personnel system. Therefore, the employer, working through the personnel department and supervisors, has to carefully review its entire personnel process, step by step, in order to pinpoint the cause of the underutilization. For example:

Are recruiting efforts inadequate?

Are selection standards too high?

How valid is each of these standards?

In practice, specific procedures with respect to all the personnel management activities discussed in this book are *potential* sources of discrimination. These activities include:

The recruitment process

Selection standards and procedures

Promotion and transfer systems

Wage and salary structure

Benefits

Termination and disciplinary policies

Union contract provisions affecting these areas

Step 6: Develop and Implement Specific Programs to Eliminate Discriminatory Barriers and Achieve Goals

Once the cause of the underutilization has been identified, the next step is to develop and implement specific programs to eliminate the problems. Some of the main steps the EEOC recommends taking to eliminate these barriers include:

In Recruitment

1. Analyze and review recruitment procedures for each job to identify and eliminate discriminatory barriers. For example, avoid recruiting primarily by "word of mouth."
2. Set objective measures to analyze and monitor the recruitment process. For example, develop an "applicant flow" record. This indicates (for each job) applicant name, race, national origin, sex, referral source, date of application, and position applied for. It should also indicate whether a job offer was or was not made. As another example, retain records of minorities and females not hired, who interviewed them, and written reasons for not hiring.
3. Train persons involved in the employment process to use valid standards and to support affirmative action goals. This includes everyone who recruits, interviews, selects, hires, places, promotes, trains, etc.
4. Institute affirmative action programs to recruit for all jobs where underutilization has been identified. For example, use minorities and females as recruiters. Do not place classified ads under "male"/"female" listings. Advertise in media directed toward minorities and women. Include the phrase "equal opportunity employer, M/F" in all advertising. Emphasize your affirmative action policy in all dealings with your employment agencies.

In Selection Standards and Procedures

1. Remember that an employer generally should not use any pre-employment enquiries or tests that disproportionately screen out minorities or females

unless they are valid predictors of job performance. Remember this also includes: biographical information on application blanks; background checks; specific educational or work experience requirements; and interviews.

2. Remember that the EEOC has also found that many common inquiries made on application forms disproportionately reject minorities and females and are *usually* not job-related. These include questions on, for example: arrest and conviction records; credit rating; marital, and family status; age and date of birth; availability for Saturday or Sunday work; and appearance (such as length or style of hair).

In Promotion and Transfer

Here again, analyze all current practices to identify and remove discriminatory barriers. For example:

1. What are the present policies or practices affecting transfer and promotion? Who makes decisions?
2. What are the requirements and procedures for promotion and transfer? Do they adversely affect minorities or females? Is the requirement a valid one?
3. Do the performance evaluations meet the requirements of the EEOC for objective selection guidelines?
4. Are adequate records kept to monitor transfers and promotions?

Wage and Salary Structure. Here, the equal pay act requires that equal wages be paid for substantially similar work performed by men and women. Similarly, Title VII requires equal pay regardless of race, national origin, religion, or sex. Therefore, make a careful review to assure nondiscrimination in compensation, benefits, and conditions of employment. Compare job descriptions and actual functions of jobs held by men and women of all racial groups.

Benefits. Review all benefits and conditions of employment to see that they are equally available without discrimination. This includes medical, hospital, accident or life insurance; retirement benefits; pension, profit sharing, and bonus plans; leave, and other terms, conditions, and privileges of employment.

Terminations and Disciplinary Actions. The standards for deciding when a person shall be terminated, demoted, disciplined, or recalled should be the same for all employees: they should not be applied differently for minorities or females. For example, courts have found a company rule calling for discharge of an employee whose wages are garnisheed to be racially discriminatory. This is because of the adverse effect on minorities and failure of the company to justify the rule on the basis of "business necessity."

Unions and Collective Bargaining. Remember that both employer and unions are responsible for nondiscrimination under Title VII. An employer cannot blame his failure to take affirmative action on barriers in the union contract.

Therefore, if the affirmative action audit finds discriminatory barriers built into a collective bargaining agreement, the union should be notified, and steps should be taken to make the necessary changes. Every collective bargaining agreement should include a nondiscrimination clause.

Step 7: Establish Internal Audit and Reporting System to Monitor and Evaluate Progress in Each Aspect of the Program

The next step in the affirmative action program should be to establish an auditing system to monitor each of the other steps in the program. The EEOC suggests that quarterly reports be provided by every manager and supervisor to the affirmative action director. These reports should cover such items as:

Survey of current employment by race, national origin, sex, job classification, salary, or wage level;

Analysis of internal and external work force availability by race, national origin, and sex;

Identification of areas of underutilization and establishment of hiring and promotion goals;

Records on applicant flow and each step of the selection process: hires, placements, promotions, requests for transfers, transfers, and training program participation by race, national origin, and sex;

Sources of referrals and hires, by race, national origin, and sex;

Resignations, layoffs, and dismissals by race, national origin, and sex;

Progress of company and subunits toward affirmative action goals.

Step 8: Develop Support of Company and Community Programs

As a final step in the affirmative action program, develop (and provide support of) company and community programs. For example, provide training for supervisors concerning their legal responsibilities with respect to affirmative action. Provide additional "support services" that may be helpful in recruiting and retaining minority and female employees, such as personal counseling, transportation, day-care facilities, and housing.

Cooperate with job-related community programs. These include the National Alliance of Businessmen, The Urban Coalition, and various community relations boards.

Affirmative Action: Two Basic Strategies [33]

When designing an affirmative action plan, personnel management can choose either of two basic strategies to pursue—the "good faith effort" strategy or the "quota" strategy—each with its own risks to the employer. The first focusses on identifying and eliminating the obstacles to hiring and promoting women and minorities, on the assumption that eliminating these obstacles will result in increased utilization of women and minorities. The quota strategy, on the other hand, mandates "bottom line" results by instituting hiring and promotion restrictions.

The Good Faith Effort Strategy.   This strategy is aimed at modifying the practices and procedures that have contributed to the exclusion or underutilization of minority groups or females. Specific actions here might include placing advertisements where they can reach target groups, supporting day-care services and flexible working hours for women with small children, and establishing a training program to enable minority-group members to better compete for entry level jobs. The basic assumption here is that if existing obstacles are identified and eliminated the desired results (improved utilization of minority members and women) will follow.

The basic risk here is that if the desired results are *not* achieved (in terms of hiring or promoting more minorities or women), the employer must then convince the EEO compliance officer that a "reasonable effort" to hire or promote specific numbers of protected individuals had taken place, and that failure to do so resulted from factors outside the employer's control. Should management fail to do this, it will find itself in an unenviable negotiating position. The EEOC compliance officer has considerable leverage in the form of economic sanctions (through contract termination) and through legal action. In the absence of results, the employer may find it has little power to resist any recommendations the compliance officer might make with respect to the employer taking additional steps to eliminate the effects of past discriminatory actions.

The Quota Strategy.   Whereas the good faith strategy attempts to eliminate obstacles and thereby get results, the quota strategy aims at mandating results through hiring and promotion restrictions. With the quota strategy, "desirable" hiring goals are operationally treated as *required* employment quotas.

Perhaps the main risk here is the possibility of being sued for "reverse discrimination." [34] Two recent supreme court decisions highlight this problem. In one, white student Allan Bakke had been denied admission to the University of California at Davis Medical School, allegedly because of the school's affirmative action quota system. In a five-four vote, the court struck down a policy that made race the only factor in considering applications for a certain number of class openings at the school, thus allowing Bakke to be admitted. In a second, industrial case, however, the court held for the company. By a five-two vote, the court rejected the claim of Brian Weber, a white employee of the Kaiser Aluminum and Chemical Company. Weber, a 32-year-old lab technician had claimed that a union-management plan that reserved 50% of certain training positions for minority workers violated the anti-discrimination provisions of the Civil Rights Act of 1964 by discriminating against white males. In its opinion, the court specifically avoided detailing "the line of demarcation between permissible and impermissible affirmative action plans." They avoided, in other words, clarifying the elements of an "acceptable" or "unacceptable" affirmative action plan,

50   focussing instead on the unique characteristics of the Kaiser situation. In its majority opinion, however, the court did state that Title VII of the Civil Rights Act of 1964 was not intended to forbid all race-related affirmative action. The effect of the court's decision was to permit Kaiser to continue allowing minorities and females with less minority than Weber (and other white males) to be admitted to the training program. Again, however, the court's decision is a narrow one, stating only that Kaiser's plan at that specific plant was permissible. The questions of when preferential treatment becomes discrimination, and under what circumstances discrimination will be temporarily permitted have yet to be answered, therefore.

A Practical Approach. [35]   According to one writer "these legal uncertainties indicate that, for the present, a strategy based on quotas should be rejected and the attention of the human resources manager directed instead toward improving the effectiveness of an affirmative action plan based on the good faith effort strategy." The viability of such a strategy, however, obviously depends on the employer engaging in activities which will in fact convince a compliance officer that a good-faith-effort to improve the status of minorities and women in the organization has indeed been made. An employer might reasonably ask, therefore, "what specific actions should I take to be able to show that I have in fact made a good faith effort?"

One recent study was aimed at answering this question. Questionnaires were sent to EEOC compliance officers who were asked to rate about 30 possible actions on their importance in evaluating the compliance effort of a hypothetical company. The company was described as having performed an acceptable work force utilization analysis that indicated underutilization in several blue collar and white collar groups. It was also assumed that acceptable goals and timetables for correcting the underutilization had been established.

As summarized in Exhibit 2.4, the results of this study indicated that there were six main areas for action:

1. Increasing the minority/female applicant flow;
2. Demonstrating top-management support for the equal employment policy;
3. Demonstrating equal employment commitment to the community;
4. Keeping employees informed;
5. Broadening the work skills of incumbent employees; and
6. Internalizing the equal employment policy.

Each of these six "areas for action," along with specific actions are presented in the exhibit. For example, *increasing minority/female applicant flow* might involve actions like "include minority colleges and universities in campus recruitment programs," and "retain applications of unhired minority/female applicants to be reveiwed as vacancies occur." In summary, this researcher suggests pursuing an effective good faith effort rather than a quota strategy, and he contends that taking actions like those listed in the exhibit (or, similarly, like those recommended by the EEOC in the 8 step program described previously) can help to insure that the good faith effort is in fact an effective one.

Exhibit 2.4   Specific Actions in a "Good Faith Effort" Strategy   51

Areas for Action	Overall Objectives	Possible Tactics
1. Increasing minority/female applicant flow	To ensure that minorities and females are not systemically excluded; and to encourage those individuals to apply.	1. Include minority colleges and universities in campus recruitment programs. 2. Place employment advertising in minority-oriented print and broadcast media. 3. Retain applications of unhired minority/female applicants to be reviewed as vacancies occur.
2. Demonstrating top-management support for EEO policy	To indicate to all employees that top management considers affirmative action and equal employment opportunity important.	1. Prepare written reports evaluating progress toward affirmative action goals as frequently as other management control reports are prepared. 2. Involve the line supervisors in the establishment of the affirmative action hiring goals. 3. Appoint an EEO coordinator who is both highly visible within the facility and from a department other than personnel.
3. Demonstrating EEO commitment to the local community	To indicate to the public and local labor market management's concern for equal employment opportunity.	1. Appoint key management personnel to serve on community relations board or similar organizations. 2. Establish a formal EEO complaint procedure within the facility. 3. Establish an on-the-job training program at the facility. 4. Establish or support existing child care facilities.
4. Keeping employees informed	To communicate to employees the specifics of the affirmative action programs, including their rights, benefits, and opportunities.	1. Discuss EEO matters, such as program success and new program efforts in internal newsletter. 2. Display EEO policy statement in work areas. 3. Explain the EEO policy, job posting procedures, tuition refund programs, and so on, during the new employee orientation procedure.
5. Broadening skills of incumbent employees	To increase the advancement opportunities and potential of employees.	1. Provide tuition refund benefits to all employees. 2. Institute a job-rotation program within work groups.
6. Internalizing the EEO policy	To encourage adherence to the EEO policy through modification of the organization's control, communication, and reward systems.	1. incorporate affirmative action progress into the performance evaluations of line supervisors. 2. Directly notify eligible employees of advancement and training opportunities as vacancies occur. 3. Formalize and communicate sanctions for violations of EEO policy.

1. Legislation barring discrimination is nothing new. For example, the fifth amendment of the U.S. Constitution (ratified in 1791) states that no person shall be deprived of life, liberty, or property without due process of law.

2. As a reaction to changing values in America; new legislation barring employment discrimination has been passed in the last two decades. This includes: Title VII of the 1964 Civil Rights Act (as amended) (which bars discrimination because of race, color, religion, sex, or national origin); various executive orders; federal guidelines (covering procedures for validating employee selection tools, etc.); the Equal Pay Act of 1963; and the Age Discrimination in Employment Act of 1967. In addition, various court decisions (such as *Griggs* v. *Duke Power Company*), and state and local laws bar various aspects of discrimination.

3. The EEOC was created by Title VII of the Civil Rights Act. It is empowered to try conciliating discrimination complaints, but if this fails the EEOC has the power to go directly to court to enforce the law.

4. A person who feels he or she has been discriminated against by a personnel procedure need only prove that the procedure has an *adverse impact* on members of his or her minority group. There are four criteria he or she can apply: disparate rejection rates, restricted policy, population comparisons, and the McDonnell–Douglas test. Once the person has shown adverse impact to the satisfaction of the court, the burden of proof shifts to the employer to prove that the qualification is job-related (and applied fairly to both minorities and nonminorities).

5. Various specific discriminatory personnel management practices that an employer should probably avoid were discussed:

In recruitment. An employer usually should not rely on "word of mouth" advertising, nor give false or misleading information to minority group members. Also, (usually) do not specify the desired sex in advertising or in any way suggest that applicants 40–65 years of age might be discriminated against.

In selection. Avoid using any educational or other requirements where (1) it can be shown that minority group members are less likely to possess the qualification, and (2) where such requirement is also not job-related. Tests that disproportionately screen out minorities and women *and that are not job-related* are deemed unlawful by the courts. Do not give preference to relatives of current employees (when most are nonminority), nor specify physical characteristics unless it can be proven they are needed for job performance. Similarly, a person's arrest record should not be used to automatically disqualify him or her for a position, nor should a person be fired whose salary has been garnisheed. Remember that one *can* use various tests and standards, but one must prove that they are job-related, or show that they're not used to discriminate against protected groups.

In promotion, transfer, layoff, and benefits: Collective bargaining agreements with requirements like "previous experience" for promotion or transfer have been held to be discriminatory.

6. There are two basic defenses an employer can use in the event of a discriminatory practice allegation. The first is "business necessity." Attempts to show that tests (or other selection standards) are valid is one example of this defense. "Bona fide occupational qualification" is the second defense. This is applied where, for example, religion, national origin, or sex is a "bona fide" requirement of the job (such as for actors or actresses). An employer's "good intentions" or a collective bargaining agreement are not defenses.

7. Eight steps in an affirmative action program (based on suggestions from the EEOC), are:

1. Issue a written equal employment *policy*.
2. *Appoint* a top official.
3. *Publicize* policy.
4. *Survey* present minority and female employment.
5. *Develop* goals and timetables.
6. Develop and implement *specific programs* to achieve goals.
7. Establish an *internal audit* and reporting system.
8. *Develop support* of in-house and community programs.

"Friendly Visits" from the EEOC*

The Synco Rubber Corporation was established during the Second World War in response to the critical shortage of natural rubber which developed when the United States was cut off from its suppliers in Malaya and the East Indies. The U.S. government had immediately created the Rubber Reserve Company to accelerate research and development of a synthetic rubber, and during the next decade of its existence Synco used this research to grow to a position of eminence in the production of synthetic rubber. When the government placed Synco up for bids in the mid-fifties, it was understandable that the bidding was very competitive. In the end, however, the several independent and friendly, but competitive, companies that had managed Synco for the government succeeded in securing its ownership.

Synco retained its home office building and main plant in Trevor City, a deep south city with a population of 200,000 which is growing due to recent industrial expansion in the area. The management of the corporation also remained relatively intact after the formal change in ownership, and very little change in management practices or personnel policies were felt by the workers out in the rubber plant operation.

In general, four main categories of jobs were present in the plant operation: operators, laboratory technicians, maintenance craftsmen, and laborers. Shortly after the change in ownership, several local unions were organized by the men in the various job categories and these unions were readily accepted by Synco's management as an example of good faith in their workers. Each union represented a craft or occupation, and each union entered into collective bargaining on its own resources.

The first three job categories, i.e., operators, laboratory technicians, and maintenance craftsmen, had been traditionally filled with white job applicants due to educational and cultural demands. The laborer jobs had always been filled with black job applicants due to these same demands and pressures. Over the earlier period of government ownership, this practice of having "racial job categories" had inadvertently become an implicitly accepted fact of life by management and workers alike. Management was concerned with "more pressing matters" when "formal" owership changed hands, so the white and black workers remained segregated in all areas that did not directly interfere with completion of their jobs; i.e., dressing rooms, eating facilities, drinking fountains, etc. In fact, when a single intelligence test was installed as a

* This case was prepared by Lee D. Stokes of Louisiana State University, Baton Rouge, under the supervision of Leon C. Megginson, as a basis for class discussion. Cases are not designed to present illustrations of either correct or incorrect handling of administrative situations. All names have been disguised. Reprinted by permission from Robert D. Hay, Edmund R. Gray, and James E. Gates, *Business and Society* (Cincinnati: Southwestern Publishing Company, 1976), pp. 236–239.

"general" hiring procedure in 1958, only white applicants for jobs were given the test. It was not until 1961 when Al Royens was hired as Training and Employment Manager that blacks could also receive the hiring test.

Early in 1966, Bob Kiligan was promoted from Labor Relations Manager to Industrial Relations Director. Bob had joined Synco's management team in 1961 at the age of 28 after working for the Teamsters Union as an organizer while he worked on his Master's Degree in Industrial Relations at one of the better universities in the East. During one of his frequent visits to one of the owner companies, Felbs & Dobbs Company, Inc., the subject of Synco's hiring procedures was discussed and Bob decided that a complete employment test battery should be developed for Synco. Shortly thereafter, Felbs & Dobbs sent in a test specialist to develop the battery. The specialist set up the battery during a period of one week based upon his objective observations and his intuitive but well trained feelings concerning the various job categories present in Synco's rubber plant operation. Both Bob Kiligan and Al Royens were pleased with their "more professional looking" test battery.

About a year later, Bob Kiligan received a visit from a representative of the United States Equal Employment Opportunities Commission (EEOC). The representative was a Negro lawyer in his late twenties, and he seemed quite friendly and open in his manner. He informed Bob that complaints had been filed in his office by two of Synco's laborers charging racial discrimination in Synco's promotion policies. Both of the employees, Sy Washington and Willie Nord, claimed that they had applied for different job categories when the job openings were advertised on the company bulletin board, a practice initiated by Al Royens to implement the policy of "promotion from within." They felt that they had been consistently passed over for these promotions in favor of white workers with the same qualifications as their own. Bob Kiligan assured the EEOC representative that he would look into the matter immediately and inform him in writing of the results of his investigation.

After the government representative had left his office, Bob decided to handle the investigation personally. He had the reputation of doing things "himself," and he put all of his "lone wolf" experience into putting together the facts available. The company records showed that Sy Washington had been employed as a laborer by Synco since 1956, and that he had indeed applied for several promotion opportunities over the last two years. Although the employment tests were one of the main criteria used in promotion decisions, Washington had never received any tests due to the fact that there were no tests when he was hired in 1956. Washington had been turned down for promotion each time he applied due to "just satisfactory" work ratings and the fact that his superior did not consider him to be "too bright."

Willie Nord, who was several years younger than Washington at age 25, had been employed as a laborer in 1961 and had received the hiring test in use at that time. Nord's applications for promotion opportunities over the last two years had been turned down due to his low test scores and his supervisor's evaluation that Nord was also not "too bright" and had to be supervised constantly.

Kiligan then checked the personnel folders of the men who had been accepted for promotion. He noted that all of these men had done well on the original test or the new test battery and that each had received many excellent ratings from their supervisors before they had been promoted.

In meeting with the supervisors of the two laborers, Kiligan inquired if they had been approached by the men themselves or their union representative concerning the

56   fact that they had not received any promotions. Both of the supervisors remembered comments by the men that they were upset due to being consistently passed over for promotion, but neither supervisor had been approached by the laborers' union questioning this consistency. Neither supervisor had felt that the discontent shown by the men was serious enough to warrant an "upward" communication. The supervisors reiterated their positions that neither Washington nor Nord were "bright" enough to deserve a promotion into another job category.

When Bob Kiligan arrived back at his office, he called Al Royens into his office and told him that he wanted all of the present employees to have a chance to take the new employment test battery. Al immediately set about accomplishing this task and completed it sooner than expected due to the fact that many of the old employees who had not been tested did not want to take the test battery regardless of its importance as a promotion criterion.

Bob Kiligan wrote the EEOC office concerning the results of his investigation and the actions he had taken to test all of the plant workers that were interested in being tested. He also informed the EEOC that the concerned laborers had taken the test battery and that their scores on the battery when combined with their supervisor's ratings still showed them to be unsuitable for promotion to a better paying job category. He assured the EEOC that all the employees who had been promoted had received much higher scores on the test battery and much better work ratings by their supervisors before they had received promotions. Kiligan ended the letter by expressing his feelings that the introduction of standard testing and ratings for all employees had corrected all possible deficits in Synco's promotion policies and that the present system was fair and non-discriminatory.

A year and a few months went by without a reply from the EEOC. Neither the laborers' union nor the concerned employees themselves were heard from concerning the promotion matter. Both Sy Washington and Willie Nord, however, had tried again, unsuccessfully, to be promoted. Bob Kiligan left Synco to accept the position of Industrial Relations Director in another company and he was replaced by Glenn Doyle.

Doyle was an "old hand" at industrial relations as he had consistently worked in one area or another concerned with industrial relations ever since he had received his law degree late in the thirties. He had the reputation of being tough, but fair, in all of his dealings with both individual employees and their unions.

One morning Glenn Doyle was studying the facts of an arbitration outcome when the lawyer from the EEOC called for an appointment. Doyle granted the appointment for an afternoon later in the week, and after he hung up the phone, he called in Al Royens to see what he knew about the matter. Al gave him the facts of the case that he had been involved with, and Doyle obtained the rest of his information from the reports and letter written by Bob Kiligan. Glenn then phoned some of his friends in industrial relations positions in other companies to obtain information about the lawyer who was to "visit." With all of this information at his disposal, Glenn formulated his strategy for dealing with the matter.

Later that week, Glenn Doyle and Al Royens both greeted the lawyer from EEOC when he arrived and all three men went into Glenn's office. Again the young lawyer was as congenial as could be expected under the circumstances and he quickly got down to business.

"Mr. Doyle, our office has investigated the discrimination complaints filed by two of your employees, Mr. Nord and Mr. Washington, and we have also taken into account the comments and actions described in a letter to our office from Mr. Kiligan, your predecessor. In the EEOC's opinion, three separate and indisputable facts stand out in this case. First, the segregation apparent in your dressing rooms, washrooms, and eating and drinking facilities tend to support an atmosphere of discrimination at Synco. Second, there are no Negroes employed by Synco in anything other than menial type jobs, and this also supports contentions of discrimination in your corporation. Third, we have noticed that the tests used as promotion criteria have not been shown to be relevant to job performance at Synco."

The young lawyer sat forward in his chair a little, looking directly into Glenn Doyle's eyes, and smiled in a friendly manner before he said, "When all of these facts are combined, we feel the evidence weighs heavily that our clients have been discriminated against at Synco in terms of promotion opportunities, if not in other areas also. Now what the EEOC wants to know is this: what does Synco plan to do to assure fair opportunities for our clients, to repay these two men for the personal injury and economic loss they have suffered, and to assure that the same situation does not occur again with other minority employees?"

Questions

[See the questions in step 2 of the Experiential Exercise below.]

EXPERIENTIAL EXERCISE

Purpose: The purpose of this exercise is to provide practice in analyzing and applying knowledge of equal opportunity legislation to a realistic problem.

Required Understanding: Be thoroughly familiar with the material presented in this chapter. In addition read "Friendly Visits" from the EEOC, the case on which this experiential exercise is based.

How to Set Up the Exercise/Instructions:

1. Divide the class into groups of four or five students.
2. Each group should develop answers to the following questions:
   a. What was wrong about the way Bob Kiligan and Al Royens handled the first visit from the EEOC?
   b. How did the EEOC lawyer prove "adverse impact?"
   c. Cite specific discriminatory personnel practices at Synco Rubber Company in various personnel management areas (recruitment, selection, etc.).
   d. How could the Synco Company defend themselves against the allegations of discriminatory practice?
3. Develop the outline of an affirmative action program for Synco Rubber Company.
4. If time permits, a spokesman from each group can present his or her group's findings. Would it make sense for this company to try to defend itself against the discrimination allegations?

DISCUSSION QUESTIONS

1. What is Title VII? What does it say?
2. What important precedents were set by the *Griggs* v. *Duke Power Company* case? The *Albemarle* v. *Moody* case?
3. What is adverse impact? How can it be proven?
4. Assume you are a supervisor on an assembly line: you are responsible for hiring subordinates, supervising them, and recommending them for promotion. Compile a list of discriminatory management practices you should avoid.
5. Explain the defenses and exceptions of discriminatory practice allegations.
6. What is the difference between affirmative action and equal employment opportunity?

NOTES

1. Portions of this chapter based on or quoted from "Principles of Employment Discrimination Law," International Association of Official Human Rights Agencies (Washington, D.C.). In addition, see W. Clay Hamner and Frank Schmidt, *Contemporary Problems in Personnel*, rev. ed. (Chicago: St. Clair, 1977), Chapter 3. Employment discrimination law is a changing field, and the appropriateness of the rules, guidelines, and conclusions in this book may also be affected by factors unique to an employer's operation; they should therefore be reviewed by the employer's attorney before implementation.

2. James Higgins, "A Manager's Guide to the Equal Employment Opportunity Laws," *Personnel Journal* (August 1976), p. 406.

3. The Equal Employment Opportunity Act of 1972, Subcommittee on Labor of the Committee on Labor and Public Welfare, United States Senate (March 1972), p. 3. In general, it is not discrimination, but *unfair* discrimination against a person merely because of that person's race, age, sex, national origin, or religion that is forbidden by Federal Statutes. In the Federal Government's uniform employee selection guidelines, "unfair" discrimination is defined as follows: "Unfairness is demonstrated through a showing that members of a particular group perform better or poorer on the job than their scores on the selection procedure (test, etc.) would indicate through comparison with how members of other groups perform. . . ." For a discussion of the meaning of "fairness" see James Ledvinka, "The statistical definition of fairness in the Federal selection guidelines and its implications for minority employment," *Personnel Psychology*, Vol. 32, (August 1979), pp. 551–562. In other words, a selection device (like a test) may discriminate—say, between low and high performers. It is *unfair* discrimination that is illegal, discrimination that is based *solely* on the persons race, age, sex, national origin, or religion.

4. "Affirmative Action and Equal Employment," U.S. Equal Employment Opportunity Commission, January 1974.

5. Thomas Dhanens, "Implications of the New EEOC Guidelines," *Personnel* (September–October 1979), pp. 32–39.

6. While most courts have given very heavy weight to these guidelines, Chief Justice Burger, in dissenting with the majority in a recent case (*Albemarle Paper Co.* v. *Moody*), recommends against requiring "slavish adherence to the guidelines. . . ." See C. Paul Sparks, "The Not So Uniform Employee Selection Guidelines," *Personnel Administrator* (February 1977), p. 37.

7. For a review, see "Principles of Employment Discrimination Law," International Association of Official Human Rights Agencies.

8. Lloyd L. Ruch, "The Impact of Employment Procedures of the Supreme Court Decision in the *Duke Power* Case," *Personnel Journal*, Vol. 50 (1971), pp. 777–783; reprinted in Hamner and Schmidt, *Contemporary Problems in Personnel*, p. 117.

9. James Ledvinka and Lyle Schoenfeldt, "Legal Developments in Employment Testing: Albemarle and Beyond," *Personnel Psychology*, Vol. 31, No. 1 (Spring 1978), pp. 1–13.

10. It should be noted that the court, in its *Albemarle* opinion, made one important modification regarding the EEOC guidelines. The guidelines required that employers using tests which screened out disproportionate numbers of minorities or women had to "validate" those tests—prove that they did in fact predict performance on the job—*and also had to prove that there was no other alternative screening device the employer could use that did not screen out disproportionate numbers of minorities or women.* This second requirement proved a "virtually impossible burden for employers." Up through the *Griggs* decision, in other words, it was not enough to just validate the test; instead, the employer also had to show that some other tests or screening tool was not available which was (1) also valid but which (2) did not screen out a disproportionate number of minorities or women. In the *Albemarle* case the court held that the burden of proof was no longer on the employer for showing that there was no suitable alternative screening device available. Instead, the burden is now on the charging party (the person discriminated against) to show that a suitable alternative *is* available. Ledvinka and Schoenfeldt, p. 4; Gary Lubben, Duane Thompson, and Charles Klasson, "Performance Appraisal: The Legal Implications of Title 7," *Personnel*, 1980, pp. 11–21. Note, however, that the *new* uniform guidelines (section 3b) still seem to insist that employers should find and use the selection procedure that has the least adverse impact. This point, therefore, is still a matter of debate.

11. James Ledvinka and Robert Gatewood, "EEO Issues with Pre-employment Inquiries," *The Personnel Administrator*, Vol. 22, No. 2 (February 1977), pp. 22–26.

12. Ruch.

13. John Klinfelter and James Thompkins, "Adverse Impact in Employment Selection," *Public Personnel Management* (May–June 1976), pp. 199–204.

14. *Ibid.*, p. 200.

15. H. John Bernardin, Richard Beatly, Walter Jensen see, "The New Uniform Guidelines On Employee Selection Procedures in the Context of University Personnel Decisions," *Personnel Psychology*, Vol. 33 (Summer 1980), pp. 301–316.

16. See Howard Bloch and Robert Pennington, "Labor Market Analysis as a Test of Discrimination," *Personnel Journal* (August 1980), pp. 649–652.

17. International Association of Official Human Rights Agencies, "Principles of Employment Discrimination Laws;" James M. Higgins, "A Manager's Guide to the Equal Employment Opportunity Laws," *Personnel Journal* (August 1976).

18. *Robinson v. Lorillard Corporation*, 444F. 2D. 791, 798, C.A. 4, 1971.

19. "Principles of Employment Discrimination Law."

20. *Ibid.*

21. *Ibid.*

22. *Ibid.*

23. Wayne Cascio, *Applied Psychology in Personnel Management* (Reston, Va.: Reston Publishing, 1978), p. 25.

24. James Ledvinka and Robert Gatewood, "EEO Issues with Pre-employment Inquiries," *The Personnel Administrator*, Vol. 22, No. 2 (February 1977), pp. 22–26.

25. This and several of the following questions are based on Ledvinka and Gatewood.

26. "Principles of Employment Discrimination Law."

27. Commerce Clearinghouse, *Employment Practices Decisions* (June 11, 1977), pp. 75–79; *Time Magazine* (June 13, 1977), p. 60.

28. This is based on Affirmative Action and Equal Employment, U.S. Equal Employment Opportunity Commission, Washington, D.C. (January 1974), 2 volumes; and Antonia Handler Chayes, "Make Your Equal Opportunity Program Court Proof," *Harvard Business Review* (September–October 1974), pp. 81–89.

29. Higgins, "A Manager's Guide to the Equal Opportunity Employment Laws," p. 410.

30. *Ibid.*

31. See Theodore Purcell, "How G.E. Measures Managers in Fair Employment," *Harvard Business Review* (November–December 1975).

32. For a discussion of this, see Howard Bloch and Robert Pennington, "Labor Market Analysis as a Test of Discrimination," *Personnel Journal*, Vol. 59 (August 1980), pp. 649–652.

33. Kenneth Marino, "Conducting an Internal Compliance Review of Affirmative Action," *Personnel* (March–April 1980), pp. 24–34.

34. See, for example, Lewis Ringler, "EEO Arrangements and Consent Decrees May Be Booby Traps!" *The Personnel Administrator*, Vol. 22 (February 1977), pp. 16–21. Reprinted in Craig Schneir and Richard Beatty, *Personnel Administrators Today* (Reading: Addison Wesley, 1978), pp. 576–583.

35. Kenneth Marino, "Conducting an Internal Compliance Review of Affirmative Action," *Personnel* (March–April 1980), pp. 24–34.

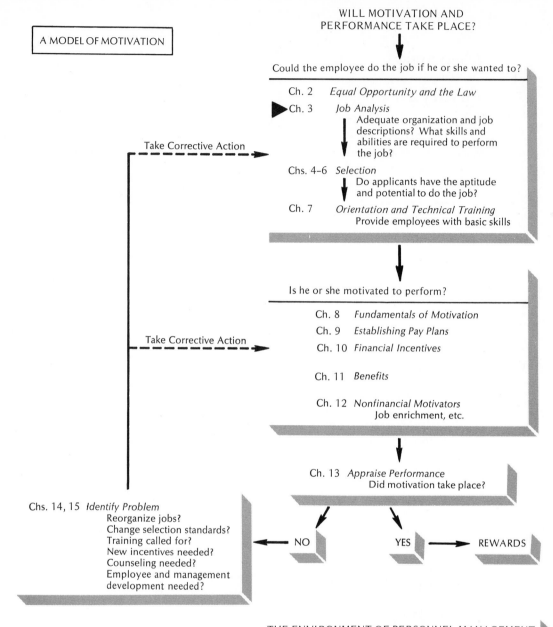

A MODEL OF MOTIVATION

WILL MOTIVATION AND
PERFORMANCE TAKE PLACE?

Could the employee do the job if he or she wanted to?

Ch. 2   *Equal Opportunity and the Law*

Ch. 3   *Job Analysis*
           Adequate organization and job
           descriptions? What skills and
           abilities are required to perform
           the job?

Chs. 4–6 *Selection*
           Do applicants have the aptitude
           and potential to do the job?

Ch. 7   *Orientation and Technical Training*
           Provide employees with basic skills

Take Corrective Action

Is he or she motivated to perform?

Ch. 8   *Fundamentals of Motivation*

Ch. 9   *Establishing Pay Plans*

Ch. 10   *Financial Incentives*

Ch. 11   *Benefits*

Ch. 12   *Nonfinancial Motivators*
           Job enrichment, etc.

Take Corrective Action

Ch. 13   *Appraise Performance*
           Did motivation take place?

Chs. 14, 15   *Identify Problem*
               Reorganize jobs?
               Change selection standards?
               Training called for?
               New incentives needed?
               Counseling needed?
               Employee and management
               development needed?

NO   YES   REWARDS

THE ENVIRONMENT OF PERSONNEL MANAGEMENT

Ch. 16   *Labor Relations and Grievances*

Ch. 17   *Employee Safety and Health*

Ch. 18   *Personnel Management and the
           Quality of Work Life*

When you finish studying

3 # Organizing and Analyzing Jobs

You should be able to:

1. *Develop an organization chart.*

2. *Compare and contrast "purpose" departmentation and "functional" departmentation.*

3. *Explain departmentation: by product,*
by customer,
by location,
by business function.

4. *Explain how to perform a "job analysis."*

5. *Explain how to prepare job descriptions and job specifications.*

6. *Compare and contrast six methods of collecting job analysis data.*

OVERVIEW

The main purpose of this chapter is to explain how to "analyze"—determine the specific duties and responsibilities of—a job. First, we discuss some basics of organization structure, including organization charts, departmentation, and span of control. We will then see that developing an overall organization structure is only the first step in "organizing." Next, "job analysis" is required. Here you determine in detail what the job entails and what kind of people should be hired for the job. We discuss several techniques for analyzing jobs and for writing job descriptions. Job analysis is in many ways the first "personnel" activity that affects performance, since it's through job analysis that one determines what the job entails, and what skills and abilities to look for in candidates for the job.

FUNDAMENTALS OF ORGANIZING[1]

The Purpose of Organization

The purpose of organization is to give each person a separate, distinct job and to ensure that these jobs are coordinated in such a way that the organization accomplishes its goals. Except on the very rarest of occasions, organizations are never ends in themselves, but are means to an end—that "end" being the accomplishment of the organization's goals. Thus:

An organization consists of people who carry out differentiated jobs that are coordinated to contribute to the organization's goals.

Organization Charts

The usual way of depicting an organization is with an organization chart, as shown in Exhibit 3.1. These are snapshots of the organization at a particular point in time and show the skeleton of the organization structure in chart form. They provide the title of each manager's position and, by means of connecting lines, show who is accountable to whom, and who is in charge of what department.

Exhibit 3.1   An Example of an Organization Chart

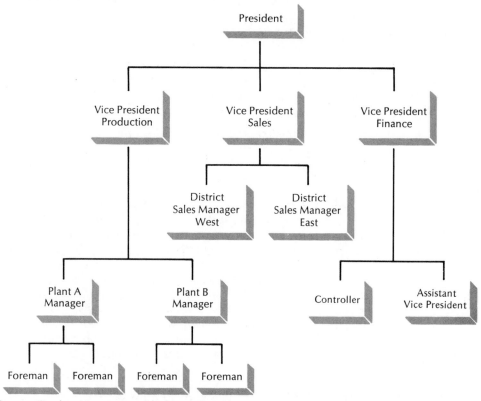

Source: Dessler, *Management Fundamentals*, p. 106.

The organization chart does not show everything about the organization, any more than a road map shows everything about the towns along its routes. Organization charts do not provide job descriptions (such as the one illustrated in Exhibit 3.2). These describe the specifics of each job in terms of the actual day-to-day activities and responsibilities the person is expected to perform. (*Job Analysis,* which we'll also discuss in this chapter, provides these job descriptions.) Nor does the organization chart show the actual patterns of communication in the organization. It also does not show how closely employees are supervised or the actual level of authority and power that each position-holder in the organization has. What it *does* show are the position titles and the "chain of command" from the top of the organization to the bottom.

Exhibit 3.2   Job Description for a Production Control Manager

TITLE	Production Control Manager
REPORTS TO	Assistant Plant Manager
SUPERVISORY RESPONSIBILITY OVER:	Assistant Production Control Manager, Production Control Supervisor, Production Control Schedulers, Clerks, Hourly employees, and such other operations as designated by Plant Manager.
JOB SUMMARY	Directs the activities of: scheduling plant production; procuring raw materials; and maintaining inventory for production and shipping.
DUTIES	Receive, review, enter and promise all orders. Schedule machinery, manpower and materials in such a way that the maximum amount of efficiency is obtained from the operating departments. Prepare production schedules in accordance with customer requirements and applicable specifications. Coordinates production control with technical and production operations and maintenance. Supervises procurement of raw materials and inventory control. Responsible for all production schedules including machine operation, overtime, vacation, etc. Prepares forthcoming schedules and advises Plant Manager, Production Manager, and Department Managers of these schedules. Supervises and coordinates packing, shipping, traffic, freight consolidation operations to insure most economical freight rates and best delivery. Confers with sales offices. Follows up rush and delinquent orders. Confers with Plant Manager, Production Manager, and Plant Accountant in maintaining accurate backlogs by product class. Assist in operations report. Receives, reviews, and compiles daily production reports of plant's progress per department. Performs special projects as required. Has authority to hire, fire, promote, demote, train, discipline and supervise employees under his jurisdiction. Responsible for plant safety, housekeeping, scrap and usage where applicable to his sphere of plant influence. Implements cost reduction and efficiency improvement programs. May be responsible for execution of Union agreement.

Most organizations have, or should have, organization charts because they are helpful in informing employees of what their jobs are and how these jobs relate to others in the organization. On the other hand, many organizations have been quite successful without organization charts, while others have failed in spite of them.

In summary: Organization charts are useful because they:

1. Show titles of each manager's job.
2. Show who is accountable to whom.
3. Show who is in charge of what department.

4. Show what sorts of departments have been established.

5. Show the "chain of command."

6. Let each employee know his job title and "place" in the organization.

But, organization charts do *not* show you:

1. Job descriptions of specific day-to-day duties and responsibilities.

2. Actual patterns of communication in the organization.

3. How closely employees are supervised.

4. The actual level of authority and power each position-holder has.

Departmentation

Every organization has to carry out certain activities in order to accomplish its goals. For a manufacturing firm, these include activities like production, selling, and accounting. Departmentation is the process through which these activities are grouped logically into distinct areas and assigned to managers: it is the organization-wide division of work. It results in "departments"—logical groupings of activities—which also often go by such names as divisions, branches, units, groups, or sections.

Departmentation is a very important process. In fact, when most people think of "organization structure" they are usually thinking about departmentation. This is because it is departments—like "production" and "sales"—that stand out on organization charts.

Departmentation is also a very common phenomenon. The work of the federal government, for example, is divided at its highest levels into the executive, judicial, and legislative branches. The executive branch itself is divided at its highest level into a number of departments, such as those for commerce, labor, and defense. Hospitals typically have such "departments" as intensive care and radiology units. Many companies, like General Motors, have separate "product divisions," such as those for Buicks or Pontiacs; and most also have separate departments for production, sales, and finance. However, though there are many ways to departmentalize organizations, most types of departments are built either around *purposes* such as "industrial customers," or *functions* like "marketing."

Departmentation by Purpose. First, there are three popular "purposes" around which one can build departments: products, customers, and locations.

Departmentation by Product. Departmentation by product is illustrated in Exhibit 3.3, which presents part of the organization chart of the General Motors Corporation. Notice how, at the operating divisions level, the car and truck group is organized around product lines. The division is managed by an executive vice president, and there are separate divisions for Buick, Oldsmobile, Pontiac, and so forth.

Exhibit 3.3   Product Departmentation at General Motors   67

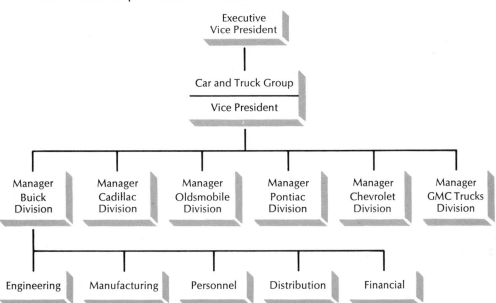

Source: Dessler, *Management Fundamentals*, p. 123.

Departmentation by Customer.   Departmentation by customer is illustrated in Exhibit 3.4, which shows the General Electric Company organization chart. Notice how the company is organized around departments which each serve different "customers." These include aerospace, construction, and consumer products customers.

Departmentation by Location or Area.   This is illustrated in Exhibit 3.5. Many agencies of the federal government are departmentalized by location. For example, the Federal Reserve System is divided into twelve geographical areas centered in cities such as Boston, New York, and San Francisco.

Departmentation by Function.   Next, there are functional types of departments; here closely related functions like advertising, selling, and sales promotion are grouped together into a single department such as marketing.

This type of departmentation is typically the basis on which a new business is organized. The head of a new company asks himself, "What basic functions will have to be performed if the business is to meet its goals?" As illustrated in Exhibit 3.6, in a manufacturing business these *"business functions"* usually would include (at least) manufacturing, sales, and finance and accounting. Thus, departmentalizing a company by business function is probably the most familiar form of departmentation, and activities are grouped around business functions such as production, marketing, and finance.

Exhibit 3.4   Customer Departmentation at General Electric

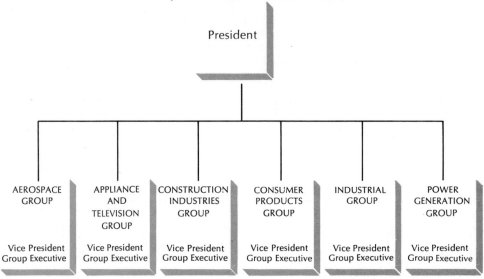

Note: Departments are built around such "customers" as aerospace, appliances and televisions, and construction.

Source: This is only a partial chart, and is adapted from *Corporate Organization Structures*, National Industrial Conference Board, Inc., No. 210 (1968), p. 59.

Exhibit 3.5   Departmentation by Area or Location

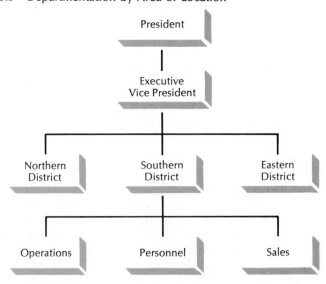

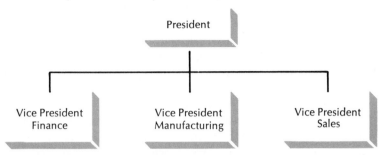

Purpose and Functional Departmentation Compared.   Purpose and function types of departmentation each have their own advantages and disadvantages.
Whether you build departments around products, customers, or locations, for
instance, *purpose* types of departmentation all result in units that are self-
contained, in that there are separate sales, production, personnel, etc., departments *for each* product, customer, or location. Here a single manager is in charge
of all functions (like sales and production) related to the purpose. For example,
the manager of a publisher's high-school division might have his own editing,
manufacturing, and distribution departments. As a result, this division could
usually respond quickly to the changing needs of high-school students since the
manager in charge does not have to rely on (or seek the approval of) editing,
manufacturing, or distribution managers who are not in his own division. The
main disadvantage here is that purpose types of departmentation breed duplication. They very fact that each product, customer, or area department is self-
contained implies that there are several production plants instead of one and
several sales forces instead of one and so on.

Functional-based departments usually have single, large departments like
sales, production, and personnel that serve *all* the company's products. As a
result, the volume of business done in each department is relatively high, and
with this volume typically come increasing returns to scale—employees become
more proficient and thus more productive, and there is less duplication, for
example. Building a department around functions therefore tends to work best
where efficiency is very important. The main disadvantage is that responsibility
for overall coordination lies squarely on the shoulders of one person, usually the
president. This may not be a serious problem when the firm is small or where
there is not a diversity of products. But as size and product diversity increases
the job of coordinating the various functions may prove too great for a single
individual: the organization can lose its responsiveness.

Span of Control

The "span of control" is the number of subordinates reporting *directly* to
a supervisor.

Arguments over what the "best" span of control is have been going on for decades. Early writers recommended a "narrow" span of only 5 or 6 subordinates. The assumption was that the boss could then keep a closer eye on each subordinate. But studies of spans in actual companies clearly show that spans are often much wider. Dale, for example, found that the number of vice presidents reporting to the chief executive in 100 companies varied from 1 to 24. Half the chief executives had spans greater than 9 and half less than 9. Only about a quarter of the companies had spans as narrow as 6.

Many factors combine to determine the best span of control. We know, for example, that the spans of control of lower level managers like foremen are usually much wider than those of top level executives. The reason seems to be that the former's jobs (and those of their subordinates) are less complex. Similarly, we know that jobs which are very routine (such as those on assembly lines or in the bookkeeping units of government bureaus) allow for much wider spans of control than nonroutine jobs (such as managing a research staff).

Delegation

Organizing departments and jobs would be impossible without delegation, which is the pushing-down of authority from superior to subordinate. This is because the assignment of responsibility for some department or job usually goes hand in hand with the delegation of adequate authority to get the task done. For example, it would be inappropriate to assign a subordinate the responsibility for designing a new product, and then tell him he cannot hire designers or choose the best design.

Decentralization

The way many people use the term, decentralization means about the same thing as delegation—simply pushing authority down to subordinates. Decentralization, according to them, is the opposite of "centralization" in which all, or nearly all, of the authority to make decisions and take action is retained by top management.

But decentralization is and was always meant to be more than simply delegation. Decentralization is a philosophy of organization and management, one that implies both selective disbursal and concentration of authority. It involves selectively determining what authority to push down into the organization (for instance, by giving a manager the authority to manage a large plant); developing standing plans (such as policies and rules) to guide subordinates who have this authority delegated to them (for instance, by telling that manager that all expenditures over $100,000 must be approved by you); and implementing selective but adequate controls for monitoring performance (for instance, by having the auditors check the manager's expenditures periodically). Thus, according to Koontz and O'Donnell:

Decentralization is a philosophy of organization and management which

involves both selective delegation of authority, as well as concentration of
authority through the imposition of policies and selective and adequate
control.

WHAT IS JOB ANALYSIS?

Developing an organization structure results in jobs that have to be staffed.
Job analysis is the procedure through which you find out (1) what the job entails, and (2) what kinds of people (in terms of skill and experience) should be
hired for the job. It provides data on job requirements that is then used to
develop *job descriptions* (what the job entails) and *job specifications* (what
kinds of people should be hired for the job).

The Uses of Job Analysis Information

The information produced by the job analysis has four main uses. It is used
for: making recruitment and selection decisions, developing compensation systems, appraising performance, and developing training programs.

Recruitment and Selection.   Job analysis provides information on what the
job entails and what "human requirements" are required to carry out these
activities. This information is the basis on which the employer decides what
sorts of people to recruit and hire.

Compensation.   A clear understanding of what each job entails is also
needed to estimate the value and appropriate compensation for each job. This
is because compensation (in the form of salary, incentives, etc.) is usually tied
to the job's required skills, educational level, safety hazards, etc. Also, many
companies and government agencies classify similar jobs into categories (such
as Secretary III, Accountant II, etc.), and two of the job analysis techniques
discussed in this chapter are especially appropriate for classifying jobs for compensation purposes.

Performance Appraisal.   Appraising performance involves comparing each
employee's actual performance with his or her desired performance. And it is
often through *job analysis* that industrial engineers determine desired performance in terms of standards to be achieved and activities to be performed.

Training.   Job analysis information is also needed for designing training
and development programs because the job description usually shows what sorts
of skills—and therefore training—is required.

The Steps in Job Analysis [2]

There are five steps involved in doing a job analysis, but before any steps
are taken decisions have to be made regarding two things: the purpose of the
job analysis; and who will perform the analysis.

Determining the purpose of the analysis is important because it helps determine how the analysis should be performed. As explained on the following pages there are many methods for collecting job analysis data (methods like interviews, and questionnaires) and some methods are uniquely suited for some purposes (like developing training objectives) but not for others (like developing tests for screening job applicants.) [3] Therefore, it is usually essential that a decision be made regarding *why* the analysis is being performed before a decision is made regarding how it will be performed.

The decision regarding *who* will perform the analysis will usually be determined partly by the specialized nature of job analysis, and partly by the specific method one chooses to use. *In general* a personnel specialist familiar with performing job analyses should be given the responsibility of coordinating the analysis. Depending on the size of the organization and its resources, he or she might be the personnel manager, an in-house job analyst, or an outside consultant, for instance.

Yet, while the specialized nature of job analysis often demands the services of a personnel staff specialist, usually the analysis also requires the active involvement of line managers and, perhaps, the workers whose jobs are being analyzed. The question of exactly who is involved depends on the specific job analysis method one chooses to use. In some instances it may be possible for the staff expert alone to observe the work being done and from these observations develop an accurate description of the duties and responsibilities of the job. In most cases, though, a line supervisor must also get involved—perhaps by filling out a questionnaire listing the activities his or her subordinate performs. And, often, the worker himself may be asked to fill out a questionnaire or answer questions about his or her job. Job analysis is thus a process that usually involves an integrated effort between the staff specialist, the line supervisor, and, perhaps, the worker.

Once the purpose of the job analysis has been clarified, and some thought has been given to who will coordinate it, the following five steps should be taken.

Step 1: Collect Background Information. First, review available background information such as organization charts, "class specifications," and existing job descriptions. *Organization charts* show how the job in question relates to other jobs and where they fit into the overall organization. *Class specifications* describe the general requirements of the *class* of jobs to which the one you are analyzing belongs. They are the classes equivalent to an individual's job description. The existing *job description* (if there is one) provides a good starting point from which to build the revised job description.

Step 2: Select Representative Positions to be Analyzed. It is usually too time-consuming (and quite unnecessary) to analyze, say, the jobs of *all* assembly line workers. Instead, one might select several *representative* positions and analyze these.

Step 3: Collect Job Analysis Data.   The next step is to actually "analyze" the job by collecting data on features of the job, required employee behaviors, and "human requirements" (the traits and abilities needed to perform the job). For this, one or more of the techniques (interviews, questionnaires, etc.) discussed in the next section can be used.

Step 4: Develop a Job Description.   Next, the information collected in Step 3 is used to develop the *job description*. This is a written statement that describes the main features of the job, as well as the activities required to perform the job effectively.

Step 5: Develop the Job Specification.   The final step is to convert the job description statements into a *job specification*. This describes the personal qualities, traits, skills, and background necessary for getting the job done. It may be a separate document, or it may be on the same document as the job description.

TECHNIQUES FOR COLLECTING JOB ANALYSIS DATA

Once background information has been collected (step 1) and the positions to be analyzed have been decided upon (step 2) the next step is to collect the data on the duties, responsibilities, and activities of the job. Various data collection techniques are available, and the most important of these are described in this section. In practice you could use any one of them or combine techniques that best fit the purpose. In those cases where there are several purposes to be served by the information from the job analysis (for example, writing job descriptions and developing a screening test for hiring new employees), combining techniques may be the only alternative because techniques suited for some purposes are often quite unsuited for others.

Basic Job Analysis Techniques [4]

First, there are four basic techniques one can use—interviews, direct observation, questionnaires, and participant logs. These are the techniques that experts have traditionally used to collect job analysis information, and even the more recent advances in job analysis techniques depend on these basic techniques.

Interviews.   The interview is probably the most widely used technique for determining the duties and responsibilities of a job, and its wide use reflects this technique's advantages. [5] Most importantly, interviewing the job incumbant allows that person to report activities and behavior that might not otherwise come to light. For example, important activities that only occur occasionally, or informal communication (between, say a production foreman and the sales manager) which wouldn't appear on the organization chart could be unearthed by a skilled interviewer. In addition, an interview can give management an opportunity to explain the need for and functions of the job analysis as well as allow the interviewee to vent frustrations or views that might otherwise go unnoticed by the organization.

Three types of interviews can be used to collect job analysis data: individual interviews (with each employee); group interviews (with groups of employees who have the same job); and supervisor interviews (with one or more supervisors who are thoroughly knowledgeable about the job being analyzed). Group interviews are normally used when a large number of employees are performing similar, if not identical work, and this group approach is therefore a quick and relatively inexpensive way of learning a lot about the job. As a rule, the workers' immediate supervisor would attend the group session; if not, it is advisable to interview the supervisor separately to get that person's perspective on the duties and responsibilities of the job in question.

The major problem with the interviewing technique is distortion of information, whether due to outright falsification or an honest misunderstanding. [6] Because job analyses are often conducted in conjunction with the implementation of new wage and salary plans there is some tendency for employees to view them as "efficiency evaluations" and as activities that may (and often will) influence their wages. There is thus a tendency for employees to exaggerate certain responsibilities while minimizing others. Obtaining valid information can therefore be a slow and painstaking process.

Although there is no universally accepted procedure for performing one of these interviews, "standard" questions usually include:

What are the major duties of your position? What exactly do you do?

What different physical locations do you work in?

What activities do you participate in?

What exactly do these involve?

What are the responsibilities you have? and

Are there any hazards or unusual working conditions you are exposed to?

There are several things to keep in mind when conducting a job analysis interview. First, the staff specialist and supervisor should work together closely in identifying those workers who know most about the job as well as workers who might be expected to be the most objective in describing their duties and responsibilities. Second, it is obviously important to establish rapport quickly with the interviewee, by knowing the person's name, speaking in easily understood language, briefly reviewing the purpose of the interview, and explaining how the person came to be chosen to be interviewed. Third, the interviewer should usually follow a structured guide or checklist, one that lists questions (like the ones above) and provides space for answers. This ensures that crucial questions can be identified ahead of time and that all interviewers (if there are more than one) cover all the required questions. (On the other hand, the interviewer should also give the worker some leeway in answering questions and provide some "open-ended" questions like "was there anything we didn't cover with our questions." This is to ensure that some important areas were not inadvertently left off the structured guide.) Fourth, when duties are not performed in a regular manner (in other words, where the worker does not perform the same job over and over again many times a day) it is advisable to ask the worker to list his duties *in order of importance* and frequency of occurrence. Finally, after completing the interview remember to verify the data. This is normally done by reviewing the information with the interviewee's immediate supervisor.

Direct Observation. Direct observation is especially useful in jobs that mainly consist of observable physical activity. Jobs like those of janitor, assembly line worker, and accounts receivable clerk are examples of these. Similarly, determining what the job entails through observation usually is *not* appropriate where the job entails a lot of unmeasurable mental activity (lawyer, design engineer) or if the employee is normally expected to engage in important activities that might occur only occasionally—such as a nurse handling emergencies.

Direct observation is often used in conjunction with interviewing. One approach it to observe the worker on the job during a complete work cycle. (This is the time it takes to complete the job—it could be a minute, an hour, a day, or more). Here the observer takes notes of all the job activities observed. Then, after accumulating as much information as possible, the worker is interviewed: here the person is encouraged to clarify points not understood and explain what additional activities he or she performs that had not been observed. Another approach is to observe and interview simultaneously, while the worker performs his or her tasks. There is some advantage to withholding questions until after observations have been made, in that it gives the observer more opportunity to *unobtrusively* observe the employee: This helps reduce the chance that the employee (who knows he or she is "under the microscope") might become anxious or in some way distort the usual routine.

Participant Diary/Logs. With the diary/log approach workers are asked to keep daily logs or lists of things they do during the day. For every activity he or she engages in, the employee records the activity (along with the time) in a log. This can provide management with a very comprehensive picture of the job, especially when it is supplemented with subsequent interviews with the worker and his or her supervisor. Again, however, there is the ever-present danger that the employee might try to exaggerate some activities and underplay others, although the detailed, chronological nature of the log tends to mediate against this.

Questionnaires. Having employees fill out questionnaires in which they describe their duties and responsibilities has long been a popular means of obtaining job analysis information. [7]

The first thing the job analyst has to decide is how structured the questionnaire should be. At one extreme some questionnaires are highly structured checklists. Each employee is presented with an inventory of 100 or more specific duties or tasks (like "change and splice wire") and is asked to indicate whether or not he performs each task and, if so, how much time is normally spent on each. [8] At the other extreme, the questionnaire can be open-ended and simply ask the employee to "describe major duties of your job" and "describe the nature of any independent decisions you make." In practice, the best questionnaire often falls between these two extremes. As illustrated in Exhibit 3.7, the typical job analysis questionnaire might have several open-ended questions, as well as some structured questions concerning, for example, the physical requirements of the job.

Any questionnaire has certain advantages and disadvantages. A main advantage is that questionnaires are a quick and efficient way of obtaining information from a large number of employees—it is usually less costly than interviewing hundreds of workers, for example. On the other hand, developing

Exhibit 3.7 A Job Analysis Questionnaire

Name	Department
Payroll Title	Name, Immediate Supervisor

Instructions: Please read the entire form before making any entries. Answer each question as accurately and carefully as possible. When completed return this form to your supervisor. If you have any questions ask your supervisor.

Your Duties

What duties and tasks do you personally perform daily?

What duties do you perform only at stated intervals such as semi weekly, weekly or monthly? Indicate which period applies to each duty.

What duties do you perform only at irregular intervals?

Supervision of Others

How many employees are directly under your supervision? (List job titles and number of people assigned to each job.)

Do you have full discretionary authority to assign work; correct and discipline; recommend pay increases, transfers, promotions and discharge; and to answer grievances?

Do you only assign work, instruct, and coordinate the activities of your subordinates?

Materials, Tools, and Equipment

What are the principal materials and products that you handle?

List the names of the machines and equipment used in your work.

List the names of the principal hand tools and instruments used in your work.

What is the Source of Your Instructions? (e.g. oral, written, blue prints, specifications, etc.)

What Contacts Are You Required to Make with Persons Other Than Your Immediate Supervisor and Departmental Associates?

   a) Give the job titles and the department or organization of those with whom you deal.

   b) Describe the nature of these contacts.

Exhibit 3.7   *(continued)*   77

Decisions

What decisions do you have to make without consulting your supervisor?

Responsibility

a) Describe the nature of your responsibility for money, machinery, equipment, and reports.

b) What monetary loss can occur through an honest error?

Records and Reports

a) What records and reports do you personally prepare?

b) What is the source of the data?

Checking of Your Work

a) How is your work inspected, checked or verified?

b) Who does this?

Physical Requirements

a) What percentage of the time do you spend in the following working positions?

Standing _____ %,   Sitting_____ %,   Walking about_____ %?

b) What weight in pounds must you personally lift and carry? _____ pounds

c) What percentage of the working day do you actually spend lifting and carrying this weight? _____ %

d) Are any special physical skills, eye-hand coordination, and manual dexterity skills required on your job?

Working Conditions

Describe any conditions present in the location and nature of your work, such as noise, heat, dust, fumes, etc., which you consider unfavorable or disagreeable.

Hazards

Describe the dangers or accident hazards present in your job.

THIS PORTION IS TO BE FILLED OUT BY YOUR SUPERVISOR.

Education Requirements

What is the lowest grade of grammar school, high school, or college required of a person starting in this job?

Previous Experience

a) What kind of previous work experience is necessary for minimum satisfactory performance for a new employee on this job?

b) Give the length of experience required.

Training

Assuming that a new employee on this job has the necessary education and experience to qualify for the work, what training is necessary after the employee is on the job to achieve an acceptable performance level? (Specify training needed and period of time to acquire it.)

_____   _____
     Date   Signature of Supervisor

Source: Dale S. Beach, Personnel (New York: Macmillan, 1970) pp. 194-5.

and testing the questionnaire (making sure the workers understand the questions, for instance) can be an expensive and time-consuming process. Therefore, the high "front end" development costs have to be compared with the time and expense that will be saved by not having to engage in an extensive interviewing program.

Summary. Interviews, observations, diary/logs, and questionnaires are four basic techniques for gathering job analysis data. Since they all provide specific, realistic information about what job incumbents *actually* do, all these techniques are useful for developing job descriptions and, possibly job specifications: In many organizations they are the *only* techniques used for collecting such data. However, when management's purpose is, for example, to group similar jobs into job classes (as it might want to do in developing a pay plan), then one of the more systematic, quantitative techniques discussed below might be more appropriate.

U.S. Civil Service Procedure

The U.S. Civil Service Commission has developed a job analysis technique that aims to provide a standardized procedure by which different jobs can be compared and classified. With this method the information is compiled on a "job analysis record sheet." Here, as illustrated in Exhibit 3.8, identifying information (like job title) and a brief summary of the job are listed first. Next, the personnel specialist lists the job's specific tasks in order of importance. Then, *for each task*, the expert specifies the:

1. Knowledge required (for example, the facts or principles the worker must be acquainted with to do his or her job).
2. Skills required (for example, the skills needed to operate machines or vehicles).
3. Abilities required (for example, mathematical, reasoning, problem solving, or interpersonal abilities).
4. Physical activities involved (for example, pulling, pushing, or carrying).
5. Any special environmental conditions (cramped quarters, vibration, inadequate ventilation, or moving objects).
6. Typical work incidents (for example, performing under stress in emergencies, working with people beyond giving and receiving instructions, or performing repetitive work) and
7. Worker interests areas (the preference the worker should have for activities dealing with "things and objects," or the "communication of data," or "dealing with people," for example). [9]

This is all illustrated in Exhibit 3.8. In this case the first task listed for a "welfare eligibility examiner" is to "decide (determine) eligibility of applicant in order to complete client's application for food stamps using regulatory policies as a guide." Beneath this task are listed the analyst's conclusions concerning the *knowledge* a welfare eligibility examiner is required to have, any *special skills* or abilities, types of *physical activities* involved in this task, special *environmental conditions*, typical *work incidents*, and the sorts of *interests* that would

Exhibit 3.8   Portion of a Completed Civil Service Job Analysis Record Sheet

JOB ANALYSIS RECORD SHEET

Identifying Information

Name of incumbent:	A. Adler
Organization/Unit:	Welfare Services
Title:	Welfare Eligibility Examiner
Date:	11/12/73
Interviewer:	E. Jones

Brief Summary of Job

Conducts interviews, completes applications, determines eligibility, provides information to community sources regarding food stamp program; refers noneligible food stamp applicants to other applicable community resource agencies.

Tasks*

1. Decides (determines) eligibility of applicant in order to complete client's application for food stamps using regulatory policies as guide.

    Knowledge required—
    —Knowledge of contents and meaning of items on standard application form
    —Knowledge of Social-Health Services food stamp regulatory policies
    —Knowledge of statutes relating to Social-Health Services food stamp program

    Skills required—
    —None

    Abilities required—
    —Ability to read and understand complex instructions such as regulatory policies
    —Ability to read and understand a variety of procedural instructions, written and oral, and convert these to proper actions
    —Ability to use simple arithmetic: addition and subtraction
    —Ability to translate requirements into language appropriate to laymen

    Physical Activities—
    —Sedentary

    Environmental Conditions—
    —None

    Typical Work Incidents—
    —Working with people beyond giving and receiving instructions

    Interest areas—
    —Communication of data
    —Business contact with people
    —Working for the presumed good of people

2. Decides upon, describes, and explains other agencies available for client to contact in order to assist and refer client to appropriate community resource using worker's knowledge of resources available and knowledge of client's needs.

    Knowledge required—
    —Knowledge of functions of various assistance agencies
    —Knowledge of community resources available and their locations
    —Knowledge of referral procedures

    Skills required—
    —None

    Abilities required—
    —Ability to extract (discern) persons' needs from oral discussion
    —Ability to give simple oral and written instructions to persons

(Continued)

Physical activities—
  —Sedentary

Environmental conditions—
  —None

Typical work incidents—
  —Working with people beyond giving and receiving instructions

Interest areas—
  —Communication of data
  —Business contact with people
  —Abstract and creative problem solving
  —Working for presumed good of people

---

*This job might typically involve 5 or 6 tasks: For *each* task, list the knowledge, skills, abilities, physical activities, environmental conditions, typical work incidents, and interest areas.

---

correspond to this task. An analyst would typically apply his or her own knowledge of the job as well as information obtained through interviews, observations, logs, or questionnaires in completing the job analysis record sheet. And, since virtually any job can be broken into its component tasks, each of which is then analyzed in terms of knowledge required, skills required, and so forth, the Civil Service method provides a relatively standardized format by which different jobs can be compared, contrasted, and classified. (In other words, the knowledge, skills, and abilities required to perform, say, an assistant fire chief's job can be contrasted with the knowledge, skills, and abilities required to perform a librarians' job, and if the requirements are similar the jobs can be classified together for pay purposes.)

The U.S. Department of Labor Procedure

The U.S. Department of Labor (DOL) Procedure is a widely used method that also attempts to provide a standardized basis by which different jobs can be compared and classified. The heart of this procedure involves describing each job in terms of what an employee does in terms of *data, people,* and *things.*

The basic procedure is as follows. As illustrated in Exhibit 3.9, a set of standard *worker functions* are provided. These describe what a worker can do with respect to data, people, and things. With respect to "data" for example, the basic functions include "synthesizing," "coordinating," and "copying." With respect to "people," the worker functions include "mentoring," "negotiating," and "supervising." With respect to "things," the basic functions include "manipulating," "tending," and "handling." Notice also that each worker function has been assigned an importance level. Thus "coordinating" is "1" while "copying" is "5." If the analyst were analyzing the job of a receptionist/clerk for example, he or she might label the job "5," "6," "7," (copying data, speaking-signaling people, and handling things). On the other hand, a psychiatric aide in a hospital

Exhibit 3.9   Basic Worker Functions

	Data	People	Things
	0 Synthesizing	0 Mentoring	0 Setting up
	1 Coordinating	1 Negotiating	1 Precision working
	2 Analyzing	2 Instructing	2 Operating-controlling
Basic Activities	3 Compiling	3 Supervising	3 Driving-operating
	4 Computing	4 Diverting	4 Manipulating
	5 Copying	5 Persuading	5 Tending
	6 Comparing	6 Speaking-signaling	6 Feeding-offbearing
		7 Serving	7 Handling
		8 Taking instructions-helping	

Note: Determine employee's job "score" on data, people, and things by observing his or her job and determining, for each of the three categories, which of the basic functions illustrates person's job. "0" is high, "6," "8," and "7" are lows in each column.

Source: U. S. Department of Labor, Manpower Administration, Handbook for Analyzing Jobs (Washington, D.C.: U.S. Government Printing Office, 1972), p. 73; reproduced in Benjamin Schneider, *Staffing Organizations* (Santa Monica: Goodyear Publishing, 1976), p. 25.

might be coded "1," "7," "5" in relation to data, people, and things. (In practice, *each task* the worker performed might be analyzed in terms of data, people, and things. Then, the highest combination (say, "4," "6," "5") would be used to identify the job.)

In addition to identifying the data/people/things quantitative score for the job, the analyst also has to identify the "work field" (like cooking) to which the job belongs. He also has to indicate the worker traits (attitudes, temperaments, interests, and so on) that seem necessary for adequate job performance.

A sample of a completed DOL job analysis form for a "dough mixer" in a bakery is presented in Exhibit 3.10. It gives a brief summary of the job and a quantitative score for the job—in this case "5," "6," "2."

One advantage of this procedure is that it results in a quantitative score for the job, and so enables management to classify jobs for compensation purposes. For example, all jobs with the score "5," "6," "2" could now be classified together and paid the same even though one job might be "dough mixer" and another "mechanic's helper." [10]

The Position Analysis Questionnaire

Researchers at Purdue University have developed an even more exacting and certainly more structured questionnaire approach for *quantitatively* describing jobs. Their position analysis questionnaire (PAQ) is usually completed by a job analyst, one who should already be acquainted with the job being analyzed.

Exhibit 3.10   Sample of End Result of Using Department of Labor Job Analysis Technique

---

Sample of the End Result of Using the Department of Labor Job Analysis Technique.

U.S. Department of Labor
Manpower Administration

JOB ANALYSIS SCHEDULE

1. Established Job Title ___ DOUGH MIXER ___

2. Ind. Assign ___ (bake prod.) ___

3. SIC Code(s) and Title(s) ___ 2051 Bread and other bakery products ___

---

4. JOB SUMMARY:

Operates mixing machine to mix ingredients for straight and sponge (yeast) doughs according to established formulas, directs other workers in fermentation of dough, and curs dough into pieces with hand cutter.

---

5. WORK PERFORMED RATINGS: (From Exhibit 3.9)

	D	P	(T)
Worker Functions	Data	People	Things
	5	6	2

Work Field ___ Cooking, Food Preparing ___

---

6. WORKER TRAITS RATINGS: (To be filled in by analyst)

Training time required

Aptitudes

Temperaments

Interests

Physical Demands

Environment Conditions

Source: Adapted from Schneider, *Staffing Organizations*, p. 27.

The PAQ has 194 items (eleven of which are presented in Exhibit 3.11). Note that each of these items (such as "written materials") represents a basic item which may or may not play an important role on the job. The job analyst decides if the item plays a role on the job, and if so to what extent. In Exhibit 3.11, for example, "written materials" received a rating of "4," indicating that written materials (like books and reports) play a *considerable* role on the job,

Exhibit 3.11 Portions of a Completed Page From the Position Analysis Questionnaire

---

INFORMATION INPUT

1 INFORMATION INPUT

1.1 Sources of Job Information

Rate each of the following items in terms of the extent to which it is used by the worker as a source of information in performing his job.

	Extent of Use (U)
NA	Does not apply
1	Nominal/very infrequent
2	Occasional
3	Moderate
4	Considerable
5	Very substantial

1.1.1 Visual Sources of Job Information

1 |4__ Written materials (books, reports, office notes, articles, job instructions, signs, etc.)

2 |2__ Quantitative materials (materials which deal with quantities or amounts, such as graphs, accounts, specifications, tables of numbers, etc.)

3 |1__ Pictorial materials (pictures or picturelike materials used as *sources* of information, for example, drawings, blueprints, diagrams, maps, tracings, photographic films, x-ray films, TV pictures, etc.)

4 |1__ Patterns/related devices (templates, stencils, patterns, etc., used as *sources* of information when *observed* during use; do *not* include here materials described in item 3 above)

5 |2__ Visual displays (dials, gauges, signal lights, radarscopes, speedometers, clocks, etc.)

6 |5__ Measuring devices (rulers, calipers, tire pressure gauges, scales, thickness gauges, pipettes, thermometers, protractors, etc., used to obtain visual information about physical measurements; do *not* include here devices described in item 5 above)

7 |4__ Mechanical devices (tools, equipment, machinery, and other mechanical devices which are *sources* of information when *observed* during use or operation)

8 |3__ Materials in process (parts, materials, objects, etc., which are *sources* of information when being modified, worked on, or otherwise processed, such as bread dough being mixed, workpiece being turned in a lathe, fabric being cut, shoe being resoled, etc.)

9 |4__ Materials *not* in process (parts, materials, objects, etc., not in the process of being changed or modified, which are *sources* of information when being inspected, handled, packaged, distributed, or selected, etc., such as items or materials in inventory, storage, or distribution channels, items being inspected, etc.)

10 |3__ Features of nature (landscapes, fields, geological samples, vegetation, cloud formations, and other features of nature which are observed or inspected to provide information)

11 |2__ Man-made features of environment (structures, buildings, dams, highways, bridges, docks, railroads, and other "man-made" or altered aspects of the indoor or outdoor environment which are *observed* or *inspected* to provide job information; do not consider equipment, machines, etc., that an individual uses in his work, as covered by item 7).

Source: From Position Analysis Questionnaire, Occupational Research Center, Department of Psychological Sciences, Purdue University. © Copyright, Purdue Research Foundation, West Lafayette, Indiana 47907. Reprinted by permission.

Note: This exhibits 11 of the "information input" questions or elements. Other PAQ pages contain questions regarding mental processes, work output, relationships with others, job context, and other job characteristics.

whereas "quantitative materials" play only an *occasional* role in the job. For convenience the 194 items (or "basic job elements") are divided on the questionnaire into 6 major sections:

1. Information input (where and how does the worker get the information that he or she uses in performing the job?)
2. Mental processes (what reasoning, decision making, planning, and information processing activities are involved in performing the job?)
3. Work output (what physical activities does the worker perform, and what tools or devices does he or she use?)
4. Relationships with other persons (what relationships with other people are required to perform a job?)
5. Job contacts (in what physical and social context is the work performed?)
6. Other job characteristics (what activities, conditions, or characteristics other than those described above are relevant to the job?)

The "bottom line" of the PAQ procedure is that it provides a quantitative score or profile of any job in terms of how that job rates on the following five basic dimensions:

1. Having decision making /communication/social responsibilities.
2. Performing skilled activities.
3. Being physically active.
4. Operating vehicles/equipment.
5. Processing information.

Computerized programs are available for scoring each job under study relative to these five dimensions. This score (really, *set* of five scores) can then be compared with standard profiles of known jobs. In this way, it is possible to compare jobs to each other within the organization, as well as to "standard" jobs outside the organization in terms of how each job rates on each of the five dimensions above (decision making, etc.). [11]

The PAQ has some distinct advantages and disadvantages. First, note that it is not a substitute for nor is it really aimed at producing a job description (which describes in detail what the worker actually does). For example, if you will review Exhibit 3.11, you will see that the PAQ does not really provide information on what *actual activities* (in terms of processing accounting forms, writing reports, or developing sales charts) the jobholder engages in. Instead, the PAQ shows the degree to which each of the 194 job elements (like "written materials") plays a role in this particular job. As a result, the PAQ's real strength is in classifying jobs. Specifically, most jobs can be described with the PAQ in terms of five common dimensions (decision making, performing skilled activities, and so on), and so management can use the PAQ to classify similar jobs into classes (such as Secretary II, III, and IV). And, since one arrives at a quantitative rating or value for each job (or class of job), a manager can use the PAQ, for example, to establish the relative worth and therefore salary levels of each job or job class. [12]

The PAQ method has been one of the most widely and carefully studied job analysis methods, and the evidence so far indicates that it can be and is a very effective one. It is *reliable* in that there is usually little variance among individual analysts who rate a job using the PAQ (assuming they understand how to fill out the questionnaire). Studies have also been carried out to determine the *validity* of the PAQ; that is, whether jobs that receive a high quantitative rating also turn out to be high paying. Results of these studies indicate that the PAQ is indeed a vaid instrument because jobs that are rated higher with the PAQ prove to be those paying higher salaries. [13]

Summary: Job Analysis Data Collection Methods Compared

After collecting background information and selecting positions to be analyzed, the next step in the job analysis is to collect data on what each job entails in terms of factors like duties, relationships, skills, and aptitudes. In this section we discussed several techniques for collecting this sort of information. These include: interviews; observations; diary/logs; questionnaires; civil service method; Department of Labor method; and position analysis questionnaire.

In comparing and contrasting these techniques we can usefully draw three conclusions. First, the techniques can be categorized as either "task-oriented" procedures like the diary/log approach (or the questionnaire presented in Exhibit 3.7), and "behavior-oriented" techniques like the PAQ, and Department of Labor methodology (DOL). The more traditional, task-oriented approaches aim at developing a list of the *actual tasks* a job incumbent performs. For an airline ticket sales agent, these might include: "confirms reservations and issues tickets," "advises on and recommends best routes," and "makes reservations for travelers," for example. These tasks, when combined, represent what the worker actually does on the job. On the other hand, "behavior-oriented" techniques like the PAQ and DOL were developed for a different purpose—to arrive at a system by which all jobs could be described in terms of standard, basic elements or *behaviors*. They therefore describe each job, not in terms of actual tasks performed, but in terms of basic, elemental behaviors like "use of written materials," or "coordinating." A first conclusion, therefore, is that these data-collection methods can be roughly classified as either task-oriented, or element/behavior-oriented. [14]

A second conclusion is that some techniques are more useful for some purposes than for others. For example, techniques like interviews, job analysis questionnaires (as in Exhibit 3.7), and, to a lesser extent, the civil service method are widely used for developing job descriptions, training curricula, and standards for appraising performance. [15] This is because they generate information concerning the *actual tasks* and activities a jobholder should engage in. On the other hand, the DOL and PAQ methods result in quantitative ratings for each job. They are therefore uniquely suited for classifying jobs for compensation purposes (since jobs of equal importance can be grouped together).

Finally, a third conclusion follows from the previous two: the best approach is often to use several techniques when there is more than one purpose to be served by the job analysis. For example, if the objectives are to develop job descriptions (for which a diary/log might be important) as well as to classify jobs for compensation purposes, then some combination of interviewing, diary/logs, and PAQ might be appropriate. [16]

The Role of Job Analysis in Equal Employment Compliance

Job analysis was once viewed as a task which "could be delegated to the lowest level technician." Today, however, the legal need for selection tests and performance appraisals that accurately predict job performance has made job analysis much more important. Federal selection guidelines (described in the previous chapter) in fact admonish the personnel specialist to do a *thorough* job analysis before selecting a personnel test or developing a measure of job performance. [17] Although the reasons for this are explained in detail in the next two chapters, one reason is that selection tests should be "content valid." This means that test items should, if possible, represent the actual on-the-job behaviors being measured, much as a typing test represents the actual behaviors required of a typist. [18] Therefore, an accurate listing of those behaviors is necessary, and this listing is usually produced by a job analysis.

DEVELOPING JOB DESCRIPTIONS

A *job description* is usually one of the tangible outcomes of a job analysis and is a written statement of *what* the jobholder actually does, *how* he or she does it, and *why* he or she does it. [19] This information can in turn be used to develop a *job specification* that lists the knowledge, abilities, and skills needed to perform the job.

There is no standard format that has to be followed in writing a job description. However, most descriptions usually include the following types of information:

Job identification. This section typically lists the title of the job, date of the job description, who wrote the description, who approved it, pay range for the job, plant/division the job is found in, and the grade level and pay range of the job. The *Dictionary of Occupational Titles* published by the U.S. Department of Labor is very useful for identifying jobs, and contains several thousand job titles (like "supervisor of data processing operations"), and standard DOL code numbers for each job.

Job summary. Next, most job descriptions contain a brief one- or two-sentence statement summarizing what the job entails.

Responsibilities, duties, and procedures. This section (as in Exhibit 3.2) describes tasks performed, required interactions with other workers, materials and machinery used, and "accountabilities"—the nature and extent of supervision given or received. (The Dictionary of Occupational Titles provides, for each title, a listing of the responsibilities, duties, and procedures for each job in the manual. As illustrated in Exhibit 3.12, for example a "Manager, Personnel" "plans and carries out policies related to all phases of personnel activities, organizes recruitment, and confers with company and union officials to establish pension and insurance plans" amongst other duties. This information can supplement an employer's own job analysis.)

Working conditions and physical environment. Here are listed any special working conditions in terms of noise level, hazardous conditions, heat, or physical locations, for example.

Exhibit 3.12   Dictionary of Occupational Titles: Description for a "Personnel Manager"

> **MANAGER, PERSONNEL** (profess. & kin.) 166.118. director, personnel; manager, employee relations; personnel supervisor. Plans and carries out policies relating to all phases of personnel activities: Organizes recruitment, selection, and training procedures, and directs activities of subordinates directly concerned. Confers with company and union officials to establish pension and insurance plans, workman's compensation policies, and similar functions. Establishes social, recreational, and educational activities. Studies personnel records for information, such as educational background, work record, and supervisor's reports, to determine personnel suitable for promotions and transfers. May represent company in negotiating wage agreements with labor representatives. May act as liaison between management and labor within organization.

Source: United States Training and Employment Service, *Dictionary of Occupational Titles*, 3rd ed. (Washington, D.C.: U.S. Government Printing Office, 1965), p. 448.

Job Descriptions and Legal Requirements [20]

Federal and state legislation have placed new emphasis on the importance of the job description. For example, the Equal Pay Act requires equal pay for all employees performing equal work (in terms of equal skill, effort, and responsibility under similar working conditions) and it is the job description that reports the skill, effort, working conditions, and responsibilities needed to perform the job. The Fair Labor Standards Act requires employers to defend their decisions regarding which of their employees are exempt and non-exempt from the provisions of the act (exempt employees like executives, for example generally do not have to be paid for overtime work). And, again, job descriptions are usually needed to support such decisions. Furthermore, a carefully developed job description provides the basis for developing selection tests and performance standards for each job; it is thus a pillar of the employer's EEO compliance program. In so far as the job description identifies hazardous working conditions, it assists in compliance with the Occupational Safety and Health Act which is aimed at protecting the health and safety of employees at work. In union-management negotiations, unions often urge uniform rates of pay for all employees, and management can use job descriptions to defend its contention that there are real differences in jobs—differences that demand differential pay. Job descriptions thus play a crucial role in an employer's legal compliance.

Job Description Guidelines. One expert [21] suggests the following as a useful set of guidelines for developing job descriptions:

1. Be clear. The job description should portray the work of the position so well that the duties are clear without reference to other job descriptions.

2. Indicate scope. In defining the position, be sure to indicate scope and nature of the work by using phrases such as "for the department," or "as requested by the manager." Include all important relationships.

3. Be specific. Select the most specific words to show: (1) the kind of work; (2) the degree of complexity; (3) the degree of skill required; (4) the extent to which problems are standardized; (5) the extent of the worker's responsibility for each phase of the work; and (6) the degree and type of accountability. Use "action" words, such as analyze, gather, assemble, plan, devise, confer, deliver, transmit, maintain, supervise, and recommend. Generally speaking, positions at the lower levels of organizations have the most detailed duties or tasks, while higher level positions deal with broader aspects.

4. Show supervisory responsibility. Show clearly whether these responsibilities are carried out by the incumbent to the position or through incumbents of other positions. The specialist or professional usually carries out the duties himself or provides technical guidance when he assigns work to other persons. The manager or supervisor generally delegates the actual work to others.

5. Be brief. Remember that brief, accurate statements will best accomplish your purpose.

6. Recheck. Finally, to check whether the description fulfills the basic requirements, ask yourself: *will a new employee understand the job if he reads the job description?*

DEVELOPING JOB SPECIFICATIONS

The job specification takes the job description and answers the question "What human traits and experience are necessary to do this job well?" It shows what kind of person to recruit for and for what qualities that person should be tested. [22]

Specifications for Trained vs. Untrained Personnel

It is useful to distinguish between specifications for trained and untrained personnel. For example, suppose you were looking for a trained bookkeeper (or trained counselor or auto mechanic). In cases like these, the job specifications would probably focus on things like length of previous service, quality of any relevant training, and so forth. Thus, it is usually not too difficult to determine the "human requirements" for placing *already trained* people on a job.

But the problems are more complex when seeking *un*trained people for jobs (probably with the intention of training them on the job). Here you need to specify qualities—like physical traits, personality, interests, sensory skills, etc.—that imply some potential for performing the job. For example, if you are recruiting for a job that entails very heavy manual labor, you might want to specify that the candidate have a minimum height and weight. If the job requires detailed manipulations, you might want to ensure that the person scores high on a test of finger dexterity. In either case your goal is to state those personal traits that *validly predict* which candidate would do well on the job and which would not. Obtaining such valid "predictors" is, in fact, the main purpose for developing job specifications. These specifications are usually set on the basis of either judgment or statistical analysis.

Job Specifications Based on Judgment

This is the more popular of the two approaches, primarily because it is the simpler of the two. It involves basing the job specifications on the educated guesses of people like supervisors and personnel managers. Here you ask them (or yourself) "What do you think it takes in terms of education, intelligence, training, etc., to do this job well?"

One of the most extensive "judgmental" approaches to developing job specifications is contained in the procedure used by the United States Department of Labor Training and Employment Service. As mentioned above, they have published a Dictionary of Occupational Titles: [23] An example is presented in Exhibit 3.12. For jobs in the dictionary, ratings have been made by various experts (job analysts, vocational counselors, etc.) of each of the following worker traits: G (intelligence); V (verbal); N(numerical); S (spacial); P (form, perception); Q (clerical perception); K (motor coordination); F (finger dexterity); M (manual dexterity); E (eye-hand-foot coordination); and C (color discrimination). [24] These ratings reflect the amount of each trait possessed by people currently working on the job (in terms of the top 10% of performers, the next highest 30%, and so on).

Job Specifications Based on Statistical Analysis

Basing the job specification on statistical analysis is the more defensible approach in terms of equal employment compliance. It is more defensible (than the judgmental approach) because equal rights legislation forbids using selection items (such as "high school diploma") that cannot be shown to distinguish between "high" and "low" job performers. Specifically, recall that items which directly or indirectly discriminate on the basis of sex, race, religion, national origin, or age may have to be shown (by you or your organization) to be good

90   "predictors," and this generally requires a statistical "validation" study—one that shows statistically that the item does predict performance. Basically, what one must do here is (statistically) determine the relationship between (1) some "predictor" or human trait (such as height, intelligence, or finger dexterity) and (2) some indicator or criterion of job effectiveness (such as performance as rated by the supervisor).

This sort of study is, of course, more difficult than just using an expert's judgment, and involves five steps: (1) analyze the job and decide how to measure job performance; (2) select personal traits which you believe should predict successful performance; (3) test job candidates for these traits; (4) measure these candidates' subsequent job performance; (5) statistically analyze the relationship between the *human trait* and *job performance*. The aim is to determine whether the former predicts the latter.

SUMMARY

1. The purpose of an organization is to give each person a separate, distinct job and to ensure that these jobs are coordinated in such a way that the organization accomplishes its goals. The usual way of depicting an organization is with an organization chart. These provide the title of each manager's position and, by means of connecting lines, show who is accountable to whom and who is in charge of what department.

2. Departmentation is the process through which the organization's basic activities (such as manufacturing) are grouped logically into distinct areas and assigned to managers: it is the organization-wide division of work. We distinguished between purpose and functional departmentation. The former includes departmentation by product, customer, and location. Departmentation by business function is an example of functional departmentation. With purpose departmentation, departments are self-contained and each can give its continuous and undivided attention to the "purpose." Function types of departments tend to be more specialized (and efficient) than purpose types.

3. *Delegation* is defined as the pushing down of authority from superior to subordinate; whereas, *decentralization* is a philosophy of organization and management. It involves both selective delegation of authority as well as concentration of authority through policies and selective controls.

4. Developing an organization structure results in jobs that have to be staffed. Job analysis is the procedure through which one finds out (1) what the job entails, and (2) what kinds of people should be hired for the job. It involves five steps: (1) collect background information; (2) select the specific positions to be analyzed; (3) collect job analysis data; (4) develop a job description; and (5) develop a job specification.

5. There are four *basic techniques* one can use to gather job analysis data: interviews, direct observation, a questionnaire, and participant logs. These are good for developing job descriptions and specifications. The *Department of Labor* and *PAQ* approaches result in quantitative ratings of each job and are therefore useful for classifying jobs.

6. The job description should portray the work of the position so well that the duties are clear without reference to other job descriptions. Always ask: Will the new employee understand the job if he reads the job description?

7. The job specification takes the job description and answers the question, "What human traits and experience are necessary to do this job well?" It tells what kind of person to recruit for and for what qualities that person should be tested. Job specifications are usually based on the educated guesses of managers; however, a more accurate statistical approach to developing job specifications can also be used.

8. Job analysis is in many ways the first "personnel" activity that effects performance. Most people can not perform a job when they do not have the ability and skills to do the job. It is through job analysis that one determines what the job entails, and what skills and abilities one should look for in candidates for the job.

Job Questionnaires

The Arkansas (Little Rock) division of the Pierce Manufacturing Co. has encountered difficulty in its job analysis program. A new industrial relations director, taking over less than a year ago, began the program by asking employees to fill out a job questionnaire. When answers came in, he asked supervisors to comment. In many cases, employees indicated that they were performing tasks that supervisors questioned. Some supervisors insisted that employees were not actually doing all they claimed. In some cases, supervisors admitted that employees were doing what they claimed but said they should not be doing some of the tasks.

The new industrial relations director now finds himself faced with a difficult problem. He sought only to find out what each job involved. Now he is being asked to settle arguments as to what should be expected of jobholders and, even more difficult, what to do about employees who insist they have long been expected to do more than their supervisors think they are doing.

Questions

1. Should the industrial relations director ignore these controversies? If so, whose word should he take as to job content? If not, how should he move to resolve the differences?
2. Did he go about the job analysis in the right way? Why? Why not? What, if anything, should he have done differently?

EXPERIENTIAL EXERCISE

Purpose: The purpose of this exercise is to give you experience in developing a job description, by developing one for your instructor.

Required Understanding: You should understand the mechanics of job analysis and be thoroughly familiar with the Job Analysis Questionnaire (Exhibit 3.7) and the Job Analysis Record Sheet (Exhibit 3.8).

How to Set Up the Exercise/Instructions: Set up groups of four to six students for this exercise. As in all the exercises in this book, the groups should be separated and should not converse with each other. Half the groups in the class will develop the job description using the Job Description Questionnaire, while the other half of the groups will develop it using the Job Analysis Record Sheet. Each student should review the questionnaire or record sheet (as appropriate) before joining his or her group.

1. Each group should do a job analysis of their instructor's job; half the groups (to repeat) will use the Job Description Questionnaire for this purpose, and half will use the Job Analysis Record Sheet.

2. Based on this information, each group will develop its own job description and job specification for the instructor.

3. Next, each group should choose a partner group, one that developed the job description and job specification using the alternate method. (A group that used the Job Description Questionnaire should be paired with a group that used the Job Analysis Record Sheet.)

4. Finally, within each of these new combined groups, compare, contrast, and criticize each of the two sets of job descriptions and job specifications. Did each job analysis method provide different types of information? Which seems superior? Does one seem more advantageous for some types of jobs than others?

DISCUSSION QUESTIONS

1. What items are typically included in the organization chart? What items are not shown on the chart?

2. Compare and contrast purpose departmentation and functional departmentation; make sure to discuss the advantages and disadvantages of each, and where each seems most appropriate.

3. Explain departmentation by: product; customer; location; business function.

4. What is job analysis? How can you make use of the information it provides?

5. We discussed several methods for collecting job analysis data. These included questionnaires, the Civil Service method, the position analysis questionnaire, etc. Compare and contrast these methods, explaining what each is useful for, and the pros and cons of each.

NOTES

1. Based on Dessler, *Management Fundamentals*, Chs. 6–8.

2. Based on "Job Analysis: A Guide for State and Local Governments." United States Civil Service Commission, Bureau of Intergovernmental Personnel Programs (Washington, D.C.: December 1973), pp. 23–26.

3. See Ernest McCormick, "Job and task analysis," in Marvin Dunnette, editor, *Handbook of Industrial and Organizational Psychology* (Chicago: Rand McNally, 1976) pp. 651–696; Erich Prien, "The Functions of Job Analysis in Content Validation," *Personnel Psychology* (Summer 1977), p. 167–174.

4. See note 2 above.

5. See Wayne Cascio, *Applied Psychology in Personnel Management* (Reston, Va.: Reston Publishing, 1978), pp. 140–141; Richard Henderson, *Compensation Management*: Rewarding Performance (Reston: Reston, 1979), pp. 154–156.

6. *Ibid.*, p. 140.

7. McCormick, p. 651.

8. *Ibid.*, p. 667.

9. A complete explanation and definition of each of these seven attributes (knowledge, skills, abilities, etc.) can be found in: U.S. Civil Service Commission, *Job Analysis*, Washington, D.C.: U.S. Government Printing Office, Dec. 1976).

10. Sidney Fine has developed a "functional job analysis" approach that is a variant of the DOL procedure. Basically, he makes some modifications to the total of 24 DOL functions that are used to scale the basic functions of data, people, and things. He has also added some scales including a "reasoning development scale" and a "mathematical scale." See Sidney Fine, *Functional Job Analysis Scales: A Desk Aid, Methods for Manpower Analysis No. 7* (Kalamazoo, Michigan: W.E. Upjohn Institute for employment research, 1973).

11. A similar approach, known as the job analysis questionnaire (JAQ) has been developed and is said to have some advantages over the PAQ. See Jerry Newman and Frank Krzystofiak, "Quantifying Job Analysis: A Tool for Improving Human Resource Management Decision Making," a paper presented at the Academy of Management meeting, Orlando, Florida, Aug. 15, 1977.

12. Similarly, for a discussion of how to use the PAQ for classifying jobs for performance appraisal, see Edwin Cornelius III, Milton Hakel, and Paul Sackett, "A Methodological Approach to Job Classification for Performance Appraisal Purposes," *Personnel Psychology* (Summer 1979), pp. 283–297.

13. See, for example Jack Smith and Milton Hakel, "Convergence among Data Sources, Response Bias, and Reliability and Validity of a Structured Job Analysis Questionnaire," *Personnel Psychology* (Winter 1979), pp. 677–692.

14. Recent evidence also indicates that task- versus behavior-oriented methods each result in different conclusions regarding, for example, how jobs should be classified. For a discussion see, for example Edwin Cornelius III, Theodore Carron, and Marianne Collins, "Job Analysis Models and Job Classification," *Personnel Psychology* (Winter 1979), pp. 693–708.

15. See Cascio, p. 145.

16. For another, technical, discussion of a related point see Edwin Cornelius III and Karen Lyness, "A Comparison of Holistic and Decomposed Judgment Strategies in Job Analyses by Job Incumbents," *Journal of Applied Psychology* Vol. 65, No. 2, (April 1980), pp. 155–163.

17. Also, the U.S. Supreme Court ruled in Albemarle Paper Company versus Moody that job analysis must be an integral part of any validation study that attempts to show a relationship between a selection device (like a test) and job performance.

18. For a more detailed discussion of job analysis and EEO compliance see, for example: Ernest McCormick, James Shaw, and Angelo DeNisi, "Use of the Position Analysis Questionnaire for Establishing the Job Component Validity of Tests," *Journal of Applied Psychology*, 1979, Vol. 64, No. 1, pp. 51–56; Erich Prien, "The Function of Job Analysis in Content Validation," *Personnel Psychology*, 1977, vol. 30, pp. 167–174; Marvin Tratner, "Task Analysis in the Design in Three Concurrent Validity Studies of the Professional and Administrative Career Examinations," *Personnel Psychology* Vol. 32, (Spring 1979), pp. 109–119.

19. Cascio, p. 134.

20. This is based on Henderson, *Compensation Management*, pp. 172–173.

21. Ernest Dale, *Organizations* (New York: AMA, 1967).

22. The remainder of this chapter, except as noted, is from Ernest J. McCormick and Joseph Tiffin, *Industrial Psychology* (Englewood Cliffs, N.J.: Prentice-Hall, 1974), pp. 56–61.

23. United States Training and Employment Service, *Dictionary of Occupational Titles*, 3rd ed. (Washington, D.C.: Superintendent of Documents, Government Printing Office, 1965).

24. McCormick and Tiffin, *Industrial Psychology*, p. 58; Marvin Dunnette, *Personnel Selection and Placement* (Belmont, Calif.: Brooks/Cole, 1966), p. 73.

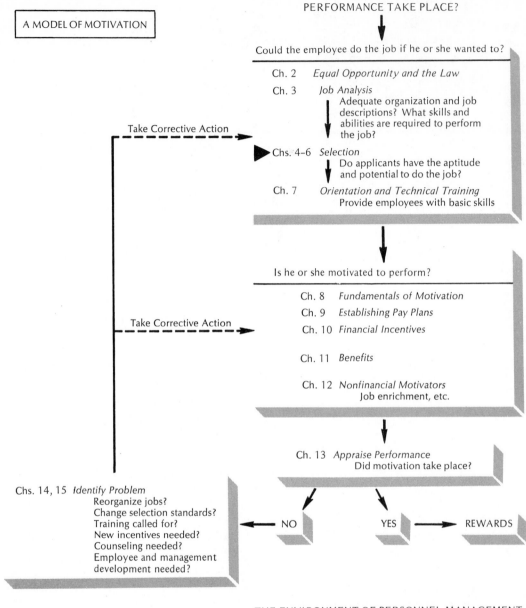

WILL MOTIVATION AND
PERFORMANCE TAKE PLACE?

A MODEL OF MOTIVATION

Could the employee do the job if he or she wanted to?

Ch. 2   *Equal Opportunity and the Law*

Ch. 3   *Job Analysis*
         Adequate organization and job
         descriptions? What skills and
         abilities are required to perform
         the job?

Take Corrective Action

Chs. 4–6 *Selection*
         Do applicants have the aptitude
         and potential to do the job?

Ch. 7   *Orientation and Technical Training*
         Provide employees with basic skills

Is he or she motivated to perform?

Ch. 8   *Fundamentals of Motivation*

Ch. 9   *Establishing Pay Plans*

Take Corrective Action   Ch. 10   *Financial Incentives*

Ch. 11   *Benefits*

Ch. 12   *Nonfinancial Motivators*
         Job enrichment, etc.

Ch. 13   *Appraise Performance*
         Did motivation take place?

Chs. 14, 15 *Identify Problem*
             Reorganize jobs?
             Change selection standards?
             Training called for?   NO   YES   REWARDS
             New incentives needed?
             Counseling needed?
             Employee and management
             development needed?

THE ENVIRONMENT OF PERSONNEL MANAGEMENT

Ch. 16   *Labor Relations and Grievances*

Ch. 17   *Employee Safety and Health*

Ch. 18   *Personnel Management and the
         Quality of Work Life*

When you finish studying

4 # Personnel Planning and Recruiting

You should be able to:

1. *Cite the steps in recruitment and placement.*
2. *Discuss the main elements in personnel forecasting.*
3. *Compare and contrast at least five sources of job candidates.*
4. *Develop an application blank.*
5. *Develop and use a "weighted" application blank.*

OVERVIEW

The main purpose of this chapter is to explain how to go about developing a pool of viable job candidates. A second purpose is to discuss developing and using application blanks and to explain a technique for using application blanks to predict success on the job. Also discussed are personnel planning and forecasting, which involve projecting personnel requirements and supply. Personnel planning and recruiting is the second step in improving performance at work. Here the employer develops a pool of qualified candidates for the job, candidates who have the skills and ability to successfully do the job. Application blanks (also discussed in this chapter) are the first step in screening the best candidates for the job.

PERSONNEL PLANNING, RECRUITMENT, AND PLACEMENT: AN OVERVIEW

In simplest terms, manpower planning, recruitment, and placement involves placing the right person on the right job. Specifically, it involves planning personnel requirements; building up a pool of acceptable candidates; interviewing and testing them to select the most promising ones; checking their backgrounds; and hiring, training, and orienting them.

Planning, recruitment, and placement are crucial functions. Managers carry out many other functions like organizing, planning, and controlling; but it is safe to say that unless you *hire the right people*, the best plans, organization charts, and control systems won't do you much good.

The Steps in Planning, Recruitment and Placement

We can conveniently assume that planning, recruitment and placement involves six steps, and the order in which we discuss them will be as follows:

Step 1: Job Analysis.   The first step is to determine what each job entails and what traits and skills are required to successfully perform it. This was discussed in the previous chapter.

Step 2: Personnel Planning and Recruiting.   This second step involves *forecasting* which positions will be open, *planning* how and by whom they'll be filled, and *recruiting* a pool of candidates. This last is an important step—in fact, much more important than most managers realize. If you have *many* candidates to choose from, you should be able to screen out all but the best. But if only one or two candidates apply for the opening, your only choice is "take them or leave them." We discuss planning and recruiting in this chapter.

Step 3: Obtain Application Blank Information.   The next step is usually to have candidates fill out application blanks. As explained in this chapter these provide basic information like name, address, previous work experience, and education.

Step 4: Interview the Candidate.   Managers use many techniques (like tests and reference checks) to screen out and select the best candidates. But virtually all managers rely on a direct, face-to-face *interview* with the candidate. This is an important selection tool, one we discuss in the next chapter.

Step 5: Test the Candidate.   Many employers also test the job candidate, to further determine his or her *competence* or *potential* to do the job. Then, as you approach the point where a hiring decision must be made, you will want to check the background and references of each candidate. We discuss testing and reference-checking in Chapter 6.

Step 6: Orient/Train.   The final step involves hiring the candidates and orienting and training them: we discuss *orientation* and *training* in Chapter 7.

PERSONNEL PLANNING AND FORECASTING

Manpower planning has been defined as "an effort to anticipate future business and environmental demands on the organization and to meet the manpower requirements dictated by these conditions." [1] It is the process through which the employer plans for the openings that inevitably develop in the organization. As such, it basically involves forecasting the demand for and supply of manpower, and developing specific manpower plans (for instance concerning who to train, and how many people to recruit for). Not all managers engage in manpower planning, of course. The other alternative is to wait for the opening

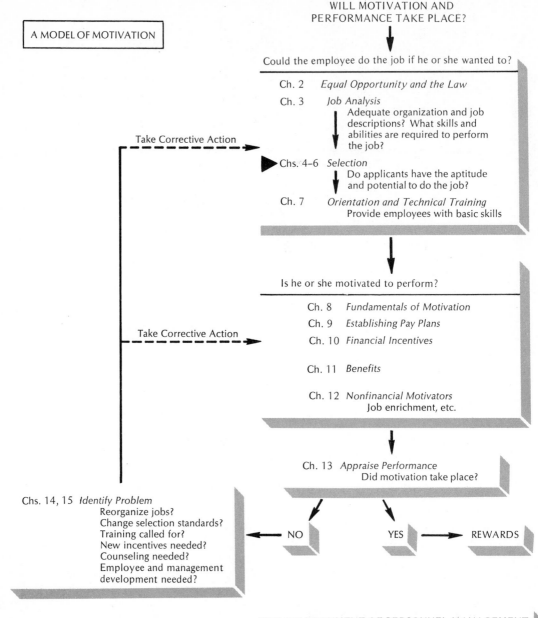

A MODEL OF MOTIVATION

WILL MOTIVATION AND
PERFORMANCE TAKE PLACE?

Could the employee do the job if he or she wanted to?

Ch. 2 *Equal Opportunity and the Law*

Ch. 3 *Job Analysis*
Adequate organization and job
descriptions? What skills and
abilities are required to perform
the job?

Chs. 4–6 *Selection*
Do applicants have the aptitude
and potential to do the job?

Ch. 7 *Orientation and Technical Training*
Provide employees with basic skills

Take Corrective Action

Is he or she motivated to perform?

Ch. 8 *Fundamentals of Motivation*

Ch. 9 *Establishing Pay Plans*

Ch. 10 *Financial Incentives*

Ch. 11 *Benefits*

Ch. 12 *Nonfinancial Motivators*
Job enrichment, etc.

Take Corrective Action

Ch. 13 *Appraise Performance*
Did motivation take place?

Chs. 14, 15 *Identify Problem*
Reorganize jobs?
Change selection standards?
Training called for?
New incentives needed?
Counseling needed?
Employee and management
development needed?

NO   YES   REWARDS

THE ENVIRONMENT OF PERSONNEL MANAGEMENT

Ch. 16 *Labor Relations and Grievances*

Ch. 17 *Employee Safety and Health*

Ch. 18 *Personnel Management and the
Quality of Work Life*

to develop and to try to fill it as best as possible. Most managers probably use this approach, and it is probably effective enough for small organizations. But for larger firms (and for managers who want to avoid last minute scurrying and mistakes), some forecasting and planning are worthwhile.

It is important to remember however that to be worthwhile manpower planning has to be *integrated* both internally and externally. This is summarized in Exhibit 4.1. *Internally,* plans for recruitment, selection, placement, training, and appraisal should be developed in such a way that, for instance, the organization's training plans reflect its plans for recruiting and selecting new employees. *Externally,* these "manpower" plans should be integrated with the organization's overall planning process, since plans to enter (or not enter) new businesses, to build (or not build) new plants, or to reduce the level of activities have significant manpower implications—in terms of recruiting, and training, for instance. [2]

Exhibit 4.1   How All Personnel Functions Impact Personnel Planning

Note: manpower planning should be integrated externally and internally. Externally it should be integrated with the organizations overall plans since, for example, opening new plants, building a new hospital wing, or reducing operations due to an impending recession all have manpower implications. Internally, manpower planning should be integrated in that planning for all the personnel functions—like recruiting, training, job analysis, and development should be integrated or coordinated: for example, hiring 50 new employees means they must be trained, and their wages budgeted for.

Manpower Forecasts.   Manpower plans are built on premises—basic assumptions about the future—and the purpose of *forecasting* is to develop these basic premises.

In terms of manpower planning, three sets of forecasts are needed: a forecast of manpower *requirements;* and forecasts for supply of *outside* candidates, and available *inside* candidates.

Factors in Forecasting Manpower Requirements

Most managers consider several factors when forecasting personnel requirements. [3] From a practical point of view, *the demand for your product or service*
is paramount. [4] Thus, in a manufacturing firm, sales are projected first. Then
the volume of production required to meet these sales requirements is determined. Finally, the manpower needed to maintain this volume of output is
estimated. But in addition to this "basic requirement" for manpower, several
other factors will also have to be considered:

1. *Projected turnover* (as a result of resignations or terminations).
2. *Quality and nature* of your employees (in relation to what you see as the
   changing needs of your organization).
3. *Decisions* to upgrade the quality of products or services, or enter into new
   markets, etc. These have implications for the nature and abilities of employees
   required; ask, for example, whether the skills of current employees are compatible with the new products your company will be producing.
4. *Technological and administrative changes* resulting in increased efficiencies:
   increased efficiency (in terms of output per man-hour) could reduce manpower needs.
5. The *financial resources* available; a larger budget allows you to hire more
   people and pay higher wages. Conversely, a projected "budget crunch" could
   mean fewer positions to recruit for and lower salary offers.

Use of Computer in Forecasting Manpower Requirements. Computers
can be useful tools in forecasting and analyzing manpower requirements. For
example, one expert has developed a computer package called Manplan which
he contends can improve the personnel manager's ability to manage (rather than
just react to) employment fluctuations. [5] As illustrated in Exhibit 4.2 a personnel
specialist, working in conjunction with line managers, programs data into the
computer in order to develop a "Manplan" forecast of manpower requirements.
As illustrated, the data to be supplied includes "direct manpower hours needed
to produce one unit of product" (a measure of productivity), and three sales
projections—minimum, maximum, and probable—for the product line in question. Based on this input Manplan generates figures on such things as "average
manpower levels required to meet product demands," as well as separate forecasts for direct manpower (such as assembly line workers), indirect manpower
(like secretaries) and exempt manpower (like executives).

As the Manplan's developer notes:

> The day of the personnel manager whose task was simply to await word
> from operation components to turn the right valve and thereby open or
> close the employment pipeline is passing quickly. A minimum data base
> and a simple computer program can today put the personnel manager of
> virtually any size business in a position to manage employment fluctuations
> rather than merely cope with them after the fact. [6]

With a system like Manplan, an organization can quickly translate estimates

Exhibit 4.2   Some of the Information Needed by Computerized Personnel
Forecasting Program

Ready
Run

Manplan LS:08EDT   Manplan L5:08EDT

Do you wish program instructions printed? Yes or No? Yes.

This is a manpower forecast program designed to guide users in developing manpower requirements directly from sales forecasts. Sales forecasts for any span of time in months, quarters or years into the immediate future on up to one hundred product lines are permissible. In addition, planned percent of productivity improvement as well as estimated overtime and absenteeism levels which are anticipated in the forecast period can be accounted for by the program. To use "Manplan", first develop sales forecasts in units of sales by product line. Determine this year's productivity improvement goal, anticipated overtime and probable absenteeism levels for the forecast period. All of your sales forecasts should be in the same time frame (one month, four months, one year, etc.).

In addition to the units of sales forecast, six other elements of data are required for each product line included in the forecast. These are:
Name of the product line (maximum ten characters)
Direct manpower hours needed to produce one unit of product
Required ratio of unapplied to applied labor manhours
Hourly manpower as a % of total (direct + indirect)
Non-exempt manpower as a % of total (direct + indirect)
Exempt manpower as a % of total (direct + indirect)
These last three percents should add to 100%.

You may either enter these elements "on line" or you may create a separate file of data and save it as "datafile". According to the following format: put all elements of data on a single "line"; begin each line with a "line number"; follow the line number with the six elements tabulated above in the order listed. These are: Line Num, Prod Name, Hrs Per Unit, Unapl/apl Ratio, % Hrly, % Non-Ex, % Exempt. An example is as follows:
10Refrig, 18.22, 48.68, 21.11
20Washers, 16.74, 51.65, 22.11
30Dryers, 11.48, 54.71, 20.9

If you do not plan to input your data on-line, you must first create your data file and store it in your time-share catalogue under the name "Datafile". If you must do that now, press the "Break" key on your keyboard to terminate this run.

After the manpower forecast has been generated, a manning schedule for up to twelve months may also be obtained provided that current manpower levels by employee classification and separations (excluding layoffs) for the last twelve months can be supplied to the program.

Source: Glenn Bassett, "Elements of Manpower Forecasting and Scheduling," *Human Resource Management*, vol. 12. (Fall 1973), pp. 35–43.

of projected productivity and sales levels to forecasts of manpower needs and can easily check the effects of *various* levels of productivity and sales on manpower demand. [7]

Forecasting the Supply of Inside Candidates

Perhaps the most important source of qualified candidates consists of people now employed by the organization. Tapping this inside supply, however, requires

102   some means of compiling information on their qualifications. These "qualifications inventories" can then be used to develop plans for promoting, transferring, or training current employees to fill the projected openings. There are two basic techniques for developing such "qualifications inventories": manual and computerized. [8]

Manual Systems and Replacement Charts. [9]   There are several types of manual systems that can be used to keep track of employees' qualifications. Many managers start with a *manning table.* This lists all the jobs in the unit (by title) and the number of workers holding each job. Some companies use *manpower replacement charts* (see Exhibit 4.3) for their most important positions. These show the present performance of each position-holder and the promotion potential of possible replacements. As an alternative, a position replacement card can be developed. This involves making up a card for each position which shows the possible replacements, as well as the training they require.

In some organizations, detailed "qualifications inventories" are developed. In terms of information, these are similar to application blanks and are updated periodically. They help ensure that employees aren't "lost in the shuffle" and neglected when manpower requirements are planned.

Computerized Information Systems.   For larger companies, maintaining qualifications inventories on hundreds (or thousands) of employees cannot be adequately managed manually. Many companies have thus computerized this information and a number of "prepackaged" systems have been developed to aid other organizations in doing the same. [10]

For example, IBM has developed the "IBM Recruiting Information System" (IRIS). Employees fill out a 12 page booklet called a data-pak in which they describe their background and experience in a uniform, computerizable language. All of this information is stored in the computer. When a manager needs a qualified person to fill a position, he or she describes the position (and the education and skills it entails). These requirements are also entered into the computer. After scanning its bank of possible candidates, IRIS then presents the manager with a computer printout of qualified candidates. Other computer companies, including Honeywell and Xerox, have similar information systems available.

Use of Mathematical Models.   Various mathematical techniques, borrowed from the field of Management Science have been used to improve an employer's ability to forecast the availability of inside job candidates. [11] *Markov-chain* analysis is one such technique. [12] Basically, Markov-chain analysis involves developing a *matrix* which shows the probability of an employee moving from one position to another. In a public accounting firm, for instance a matrix (shown in Exhibit 4.4) was developed based on five years of personnel transfer data. This matrix (which shows the end result of the statistical analysis) indicates

Exhibit 4.3 Management Manpower Replacement Chart

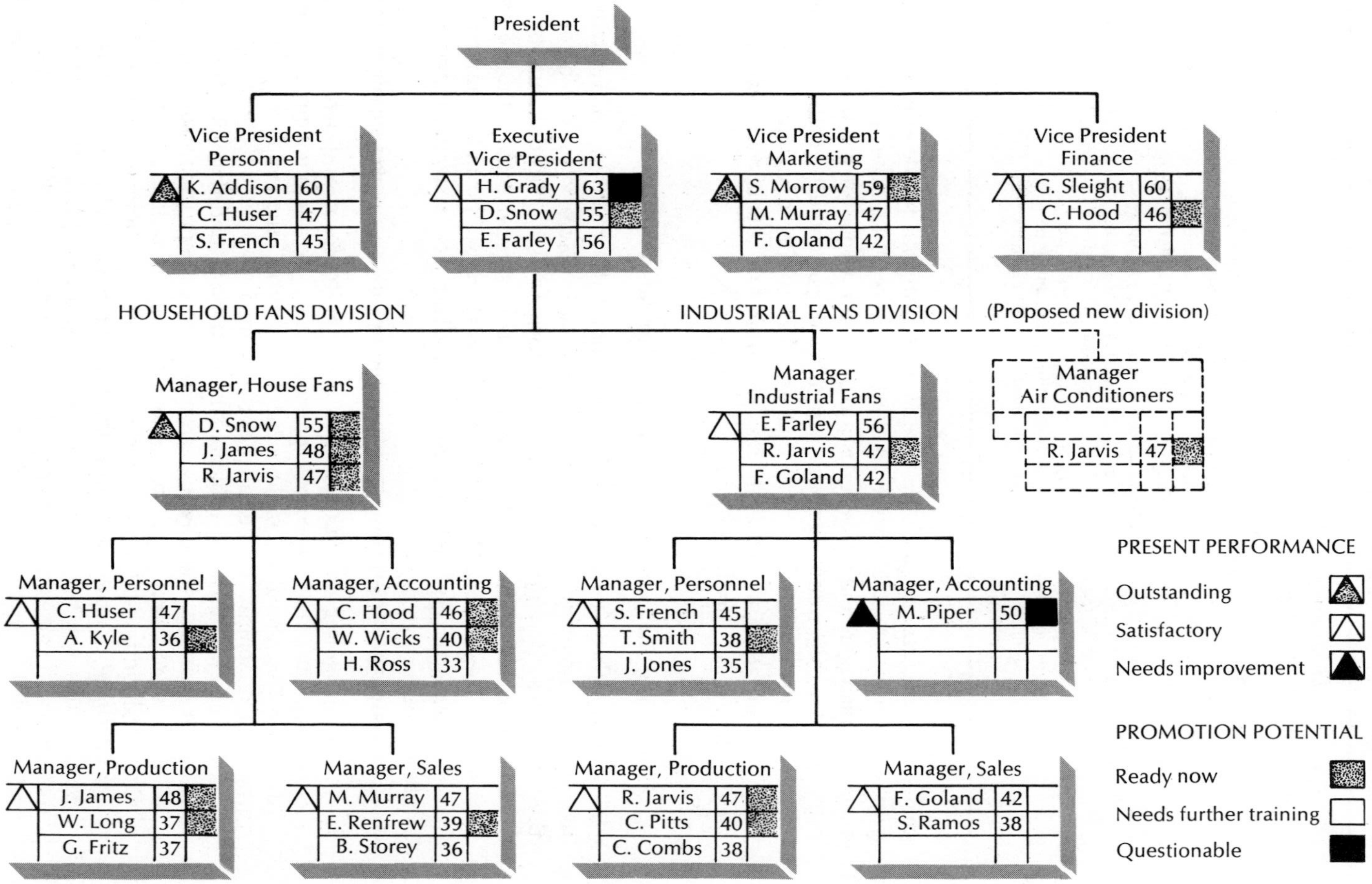

President

Vice President Personnel
K. Addison	60
C. Huser	47
S. French	45

Executive Vice President
H. Grady	63
D. Snow	55
E. Farley	56

Vice President Marketing
S. Morrow	59
M. Murray	47
F. Goland	42

Vice President Finance
G. Sleight	60
C. Hood	46

(Proposed new division)

Manager Air Conditioners
R. Jarvis	47

HOUSEHOLD FANS DIVISION

INDUSTRIAL FANS DIVISION

Manager, House Fans
D. Snow	55
J. James	48
R. Jarvis	47

Manager, Personnel
C. Huser	47
A. Kyle	36

Manager, Accounting
C. Hood	46
W. Wicks	40
H. Ross	33

Manager, Sales
M. Murray	47
E. Renfrew	39
B. Storey	36

Manager, Production
J. James	48
W. Long	37
G. Fritz	37

Manager, Industrial Fans
E. Farley	56
R. Jarvis	47
F. Goland	42

Manager, Personnel
S. French	45
T. Smith	38
J. Jones	35

Manager, Accounting
M. Piper	50

Manager, Production
R. Jarvis	47
C. Pitts	40
C. Combs	38

Manager, Sales
F. Goland	42
S. Ramos	38

PRESENT PERFORMANCE
Outstanding
Satisfactory
Needs improvement

PROMOTION POTENTIAL
Ready now
Needs further training
Questionable

103

Exhibit 4.4   Example of Use of Markov Chain Analysis in Personnel Planning

*Number of Years Spent
at this Level:*

Junior	Senior	Manager	Partner		
2.4	1.4	1.3	1.3	Junior	
0	2.3	2.1	2.1	Senior	*Level when*
0	0	5.4	5.4	Manager	*entering firm*
0	0	0	22.9	Partner	

Note: A person who entered the firm as, say, a junior, would spend 2.4 years as a junior, 1.4 as a senior, 1.3 as a manager, and 1.3 as a partner. This information, in turn, can help a firm plan its manpower needs, by showing how many juniors, etc. must be hired if the firm knows it will need, say, 50 partners six years from now.

that *on the average* an employee entering the firm as a junior (the entry level position) could expect to spend 2.4 years as a junior, 1.4 years as a senior, 1.3 years as a manager, and 1.3 years as a partner for a total of 6.4 years with the firm. [13] From this information the personnel officer could predict the number of partners, managers, and seniors that would be available within the firm, say, three years in the future and from this (and from forecasts of manpower requirements) deduce the number of juniors that had to be hired.

Forecasting the Supply of "Outside" Candidates

Assuming there are not enough inside candidates to fill manpower requirements most employers next have to forecast the supply of outside candidates—those not currently employed by the organization. This "outside" forecast provides an important input for the manpower plans, since it enables the employer to anticipate the number of outside candidates there will be and to immediately take measures (make plans) to increase recruiting efforts should a shortfall of candidates be projected.

There are three main components in the outside manpower supply forecast:

1. *General economic conditions.* First, one has to forecast general economic conditions and the (expected) prevailing rate of unemployment. Usually, the lower the rate of unemployment, the "tighter" the supply of labor, and the more difficult it will be to recruit personnel.

2. *Local market conditions.* Projected local market conditions are also important. For example, the phasing down of aerospace programs some years ago resulted in relatively high unemployment in cities like Seattle and Cape Canaveral, quite aside from general economic conditions in the country.

3. *Occupational market conditions.* Finally, the personnel specialist has to ask what are (or will be) the market conditions for people in the specific occupations (drill press operators, engineers, draftsmen, and so forth) the organization will be recruiting for. For the past few years, for example there has

been an undersupply of accountants, physicians, and (more recently) engineers. On the other hand, in most cities there tends to be an oversupply of available grade school and high school teachers.

There is a great deal of published information that can help an employer develop Economic, Market, and Occupational forecasts. In December of each year, *Business Week* magazine presents its economic forecasts for the following year; and each week it presents a snapshot of the economy on its "outlook" page. *Fortune* magazine has a monthly forecast of the business outlook that is usually buttressed in its January issue with a forecast for the coming year. Many banks, such as First National City of New York, Manufacturers Hanover Trust, and Chase Manhattan, publish periodic analyses and forecasts of the economy. Each December the Prudential Insurance Company publishes an economic forecast for the coming year.

Several agencies of the Federal Government also make available a wide variety of economic activity information. The U.S. Council of Economic Advisors prepares "economic indicators" each month which shows the trend to date of a variety of economic indicators. The Federal Reserve Bank of St. Louis also publishes monthly summaries of various economic indicators. The Bureau of Labor Statistics of the U.S. Department of Labor, the Engineering Manpower Commission, and the National Science Foundation regularly forecast labor market conditions and future occupational supplies, as do the Public Health Service, the U.S. Employment Service, and the Office of Education.

SOURCES FOR RECRUITING CANDIDATES

Once a decision has been made to fill a position (and permission to do so has been granted) the next step is to develop a pool of applicants using one or more of the sources described below. Recruiting is an extremely important personnel function because the greater the number of applicants the more selective an organization can be in its hiring. If only two candidates appear for two openings, then the organization may have little choice but to hire them. On the other hand, if 10 or 20 applicants appear, then the organization can employ various techniques like interviews and tests to screen out all but the best. [14]

Recruitment is one area in which line-staff cooperation is essential, and there are several reasons for this. First, from a practical point of view the specialist who recruits (and screens) for the vacant job is seldom the one responsible for supervising its performance. [15] Therefore, the personnel specialist should have as clear a picture as possible of what the job entails, and this almost always demands interviewing the supervisor involved. For example, the personnel specialist might want to know something about the behavioral "style" of the supervisor and the members of the work group—is it a "tough" group to get along with? for instance. The personnel specialist might also want to visit the

106   work site and review the job description with the supervisor to ensure that the job has not changed since the description was last updated. Furthermore, the supervisor may be able to supply additional insights into the skills and talents the new worker will need. For reasons like these, personnel planning in general and recruitment in particular require close and ongoing cooperation between line and staff personnel.

Equal Rights and Recruiting

Recent equal rights legislation (which we discussed at length in chapter 2) draws important limits around what every manager (not just personnel managers) can do in recruiting. These laws influence what can be asked in interviews and application blanks; what can be said in recruiting advertisements; the job specifications set; and the recruiting and hiring records kept, for example. [16] [17]

These laws, combined with guidelines on selection procedures published by various government agencies, and a recent Supreme Court decision (*Griggs v. Duke Power Company*) basically boil down to this: *if* your recruiting technique or selection device is called into question, then the requirements set as prerequisites to being hired can be legimately used in hiring only if it can be proved they are related to success or failure on the job. [18] The burden of proof rests with the employer. *The employer* must demonstrate the validity and fairness of the allegedly discriminatory item.

What does this mean in practice? For one thing, it means that certain employer actions are frowned upon by the EEOC, and that an organization using any of these will have the burden of proving that the action was *not* unfairly discriminatory. For example, as explained in Chapter 2, an employer usually should not advertise a job as "Man Wanted" (or "Gal Friday") *unless* sex (or national origin or religion) is a legitimate requirement of the job. (Thus you could legitimately advertise for a female masseuse to work in a women's health spa although many men are liable to apply anyway.) Similarly, it is usually not wise to request photographs of candidates prior to employment. An employer can require proof of age, but only after hiring. Also keep in mind that any question (such as "Any prior arrests?") that may unfairly discriminate against some group may be illegal. Similarly, it's usually best not to make any inquiry directly or indirectly into the person's religion, birthplace, race, or age prior to hiring. (Remember, though, as discussed in Chapter 2, that under the Griggs decision it is generally not the *intrinsic nature* of an employer's personnel policies or practices that the courts object to. Instead, it is the *results* of applying a policy or practice in such a way that it has an adverse impact on some protected group. You could, therefore, demand pictures or age, for instance, before hiring but only if you are ready to *prove* the information was not used to discriminate unfairly—based on the person's age, sex, race, religion, or national origin.)

Internal Sources of Candidates

"Promotion from within" has become a very popular policy in the last few years. Some surveys indicate that up to 90% of all management positions are filled internally, compared with only 50% in the 1950s. [19]

Filling open positions with inside candidates is said to have some benefits. Employees see that competence is rewarded with promotion, so morale and performance are supposedly enhanced. Inside candidates (having already been with the organization for some time) may be more committed to its goals and less likely to leave. They may also require less orientation and training.

Yet promotion from within can also backfire. Those employees who apply for jobs and do not get them may become discontented: informing unsuccessful applicants of why they were rejected and what remedial actions they might take to be more successful in the future is therefore essential. [20] And many organizations *require* managers to post job openings and interview all inside candidates. Yet very often the manager knows ahead of time exactly who he wants to hire and requiring him to interview a stream of unsuspecting inside candidates is therefore a waste of time for all concerned. We also know that groups may not be as satisfied when their new boss is appointed from within their own ranks as when he or she is a newcomer. [21]

In any case, promotion from within seems here to stay and many organizations have established policies to help assure its smooth implementation. One such policy states that job openings must be posted and circulated (as in Exhibit 4.5). [22] Qualifications inventories and computerized systems like IRIS (discussed above) can help ensure that qualified internal applicants are considered for the opening.

Advertising as a Source of Candidates

Advertising is another popular technique for attracting candidates. It is very useful for recruiting blue-collar and hourly workers, [23] as well as scientific, professional, and technical employees. [24] The local newspaper can be a good source of blue-collar help, clerical employees, and lower-level administrative employees. [25] For specialized employees you can advertise in trade and professional journals like the *American Psychologist*. Each industry also usually has its own periodical, such as the *Journal of Higher Education*. The *Wall Street Journal* has a classified section called "The Mart." Here employers place ads for higher level administrative and managerial personnel.

Employment Agencies [26] as a Source of Candidates

Employment agencies—both public and private—are useful sources of personnel.

JOB POSTINGS

35

JOB CODE NO.	JOB DESCRIPTION	WORKING SCHEDULE	JOB RATE
11-75	OFFICE SUPERVISOR (REQ. NO. 16904) ONE Supervise 10-15 people engaged in clerical activities related to the following: 1. Receiving, scheduling, routing and controlling of orders through the planning, estimating, scheduling and requisitioning cycle. 2. Auditing and processing of documents required for accounting and cost control. 3. Typing of numerical control program tapes, planning and control documents, memoranda, etc. Technical school graduate or equivalent, familiar with mechanical trades, shop processes and shop control procedures from engineering release through shipping. Three to five years' experience in areas of material or production control; shop planning methods or estimating; and supervisor or functional work direction of others. Supervisor: J. Doe Department 981	8:00 a.m. 4:30 p.m.	Open
11-76	METHODS PLANNER/ESTIMATOR (REQ. NO. 16908) ONE 1. Review prints for completeness and add manufacturing instruction. 2. Determine economic methods of fabrication. 3. Prepare operation sheets and program instructions. 4. Estimate labor requirements. 5. Determine material requirements and specify cutting dimension. 6. Estimate costs of all fabrication. 7. Assist in other planning scheduling activities. Background in shop math, including geometry, trigonometry and drafting. Minimum of 4 years' combined experience in machine shop, sheet metal fabrication and assembly, or equivalent. Must be able to read complex blueprints. Supervisor: J. Doe Department 981 FOR THE ABOVE POSTINGS PLEASE CALL EXT. 852	8:00 a.m. 4:30 p.m.	Open

It is our general policy to fill job openings from within the company when there are qualified candidates among our own people. If you are interested in any of the above jobs, please tell your supervisor or contact Personnel *immediately*. Jobs will be posted for three days before being filled. Occasional exceptions may be made when particular speed is necessary in filling the vacancy, and recent postings of similar jobs have brought no response. The details of how the Job Posting System operates are contained in Personnel Instructions 52-12 which your Supervisor can show you

POSTING DATE: 11/15/65 – 11/19/65

Source: Reprinted by permission of the publisher from *Book of Employment Forms,* American Management Association, copyright © 1967 by the American Management Association, p. 35.

Public ("State Employment Service") agencies exist in every state. They are aided and coordinated by the United States Employment Service of the United States Department of Labor, which also has recently developed a nationwide computerized *job bank* to which all state employment offices will some day be connected. Using the computer-listed job bank information, an agency interviewer will be better able to counsel job applicants concerning available jobs in their own, and other geographical areas.

These public agencies are a major source of hourly blue-collar workers, although the experience of many employers with these agencies has been mixed. Applicants for unemployment insurance are required to register with these agencies and make themselves available for job interviews in order to collect their unemployment payments. Some of these people are not anxious to get back to work, and employers can end up with applicants who have little or no real interest in obtaining immediate employment.

Private employment agencies are important sources of clerical, white-collar, and managerial personnel. (Most personnel managers use a few selected agencies for each of their job categories—secretarial, technical, etc.) Private agencies charge fees for each applicant they place and these fees are usually set by state law and posted in their offices. Whether the company or the candidate pays the fee is mostly determined by market conditions. (Thus, if there's a "tight" market for qualified secretaries, there might be an increase in the number of "fee-paid" jobs.) Many organizations have voluntarily decided to pay most fees themselves. They assume that the most qualified candidates are presently employed and would not be as willing to switch jobs if they had to pay the fees themselves. Finally, many private agencies now offer (or specialize in) *temporary help* service, and provide secretarial, clerical, or semi-skilled labor on a per diem basis. These agencies can be useful in helping an organization cope with peak loads, and fill in for vacationing employees, for example.

Executive Recruiters as a Source of Candidates

Executive recruiters (also known as "head-hunters") are an important source of top management candidates. The percentage of an organization's positions filled by these services might be small, but these jobs would include the most crucial executive and technical positions: for executive positions "head-hunters" may be the *only* source.

Their fees are usually equal to about 25% of the hired candidate's first-year compensation, to which is added about $300 per day for expenses. The fees (in virtually all instances) are paid by the organization doing the recruiting.

These firms can be very useful. They have many contacts and are especially adept at contacting qualified candidates who are employed and "not looking" to change jobs. They can also keep the employer's name confidential until late into the search process.

But there are some pitfalls. As an employer, it is essential to explain completely what sort of candidate is required—and why. Also, some "head-hunters" are more salesmen than professionals. They may be more interested in persuading an employer to hire a candidate than finding one they believe will really do the job. Executive recruiters also claim that what their client *says* he wants is often not really what he needs; therefore, employers should be prepared for some in-depth "dissecting" of their requests.

If you are a candidate, keep in mind that most of these firms pay little heed to unsolicited resumes: they usually ferret out their own candidates. Some firms have also been known to present an unpromising candidate to a client simply to make the other one or two candidates look that much better. Some eager clients may also jump the gun, checking your references (and thereby undermining your present position) prematurely. Also, keep in mind that executive recruiters (and clients) are much more impressed with candidates who are obviously "not looking" for a job; eagerness to take the job has been the downfall of many a candidate. [27]

College Recruiting as a Source of Candidates

We have already seen that promotion from within is a major source of management candidates. Many of these "promotable" candidates are originally hired through college recruiting which is therefore an important source of management trainees, as well as of both professional and technical employees.

There are two main problems with on-campus recruiting. First, it is usually both expensive and time-consuming from the point of view of the individuals doing the recruiting. To be done right, schedules have to be set well in advance, company brochures printed, records of interviews kept, and much recruiting time spent on campus. A second problem is that recruiters themselves are sometimes ineffective (or worse). [28] Some students probably have found that recruiters are unprepared, show little interest in the candidate, and act superior. Similarly, many recruiters don't effectively screen their student candidates. For example, students' physical attractiveness often outweighs other, more valid traits and skills. [29] Some recruiters also tend to assign females to "female-type" jobs and males to "male-type" jobs. [30] One suggestion is to use a structured interview form (one that forces interviewers to follow a standard and proven set and sequence of questions) and to train recruiters before sending them to the college campus. [31]

Referrals and Walk-ins as a Source of Candidates

Particularly for hourly workers, "walk-ins"—direct application at your office —are a major source of applicants. [32] Some organizations encourage such applicants by mounting an "employee referrals" compaign. Announcements of openings and requests for referrals are made in the organization's bulletin and posted on bulletin boards: Prizes are offered for referrals that culminate in hirings. This sort of campaign can cut recruiting costs by eliminating advertising and agency fees. It can also result in higher quality candidates (since many people

are reluctant to refer less qualified candidates). But the success of the campaign   111
depends largely on the morale of employees. [33] And the campaign can boomer-
ang if an employee's referral is rejected and the employees become dissatisfied.
Using referrals exclusively may also be judged to be discriminatory where most
of the current employees are either white or male.

DEVELOPING AND USING APPLICATION BLANKS

The Purposè of Application Blanks

Once you have a pool of applicants you can begin the process of selecting
the person you want to hire, and in most organizations the application blank
is the first step in the selection process. (Some firms first require a brief, screening interview.) The application blank (or form) is a good means of quickly
collecting verifiable (and therefore fairly accurate) basic historical data from
the candidate: it usually includes information on such things as education, prior
work history, and hobbies.

A filled-in form can provide four types of information. [34] First, you can
make judgments on *substantive* matters, such as "does the applicant have the
education and experience to do the job?" Second, you can draw conclusions
about the applicant's previous *progress and growth* (this is especially important
for management candidates). Third, you can also draw some *tentative* conclusions concerning the applicant's *stability* based on his previous work record.
(Here, be careful not to assume that an unusual number of job changes necessarily reflects on the applicant's stability. Check the reasons for the job changes:
Did his previous employer have to lay-off large numbers of employees? Did the
applicant simply make a mistake in accepting his previous job? etc.) Fourth,
you may be able to use the data in the application to *predict* which candidates
will succeed on the job and which will not (we will discuss this in a moment).

In practice, most organizations use several different application forms. For
technical and managerial personnel, for example, the form may require detailed
answers to questions concerning such things as the applicant's education. The
form for hourly factory workers might focus on the tools and equipment the
applicant has used. An example of an application form is presented in Exhibit
4.6 .

Equal Rights and Application Blanks

Again, remember that questions concerning race, religion, age, sex, or national origin are not illegal, per se, under the federal laws (but may be under
some state laws). But, they *are* viewed with "disfavor" [35] by the EEOC, and the
burden of proof will always be on the employer to prove that they are *both*
related to success or failure on the job *and* not unfairly discriminatory. (Similarly,
remember that it may be ill-advised to request photographs prior to employ-

112 ment.) The point is that while an item (like "have you ever been arrested?") may not be illegal *per se* under federal laws an unsuccessful applicant might establish a *prima facie* case of unfair discrimination by demonstrating that the item produces an adverse impact, say, on blacks. Having so demonstrated, the burden of proof would rest with the employer to show that the item is valid (in terms of predicting job performance), and is applied fairly to all applicants.

Exhibit 4.6   Application for Professional Employment

RETURN THIS FORM TO:

(NAME OF COMPANY REPRESENTATIVE)   DATE OF APPLICATION

APPLICATION FOR PROFESSIONAL EMPLOYMENT

NAME OF APPLICANT (LAST, FIRST AND MIDDLE)				SOCIAL SECURITY NO.	

ADDRESS (STREET, CITY AND STATE)   PHONE NO. (TEMPORARY)
TEMPORARY

ADDRESS (STREET, CITY AND STATE)   PHONE NO. (PERMANENT)
PERMANENT

TYPE OF POSITION DESIRED

SALARY EXPECTED   POSITION TO BE   WHEN AVAILABLE FOR WORK
TO START   ☐ PERMANENT   ☐ TEMPORARY

LOCATION PREFERENCES OR RESTRICTIONS

EDUCATION

SCHOOL	NAME AND LOCATION	YRS. ATTENDED		DIPLOMA OR DEGREE	MAJOR SUBJECTS	UPPER MIDDLE OR LOWER $\frac{1}{3}$ OF CLASS
		FROM	TO			
HIGH OR PREPARATORY						
COLLEGE						
GRADUATE WORK						
OTHER						

HONORS RECEIVED

LIST THESIS, PUBLISHED ARTICLES AND YOUR PATENTS, IF ANY

DID YOU HAVE A SCHOLARSHIP   IF YES, WHAT TYPE OR KIND
☐ YES   ☐ NO

DID YOU EARN ANY OF YOUR EXPENSES   IF YES, WHAT % OF TOTAL EXPENSE AND HOW EARNED
☐ YES   ☐ NO

WHAT ACADEMIC WORK DID YOU ENJOY MOST

WHAT SUBJECT ARE YOU NOW PURSUING, OR WHAT PLANS DO YOU HAVE FOR CONTINUING YOUR EDUCATION

WHAT STUDENT ACTIVITIES DID YOU PARTICIPATE IN

HOBBIES OR FAVORITE RECREATION   COLLEGE POINT OR LETTER GRADE AVERAGE
BASED ON

U. S. MILITARY SERVICE

ARE YOU A VETERAN OF UNITED STATES MILITARY SERVICE ☐ YES ☐ NO   BRANCH OF SERVICE   PERIOD OF SERVICE
FROM   TO

TYPE OF DISCHARGE   RANK ATTAINED   RESERVE STATUS

NATURE OF SERVICE ASSIGNMENTS

Exhibit 4.6 *(continued)*   113

List Last Position First

EMPLOYMENT DATES		COMPANY AND ADDRESS	*POSITION OR TYPE OF WORK	SALARY OR WAGE	REASON FOR LEAVING
FROM	TO				

EMPLOYMENT HISTORY

WHY ARE YOU SEEKING A JOB CHANGE (IF APPLICABLE)

CAN WE CONTACT YOUR PRESENT EMPLOYER WITHOUT JEOPARDIZING YOUR POSITION   ☐ YES   ☐ NO

HAVE YOU EVER BEEN EMPLOYED BY THIS COMPANY   ☐ YES   ☐ NO   WHEN   WHERE

IN WHAT CAPACITY

NAME ACQUAINTANCES IN OUR EMPLOY

Use this space to describe in detail above Work Experience

REFERENCES

List 2 persons acquainted with your academic preparation or business experience.

NAME	BUSINESS OR PROFESSION	ADDRESS

APPLICANT'S STATEMENT & AGREEMENT
Read the following carefully before signing this application for employment.

1. I AM NOT A MEMBER OF ANY ORGANIZATION WHICH ADVOCATES THE FORCEFUL OVERTHROW OF THE UNITED STATES GOVERNMENT.

2. I UNDERSTAND THAT UNLESS ACTED UPON THIS APPLICATION WILL BECOME INACTIVE AFTER NINETY DAYS.

3. I UNDERSTAND THAT ANY FUTURE OFFER OF EMPLOYMENT IS CONTINGENT UPON MY PASSING THE COMPANY'S STANDARD PHYSICAL EXAMINATION.

4. I HEREBY CERTIFY THAT THE FOREGOING ANSWERS ARE CORRECT TO THE BEST OF MY KNOWLEDGE AND BELIEF. I UNDERSTAND THAT MISREPRESENTATION WILL BE CONSIDERED AS JUST CAUSE FOR REJECTION OF THIS APPLICATION OR DISMISSAL FROM EMPLOYMENT.

SIGNATURE OF APPLICANT_____   DATE _____

ATTACH ANY ADDITIONAL INFORMATION OR DOCUMENTS TO THIS APPLICATION

Source: Reprinted by permission of the publisher from *Book of Employment Forms,* American Management Association, copyright © 1967 by the American Management Association, p. 147.

Using Application Forms to Make Predictions

Most managers just use application forms to obtain basic background data, while other managers put their forms to better use. Through a fairly simple procedure (explained in the appendix to this chapter) they find the relationship between (1) responses on the application and (2) measures of success on the job. They can then use their application forms to *predict* which candidates will be successful and which will not. For example:

Using Application Blanks to Predict Job Tenure. [36]   A researcher obtained the application blanks of 160 female clerical employees from the personnel file of a large insurance company. At the time the company was experiencing a 48% turnover rate among its clerical personnel. (Thus, for every two employees hired at the same time, there was about a 50–50 chance that one of the two would not remain with the company 12 months or longer.)

The researcher split the application blanks into two categories: those representing "long tenure" employees and those representing "short tenure." He then found that some responses were highly related to tenure. By giving these responses appropriate weights he was able to use the company's application blanks to predict which of the company's *new* applicants would stay on the job and which would not. In addition, some of the items on the application blanks concerned age and marital status. (Remember that while there are no legal barriers to *asking* such questions, the employer may have to be able to *prove* that they predict success or failure on the job.) In this case the researcher was able to prove that these items *did* predict success or failure on the job (long tenure vs. short tenure). [37]

Predicting Success on the Job with Application Blanks.   Application blanks have also been used to predict job success. [38] In one study, for example, the researcher was able to predict success in the military (in terms of "military rank when released"). He found that a number of items (like father's country of origin, father's occupational level, and high school major) were related to success in the Israeli army. Other studies have been able to predict success as a life insurance salesman. [39]

Using Application Blanks to Predict Employee Theft.   Losses due to shoplifting, worker pilferage, etc., range up to $16 billion per year. [40] Special tests which supposedly predict stealing are available, but tend to be "in-depth" tests of personality. They are difficult and time-consuming to administer and even more difficult to evaluate.

Application blank information may provide a simpler alternative, since researchers have used firms' application blanks to successfully identify potential "stealers." In one case, the researcher carried out studies for both a mass merchandiser and a supermarket in Detroit. He found that some items (like "not living with parents" and "does not own automobile") were highly related to

whether or not the employee was "caught stealing," [41] and he was therefore able
to identify potential stealers.

SUMMARY

1. Manpower planning, recruitment, and placement involves placing the right man (or woman) on the right job. We said it requires six steps as follows: (1) job analysis; (2) personnel planning and recruiting; (3) obtain application blank information; (4) interview the candidate; (5) test the candidate and check references; and (6) orient and train the person.

2. Developing personnel plans requires three forecasts: one for personnel *requirements,* one for the *supply* of outside candidates, and one for the *supply* of inside candidates. Predicting the need for personnel usually first requires projecting the demand for the product or service ("sales"). Next, project the volume of production required to meet these sales estimates; finally, relate manpower needs to these production estimates.

3. Once personnel needs are projected, the next step is to build up a pool of qualified applicants. We discussed several sources of candidates including "internal" sources (or "promotion from within"), advertising, employment agencies, executive recruiters, college recruiting, and referrals and walk-ins. Remember that it's unlawful to discriminate against any individual with respect to employment because of race, color, religion, sex, national origin, or age, (unless religion, sex, or origin are BFOQ's).

4. The initial selection screening in most organizations begins with an application blank. Most managers just use these to obtain background data. However, you can use application blank data to make *predictions* about the applicant's future performance. For example, application blanks have been used to predict job tenure, job success, and employee theft.

5. Using application blanks to predict success (or some other criteria) assumes you can "weight" the more important items. In the appendix we present a seven-step method for doing this: (1) decide on a measure of success; (2) pull the applications of "highs" and "lows"; (3) for each response on the application determine the percentage of "highs" and the percentage of "lows"; (4) compute percentage differences for each item; (5) convert these percentage differences to weights; (6) add up the applicant's total score; and (7) find the "ideal" total score.

6. Manpower planning and recruiting directly affect employee performance. This is because performance depends on hiring employees who have the aptitude to do the job well. And, the more qualified applicants you have, the higher your selection standards can be. Then, once a pool of qualified applicants is available you can turn to selecting the best. This process usually begins with effective interviewing, to which we now turn.

Phillips Foods*

Jack Billings, an employee in the purchase order department of Phillips Foods, entered the office of Personnel Manager Bill Fischer one morning and requested that he be able to remain in his present position. Mr. Fischer felt that this was an unusual request since Jack had recently notified him that he was going to leave Phillips and accept a sales position in a Louisville photographic equipment supply firm.

Mr. Fischer asked "Jack, why have you suddenly decided that you want to stay?"

"Well, the firm I was going to work for in Louisville was sold yesterday. The owner said he was sorry that the job fell through, but that doesn't help me now."

Mr. Fischer told Jack that he could not give him an immediate answer, since he would first have to check with Howard Byers, head of the purchase order department, and Bill Simmons, regional manager, before a decision could be made.

Mr. Fischer knew that Jack, who was twenty-four years old, had been with Phillips in the order department for three years and had recently been married. Jack had previously spent two years in the armed forces after graduating from high school.

The order department had always been considered a "pressure" job by Mr. Fischer although it was often routine. Whenever an order was phoned in, the person in the order department who answered would have to write the order, call the production manager and inform him of any unusual order or special request, notify the shipping department and confirm the copy of the order, and finally tell the transportation department of the need for a carrier to deliver the order. In addition, the members of the order department would have to follow up on all orders and make necessary corrections. The number of calls kept the department constantly busy.

Since the operations were basically mechanical, Mr. Fischer felt that men with high school educations or men who had not completed college were suitable for the position. Mr. Fischer had previously concluded that women simply did not like the high degree of "pressure" the job demanded and also didn't accept the hours of overtime that were necessary.

The order department had always had a high degree of turnover. Mr. Fischer concluded that it was simply not the type of job that a person would like to make his lifetime work. In the past there had been very little advancement from this position.

As his investigation of the possibilities of Jack's remaining continued, Mr. Fischer learned that the salesmen who phoned their orders into the order department often specifically requested to talk to Jack so that they could be sure that the

* Arno F. Knapper, *Cases in Personnel Management*, (Columbus, Ohio: Grid, Inc., 1977) pp. 19–20.

orders would be written correctly and that the proper supply of each item was
actually on hand. Mr. Fischer also found out that the shipping and transportation
departments would consult Jack about various order questions when Howard Byers
was not present or was too busy to handle them immediately.

After talking to Howard Byers, the personnel manager's opinion that Jack was
the best of the eight men in the department was substantiated. As far as Howard
Byers was concerned, Jack's continuance as a member of the department would
certainly be welcome.

Mr. Fischer then talked to Mr. Simmons, who felt that it would be wise to
retain a man of Jack's ability, especially since there had always been a high turnover in the order department.

After reviewing the situation, Mr. Fischer was prepared to let Jack continue,
when John Rockwell, head of industrial sales, requested that Jack be transferred to
his department to begin training as a salesman. Although most of the other salesmen
had college degrees in chemistry, Mr. Rockwell felt that Jack, through his past performance, could handle the job even without a college education.

Mr. Fischer talked to Jack about the possible change, "Jack, do you believe that
you would like to sell for Phillips?"

"Of course I would. I'm sure that I could handle the job. Working in the order
department gave me an excellent opportunity to observe the entire operation here
at Phillips. I'd like the challenge."

Questions

1. Should Jack be retained by Phillips Food? If so, in what position?
2. If Jack succeeds in his job as salesman, should the job qualifications be changed?
   Why? Why not? Is experience a good substitute for education in qualification
   requirements?
3. What did Phillips Foods do wrong in *planning* for this opening? In *screening* for
   this position? In setting up selection standards?
4. How (specifically) might Phillips Foods improve their staffing (job analysis, recruitment, selection, orientation) procedures?

EXPERIENTIAL EXERCISE

Purpose. The purpose of this exercise is to give you practice in developing an application blank.

Required Understanding. The reader will want to be familiar with personal history items useful in developing an application blank (Exhibit 4.10), and the job description presented in Exhibit 3.2. (from Chapter 3). Your objective is to develop an application blank for a production control manager.

How to Set Up the Exercise.

1. Set up groups of three or four students.

2. Before joining his or her group, each student should carefully read through the exhibits referred to above. The exercise should take about one hour.

Instructions for the Exercise. Form into assigned groups and compile a list of the application blank items you wish to include in your form. Next, sketch out a rough application blank, showing where each of your items would appear on the page(s).

Each group should then choose a spokesman and list his or her group's items on the blackboard. Which items appeared most often? What items seem to be missing? Which items do you think would be most useful it you wanted to develop a weighted application? Which items do you think would be most predictive of the applicant's performance?

DISCUSSION QUESTIONS

1. Compare and contrast at least five sources of job candidates.
2. What types of information can an application blank provide you with?
3. Explain how you would go about weighting an application blank.
4. Discuss some of the ways in which equal rights legislation limits what you can do in recruiting.

NOTES

1. Wayne Cascio, *Applied Psychology in Personnel Management* (Reston, Va.: Reston Publishing, 1978), p. 158.

2. For a discussion of this see Cascio, pp. 156–158.

3. Herbert G. Heneman, Jr. and George Seitzer, "Manpower Planning and Forecasting in the Firm: An Exploratory Probe," in Elmer Burack and James Walker, *Manpower Planning and Programming* (Rockleigh, N.J.: Allyn, 1972), pp. 102–120; Sheldon Zedeck and Milton Blood, "Selection and Placement," from *Foundations of Behavioral Science Research in Organizations* (Monterey: Brooks/Cole, 1974) in J. Richard Hackman, Edward Lawler III, and Lyman Porter, *Perspectives on Behavior in Organizations* (New York: McGraw-Hill, 1977), pp. 103–119. For a discussion of equal employment implications of manpower planning see James Lispunicia, "Technical Implications of Equal Employment Law for Manpower Planning," *Personnel Psychology*, Vol. 28 (Autumn 1975).

4. Roger Hawk, *The Recruitment Function* (New York: American Management Association, 1967).

5. Glenn Bassett, "Elements of Manpower Forecasting and Scheduling," *Human*

Resource Management, Vol. 12, No. 3, Fall 1973, pp. 35–43, reprinted in Richard Peterson, Lane Tracy, and Allen Cabelly, *Systematic Management of Human Resources,* (Reading, Mass.: Addison-Wesley, 1979), pp. 135–146.

6. Peterson et al., p. 142.

7. For an example of a computerized system in use at Citibank, see Paul Sheiber, "A Simple Selection System Called "Jobmatch," *Personnel Journal* (January 1979), pp. 26–54.

8. For a discussion, see Don Bryant, Michael Maggart, and Robert Taylor "Manpower Planning Models and Techniques: A Descriptive Survey" *Business Horizons,* Vol. 16, No. 2 (April 1973), pp. 69–78.

9. Based on William F. Glueck, *Personnel: A Diagnostic Approach* (Dallas: Business Publications, Inc., 1974), pp. 108–110.

10. See Elizabeth Marting, A.M.A. *Book of Appointment Forms* (New York: American Management Association, 1967), pp. 671–692.

11. For a discussion of these see Elmer Burack and James Walker, *Manpower Planning and Programming* (Boston: Allyn and Bacon, 1972), pp. 122–142.

12. See Cascio, pp. 167–171.

13. J. F. Gillespie, W. E. Leieinger, and H. Kahalas, "A Human Resource Planning and Valuation Model," *Academy of Management Journal,* Vol. 19, 1976, pp. 650–656.

14. In line with this, Cascio points out yield ratios should always be computed before any recruiting begins. Yield ratios are the ratios of leads to invites, invites to interviews, interviews (and other selection instruments) to offers, and offers to hires obtained over some specified time period like 6 months or a year. Cascio, p. 187.

15. Henderson, *Compensation Management,* pp. 170–171.

16. See J. D. Dunn and E. C. Stephens, "Federal Laws Affecting Personnel Management," based on *Management of Personnel: Manpower Management and Organizational Behavior* (New York: McGraw-Hill, 1972) in W. Clay Hammer and Frank Schmidt, *Contemporary Problems in Personnel* (Chicago: St. Clair, 1974), p. 25.

17. See Richard Henderson, *Compensation Management* (Reston, Va.: Reston Publishing, 1976), pp. 444–446.

18. See, for example, Wayne Cascio, "Turnover, Biographical Data, and Fair Employment Practice," *Journal of Applied Psychology,* Vol. 61 (October 1976); other defenses, such as "Business Necessity," were discussed in Chapter 2.

19. John Campbell, Marvin Dunnette, Edward Lawler III, and Karl Weick, Jr., *Managerial Behavior, Performance, and Effectiveness* (New York: McGraw-Hill, 1970), p. 23.

20. David Dahl and Patrick Pinto, "Job Posting: An Industry Survey," *Personnel Journal,* Vol. 56, No. 1 (January 1977), pp. 40–41.

21. Jeffrey Daum, "Internal Promotion—Psychological Asset or Debit? A Study of the Effects of Leader Origin," *Organizational Behavior and Human Performance,* Vol. 13 (1975), pp. 404–413.

22. For a discussion of current job posting practice see "Employee Promotion and Transfer Policies," PPF survey No. 20 (Washington, D.C. The Bureau of National Affairs) January 1978.

23. National Industrial Conference Board, "Personnel Practices in Factory and Office: Manufacturing," *Studies in Personnel Policy,* No. 194 (1964), p. 8; Wendell French, *The Personnel Management Process* (Boston: Houghton Mifflin, 1974), p. 259.

24. Bureau of National Affairs, "Solving the Shortage of Specialized Personnel," Survey #62 (September 1961), p. 1; in French, p. 259.

25. Arthur Pell, *Recruiting and Selecting Personnel* (New York: Regents, 1969), p. 16.

26. Based on Pell, *Recruiting and Selecting Personnel*, pp. 34–42.

27. *Ibid.*; Alan J. Cox, *Confessions of a Corporate Head Hunter* (New York: Trident, 1973).

28. See, for example, Richard Becker, "Ten Common Mistakes in College Recruiting—or How to Try Without Really Succeeding," *Personnel*, Vol. 52, No. 2 (March–April 1975), pp. 19–28.

29. Robert Dipboye, Howard Fronkin, and Ken Wiback, "Relative Importance of Applicant Sex, Attractiveness and Scholastic Standing in Evaluation of Job Applicant Resumes," *Journal of Applied Psychology*, Vol. 61 (1975), pp. 39–48.

30. Dipboye, Fronkin, and Wiback, "Relative Importance of Applicant Sex, Attractiveness and Scholastic Standing in Evaluation of Job Applicant Resumes," pp. 39–48.

31. *Ibid.* See also, "College Recruiting," in *Personnel*, May–June 1980.

32. "Personnel Practices," p. 9, in French, p. 259.

33. Pell, *Recruiting and Selecting Personnel*, p. 13.

34. *Ibid.*, pp. 96–98. See also Wayne Cascio, "Accuracy of Verifiable Biographical Information Blank Responses," *Journal of Applied Psychology*, Vol. 60 (December 1975) for a discussion of accuracy of bio-data.

35. See French, "The Personnel Management Process," p. 267.

36. For other representative studies see, for example, J. J. Asher, "The Biographical Item: Can it Be Improved?" *Personnel Psychology*, Vol. 22 (1972), pp. 251–269; A. J. Schuh, "The Predictability of Employee Tenure: A Review of the Literature," *Personnel Psychology*, Vol. 20 (1967), pp. 139–152; for a contrasting view, see D. P. Schwab and R. L. Oliver, "Predicting Tenure with Biographical Data: Exhuming Buried Evidence," *Personnel Psychology*, Vol. 27 (1974), pp. 125–128.

37. Wayne Cascio, "Turnover, Biographical Data, and Fair Employment Practice," *Journal of Applied Psychology*, Vol. 61 (October 1976).

38. Barukh Nevo, "Using Biographical Information to Predict Success of Men and Women in the Army," *Journal of Applied Psychology*, Vol. 61 (1976), pp. 106–108.

39. Tiffin and McCormick, *Industrial Psychology*, pp. 70–71.

40. Quotes in Richard Rosenbaum, "Predictability of Employee Theft Using Weighted Application Blanks," *Journal of Applied Psychology*, Vol. 61 (1976), pp. 94–98.

41. Rosenbaum, "Predictability of Employee Theft Using Weighted Application Blanks," pp. 94–98.

42. Based on David J. Weiss, "Multivariate Procedures," in Marvin Dunnette, *Handbook of Industrial and Organizational Psychology* (Chicago: Rand-McNally, 1967), pp. 345–346.

43. For purposes of proving conformity to equal rights legislation, you'd probably have to use a somewhat more sophisticated statistical technique to find your ideal total score. For a further explanation, see G. W. England, *Development and Use of Weighted Application Blanks*, rev. ed. (Minneapolis: University of Minnesota, Industrial Relations Center, 1971). See also Larry Pace and Lyle Schoenfeldt, "Legal Concerns in the Use of Weighted Applications," *Personnel Psychology*, Vol. 30 (Summer 1977), pp. 159–166.

44. Paraphrased from Larry Pace and Lyle Schoenfeldt, "Legal Concerns in the Use of Weighted Applications," *Personnel Psychology*, Vol. 30, No. 2, (Summer 1977).

45. Pace and Schoenfeldt, p. 160.

46. R. W. Rosenbaum, "Predictability of Employee Theft Using Weighted Application Blanks," *Journal of Applied Psychology*, Vol. 61 (1976), pp. 94–98.

HOW TO WEIGHT APPLICATION BLANKS[42]

Using application blanks to predict success assumes that some responses are more predictive of success than others. For example, suppose you find that most who check the response "age 21–25" quit within one year, while most who check the box "age 31–35" stay with the company *more* than one year. What you'll need is some method for giving more weight to the latter response, since there will then be more chance of an applicant between 31 and 35 years of age being offered a position. The following is one technique for "weighting" application blank items. (Note: you will have to follow Exhibits 4.7, 4.8, and 4.9 carefully.)

Step 1: Decide on Measure of Success.   First, decide on what your measure of success will be (this is usually called the "criterion"). It might be tenure on the job, performance, employee theft, etc. Then, decide on a *standard*—such as "stayed on the job one year or more," if job tenure is your criterion.

Step 2: Pick Out "High" and "Low" Performers.   Next, for some period (say those hired in 1978) pull out the application blanks for those employees who stayed one year or more (the "long tenures"); and pull out those who stayed less than one year (the "short tenures"). (If there are too many employees involved, some scheme for randomly selecting a sample of employees could be used, although for statistical purposes it is often useful to have as large a sample as practical.)

Step 3: For Each Response Determine the Percentage "Highs" and the Percentage "Lows."   Let's say you decide to focus on 10 application blank items, four of which are presented in Exhibit 4.7. And, again, let's assume that your measure of success (your criterion) is "short tenure" versus "long tenure."

Step 3 would be to indicate for each application blank response (such as "under 20" for the item "Age") the percentage of "short tenure" applicants that checked that response (40% in Exhibit 4.7) and the percentage of "long tenure" applicants that checked that response (10% in Exhibit 4.7). As an example, we've listed these percentages for the responses for each of the four items in Exhibit 4.7.

Step 4: Compute Percent Differences.   Next, compute the percent differences (between the long and short tenure percentages) for each response. For the "previous salary" item in Exhibit 4.7, for example, 50% minus 20% is a difference of 30%; 20% minus 40% equals −20%; 20% minus 20% equals 0%; and 10% minus 20% equals −10%.

Exhibit 4.7 Comparison of Responses by Long and Short Tenure Employees

Application Blank Items (Predictors)	% Short Tenure*	% Long Tenure*	% Differences	Weights
Local Address				
within city	40%	70%	-30%	-3
outlying suburbs	60%	30%	30%	3
	100%	100%		
Age				
under 20	40%	10%	30%	3
21-25	20%	30%	-10%	-1
26-30	20%	20%	0%	0
31-35	10%	20%	-10%	-1
35 and over	10%	20%	-10%	-1
	100%	100%		
Previous Salary				
under $3,000	50%	20%	30%	3
$3,000-$4,000	20%	40%	-20%	-2
$4,001-$5,000	20%	20%	0	0
Over $5,000	10%	20%	-10%	-1
	100%	100%		
Age of Children				
preschool	40%	20%	20%	2
public school	20%	30%	-10%	-1
high school or older	40%	50%	-10%	-1
	100%	100%		

*EXAMPLE: 40% of short-tenure (employees had a "within City" address; 60% of them had a "Suburbs" address).

Exhibit 4.8 Weighted Score of Applicant

APPLICATION FOR EMPLOYMENT

	Code:* (for use by Personnel Department)
Name: Harvey Hooley	
Address: 108 Elm Street, Springfield	within -3
Age: 23	21-25 -1
Salary on last job: $5,800	over $5,000 -1
Age of children: 4, and 5 . . . . (if any)	Public -1
Duties on last job:	
Educational history:	
Reason for leaving last job:	
	TOTAL -6

*See Exhibit 3.6 for code.

Step 5: Convert Percent Differences to Weights.　The next step is to convert these percent differences to integer weights. (This makes them more convenient to use.) Thus the 30% difference would be given a weight of +3. The —10% difference would be given a weight of —1, and so on.

Step 6: Add Up Each "Applicant's" Total Score.　Your next step is to compute the total score for each of the long and short tenure "applicants." You do this for each applicant by finding his response to each item and then adding up the weights for these responses. For the applicant shown in Exhibit 4.8 the total score would be —6.

Step 7: Find the "Ideal" Total Score.　Next you find the "ideal" total score. (In our case this is the score *that best differentiates between short and long tenure employees.*) One way to do this is illustrated in Exhibit 4.9. Let's say that in our study of long versus short tenure employees we found that total scores for applicants ranged from —10 to +21. (There may be several people with each total score.) For each total score, list the percentage of "long" and "short" tenure applicants reaching that score. Then, in the last column, show the difference between the former and the latter (as in Exhibit 4.9).

In this case our "ideal" score is +4. We arrived at "+4" as follows. Run your finger down the last column in Exhibit 4.9. Halt when the numbers stop climbing and start falling. This is the point at which you draw a horizontal line and find your "ideal" total score. [43] It is the cutoff for the "ideal" score, because at this point there is the *maximum difference* between percentage of long tenure employees (column A) and percentage of short tenure employees (column B): recall you were looking for the score that *best differentiates* between long and short tenure employees.

A List of Useful Application Blank Items.　George England has reviewed a number of studies of weighted application blanks. From his review, he has compiled a list of application blank items that have been found to predict various measures of success on the job. These are presented in Exhibit 4.10. They include items like "age," "education," and "college grades." A manager can use these as a "menu" for developing a weighted application blank.

Summary.　Developing a weighted application blank basically involves determining the relationship between (1) an application blank item (like age) and (2) job performance and then determining the "weight" to be applied to various degrees of that item (such as age 21–30, 31–40, and 41–50). According to two experts, weighted application blanks present an attractive alternative to the use of tests for employment decisions, and this attractiveness stems from several sources:

1. Most applicants *expect* to be asked to complete an application form.
2. The weighted application form need have no distinguishable differences from an unscored form.
3. Filling in a blank with verifiable information about one's personal history is

less noxious (to most people) than taking a test in which it is usually presumed that the test score will have something, perhaps everything, to do with whether one is offered employment.

4. Finally, weighted applications are developed on the basis of their statistically proven relationship to performance and should therefore be permissible from a legal (EEOC) standpoint. [44]

Exhibit 4.9   Obtaining a Cutting Score

	Total Score	Percentage of Subjects at or above a Given Score		Index of Differentiation (A minus B)	
		A Percentage of Long-Tenure Employees	B Percentage of Short-Tenure Employees		
	21	4	0	4	
	20	4	0	4	
	19	4	0	4	
	18	12	0	12	
	17	16	0	16	
	16	20	0	20	
	15	20	0	20	
	14	24	0	24	
	13	24	3	21	
	12	28	3	25	
	11	32	5	27	
	10	36	8	28	
	9	40	10	30	
	8	40	14	26	
	7	44	15	29	
	6	48	17	31	
Cutting	5	60	20	40	
Score	4	68	22	46	Point of Greatest Differentiation
	3	72	27	45	
	2	72	32	40	
	1	72	39	33	
	0	80	42	38	
	-1	80	46	34	
	-2	80	54	26	
	-3	84	66	18	
	-4	92	68	24	
	-5	92	76	16	
	-6	92	85	7	
	-7	96	90	6	
	-8	96	94	2	
	-9	100	98	2	
	-10	100	100	0	

Source: Edwin A. Fleishman and Alan R. Bass, *Studies in Personnel and Industrial Psychology,* 3rd ed. (Homewood, Ill.: The Dorsey Press, 1974), p. 90.

Note: Moving down last column, numbers *rise* till reach cutting point, and then start *falling,* since it is at this point that there is the *greatest difference* between column A (long-tenure) and column B (short-tenure).

Exhibit 4.10   Personal History Items Useful in Developing an Application Blank   125

PERSONAL
Age *
Age at hiring
Marital status *
Number of years married
Dependents, number of
Children, number of
Age when first child born
Physical health
Recent illnesses, operations
Time lost from job for certain previous period
  (last 2 years, etc.)
Living conditions, general
Domicile, whether alone, rooming house, keep
  own house, etc.
Residence, location of
Size of home town
Number of times moved in recent period
Length of time at last address
Nationality *
Birth place *
Weight and height
Sex

GENERAL BACKGROUND
Occupation of father
Occupation of mother
Occupation of brothers, sisters, other relatives
Military service and rank
Military discharge record
Early family responsibility
Parental family adjustment
Professionally successful parents
Stable or transient home life
Wife does not work outside home

EDUCATION
Education
Educational level of wife
Educational level of family relatives
Education finances—extent of dependence on
  parents
Type of course studied—grammar school
Major field of study—high school
Specific courses taken in high school or college
Subjects liked, disliked in high school
Years since leaving high school
Type of school attended, private/state
College grades
Scholarship level, grammar school and high school
Graduated at early age compared with classmates

*Some items such as these may violate fair employ-
ment practice legislation. See explanation in text.

EMPLOYMENT EXPERIENCE
Educational—vocational consistency
Previous occupations (general type of work)
Held job in high school (type of job)
Number of previous jobs
Specific work experience (specific jobs)
Previous (selling) experience
Previous (life insurance sales) experience
Total length of work experience (total years,
  months)
Being in business for self
Previous employee of company now considering
  application
Seniority in present employment
Tenure on previous job
Minimum current living expenses
Salary requests, limits set for accepting job
Earnings expected (in future, 2 yrs., 5 yrs.,
  etc.)

SOCIAL
Club memberships (social, community, campus,
  high school)
Frequency of attendance at group meetings
Offices held in clubs
Experience as a group leader
Church membership

INTERESTS
Prefer outside to inside labor
Hobbies
Number of hobbies
Specific type of hobbies, leisure time activities
  preferred
Sports
Number of sports active in
Most important source of entertainment

*PERSONAL CHARACTERISTICS,
ATTITUDES EXPRESSED*
Willingness to relocate or transfer
Confidence (as expressed by applicant)
Basic personality needs (5 types) as expressed by
  applicant in reply to question on application
  blank
Drive
Stated job preferences

MISCELLANEOUS
Time taken for hiring negotiations between appli-
  cant and company
Former employer's estimate of applicant

Source: George W. England, *Development and Use of Weighted Application Blanks*, rev. ed.
(Minneapolis: Industrial Relations Center, University of Minnesota, 1971), pp. 16–19.

126   *Legal Concerns in the Use of Weighted Applications.*   Although weighted application blanks can be effective screening devices, they can also lead to illegal employment decisions or to decisions that, while not against the equal employment laws in a literal sense violate the spirit of a law. [45]

The legal pitfalls in the use of weighted application blanks derive largely from two things: (1) the relative ease with which persons other than experienced personnel psychologists can develop weighted application blanks, and (2) the fact that many items on the application blank (concerning race or age, for instance) necessarily have an adverse impact on protected groups but are also routinely weighted in the weighting process. Application blank items concerning race, sex, religion, age, or national origin *could* be included, of course, even if they do have an adverse impact, as long as their job relatedness and fairness is provable. Again, however, the problem is that they are "red flags" to the EEOC. Furthermore, the ease with which nonspecialists can develop weighted applications creates the possibility that undesirable items may inadvertently be included by nonexperts who are not fully cognizant of the legal requirements or statistical validation procedures to be used. [46] One implication seems to be that those developing weighted application blanks would do well to steer clear of items (concerning race, and religion, for instance) that clearly have an adverse impact. Instead, they should seek out items which, based on a thorough job analysis, seem to be obvious and reasonable prerequisites for success on the job. A second implication is that those who are not experienced personnel psychologists should use this technique (and all testing techniques) with considerable caution.

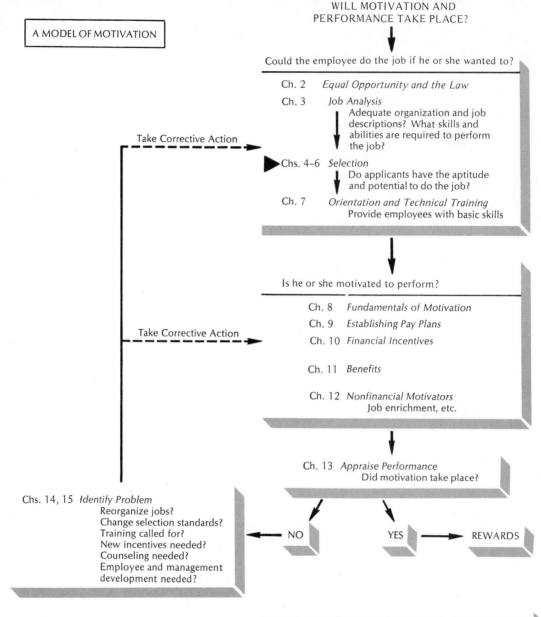

A MODEL OF MOTIVATION

WILL MOTIVATION AND
PERFORMANCE TAKE PLACE?

Could the employee do the job if he or she wanted to?

Ch. 2   *Equal Opportunity and the Law*

Ch. 3   *Job Analysis*
Adequate organization and job descriptions? What skills and abilities are required to perform the job?

Chs. 4–6 *Selection*
Do applicants have the aptitude and potential to do the job?

Ch. 7   *Orientation and Technical Training*
Provide employees with basic skills

Is he or she motivated to perform?

Ch. 8   *Fundamentals of Motivation*

Ch. 9   *Establishing Pay Plans*

Ch. 10 *Financial Incentives*

Ch. 11 *Benefits*

Ch. 12 *Nonfinancial Motivators*
Job enrichment, etc.

Ch. 13 *Appraise Performance*
Did motivation take place?

Take Corrective Action

Take Corrective Action

Chs. 14, 15 *Identify Problem*
Reorganize jobs?
Change selection standards?
Training called for?
New incentives needed?
Counseling needed?
Employee and management development needed?

NO   YES ⟶ REWARDS

THE ENVIRONMENT OF PERSONNEL MANAGEMENT

Ch. 16 *Labor Relations and Grievances*

Ch. 17 *Employee Safety and Health*

Ch. 18 *Personnel Management and the Quality of Work Life*

When you finish studying

5 Interviewing Job Candidates

You should be able to:

1. *Discuss the findings regarding how useful most interviews are.*

2. *Explain at least six factors that affect the usefulness of interviews.*

3. *Explain each of our nine guidelines for being a more effective interviewer.*

4. *Cite at least fifteen questions you can ask interviewees.*

5. *List some important "guidelines for interviewees."*

6. *Effectively interview a job candidate.*

OVERVIEW

The purpose of this chapter is to improve your ability to interview job candidates. We first discuss the pros and cons of interviewing and then turn to some of the factors we know affect the usefulness of interviews. We then present some specific guidelines for improving one's effectiveness as an interviewer—and as an interviewee. Interviews are an important way to screen candidates and to select those who are enthusiastic and who also have the skills and abilities to do the job (and therefore are qualified to do so). Selection interviews are thus the next "Personnel" activity that has an influence on employee performance.

INTRODUCTION

Selection tools like applications and tests can be useful, but the screening tool that is used most often (and sometimes exclusively) is the *selection interview*, and there's good reason for this. Interviews provide a chance to personally "size up" the candidate, and to pursue questioning in a way that tests cannot. They provide an opportunity to make judgments on the candidate's enthusiasm, and intelligence. And, they provide an opportunity to assess "subjective" aspects of the candidate—facial expressions, appearance, nervousness, and so forth. Interviews can be, in other words, a *very* potent screening tool

The trouble is that interviews are often not used to their best advantage. The interviewer may be nervous, and pertinent questions aren't asked, for instance. The result is that the findings on the "reliability" and "validity" of interviews could lead one to believe that interviews are worthless, when in fact it's not the interview but the ineptness of the interviewer that creates the problem. In considering the following findings, therefore, (on reliability and validity of interviews) keep in mind that interviews are (or can be) potentially very useful.

How "Reliable" Are Interviews?

The word "reliability" means something specific to researchers, and refers to how *consistently* a test (or a questionnaire or an interview, etc.) measures the traits it is supposed to be measuring. For example, most students applying to graduate school take a graduate admissions test, and it is important that this test be "reliable." Thus, a student who scores very low in March should not score very high when he or she retakes the test in August. With respect to interviews, reliability means that if several people interview a candidate, they should all draw about the same conclusions concerning his or her potential for the job.

The evidence suggests that interviews are often not too "reliable," since interviewers usually disagree with each other concerning how well the candidate would (or would not) perform on the job.

As an example, one study involved 42 manager–interviewers. [1] They watched films and videotapes simulating an interview and were then given a detailed written summary of the interview. The interview lasted almost three hours and covered things like the interviewee's work history, work experience, education, family life, etc. Each "interviewer" was then asked to make predictions about how the interviewee would perform as an insurance salesman. For example, "Could he use the telephone for business purposes?," and, "Could he make 'cold' calls?"

The researchers found little or no agreement among the interviewers. Thus, even though the interviewers had all watched the same simulated interview and had a chance to "study" the candidate firsthand, the interviewers came to different conclusions as to how he would perform on the job. In this case, they couldn't agree as to whether he could make the all-important "cold" calls, or whether he could use the telephone to develop new business, for example. Other researchers have come to similar conclusions. [2]

How "Valid" Are Interviews?

The word "validity" also has a specific meaning for scientists. It refers to the extent to which some device (like a test) measures what it is purported to measure. (Thus an "I.Q." test should measure intelligence, and a scholastic aptitude test should measure one's ability to do schoolwork.) An interview would be valid as a selection tool if the interviewer could accurately predict how the interviewee would perform on the job. Here the results are mixed, but generally suggest that most interviewers do not accurately predict the candidate's performance. [3]

These results could lead one to believe that interviews are a waste of time, but in fact that's not the case. They can be very useful, if you know the common interviewing problems, and how to avoid them. We should therefore start by reviewing these problems, and then present some guidelines for effective interviewing.

FACTORS THAT AFFECT THE USEFULNESS OF INTERVIEWS

Several factors—including a tendency to make premature decisions early in the interview, and to let unfavorable information from the interviewee dominate your opinions—have been shown to undermine the usefulness of interview.

Premature Decisions

First, we know that interviewers often make up their minds about candidates during the first few minutes of the interview: prolonging the interview past this point usually adds little to change these decisions. One researcher even found that in 85% of the cases the interviewer had already made up his mind about the candidate *before* the interview even began (on the basis of an application form and the applicant's personal appearance).

Similarly, getting negative feedback about the candidate *before* the interview starts also seems to color the interviewer's opinion. In one study, for example, three groups of subjects had to evaluate an interviewee: 24 subjects first received a favorable letter of reference on the person, 24 received an unfavorable reference, and 24 received a neutral letter. The researchers found that interviewer/subjects who received the unfavorable letters (and thus formed an early unfavorable expectation concerning the applicants' abilities) were likely to give the candidate less credit for past successes and to hold the person more personally responsible for past failures. The final decision to accept or reject an applicant was also closely related to what the interviewer/subject *expected* of the person, based on the references. [4]

Unfavorable Information Predominates

We also know that interviewers are influenced more by unfavorable than favorable information. [5] Furthermore, interviewers' impressions are much more likely to change from favorable to unfavorable than from unfavorable to favorable: in fact, the interview itself is often mostly a search for negative information. And, as often as not, finding one unfavorable trait can result in a "reject" decision. Some say these problems occur because interviewers put *less weight on favorable* information. Some say they put *more weight on unfavorable* information. In any case, unfavorable information predominates.

Also remember (as noted above) that interviewers tend to make their decisions during the first few minutes of the interview. Combine this with the dominance of unfavorable information, and you can see why first impressions are so important. An interviewee who is initially rated "high" could eventually end up with a low rating, but it's not too likely. But an interviewee who initially starts off with a "poor" rating will find it very difficult to overcome that first bad impression during the interview.

Do You Know the Job?

We also know that interviewers who clearly understand what the job entails give more reliable and more valid interviews. In one study, 30 professional interviewers were used. [6] Half of them were just given a brief description of the jobs for which they were "recruiting." They were told "the eight applicants here represented by their application blanks are applying for the position of secretary." In contrast, the other fifteen interviewers were given much more explicit job information:

> The eight applicants . . . are applying for the position of executive secretary. The requirements are typing speed of 60 w.p.m., stenography speed or 100 w.p.m., dictaphone use, and bilingual ability in either French, German, or Spanish . . . Salary: $10,000 per year.

The results were clear. The 15 interviewers who had more job information generally agreed among themselves about each candidate's potential; those without the complete job information did not. (Thus, the formers' interviews were more "reliable.") Interviewers who did not have full job information also didn't discriminate very well among the applicants: there was a tendency to give them all high ratings.

Pressure to Hire

Being under pressure to hire can also undermine the usefulness of the interview. For example, [7] a group of managers was told to assume that they were behind in their recruiting quota and that the home office had just called. Another group was "ahead" of quota; for a third group, no quota situation existed. All three groups of managers evaluated descriptions of the same job applicants.

The recruiters who were "behind" their recruiting quota evaluated the recruits much more highly than did the other two groups of managers. Specifically, they said they would offer more employment contracts than did managers in the other two groups.

The "Contrast" Effect: Standards of Comparison

The *order* in which the interviewer sees applicants can also affect how he or she rates them. In one study, managers were asked to evaluate a candidate who was "just average" after first evaluating several "unfavorable" candidates. The average candidate was evaluated much more favorably than he might otherwise have been, [8] since, in *contrast* to these unfavorable candidates, the "average" one looked much better than he actually was.

This "contrast" effect can be a major problem; in some studies, only a small part of the interviewee's rating was based on his *actual* potential. Most of his or her rating was based on the "contrast" effects of following very favorable (or unfavorable) candidates. [9]

Similarly, many interviewers seem to have an "ideal" applicant against which each interviewee is evaluated. This *stereotype* may or may not make sense in terms of the job being recruited for. But whether it does or not, it may still affect the rating given the interviewee. [10]

Visual Cues and Traits

Interviewers' ratings are also affected by "visual cues." In fact, visual cues like enthusiasm, manner, facial expression, and personal appearance *sometimes* have a greater effect on the interviewer than does the factual information obtained during the interview. [11]

Another facet of this problem is the role played by the applicant's *attractiveness,* and whether the person is male or female. [12] In one recent study, for example, researchers found that whether attractiveness was a help or a hindrance to job applicants depended upon the sex of the applicant and the nature of the job he or she was seeking. Attractiveness consistently proved to provide an advantage for male applicants seeking white collar jobs, for instance. Yet attractiveness was an advantage for female interviewees only when the job was a *non*managerial one. When the position the woman was being interviewed for was a managerial one, there was, in fact, a tendency for the person's attractiveness to work against her—in terms of recommendations for hiring, and suggested starting salary, for example. While the reason for this last finding isn't clear, it seems to be a result of interviewers' tendencies to equate "attractiveness" with "femininity": the result is that attractive ("more feminine") women are seen as less fit for "masculine-type" jobs (like that of manager) quite aside from the women's actual qualifications, or the talents actually needed for the job, on the erroneous assumption that attractiveness, performance, and femininity are related. [13]

Finally, note also that certain traits are more easily measured in the interview setting than are others. For example, interviewers can generally rate the *intelligence* of interviewees with good degrees of reliability and validity. [14] And, most importantly, the interviewee's *"personal relations"* abilities and his or her *"motivation* to work" can both be assessed with some accuracy in the interview. [15]

Structured vs. Unstructured Interviews

Interviews can be either structured or unstructured. In the *unstructured*

134   interview, the interviewer asks questions as they come to mind: there is no special format to follow, and the conversation can wander off in different directions. In a *structured* interview, a form like that in Exhibit 5.1 is used to guide or "structure" the discussion. Note that it guides the interviewer's questions, requiring the person to ask "standard" questions like "why are you applying for this position?" and "how was your last job obtained?"

Research findings suggest that structured interviews are superior. In one study, for example, experienced interviewers were assigned to three groups. [16] The *structured* group was *not* permitted to deviate from the predetermined interview format. The same format was used for the *semi-structured group*, but deviations *were* permitted. The *unstructured* group was free to interview applicants in any manner. The basic question was "Would one group's ratings be more reliable than another's?"

In this study *only* the structured interview resulted in information that enabled interviewers to agree with each other about candidates. With the structured approach each interviewer seemed to know what to ask and what to do with the information he received. And each interviewer applied the same frame of reference to each applicant since he covered the same areas for each. This was not the case with the less structured interviews.

A related problem is that in the unstructured interview the interviewer talks more than the interviewee. (Remember that interviewers tend to make premature decisions and emphasize unfavorable information. Combine this with the fact that in unstructured interviews the interviewer ends up doing most of the talking, and you can see that in many cases the interviewee probably never had a chance.) [17]

The Interviewer's Experience

Are experienced interviewers any more adept at avoiding some of the problems we just discussed? Are their ratings more reliable or valid than those of inexperienced interviewers? The answer in both cases seems to be "no."

In one study, for example, experienced interviewers did not agree with each other any more than did less experienced interviewers (on how they would rate candidates). [18] But the "experienced" interviewers *were* more resistant to "quota" pressure than were inexperienced interviewers.

Summary: Things that Affect the Usefulness of Interviews

We have discussed eight important factors that affect the usefulness of interviews. These are:

1. *Premature decisions.* Interviewers tend to make their decisions during the first few minutes of the interview (and often before the interview even starts!).
2. *Unfavorable information predominates.* Interviewers emphasize unfavorable

Exhibit 5.1   Structured Interview Form—Executive Position   135

PATTERNED INTERVIEW FORM — EXECUTIVE POSITION

Date_____19_____

SUMMARY

Rating: [1] [2] [3] [4]   Comments:_____
In making final rating, be sure to consider not only what the applicant can do but also his stability, industry,

perseverance, loyalty, ability to get along with others, self-reliance, leadership, maturity, motivation, and domestic situation and health.

_____

_____

_____

Interviewer:_____Job considered for:_____

Name_____   Date of birth_____Age_____; Phone No. _____

Present address_____City_____State_____How long there?_____
Is this a desirable neighborhood? Too high class? Too cheap?

Previous address_____City_____State_____How long there?_____
Is this a desirable neighborhood? Why did he move?

What kind of a car do you own?_____Age_____Condition of car_____
Will he be able to use his car if necessary?

Were you in the Armed Forces of the U. S.? Yes, branch_____Dates_____19_____to_____19_____

_____19_____to_____19_____

If not, why not?_____

Are you employed now? Yes ☐   No ☐. (If yes) How soon available?_____
What are his relationships with present employer?

Why are you applying for this position?_____
Is his underlying reason a desire for prestige, security, or earnings?

WORK EXPERIENCE. Cover all positions. This information is very important. Interviewer should record last position first. Every month since leaving school should be accounted for. Experience in Armed Forces should be covered as a job.

LAST OR PRESENT POSITION

Company_____City_____From_____19_____to_____19_____
Do these dates check with his application?

How was job obtained?_____Whom did you know there?_____
Has he shown self-reliance in getting his jobs?

Nature of work at start_____Starting salary_____
Will his previous experience be helpful on this job?

In what way did the job change?_____
Has he made good work progress?

Nature of work at leaving_____Salary at leaving_____
How much responsibility has he had?   Any indication of ambition?

Superior_____Title_____What is he like?_____
Did he get along with superior?

How closely does (or did) he supervise you?_____What authority do (or did) you have?_____

Number of people you supervised_____What did they do?_____
Is he a leader?

Responsibility for policy formulation_____
Has he had management responsibility?

To what extent could you use initiative and judgment?_____
Did he actively seek responsibility?

Form No. EP-302-R   Copyright, 1975, The Dartnell Corporation, Chicago, Ill. 60640. Printed in U.S.A.
                                               Developed by The McMurry Company

---

Source: Published by the Dartnell Corporation, Chicago; reprinted by permission in Dessler, *Management Fundamentals*, p. 198.

information. And it's harder for an interviewee to overcome an initially "un-favorable" impression than a "favorable" one.

3. *Do you know the job?* Interviewers who had more information about what the job entails held more reliable interviews.

4. *Pressure to hire.* Interviewers who had a quota (and were under pressure to hire) rated candidates higher than interviewers who were not under such pressure.

5. *Contrast effects: standards of comparison.* The same candidate is often rated higher if he follows several unfavorable candidates than if he follows several favorable ones into the interview. The interviewer also often has an ideal stereotype of the "perfect" candidate.

6. *Visual cues and traits.* Interviewers tend to make decisions on the basis of facial expressions, etc. Interviewers can more easily rate "intelligence," "motivation," and "personal relations aptitude."

7. *Structured vs. unstructured interviews.* Structured interviews consistently result in more reliable and more valid interviews than do unstructured ones.

8. *Interviewing experience.* Interviews held by "experienced" interviewers are usually neither more reliable nor more valid than those of "inexperienced" interviewers.

These are eight factors we know represent some of the main problems that undermine the usefulness of interviews. The first step in becoming a better interviewer is to fully understand the nature of each of these problems, as you should by now. The next step is to turn to some specific implications and guidelines for how to be a better interviewer.

IMPLICATIONS AND GUIDELINES FOR INTERVIEWERS

1. Use a Structured Guide

First (to repeat), interviews based on structured guides (as in Exhibit 5.1) are usually the most useful. For one thing, they help you accurately record and recall information gathered during the interview. (This can be very important; in one study half the interviewers could not accurately recall the information produced in a 20-minute interview, for example.) [19] A structured guide also insures that you consistently touch on all important questions. You will tend to talk less in the structured interview, while the interviewee talks more. You can review all the interviewees' answers after the interview, so there is less chance of making a snap, premature decision. And the structured guide reduces the large amount of information developed from an interview to a manageable number of constant dimensions. This in turn can help reduce contrast effects, since you're evaluating each candidate by the same standards instead of relative to each other.

The structured guide also helps to reduce one's tendency to let unfavorable information predominate. You decide ahead of time which important areas you are going to delve into during the interview. Thus, there is less chance that an unfavorable response to one or two questions will override "favorable" responses to other questions, as they might in an unstructured interview. [20]

2. Know the Requirements of the Job

Second, understand clearly what the job entails and what its requirements are. This will help you avoid putting too much weight on irrelevant information, and also helps reduce the chance that candidates will be compared with an erroneous "stereotype." As two researchers concluded:

> . . . by availing the interviewer of rather extensive information about the job to be filled, such as that provided by detailed job descriptions and job titles, reliability of employment selection decisions can be increased. Equally as evident are the consequences of depriving personnel interviewers about the details of the job they are screening for—a lack of discrimination among applicants ensued. . . . [21]

3. Provide Training for Interviewers

Third, we know that managers can be trained to avoid problems such as contrast effects. In one study, for example, interviewer/trainees were asked to watch three videotaped employment interviews. After watching an applicant, the interviewer–trainees each rated the interviewee on a 9-point scale, and then announced their rating to the group. Each trainee explained to the group his reasons for giving that particular rating, and the trainees also discussed possible reasons for the discrepancies among their ratings. During these discussions, the trainers announced the "correct" rating for the particular interviewee. At the same time, they referred to various types of rating errors, including; leniency (rating all candidates high); halo (rating an applicant high [or low] on all traits based on how he rated on one important trait); central tendency (the tendency to rate all candidates as "average"); contrast effect; and stereotyping. It was found that many of these errors were reduced due to the workshop; contrast effect errors were almost eliminated. [22]

(This type of training is one area in which a concerted personnel staff-line management effort is essential. In virtually all instances an applicant will be interviewed by both a personnel specialist *and* by the supervisor of the job, and so both specialists and line manager have to be adept at interviewing. Yet developing interviewer–training programs (and structured interview forms) are tasks best accomplished by the personnel specialist, who also has to work closely with the supervisor in developing a clear picture of what demands are to be made of the prospective job incumbent.)

4. Focus on Traits that are More Accurately Evaluated

Some traits are more accurately assessed during interviews than others. These include "intelligence," "personal relations aptitude," and, especially "motivation to work." As two researchers suggest:

The results rather consistently indicate two areas which both contribute heavily to interviewer decisions and show greatest evidence of validity. These two areas of assessment may be described roughly as *personal relations* and *motivation to work*. In other words, perhaps the interviewer should seek information on two questions: "what is the applicant's motivation to work?", and "would he adjust to the social context of the job?" Such an approach would leave the assessment of abilities, aptitudes, and biographical data to other, and, in all likelihood, more reliable and valid sources. [23]

An interviewer also has to keep in mind that traits which are generally *un*-related to job performance—such as the applicant's attractiveness—can distort the way the applicant is evaluated. Recall that attractive males are usually rated higher for managerial jobs, for instance, and that attractive females are usually rated lower for such jobs, quite aside from the applicant's actual qualifications.

5. Get the Interviewee to Talk

The main (but not only) reason for the interview is usually to find out about the applicant—about the person's motivation, and ability to work with others, for instance—and it is therefore essential that the applicant—and not the interviewer—do most of the talking.

There are several ways to accomplish this. First, using a structured interview guide helps ensure that the interviewer "touches all bases" in the interview, and that he or she does not have to fill long voids in the discussion with idle chatter. It is also useful to remember that the applicant should be made to feel at ease early in the interview, perhaps with some general comments about the organization and job. Finally, most people tend to "clam up" when asked too many direct questions; some successful interviewers find they can "draw out" an applicant's opinions and feelings by just repeating the person's last comment as a question (such as, "you didn't like your last job?"), or by just nodding agreement on making some comment like, "you didn't?" when the person, says, for example, that he didn't like his last job. Some sample interview questions (such as "why do you feel qualified for this job?" and "what attracts you to us?") are presented in Exhibit 5.2.

6. Delay the Decision

We saw that interviewers often make accept/reject decisions during the first few minutes of the interview, and that the ensuing discussion often does little to change the interviewer's decision. In fact, interviewers often make their decisions *before* they ever see the candidate—on the basis of his or her application blank, or references, for example. [24]

There are several factors that influence the time it takes an interviewer to arrive at an accept/reject decision about a candidate. First, from a practical

Openers

- May I see your résumé?
- What can I do for you?
- Why are you interested in joining our company?
- Why do you feel qualified for this job?
- What do you think you can do for us?
- What attracts you to us?
- Tell me about your experience.
- What pay do you have in mind? (Try tactfully to avoid answering this one early in the interview.)

Regarding motivation

- Is your present employer aware of your interest in a job change?
- Why do you want to change jobs?
- What caused you to enter your job field?
- Why do you want to change your field of work?
- Why are you leaving military service at this point?
- What would you like to be doing five years from now? When you retire?
- What is the ideal job for you?
- If you had complete freedom of choice to be a great success in any job field, which would you choose? Why?

Regarding education

- Describe your education for me.
- Why did you pick your major?
- What was your class standing?
- What were your activities?
- What honors did you earn?
- What were your average grades?
- Did your grades adequately reflect your full capability? Why not?
- What courses did you like best/least and why?
- Have you had any special training for this job?

Regarding experience

- Why should I hire you?
- How do you fit the requirements for this job?
- What did you do in military service?
- What would you do to improve our operations?
- Who has exercised the greatest influence on you? How?
- What duties performed in the past have you liked best/least and why?
- What are your greatest strengths/limitations for this job?
- What are the strongest limitations you have found in past supervisors?
- Which supervisor did you like best and why?
- What kinds of people appeal most/least to you as work associates?
- How many people have you supervised? What types?
- What are your greatest accomplishments to date?
- What equipment can you work with?
- Why have you changed jobs so frequently?
- Have you ever been fired or asked to resign?
- Describe the biggest crisis in your career.
- What were you doing during the period not covered in your résumé?
- Why were you out of work so long?
- What was the specific nature of your illness during your extended hospitalization?
- Why did you leave your previous jobs?
- Could I see samples of your work?

Regarding pay

- What do you require?
- What is the *minimum* pay you will accept?
- What is your pay record for the last five years?
- Why do you believe you are qualified for so much more?
- We can't pay the salary you should have. Would you be willing to start lower and work up to that figure?
- What do you expect to be earning five years from now?

Source: Adapted from Richard Lathrop, *Who's Hiring Who* (Reston, Va.: Reston Publishing Company, 1976), pp. 169–171.

point of view, just *being aware* (perhaps through training) of the tendency to make early, snap judgments about applicants can help the interviewer guard against making premature decisions. Researchers have also found that the *quality of the applicant* influences how long the interviewer takes to make a decision, with the quickest decisions being made on the "worst" applicants—those that get off to the worst start, in terms of their answers to the interviewer's questions. [25] Another, easily manipulated factor is *the time allotted for the interview*: studies indicate that allotting more time for a given interview will make the interviewer less likely to make a premature decision. [26] At one time, it was also believed that withholding information on an applicant (such as the person's application blank and references) would delay the interviewer's decisions because he or she would be "in the dark" about the applicant's credentials, and would therefore have to pursue more questioning in the interview. [27] Today the results, while somewhat contradictory, seem to refute this. [28] Specifically, researchers have found that interviewers without access to applicant's application forms did not take any more (or less) time to arrive at a decision about the person than did those receiving a copy of the form. In this study the researchers had also hypothesized that interviewers *without* access to the application forms would make their decisions based on more relevant information, on the assumption that they would have to rely more on intensive interviewing. In fact, though, the researchers found just the opposite: interviewers *with* the application seemed to be able to zero right in on important facts presented in the application, while those without access to the applications had to spend interview time unearthing facts already on the application.

7. *Accentuate the Positive (or Deemphasize the Negative)*

Remember that there is a tendency for interviewers to put more weight on unfavorable (or less weight on favorable) information. Interviews, in fact, are often mostly searches for negative data, and there is much more chance of your impression changing from favorable to unfavorable than from unfavorable to favorable. [29] Therefore, an interviewer should go out of his or her way to find positive cues, and to not give undue weight to negative ones.

8. *Remember: Applicants Also Evaluate Interviewers*

Interviewees form overall impressions of the "goodness" or "badness" of an interviewer, and this in turn effects their decision to join (or not join) the organization. Based on one study, for example, we know that some of the things interviewees look for include: Are you calm and relaxed? Do you use a lot of "ums" and "ahs"? Do you seem well acquainted with the potential job? Are you capable of answering questions? Do you understand the interviewee's view of work? and, Do you provide information about supervision in the company? [30]

9. Remember EEOC Requirements

Employers are legally responsible for showing that their selection procedures (including interviews) are job-related. [31] Keep in mind that the employer
may be called upon to explain the selection procedures used in the interview.
Therefore, an employer should be alert to bias, and make periodic checks on
the number of minorities hired or recommended, along with the jobs they are
recommended for. [32] Using a structured interview form is advisable: it can be
standardized and validated as a selection tool for EEOC purposes. [33]

As explained in Chapter 2, *federal* EEO laws generally do not prohibit
interviewers from asking anything, but the EEOC does look with suspicion on
certain types of inquiries. [34] As we explained, "problem" questions include
those concerning: marital status, childcare, availability for Saturday or Sunday
work, arrest record, garnishing of salary, national origin, age, or education.
Questions concerning topics like these have an adverse impact on protected
groups (some minorities have higher arrest records, for instance) and so they
should generally only be used where their use is justified, and where it is made
clear that they will not be used to discriminate between applicants.

GUIDELINES FOR INTERVIEWEES

Introduction: What Interviewers Look For

Research findings like those described in this chapter can also help *interviewees* raise their effectiveness in the interview and (since most employees first
have to be interviewed themselves before they are able to interview others) it
would be appropriate to end this chapter with some information for interviewees.

What do interviewers look for in interviewees? [35] The first thing to understand is that job interviews are used primarily to help employers determine what
the candidate is like as a person. In other words, (as noted above) information
concerning how the candidate gets along with other people and his or her desire
to work is of prime importance in the interview, since the applicant's skills and
technical expertise are usually best determined through the use of tests, and a
careful study of the applicant's work history. The bottom line is that superior
interpersonal behavior in the interview may give a candidate that extra edge that
sets the person apart from equally qualified applicants. [36]

What exactly can an applicant do to get this "extra edge"? One recent study
sheds some light on this question. [37] The researchers divided an interviewee's
behavior into three categories: verbal, articulative, and nonverbal. They define
each of these three types of behavior as follows:

1. *Nonverbal.* In the study, nonverbal behavior consisted of three elements:
(1) *eye contact*: "generally maintained appropriate eye contact when speaking or listening to the interviewer"; (2) *body posture*: "sat erect, used appropriate hand gestures, facial expression appropriate to verbal message"; (3)
personal appearance: "*neat and clean* in appearance, and appropriately

dressed"; *composure*: appeared *at ease* during the interview, comfortable and relaxed."

2. *Articulative.* This consisted of two elements: (1) *loudness* of voice: "spoke with clarity and appropriately loud without whispers or shouts"; and (2) *fluency* of speech: "spoke spontaneously, used words well, was able to articulate thoughts clearly."

3. *Verbal.* This reflected the "appropriateness of content" of the person's responses: "responded concisely, cooperated fully in answering questions, stated personal opinions when relevant, and kept to the subject at hand." [38]

In this study, findings indicated that *appropriateness of content* was the single most important variable: Superior candidates were those that responded concisely, cooperated fully, stated relevant personal opinions, and kept to the subject at hand. Fluency of speech ("used words well," etc.) and composure ("appeared at ease") were ranked as second and third in importance, respectively. Other elements like eye contact, body posture, loudness of voice, and personal appearance also contributed to the interviewers' decisions but much less strongly than the first three elements. In other words, the appropriateness of the content of the interviewee's answers—whether the person responded concisely, cooperated fully in answering questions, stated personal opinions when relevant, and kept to the subject at hand—was by far the most important element in influencing the interviewer's decision. The applicant's ability to use words well and to articulate thoughts, and the person's composure were important as well. These findings suggest the following implications for interviewees:

1. Preparation is Essential

Perhaps the clearest implication of these findings is that while fluency and various nonverbal behaviors are important, the ability of the candidate to respond concisely and answer questions fully is of prime importance, and doing so demands meticulous preparation on the candidate's part. The person should try to find out all he or she can about the organization, the job that is being applied for, and the persons doing the recruiting.

2. Think Before Answering

Fluency of speech—using words well, and articulating thoughts clearly—was also important and this indicates that an applicant should develop his or her ability to give well-organized and focused answers. Studies indicate, in fact, that training an applicant to pause before answering, focus on the key words in the interviewer's question, and briefly organize his or her answer before responding is useful in decreasing speech disturbances and improving speech fluency. [39] The basic process, therefore, is one of pause-think-speak and it appears that a person can be trained to become more fluent and articulate by following (and being trained in) this process.

144   *3. Appearance and Enthusiasm are Important*

While the applicant's ability to respond intelligently and fluently to questions is of prime importance, appearance and enthusiasm are important as well. Here, one expert suggests paying attention to the following "key interviewing considerations":

1. Appropriate clothing.
2. Good grooming.
3. A firm handshake.
4. The appearance of controlled energy.
5. Pertinent humor and readiness to smile.
6. A genuine interest in the employer's operations and alert attention when the interviewer speaks.
7. Pride in past performance.
8. An understanding of the employer's needs and a desire to serve them.
9. The display of sound ideas.
10. Ability to take control when employers fall down on the interviewing job. [40]
    Having this ability can help fill embarrasing voids in the interview; some questions an interviewer can ask are presented in Exhibit 5.3, and include "would you mind describing the job for me?", and "could you tell me about the people who would be reporting to me?"

Exhibit 5.3 Questions For The Employer

Openers

- (After the usual cordialities:) Have you had a chance to review my qualifications brief?
- Did it raise any questions about my qualifications that I can answer?
- Did (the previous interviewer) give you the full story on my experience?

Regarding job content

- Would you mind describing the duties of the job for me, please?
- Could you show me where it fits in the organization?
- Is this a new position?
- What do you consider ideal experience for this job?
- Was the previous incumbent promoted?
- Could you tell me about the people who would be reporting to me?
- How does their pay compare with that in other sections/companies?
- Are you happy with their performance?
- Have there been any outstanding cases of dissatisfaction among them?

- What is the largest single problem facing your staff now?
- Is there anything unusually demanding about the job I should know about?
- What have been some of the best results produced by people in this job?
- Could you tell me about the primary people I would be dealing with?
- What are their strengths and limitations as you see them?
- What are the primary results you would like to see me produce?
- May I talk with the person who last held this job? Other members of the staff?

Regarding your bid for the job, pay, and other closing questions

- Is there anything else I can tell you about my qualifications?
- I can be ready to go to work in –– days. Should I plan on that?
- Based on my qualifications, don't you think $––– a year would be appropriate for me in this job?
- Would you mind telling me the pay *range* the company has in mind for this job?
- Do you think more could be justified in light of my particular experience?
- Can you tell me the prospects for advancement beyond that level?
- I greatly appreciate your offer. How soon do you need a decision?
- Will it be all right if I let you know by (date)?

Regarding benefits
(Raise only after it looks like you will be offered the job—or separately with the personnel department)

- Could you tell me briefly about your benefits program? (Vacations, insurance, retirement, profit sharing, bonuses, hospitalization, etc.)

If the employer finally says "no"

- Do you know of others in the organization or elsewhere who would be interested in my experience?
- I very much like what you are doing. Could you keep my qualifications brief on hand for other openings in your office or referral to others?

Source: Adapted from Lathrop, *Who's Hiring Who*, pp. 171–173

Interviewers Make Premature Decisions and
        Let Unfavorable Information Predominate

Finally, remember that the game will probably be won or lost during the first few minutes of the interview. If you enter making a good impression and start off well, this first good impression *may* be changed by the interview, but it's unlikely. But if you start off with an initial unfavorable impression, it may be all but impossible to overcome it during the interview.

SUMMARY

1. Interviews often contribute very little to improved selection decisions. Two (or more) interviewers usually don't agree on which interviewee is "good" and which is "bad" (poor reliability). And predictions of job success based on the interview are usually quite inaccurate (validity). But, often this is more a function of the ineptness of the interviewer than of the interview itself.

2. We discussed several factors and problems that can undermine the usefulness of an interview. These are: making premature decisions; the fact that unfavorable information predominates; the extent to which the interviewer knows the requirements of the job; being under pressure to hire; the contrast effect (standards of comparison); visual cues and traits such as enthusiasm; and structured versus unstructured interviews.

3. These suggest a number of implications and guidelines for interviewers: use a structured guide; know the requirements of the job; train yourself (and your subordinates) in the art of interviewing; focus on traits you can more accurately evaluate (like motivation); let the interviewee do most of the talking; delay your decision; accentuate the positive; try to do some "selling" during the interview; and remember the EEOC requirements.

4. As an interviewee, keep in mind that: interviewers tend to make premature decisions and let unfavorable information predominate; your appearance and enthusiasm are important; you should get the interviewer to talk; it is important to prepare—before walking in, get to know the job and the problems the interviewer wants solved; and you should stress your enthusiasm and motivation to work.

5. Effective interviewing can contribute directly to increasing the performance in your organization. First, it helps you select the best qualified candidates —ones who have the ability and potential to do the job. Second, a candidate's motivation is one of the traits most accurately measured during an interview.

Vice-President For Discouragement

The selection program in a medium-sized manufacturing firm has, for several years, maintained a panel-type interviewing procedure, one interview following another, for all applicants who are believed likely to move into supervisory and managerial positions. After a preliminary screening interview by a recruiter, candidates meet with each of six company officers, including one representative of the industrial relations department.

One vice-president is insistent that he be included on all such panels. He is impressed with what he regards as a tendency of modern business to "coddle" and "baby" new recruits. He says they should know the basic "economic facts of life." He thinks they should be told to expect to work long hours and to encounter many frustrations and discouragements. Accordingly, in his visits with candidates, he "gets rough" and "gives them the works."

The effects of his interviewing are readily apparent. Several candidates regarded by other interviewers as most promising have decided against joining the firm. Some of them have said bluntly that they don't want to work with an outfit that has such a vice-president. One candidate advised two panel members that they ought to leave the firm on this account.

Questions

1. Do you think this firm has a good interviewing/screening procedure? Why? Why not?
2. Do you think these "realistic" job previews are a good idea? Why? Why not?
3. What should be done about this person someone has dubbed the "vice-president for discouragement?" He has several years to serve before retirement. Would it be fair, if it is possible, to keep him off the panels? Could he be encouraged to change his tactics? What approach would you suggest?

EXPERIENTIAL EXERCISE

Purpose: The purposes of this exercise are:

1. To give you practice in developing a structured interview form, and
2. To give you practice in using this form.

Required Understanding: The reader should be familiar with the interviewing problems we discussed, and with the example of the structured interview form presented in Exhibit 5.1.

How to Set Up the Exercise/ Instructions:

1. Set up groups of four or five students. One student will be the "interviewee" while the other students in the group will develop the structured interview form and, as a group, interview the interviewee.

2. Instructions for the *interviewee*: Please do not read the exercise beyond this point (you can leave the room for a few minutes).

3. Instructions for the *interviewers*. You may be a plant manager, assistant plant manager, or assistant production control manager, but in any case you have to interview a candidate for production control manager in about an hour. Each of you knows you'd be best off using a structured interview form to guide the interview, so you're now meeting for about half an hour *to develop such a form,* based in part on the "job description for a production control manager" presented in Exhibit 3.2, and on the example in Exhibit 5.1. (Hint: Start by listing the most relevant abilities and then rate these in importance on a 5-point scale. Then use the high-rated abilities on your interview form.)

4. As soon as you have completed your structured interview form, call in your interviewee and explain to him that he is a candidate for the job of production control manager and that the plant manager, the assistant plant manager (who the candidate will report to if hired), and one or more assistant production control managers will interview him as a group. You may tell the interviewee that his or her job summary calls for the production control manager to "direct the activities of: scheduling plant production; procuring raw materials; and maintaining inventory for production and shipping."

Next, interview the candidate, with each interviewer separately keeping notes on his or her own copy of the group's structured interview form. Each interviewer can take turns asking questions.

After the interview, discuss the following questions in the group: Based on each interviewer's notes, how similar were your perceptions of the candidate's responses? Did you all agree on the candidate's potential for the job? Did the candidate ask good questions of his interviewers? Did any of the interviewers find themselves jumping to conclusions about the candidate?

DISCUSSION QUESTIONS

1. Do interviews have to be a waste of time? Why? Why not?
2. Explain at least six factors that affect the usefulness of interviews.
3. Discuss at least eight of our guidelines for being a more effective interviewer.
4. Write a short presentation entitled "How to Be Effective as an Interviewee."

NOTES

1. Robert E. Carlson, et al., "Improvements in the Selection Interview," *Personnel Journal*, Vol. 50 (April 1971), pp. 268–275; in W. Clay Hamner and Frank L. Schmidt, *Contemporary Problems in Personnel: Readings for the 70's* (Chicago: St. Clair, 1974), pp. 93–101.

2. For a recent summary, see Neal Schmitt, "Social and Situational Determinants of Interview Decisions: Implications for the Employment Interview," *Personnel Psychology*, Vol. 29 (Spring 1976), pp. 79–101.

3. Lynn Ulrich and Don Trumbo, "The Selection Interview Since 1949," *Psychological Bulletin*, Vol. 63 (1965), pp. 100–116; for one recent exception, see Frank Landy, "The Validity of the Interview in Police Officer Selection," *Journal of Applied Psychology*, Vol. 61 (1976), pp. 193–198.

4. Eugene Mayfield, "The Selection Interview—A Re-evaluation of Published Research," *Personnel Psychology*, Vol. 17 (Autumn 1964), pp. 239–260; Schmidt, "Social and Situational Determinants," pp. 82–83; Thomas Hollmann, "Employment Interviewers Errors in Processing Positive and Negative Information," *Journal of Applied Psychology*, Vol. 56 (1972), pp. 130–134; S. W. Constantin, "An Investigation of Information Favorability in the Employment Interview," *Journal of Applied Psychology*, Vol. 61 (1976), pp. 743–749. It should be noted that a number of the studies discussed in this chapter involve having interviewers evaluate interviewees based on written transcripts of interviews (rather than face to face), and that a recent study suggests that this procedure may *not* be equivalent to having interviewers interview applicants directly. See Charles Gorman, William Grover, and Michael Doherty, "Can We Learn Anything About Interviewing Real People from "Interviews" of Paper People? The Study of the External Validity Paradigm," *Organizational Behavior and Human Performance*, Vol. 22, No. 2 (October 1978), pp. 165–192.

5. David Tucker and Patricia Rowe, "Relationship Between Expectancy, Causal Attributions, and Final Hiring Decisions in the Employment Interview," *Journal of Applied Psychology*, Vol. 64, No. 1 (Feb. 1979), pp. 27–34.

6. John Langdale and Joseph Weitz, "Estimating the Influence of Job Information on Interviewer Agreement," *Journal of Applied Psychology*, Vol. 57 (1973), pp. 23–27.

7. R. E. Carlson, "Selection Interview Decisions: The Effects of Interviewer Experience, Relative Quota Situation, and Applicant Sample on Interview Decisons," *Personnel Psychology*, Vol. 20 (1967), pp. 259–280; Robert E. Carlson, et al., "Improvements in the Selection Interview," *Personnel Journal*, Vol. 50 (April 1971), p. 95.

8. R. E. Carlson, "Effects of Applicant's Sample on Ratings of Valid Information in an Employment Setting," *Journal of Applied Psychology*, Vol. 54 (1970), pp. 217–222; Carlson, et al., p. 95.

9. K. N. Wexley and W. F. Nemeroff, "Effect of Racial Prejudice, Race of Applicant, and Biographical Similarity on Interviewer Evaluations of Job Applicants," *Journal of Social and Behavioral Sciences*, Vol. 20 (1974), pp. 66–78; Schmitt, "Social and Situational Determinants," p. 88.

10. E. C. Mayfield, and R. E. Carlson, "Selection Interview Decisions: First Results From a Long Term Research Project," *Personnel Psychology*, Vol. 19 (1966), pp. 41–55; Neal Schmitt, "Social and Situational Determinants," p. 90.

11. Mayfield, "The Selection Interview—A Re-evaluation of Published Research," p. 254; E. Valenzi and I. R. Andrews, "Individual Differences in the Decision Process of Employment Interviews," *Journal of Applied Psychology*, Vol. 58 (1973), pp. 49–53. See also John Sterrett, "The Job Interview: Body Language and

150   Perceptions of Potential Effectiveness," *Journal of Applied Psychology*, Vol. 63, No. 3 (June 1978), pp. 388–390.

12. Madeline Heilman and Lewis Saruwatari, "When Beauty is Beastly: The Effects of Appearance and Sex on Evaluations of Job Applicants for Managerial and Nonmanagerial Jobs," *Organizational Behavior and Human Performance*, Vol. 23 (June 1979), pp. 360–372.

13. Heilman and Saruwatari, pp. 360–361.

14. Mayfield, "Selection Interview—A Re-evaluation of Published Research," p. 252.

15. Lynn Ulrich and Don Trumbo, "The Selection Interview Since 1949," pp. 100–116.

16. R. E. Carlson, D. P. Schwab, and H. G. Henneman III, "Agreement among Selection Interview Styles," *Journal of Industrial Psychology*, Vol. 5 (1970), pp. 8–17; Carlson, et al., "Improvements in the Selection Interview," p. 100; Schwab and Henneman, "Relationships Between Interview Structure and Interviewer Reliability in an Employment Setting," *Journal of Applied Psychology*, Vol. 53 (1968), pp. 214–217.

17. See Mayfield, "The Selection Interview—A Re-evaluation of Published Research," pp. 249–253, for a good review of this evidence. Richard Nehrbass and Dominguez Hills, "Psychological Barriers to Effective Employment Interviewing," *Personnel Journal*, Vol. 55 (December 1976).

18. Carlson, "Selection Interview Decisions: The Effect of Interviewer Experience, Relative Quota Situations and Applicant Sample on Interviewer Decisions," p. 279.

19. Carlson, et al., "Improvements in the Selection Interview," p. 96.

20. These and the other implications are based partly on Schmitt, "Social and Situational Determinants," p. 97.

21. John Langdale and Joseph Weitz, "Estimating the Influence of Job Information on Interviewer Agreement," *Journal of Applied Psychology*, Vol. 57 (1963), pp. 23–27.

22. Kenneth Wexley, Raymond Sanders, and Gary Yukl, "Training Interviewers to Eliminate Contrast Effect in Employment Interviews," *Journal of Applied Psychology*, Vol. 57 (1973), pp. 233–236. For description of another training program see Carlson, et al., "Improvement of the Selection Interview," p. 100.

23. Ulrich and Trumbo, "The Selection Interview Since 1949," p. 113; Frank Landy and Don Trumbo, *Psychology of Work Behavior* (Homewood, Ill.: Dorsey, 1976), p. 185.

24. Mayfield, "The Selection Interview—A Re-evaluation of Published Research," p. 254. Some propose not letting the interviewer consult the candidate's application blank as one way to "delay" the interviewer's decision. There's debate as to whether this is effective; David Tucker and Patricia Rowe, "Consulting the Application Form Prior to the Interview: An Essential Step in the Selection Process," *Journal of Applied Psychology*, Vol. 62, No. 3, pp. 283–287, 1977.

25. William Tullar, Terry Mullins, and Sharon Caldwell, "Effects of Interview Length and Applicant Quality on Interview Decision Time," *Journal of Applied Psychology*, Vol. 64, No. 6 (December 1979), pp. 669–674.

26. Tullar, et al., p. 674.

27. E. C. Webster, *Decision Making in the Employment Interview* (Montreal, Canada: McGill University Industrial Relations Center, 1964).

28. David Tucker and Patricia Rowe, "Consulting the Application Form Prior to the Interview: An Essential Step in the Selection Process," *Journal of Applied Psychology*, 1977, Vol. 62, No. 3, pp. 283–287.

29. Mayfield, "The Selection Interview—A Re-evaluation of Published Research," p. 253.   151

30. Neal Schmitt and Bryan Coyle, "Applicant Decisions in the Employment Interview," *Journal of Applied Psychology*, Vol. 61 (1976), pp. 184–192.

31. Schmitt, "Social and Situational Determinants," p. 79.

32. *Ibid.*, p. 97.

33. Robert Dipboye, Richard Arvey, and David Terpstra, "Equal Employment and the Interview," *Personnel Journal*, Vol. 55 (October 1976).

34. James Ledvinka and Robert Gatewood, "EEO Issues with Preemployment Inquiries," *The Personnel Administrator*, Vol. 22, (February 1977) pp. 22–26; reprinted in Gregg Eric Schneir and Richard Beatty, *Personnel Administration Today* (Reading: Addison-Wesley, 1978) pp. 233–239.

35. This is based largely on James Hollandsworth Jr., Richard Kazlskis, Joanne Stevens, and Mary Edith Dressel, "Relative Contributions of Verbal, Articulative, and Nonverbal Communication to Employment Decisions in the Job Interviewing Setting," *Personnel Psychology*, Vol. 32, No. 2, (Summer 1979), pp. 359–367.

36. Hollandsworth et al., p. 59.

37. Hollandsworth et al., p. 360.

38. Hollandsworth et al., p. 362

39. J. G. Hollandsworth, R. C. Ladsinski, and M. H. Russell, "Use of Social Skills Training and the Treatment of Extreme Anxiety and Deficient Verbal Skills of a Job Interview Setting," *Journal of Applied Behavior Analysis*, 1978, Vol. 11, pp. 259–269.

40. Richard Lathrop, *Who's Hiring Who* (Reston, Va.: Reston Publishing, 1976), pp. 166–167.

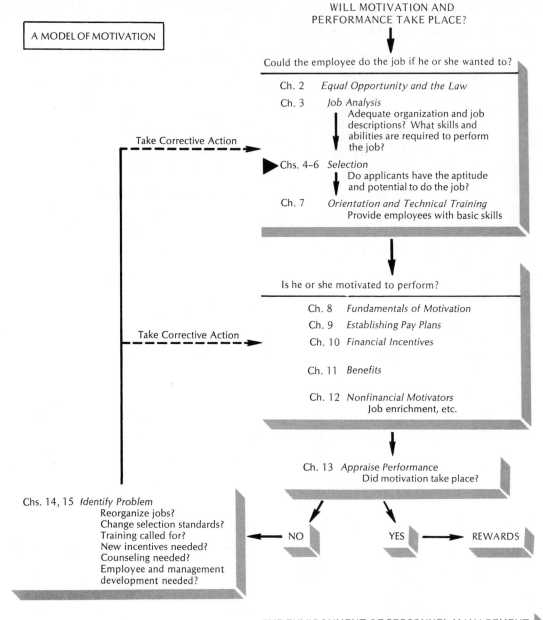

A MODEL OF MOTIVATION

WILL MOTIVATION AND
PERFORMANCE TAKE PLACE?

Could the employee do the job if he or she wanted to?

Ch. 2   *Equal Opportunity and the Law*

Ch. 3   *Job Analysis*
Adequate organization and job descriptions? What skills and abilities are required to perform the job?

Chs. 4–6   *Selection*
Do applicants have the aptitude and potential to do the job?

Ch. 7   *Orientation and Technical Training*
Provide employees with basic skills

Take Corrective Action

Is he or she motivated to perform?

Ch. 8   *Fundamentals of Motivation*

Ch. 9   *Establishing Pay Plans*

Ch. 10   *Financial Incentives*

Ch. 11   *Benefits*

Ch. 12   *Nonfinancial Motivators*
Job enrichment, etc.

Take Corrective Action

Ch. 13   *Appraise Performance*
Did motivation take place?

Chs. 14, 15   *Identify Problem*
Reorganize jobs?
Change selection standards?
Training called for?
New incentives needed?
Counseling needed?
Employee and management development needed?

NO   YES → REWARDS

THE ENVIRONMENT OF PERSONNEL MANAGEMENT

Ch. 16   *Labor Relations and Grievances*

Ch. 17   *Employee Safety and Health*

Ch. 18   *Personnel Management and the Quality of Work Life*

When you finish studying

6 Other Selection Techniques

You should be able to:

1. *Explain what is meant by "reliability," and "validity."*
2. *Discuss six types of tests.*
3. *Explain how you would go about validating a test.*
4. *Give examples of some of the ethical and legal considerations in testing.*
5. *Cite our nine testing guidelines.*
6. *Explain the work sampling procedure.*
7. *Explain what an assessment center is.*

OVERVIEW

The purpose of this chapter is to explain how to use four employee selection techniques: testing; assessment centers; work sampling; and reference checks. First we discuss testing, and the concepts of validity and reliability. We talk about different types of tests, including intelligence tests and achievement tests, and explain an "ideal" procedure for deciding what tests to use. "Work sampling" is another selection tool that helps managers formalize a selection criteria they've long used—prior work experience. Finally, we discuss the pros and cons of "assessment centers," and also present some pointers on background and reference checking. Like applications and interviews, these four selection techniques improve performance by helping to select only those candidates who have the skills and abilities to do the job.

WHERE WE ARE NOW

One of a manager's most important jobs involves recruitment and placement—finding the right person for the right job and hiring that person. This requires screening candidates, and so we've discussed the two main screening techniques (application blanks and interviews). But most managers also use (or have used on them) other selection tools for screening. These include tests, prior work experience, assessment centers, and reference checks, and in this chapter we discuss these other selection tools. (Then, once the person has been selected and hired, the next steps involve orientation and training, steps we address in the next chapter.)

TESTING FOR EMPLOYEE SELECTION

Introduction: The Use of Tests

As illustrated in Exhibit 6.1 many organizations use tests for hiring, promotion, or both, but their use has been diminishing in recent years. In one study, for example, about 90% of companies responding in 1963 said they used tests for screening applicants, but by 1975 only about 42% reported doing so. [1]

Exhibit 6.1 Use of Testing For Hiring and Promotion (By Size of Employer)

	Test for Hiring	Test for Promotion	Not Test
Fewer than 100 Employees	30.4%	17.9%	61.0%
100 to 499 Employees	43.4	17.3	49.2
500 to 999 Employees	46.8	24.0	45.1
1,000 to 4,999 Employees	55.4	29.3	40.3
5,000 to 9,000 Employees	62.7	27.4	32.9
10,000 to 25,000 Employees	54.9	32.7	38.4
More than 25,000 Employees	57.1	32.4	39.6
All Respondents	49.1	24.0	36.5

Source: Reprinted with permission from *Personnel Management: Policies and Practices Report* #22, 4-2-75, published by Prentice-Hall, Inc., Englewood Cliffs, N.J. 07632. © 1975 by Prentice-Hall, Inc.; reprinted in Robert L. Mathis and John H. Jackson, *Personnel: Contemporary Perspectives and Applications* (St. Paul: West Publishing Company, 1976).

Several things account for the diminishing use of tests, but by far the most important is probably the new, more stringent equal employment laws and regulations. As explained in Chapter 2, these laws have had the effect of requiring that rigorous procedures be followed in developing and using tests. Furthermore, recent "truth in testing" laws (which are aimed at requiring organizations to provide tests-takers with itemized answers to questions missed as well as other related data) may also have inhibited the use of tests. [2] In summary, "tests are under attack today, as they have been throughout most of this decade" [3] and the problems of validating and safeguarding tests have probably contributed to their diminished use, by increasing the costs to the organization of using them.

Yet there are several excellent reasons for using and studying the use of tests. First, while their use has diminished, about half of all organizations still use testing for either hiring, promotion, or both, so it would be inaccurate to assume their demise is imminent. Furthermore, employers can develop and implement testing programs that do not unfairly discriminate, and which comply with requirements of equal employment regulations. [4] A knowledge of testing can also help a person get the most out of his or her organization's testing program by helping the person keep tests results in perspective. And, having oneself tested can help a person make better career decisions by highlighting aptitudes, interests, and skills that may not have been obvious before.

Last, but not least, we know that a testing program can also substantially improve an organization's productivity and profitability. [5] One study that illustrates this focussed on the selection of computer programmers. The researchers asked supervisors (in the U.S. Federal Government) to estimate the value to his or her agency of a low performing, average, and high performing computer programmer in dollars per year. Based on this information, the researchers concluded that the U.S. Government (which hires about 600 programmers per year) could gain over $6 million per year in increased productivity by using a special "programmer aptitude test" for selecting high-potential programmers. [6]

Basic Testing Concepts [7]

What Is a Test?   A test is basically a *sample* of a person's behavior. In some cases the behavior you're sampling is obvious from the test itself: A typing test is an example of one where the test clearly corresponds to some behavior (in this case typing).

At the other extreme there may be no apparent relationship between the items on the test and the behavior. This is the case with projective personality tests, for example. Thus in the "thematic apperception" test (Exhibit 6.5) the person is asked to explain what he or she "sees" in the blurred picture. The person's interpretation is then used to draw conclusions about his or her personality and behavior.

In summary, some tests are more clearly representative of the behavior they are supposed to be measuring than others. Because of this, it is much harder to "prove" that some tests are measuring what they are purported to measure— that they are *valid*.

Validity.   We touched on the concepts of validity and reliability in the last chapter. Since these are very important concepts in testing, we now discuss them more fully.

Validity refers to the extent to which a test measures what it purports to measure or carries out the function it was designed for.

There are several types of validity. One is *empirical validity*. This refers to the accuracy with which a test (like a college admissions test) predicts some measure of performance (like college grades). The test score is usually called a "predictor." The measure of performance is usually called a "criterion."

Content validity is a second type of validity. It refers to the extent to which the items in the test are an unbiased representation of the trait being measured. Thus a typing test might be representative of what a typist does, but would not by itself be a content valid test of an executive secretary's duties. *Face* validity is very similar to content validity and refers to whether the test "looks" like it measures what it's supposed to measure. (A test of French vocabulary in which you are asked to define several French words would probably have high "face

156   validity.") Both content and face validity are usually based on the judgments of experts, rather than on statistical analysis.

Construct validity is the most difficult type of validity to understand and to prove. It reflects the extent to which the test measures the psychological quality—like "intelligence" or "introversion"—it is supposed to measure. It is the most "theoretical" type of validity since it's aimed at measuring the relationship between a test and an artificial abstraction or "construct" such as intelligence.

Reliability.   Validity is the most important characteristic of a test since, if the test doesn't measure what it's supposed to measure, it is probably of little use. *Reliability* is the second important requirement of a test. As used by psychologists, the term reliability always means consistency. Test reliability is "the consistency of scores obtained by the same persons when retested with the identical test or with an equivalent form of the test." [8] Test consistency is very important: if a person scores 90 on an intelligence test on Monday and 130 when retested on Tuesday you probably couldn't have much faith in the test.

There are several different ways to measure reliability. One could, for example, administer the same test to the same people at two different points in time, comparing their performance at time two with that at time one. Or, one could administer a test and then administer what experts believe to be an equivalent test at a later date.

A test's "internal consistency" is another measure of its reliability. For example, suppose you have 10 items on an attitude test, all of which are supposed to measure "satisfaction with your supervisor." Administer the test and then (statistically) analyze the degree to which responses to these 10 items vary in unison. This would provide a measure of the internal reliability of the test, and is why one often finds questions which apparently are repetitive on some questionnaires.

Types of Tests [9]

Intelligence Tests.   Intelligence tests measure a person's "I.Q." or "Intelligence Quotient." As it was originally used, I.Q. was literally a quotient. You divided a child's mental age (as measured by the intelligence test) by his or her chronological age, and then multiplied the result by 100. Thus, if an eight-year-old child answered questions as a 10-year-old might, his or her I.Q. would be $10 \div 8, \times 100$, or 125.

For adults, of course, the notion of mental age divided by chronological age wouldn't make much sense; for example, we wouldn't necessarily expect, say, a 30-year-old man to be more intelligent than a 25-year-old man. Therefore, an adult's "I.Q." score is actually a *derived* score. It reflects the extent to which the person is above (or below) the "average" adult's intelligence score.

Some intelligence tests are written tests administered to groups of people.

Others, like the "Wechsler," must be administered to individuals by trained personnel, as in Exhibit 6.2.

Exhibit 6.2   Material Used in Testing Intelligence with the Wechsler

Source: Courtesy of The Psychological Corporation; reprinted in Leona E. Tyler, *Tests and Measurements,* 2nd ed. (Englewood Cliffs, N.J.: Prentice-Hall, Inc., 1963), p. 44.

Tests of Physical Skills.   Tests of physical skills are very important for some jobs, particularly those in the production shop. One example is the "Stromberg Dexterity Test." This measures the speed and accuracy of simple judgment as well as speed of finger, hand, and arm movements (see Exhibit 6.3). There are also various tests to measure visual skills, such as color vision, and distance-acuity.

For most jobs, the minimum required physical skills can be developed through technical training. The physical skills test provides an indicator of how long it will take the applicant to learn the skills, as well as the accuracy with which he or she will perform them. It can also help screen out those people who (for one reason or another) might never be able to perform satisfactorily. [10]

158   **Exhibit 6:3**   Minnesota Rate of Manipulation Test *(top)*, and Stromberg Dexterity
                   Test *(bottom)*

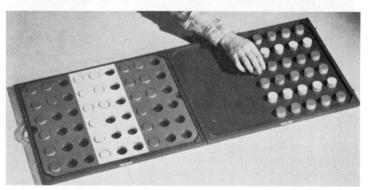

Source: Educational Test Bureau and The Psychological Corporation; reprinted in C. H.
Lawshe and Michael J. Balma, *Principles of Personnel Testing* (New York: McGraw-Hill Book
Company, 1966), p. 123.

Tests of Achievement: Job Knowledge and Mechanical Abilities.   Most of
the tests one takes in school are achievement tests. These test "job knowledge"
in areas like economics, marketing, or personnel management.

Achievement tests are also widely used in the public and private sectors.
For example, the Purdue test for machinists and machine operators tests the
job knowledge of (supposedly) experienced machinists with questions like
"What is meant by 'tolerance'?" Other tests are available for electricians,

welders, carpenters, and so forth. Similar tests are available to measure the *abilities* of candidates. A typing test is one example.

Aptitude Tests.   Other tests measure the applicant's aptitudes for the job in question. One example is the mechanical comprehension test illustrated in Exhibit 6.4. This particular test is used to predict success in mechanical type jobs (like that of maintenance mechanic).

Exhibit 6.4   Two Problems From the Test of Mechanical Comprehension, Forms S & T

Look at Sample X on this page. It shows two men carrying a weighted object on a plank, and it asks, "Which man carries more weight?" Because the object is closer to man "B" than to man "A," man "B" is shouldering more weight; so blacken the circle under "B" on your answer sheet. Now look at Sample Y and answer it yourself. Fill in the circle under the correct answer on your answer sheet.

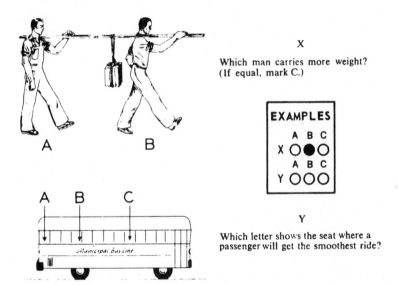

X

Which man carries more weight?
(If equal, mark C.)

Y

Which letter shows the seat where a passenger will get the smoothest ride?

Interest Inventories.   Interest inventories compare a person's interests with those of people in various occupations. Thus, if a person takes the "Strong–Campbell" inventory he or she would receive a report showing where the person's interests lie in relation to those of people already in occupations such as accountant, engineer, manager, forestry, or medical technician, for example.

Interest inventories can be useful in career planning, since a person will likely do better on jobs that involve activities he or she is more interested in. For much the same reasons these tests can be useful as selection tools. Clearly, if you can select people whose interests are roughly the same as those of success-

160 ful incumbents in the jobs you are recruiting for, you could be that much ahead of the game. [11]

Personality Tests.   Personality tests are used to measure basic aspects of an applicant's personality, aspects like introversion, stability, and motivation. Many personality tests are *projective:* an ambiguous stimulus (an ink blot, a clouded picture, etc.) is presented to the person taking the test, and he or she is asked to interpret or react to it. These pictures are not a clear picture of anything, so the person's *interpretation* must come from "within" himself—be *projected.* Thus, he or she supposedly *projects* into the picture his or her own emotional attitudes and ideas about life: Thus, a security-oriented person might describe the man in Exhibit 6.5 as "worrying about how he'll feed his family if he's fired from his job." [12]

Personality tests are the most difficult tests to evaluate and use. An expert has to assess the test-taker's interpretations and reactions and infer from them the makeup of his or her personality. And the usefulness of such tests in selection assumes that you are able to find a relationship between measurable personality traits (like introversion) and success on the job.

A Suggested Test Procedure

What makes a test like the Graduate Record Examination useful for college admissions directors? What makes a mechanical comprehension test useful for a manager trying to hire a machinist?

The answer to both questions, of course, is that people's scores on these tests have been shown to be *predictive* of how they perform. Thus, other things being equal, students who score high on the graduate admissions tests also do better in graduate school. Applicants who score higher on the mechanical comprehension test perform better as machinists.

In order for any selection test to be useful, an employer has to be fairly sure that scores on the test are related in a predictable way to performance on the job. In other words, it is imperative that you *validate* the test before using it: the employer has to be sure that test scores are a good *predictor* of some *criterion* like job performance. The *validation process* usually requires the expertise of an industrial psychologist and is coordinated by the personnel department. Line management's contribution comes in clearly describing the job and it's requirements, so that the human requirements of the job, and the job's standards of performance are clear to the psychologist. This *validation process* consists of six steps, as follows:

Step 1: Analyze the Job.   The first step is to analyze the job in order to develop job descriptions and job specifications. Here specify the human traits and skills believed necessary for adequate job performance. For example: Must an applicant be aggressive? Is shorthand required? Must the person be able to assemble small, detailed components? These requirements become the *predictors.*

Exhibit 6.5   Page From a Projective Personality Test

JUST LOOK AT THE PICTURE BRIEFLY (TEN TO FIFTEEN SECONDS),
TURN THE PAGE, AND WRITE THE STORY IT SUGGESTS.

Source: David A. Kolb, Irwin M. Rubin, and James M. McIntyre, *Organizational Psychology: An Experiential Approach,* 2nd ed. (Englewood Cliffs, N.J.: Prentice-Hall, Inc., 1971), p. 57. Reprinted by permission.

They are the human traits and skills believed to be predictive of success on the job. In this first step, you also have to define what you mean by "success on the job," since it is this success you seek *predictors* for. The standards of success are called "criteria." One can focus on *production-related criteria* (quantity, quality, etc.); *personnel data* (absenteeism, length of service, etc.); or *judgments* (of persons like supervisors).

   Step 2: Choose the Test.   Next, choose tests which seem to measure the attributes (predictors) that are important to job success. This choice is usually based on experience, previous research, and "best guesses," and the expert usually won't start off with just one test. Instead, he or she chooses several tests, combining them into a *battery*. These are aimed at measuring a variety of possible predictors, such as aggressiveness, extroversion, and numerical ability.

Step 3: Administer Test.   Next, administer the selected test to employees. You have two choices at this point. First, you can administer the tests to employees presently on the job. You then would compare their test scores with their *current* performance; this is called "con*current*" validation. Its main advantage is that data on performance is readily available. The disadvantage is that the current employees may not be representative of new job applicants (who are really the ones you are interested in screening with the tests): current employees have already received on-the-job training and have already been screened by your existing selection techniques, for example.

The most dependable way of validating tests is to administer them to *applicants* before they are hired. Then hire these applicants using only existing selection techniques (*not* the test results). Then, after these people have been on the job for some time, measure their performance *and* compare it to their earlier test results. This is called "predictive" validation.

Step 4:   Next, measure employee job performance using the performance criteria developed from step 1.

Step 5: Relate Test Scores and Criteria.   The next step is to determine if there is a significant relationship between test scores (the predictor) and performance (the criteria). [13] First, gauge the degree of relationship between the test (predictor) and performance (criteria) through *correlation analysis*. Here you compute a "correlation coefficient" (in this case usually called a "validity coefficient") which shows the degree of relationship.

Next, if desired (and if the test and performance *are* correlated), an "expectancy chart" can be developed as an aid to graphically present the relationship between the test and job performance. To do this, split the employees into, say, five groups by test score (those scoring highest fifth on the test, second highest fifth, third highest fifth, etc.). Then compute the percentage of high job performers *in each of these five test score groups* and present the data in an expectancy chart such as in Exhibit 6.6. As illustrated, this shows the "odds" of an employee being rated a high performer if he or she scores in each of the five test score groups: Thus, a person in the top 20% of the test has a 97% chance of being rated a "high performer," while one scoring in the lowest 20% has only a 29% chance of being rated a "high performer." [14]

Step 6: Cross Validation and Revalidation.   Finally (before putting the test into use), you may want to check it by "cross validating"—by again performing steps 3, 4, and 5 on a new sample of employees. At a minimum, an expert should revalidate the tests periodically (say every year or two) to make sure they continue to accurately distinguish between high and low performers.

Ethical and Legal Considerations in Testing

Equal Rights Legislation.   As explained in Chapter 2, various federal and

Exhibit 6.6   Expectancy Chart   163

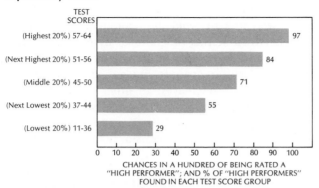

TEST
SCORES

(Highest 20%) 57-64 97
(Next Highest 20%) 51-56 84
(Middle 20%) 45-50 71
(Next Lowest 20%) 37-44 55
(Lowest 20%) 11-36 29

0   10   20   30   40   50   60   70   80   90   100

CHANCES IN A HUNDRED OF BEING RATED A
"HIGH PERFORMER"; AND % OF "HIGH PERFORMERS"
FOUND IN EACH TEST SCORE GROUP

Note: Expectancy chart showing the relation between scores made on the Minnesota Paper Form Board and rated success of junior draftsmen in a steel company. Example: persons who score between 37 and 44 have a 55% chance of being rated above average; those scoring between 57 and 64 have a 97% chance. Therefore, the higher the score, (probably) the higher the person's performance rating on the job. This is because, previously, 55% of those with scores between 37 and 44 were high performers; while 97% of those with scores between 57 and 64 were high performers.

Source: Ernest J. McCormick and Joseph Tiffin, *Industrial Psychology*, 6th ed. (Englewood Cliffs, N.J.: Prentice-Hall, Inc., 1974), p. 105. Reprinted by permission.

state laws (including the 1964 Civil Rights Act and 1967 Age Discrimination in Employment Act) bar discrimination with respect to race, color, age, religion, sex, and national origin. These laws were bolstered by the Equal Employment Opportunity Act of 1972, by guidelines published by the EEOC, and by several court decisions. With respect to testing, these laws boil down to this: (1) your organization must be able to *prove* that its tests are related to success or failure on the job (validity); and (2) it must be able to *prove* that its tests don't unfairly discriminate against either minority or nonminority subgroups. The burden of proof rests on the employer once adverse impact (the tendency of a test or other selection tool to screen out more of a protected group) has been shown: the employer is presumed "guilty" until proven innocent and may have to demonstrate the validity and selection fairness of the allegedly discriminatory item.

Yet the fact remains that the results of at least one survey indicate that a sizable proportion of companies have not conducted validation studies of their personnel selection procedures. [15] Specifically, less than half of those employers with less than 10,000 employees had conducted validation studies and less than one-fourth of those with less than 1,000 employees had done so. These findings suggest that (as of this 1975 survey) there was widespread noncompliance with the EEOC selection guidelines.

The main reason for noncompliance, apparently, is not that the guidelines are unfeasible but that compliance can be, for the employer, an expensive inconvenience. [16] For instance, employers are faced with the expense and inconvenience of implementing a validation study, of developing an objective

164   performance appraisal method (so that objective criteria of performance are available), and of doing a thorough job analysis.

Yet employers who seek to avoid the rigorous requirements of EEO legislation by phasing out their testing programs or by not complying are probably operating under a misapprehension. The fact of the matter is that EEO guidelines and related court decisions apply to any and *all* screening devices including interviews, applications, and references. In other words, the same burden of proving job-relatedness and fairness falls on interviews and other techniques that falls on tests, and employers must be ready to prove the validity and fairness of *any* screening tool which has been shown to have an adverse impact on a protected group:

> It is easy to forget that the function of personnel selection methods—interviewing as well as testing—is to measure people for jobs. The need for adequate measurement does not disappear when employers give up testing. As long as selection continues to affect women and minorities adversely, the government will continue giving the selection method close scrutiny. [17]

Implications of Equal Rights Legislation for Testing. Equal rights legislation and court decisions like *Albemarle* have a number of practical implications for testing. First, it is useful to keep in mind that these laws and regulations apply to all screening items—not just tests. An employer who sought to avoid having to comply with these laws and regulations by dropping its testing program would therefore be misinterpreting the legislation, and could find itself in the unenviable position of having to defend the validity and fairness of more subjective tools like interviews. Second (particularly in light of the apparent widespread noncompliance) employers, through their personnel staffs, should embark on validation studies aimed at determining the job-relevance of their selection tests (and other screening tools). Related to this, employers have to develop objective, defensible performance appraisal rating methods, and to train supervisors in their use. Furthermore, employers should ensure that any tests being administered have been validated *for the position the candidate is being screened for, and on a group that is representative of applicants.* (In the *Albemarle* case, which the employer lost), the company had validated its screening tests not on the entry-level job the applicants were recruiting for but on higher level jobs which applicants might some day hope to obtain. Furthermore, their validation study used only experienced, white workers while applicants who took the test were generally younger, largely inexperienced, and often nonwhite. Finally, remember that valid, fair testing demands close cooperation between line managers and personnel specialists. The personnel department's job is to establish procedures for and coordinate the necessary job analyses, performance appraisals, and validation study, and it is usually the personnel manager who will seek out and retain the services of an outside industrial psychologist, if no qualified person is available in-house. Line managers have to provide accurate information about the nature of the job and its human requirements, and are responsible for doing objective, defensible performance appraisals.

The Problem of Test Unfairness. A test might be valid when all applicants are considered, but still discriminate unfairly against *sub*groups of applicants. Thus, suppose a test is administered to 100 applicants, 60 of whom are white and 40 black. You find that for the 100 applicants the test is valid. But on closer examination it turns out that 80% of the whites are selected, while only 20% of the blacks are selected. The fact that a lower proportion of blacks are selected puts the burden of proof on the employer to prove that the blacks are not being unfairly discriminated against by the test. The employer could be required to validate the test separately for *both* blacks and whites.

Suppose the employer makes separate validation studies and finds the test is in fact valid for both blacks and whites. Then even though the test results in a larger proportion of rejects among blacks than whites, the test is, generally speaking, still legally acceptable. While it *does* "discriminate" between black and white candidates, it probably does not do so *unfairly* since it is valid (it predicts performance) for both groups.

It occasionally happens, however, that while a person's score on the test is a valid predictor of his or her performance on the job, members of one group consistently score better (or worse) than do members of another group, and are therefore more likely to be hired. For example, assume an employer decides to hire applicants who will perform on-the-job in a "good" manner (equivalent to supervisor performance ratings of 70–80). Further assume that the selection test is validated separately for whites and non-whites and found to be valid for both. However, non-whites who score 60 on the test tend to get "good" on-the-job performance ratings, while whites who score 80 on the test tend to get the "good" ratings.

If the employer decided to use the higher test score (80) as his cut-off score, then mostly whites would be hired, since relatively few non-whites (for whom 60 was a high score) probably achieved scores as high as 80. (Perhaps non-whites can't read as well, for instance, and thus do more poorly, overall, than whites on the test, although once on the job the non-white who scores 60 will perform as well as the white who scores 80.)

Such a situation could be *unfairly discriminatory* to the non-whites. Unfair discrimination exists when persons with equal probabilities of success on the job have unequal probabilities of being hired. In our case, a non-white who scores 60, and a white who scores 80 both have equal probabilities of being "good" performers. But since the employer chose to use the higher test score (80) as a cut-off, whites, primarily, were hired, thus unfairly discriminating against those non-whites (who scored 60) *who had the same probability as the whites who scored 80 of performing in a "good" manner.*

There are two implications. First, employers should, whenever feasible, validate tests separately for both minorities and non-minorities, both to ensure that the test is valid for both, and to ascertain whether different cut-off scores for each group might be appropriate. [18] Second, an employer can generally use different cut-off scores for each group (like 80 for whites and 60 for non-whites) *as long as each cut-off score corresponds to the same level of on-the-job performance* (in our case "good"). [19]

Quota Systems. From a practical point of view the time and cost involved in validating tests separately for minorities and nonminorities (and then possibly dealing with questions of differential cut-offs) are considerable. Therefore many managers have opted for a "quota" system for selection. For example, if they hire 30% of their white applicants, they also hire 30% of their black applicants. They thereby avoid the problem of having to prove that rejecting a higher proportion of minority candidates is valid and does not unfairly discriminate.

Keep in mind, though, that even with this sort of quota system an employer may still need selection tests. Even if a company decides to hire some fixed percentage of minority and nonminority candidates, it should still ensure that it selects the "best" 30% or 40%, for instance. It will still, therefore, need tests. However, it will avoid the legal need for validating tests separately for minorities and nonminorities.

Individual Rights of Test Takers and Test Security. Under the American Psychological Association's standards for educational and psychological tests, and ethical standards for psychologists, test takers have certain rights to privacy and information that should be complied with. These may be summarized as follows: [20]

1. *The individual test taker has the right to the confidentiality of the test results and the right to informed consent regarding the use of those test results.* In other words, psychologists are obligated to safeguard information obtained about an individual, in an attempt to avoid any undue invasion of the person's privacy. Furthermore, psychologists and test administrators are charged with fully informing the test taker about the purpose of the test and about how test results would be used by organizational personnel who had a legitimate need for the scores.
2. *The individual has the right to expect that only people qualified to interpret the scores will have access to those scores, or that sufficient information will accompany the test scores to ensure their appropriate interpretation.* In other words, test scores should ordinarily be reported only to people who are qualified to interpret them, and scores, if reported, should be accompanied by explanations sufficient for the recipient to interpret the scores correctly.
3. *The individual has the right to expect that the test is equally fair to all test takers in the sense of being equally familiar or unfamiliar, so that the test results reflect the test taker's true abilities.* In particular, this means that the test should be *secure* in that no person taking the test should have been able to have obtained information concerning the questions or answers on the test.

Legislation has been introduced at both the Federal and State levels which could make compliance with the third standard—that dealing with test security— more difficult to accomplish. Basically, these "truth in testing" bills contain two elements. [21] The first element, already covered by the psychologists' standards of ethics, holds that students (these bills, at present, have generally been aimed at protecting the rights of students taking admissions tests) be informed of their scores and evaluations. A second feature of these bills, however (and one that may violate standard three above) may be called "open testing" and demands that students (or applicants) be provided with, in advance, a detailed description of the aptitude test, and that upon the applicant's request, he or she will also be notified of his specific score on each subject tested, the passing score, and information including a copy of the test questions, his own answer sheet, and a copy of the answer key. Psychologists, testing services, personnel specialists, and other interested parties are generally resisting "open testing" legislation on the grounds that it could breach test security, give an unfair advantage to some applicants, invalidate the selection procedure, and necessitate the creation of a large number of replacement tests. At the present time one state, New York, has already passed such a bill (the "LaValle bill").

Some Basic Testing Guidelines [22]

Our explanation of testing suggests the following testing guidelines:

1. Use Tests as Supplements.   Do not use tests as the only selection technique; instead, use them to supplement other techniques like interviews and background checks.

There are several reasons for this. First, tests are far from infallible. Even in the best of cases the test score usually only "accounts" for or explains a small part of the person's actual performance. In addition, tests are usually better at predicting which candidates will fail (because they don't have the necessary qualifications) than which will succeed—even those with all qualifications often fall down on the job due to "circumstances beyond their control," for instance.

2. Perform a Thorough Job Analysis.   Both legislation and common sense demand that any validation study be based on a thorough job analysis, one in which the requirements of the job are carefully ascertained.

3. Develop an Effective Performance Appraisal System.   Performance appraisal (explained in Chapter 13) is a cornerstone of a valid testing procedure. In one case, for example, the court held that instructions supervisors received concerning how to appraise performance were too vague and that, furthermore, employees were compared with one another although performing substantially different job duties. As a result, the court held that the criteria against which the company's selection test was validated was inadequate, and therefore found for the plaintiff.

4. Validate the Tests for the Appropriate Organization, Jobs, and Groups. At a minimum, those responsible for an employer's testing program have to ensure that the test has been validated in their own organization, for the job or jobs that the test will be used to screen for, and for groups that are representative of actual job applicants. The fact that the same tests have been proven valid in similar organizations is generally not sufficient. Furthermore, as we explained above, conducting a validation study using, for example, job-experienced, white workers while the applicants who are required to take the test are younger, inexperienced, and often non-white was found in at least one instance (the *Albemarle* case) to be unacceptable. Similarly, a test used to screen applicants primarily for entry level jobs should usually be validated for those entry level jobs, rather than for higher level jobs which the employees might someday obtain. [23]

5. Analyze All Current Hiring and Promotion Standards. Specifically, ask questions like: "What proportion of applicants both minority and nonminority are being rejected at each stage of the hiring process?", and "Why are we using this standard—what does it mean in terms of actual behavior on the job?" Remember that the burden of proof is always on the employer to prove that the predictor (such as intelligence) is related to success or failure on the job.

6. Keep Accurate Records. It is important to keep accurate records of why each applicant was rejected. For purposes of the EEOC, the general note of "not sufficiently well-qualified" would not be enough. State, as objectively as possible, why the candidate was rejected. Remember that your reasons for rejecting the candidate may be subject to validation at a later date.

7. Use of Certain Tests Questionable. Certain intelligence tests (like the Wonderlic and Otis) have been so misused that the EEOC is prejudiced against them. The evidence provided on their validity in your organization would have to be overwhelming to permit their use.

8. Use a Certified Psychologist. The development, validation, and use of selection standards (including tests) generally requires the assistance of a qualified psychologist. Most states require that persons who offer psychological services to the public be certified or licensed. [24] Persons engaged in test validation generally belong to the American Psychological Association and probably to Division 14 (Division of Industrial and Organizational Psychology) as well. Most industrial and organizational psychologists hold the Ph.D. degree (the Bachelor's degree is never sufficient). Potential consultants should be able to provide evidence of similar work and experience in the area of test validation. He or she should be familiar with the standards for psychological tests and manuals published by the APA. And the consultant should demonstrate familiarity with existing federal and state laws and regulations applicable to equal rights. The names of previous clients should be provided so you can verify them. Competent professionals generally will not make any claims for extraordinary results nor guarantee certain, positive outcomes. Fees vary and no fee rate has been established.

9. Test Conditions are Important. Any student that has ever tried to take a test with less-than-perfect test conditions knows how important good test conditions can be. The place where tests are administered should be reasonably private as well as quiet, well lighted and ventilated. All applicants should take the tests under the same test conditions, and test security should not be allowed to be violated.

10. Avoid Invasions of Privacy. Remember that most test results are personal and should be held in the strictest confidence. Where necessary, tests should be administered and evaluated by experts.

WORK SAMPLING FOR EMPLOYEE SELECTION [25]

Work sampling is a second technique for screening job candidates.

Work Sampling—What and Why

Some psychologists believe that the "classic" validity procedures we discussed in the last few pages are inadequate. They say there is a tendency to overemphasize "predictors" like human traits (i.e.: intelligence, etc.) and to deemphasize the *actual* behaviors required by the job. For example, if you were recruiting insurance salesmen, you might focus on a predictor like "extroverted." But "extroverted" is really just a means to an end: what you are *really* interested in is the salesman's behavior *on the job*—whether he gets along well with people; whether he is able to make "cold" calls; whether he can carry on a good conversation over lunch with a client; etc. The "classic" validity model tends to disregard such on-the-job behavior, focusing instead on "predictors" of job behavior (like extroversion). While these predictors *are* often related to job performance, the relationships are often not too strong.

Therefore, some psychologists have suggested a different approach. Basically, they say that "the best indicator of future performance is past performance." They recommend using the person's actual performance on the same (or very similar) job to predict the person's future job performance. Many managers, of course, have long used a very informal version of this system for selecting employees. They have done this by inquiring about the candidate's "prior work experience," intuitively relating prior work experience to performance on the job they are recruiting for.

The Basic Work Sampling Procedure

The basic procedure involves choosing several specific tasks that are crucial to performing the job being recruited for. Then applicants are tested on these specific tasks. Their performance (on these tasks) is then used as a predictor of their performance on the job. The following is an outline of the procedure, based on an actual example.

Step 1: Analyze applicants' previous work experience. Several people familiar with the job (of "maintenance mechanic") analyzed the previous work experience of the maintenance mechanic applicants.

Step 2: Have experts list tasks. Then, these experts listed all possible tasks (like "install pulleys and belts") that maintenance mechanics would be required to perform. For each task they were asked to indicate frequency of performance and evaluate its relative importance to the job.

Step 3: Develop basic dimensions of work behavior. Next, the experts reviewed these tasks and classified them into *major dimensions* of work behavior that they felt discriminated between effective and ineffective performance on the job. The experts then pooled their information, discussed differences, and decided on two crucial dimensions: "use of tools" and "accuracy of work."

Step 4: Select "crucial" tasks as work sample measures. Next, the experts had to choose several tasks (from step 2) that were crucial for the maintenance mechanic jobs. These tasks also had to "make sense" in terms of the applicants' prior work experience (which they analyzed in step 1). *And, the tasks had to be representative of the two "basic dimensions" that had been chosen in step 3:* "use of tools" and "accuracy of work." In this case, four tasks were selected: installing pulleys and belts; disassembling and installing a gear box; installing and aligning a motor; and pressing a bushing into a sprocket.

Step 5: Break down tasks into steps. Next, these four tasks (installing pulleys and belts, etc.) were broken down into the steps needed to complete them. Each step was then analyzed to determine the different ways each step could be accomplished. Some approaches were better than others; therefore, the experts gave different weights to different approaches.

For example, shown on top of Exhibit 6.7 is one of the steps required for "installing pulleys and belts": "checks key before installing." Different possible approaches here include checking the key against the (1) shaft, or (2) the pulley, or (3) against neither. Weights reflecting the "goodness" of each of these three approaches are shown on the right.

Step 6: Test the applicant. Next, each applicant was required to perform each of the steps. A test administrator watched the applicant and checked off (on a questionnaire like that illustrated in Exhibit 6.7) the approach the applicant used.

Step 7: Relate work sample score and applicant's performance on the job. The final step is to determine the relationship between the applicant's score on his "work samples" and his actual performance on the job. Then, once they were sure the work sample was a valid predictor of job success, the employer could begin using it for selection.

Advantages. There are several advantages to using work sampling as a

Exhibit 6.7 Work Sampling Questions

"Crucial Tasks" and Sample Questions for Maintenance Mechanics

		Scoring Weights
	Installing Pulleys and Belts	
1.	Checks key before installing against:	
	_____ shaft	2
	_____ pulley	2
	_____ neither	0
	Disassembling and Repairing a Gear Box	
10.	Removes old bearing with:	
	_____ press and driver	3
	_____ bearing puller	2
	_____ gear puller	1
	_____ other	0
	Installing and Aligning a Motor	
1.	Measures radial misalignment with:	
	_____ dial indicator	10
	_____ straight edge	3
	_____ feel	1
	_____ visual or other	0
	Pressing a Bushing Into Sprocket and Reaming to Fit a Shaft	
4.	Checks internal diameter of bushing against shaft diameter:	
	_____ visually	1
	_____ hole gauge and micrometers	3
	_____ Vernier calipers	2
	_____ scale	1
	_____ does not check	0

Source: James E. Campion, "Work Sampling for Personnel Selection," *Journal of Applied Psychology*, Vol. 56 (1972). Copyright 1972 by the American Psychological Association. Reprinted by permission.

selection tool. The emphasis is on samples of actual behavior, so it is harder to "fake" answers (as a person might on aptitude or interest tests). The work sample is more clearly relevant to the job you are recruiting for. The content of the work sample is not as likely to be "unfair" (or to emphasize middle class concepts and values) as some psychological tests might. [26] And, since it doesn't delve into the applicant's background and personality, there's almost no chance of the work sample being viewed as an invasion of privacy.

MANAGEMENT ASSESSMENT CENTERS FOR EMPLOYEE SELECTION

Assessment centers are a third device for screening job candidates.

What are managment assessment centers?

Many organizations are beginning to use "management assessment centers" for employee selection and many employees now find themselves participating in one as a prerequisite to being hired (or promoted). In the typical assessment center, the applicant is exposed to a series of "real life" exercises. His or her performance is observed and assessed by experts, who then check on their assessments by watching the participant once he is back at his old job. Examples of such real life exercises include:

The in-basket. [27]   In a typical in-basket exercise the candidate is faced with an accumulation of reports, memos, notes of incoming phone calls, letters, and other materials supposedly collected in the "in-basket" of the job he or she is to take over. The candidate is asked to take appropriate action on each of these materials by writing letters, notes, agenda for meetings, and so on. The results of the person's actions are then reviewed by a trained rater.

The leaderless group discussion.   Participants in a leaderless group discussion are usually given a discussion question and instructed to arrive at a group decision. Topics may include such things as promotion decisions, or business expansion problems, for example. Here, trained raters can evaluate each participant's interpersonal skills, acceptance by the group, leadership, and individual influence.

Management games.   Management games usually require participants to engage in realistic problem solving, perhaps as members of two or more simulated companies that are competing in the market place. Decisions might have to be made about matters like how much to advertise, how much to manufacture, and how much inventory to keep in stock. Participants can exhibit organizational abilities, interpersonal skills, and leadership abilities.

Individual presentations.   Here a participant's communication skills and persuasiveness are evaluated by giving the person time to make an oral presentation on a particular topic or theme.

Objective test.   All types of paper and pencil tests of personality, mental ability, interests, and achievements might be a part of an assessment center.

An interview.   Most assessment centers also have an interview between at least one assessor and the participant in which the latter's current interests, background, past performance, and motivation are investigated.

An example.   An assessment center was set up to assess first line managers' potential for middle management positions. Twelve participants were nominated by their immediate supervisors as having potential (based on their current job performance). For two days, participants took part in exercises aimed at exposing behaviors deemed important in this particular organization. For example, participants played a simulated business game, completed an "in-basket" exercise and participated in group discussions. They also had to take several individual tests and exercises and be interviewed.

Six experts observed and assessed each participant's behavior and took
notes on special forms. After the two days of exercises, the participants went
back to their jobs and the assessors spent two days comparing their observations
and making a final evaluation of each participant. A summary report was then
developed on each participant: This outlined his or her potential and defined
development action appropriate to both the organization and the individual.

Effectiveness.   Findings concerning the effectiveness of such centers (which
were first used in the Bell System) are spotty. The results of some studies indicate that a thorough evaluation of a participant's personnel file and an interview
will provide information comparable to the results of the assessment center. Yet
many studies (including all those in the Bell System) suggest that assessment
centers *are* useful for predicting success in management positions. [28] Studies
also indicate that assessment centers, insofar as they sample "actual" job behavior, have been shown to be valid, unbiased selection tools. [29]

In any case, they have some disadvantages. They can be expensive and time-
consuming to organize and run. Employees who are not nominated (or who
are nominated, but not promoted) can become morale problems. The centers
rely on the supervisor to nominate employees for participation and otherwise
"high potential" employees may never be nominated because of qualities like
aggressiveness. Many participants feel they can't really "get to show what I can
do" in assessment centers. Anxiety at any assessment center can also be a
problem. [30]

BACKGROUND AND REFERENCE CHECKS

Background and reference checks are a fourth device for screening job
candidates, and almost all companies carry out some sort of reference check
on their candidates. The problem, though, is that most people prefer not to
give bad references and the ones received are often unrevealing (at best). Therefore, the reference check may not be very useful for evaluating a person's strong
points. But, given the fact that most people do not like giving bad references,
receiving some negative comments can provide a good "red flag."

Structured Background Checks

In order to make their background checks more useful, many organizations
now use questionnaires, as in Exhibit 6.8. In one such questionnaire, evaluators
rate a job candidate on job factors including *occupational ability*, *character*, and
reputation. Studies suggest that this questionnaire is useful—at least for describing the applicant's character and reputation. [31]

Generally speaking, the use of questionnaires seems to result in more useful
information (than not using them), although this is not always so. Part of the
problem (to repeat) is that many people prefer not to give bad references.

TELEPHONE OR PERSONAL INTERVIEW

☐ **FORMER EMPLOYER**
☐ **CHARACTER REFERENCE**

COMPANY   ADDRESS   PHONE

NAME OF PERSON   POSITION
CONTACTED   OR TITLE

1. I WISH TO VERIFY SOME FACTS GIVEN BY

    (MISS, MRS.)

    MR.

    WHO IS APPLYING FOR EMPLOYMENT WITH OUR FIRM. WHAT
    WERE THE DATES OF HIS EMPLOYMENT BY YOUR COMPANY?   FROM   19   TO   19

2. WHAT WAS THE NATURE OF HIS JOB?   AT START

                                         AT LEAVING

3. HE STATES THAT HE WAS EARNING $ PER
    WHEN HE LEFT, IS THAT CORRECT?   YES   NO $

4. WHAT DID HIS SUPERIORS THINK OF HIM?

    WHAT DID HIS SUBORDINATES THINK OF HIM?

5. DID HE HAVE SUPERVISORY RESPONSIBILITY?   YES   NO

    (IF YES) HOW DID HE CARRY IT OUT?

6. HOW HARD DID HE WORK?

7. HOW DID HE GET ALONG WITH OTHERS?

8. HOW WAS HIS ATTENDANCE RECORD?   PUNCTUALITY?

9. WHAT WERE HIS REASONS FOR LEAVING?

10. WOULD YOU REHIRE HIM? (IF NO) WHY?
                                         YES   NO

11. DID HE HAVE ANY DOMESTIC, FINANCIAL OR PERSONAL
    TROUBLE WHICH INTERFERED WITH HIS WORK?   YES   NO

12. DID HE DRINK OR GAMBLE TO EXCESS?   YES   NO

13. WHAT ARE HIS STRONG POINTS?

14. WHAT ARE HIS WEAK POINTS?

REMARKS:

Source: Reprinted by permission of the publisher from *Book of Employment Forms,* American Management Association, copyright © 1967 by the American Management Association, p. 228.

Another problem is that references are, as their name implies, *referred* to you by the job applicant. Therefore, many managers use the applicant's suggested references as a source for other references who may know of the applicant's performance. Thus you might want to ask each of your applicant's references, "Could you please give me the name of another person who might be familiar with the applicant's performance?" In that way you begin getting information from references other than those referred by the applicant himself.

The Importance of Following Up Quickly on Candidates

Finally, whichever selection tools are used (interviews, tests, etc.) it is important to minimize the time lag between the date the candidate applies for the job and the date of the first selection procedure. A longer delay results in more candidates dropping out, and this may be especially true of minority candidates. [32]

SUMMARY

1. In this chapter we discussed four techniques for screening and selecting job candidates: the first was testing.

2. Test validity refers to the extent to which the test measures what it purports to measure or carries out the function it was designed for. We discussed empirical validity, content validity, face validity, and construct validity.

3. As used by psychologists, the term reliability always means consistency. One way to measure this is to administer the same (or equivalent) test to the same people at two different points in time. Or, you could focus on "internal consistency." Here, compare the responses to roughly equivalent items on the same test.

4. There are many types of personnel tests in use, including intelligence tests, tests of physical skills, tests of achievement, aptitude tests, interest inventories, and personality tests.

5. In order for a selection test to be useful, scores on the test should be related in a predictable way to performance on the job: you must *validate* the test. This involves six steps: (1) job analysis; (2) choose your test; (3) administer the test; (4) measure performance; (5) relate test scores and criteria; and (6) cross validate and revalidate the test.

6. Under equal rights legislation, an employer may have to be able to prove that his tests are predictive of success or failure on the job. This usually involves a predictive validation study, although other means of validation are acceptable.

7. Some basic testing guidelines include: (1) use tests as supplements; (2) perform a job analysis; (3) develop an effective performance appraisal system; (4) validate the tests for appropriate jobs; (5) analyze all current hiring and promotion standards; (6) keep accurate records; (7) beware of certain tests; (8) use a certified psychologist; (9) maintain good test conditions; and (10) avoid invasions of privacy.

8. The work sampling selection technique is based on the assumption that "the best indicator of future performance is past performance." Here one uses the applicant's actual performance on the same (or very similar) job to predict his or her future job performance. The steps are: (1) analyze applicant's previous work experience; (2) have experts list component tasks for jobs being recruited for; (3) classify these into basic dimensions of work behavior; (4) select crucial tasks as work sample measures; (5) break down these tasks into steps; (6) test the applicant; and (7) relate the applicant's work sample score to his performance on the job.

9. Management assessment centers are a third screening device, and involve exposing applicants to a series of "real life" exercises. Performance is observed and assessed by experts, who then check on their assessments by watching the participants when they are back at their jobs. Examples of "real life" exercises include a simulated business game, an "in-basket" exercise, and group discussions.

10. Even though most people prefer not to give bad references, most companies still carry out some sort of screening reference check on their candidates. These can be useful in raising "red flags," and structured questionnaires can improve the usefulness of the responses you receive.

11. Employee selection is directly related to employee performance. Your aim is to select those who have the ability and potential to successfully perform the job. In this chapter we discuss a variety of tools—tests, previous experience, assessment centers, etc.—that can help an employer choose the best qualified, most highly motivated candidates—those with the potential to do the job. The next step is to hire, orient, and train the new employees, to which we now turn.

Use of References

The X-Press Company requires all applicants for employment to give the names of three former employers as references. In practice, in the selection procedure, one of the three is queried about the facts of earlier employment described on the application form.

Recently, the staff has speculated about the soundness of this practice. Some staff members have raised questions about the implications of this "sampling" procedure. They suggest that inquiries directed to one or the other of the two remaining names might produce quite different evidence. They argue that all three should be questioned if heavy reliance is to be placed on references as a basis for acceptance or rejection.

Another staff member has suggested that the entire procedure should be discarded. He argues that, in the first place, the statements made in reply to such inquiries are not reliable, that references do not disclose the most important facts. Second, he insists that staff members can and do place a wide range of interpretations on these statements.

The personnel manager has been concerned by these criticisms. He is particularly worried because of a recent experiment. In that test, all his staff members were asked to examine references for fifty recent applicants and to rank each for acceptance or rejection. Names of applicants were deleted. Staff members disagreed on more than thirty of the fifty references.

Questions

1. Do you agree that the firms should stop asking for references? Why? Why not?
2. What are they doing wrong now with respect to requesting and checking references?
3. What might the firm do to improve its reference procedures?

EXPERIENTIAL EXERCISE[33]

Purpose. The purpose of this exercise is to give you practice in developing a test to measure *one specific ability* for the job of directory assistance operator in a telephone company. If time permits you will also be able to combine your tests into a test battery, and validate it.

Required Understanding. The reader should be fully acquainted with the procedure for developing a personnel test and should read the following description of a directory assistance operator's duties:

Customers contact directory assistance operators to obtain the telephone numbers of persons whose numbers are not yet listed, whose listings have changed, or whose numbers are unknown to the customer. These operators look up the requested number in telephone books issued daily and transmit numbers to the customers. A number must be found quickly so that the customer is not kept waiting. It is often necessary to look under various spellings of the same name since customers frequently give incorrect spellings.

You may assume that one-third of the applicants seen will become directory assistance operators. You wish for a test that will aid in selecting the best third of those available.

How to Set Up the Exercise.   First, divide the class into teams of five or six. The instructor will then assign procedures I and II to different teams.

Procedure I: Select an important ability (for a directory assistance operator) and develop a test to measure it. Only the materials available in the room are to be used. Telephone directories may not be furnished. The test should permit quantitative scoring and may be an individual or a group test.

Procedure II: Select an important ability that is susceptible to rating by means of an interview. Develop a patterned (structured) interview form as well as a method for scoring it.

Instructions for the Exercise.   The students should go to their preassigned groups and (as per our discussion of test development in this chapter), each group should make a list of the abilities that seem relevant to success on the operators' job. Each group should then rate the importance of these abilities on a five point scale. Then, develop either a test (procedure I) or an interview form (procedure II) to measure this ability.

Next, each team should be given a chance to demonstrate their tests on one of the other teams.

If time permits, the various tests (from each team) should be combined to form a test battery. (The instructor will want to provide some guidelines on which tests would make up the best battery.) Next, a group of eight to ten students take the test battery. Then, supply telephone directories to these students and have one person call out the names of persons whose numbers are to be looked up. If you use a time limit, success could be measured by the number of correct responses each of the eight to ten students obtains. Finally, relate these scores to the students' test results. Did the test distinguish between high and low performers? What part of the job was not measured by the test?

DISCUSSION QUESTIONS

1. Explain what is meant by reliability and validity. What is the difference between them? In what respect(s) are they similar?
2. Explain how you would go about validating a test. How can this information be useful to a manager?
3. Write a short essay discussing some of the ethical and legal considerations in testing.
4. Explain why you think a certified psychologist should (or should not) always be used by a company developing a personnel test battery.

NOTES

1. Selection Procedures and Personnel Records, Personnel Policies Form Survey, No. 114 (Washington, D.C.: The Bureau of National Affairs, Inc., 1976), p. 7.

2. For a discussion of this see, for example Joel Lefkowitz, "Pros and Cons of 'Truth in Testing' Legislation," *Personnel Psychology*, Vol. 33 (Spring 1980), pp. 17–24.

3. Barbara Lerner, *Personnel Psychology*, Vol. 33 (Spring 1980), p. 11–16.

4. See for example John B. Miner, "Psychological Testing and Fair Employment Practices: A Testing Program That Does Not Discriminate," *Personnel Psychology*, Vol. 27 (1974), pp. 49–62.

5. This is based on Frank Schmidt, John Hunter, Robert McKenzie, and Tressie Muldrow, "Impact of Valid Selection Procedures on Work Force Productivity," *Journal of Applied Psychology*, Vol. 64 (December 1979), pp. 609–626.

6. Based on the supervisor's estimates, the mean estimated difference in dollar value of yearly job performance between programmers at the 85 and 50 percentiles in job performance was $10,871. The figure for the difference between the 50 and 15 percentiles was $9,955.

7. See Anne Anastasi, *Psychological Patterns* (New York: Macmillan, 1968), reprinted in Hamner and Schmidt, *Contemporary Problems in Personnel* (Chicago: St. Clair, 1974), pp. 102–109; Leona Tyler, *Tests and Measurements*, pp. 25–31; Tiffin and McCormick, *Industrial Psychology* (Englewood Cliffs, N.J.: Prentice-Hall, 1974), pp. 101–125; Lawshe and Balma, *Principles of Personnel Testing* (New York: McGraw-Hill, 1966), pp. 53–69. For an excellent series of recent papers in the areas covered in this chapter, see W. Clay Hamner and Frank L. Schmidt, *Contemporary Problems in Personnel*, rev. ed. (Chicago: St. Clair, 1977), pp. 60–131.

8. Anastasi, *Psychological Patterns*, p. 107.

9. See Tyler, *Tests and Measurements*, pp. 38–79; Lawshe and Balma, *Principles of Personnel Testing*, pp. 83–164.

10. See, for example, Richard Reilly, Sheldon Zedeck, and Mary Tenopyr, "Validity and Fairness of Physical Ability Tests for Predicting Performance in Craft Jobs," *Journal of Applied Psychology*, Vol. 64, No. 3 (June 1979), pp. 262–274.

11. For a study describing how matching (1) task and working condition *preferences* of applicants with (2) actual job and working conditions, see Ronald Ash, Edward Levine, and Steven Edgell, "Study of a Matching Approach: The Impact of Ethnicity," *Journal of Applied Psychology*, Vol. 64, No. 1 (February 1979), pp. 35–41.

12. Tyler, *Tests and Measurements*, p. 74.

13. Based on Tiffin and McCormick, *Industrial Psychology*, pp. 104–105; Lawshe and Balma, *Principles of Personnel Testing*.

14. Experts sometimes have to develop expectancy charts and "cutting points" for minorities and non-minorities if the validation studies indicate that "high performers," from either group (minority or non-minority) score lower (or higher) on the test. See our discussion of differential ability.

15. Prentice-Hall, Inc. PH/ASPA Survey: Employee Testing Procedures—Where are They Headed? *Personnel Management: Policies and Practices*, April 22, 1975; described in James Ledvinka and Lyle Schoenfeldt, "Legal Developments in Employment Testing: Albemarle and Beyond," *Personnel Psychology*, Vol. 31, No. 1 (Spring 1978), p. 9.

16. Ledvinka and Schoenfeldt, p. 9.

17. Ledvinka and Schoenfeldt, p. 12.

180   **18.** David Robertson, "Update on Testing and Equal Opportunity," *Personnel Journal*, Vol. 56, No. 3 (March 1977) reprinted in Craig Schneier and Richard Beatty, *Personnel Administration Today* (Reading, Mass.: Addison Wesley, 1978), p. 300.

19. Virginia R. Boehm, "Negro–White Differences in Validity in Employment and Training Selection Procedures: Summary of Research Evidence," *Journal of Applied Psychology*, Vol. 56 (1972), pp. 33–39; in Hamner and Schmidt, *Contemporary Problems in Personnel*, pp. 126–134. See also John Hunter and Frank Schmidt, "Differential and Single Group Validity of Employment Tests by Race: A Critical Analysis of Three Recent Studies," *Journal of Applied Psychology*, 1978, Vol. 63, No. 1, pp. 1–11. Note that the need for differential test scores is a separate problem from that of *differential validity*. Differential validity exists when the validity coefficients for two groups are significantly different in a statistical sense. Differential validity thus refers to the predictive capability of the test for each group. When a test is validated separately for two groups—say, white and non-white—it could thus turn out that: (1) The test is *differentially valid*, in that the validity coefficients (the correlation between test score and job performance) are different for the two groups; *and/or* (2) different cutting scores are needed for each group, since using the same cutting score might be unfairly discriminatory to one group. In practice, *differential validity* is generally not a serious problem. Finally, also note that while the need for different cutting scores is an important source of test unfairness, there are other ways to use a test unfairly. One could, for instance (to use an extreme example) give non-minority candidates the test answers ahead of time.

20. This is based on Marilyn Koch Quaintance, "Test Security: Foundation of Public Merit Systems," *Personnel Psychology*, Vol. 33, No. 1 (Spring 1980), pp. 25–32.

21. This is based on William Roskind, "Deco versus NLRB, and the Consequences of Open Testing in Industry," *Personnel Psychology*, Vol. 33, No. 1 (Spring 1980), pp. 3–9.

22. See Floyd L. Ruch, "The Impact on Employment Procedures of the Supreme Court Decision in the Duke Power Case," *Personnel Journal*, Vol. 50, No. 4 (October 1971), pp. 777–783; in Hamner and Schmidt, *Contemporary Problems in Personnel*, pp. 117–123; Dale Beach, *Personnel* (New York: Macmillan, 1970); Hubert Field, Gerald Bagley, and Susan Bagley, "Employment Test Validation for Minority and Nonminority Production Workers," *Personnel Psychology*, Vol. 30, No. 1 (Spring 1977), pp. 37–46; M. K. Distefano, Jr., Margaret Pryer, and Stella Craig, "Predictive Validity of General Ability Tests with Black and White Psychiatric Attendants," *Personnel Psychology*, Vol. 29, No. 2 (Summer 1976). Also, see the Winter 1976 issue of *Personnel Psychology*, Vol. 2, No. 4.

23. EEOC guidelines require that the validation study be conducted on higher level employees only if "new employees will probably, within a reasonable period of time and in a great majority of cases, progress to a higher level." See Ledvinka and Schoenfeldt, p. 5.

24. These points based on "Proposed Guidelines for Choosing Consultants for Psychological Selection, Validation Research and Implementation," Professional Affairs Committee, Division 14, American Psychological Association.

25. Paul Wernamont and John P. Campbell, "Signs, Samples, and Criteria," *Journal of Applied Psychology*, Vol. 52 (1968), pp. 372–376, and James Campion, "Work Sampling for Personnel Selection," *Journal of Applied Psychology*, Vol. 56 (1972), pp. 40–44, both reprinted in Hamner and Schmidt, *Contemporary Problems in Personnel*, pp. 168–180; Dunnette, *Handbook of Industrial and Organizational Psychology*, p. 515; Sidney Gael, Donald Grant, and Richard Ritchie, "Employment Test Validation for Minority and Nonminority Clerks with Work Sample

Criteria," *Journal of Applied Psychology*, Vol. 60, No. 4 (August 1974); Frank Schmidt, Alan Areenthal, John Hunter, John Berner, and Felecia Seaton, "Job Sample vs. Paper and Pencil Trades and Technical Tests: Adverse Impacts and Examinee Attitudes," *Personnel Psychology*, Vol. 30, No. 7 (Summer 1977), pp. 187–198.

26. See for example George Brugnoli, James Campion, and Jeffry Bisen, "Racial Bias in The Use of Work Samples for Personnel Section," *Journal of Applied Psychology*, Vol. 64, No. 2 (April 1979), pp. 119–123.

27. This section based on Ann Howard, "An Assessment of Assessment Centers," *Academy of Management Journal*, Vol. 17, 1974, pp. 115–34. See also Louis Olivas, "Using Assessment Centers for Individual and Organizational Development," *Personnel*, Vol. 57, (May–June 1980), pp. 63–67.

28. For other evidence see, for example, John Hinrichs, "An Eight Year Follow-up of a Management Assessment Center," *Journal of Applied Psychology*, Vol. 63, No. 5 (October 1978), pp. 596–601; Larry Alexander, "An Exploratory Study of the Utilization of Assessment Center Results," *Academy of Management Journal*, Vol. 22, No. 1 (March 1979), pp. 152–157; Wayne Cascio and Val Silby, "Utility of the Assessment Center as a Selection Device," *Journal of Applied Psychology*, Vol. 64, No. 2 (April 1979), pp. 107–118.

29. For a discussion of this see Steven Norton, "The Empirical and Content Validity of Assessment Centers Versus Traditional Methods of Predicting Management Success," *Academy of Management Review*, July 1977, pp. 442–53.

30. See William Byham, "The Assessment Center as an Aid in Management Development," *Training and Development Journal* (December 1971), and Douglas W. Bray and Richard Campbell, "Selection of Salesmen by Means of an Assessment Center," *Journal of Applied Psychology*, Vol. 52 (1968), pp. 36–41. The former reprinted in Hamner and Schmidt, *Contemporary Problems in Personnel*; the latter reprinted in Fleishman and Bass, *Studies in Personnel and Industrial Psychology*; James Huck and Douglas Bray, "Management Assessment Center Evaluations and Subsequent Job Performance of White and Black Females." *Personnel Psychology*, Vol. 29, No. 1 (Spring 1976).

31. Tiffin and McCormick, *Industrial Psychology*, pp. 78–79.

32. Richard Arvey, Michael Gordon, Douglas Massengill, and Stephen Mussio, "Differential Dropout Rates of Minority and Majority Job Candidates Due to Time Lags Between Selection Procedures," *Personnel Psychology*, Vol. 28, No. 2 (Summer 1975).

33. This is based on "Matching People and Jobs," in Norman R. F. Maier, *Psychology in Industrial Organizations* (Boston: Houghton Mifflin, 1973), pp. 232–233.

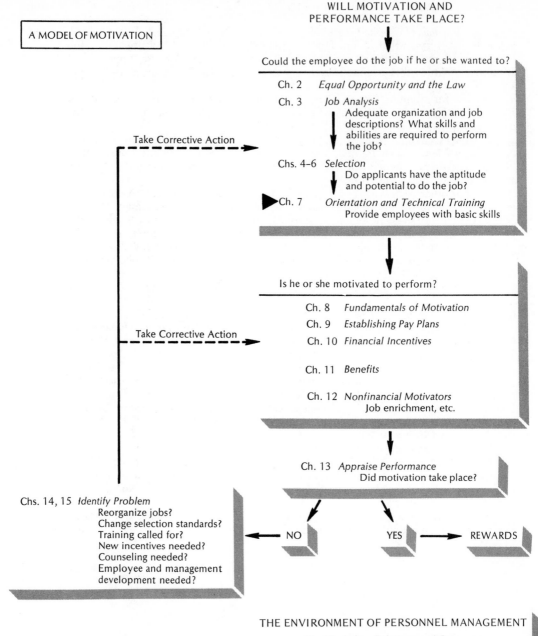

A MODEL OF MOTIVATION

WILL MOTIVATION AND
PERFORMANCE TAKE PLACE?

Could the employee do the job if he or she wanted to?

Ch. 2 *Equal Opportunity and the Law*

Ch. 3 *Job Analysis*
Adequate organization and job descriptions? What skills and abilities are required to perform the job?

Chs. 4–6 *Selection*
Do applicants have the aptitude and potential to do the job?

Ch. 7 *Orientation and Technical Training*
Provide employees with basic skills

Take Corrective Action

Is he or she motivated to perform?

Ch. 8 *Fundamentals of Motivation*

Ch. 9 *Establishing Pay Plans*

Ch. 10 *Financial Incentives*

Ch. 11 *Benefits*

Ch. 12 *Nonfinancial Motivators*
Job enrichment, etc.

Take Corrective Action

Ch. 13 *Appraise Performance*
Did motivation take place?

Chs. 14, 15 *Identify Problem*
Reorganize jobs?
Change selection standards?
Training called for?
New incentives needed?
Counseling needed?
Employee and management development needed?

NO   YES   REWARDS

THE ENVIRONMENT OF PERSONNEL MANAGEMENT

Ch. 16 *Labor Relations and Grievances*

Ch. 17 *Employee Safety and Health*

Ch. 18 *Personnel Management and the Quality of Work Life*

When you finish studying

7 Orientation and Technical Training

You should be able to:

1. *List the important factors in an employee orientation program.*
2. *Explain how to develop and implement a training program.*
3. *Explain how to distinguish between "training" problems and those not amenable to training.*
4. *Discuss three training techniques.*
5. *Explain how you would go about identifying training requirements.*
6. *List seven principles of learning.*
7. *Prepare a "job instruction training" chart for a job.*

OVERVIEW

The main purpose of this chapter is to explain the process and techniques of training, including the assessment, implementation, and evaluation of training programs. A second purpose is to explain orientation which (with training) is used to assimilate the new employee into the organization. These are, therefore, the final steps in recruiting and placing employees, as well as a final step in seeing to it that employees have the ability required to do the job.

INTRODUCTION

Once employees have been screened and selected, the next step is to orient and train them: orientation and training provides them with the basic information and skills they need to be successful on their new jobs.

As illustrated in our model, orientation and training are important factors in performance. For performance to take place employees must have the basic skills required to do their jobs. And it is through orientation and training that they are provided with the basic knowledge and skills they need to successfully carry out their tasks.

The Functions of Orientation

Orientation serves three functions in organizations. First, it is during orientation that new employees are provided with basic information about the employer, information that they require to perform their jobs satisfactorily. This basic information includes, for example, how to get on the payroll, how to obtain identification cards, what the working hours are, and who the new employee will be working with.

Orientation also serves a second, equally important function: it can help the new employee feel more like "one of the family," and thus help him overcome his "first day jitters," and feel more comfortable on the job. Almost everyone who has started a new job has probably experienced these sorts of "jitters," and, in fact, they are typical of new employees. For example, in one study at the Texas Instruments Company, researchers discovered the following about new employees: [1]

—The first days on the job were anxious and disturbing ones.
—"New employee initiation" practices by peers intensified anxiety.
—Anxiety interfered with the training process.
—Turnover of newly hired employees was caused primarily by anxiety.
—The new workers were reluctant to discuss problems with their supervisors.

Employee orientation is aimed at minimizing such problems. Its second function, in other words, is to introduce the new employee and the organization to each other, to help them become acquainted, and to help them accommodate each other.

Finally, there is a third reason for orientation: it helps minimize what might be called the "reality shock" some new employees undergo. [2] This reality shock, according to Hall, is caused by the incompatibility between what the employees *expect* in their new jobs (in terms of challenge, for instance,) and the realities they are often confronted with (in terms of boring first jobs, for instance). Orientation can help minimize this "shock" by showing employees the reasons for their job assignments, and what they can expect in terms of future career moves in the organization. [3]

What Orientation Entails

Orientation programs range from brief informal introductions to lengthy, formal programs. In the latter, the new employee is usually given a handbook or printed materials (which cover matters like working hours, performance reviews, getting on the payroll, and vacations) as well as a tour of the facilities.

The information provided in orientation programs typically covers things like employee compensation benefits, personnel policies, the employee's daily routine, company organization and operations, and safety measures and regulations. The new employee's supervisor is often given an orientation checklist similar to that in Exhibit 7.1. [4] This helps to insure that the supervisor has covered all of the necessary orientation steps like "explain organization," and "introduce to fellow workers." In most organizations the preliminary part of the orientation is performed by the personnel specialist, who explains matters such as working hours and vacations. The employee is then introduced to his or her new supervisor, who continues the orientation by explaining the exact nature of the job, introducing the new employee to his or her co-workers, and familiarizing the person with the workplace.

Some companies have also found it useful to provide new employees with special "anxiety-reduction seminars." For example, when the Texas Instruments Company found out how high the anxiety level of its new employees was, they initiated special full-day seminars. These focused on information about the company and the job and allowed many opportunities for questions and answers. The new employees were also told what to expect in terms of rumors and hazing from old employees. They were also told that it was very likely they'd succeed on their jobs. These special seminars proved to be very useful. By the end of the first month, the new employees who had participated in the seminar were performing much better than those who had not. [5]

THE NATURE OF TRAINING IN ORGANIZATIONS

Training is an important prerequisite for performance. In analyzing performance problems, for example, it is useful to ask, "Could the person do this job if he or she wanted to?" and, often, without training, the answer is "no." Often, in other words, when a person is performing poorly, it is not because he or she does not *want* to do better, but, rather, because the person hasn't the skills to do the job well: training can often rectify such a problem.

Types of Training

Any training is a learning experience aimed at bringing about some desirable change in the employee and/or organization. We can distinguish, however, between two types of training: technical training and employee and management development. Technical training (explained in this chapter) is aimed at providing the new employee with the skills the person needs to perform his or her current job adequately. Employee and management development (explained in chapter 15) is training of a more long-term nature: its aim is to develop the employee for some future job with the organization, or to solve some organizational problem concerning, for instance, inadequate departmental communication.

Who Should Train?

In most organizations line managers and personnel specialists both have training responsibilities. The personnel specialist (and, in larger organizations

    Exhibit 7.1 Supervisor's Orientation Checklist

Employee's Name:	*Discussion Completed* *(please check each* *individual item)*

I.   Word of welcome   _____

II.   Explain overall departmental organization and its relationship to other activities of the company

III. Explain employee's individual contribution to the objectives of the department and his starting assignment in broad terms _____

IV. Discuss job content with employee and give him a copy of job description (if available) _____

V.   Explain departmental training program(s) and salary increase practices and procedures _____

VI. Discuss where the employee lives and transportation facilities _____

VII. Explain working conditions:
      a. Hours of work, time sheets
      b. Use of employee entrance and elevators
      c. Lunch hours
      d. Coffee breaks, rest periods
      e. Personal telephone calls and mail
      f. Overtime policy and requirements
      g. Paydays and procedure for being paid
      h. Lockers
      i. Other _____ _____

VIII. Requirements for continuance of employment—explain company standards as to:
      a. Performance of duties
      b. Attendance and punctuality
      c. Handling confidential information
      d. Behavior
      e. General appearance
      f. Wearing of uniform _____

IX. Introduce new staff member to manager(s) and other supervisors.
Special attention should be paid to the person to whom the new employee will be assigned. _____

X.   Release employee to immediate supervisor who will:
      a. Introduce new staff member to fellow workers
      b. Familiarize the employee with his work place
      c. Begin on-the-job training _____

If not applicable, insert N/A in space provided.

Employee's Signature	Supervisor's Signature
Date	Division

Form examined for filing:

Date	Personnel Department

Source: *Handbook of Modern Personnel Administration* by Joseph Famularo. Copyright © 1972 by McGraw-Hill Inc. Used with permission of McGraw-Hill Book Company.

the training manager) is usually responsible for such matters as scheduling training programs, ensuring attendance, administering performance tests, obtaining outside instructors and consultants, certifying and qualifying program graduates, and administering payroll and travel expenses. [6] In addition to managing the training function, however, it is not unusual to find organizations in which "in-house" personnel specialists act as resource persons and actually train employees by holding lectures, seminars, and similar activities. And, of course, the personnel or training specialist would also be expected to obtain, design, and make available the pedagogical tools needed for the organization's various training programs, including, for example workbooks, films, and experiential exercises.

Line managers also have (or should have) an important role to play in training. For many of the most important types of training—like the "on the job training" described below—there is simply no substitute for having the employee's supervisor do the actual training. And of course in many smaller organizations the entire training function—designing it, a finding speakers, for instance—may be relegated to line managers.

The Basic Steps in Training

There are three basic steps or phases in any training program: assessment; training; and evaluation. The purpose of the assessment phase is to determine if there is a need for training. In other words, the main purpose of this phase is to determine whether any observed performance deficiencies can be rectified by training. In the second, "training" phase the actual training method and media to be used are chosen, and the training is conducted. The purpose of the final, evaluation phase is to determine if the trainee's performance has improved as expected and the extent to which the training program contributed to this improvement. Each of these phases will be explained more fully in the remainder of this chapter. First, however, because training is essentially a learning process, it would be useful to begin our discussion with an explanation of how people learn.

PRINCIPLES OF LEARNING

Training is essentially a learning process and so to train employees, one should understand something about how people learn. Research into why people learn (and how to get them to learn) has been going on for years and there are still no sure-fire answers. But there are some findings that are useful, and we discuss these "principles" of learning in this section.

Make the Material Meaningful

First, it is easier for trainees to understand and remember material that is *meaningful*. And, there are at least six ways in which training materials can be made more meaningful: [7]

188

1. At the start of training, provide trainees with a *bird's eye view* of the material to be presented. Knowing the overall picture and understanding how each part of the program fits into it helps make the entire program more meaningful.

2. Make sure to use a variety of *familiar examples* when presenting material to the trainees.

3. *Organize the material* so that it is presented in a logical manner and has meaningful units.

4. Split the material up into *meaningful chunks* rather than presenting it all at once.

5. Try to use terms and concepts that are already *familiar* to the trainees.

6. Use as many *visual* aids as possible to augment "theoretical" materials.

Make Provision for Transfer of Learning

Training often takes place away from the jobsite (perhaps in a classroom) and, if so, it is important to make sure that what is learned is transferred back to the job. Some guidelines for accomplishing this include: [8]

1. *Maximize the Similarity between the Training Situation and the Work Situation.* For example, if the employee will have to work in a noisy enviroment, make sure the person gets some practice during training under noisy conditions.

2. *Provide Adequate Experience with the Tasks during Training.* As a rule, the more the employee can practice the task, the better will be his or her transfer of learning back to the job.

3. *Provide for a Variety of Examples when Teaching Concepts or Skills.* For example, if trying to "get across" a concept, present examples of instances which represent and do not represent the concepts—like the right and wrong way of doing some task.

4. *Label or Identify Important Features of the Task.* For example, if training a machine operator, it is useful to give each important part of the machine a label (e.g., starter switch); and to label each step of the procedure (e.g., start machine; place tube in press; etc.).

5. *Make Sure the Trainee Understands General Principles.* This is really a variation on the idea that the material should be made as meaningful as possible. Thus, if the trainee understands the general principles underlying what is being taught, it will probably make more sense than will a memorized series of isolated steps.

Provide Feedback

Trainees who receive feedback on their progress and frequent reinforcement usually learn faster and perform better than those who do not. As a rule, feedback should be fast and frequent. This is especially so for lower-level jobs which are often routine and quickly completed.

Motivate the Trainee

Educational psychologists know that to get students (or trainees) to learn, it is best to first get them to *want* to learn. And if you think about classes in which you have done especially well (or badly), you will probably agree that this is so.

Some of the learning guidelines we just discussed are relevant here. For example, making the material *meaningful* and providing *quick feedback* and *reinforcement* will help motivate your trainee. The reinforcement aspect is especially important: provide quick, positive reinforcement (this might just take the form of a "reward" like a compliment for "a job well done").

Provide for Practice and Repetition

Practice and repetition are important for learning new skills. Skills that are practiced often are better learned and less easily forgotten.

Summary: Six Guidelines

Based on these principles and the work of educational psychologists, six guidelines for improving learning include: [9]

1. *Trainees learn best by doing.* Try to give them as much "real life" practice as possible.
2. *Provide reinforcement as quickly and frequently as possible.* Don't wait until the end of the day to tell trainees they've "done well." Instead, reinforce frequently, whenever they do something right.
3. *Provide for practice in a variety of settings.* This helps ensure that trainees become familiar with performing the task in a setting similar to the one they'll find "on the job." It also helps them apply their learning in a variety of settings.
4. *Motivate your trainees.* Trainees who are motivated are more likely to learn and apply their new knowledge and skills than those who are unmotivated. Make sure they see how the training will affect their success and rewards.
5. *Make the learning meaningful* by using familiar examples and summaries and by intelligently organizing the material.
6. Finally, we know that trainees learn better when they *learn at their own pace*. Think about how you would feel with someone looking over your shoulder as you try to learn a new subject. Most people don't learn well under these conditions. Instead, they learn best when they are allowed to proceed at their own pace.

THE ASSESSMENT PHASE: HOW TO DETERMINE WHAT TRAINING IS REQUIRED

In determining what training is required, it is useful to distinguish between the training needs of *new* employees, and of *present* employees.

Assessing the Training Needs of New Employees

Assessing the training needs of new employees is perhaps the easier task. Here, particularly with lower echelon workers, it is common to hire inexperienced personnel and train them—give them the necessary skills to perform the task. For such people the training needs are fairly obvious. [10] Here the aim is to develop the skills and knowledge required for effective performance, and so the training is usually based on a detailed study of the job itself to determine what specific skills and knowledge are required.

Job description and analysis is helpful in this regard. Recall that job analysis is aimed at determining what constitutes the job, the methods that are used on the job, and the human skills required to perform the job adequately. This analysis leads to a *job description* (which lists the actual duties to be performed), and a *job specification* (which lists the human skills and knowledge required). This list of duties and required skills then becomes the basic reference point in developing the training program for the job.

Task Analysis. In developing a training program, some experts suggest going beyond the job analysis and developing a *task analysis record form* which is specifically aimed at taking job analysis-type data and presenting it in a form most useful for trainers. As illustrated in Exhibit 7.2, a task analysis record form contains 6 types of information. In the first column the job's *major tasks and subtasks* should be listed. For example, if one major task is "operate paper cutter" subtasks 1.1 through 1.5 might include "start motor," "set cutting distance," "place paper on cutting table," "push paper to cutter," and "grasp safety release with left hand." In column 2 the trainer indicates the *frequency* with which the task (and subtasks) are performed. For example, is it performed only once—at the beginning of the shift, or many times, hour after hour? In column 3 indicate the *standards of performance* for the particular task and subtasks. Since these show the level to be obtained by the trainee they should be as specific as possible and should be expressed in measurable terms like "plus or minus tolerance of 0.005," "12 units per hour," or "within 2 days of receiving the order," for example. In column 4 indicate the *conditions* under which the tasks and subtasks are to be performed. This is especially important if the conditions are critical to the training—for example where, as in the case of an air traffic controller, the person normally has to work under conditions of great turmoil and stress. In column 5 indicate the *skills or knowledge* required for each of the tasks and subtasks. This column should be based on the job specification and is used to report the kinds of aptitudes, skills, or knowledge required to perform each task. For example, if a subtask requires that certain measurements be made on a piece of wood, then the employee would at a minimum have to know how to use the measuring instrument. Finally, in column 6 make a decision concerning whether the task is learned best *on or off the job*. The decision here will be based on several considerations. Safety is one: for example, prospective jet pilots must learn something about the plane off the job, in a simulator, before

Exhibit 7.2 Task Analysis Record Form

Task List	When and How Often Performed	Quantity and Quality of Performance	Conditions under which Performed	Skills or Knowledge Required	Where Best Learned
1. Operate Paper Cutter	4 times per day		Noisy press-room: distrac-tions		
1.1 Start Motor					
1.2 Set Cutting Distance		± tolerance of 0.007 in.		Read gauge	On the job
1.3 Place Paper on Cutting Table		Must be com-pletely even to prevent uneven cut		Lift paper correctly	"
1.4 Push Paper up to Cutter				Must be even	"
1.5 Grasp Safety Release with Left Hand		100% of time, for safety		Essential for safety	On the job but practice first with no distractions
1.6 Grasp Cutter Release with Right Hand				Must keep both hands on releases	"
1.7 Pull Cutter Re-lease with Right Hand				"	"
1.8 Wait for Cutter to Retract		100% of time, for safety		"	"
1.9 Retract Paper				Wait till cutter retracts	"
1.10 Shut Off		100% of time, for safety			"
2. Operate Printing Press 2.1 Start Motor . . .					

NOTE: Task analysis record form showing some of tasks and subtasks performed by printing pressman

actually getting behind the controls. On the other hand, some jobs are so simple that they can be observed once and then done correctly. Another consideration is whether there is some "book learning" that should take place off the job before the person actually begins his or her work. For example, a computer salesman might be expected to spend several days in a classroom learning about the specifications of the company's computers before actually calling on customers. [11]

Assessing the Training Needs of Present Employees

Assessing the training needs of *present* employees is often more complex. Here the need for training is usually prompted by problems (like excess scrap) or by supervisors' requests, and so those in charge of training have the added task of deciding—perhaps through interviews, observations, or questionnaires—if "training" is in fact the solution. Often, for example, performance is down because standards are not clear, or because rewards are inadequate.

Analyzing performance problems entails four basic steps:

1. Identify a performance improvement area (it might be a single job, or the whole quality control system, for instance), and determine acceptable performance standards;
2. Next, measure *actual* performance, and identify discrepancies between actual and acceptable performance;
3. Next, analyze the cause of the problem: could the employee do a better job if he or she wanted to? Has the person the skills to do the job? Is the person just not motivated? Is the problem being caused by some factor other than the employee—a factor like worn out machinery, for instance?
4. Finally, take remedial action, action which might (and might not) involve training.

A typical analysis might be as follows:

First, it comes to the attention of those in charge of training that there is some sort of problem. For example, there may be *obvious problems* like: work standards not being met; accidents; excessive scrap; high turnover; too many low ratings on performance evaluation reports; fatigue; or deadlines not being met. In most cases first line supervisors are the first to notice such problems, and so *management requests* for training begin making their way to the training department, on the (often erroneous) assumption that "better training" is the solution. Then:

1. Having determined that a problem may exist, those in charge of training begin to analyze the problem. First, they list the duties and tasks of the job under consideration (using the job description and task analysis as a guide), as well as the acceptable standards of work performance.
2. Next, they interview and closely observe the employees involved, and determine their *actual* present performance. If actual performance is significantly below the acceptable standards for the job, a *performance deficiency* or problem does in fact exist.
3. The next step is to analyze the cause of the problem, and here it is especially important to distinguish between "can't do" and "won't do" problems. Some problems are "won't do" problems—they arise because for one reason or another employees are just not motivated to perform up to standards. Here it is useful to ask "what are the consequences of good performance?" For instance, "does the person get rewarded whether or not he or she does a good job?" And, "does the worker actually get punished for doing a good job—perhaps by having his or her performance standard raised?"

4. On the other hand there are many instances in which the employee *could not do a good job even if he or she wanted to*. Here, it is important to determine what parts of the job are giving the person trouble. Sometimes the person just does not know what is expected in terms of good performance, and the solution may be as simple as setting clear and attainable performance goals. Other times you might find that the person could not do the job if he or she wanted to because materials do not arrive at the job site on time, or because required tools are not available. Often, however, you will find that the person can not do the job because he or she does not have the skills or knowledge to perform the job: in such a case, training might be indicated. (This assumes, of course, that the organization's employee selection decision was correct, and that the person in fact has the aptitude to learn the job.)

5. Next, having identified the cause of the problem, one can plan and implement the necessary change.

Often, in other words, the solution *does* turn out to be training, and so in the rest of this chapter we discuss how to train employees, focussing particularly on technical, entry-level training. Remember, however, that the problem often lies not in the employee's skills, but in the fact that he or she does not know what is expected, or that materials do not arrive at the person's station on time, or that the consequences of performing are negative or inadequate. In other words, there may in fact be a need for training—the person does not have the skills to do the job. But on the other hand, the solution often lies in setting clearer standards, removing organizational impediments to performance, or providing positive rewards. With that in mind, we can turn to a discussion of training techniques.

TRAINING TECHNIQUES

Job Instruction Training

Many jobs consist of a logical sequence of steps and are best taught in this manner—step-by-step. This step-by-step learning has been called job instruction training (JIT).[12] It involves listing all necessary steps in the job, each in its proper sequence. Alongside each step is listed a corresponding *key point* (if any). The steps show *what* is to be done, while the key points show *how* it is to be done—and *why*. The following is an example of a job instruction training sheet for teaching a trainee how to operate a large motorized paper cutter (these are used in printing factories):

Steps	Key Points
1. Start motor	None
2. Set cutting distance	Carefully read scale—to prevent wrong-sized cut
3. Place paper on cutting table	Make sure paper is even—to prevent uneven cut

Steps	*Key Points*
4. Push paper up to cutter	Make sure paper is tight—to prevent uneven cut
5. Grasp safety release with left hand	Do not release left hand—to prevent hand from being caught in cutter
6. Grasp cutter release with right hand	Do not release right hand—to prevent hand from being caught in cutter
7. Pull cutter release with right hand	Keep both hands on corresponding releases —to avoid hands being on cutting table
8. Wait for cutter to retract	Keep both hands on releases—to avoid having hands on cutting table
9. Retract paper	Make sure cutter is retracted; keep both hands away from releases
10. Shut off motor	None

On-the-Job Training (OJT)

Virtually every employee, from mail-room clerk to company president, gets some "on-the-job training" when he or she joins a firm. This is why one expert calls it "the most common, the most widely accepted, and the most necessary method of training employees in the skills essential for acceptable job performance." [13] In many companies, OJT is the *only* type of training available to employees.

There is a variety of OJT methods. Probably the most familiar is the *"coaching"* or *"understudy"* method. Here the employee is trained on the job by his or her immediate superior. At lower levels, the coaching may simply involve having the trainee observe his supervisor so as to develop the skills necessary for running a machine. But this technique is also widely used at top management levels. Here the positions of "assistant" and "assistant to" are often used for the purpose of training and developing the company's future top executives. [14] Some guidelines for using OJT, such as "put the learner at ease," and "create interest" are summarized in Exhibit 7.3.

Job rotation, in which the employee (usually a management trainee) moves from job to job at planned intervals, is another OJT technique. The jobs usually vary in content, and the trainee might be moved periodically from production, to finance, to sales, and so on.

Special assignments and *committees* are OJT techniques used to provide lower level executives with first-hand experience in working on actual problems. Executives from various functional areas serve on "boards" and are required to analyze problems and recommend solutions to top management. [15]

Vestibule Training

Vestibule training is a training approach that aims to obtain the advantages

Exhibit 7.3   The Four Step Method of On-the-Job Training: Guidelines

STEP 1:   *Preparation of the Learner*

    1. Put the learner at ease—relieve the tension.
    2. Explain why he is being taught.
    3. Create interest, encourage questions, find out what the learner already knows about his job or other jobs.
    4. Explain the why of the whole job, and relate it to some job the worker already knows.
    5. Place the learner as close to his normal working position as possible.
    6. Familiarize him with the equipment, materials, tools, and trade terms.

STEP 2:   *Presentation of the Operation*

    1. Explain quantity and quality requirements.
    2. Go through the job at the normal work pace.
    3. Go through the job at a slow pace several times, explaining each step. Between operations, explain the difficult parts, or those in which errors are likely to be made.
    4. Go through the job at a slow pace several times, explain the key points.
    5. Have the learner explain the steps as you go through the job at a slow pace.
    6. Have the learner explain the key points as you go through the job at a slow pace.

STEP 3:   *Performance Tryout*

    1. Have the learner go through the job several times, slowly, explaining to you each step. Correct his mistakes, and, if necessary, do some of the complicated steps for him the first few times.
    2. You, the trainer, run the job at the normal pace.
    3. Have the learner do the job, gradually building up skill and speed.
    4. As soon as he demonstrates that he can do the job put him on his own, but don't abandon him.

STEP 4:   *Follow Up*

    1. Designate to whom the learner should go for help if he needs it, or if he needs to ask questions.
    2. Gradually decrease supervision, checking his work from time to time against quality and quantity standards.
    3. Correct faulty work patterns that begin to creep into his work, and do it before they become a habit. Show him why the learned method is superior.
    4. Compliment good work; encourage him and keep him encouraged until he is able to meet the quality/quantity standards.

Source: William Berliner and William McLarney, *Management Practice and Training* (Homewood, Ill.: Richard D. Irwin, 1974), pp. 442–43. Reproduced by permission of the publisher.

of both "off-the-job" methods (like classroom training), and realistic "on-the-job training." In vestibule training the trainee gets realistic practice in using required machinery and controls, but the training is done off-the-job. For example, a "mock-up" of an assembly line might be set up in a separate section of the plant for the trainees; cockpit simulators used by airline pilots are another example.

Vestibule training has some clear advantages and disadvantages relative to other types of training. In terms of advantages it is useful where (as on the assembly line) putting trainees right to work could drastically slow production. And where safety is concerned—as with pilots—it may be the only practical alternative. Its disadvantages revolve around the dual questions of realism and transfer of learning. Even with sophisticated simulators the actual stress and working conditions are usually impossible to duplicate perfectly off the job. As a result the trainee's performance in the simulated situation will not necessarily be the same as his or her performance on the job.

EVALUATING THE TRAINING EFFORT

Evaluating the results of the training effort is the third and final phase of a training program.

Ideally, the best method to use in evaluating a training effort involves *controlled experimentation*. In a controlled experiment both a training group and a control (no training) group are used. Relevant data (for instance on quantity of production, quality of production, or attitudes) should be obtained both before and after the training effort in the group exposed training, and before and after a corresponding work period in the control group. In this way, it is possible to determine to what extent any change in performance in the training group resulted from the training itself, rather than from some company-wide change (like a raise in pay); the latter, one assumes, would have affected employees in both the training, and control groups. [16] In terms of current practices, one survey found that something less than half the companies responding attempted to obtain before and after measures from trainees but that the number of organizations using control groups was negligible. [17]

What Training Effects to Measure

There are four basic categories of training outcomes or effects that can be measured: [19]

1. *Reaction.* First, evaluate trainees' reactions to the program. Did they like the program? Did they think it worthwhile? etc.
2. *Learning.* Did trainees learn the principles, skills, and facts that they were to learn?
3. *Behavior.* Next, ask whether the trainees' behavior on the job changed because of the training program.
4. *Results.* Last (but probably most important) ask: What final results were achieved? Did the trainee learn how to work the machine? Did scrappage costs decrease? Was turnover reduced? Are production quotas now being met? and so forth. This last outcome is especially important. The training program may succeed in terms of the reactions from trainees, increased learning, and changes in behavior. But if the *results* aren't achieved then, in the final anal-

ysis, the training has probably failed. Perhaps the training was not effective.
Remember, however, the results may be inadequate because it was not a
"training" problem in the first place.

Conclusion: Training in Industry. [18]   Which training techniques are used
most often in industry? Results of one survey indicate that in manufacturing
firms, job instruction training, training conferences or discussions, apprenticeship training, and job rotation were most prevalent. In non-manufacturing firms
the top techniques were job instruction training, conferences or discussions, and
job rotation.

SUMMARY

1. In this chapter we focused on technical, "skills" training for new employees and for present employees whose performance is deficient. For either,
uncovering training requirements involves analyzing the cause of the problem
and determining what (if any) training is needed. Remember to ask, "Is it a
training problem?" Make sure the "problem" is not being caused by some more
deep rooted problem like poor selection or low wages.

2. We discussed some principles of learning that should be understood by all
trainers. The guidelines include: make the material meaningful (by providing a
bird's eye view, familiar examples, organizing the material, splitting it into meaningful chunks, and using familiar terms and visual aids); make provision for
transfer of training; provide feedback; try to motivate your trainee; provide for
practice and repetition; and follow the six guidelines (such as "trainees learn
best by doing").

3. We discussed three training techniques. *Job instruction training* is useful
for training on jobs that consist of a logical sequence of steps. *Vestibule* training
combines the advantages of on- and off-the-job training.

4. On-the-job training is a third technical training technique. It might involve the "understudy" method, job rotation, or special assignments and committees. In any case, it should involve four steps: preparing the learner; presenting
the operation (or nature of the job); performance tryouts; and a follow-up.

5. Most managers don't spend time evaluating the effects of their training
program although this should be an important consideration. In measuring the
effectiveness of a training program there are four categories of outcomes one
can measure: reaction, learning, behavior, and results. In some cases where
training seems to have failed, it may be because "Training" was not the appropriate solution.

Charlie, The Railroad Agent

Charlie Bagley was employed by a railroad in Farlin, Kansas, a city of about 30,000 people. As the railroad agent, Charlie was in charge of all the company's operations in the community. Before becoming agent in Farlin, Charlie had been an agent in a small one-man agency for approximately forty years. When the one-man agency was closed, Charlie asserted his seniority rights and became agent in Farlin.

At the present location, Charlie had approximately thirty-five men for whom he was either directly or indirectly responsible. At age seventy-two, Charlie was still working full time since the company had no mandatory retirement age for agents. Because of Charlie's age, though, the company preferred that he retire; but he had maintained his present position for twelve years with no major difficulties.

One September evening, an unidentified automobile driver crossing the railroad tracks ran off the crossing, into a switch stand, back onto the road, and drove off. The accident was witnessed and reported by an employee of the company. The telegrapher on duty called the section foreman directly responsible for the condition of the tracks.

The foreman inspected the tracks and the switch stand and called Charlie. He told Charlie there was no damage to the tracks but there was about $5 damage to the switch stand. He also said that he could repair the stand the following day and that no report was necessary. Charlie did not make a report as was technically required by the rules and regulations and forgot about the incident. This was not an abnormal practice when everyone agreed to cover up an accident and save several hours required in filling out the long accident reports used by the company.

At the end of the month the section foreman turned in a claim for overtime for making the inspection, thereby bringing to the attention of the division headquarters that an accident had not been reported. The section foreman absolved himself of any responsibility by denying he had told Charlie that a report was unnecessary. Giving due consideration to the fact that Charlie had more than fifty years of service to the company and the fact that Charlie had two sons employed as agents, the superintendent asked Charlie to retire and take his pension. Charlie refused and replied that, after fifty years of service, working from eight to ten hours a day, six days a week, he had no other interests and that he was also financially committed to purchase a home, which would be impossible with only the income from a pension.

The incident prompted a formal investigation by the superintendent with union officials present; they decided that Charlie should be fired. Charlie was fired and

SOURCE: Arno Knapper, *Cases in Personnel Management* (Columbus: Grid, 1977), pp. 14–15.

signed up for his pension. Since Charlie had always maintained his membership in the telegraphers' union, the local chairman for the union instigated a claim for Charlie's reinstatement. After two years, the full process of labor-management grievance procedures had been exhausted, and the case went to arbitration. The arbitrator's decision stated that an accident so trivial as this was insufficient cause to dismiss an employee of fifty years' service. The arbitrator ordered that Charlie be reinstated in his job as agent, that he receive full back pay from the date of his dismissal two years ago, and that a comparable place be found for the man who had been working Charlie's job.

Questions

1. Is there a need for training in this company? If so, who needs training? If needed, what should the nature of the training be?
2. Do you think the facts of this case support the need for a mandatory retirement age?
3. How would you go about convincing employees of the need to follow rules and regulations?

EXPERIENTIAL EXERCISE

Purpose. The purpose of this exercise is to give you practice in developing a training program.

Required Understanding. You should be thoroughly familiar with the training methods we discussed in this chapter: job instruction training; vestibule training; and on-the-job training. Since you'll be developing a training program for directory assistance operators you should read the following description of a directory assistance operator's duties:

Customers contact directory assistance operators to obtain the telephone numbers of persons whose numbers are not yet listed, whose listings have changed, or whose numbers are unknown to the customer. These operators look up the requested number in telephone books issued daily and transmit numbers to the customers. A number must be found quickly so that the customer is not kept waiting. It is often necessary to look under various spellings of the same name since customers frequently give incorrect spellings.

Next, read this: imagine you are the supervisor of about ten directory assistance operators in a small regional phone company that has no formal training program for new operators. Since you get one or two new operators every few months you think it would raise efficiency for you to develop a "new directory assistance operator's training program" for your own use in your department. Consider what such a program would consist of before proceeding to your assigned group.

How to Set Up the Exercise. Divide the class into groups of four or five students.

Instructions

In keeping with the procedure we discussed for setting up a training program, your group should, at a minimum, go through the following steps:

1. List the duties and responsibilities of the job (of directory assistance operator) using the description provided above.

2. List some assumed standards of work performance for the job.

3. Within your group, develop some assumptions about what parts of the job give new employees the most trouble (you'd normally be able to do this based on your experience as the operators' supervisor).

4. Determine what kind of training is needed to overcome these difficulties.

5. Develop a "new directory assistance operator's training package." In this you'll provide two things. First, you will provide a one-page outline showing the type(s) of training each new operator in your unit will go through. (For example, you might indicate that the first two hours on the job will involve the new operator observing existing operators; then four hours of lectures, etc.) Second, in this package, you'll also expand on exactly what each training technique will involve. For example if you are going to use job instruction training, show the steps to be included; if you're going to use lectures, provide an outline of what you'll discuss; etc.

If time permits, a spokesman from each group can put his or her group's training program outline on the board, and the class can discuss the relative merits of each group's proposal.

DISCUSSION QUESTIONS

1. "A well thought out orientation program is especially important for employees (like recent graduates) who have had little or no work experience." Explain why you agree or disagree with this statement.

2. You're the supervisor of a group of employees whose task it is to assemble tuning devices that go into radios. You find that quality is not what it should be and that many of your groups' tuning devices have to be brought back and reworked: your own boss says that "You'd better start doing a better job of training your workers."

   a. What are some of the "staffing" factors that could be contributing to this problem?

   b. Explain how you would go about assessing whether it is in fact a training problem.

3. Explain how you would apply our "principles of learning" in developing a lecture, say, on "orientation and training."

4. Pick out some task with which you are familiar—mowing the lawn, tuning a car, etc.—and develop a job instruction training sheet for it.

NOTES

1. Earl Gomerjail and M. Scott Meyers, "Breakthrough in On-The-Job Training," *Harvard Business Review* (July–August 1966).

2. For an interesting explanation of this see, for example, Meryl Reis Louis, "Surprise and Sense Making: What New Comers Experience in Entering Unfamiliar Organizational Settings," *Administrative Science Quarterly*, Vol. 25, No. 2 (June 1980), pp. 226–251.

3. Based on Hall, *Careers in Organizations*, pp. 65–71.

4. William Glueck, *Personnel: A Diagnostic Approach* (Dallas: Business Publications, Inc., 1974); Famularo, *Handbook of Modern Personnel Management*, p. 238. See also John Wanous, "Organization Entry: The Individual's Viewpoint," in J. Richard Hackman, Edward Lawler III, and Lyman Porter, *Perspectives on Behavior in Organizations* (New York: McGraw-Hill, 1977), pp. 126–135.

5. See also Walter St. John, "The Complete Employee Orientation Program," *Personnel Journal* (May 1980), pp. 373–378.

6. Joseph Famularo, *Handbook of Modern Personnel Administration* (New York: McGraw-Hill, 1972), p. 18–5.

7. Based on Kenneth Wexley and Gary Yukl, *Organizational Behavior and Personnel Psychology* (Homewood, Ill.: Richard D. Irwin, 1977), pp. 289–95; McCormick and Tiffin, *Industrial Psychology*, pp. 232–240.

8. Adapted by Wexley and Yukl, *Organizational Behavior*, from H. C. Ellis, *The Transfer of Learning* (New York: Macmillan, 1965).

9. R. E. Silverman, *Learning Theory Applied to Training* (Reading, Mass.: Addison-Wesley, 1970), ch. 8, in McCormick and Tiffin, *Industrial Psychology*, pp. 239–240.

10. E. J. McCormick and J. Tiffin, *Industrial Psychology* (Englewood Cliffs, Prentice-Hall, 1974), p. 245.

11. This was based on Donald Michalak and Edwin Yager, *Making the Training Process Work* (New York: Harper & Row, 1979), pp. 43–65.

12. Berliner and McLarney, *Management Practices*, pp. 441–442.

13. Tracey, *Designing*, p. 30.

14. Robert J. House, *Management Development* (Ann Arbor: University of Michigan), p. 74.

15. House, *Management Development*, p. 75.

16. If using "before" measures or control groups is impractical, various other "experimental designs" are available, and while they may not provide the same unambiguous results, they are better than no evaluation at all. For a good explanation of some of these see Wayne Cascio, *Applied Psychology in Personnel Management*, pp. 297–314; for a description of an actual training evaluation see Kerry Bunker and Stephen Cohen, "The Rigors of Training Evaluation: Discussion and Field Demonstration," *Personnel Psychology*, Vol. 30, No. 4 (Winter 1977), pp. 525–542.

17. R. E. Catalanello and D. L. Kirkpatrick, "Evaluating Training Programs— the State of the Art," *Training and Development Journal*, Vol. 22, No. 5 (May 1968), pp. 2–9.

18. Robert Wenig and William Wolansky, *Review and Synthesis of Literature on Job Training in Industry* (Columbus: ERIC Clearinghouse, 1972), p. 23.

Part Two

Compensation and Motivation

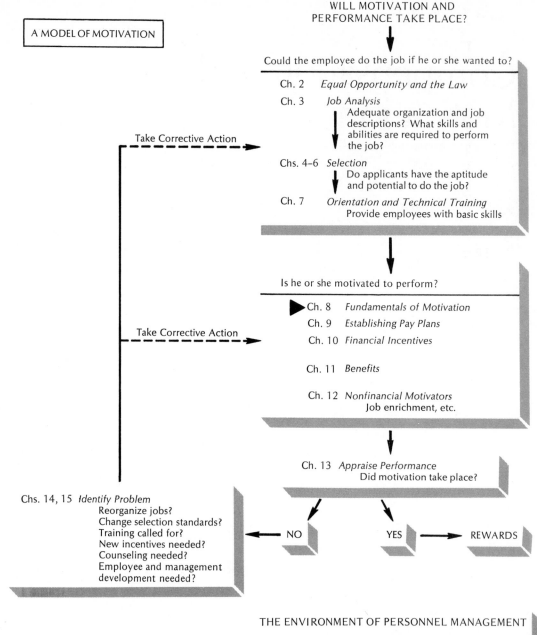

A MODEL OF MOTIVATION

WILL MOTIVATION AND
PERFORMANCE TAKE PLACE?

Could the employee do the job if he or she wanted to?

Ch. 2   *Equal Opportunity and the Law*

Ch. 3   *Job Analysis*
         Adequate organization and job
         descriptions? What skills and
         abilities are required to perform
         the job?

Chs. 4–6   *Selection*
            Do applicants have the aptitude
            and potential to do the job?

Ch. 7   *Orientation and Technical Training*
         Provide employees with basic skills

Take Corrective Action

Is he or she motivated to perform?

Ch. 8   *Fundamentals of Motivation*
Ch. 9   *Establishing Pay Plans*
Ch. 10 *Financial Incentives*

Ch. 11 *Benefits*

Ch. 12 *Nonfinancial Motivators*
         Job enrichment, etc.

Take Corrective Action

Ch. 13 *Appraise Performance*
         Did motivation take place?

Chs. 14, 15 *Identify Problem*
              Reorganize jobs?
              Change selection standards?
              Training called for?
              New incentives needed?
              Counseling needed?
              Employee and management
              development needed?

NO   YES   REWARDS

THE ENVIRONMENT OF PERSONNEL MANAGEMENT

Ch. 16 *Labor Relations and Grievances*
Ch. 17 *Employee Safety and Health*
Ch. 18 *Personnel Management and the
         Quality of Work Life*

When you finish studying

8 Fundamentals of Motivation

You should be able to:

1. *Explain why human needs are the "mainsprings of motivation."*
2. *Discuss three "needs" theories of motivation.*
3. *Give examples of how perceived equity (or inequity) affects performance.*
4. *Explain the expectancy theory of motivation.*
5. *Present several implications of these motivation theories.*

OVERVIEW

This chapter starts a new section in this book, the section on motivating and compensating employees. In Chapter 1 we introduced our performance model, and said that people should perform effectively if they have both the ability and motivation to do the task. In Section I—Recruitment and Placement—we discussed techniques aimed at ensuring that employees have the skills and abilities to do their jobs.

In the present section, we turn to the second aspect of performance—motivation—and to a discussion of rewards and their relationship to motivation. We devote four chapters (8-11) to the question of rewards, but before going on to these chapters we turn to the fundamentals and mechanics of motivation—what it is, what rewards people find important, etc.

The main purpose of this chapter is to explain some important theories of motivation. These include needs *theories (which assume that people are motivated to satisfy important personal needs),* equity *theory (which assumes they are motivated to obtain equitable rewards), and* expectancy *theory (which assumes that for motivation to occur a person must believe he or she can in fact obtain a valued reward).*

WHAT IS MOTIVATION?

Motivating—Simple Yet Complex

Motivating is both one of the simplest and most complex of management jobs. It is simple because people are basically motivated or driven to behave in a way that they feel leads to rewards. [1] So motivating someone should be easy: just find out what he or she wants and hold it out as a possible reward (or "incentive").

But this is where many experts believe that the complexity of motivating comes in. For one thing, what one person considers an important reward, another person might consider useless. For example, a glass of water would probably be a lot more "motivating" to a person who has just spent three hours on a hot beach, than it would be to someone who had just downed three Cokes. And even holding out a reward that *is* important to someone is certainly no guarantee that it will motivate him. The reason is that the reward itself (the glass of water, a date with some movie star, a promotion, and so on) will not motivate him unless he feels that effort on his part will probably lead to his obtaining that reward. People differ greatly in how they size up their chances for success on different jobs. So you can see that a task that one person might feel *would* lead to rewards, might be viewed by another as impossible.

But, the complexities of motivation notwithstanding, there is no doubt that motivation is very much the "bottom line" of management. Managers get things done through people, and if you can't somehow motivate your people, you will probably not make it in management. Therefore, let us accept the complexity of motivation as a fact of life and instead examine what *is* known about motivating employees.

Some Basic Terminology

Before proceeding, we should review some basic terminology. Most writers agree that some sort of "internal tensions" are at the root of motivation, and that motivated behavior is aimed at reducing these tensions. [2] For example, everyone has a need to eat. But right after finishing a big meal, this need would probably be satisfied. Thus someone could not "motivate" you by offering you a steak dinner. But after not eating for a few days, the need to eat would again become activated. An internal tension would develop: on the one hand, there is that basic need to eat, but on the other hand, you haven't eaten for days. At that point, if someone were to offer you a steak dinner (an incentive or reward), you might be motivated to obtain it.

Now suppose there is a barrier (for example, a fence) between you and that steak dinner. You would find your path to the goal (the steak dinner) blocked by the fence and would probably become frustrated. Frustrated or not, of course, if the goal were important enough, you might find some ingenious way of getting around the fence. But what is found more often in industry is that when the paths of workers are blocked, they often just "give up." *Morale* drops; they sit around with their friends and gripe, and, in some cases, retaliate by throwing a wrench (sometimes literally) into the machinery. This terminology is summarized in Exhibit 8.1.

HUMAN NEEDS AND MOTIVATION

Human needs are the mainsprings of motivation. All motivation ultimately derives from a tension that results when one or more of our important needs are unsatisfied: a person who is hungry is motivated to find food; a person who

Exhibit 8.1   How Motivation, Incentives, and Frustration Are Related

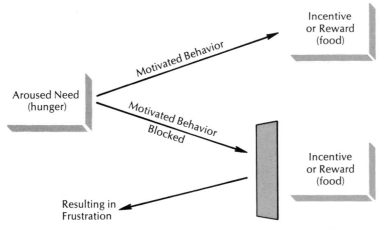

Note: Motivation takes place when you see an incentive or reward that can satisfy an *AROUSED* need. Frustration occurs when a barrier is placed between you and that incentive or reward.

needs security is motivated to find it; and a person with a compelling need to accomplish challenging tasks might try to conquer a mountain, for example. The work of three psychologists—Abraham Maslow, Frederick Herzberg, and John Atkinson—is closely associated with human needs and motivation, and their work is discussed in this section.

Abraham Maslow and the Needs Hierarchy

Maslow says that man has five basic categories of needs: physiological, safety, social, ego, and self-actualization needs. [3] He says these needs form a hierarchy or ladder (as in Exhibit 8.2) and that each need becomes active or aroused only when the next lower level need is reasonably satisfied.

Physiological Needs.   The lowest level in Maslow's hierarchy contains the physiological needs. These are the most basic needs everyone has, for example, the needs for food, drink, shelter, and rest.

Safety Needs.   When the physiological needs are reasonably satisfied— when one is no longer thirsty, has had enough to eat, has a roof overhead, and so forth—then the safety needs become activated. They become the needs which the person tries to satisfy, the needs that motivate him. These are the needs for protection against danger or deprivation and the need for security.

Social Needs.   Once a person's physiological and safety needs are satisfied, according to Maslow, they no longer motivate behavior. Now the social needs

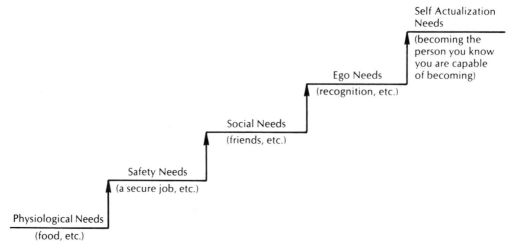

Note: Each higher order needs become active only when succeedingly lower level needs are fairly well satisfied.

become the active motivators of behavior—needs such as for affiliation, for giving and receiving affection, and for friendship.

Ego Needs.   Next in the hierarchy are the ego needs, which McGregor has interpreted as:

1. Those needs that relate to one's self-esteem—needs for self-confidence, for independence, for achievement, for confidence, for knowledge, and
2. Those needs that relate to one's reputation—needs for status, for recognition, for appreciation, for the deserved respect of one's fellows.

One of the big differences between these ego needs and the physiological, safety, and social needs is that the ego needs (and the self-actualization needs discussed next) are rarely satisfied. Thus, according to Maslow, people have a constant, infinite craving for more achievement, more knowledge, and more recognition. On the other hand, the physiological, safety, and social needs are finite: they can be and often are fairly well satisfied. As with all needs, ego needs only motivate behavior, says Maslow, once the lower level needs are reasonably satisfied.

Self-actualization Needs.   Finally, there is an ultimate need; a need that only begins to dominate a person's behavior once all lower level needs are reasonably satisfied. This is the need for self-actualization or fulfillment, the need we all have to become the person we feel we have the potential for becoming. This is the need that drives an artist to express herself on canvas, the need that motivates a student to work all day and then take a college degree in night school. This need, as with the ego needs, is rarely if ever satisfied.

Discussion. How valid is the idea that needs form a hierarchy as Maslow proposed? The Maslow theory is very difficult to test, since technically it would be best to test it at different points in time as the subjects satisfy their lower and their higher level needs. Researchers who have attempted to test the theory in this way have generally not found much support for it. [4] Maslow himself, by the way, never carried out any experiments to test his theory and, in fact, developed it based on the observations he made as a clinical psychologist. Other experts, noting the unlikelihood of finding that needs form a neat five-step hierarchy have attempted to reformulate Maslow's theory in various ways. Alderfer, for example, classifies needs as either *existence* (food and shelter), *relatedness* (affiliation), or *growth* (achievement, self-actualization) needs and reports that such a three-step hierarchy seems to make sense. [5] Based on studies of the Maslow theory, the following conclusions appear to be warranted:

> *In practice, the needs probably form a two-, not a five-, level hierarchy.* Based on a variety of studies, psychologists today believe that needs are arranged in a two-level hierarchy. At the lower level are physiological and security needs. At the higher level are social, esteem, achievement, and self-actualization needs. These include needs to feel important and to be treated as a capable individual. Needs apparently do not fall into a neat five-step hierarchy the way Maslow proposed. It is more useful to assume a two-level hierarchy, in which the higher level needs become aroused only when the lower level needs for food, security, and so on are reasonably satisfied. Thus a person won't start craving achievement, recognition, or a more interesting job until (from his or her point of view) the lower level needs for existence and security are fairly well fulfilled. [6]

> *Blue collar workers (and many white collar workers) still seem to value "existence" needs like security more highly than needs for achievement or self-actualization.* Particularly in more developed countries, one might assume that because of unions, welfare, and so on, existence needs like those for shelter, food, security, and so on are already well satisfied and that as a result it is the higher level needs—such as for achievement—that workers most value. The findings suggest, however, that workers still seem to value "bread and butter" issues like security and pay much more highly than non-economic factors like how much challenge the job provides. [7] In one study the researcher found that "type of work" had in fact become an important consideration in determining what made a job good or bad from the point of view of employees, but that job security was by far the most important factor. In other studies researchers have similarly found that issues like pay, security, and good working conditions are all valued more highly by workers than are "high level needs satisfiers" like challenging work. [8]

Frederick Herzberg and the Motivator-Hygiene Theory

Frederick Herzberg argues that man has two different sets of needs. [9] One set derives from man's desire to avoid pain and satisfy his basic needs. These include the needs for such things as food, clothing, and shelter, as well as the need for money to pay for these things. The "lower level" set is similar to Maslow's physiological and safety needs.

Herzberg states that people also have a "higher level" set of needs. This other set of needs "relates to that unique human characteristic: the ability to achieve, and to experience psychological growth." Included here are the needs to achieve a difficult task, to obtain prestige, and to receive recognition. This set is similar to Maslow's social, ego, and self-actualization needs.

Herzberg has carried out studies to more precisely determine what people want and what motivates them. In one study he asked several hundred engineers and accountants to explain things about their jobs that they found "exceptionally good" (and therefore motivating) or "exceptionally bad."

His findings are summarized in Exhibit 8.3. According to Herzberg, these findings mean that the work factors that lead to job satisfaction and motivation (the *motivators*) are different from those (the *hygienes*) that lead to job dissatisfaction. Specifically, if these hygiene factors (like better working conditions, salary, supervision) that appear on the left of Exhibit 8.3 are absent, employees become dissatisfied. But—and this is extremely important—adding more and more of these hygiene factors (like salary) to the job will not motivate employees once the factor (like salary) is adequate: these hygienes can only keep the employees from becoming dissatisfied.

On the other hand, the "job content" or motivator factors on the right of Exhibit 8.3 (achievement, recognition, etc.) *can* motivate employees. Thus, according to Herzberg, if you continue to build more opportunities for achievement and recognition into (and thus "enrich") the job, then your employees should become more motivated. But, says Herzberg, if motivators like opportunities for achievement are missing from the job, workers will not necessarily be dissatisfied; they just will not be highly motivated.

Discussion. Research findings suggest that Herzberg's theory is probably a useful but oversimplified explanation of how needs influence motivation in organizations. [10] [11] [12] On the one hand, Herzberg's contention that (1) hygienes only prevent dissatisfaction while (2) the absence of motivators cannot cause dissatisfaction is clearly indefensible. [13] [14] Studies have shown that hygienes like pay *can* satisfy needs and increase motivation and that the absence of motivators like recognition *does* mean that important needs will be unsatisfied, and the person dissatisfied. On the other hand, Herzberg's work helps to emphasize that lower level needs (the ones satisfied by hygienes like pay and security) are relatively finite and quickly satisfied. However, higher level needs (those satisfied by recognition, challenging work, and so on) are rarely satisfied. As a result, building "motivators" into the work by making it more interesting and challenging should have a powerful and lasting effect on motivation, especially for employees whose lower level needs are fairly well satisfied. [15]

Exhibit 8.3   Summary of Herzberg's Motivation Hygiene Findings   211

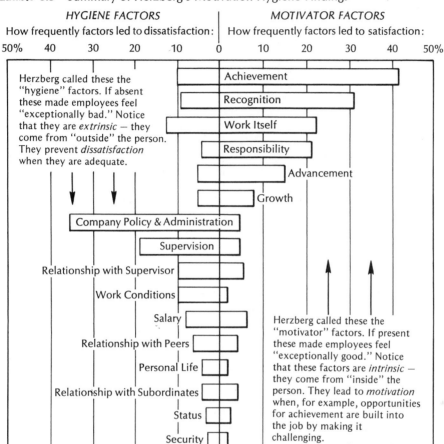

HYGIENE FACTORS | *MOTIVATOR FACTORS*

How frequently factors led to dissatisfaction: | How frequently factors led to satisfaction:

50%   40   30   20   10   0   10   20   30   40   50%

Herzberg called these the "hygiene" factors. If absent these made employees feel "exceptionally bad." Notice that they are *extrinsic* — they come from "outside" the person. They prevent *dissatisfaction* when they are adequate.

Achievement
Recognition
Work Itself
Responsibility
Advancement
Growth
Company Policy & Administration
Supervision
Relationship with Supervisor
Work Conditions
Salary
Relationship with Peers
Personal Life
Relationship with Subordinates
Status
Security

Herzberg called these the "motivator" factors. If present these made employees feel "exceptionally good." Notice that these factors are *intrinsic* — they come from "inside" the person. They lead to *motivation* when, for example, opportunities for achievement are built into the job by making it challenging.

Source: Adapted from Frederick Herzberg, "One More Time: How Do You Motivate Employees," *Harvard Business Review* (January-February 1968).

Need Achievement Theory

In its simplest form, need achievement theory aims at predicting the behavior of those who rank high or low in achievement motivation, which has been defined as a "predisposition to strive for success." [16] Basing his ideas on a projective personality test known as the Thematic Apperception Test (TAT), psychologist John Atkinson formulated the concept of the "need to achieve," arguing that it is a personality trait. [17] People who are high in need achievement are highly motivated to strive for the satisfaction that is derived from accomplishing (or achieving) some challenging task or goal. They prefer tasks for which there is a reasonable chance for success and avoid those that are either too easy or too difficult. Relatedly, such people prefer obtaining specific, timely criticism and feedback about their performance.

Most of the studies in this area have been carried out by Atkinson and his colleagues and suggest that there is a strong relationship between achievement motivation (a high need to achieve) and both economic and entrepreneurial success. They have found, for example, that societies high in achievement motivation had relatively high economic growth rates and those low in achievement motivation had lower rates. They have also found that the proportion of students entering entrepreneurial occupations was greater among those with high needs to achieve, and that achievement motivation training produced significant increases in entrepreneurial activity. [18] Others have found that achievement motivation can be learned, and that trainees who do increase in this trait perform better than those who do not. [19] Taken as a whole, the research findings suggest three conclusions:

1. People have different degrees of achievement motivation.
2. Through training, a person's achievement motivation can be increased.
3. Achievement motivation is directly related to performance at work.

Is There an "Ultimate Need"?

Management expert Saul Gellerman agrees that everyone has needs for things like money, status, achievement, and recognition. And he agrees that if one of these needs is not satisfied, then a person will be motivated to satisfy it. But he also says that we do not only seek money, or status, or achievement for its own sake. Instead, these are only vehicles that the person uses in his constant quest to be himself, or to be the kind of person he thinks he should be. [20]

> The ultimate motivation is to make the self-concept real: to live in a manner that is appropriate to one's preferred role, to be treated in a manner that corresponds to one's preferred rank, and to be rewarded in a manner that reflects one's estimate of his own abilities. Thus we are all in perpetual pursuit of whatever we regard as our deserved role, trying to make our subjective ideas about ourselves into objective truths.

Gellerman argues that, above all, most people have a need to be treated as valuable individuals and to become, in Maslow's terms, the person they are capable of becoming. Each has his or her own concepts of who he is, and what he deserves, and each wants to be treated in a manner that supports this self-concept. Each person is strongly motivated to behave in a way that satisfies that need.

This is also, in large part, what Maslow and the other psychologists discussed are saying. Whether called the need for self-actualization, or for achievement, or for recognition, each is saying that over and above the lower-level physiological or safety needs, most people have this continuing need to be treated as valuable individuals.

Summary: Human Needs and Motivation

People have many different needs. These include a number of existence or physiological needs, (including those for food, shelter, warmth, and so on) and needs for security, affiliation, esteem and recognition, self-control and independence, competence, achievement, and self-actualization. The needs fall into a rough two-level hierarchy, with existence and security needs on the bottom and needs for affiliation, achievement, and so on on the top. The lower level needs are finite and are relatively easy to satisfy. The higher level needs, such as achievement, are never completely satisfied. The lower level needs are satisfied primarily by outcomes that are concrete and *external* to the person. These external (or hygiene) outcomes include things such as food, money, and praise. On the other hand, "the need for self-actualization and competence seems to be satisfied only by outcomes given *intrinsically* by persons to themselves." [21] Thus, many believe that to appeal to a person's higher order needs, the "rewards" you provide will have to be such that the person himself derives a sense of accomplishment from performing a difficult task: here, in other words, complexity and challenge will have to be built into the job as "rewards."

EQUITABLE REWARDS AND HUMAN MOTIVATION

Equity Theory

The equity theory of motivation assumes that individuals are strongly motivated to maintain a balance between what they perceive as their inputs, or contributions, and their rewards. The theory focuses on the exchanges that take place between the organization and the individual, in terms of the inputs made by the latter (such as effort), and the outcomes he or she receives for these in terms of pay, recognition, or promotion. In equity theory, the net "value" of the exchange (to the person) may then be expressed as a ratio of inputs to outputs or rewards. A perceived equity or inequity then results when the person compares his input/reward ratio with those of others in the organization (or what he believes are the ratios of others in the organization). Basically, if a person perceives an inequity, the theory states a tension or drive will develop in the person's mind, and the person will be motivated to reduce or eliminate the tension and perceived inequity.

Impact on Performance

According to equity theory, exactly *how* the person goes about reducing what he perceives as an inequity depends on whether he is paid on a piece-rate basis or on a straight salary basis. Furthermore, while equity theory could supposedly be used to explain a variety of input/reward inequities, most studies have focused on the relationship between a person's performance and his *financial* rewards—especially under- or overpayment. Some conclusions concerning the impact of equity on performance are as follows:

1. If a person is paid on a *piece-rate* basis and thinks he is *overpaid,* the quantity the person produces should stay the same or may decrease, since producing *more* would simply increase the financial rewards to the person and therefore increase his perceived inequity even more. However, quality should increase since this should allow an increase in the inputs a person sees himself as providing, thus reducing his perceived inequity.

2. On the other hand, if the person is paid per piece and views himself as *underpaid,* the quality of his work should go down, and the quantity he produces will probably increase, depending upon how much the person is paid per unit he produces.

3. If the person is paid a *salary,* regardless of his output, and he views himself as *overpaid,* then either the quantity or quality of his work should increase since this will reduce the perceived inequity.

4. However, if the person is paid a salary and believes he is underpaid, then his quantity and quality should both decrease. These findings are summarized in Exhibit 8.4.

Exhibit 8.4   The Effects of a Perceived Inequity on Performance

	Employee thinks he is underpaid	Employee thinks he is overpaid
Piece-rate Basis	Quality down Quantity the same or up	Quantity the same or down Quality up
Salary Basis	Quantity or quality should go down	Quantity or quality should go up

Research Findings

The prevailing evidence supports most of these conclusions concerning the equity theory of motivation. [22] In one study, subjects being paid on an hourly basis believed they were being overpaid; they significantly outperformed those who saw their pay as equitable. In a follow-up study, subjects who were paid a piece-rate basis and who believed they were being overpaid reacted by producing less than did those who viewed their pay is equitable, therefore effectively lowering their pay. The "equity" effects are usually most dramatic when the person believes he or she is being *underpaid.* A person who is being paid on an hourly basis can be expected to drastically curtail both the quantity and quality of his work if he perceives himself as being underpaid. If an underpaid person is being paid on an incentive, piece-rate basis, then quality can be

expected to go down; quantity will generally increase, assuming that producing
more units will reduce the inequity from the point of view of the employee.

EXPECTANCIES AND HUMAN MOTIVATION

Many psychologists believe that to motivate people, it is not enough to
offer them something to satisfy their important needs. The reason for this is
that (even if the reward is perceived as important and equitable) for the
person to be motivated, he will also have to believe he has the *ability* to obtain
the reward. For example, telling a person she will be appointed salesmanager
if she increases sales in her district will probably not motivate her if she
knows the task is virtually impossible.

Expectancy Theory

The *expectancy theory of motivation* assumes that a person's motivation
to exert effort is based on his or her expectations for success. [23] Probably the
most popular version of expectancy theory was formulated by Vroom and is
based on three concepts: valence, instrumentality, and expectancy. [24] Other
valence-instrumentality-expectancy (VIE) theories of motivation have been
proposed, but they are all similar to Vroom's theory in their concepts and
implications.

Valence represents the value or importance that a particular outcome
has for a person. It reflects the strength of a person's desire for, or attraction
toward, the outcomes of particular courses of action. Perhaps the simplest
way to interpret valence is to assume that outcomes represent rewards such
as pay, promotion, and recognition. The valence of each outcome or reward
then represents the positive or negative value ascribed by the individual to
each outcome or reward.

Instrumentality reflects the person's perception of the relation between a
"first level outcome" (such as high performance) and a "second level outcome"
(such as a promotion). For example, it might reflect the extent to which a
person believes that performance on his part will be instrumental in getting
him a promotion. *Expectancy* refers to the perceived relationship between a
given level of effort and a given level of performance. In other words, it refers
to the extent to which the person feels that his efforts will, in fact, lead to the
first level outcome, in this case, performance. The Vroom model attempts to
predict (a) what task a person will choose and (b) what level of effort he will
put forth on that task, based upon a knowledge of the valences, instrumentalities,
and expectancies involved.

In sum, Vroom argues that motivation involves a three-step process:

1. Does the person feel that the second level outcome, such as promotion, is
   important to him, or high in valence?

2. Does he feel that high performance—the first level outcome in this case—will be *instrumental* in getting him his promotion?

3. Does he feel that exerting *effort* will in fact result in increased performance?

In summary, the strength of a person's motivation to perform effectively depends on two things: (1) the person's belief that effort can be converted into performance and (2) the net attractiveness of the outcomes (rewards) that are perceived to stem from good performance. [25]

Conclusions and Implications

There are some useful implications to be drawn from expectancy theory. Of these, perhaps the most obvious is that pay and other rewards should be made contingent on performance. [26] The expectancy theory research findings indicate that high-performing employees are those that see a strong relationship between performing their jobs well and receiving rewards they value. [27] Therefore, according to many experts, organizations should put more emphasis on rewarding people (through pay, promotion, better job opportunities, etc.) *contingent on their performances*. And, these experts argue, that if an organization *does* decide to reward employees on the basis of their performance, it would be self-defeating to keep such rewards a secret; instead, *rewards should be publicized* so that all employees can develop a clearer understanding of the relationship (instrumentality) between performance and reward.

MOTIVATION THEORIES: MODEL AND IMPLICATIONS

A Model of Motivation

It would be useful to summarize and integrate these motivation theories, and to do so one can use the model illustrated in Exhibit 8.5. As can be seen, motivation can be thought of within an expectancy theory framework. Expectancy theory states that motivation will occur if the incentive is of value to the person and if the person is reasonably sure that effort on his or her part will result in accomplishing the task and obtaining the incentive.

Therefore, as shown in the model, for motivation to take place, several things must occur. First, the incentive must be important to the person. Here, theorists like Maslow, Herzberg, and Atkinson would suggest that certain needs—such as for recognition, esteem, and achievement—are the most important in our society. Related to this, the incentive cannot just be important, but must also be viewed as equitable if it is to elicit the desired motivation. (An *inequitable* reward can also elicit motivation if, for example, a person paid a salary believes that she is overpaid.) Furthermore, the person must feel that effort *will in fact lead* to rewards. Here, other, "nonmotivational" matters must

Exhibit 8.5 A Model of Motivation

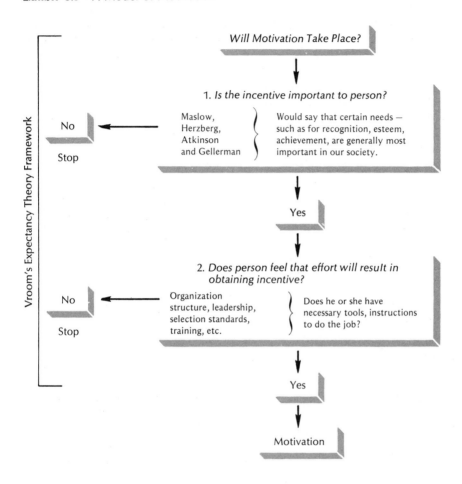

be addressed, including individual factors like skills, organizational factors like organization structure, and "change" factors like adequate training, so as to ensure there are no impediments to performing.

Implications of Motivation Theories

Rewards Should Be Tied to Performance. Expectancy theory assumes that motivation is greatest when obtaining rewards is contingent on performance. For those tasks and people for whom pay is the most obvious reward, this would argue for an emphasis on incentive bonuses and piece-rate pay plans. For *all* jobs, it would argue for tying *non*financial rewards (like advancement, recognition, and praise) to performance.

Outcomes or Rewards Should Be Equitable. Evidence from studies of equity theory suggests that whether or not the reward is perceived as equitable has important implications for one's motivation. For example, employees who are paid on a straight salary basis but who feel they are underpaid will reduce the quality or quantity of their performance, while those who believe they are being overpaid will improve their performance.

A Person Should Have the Ability to Accomplish the Task or to Be Motivated to Do So. Evidence from studies of expectancy theory and need achievement theory suggest that if a person believes there is little or no chance of successfully completing a task (and therefore obtaining the reward), that person will probably not be motivated to accomplish it. Thus, always ask, *"Could the employee do the job if he or she wanted to?"*

It is Useful to Distinguish Between Lower Level "Existence" Needs and Higher Level "Psychological" Needs. Existence needs are those people have for food, clothing, shelter, and security. Existence needs are most often satisfied by extrinsic rewards such as money. Psychological needs are the needs people have for recognition, achievement, and self-actualization. These are satisfied primarily by *intrinsic* rewards like the feeling of accomplishment a challenging job provides. In general, psychological needs satisfaction must come from within the person and be derived from an interaction between the person and the task: scientists developing a new vaccine, craftsmen producing a product, and the weekend hobbiest building a stereo set are all examples of those who are driven to satisfy psychological needs. It is useful to think of the existence and psychological needs as forming a two-level hierarchy, so that psychological needs only become activated as the existence needs become fairly well satisfied. This suggests that trying to tap employees' psychological needs (say, by giving them enriched, more challenging jobs) may be ineffective as long as basic needs like those for adequate salary and security are not satisfied.

SUMMARY

1. Basically, people are motivated or driven to behave in a way that they feel leads to rewards. Thus, there are two basic requirements for motivating someone: (1) the incentive or reward must be important to the person and (2) he or she must feel that effort will probably lead to obtaining the reward. This is the essence of Vroom's expectancy theory of motivation.

2. Maslow says that people's needs can be envisioned in a hierarchy. Each succeedingly higher level need does not become aroused until the next lower level need is fairly well satisfied. Working up the hierarchy, the five Maslow needs are: physiological, safety, social, ego, and self-actualization.

3. Herzberg says that the work factors involved in producing job satisfaction and motivation are separate and distinct from those that lead to job *dissatisfac-tion*. Those leading to job dissatisfaction (if they are absent) are the hygiene

factors. These include extrinsic factors such as supervision, working conditions, and salary. The factors leading to satisfaction and motivation (if they are present) include intrinsic job factors such as achievement and recognition.

4. In its simplest form, need achievement theory aims at predicting the behavior of those who rank high or low in achievement motivation. People who are high in need to achieve are highly motivated to strive for the satisfaction that is derived from accomplishing (or achieving) some challenging task or goal.

5. Researchers today believe needs form a rough two-level hierarchy, with existence and security needs on the bottom, and needs for affiliation, achievement, and self-actualization on the top. The lower level needs are finite and are relatively easy to satisfy. The higher level needs are never completely satisfied.

6. The equity theory of motivation assumes that people are motivated to maintain a balance between what they perceive as their input (or contributions), and their rewards. The theory has received a good deal of support and we know, for example, that people paid on an hourly basis who believe they are underpaid generally reduce both the quantity and quality of that which they are producing.

7. According to Vroom, the strength of a person's motivation to perform depends on two things: the person's belief that effort can be converted into performance, and the net attractiveness of the outcomes (rewards) that are perceived to stem from good performance.

A Case of Motives and Behavior*

Jack Dixon is the district sales manager for the eastern division of Colinary Stove, Inc., a medium-sized manufacturer of kitchen appliances, including electric and gas ranges, refrigerators, microwave ovens, dishwashers, trash compactors, and disposals. His district covers the New England states, New Jersey, New York, Pennsylvania, Ohio, Delaware, and Maryland. Job assignments of sales representatives reporting to him tend to fall into two distinct categories: (1) assignment to a large metropolitan area where traveling is at a minimum and there are many established accounts that bring in a great deal of repeat orders; and (2) assignment to broad geographical areas outside of the metropolitan areas, where the company presently does not have many established accounts and desires to expand aggressively.

The company has established a policy to attract their sales representatives into the second type of job assignment. The policy essentially establishes a bonus commission for new sales in the nonmetropolitan areas. All sales representatives are paid a straight 5 percent commission on sales credited to them. Sales in the expansion areas, however, will also receive an additional 3 percent commission. Thus, sales representatives will receive a total of an 8 percent commission on sales in the new areas. The company has estimated that, because of population growth and new industry moving into the area, an aggressive sales representative might be able to increase his or her annual income by as much as 30 percent.

Jack assumed that job assignments in the new areas would be extremely attractive to all the sales representatives. When a position became open last month, therefore, he presumed that he would have no trouble finding a person who wanted the job. He decided to offer the job first to the individual who had a combination of experience representing the firm and a high rate of performance measured by the annual sales he or she generated. Bob Jordan seemed to be a natural choice for the opening. He had fifteen years experience with the company and had recorded the highest level of sales in the district three out of the past five years.

Jack called Bob into his office in the morning and offered the position to him after explaining it and pointing out its advantages. He fully expected Bob to jump at the offer. Instead he was shocked by Bob's reply:

"I appreciate your offer, Jack, but I'm really going to have to think about it. My answer will probably be no. You know, the kids are in high school now and pretty used to their surroundings. Doris and I have a good circle of friends we would hate to leave. We like our house and would not like to leave our neighborhood. In

---

* John M. Ivancevich, Andrew D. Szilagyi, Jr., and Marc J. Wallace, Jr., *Organizational Behavior and Performance* (Santa Monica, California: Goodyear Publishing Company, Inc., 1977), pp. 71–72.

addition, I've got a good shot at running for a position on our town council. I'd   221
like to start devoting more of my time to township matters. I'm not sure what I'd
do with the extra money. Sure, I can always use more money, but what the heck
do I really need? Another car? A vacation? All in all, I'm pretty satisfied right
where I am."

Questions

1. What kinds of needs would you attribute to Bob in his reaction to the job offer?
2. What kinds of needs do you think Jack Dixon *assumed* Bob would have in reacting to the offer?
3. What are the differences in these needs and how might such differences explain what happened?
4. Do you think Bob might have been operating under a different set of needs ten years ago, and would have reacted differently to such an offer?
5. How would you go about trying to get Bob to accept the job offer and make the change?

EXPERIENTIAL EXERCISE

Purpose. The purposes of this exercise are:

1. To provide you with information on what your needs are.
2. To give you information on what behaviors characterize people with different needs.

Required Understanding. This exercise can be used either prior to or after reading this chapter.

How to Set Up the Exercise. Readers should work on this exercise individually.

Instructions. First, fill in the following questionnaire:

	Yes	No
1. When you start a task, do you stick with it?		
2. Do you try to find out how you are doing, and do you try to get as much feedback as possible?		
3. Do you respond to difficult, challenging situations? Do you work better when there is a deadline or some other challenge involved?		
4. Are you eager to accept responsibility? Do you set (and meet) measurable standards of high performance?		
5. Do you seem to enjoy a good argument?		
6. Do you seek positions of authority where you can give orders rather than take them? Do you try to take over?		
7. Are status symbols especially important to you, and do you use them to gain influence over others?		
8. Are you especially eager to be your own boss, even when you need assistance, or when joint effort is required?		

9. Do you seem to be uncomfortable when you are forced to work alone?
10. Do you interact with other workers, and go out of your way to make friends with new workers?
11. Are you always getting involved in group projects, and are you sensitive to other people (especially when they are "mad" at you)?
12. Are you an "apple polisher," and do you try hard to get personally involved with your superiors?

Second, score your answers. According to Litwin and Stringer, "Yes" answers to questions 1–4 mean that you have a high need to achieve. You prefer situations which have moderate risks, in which you can identify your own contribution, and in which you receive concrete feedback concerning your performance.

"Yes" answers to questions 5–8 mean that you have a high need for power. You prefer situations in which you can get and maintain control of the means for influencing others.

Finally, "Yes" answers to questions 9–12 mean that you have a high need for affiliation. You have a strong desire to maintain close friendships and positive emotional relationships with others. (Keep in mind that a quick test like this can give you only the roughest guidelines about what your needs are.)

Next, if time permits, each student can write down on a sheet of paper the number of questions he or she answered "Yes" to for each of the three needs (achievement, power, affiliation). It is not necessary to sign your names. Pass these sheets on to your instructor.

Your instructor can then list respondents vertically on the board (No. 1, No. 2, etc.) and the number of "Yes" answers (for each respondent) in each of three columns headed achievement, power, and affiliation. (Student 1, for example, might show 2, 2, and 4 in the respective columns.) Did the test appear to distinguish between students on the basis of their needs? Do you think you could identify people in your class who have high needs to achieve? For power? For affiliation? What does this exercise tell you about the factors that characterize people who are high (or low) on each of these three needs? How do you think this information could help you as a supervisor?

DISCUSSION QUESTIONS

1. Why are human needs the "mainsprings of motivation"?
2. Explain Maslow's hierarchy of needs theory. Describe a practical example that seems to support his theory. (The class might want to break into groups of four or five students and develop examples within the groups.)
3. Compare and contrast the Maslow and Herzberg motivation theories.
4. What is "need achievement theory"? How does it compare with the Maslow and Herzberg theories?
5. Explain equity theory—what it is and its implications. Do you think that people are really motivated by perceived inequities? Give some examples to support your position.

6. "I don't need to know about any fancy motivation theories," your boss tells you. "What they all come down to is that you should practice the golden rule—do unto others as you would have others do unto you." Explain why you agree or disagree with this statement and why.

7. Working individually, think of some jobs that you were especially motivated to carry out. What was it about the job, your manager (if any), and the way you felt that so motivated you? Discuss your answers in class.

NOTES

1. Edward Lawler III and John Grant Rhode, *Information and Control in Organizations* (Pacific Palisades: Goodyear, 1976).

2. See, for example, Joel Leidecker and James Hall, "Motivation: Good Theory-Poor Application," *Training Development Journal* (June 1974), pp. 3–7.

3. This section is based on Douglas McGregor, "The Human Side of Enterprise," *The Management Review* (November 1957), pp. 22–28, 88–92, reprinted in Max Richards and William Nielander, *Readings in Management* (Cincinnati: Southwestern, 1974), pp. 433–441.

4. See, for example, Mahmoud Wahba and Lawrence Bridwell, "Maslow Reconsidered: A Review of Research on the Needs Hierarchy Theory," *Organizational Behavior and Human Performance*, Vol. 15, No. 2 (April 1966), pp. 212–240.

5. Clay Alderfer, *Existence, Relatedness, and Growth: Human Needs in Organizational Settings* (New York: The Free Press, 1972).

6. For some examples of studies in this area see: Mahmoud Wahba and Lawrence Bridwell, "Maslow Reconsidered: A Review of Research on the Needs Hierarchy Theory," *Organizational Behavior and Human Performance*, 15, No. 2 (April 1976), pp. 212–240; Vance Mitchell and Pravin Moudgill, "Measurement of Maslow's Needs Hierarchy," *Organizational Behavior and Human Performance*, 16, No. 2 (August 1976), pp. 334–349; John P. Wanous, "A Cross-Sectional Text of Need Hierarchy Theory," *Organizational Behavior and Human Performance*, 18, No. 1 (February 1977), pp. 78–97.

7. Chester Schriesheim, "Job Satisfaction, Attitudes Toward Unions, and Voting in a Union Representation Election," *Journal of Applied Psychology*, 63, No. 5 (October 1978), pp. 548–552.

8. See, for example, M. Schwartz, E. Jenusaitis, and H. Stork, "A Comparison of the Perception of Job Related Needs in Two Industry Groups," *Personal Psychology* (Summer 1966).

9. See, for example, Frederick Herzberg, "One More Time: How Do You Motivate Employees?" *Harvard Business Review* (January–February 1968).

10. Victor Vroom, *Work and Motivation* (New York: John Wiley & Sons, 1964); a group of psychologists recently found that Vroom seems to be correct. See Ann Harlan, Jeffrey Kerr, and Steven Kerr, "Preference for Motivator and Hygiene Factors in a Hypothetical Situation: Further Findings and Some Implications for Employment," *Personnel Psychology*, 30, No. 4 (Winter 1977).

11. See, for example, M. Scott Myers, "Who Are Your Motivated Workers?" *Harvard Business Review*, 42 (January–February 1969), pp. 73–88.

12. H. H. Soliman, "Motivator-Hygiene Theory of Job Attitudes," *Journal of Applied Psychology*, 54 (1970), pp. 452–456.

13. See, for example, Marvin Dunnette, John Campbell, and Milton Hakel, "Factorial Contributions to Job Satisfaction in Six Occupational Groups," *Organizational Behavior and Human Performance*, 2 (1967), pp. 143–174.

224

14. Edwin Locke, "Nature and Causes of Job Satisfaction," in Marvin Dunnette's *Handbook of Industrial and Organizational Psychology* (Rand McNally, 1976), p. 1315.

15. For findings that do not support Herzberg's theory see, for example, Locke, "Nature and Causes," p. 1318. For a paper that supports Herzberg's theory, see, for example, Steven Kerr, Ann Harlan, and Ralph Stogdill, "Preference for Motivator and Hygiene Factors in a Hypothetical Interview Situation," *Personnel Psychology*, 27 (1974), pp. 109–124; Harlan et. al. have found that employees do tend to favor motivators when discussing jobs: see Anne Harlan, Jeffrey Kerr, and Steven Kerr, "Preference for Motivator and Hygiene Factors in a Hypothetical Interview Situation: Further Findings and Some Implications for the Employment Interviews," *Personnel Psychology*, Vol. 30, No. 4 (Winter 1977).

16. John Campbell and Robert Pritchard, "Motivation Theory in Industrial and Organizational Psychology," in Dunnette, *Handbook*, pp. 63–130.

17. See John W. Atkinson, "Motivational Determinants of Risk-Taking Behavior," *Psychological Review*, 64 (1957), pp. 359–372.

18. David McClelland, *The Achieving Society* (New York: Van Nostrand Rinehold Co., 1961).

19. Douglas Durand, "Effects of Achievement Motivation and Training on the Entrepreneurial Behavior of Black Businessmen," *Organizational Behavior and Human Performance*, 14 (August 1975), pp. 76–90.

20. Saul Gallerman, *Motivation and Productivity* (New York: American Management Association, 1963), p. 290.

21. Edward Lawler III and John Grant Rhode, *Information and Control in Organizations* (Pacific Palisades: Goodyear, 1976), p. 14.

22. See, for example, J. Stacey and Adams and William Rosenbaum, "The Relationship of Worker Productivity to Cognitive Dissonance About Wage and Equity," *Journal of Applied Psychology*, 46 (1962), pp. 161–164; Laurie Larwood, Michael Kavanagh, and Richard Levine, "Perceptions of Fairness with Three Alternative Economic Exchanges," *Academy of Management Journal*, Vol. 21, No. 1 (March 1978), pp. 69–83; Michael Carrell, "A Longitudinal Field Assessment of Employee Perceptions of Equitable Treatment," *Organizational Behavior and Human Performance*, Vol. 21, No. 1 (February 1978).

23. David Nadler and Edward Lawler III, "Motivation: A Diagnostic Approach," in J. Richard Hackman, Edward Lawler III, and Lyman Porter, *Perspectives on Behavior in Organizations* (New York: McGraw-Hill, 1977), pp. 26–38.

24. Victor Vroom, *Work and Motivation*. For other versions see, for example, G. Graen, "Instrumentalities Theory of Work Motivation: Some Experimental Results and Suggested Modifications," *Journal of Applied Psychology Monograph*, 53 (1969), pp. 1–25; Lyman Porter and Edward Lawler III, *Managerial Attitudes and Performance* (Homewood, Ill.: Dorsey Press, 1968); Campbell and Pritchard, "Motivation Theory," pp. 79–84.

25. David Nadler and Edward Lawler, "Motivation," p. 35.

26. Based on Nadler and Lawler, "Motivation," p. 35.

27. Nadler and Lawler, "Motivation," pp. 29, 32.

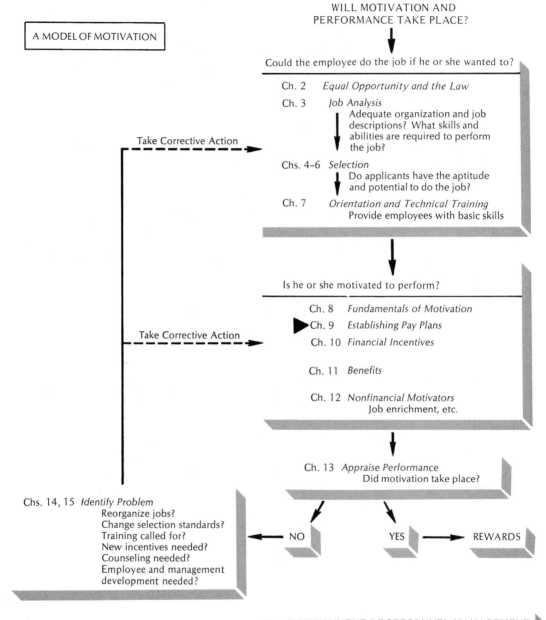

A MODEL OF MOTIVATION

WILL MOTIVATION AND
PERFORMANCE TAKE PLACE?

Could the employee do the job if he or she wanted to?

Ch. 2   *Equal Opportunity and the Law*

Ch. 3   *Job Analysis*
         Adequate organization and job
         descriptions? What skills and
         abilities are required to perform
         the job?

Chs. 4–6 *Selection*
         Do applicants have the aptitude
         and potential to do the job?

Ch. 7   *Orientation and Technical Training*
         Provide employees with basic skills

Take Corrective Action

Is he or she motivated to perform?

Ch. 8   *Fundamentals of Motivation*
Ch. 9   *Establishing Pay Plans*
Ch. 10   *Financial Incentives*

Ch. 11   *Benefits*

Ch. 12   *Nonfinancial Motivators*
         Job enrichment, etc.

Take Corrective Action

Ch. 13   *Appraise Performance*
         Did motivation take place?

Chs. 14, 15 *Identify Problem*
         Reorganize jobs?
         Change selection standards?
         Training called for?
         New incentives needed?
         Counseling needed?
         Employee and management
         development needed?

NO   YES   REWARDS

THE ENVIRONMENT OF PERSONNEL MANAGEMENT

Ch. 16   *Labor Relations and Grievances*
Ch. 17   *Employee Safety and Health*
Ch. 18   *Personnel Management and the
         Quality of Work Life*

When you finish studying

9 Establishing Pay Plans

You should be able to:

1. *Describe the job evaluation process.*

2. *Discuss the legal considerations in compensation.*

3. *Explain what is meant by "compensable" factors.*

4. *Perform a job evaluation using: "the ranking" method and "the point" method.*

5. *Develop a wage curve.*

6. *Price jobs using job evaluation results and a wage curve.*

OVERVIEW

The main purpose of this chapter is to explain how to establish a pay plan, one in which specific salaries or pay ranges are attached to each of the organization's jobs. Developing a pay plan involves evaluating the relative worth of jobs (through the technique of "job evaluation"), and then pricing each job using "wage curves" and "pay grades." In this chapter four evaluation methods ("ranking," "classification," "point," and "factor comparison") are explained, as is the process for developing wage curves and pay grades. Salaries or wages are the most widely used rewards for motivating performance but to motivate they must be adequate and equitable—and job evaluation and wage curves help make them so.

BASIC ASPECTS OF COMPENSATION

Money and Motivation

Psychologists know that people have many needs, only some of which can be satisfied directly with money. Other needs—for achievement, for affiliation, for power, to self-actualize, etc.—also motivate behavior but can only be satisfied indirectly (if at all) by money.

Yet even with all our more "modern" motivation techniques (like "job enrichment") there's no doubt that money is still the most important "motivator." As three experts put it:

Pay, in one form or another is certainly one of the mainsprings of motivation in our society. . . . The most evangelical human relationist insists it is important, while protesting that other things are too (and are, perhaps in his view, nobler). It would be unnecessary to belabor the point if it were not for a tendency for money drives to slip out of focus in a miasma of other values and other practices. As it is, it must be repeated: pay is the most important single motivator used in our organized society.

Bases for Determining Pay

There are essentially two bases on which to pay employees: increments of time and volume of production.

Compensation Based on Time. Most employees are paid on the basis of the time they put in on the job. For example, blue collar workers are usually paid hourly or daily *wages*: this is often called *day work*. Some employees— managerial, professional, and usually secretarial and clerical—are *salaried*. They are compensated on the basis of a set period of time (like a week, month, or a year) rather than hourly or daily.

Pay based on time (discussed in this chapter) occupies a unique if somewhat confusing position as a motivation tool. On the one hand, most employees are paid wholly or in part on the basis of time, and most surveys indicate that they prefer to be. [1] Yet, most experts would also agree that rewards that are not performance-based do not motivate performance. [2] No one would argue, of course, that people would come to work if they were *not* paid because most people obviously work to earn a living. The experts simply argue that pay based on time merely ensures that workers will show up for work but that only performance-based pay can motivate a more than average performance.

There are, however, several explanations for why a time-based plan can motivate performance. [3] [4] First, Herzberg argues that unless "hygienes" like pay are at least adequate the worker will be dissatisfied, and it will be unlikely that even a "fair day's work" will result, or that techniques (like "job enrichment") that are aimed at motivating employees by tapping their "higher level" needs will be effective. Second, the equity theory findings indicate that how the person views his or her *relative* pay effects the person's performance: for example, when a person is paid on a straight salary basis a perception that he is being overpaid can, and probably will, improve his or her performance. [5]

Piecework. The second basis on which employees are paid is called piecework. Piecework (explained in Chapter 10) ties compensation directly to the amount of production (or number of "pieces") the worker produces; its relation to performance is therefore clear. It is therefore most popular as an incentive pay system. In one simple version, for example, a worker's hourly wage is divided by the standard number of units he or she is expected to produce in one hour. Then for each unit he produces over and above this standard he is paid an incentive rate (per piece). Salesmen's commissions are another example of compensation tied to "production" (in this case, sales).

LEGAL AND UNION CONSIDERATIONS IN COMPENSATION

Legal Considerations.   A number of laws have been enacted that affect an employer's compensation decisions, in terms of minimum wages, overtime rates, and benefits, for example. The most important of these laws include: [6]

1931—The Davis-Bacon Act.   This act provided for the Secretary of Labor to set wage rates for laborers and mechanics employed by contractors working for the federal government. Amendments to the act provide for employee benefits. And, they require contractors or subcontractors to make necessary payments for these benefits.

1936—The Walsh-Healey Public Contract Act.   This act set basic labor standards for employees working on any government contracts which amount to more than $10,000. The law contains minimum wage, maximum hours, and safety and health provisions. It requires that time-and-a-half be paid for work over eight hours a day (and 40 hours a week).

1938—The Fair Labor Standards Act.   This act, originally passed in 1938 and since amended many times, contains minimum wage, maximum hours, overtime pay, equal pay, recordkeeping, and child provisions covering the majority of American workers—virtually all those engaged in the production and/or sales of goods for interstate and foreign commerce. In addition, agricultural workers, and those employed by certain larger retail and service companies are also included. By 1978, approximately 72 million American workers were covered by the Fair Labor Standards (or "wage and hour") Act.

The act has several provisions. First, it states that overtime must be paid at a rate at least 1 and ½ times normal pay for any hours worked over 40 in a work week. Thus, if a worker covered by the act works 44 hours one week, he or she must be paid for 4 of those hours at a rate equal to 1 and ½ times the hourly or weekly base rate the person would have earned for working 40 hours. For example, if the person earns $5 an hour (or $200 for a 40 hour week) he or she would be paid at the rate of $7.50 per hour ($5 $\times$ 1.5) for each of the 4 overtime hours worked, or a total of $30.00 extra. If the employee instead receives time off for the overtime hours, the number of hours granted off must also be computed at the 1 and ½ times rate so that, for example, a person working 4 hours overtime would be granted 6 hours off, in lieu of overtime pay. The act also establishes a minimum wage for those covered by the act, a minimum wage that not only sets a floor or base wage for employees covered by the act, but also serves as an index that usually leads to increased wages for practically all workers, whenever the minimum wage is raised. [7] The minimum wage in 1980 is $3.10 per hour for the majority of those covered by the act, and is scheduled to increase $3.35 in 1981. The act also contains child labor provisions that prohibit employing minors between 16 and 18 years of age in hazardous

230 occupations (such as mining), and carefully restricts employment of those under 16.

Exempt vs. Nonexempt Jobs.   Certain categories of employees are exempt from the act (or certain provisions of the act), and particularly from the act's overtime provisions. Employee exemption depends on responsibilities, duties, and salary. Generally, bona fide executives, administrative, and professional employees are exempt from the minimum wage and overtime requirements of the act. [8]

In practice, employees paid on either of the two bases discussed (time or piecework) might be either exempt or nonexempt. Hourly or daily wage earners are usually nonexempt, but this is changing rapidly, and many organizations are even taking factory workers off hourly pay systems, and putting them on a salary. [9] Thus, it is becoming difficult to generalize about whether salaried or piecework employees are exempt or not.

1963—The Equal Pay Act.   This act (an amendment to the Fair Labor Standards Act), requires "equal pay for equal work." It states that employees of one sex may not be paid wages at a rate lower than that paid to employees of the opposite sex who are doing roughly equivalent work. Specifically, if the work requires equal *skill, effort,* and *responsibility* and is performed under similar *working conditions,* employees of both sexes must receive equal pay.

1964—The Civil Rights Act.   Title VII of this act is known as the Equal Employment Opportunity Act of 1964. It established the Equal Opportunity Employment Commission (EEOC), and it makes it an unlawful employment practice for an employer to discriminate against any individual with respect to hiring, compensation, terms, conditions, or privileges of employment because of *race, color, religion, sex,* or *national origin.* In 1967, *age* discrimination was also made illegal.

1974—Employee Retirement Income Security Act (ERISA).   This act, in effect, renegotiated every pension contract in the country. It provides for the creation of government-run employer-financed corporations that will protect employees against a failing pension plan. In addition, it set regulations regarding vesting rights. (Vesting refers to the equity the employees build up in their pension plan should their employment be terminated before retirement.) It also covers portability rights (the transfer of an employee's vested benefits from one organization to another) and contains fiduciary standards to prevent dishonesty in the funding of pension plans.

Other Legislation Affecting Compensation. [10]   Various other laws directly or indirectly impact an employer's compensation decisions. *The Age Discrimination in Employment Act of 1967* prohibits discrimination in hiring individuals between 40 and 65 years of age, and covers employers with 25 or more employees (and labor organizations with 25 or more members) in industries involved in interstate commerce. *The Equal Employment Opportunity Act of 1972* empowered the equal employment opportunity commission to prevent any person from engaging in any unlawful employment practices (including discriminating on the basis of sex, age, race, religion, or national origin when making pay decisions) as described in Title VII of the Civil Rights Act of 1964. [11] *The Rehabilitation Act of 1973* prohibits employers performing under Federal contracts or subcontracts exceeding $25,000 from discriminating against handicapped persons. The *Vietnam Era Veterans Readjustment Act of 1974* protects the rights of employees to return to their former jobs after engaging in military service. *The Mandatory Retirement Age Law of 1978* prohibits forced retirement of any employee under 70 years of age (college professors and top business executives are exempt from this law, as are employees who have certain bona fide occupational qualifications). *Each of the 50 states currently has its own workers' compensation* laws which today cover over 85 million workers. Among other things, the aim of these laws is to provide a prompt, sure, and reasonable income to victims of work-related accidents. *The Social Security Act of 1935* has been amended several times, and is aimed at protecting American workers from total economic destitution in the event of termination of employment beyond their control. Employers and employees contribute equally to the benefits provided by this act. *This act also provided for unemployment compensation*—joblessness benefits—for workers unemployed through no fault of their own for up to 26 weeks in duration. The Federal wage garnishment law limits the amount of an employee's earnings that can be garnisheed in any one week, and protects the worker from discharge due to garnishment.

Union Influences on Compensation Decisions [12]

Labor relations laws and court decisions also impact compensation decisions. The National Labor Relations Act of 1935 (or "Wagner Act") and associated legislation and court decisions legitimatized the labor movement, gave it legal protection, and gave employees the right to self-organization, to bargain collectively, and to engage in concerted activities for the purpose of collective bargaining or other mutual aid or protection. Historically, the wage rate has been the main issue in collective bargaining, although other issues including time off with pay, income security (for those in industries with periodic layoffs), cost-of-living adjustment, and various benefits—like health care—have also been important.

In addition, the National Labor Relations Board (NLRB)—the group created by the National Labor Relations Act to oversee employer practices and to ensure that employees receive the rights granted under the act—has made a series of rulings that underscore the need to involve union officials in developing the compensation package. For example, the employees' union must be provided with a written explanation of an employer's "salary curves"—the graph that relates jobs to pay rate—and is also entitled to know the salary of each employee in the bargaining unit. [13]

Union Attitudes Toward Compensation Decisions. Several studies shed some light on union attitudes toward compensation plans, and underscore a number of commonly held union fears. [14] Many union leaders fear that any technical systems (like "time and motion study") used to evaluate the worth of a job can quickly become a tool for management malpractice. They tend to feel that no one can judge the relative value of jobs better than the workers themselves. And, they feel that management's usual method of using several "compensable factors" (like "degree of responsibility") to evaluate and rank the worth of jobs can be a manipulative device aimed at restricting or lowering the pay of workers. The methods used to evaluate the worth of jobs require training and practice, training that is often not available to unions at the local level: union members thus sometimes feel at a disadvantage in discussing the relative worth of jobs. One implication seems to be that the best way to gain the cooperation of union members in evaluating the worth of jobs is to request and use their active involvement in the process of evaluating the relative worth of jobs, and in assigning fair rates of pay to these jobs. On the other hand, management has to ensure that its prerogatives—such as to use the appropriate "job evaluation" technique to assess the relative worth of jobs— are not surrendered.

JOB EVALUATION METHODS

The Purpose of Job Evaluation

Whether time or piecework is used as a basis for paying employees, management has to have some method for determining specifically how much (or at what rate) to pay them. For example, is the job worth $4 per hour? Or $5? Or $6? Should it pay $2 per widget produced? Or $4? Or more?

Job evaluation is aimed at determining the relative worth of a job. It involves a formal and systematic comparison of jobs in order to determine the worth of one job relative to another, and eventually results in a wage or salary hierarchy. The basic procedure of job evaluation is to compare the *content* of jobs in relation to one another, for example, in terms of their effort, responsibility, or skills. This job content, in terms of responsibility, etc., is obviously an important factor in the wage or salary rate assigned to each job. But we'll see that other factors—like market conditions—also must be considered. Job evaluation entails essentially four steps:

Evaluate the job. Find the "value" of the job in relation to other jobs, using one of the job evaluation methods described in this chapter.

Develop wage grades. Classify the jobs into various wage grades, such as secretary II, secretary III, and secretary IV. This permits management to slot jobs with similar requirements into grades for pay purposes.

Use wage curves. Develop and use wage curves to relate jobs and grades to wages.

Price the jobs. "Fine-tune" the prices to be paid for each of the jobs in the
organization. This typically involves making wage surveys to find out what
competitors are paying, establishing compensation policies, and reviewing
a number of other factors, as explained below.

Compensable Factors

Job evaluation involves comparing jobs to one another based on their content. But what exactly do we mean by "content?"

There are two basic approaches that can be used for comparing several jobs.
First, one can take a more intuitive, "overview" approach. For example, you
might decide that one job is "more important" than another, and not dig any
deeper into why—in terms of specific job-related factors.

A second alternative is to compare the jobs to one another by focussing on
certain basic factors each of the jobs have in common. In compensation management, these basic factors are called "compensable factors." They are the
factors which determine how "job content" is defined; they are the basic factors
that determine how the jobs compare to each other; and they are the basic
factors that help determine the compensation paid for each job.

Example.   While an employer could develop his own compensable factors,
most use the factors contained in "packaged" job evaluation systems or federal
legislation. For example, the "Equal Pay for Equal Work" act focuses on four
compensable factors: *skills, effort, responsibility,* and *working conditions.* The
popular "Hay system" for job evaluation focuses on *know-how, problem solving,*
and *accountability.*

Most managers choose several basic factors and then subdivide these into
"subfactors." This is illustrated in Exhibit 9.1. Notice how the factor "knowledge" is comprised of three subfactors (education, experience, and skill). Each
subfactor, in turn, contains a number of degrees. For example, the job's "education" subfactor may be rated from first degree (low) to eighth degree (high).

Identifying compensable factors is at the core of most job evaluation
methods. Each job is compared with all the others *using the same factors,* sub-
factors, and number of degrees. You thus evaluate the same "content" for each
job, and are then able to compare jobs to each other—for example, in terms of
knowledge, problem solving, and decision making required.

Compensable Factors and Job Specifications.   Job analysis (discussed in
Chapter 3) provides information for job descriptions and job specifications.
Some managers have the foresight to identify compensable factors before doing
the job analysis. They can thus base their job specifications on these factors,
stating the "human requirements" of the job in terms of compensable factors
like education, experience, skills, problem solving, and decision making. [15] This
greatly facilitates the process of evaluating different jobs, and of determining
the relative worth of each.

Exhibit 9.1 Compensable Factors

Universal Factors	Subfactors	Number of Degrees
Knowledge	Education	(8)
	Experience	(8)
	Skill	(8)
Problem-solving	Interpretation	(6)
	Compliance	(6)
	Communication	(6)
Decision-making	Interpersonal	(7)
	Managerial	(7)
	Asset	(7)

Source: Richard I. Henderson, *Compensation Management* (Reston, Va.: Reston Publishing Company, 1976), p. 115.

Installing a Job Evaluation Program [16]

Implementing a job evaluation program—a program in which the relative worth of the organization's jobs are established, and each is assigned a wage rate—is primarily a judgmental process, one that demands close cooperation between management, the personnel specialist, and the employees and their union representatives. The main steps involved in implementing such a program include identifying the need for the program, getting cooperation, and choosing an evaluation committee; the latter then carries out the actual evaluation.

Identifying the Need. Not having an orderly, systematic structure of jobs and pay rates often results in characteristic symptoms. With respect to employees, for example, dissatisfaction—as evidenced by turnover, work stoppages, or arguments and fights—may result from the inequities of paying individuals different rates for similar jobs. [17] Similarly, managers may express uneasiness with the current, informal way of assigning pay rates to jobs, accurately sensing that a more systematic means of assigning pay rates would be more equitable and manageable because rules, procedures, and an accepted method could be used for deciding how much to pay for each job. The personnel department or its compensation specialist is usually responsible for crystallizing and studying the need for the job evaluation.

Getting Employee Cooperation. Nash and Carroll contend that if the personnel department has done a good job of identifying the need for job evaluation ". . . it should not be too difficult to convince top management and the employees of the desirability of job evaluation." [18] Employees can be told that as a result of the impending job evaluation program, wage-rate decisions will no longer be made exclusively by management whim, that job evaluation will provide a mechanism for considering the complaints they have been expressing, and that no present employee's wage will be adversely affected as a result of the job evaluation. [19]

Choosing the Evaluators: The Evaluation Committee. There are two reasons for using an *evaluation committee* for evaluating and comparing jobs. First, it brings to bear the points of view of several people who are familiar with the jobs in question, each of whom may have a unique and valuable point of view with respect to the nature of the jobs. Second, (if the committee is composed at least partly of representatives of the employees who will be affected by the evaluation) the committee approach can help to ensure greater acceptance by employees of the results of the job evaluation.

There are several things to consider in choosing committee members. While committees typically consist of 5 to 12 members, [20] five is about optimal: adding more members seems to add little in the way of accuracy to the results, and may in fact make it more difficult for the committee to act as a close-knit cooperative unit. [21] One possibility is to use a revolving membership so that employees are included on the committee only for evaluation of jobs in which they are most interested. In any case, the employees themselves—generally those felt by their supervisors to be intelligent, usually and widely respected—form a majority of the committee. Union representation is possible but in most cases the union's position seems to be one of simply accepting job evaluation as an initial decision technique and then reserving the right to appeal the actual job-pricing decisions through grievance or bargaining channels: [22] While management has every right to serve on such a committee, their presence could be viewed by suspicion by employees and ". . . it is probably best not to have managerial representatives involved in committee evaluation of nonmanagerial jobs. . . ." [23] On the other hand, a personnel specialist can usually be justified on the grounds that he or she has a more impartial image (than line managers), and can provide expert assistance in the job evaluation: one alternative is to have this person serve in a nonvoting capacity.

Because individuals who are inexperienced in job evaluation usually comprise the committee, training of the committee becomes an important matter. [24] In general, each committee member should receive a manual explaining the job evaluation process, and instructions concerning how to identify jobs to be evaluated, how to develop, select, or approve compensable factors, and how to assign fair and equitable wage scales. (These matters are explained below.) In addition, the manual should contain a brief description of the employer's compensation policies—such as whether it wants to be a salary "leader," paying somewhat higher wages in general then comparable companies in the community.

The evaluation committee should serve at least three basic functions. First, they should be involved in *identifying "key" or "benchmark"* jobs. As their name implies, benchmark jobs (15 are usually enough) are the first jobs to be evaluated; they serve as the anchors or benchmarks against which the relative importance or value of all other jobs can then be compared and slotted

236   into the hierarchy of jobs. Selecting benchmark jobs is usually accomplished in conjunction with the compensation (or personnel) specialist, who screens all benchmark jobs to ensure that they represent a wide range of technological and interpersonal skills, as well as rates of pay ranging from lowest to highest. A detailed job description for each job should be available.

The committees' second function involves selecting compensable factors. In many cases the personnel department has already chosen a specific job evaluation method, one it believes is most appropriate for the organization. At the same time, it is common for the personnel or compensation specialist to develop a list of recommended compensable factors. Their pros and cons are explained to the committee, which sometimes makes the final decision on which factors to use in evaluating the jobs.

Finally, the committee turns to its most important function, actually evaluating job worth. For this, the committee will probably use one of the job evaluation methods we now turn to, such as the *ranking method*, the job *classification method*, the *point method* or (as discussed in the appendix to this chapter), the *factor comparison method*.

The Ranking Method of Job Evaluation

The simplest job evaluation method involves ranking each job relative to all other jobs, as illustrated in Exhibit 9.2. The steps involved are as follows:

Step 1: Obtain Job Information. The first step is job analysis. Job descriptions for each job are prepared and these are (usually) the basis on which the rankings are made. (Sometimes job specifications also are prepared, but the job-ranking method usually ranks jobs according to "the whole job" rather than a number of compensable factors. Therefore, job specifications are not quite as necessary with this method as they are for other job evaluation methods.)

Step 2: Select Clusters of Jobs to be Rated. Because the nature of jobs can vary widely from department to department, it is often not practical to make just one ranking of all jobs in an organization. The more usual procedure involves ranking jobs *by department* or in "clusters" (for instance, factory workers, scientific and technical workers, and clerical workers). This eliminates the need for having to compare directly, say, factory jobs and clerical jobs.

Step 3: Select Compensable Factor(s). In the ranking method, it is common to use just one factor (such as "job difficulty") and to rank jobs on the basis of this one factor, or on the basis of "the whole job." Regardless of the number of factors chosen, however, it is advisable to carefully explain the definition of the factor(s) to the raters so that they evaluate the jobs consistently.

Olympia Health Care, Inc. ranked the following seven jobs:

Ranking Order	Annual Pay Scale
1. Office Manager	$12,500
2. Chief Nurse	10,000
3. Bookkeeper	9,000
4. Nurse	8,500
5. Cook	6,500
6. Nurse's Aide	6,000
7. Maid	5,200

After ranking, it becomes possible to slot additional jobs between those already ranked and to assign an appropriate wage rate.

Source: Henderson, *Compensation Management*, p. 150.

Step 4: Rank Jobs. Next, the jobs are ranked. The simplest way to do this involves giving each rater a set of index cards, each of which contains a brief description of a job. These cards are then ranked from lowest to highest. Some managers use an "alternation ranking method" for making the procedure more accurate. Here you take the cards, first choosing the highest, and then the lowest, then the next highest and next lowest and so forth until all the cards have been ranked. Since it's usually easier to choose extremes, this approach facilitates the ranking procedure.

Step 5: Combine Ratings. It is usual to have several raters rank the jobs independently. Then, once this is accomplished, the rating committee can simply average the rankings.

Pros and Cons. This is the simplest job evaluation method, as well as the easiest to explain. And, it usually takes less time to accomplish than other methods.

Some of its drawbacks derive more from how it is used than the method itself. For example, there is a tendency to disregard compensable factors and rely too heavily on "guestimates." Similarly, ranking provides no yardstick for measuring the value of one job relative to another. For example, job No. 4 may in fact be five times "more valuable" than job No. 5, but with the ranking system all you know is that one job ranks higher than the other. Ranking is probably more appropriate for small organizations that can't afford the time or expense of developing a more elaborate system.

The Job Classification Method

This is a simple, widely-used method in which jobs are categorized into groups. The groups are called *classes* if they contain similar jobs (like all "fiscal assistant IV's"), or *grades* if they contain jobs that are similar in "difficulty" but otherwise different (thus in the federal government's pay grade system a "press secretary" and a "fire chief" might both be graded "GS 10").

Categorizing jobs is a fairly straightforward matter and one of two methods are traditionally used. One is to draw up "class descriptions" (the analogues of job descriptions) and place jobs into classes based on their similarity to these descriptions. The second is to draw up a set of classifying rules for each class (e.g., "Jobs in this class demand much independent judgment, little physical effort, and moderate skill.") and then categorize the jobs according to these rules.

Job classification is simple, and, as we will see, most firms end up categorizing jobs, *whichever* job evaluation technique they use (to cut down on having to work with an unmanageable number of jobs). However, this method (like ranking) is *non*quantitative and depends wholly on subjective judgments of raters.

The Point Method of Job Evaluation

The point method is widely used. Basically, it requires identifying several compensable factors (like skills, and responsibility), each with several degrees, and also the *degree* to which each of these factors is present in the job. A different number of points is usually assigned for each degree of each factor. So once you determine the degree to which each factor is present in the job, you need only add up the corresponding number of points for each factor and arrive at an overall point value for the job. Here are the steps:

Step 1: Determine Clusters of Jobs to be Evaluated. Again, because jobs vary widely by department, you usually will not use one point rating plan for all jobs in the organization. Therefore, the first step is usually to *cluster* jobs, for example into shop jobs, clerical jobs, sales jobs, etc. Then, the committee will generally develop a point plan for one group (or cluster) at a time.

Step 2: Collect Job Information. This involves job analysis, and writing job descriptions and job specifications.

Step 3: Select Compensable Factors. Here, select compensable factors, like education, physical requirements, or skills. (Often, each cluster of jobs may require its own compensable factors.)

Step 4: Define Compensable Factors. Next, carefully define each compensable factor. This is to ensure that the evaluation committee members will each apply the factors with consistency. Some examples of definitions are presented in Exhibit 9.3. The definitions are often drawn up or obtained by the personnel specialist.

Step 5: Define Factor Degrees. Next, define each of several degrees for

Exhibit 9.3   Two Factors and Their Degree Definitions (From a Five-Factor   239
                  Point Plan) *

FACTOR 1: COMPLEXITY OF JOB

Refers to amount of judgment, planning, and initiative required. Consider the extent to which the job requires the exercise of discretion and the difficulty of the decisions that must be made. It is not necessary that all qualifications noted in a degree definition be present in order for a job to qualify for that degree. The best fit is used for assigning degrees.

1st Degree   35 points
Covers jobs that are so standardized as to require *little or no choice* of action including repetitive jobs that do not need close supervision.

2nd Degree   70 points
Follows detailed instructions and standard practices. Decisions are limited strictly to *indicated choices between prescribed alternatives* which *detail course of action.*

3rd Degree   105 Points
Follows detailed instructions and standard practices, but, due to variety of factors to be considered, decisions require *some judgment, or planning to choose prescribed alternatives* which *detail course of action.*

4th Degree   140 points
General instructions and standard practices usually applicable. Due to variety and character of factors to be considered, decisions require some *initiative as well as judgment and planning to choose pre-scribed alternatives* which in turn require use of *resourcefulness or judgment to adapt to variations* in problems encountered.

FACTOR 2: RESPONSIBILITY FOR RELATIONSHIPS WITH OTHERS

This factor measures the degree to which the job requires the employee to get results by working with or through other people. Consider the extent to which the job involves responsibility for the work of others, and for contacts within and outside the company. The primary consideration is the nature of contact. Frequency of contact is contributory only.

1st Degree   15 points
Requires employee to get along harmoniously with fellow workers. Covers jobs with simple personal contacts within and outside own department involving little responsibility for working with or through other people, and simple telephone calls involving identification, referral of calls, taking or giving simple messages without discussion.

2nd Degree   30 points
Requires routine personal, telephone, or written contacts with others in or out of the company involving exchange and explanation of information calling for courtesy to avoid friction.

3rd Degree   45 points
Requires personal, telephone, or written contacts with others in or out of the company involving exchange and discussion of information calling for tact as well as courtesy to get cooperation or to create a favorable impression.

4th Degree   60 points
Requires personal, telephone, or written contacts with others in or out of the company involving the exercise of persuasion, discretion, and tact to get willing action or consent on a non-routine level.

Source: Famularo, *Handbook of Modern Personnel Administration,* pp. 28–29. Copyright ©
1972 by McGraw-Hill Inc. Used with permission of McGraw-Hill Book Company.

---

each factor so that raters may judge the amount or "degree" of a factor existing in a job. Thus, for the factor "complexity" you might choose to have four degrees, ranging from "job is repetitive" through "requires initiative" (definitions for each degree are shown in Exhibit 9.3). The number of degrees usually does not exceed five or six, and the actual number depends mostly on judgment. Thus, if all employees either work in a quiet, air conditioned office, or in a noisy, hot factory, then two degrees would probably suffice for the factor "working conditions." One need not have the same number of degrees for each factor, and should limit degrees to the number necessary to distinguish among jobs.

Step 6: Determine Relative Values of Factors. The next step is to decide how much weight (or how many total points) to assign to each factor. This is important because for each cluster of jobs some factors are bound to be more important than others. Thus, for executives the "mental requirements" factor would carry far more weight than would "physical requirements." The opposite might be true of factory jobs.

So, the next step is to determine the relative values or "weights" that should be assigned to each of the factors. Assigning factor weights is generally done by the evaluation committee. The committee members carefully study factor and degree definitions, and then determine the relative value of the factors for the cluster of jobs under consideration. Here is one method for doing this:

a. First, assign a value of 100% to the highest ranking factor. Then assign a value to the next highest factor *as a percentage of its importance to the first factor*, and so forth. For example:

Decision making	100%
Problem solving	85%
Knowledge	60%

b. Next, sum up the total percentage (in this case 100% + 85% + 60% = 245%). Then convert this 245% to a 100% system as follows:

Decision making:	100 ÷ 245 = 40.82 = 40.8%
Problem solving:	85 ÷ 245 = 34.69 = 34.7%
Knowledge:	60 ÷ 245 = 24.49 = 24.5%
Totals	100 %

Step 7: Assign Point Values to Factors and Degrees. In step 6 total weights were developed for each factor, in percentage terms. Now assign points to each factor, as in Exhibit 9.4. For example, suppose it is decided to use a total number of 500 points in the point plan. Then since the factor "decision making" had a weight of 40.8%, it would be assigned a total of 40.8% × 500 = 204 points.

Thus it was decided to assign 204 points to the "decision making" factor. *This automatically means that the highest degree for the decision making factor would also carry 204 points.* Then assign points to the other degrees for this factor, usually in equal amounts from the lowest to the highest degree. For example, divide 204 by the number of degrees (say, 5); this equals 40.8. Then the lowest degree here would carry about 41 points. The second degree would carry 41 plus 41, or 82 points. The third degree would carry 123 points. The

Exhibit 9.4 Evaluation Points Assigned to Factors and Degrees

	1st degree Points	2nd degree Points	3rd degree Points	4th degree Points	5th degree Points
Decision making	41	82	123	164	204
Problem solving	35	70	105	140	174
Knowledge	24	48	72	96	123

fourth degree would carry 164 points. Finally, the fifth and highest degree would carry 204 points. Do this for each factor (as in Exhibit 9.4).

Step 8: Write the Job Evaluation Manual.   Developing a point plan like this usually culminates in a "point manual" or "job evaluation manual." This simply consolidates the factor and degree definitions and point values into one convenient manual.

Step 9: Rate the Jobs.   Once the manual is complete, the actual evaluations can begin. Raters (usually the committee) use the manual to evaluate jobs. Each job, based on its job description and job specification, is evaluated factor by factor to determine the number of points that should be assigned to it. First, committee members determine the *degree* (1st degree, 2nd degree, etc.) to which each factor (like decision making) is present in the job. Then they note the corresponding *points* (see Exhibit 9.4) that were previously assigned to each of these degrees (in step 7). Finally, they add up the points for all factors, arriving at a *total point value* for the job. Raters generally start with rating key jobs, obtaining consensus on these. Then they rate the rest of the jobs in the cluster.

"Packaged" Point Plans.   Developing a point plan of one's own can obviously be a time-consuming process. For this reason a number of groups (such as the National Electrical Manufacturer's Association and the National Trade Association) have developed standardized point plans. These have been used or adapted by thousands of organizations. They contain ready-made factor and degree definitions and point assignments for a wide range of jobs, and can often be used with little or no modification. One survey of U.S. companies found that 93% of those using a ready-made plan rated it successful. [25]

Pros and Cons.   Point systems have their advantages, as their wide use suggests. This is a quantitative technique that is easily explained to and used by employees. On the other hand, it can be difficult to develop a point plan, and this is one reason many organizations have opted for ready-made plans. In fact, the availability of a number of ready-made plans probably accounts in part for the wide use of point plans in job evaluation.

DEVELOPING PAY GRADES

Why Grades Are Necessary

Once a job evaluation method has been used to show the relative worth of each job, the committee can turn to the task of assigning wage or salary rates to each job.

If it used the ranking, point method (or the factor comparison method presented in the appendix of this chapter) it *could* assign wage or salary rates to *each* individual job. But in a large organization such a system could be difficult to administer, since there might be different wages for hundreds or even thousands of jobs. And even in smaller organizations there is a tendency on the part of management and unions to simplify wage and salary structures as much as possible.

As a result, the committee will probably want to group similar jobs (similar in terms of skills, responsibility, demands, etc.) into grades for pay purposes. Then, instead of having to deal with hundreds of job rates, it might only have to focus on, say, ten or twelve pay grades. [26]

A pay (or wage) grade is comprised of jobs of approximately equal difficulty or importance as determined by job evaluation. If you **used** the *point* method of job evaluation, the pay grade consists of jobs falling within a range of points. If the ranking plan was used, the grade consists of a specific number of ranks. If you used the classification system, then of course the jobs are already categorized into classes (or grades). (If the *factor comparison* plan [explained in the appendix] was used, the grade consists of a range of evaluated wage rates.)

Determining the Number of Pay Grades

It is standard practice to establish grades of equal width or point spread. (In other words, each grade might include all those jobs falling between 50 and 100 points, 100 and 150 points, 150 and 200 points, etc.) Since each grade is the same width, the main problem involves determining *how many* grades to have. There doesn't seem to be any optimum number, although 10 to 16 grades for a given job cluster (shop jobs, clerical jobs, etc.) seem to be common.

There are three things to consider when deciding how many pay grades to have. The first is organization size: clearly, more pay grades are needed if there are 1,000 jobs to be graded, than if there are only 100.

A second thing to consider is the broadness of the job clusters. Remember that it is common (especially when the point method is used) to develop wage structures for one job cluster at a time—such as shop jobs, clerical jobs, etc.). And, one would need more pay grades if the job cluster included *all* factory jobs, than if one had separate job clusters for assembly-line jobs and maintenance jobs.

Third, some find it useful to plot the jobs on a chart, as in Exhibit 9.5.

Once this is done, you may find that a certain point spread (say, 60 points per
grade) is satisfactory. Judgment is needed though. For example, in Exhibit 9.5
it would not make sense to split the groupings in the middle into two pay
grades.

Exhibit 9.5   Plotting Job Wage Rates on a Chart

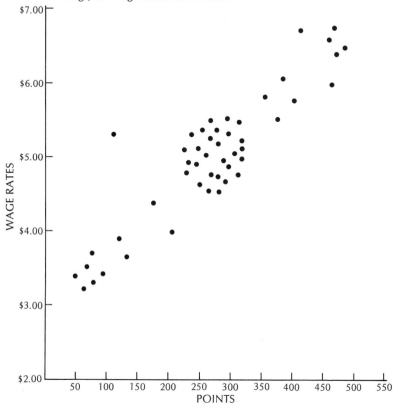

Source: Belcher, *Compensation Administration,* p. 259. Reprinted by permission.

USING WAGE CURVES

The committee now has two important inputs for the job pricing decision.
First, a job evaluation method was used to develop a job structure—a hierarchy
of jobs based upon their difficulty, importance, or some other compensable
factors. Second, this hierarchy of jobs has been divided up into grades. Thus,
instead of dealing with, say, 100 separate jobs, one can now focus on, say, 10
pay grades.

The next step involves assigning wage or salary rates to each of these pay
grades. (Of course, if one chose *not* to slot jobs into pay grades, wage or salary
rates would instead have to be assigned to each individual job.) Assigning pay
rates to each pay grade (or to each job) usually begins with a wage curve.

Steps in Using Wage Curves

The wage curve depicts graphically the wage rates currently being paid for jobs relative to the points assigned to each job (as determined by the job evaluation). An example of a wage curve is presented in Exhibit 9.6; note that wage rates are shown on the vertical axis while the pay grades (in terms of points) are denoted along the horizontal axis. The purpose of the wage curve is to show the relationship between (1) the "value" of the job (as determined by one of the job evaluation methods) and (2) the average wage rates of these grades (or jobs). (The wage rates are usually the present wage rates paid by the organization. Adjustments based on other factors—like market conditions—can be made at a later point.) Here are the steps in drawing a wage curve.

Step 1: Find average pay for each pay grade. Each of the pay grades contains several jobs. Chances are that each of these jobs is currently being paid a different rate. So, the first step is to find the average of these pay rates and obtain an average pay rate for each pay grade.

Step 2: Plot wage rates for each pay grade. Next, as in Exhibit 9.6, plot the average wage rate for each pay grade.

Step 3: Draw wage line. Next, fit a "wage line" through the points just plotted. The lines may be straight or curved; if the pay grades comprise a single job cluster, one can usually employ a straight line.

One can either fit a line through the plots freehand, or use the "least squares" method. The easiest alternative is to draw a freehand line, trying to minimize the vertical deviations of the plotted points from the line. With the least squares method these deviations are minimized mathematically. (Any introductory statistics textbook will explain this procedure.)

Step 4: Price jobs: wages along the wage line are the target wages or salary rates for the jobs in each pay grade. You may find (as in Exhibit 9.6) that some of the plotted points fall well off the wage line. This means that the average for that pay grade is currently too high (or too low), given the pay rates for the other grades. If the plot falls well below the line, raises for jobs in this pay grade may be required. If the plot falls well above the wage line, pay cuts or a pay freeze may be necessary, as explained below.

PRICING THE JOBS

The wage curve provides the basic information around which to build the new wage structure. However, in most cases more information will be needed before arriving at a final wage or salary rate for each job (or pay grade). In this section some of the factors are discussed that will modify and influence the wages or salaries ultimately paid; these factors include prevailing market wages, and compensation policies.

Exhibit 9.6 Plotting a Wage Curve

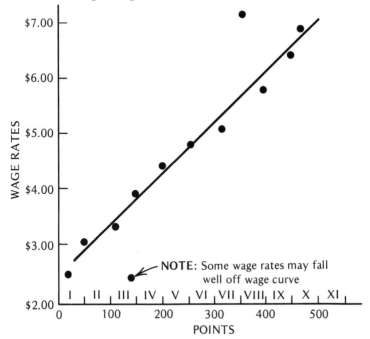

Note: The average pay rate for jobs in each grade (Grade I = 0—50 points, Grade II = 50—100 points, Grade III = 101—150 points, etc.) are plotted, and the wage curve fitted in.

Prevailing Market Wages

The wages or salaries being paid by other organizations in the area are one important consideration, and the usual method for obtaining this data is a *compensation survey*.

There are several ways to make such a survey. First, there are packaged surveys available. [27] The Bureau of Labor Statistics annually conducts area wage surveys, industry wage surveys, and professional, administrative, technical, and clerical surveys. These surveys provide (by industry) information such as pay ranges, average pay, paid holidays and vacations, and pension plan data. The American Management Association of New York furnish executive, managerial, and professional compensation data. Some Federal Reserve banks conduct compensation surveys semiannually, and this data is often available upon request. [28]

Another alternative is for the employer to collect his own survey data. Telephone surveys are useful if focussing on a number of small, easily identified jobs. (For example, one can survey other managers and personnel agencies to determine prevailing wages for certain secretarial positions.) A mailed questionnaire is the most common technique for collecting survey data. Personal interviews with compensation managers are another possibility.

Compensation Policies

The organization's *compensation policies* will also influence the final wages and salaries paid because they provide the fundamental compensation guidelines in a number of important areas. One area concerns whether the organization wants to be a leader or a follower regarding pay. For example, one hospital might have a policy of starting nurses at a wage at least 20% above the prevailing market wage; this policy would obviously influence nurses' wage rates. Other policies might cover matters like how foreign-based employees of the company will be paid, which employees will be paid on an hourly versus a weekly basis, and how much variation in salary is permissible within each pay grade. Policies concerning across-the-board versus merit pay increases, and concerning probationary periods and what increase if any should be awarded to employees that complete their probation are other examples of compensation policies.

Compensation policies are generally written by the organization's personnel (or compensation) director, in conjunction with top management. [29] Ideally, these policies should reflect top management's philosophy, and should be contributed to and critiqued by key supervisors from various echelons in the organization.

Rate Ranges

Based on the compensation survey, and policies, a discrepancy may be found between market rates and the evaluated rates, and there are several ways to deal with this problem. One, (as explained above) is to develop *several* wage structures, one for each type of job or job cluster. [30] Then a job cluster that must be tied closely to the labor market can be so tied without seriously disturbing other wage and salary structures.

Some organizations deal with the problem by maintaining a flexible stance in regard to pay rates. As it becomes increasingly difficult to hire qualified workers, they may abandon their current wage structure (at least for a particular job cluster). Or, they may set new compensation policies that bring their own wage structures in line with the market.

Most organizations maintain flexible wage structures through the use of *rate ranges*. Here (as in Exhibit 9.7) there is a *range* of possible pay rates within each pay grade.

There are several benefits to using rate ranges for each pay grade. First, the employer can take a more flexible stance with respect to the labor market. (For example, it makes it easier to attract experienced, higher paid employees from other organizations.) Rate ranges also help ensure that there is an overlap between the companies pay rates and those prevailing in the labor market. And, using rate ranges also allows the employer to provide for performance differences between employees within the same wage grade, or between those with differing seniorities.

Exhibit 9.7   Wage Structure

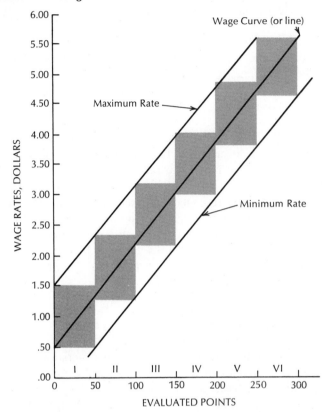

Note: This shows overlapping wage classes (I-VI) and maximum — minimum wage ranges.

Developing Rate Ranges. There are several approaches one can use for developing rate ranges, but most start with the wage curve. One alternative is to somewhat arbitrarily decide on a maximum and minimum rate for each grade, such as 15% above and below the wage line. These maximum and minimum lines are then drawn on the wage curve (as in Exhibit 9.7) and the rate ranges are then drawn in. As an alternative, one could allow the range to become wider for the higher pay grades. This reflects the greater demands (and performance variability) inherent in jobs in these grades.

As in Exhibit 9.7, most organizations structure their rate ranges to overlap a bit. Thus a person who has been on the job longer and is more experienced may earn more than an entry level person in the next higher pay grade.

Correcting Out of Line Rates

At this point one should identify overpaid (and underpaid) employees—

248   those whose pay rates fall (when they are plotted) above the maximum (or below the minimum) for their grade. The next step is to bring their pay within the new rate ranges.

Underpaid Employees.   The problem here is fairly easy to solve. Underpaid employees (assuming one wants to retain them and has the funds) should have their wages raised to the minimum of the rate range. This can be done either immediately, or in one or two steps. [31]

Overpaid Employees.   Rates being paid to overpaid employees are often called "red circle," "flagged," or "overrates." They would be conspicuous on the wage curve, being well above the maximum rate for their grade.

There are several ways to cope with this problem. One is to simply freeze the rate paid to this person until general salary increases bring the other jobs in line with it. A second alternative is to transfer or promote the employee to a job where he or she can "legitimately" be paid his or her current rate. The third alternative is to freeze the rate for six months, during which time you try to transfer or promote the employee; if you cannot, then the rate at which he or she is being paid is cut to the maximum in the pay grade.

Compensation of Managers and Scientific Employees [32]

Developing a compensation plan to pay executive, managerial, and engineering/science personnel is similar in many respects to developing a plan for any employees. For one thing, the basic aims of the plan are the same, in that the objective is to attract good employees and maintain their commitment. Furthermore, the basic methods of job evaluation—classifying jobs, ranking them, or assigning points to them, for instance—are generally about as applicable to managerial and professional jobs as they are to production and clerical jobs.

Yet for managerial and professional jobs, job evaluation usually provides only a partial solution to the question of how these employees are to be paid because these kinds of jobs differ in some important respects from production and clerical jobs. For one thing, managerial and professional jobs tend to emphasize judgment and problem solving much more heavily than do production and clerical jobs. A second difference is the tendency to pay managers and professionals based on ability—based on what they can do—rather than on the basis of "job demands" like working conditions. As a result of these differences (and others explained below) developing compensation plans for managers and professionals tends to be a relatively complex matter, one in which job evaluation, while still important, often plays a secondary role to non-salary issues like bonuses, incentives, and benefits. With this in mind, it would be useful to briefly describe some of the unique aspects of managerial, and professional compensation.

Executive and Managerial Compensation.   Executive and managerial jobs
differ in many respects from most other jobs in the organization, and so their
compensation plans must differ as well. [33] For one thing, executives and managers typically have greater latitude to "make their own jobs" than most other
employees: in other words, their jobs tend to grow (or diminish) as a direct
result of their own efforts. Heads of departments, for example, become more
important as the activities they direct expand, and staff managers become more
important and influential as they gain acceptance. Another difference is that
company results (as well as those of separate "profit centers" or departments)
are more likely to reflect the personal contributions of executives and managers
than do those of employees at lower levels. As a result, executive and managerial compensation is much more likely to be tied to "results" and paid in the
form of a combination of base salary plus annual incentive awards or bonuses.
Another difference is that executives and managers tend to be subject to much
higher personal income tax rates than are lower level employees. Tax considerations therefore play a significant role in the manager's compensation plan, and
remuneration in terms of stock options and differed compensation become more
important as well. The net affect of this is that compensation plans for executives and managers almost always tend to emphasize results and to provide for
compensation based on a combination of salary plus incentive bonuses.

Yet even with these types of jobs, job evaluation still plays an important
role, at least in most organizations. According to one expert, "the basic approach used by most large companies to ensure some degree of equity among
various divisions and departments is to classify all (executive and management)
positions into a series of grades, to which a series of salary ranges is attached." [34]
As with other types of jobs, one alternative is just to rank the executive and
management positions in relation to each other, grouping those of equal value.
On the other hand, the job classification, and point evaluation methods are
also used, with compensable factors that focus on the scope of the position, its
complexity, difficulty, and creative demands, and on the requirements of the
position in terms of knowledge and skill. Yet, if the executive/managerial group
is small (up to 20 or 30) and one person—say, the chief executive—works closely
with all members of that group he or she might be able to make compensation
decisions unilaterally, based on his or her perceptions of each member's individual contribution and market value.

Compensation for Engineers and Scientists.   There are several aspects of
engineer/scientist jobs that should be considered in developing a compensation
plan for such positions. [35] First, work of this kind is concerned with investigation and puts a very heavy premium on creativity and problem solving. Second,
the scientist's economic impact (on the company) is often related only indirectly to the person's actual contributions. This is partly because the economic impact of the project to which the person is assigned is usually fore-
ordained by management (who has probably carried out feasibility studies

250   before giving the "go ahead" for the project—and partly because the success of the end product depends on many other factors like how well it is produced and marketed. As a result, compensation plans (like bonuses) that tie remuneration directly to results are not widely used for scientific employees.

Generally speaking, the job evaluation methods explained above can be and are widely used for evaluating engineering and scientific jobs. As one might expect, the compensable factors here tend to focus on problem solving, creativity, job scope, and technical knowledge and expertise. The point method of job evaluation, as well as the factor comparison method (explained in the appendix) have both been used for engineering and scientific positions. The job classification method seems most popular, however. Here (as explained above) a series of grade definitions are written and then a position or individual is slotted into the grade having the most appropriate definition.

The Issue of Pay Secrecy

There are basically two opposing points of view with respect to the question "should employees know what other employees in the organization are being paid?" The basic argument *for* "open pay" is that it improves employee motivation, and the basic thinking here is as follows. According to the expectancy theory of motivation (explained in Chapter 8) an employee's perception of how (and if) pay results from effort has a direct bearing on his or her motivation. In other words, if employees believe that greater effort does not result in greater rewards then, generally speaking, greater effort (and therefore motivation) will not be forthcoming. On the other hand, if employees do believe that there is a direct relationship between effort and rewards then greater effort should result. Proponents of "open pay" contend that where workers do *not* know each other's pay they cannot easily (or at all) assess how effort and rewards are related, and as a result of this uncertainty motivation tends to suffer. (They cannot, for example, say "Smith doesn't work hard, so is paid less than Jones, who works hard.") A related argument is based on equity theory. Specifically, Lawler contends that pay secrecy can and does result in misperceptions of salary levels and, consequently, in feelings of inequity. In one study he found that managers underestimated their superiors' pay and overestimated the pay of their subordinates, the effect of which was that these managers were left feeling somewhat underpaid. And, as we explained, salaried employees who feel underpaid will reduce their effort so as to reduce the perceived inequity. Lawler believes that by following an "open pay" policy, organizations can reduce such misperceptions, by showing employees that they are in fact equitably paid.

The opposing argument is that in practice there are usually real inequities in the pay scale, perhaps because of the need to hire someone "in a hurry," or because of the superior salesmanship of a particular applicant. And even if the employee in a similar job who is being paid more actually deserves the higher salary because of his effort, skill, or experience, it is possible that his lower paid colleagues, viewing the world through their own point of view, may still convince themselves that they are underpaid relative to this person.

The research findings to this point are sketchy. In one study a researcher found that managers' satisfaction with their pay increased following their firms' implementation of an open pay policy. [36] A survey conducted by the Bureau of National Affairs found that less than half the firms responding gave employees access to salary schedules. Those not providing such information indicated, among other things, that "secrecy prevents much quibbling . . . ," "salary is a delicate matter . . . ," open pay "could well lead to unnecessary strain and dissatisfaction among managers . . . ," and "open systems too often create misunderstandings and petty complaints." The author of this study notes that "whether the inequities result from a growth situation or some other factor, it is clear that some inequities and openness are incompatible." [37] The implication for compensation management seems to be that a policy of open pay can, under the best of conditions, improve employees' satisfaction with their pay and (possibly) their effort as well. On the other hand, if conditions are not right—and especially if there are any lingering inequities in the employer's pay structure—moving to an open pay policy is probably not advisable.

SUMMARY

1. There are two bases on which to pay employees compensation: increments of time and volume of production. The former includes hourly or daily wages and salaries. Basing pay on volume of production ties compensation directly to the amount of production (or number of "pieces" the worker produces).

2. The job evaluation process includes four basic steps: (1) evaluate the job; (2) develop wage classes; (3) use wage curves; and (4) price your jobs. We discussed a number of legal and union considerations, including the Equal Pay Act, the Civil Rights Act, and the Fair Labor Standards Act.

3. Job evaluation is aimed at determining the relative worth of a job. It involves comparing jobs to one another based on their content, which is usually defined in terms of compensable factors like skills, effort, responsibility, and working conditions.

4. The ranking method of job evaluation involves five steps: (1) obtain job information; (2) select clusters of jobs to be rated; (3) select compensable factors; (4) rank jobs; and (5) combine ratings (of several raters). This is a simple method to use but there is a tendency to rely too heavily on "guesti-mates." The classification (or grading) method is a second qualitative approach that involves categorizing jobs based on a "class description" or "classification rules" for each class.

5. The point method for job evaluation requires identifying a number of compensable factors and then determining the degree to which each of these factors is present in the job. It involves nine steps: (1) determine types of jobs to be evaluated; (2) collect job information; (3) select compensable factors; (4) define compensable factors; (5) define factor degrees; (6) determine relative

252 weights of factors; (7) assign point values to factors and degrees; (8) develop a job evaluation manual; and (9) rate the jobs. This is a quantitative technique and many "packaged" plans are readily available.

6. Most managers group similar jobs into wage or pay grades for pay purposes. These are comprised of jobs of approximately equal difficulty or importance as determined by job evaluation.

7. The wage curve (or line) shows the average target wage for each pay grade (or job). It can help show you what the average wage for each grade *should be*, and whether any present wages (or salaries) are out of line. Developing a wage curve involves four steps: (1) find the average pay for each pay grade; (2) plot these wage rates for each pay grade; (3) draw the wage line; and (4) price jobs, after plotting present wage rates.

8. The wage curve is usually drawn using the organization's current wage or salary rates. But in actually pricing jobs, wage curve results will have to be modified to take into consideration market wages and your organization's compensation policies.

9. The factor comparison method (as explained in the appendix) is a quantitative job evaluation technique that entails deciding which jobs have more of certain compensable factors than others. It is one of the most widely used job evaluation methods and entails eight steps: (1) obtain job information; (2) select key jobs; (3) rank key jobs by factors; (4) distribute wage rates by factors for each job; (5) rank jobs by wage rates; (6) compare the two sets of rankings to screen out unusable key jobs; (7) construct the job comparison scale; and (8) use the job comparison scale. This is a systematic, quantifiable method. However, it is also a difficult method to implement. Steps 5 and 6 can be skipped if one prefers.

10. In Chapters 3 through 7 we discussed recruitment and placement—finding and selecting employees who have the ability and potential to get the job done. In this chapter we focused on the second component of performance—providing important rewards—in this case, wages and salaries. In the next three chapters we discuss other types of rewards, starting with financial incentives, to which we now turn.

CASE INCIDENT

*The Pressroom**

In the years prior to passage of the equal pay amendments to the Fair Labor Standards Act, the General Machine Tool Corporation classified press operators as male (M) and female (F) with a wage differential in favor of male operators. After the company became organized by the union, the classifications were renamed type I and type II, putting a supposed end to discrimination by sex. This was the pay-maintenance problem that Henry Baker was assigned to look into, namely, were there meaningful differences today between the work customarily completed by type I and type II operators?

In order to diagnose the problem thoroughly and propose a workable and lawful solution, Henry conducted a personnel study that yielded much useful information. He found that the pressroom at GMTC manufactured literally dozens of pressed steel products (called "stampings") in relatively small lots to meet customers' specific requirements. The pressroom was in effect a "job shop" because the stampings generally were component parts for larger products manufactured by GMTC's customers. Henry learned also that a job shop is more difficult to schedule, operate, and manage than a continuous production shop. The difficulty is caused by continual setup and takedown. For example, a machine may be set up for a job in the morning. After a few hundred parts are stamped, the machine may be taken down at midday and set up for another job that afternoon. The machine operator might not perform a task on the machine for a sufficient length of time to achieve the maximum production rate. Hence, a press operator may never become proficient at a given task. Personnel and machine changeovers prevented GMTC from achieving the maximum utilization of resources and the maximum efficiency theoretically possible.

Henry observed that the pressroom was sizable: it had 15 large and small presses. The large presses were manned by several operators organized as a team, whereas each smaller one was run by a single operator. Some of the smaller presses were operated in a series: a sequence of operations were performed on the same part as it progressed through the series of presses.

Operations were classified as type I and type II in the following manner. The company studied the manufacturing processes for each particular part and assigned the job to a type I or a type II operator depending upon the complexity of the operation to be performed. If the operation traditionally was assigned a type I

* This case is based upon some facts in Burton v. Dean *et al.*, "Job Evaluation Upholds Discrimination Suit," *Industrial Engineering*, Vol. 3, No. 2 (March 1971), pp. 28–31. Reprinted by permission from Thomas H. Patten, Jr., *Pay: Employee Compensation and Incentive Plans* (New York: The Free Press, 1977), pp. 339–342.

classification, then only a type I operator could perform it. If the operation was assigned a type II classification, then the operation could be performed by either a type I or a type II operator. The managerial preference was to assign a type II operator whenever possible because there was a significant wage differential in favor of type I operators.

Henry was told by top management that the official company position was that the bases for the wage differential were the additional employee skill, effort, and responsibility the job demanded as well as the more demanding job conditions of the type I operators. Henry was not convinced that what top management was telling him was true. He believed the differentials were based upon the operator's sex and that somehow this weighty consideration had been forgotten, buried, or deliberately falsified.

In order to evaluate the pressroom jobs anew and to obtain a better grasp of the problem, Henry designed a study of the jobs using a well-known point-factor job evaluation plan applicable to manual jobs that had not been used before at GMTC. The plan was based upon the four job factors of skill, effort, responsibility, and job conditions. The job factors were expressed in terms of 11 sub-factors, which in turn were subdivided into degrees of varying points.

To apply the point-factor plan, Henry evaluated each of 12 customers' jobs in a sample of 5 type I and 7 type II jobs. He completed a job rating specification sheet for each of these jobs in order to get data. He then selected each sub-factor and categorized the job according to the degree points for each sub-factor. The degree was determined by comparing the particular job to the list of degree descriptions in the job evaluation manual. Degree determination was easily accomplished. For example, none of the pressroom jobs required the use of any mathematics. Consequently, under the sub-factor of education, all die pressroom jobs were classified as degree I. The manner in which the job evaluation plan set forth degrees for the sub-factors made it very unlikely that the evaluator could err in judging the proper assignable degree by more than one level. Once the degree level was assigned to a particular job factor, Henry added the number of points to the points of other sub-factors to obtain a total score. When the total score was obtained, the job was considered evaluated vis-à-vis the other jobs in GMTC included in the study. The result was an array of jobs with quite similar point values, although there was some rather narrow spread.

In conducting the study, Henry asked a job analyst at GMTC, Bob Clancy, to conduct an identical evaluation of the type I and type II jobs so that Henry's results could be compared with those of someone else. Bob duplicated Henry's study completely but performed the actual job evaluation one factor at a time across all jobs, whereas Henry performed the evaluations one job at a time. The resultant job evaluation pairs were, however, found to have a significant positive correlation in every case. Henry and Bob found that the type I and type II jobs (considered in terms of the job evaluation plan used) revealed no basis for a separate classification. In some instances, type II jobs scored as high or higher than some type I jobs by the individual factors. There were some type II jobs whose overall score was actually higher than that of some type I jobs. Thus, it appeared that there was no basis for the two classifications in terms of skill, effort, responsibility, and working conditions.

Henry reported his and Clancy's findings to the personnel director, who in turn reported them to the top-management administration committee at its next regular

Monday morning meeting. At that meeting, the president directed the controller to estimate the additional labor costs that would be involved in making all press operators type I and ceasing to use the type II operator classification.

The union soon heard about the results of the study and demanded retroactive pay for the type II operators. The union threatened to take the case to court unless the company negotiated retroactivity and immediately adjusted all press operators' rates.

Henry was asked to explain how "male" and "female" had become "type I" and "type II" and the rationale by which the union had gone along with the sexually discriminatory action over the years. He was asked to give facts to the controller for "costing out" the changes in rates. He was asked also to set up procedures so that in the future discriminatory pay practices would be forestalled. Last, he was asked to think through what the company's strategy and controls should be if grievances and complaints about classifications started flooding the personnel office. He was told that this strategy should be both a short-range holding action and a long-range preventive action.

Questions

1. How appropriate was Henry's approach to studying the differences between type I and type II operators?
2. If it were desirable to identify two classes of press operators, how could this be done based upon the facts in the case (and, of course, lawfully)?
3. How should the union's demands be met?
4. What types of controls could be set up in the future to maintain the classification and rate structures?
5. What should be the short-range and long-range strategies that Henry has been asked to identify?

EXPERIENTIAL EXERCISE

Purpose. The purpose of this exercise is to give you experience in performing a job evaluation using either the ranking method or the point method.

Required Understanding. You should be thoroughly familiar with both the ranking and the point methods of job evaluation and with the five job descriptions presented at the end of this exercise. It would be helpful to have completed Discussion Question 6.

How to Set Up the Exercise/Instructions

1. Divide the class into groups of four or five students. Half the groups will perform a job evaluation of the clerical positions described at the end of this exercise using the ranking method; the other half will do so using the point method.

2. *Groups using the ranking method.* Perform a job evaluation by ranking the jobs described at the end of this exercise. You may use one or more compensable factors.

3. *Groups using the point method.* Perform a job evaluation on the jobs described at the end of this exercise using the point method. This should include selecting compensable factors, defining these factors, defining factor degrees, determining the relative values of factors, assigning point values to factors and degrees, and rating the jobs. Since all the jobs you are evaluating are clerical they already comprise just one "cluster."

4. If time permits, a spokesman from each "point method" group can put his or her group's factors, points, and ratings on the board. Did the "point method" groups end up with about the same results? How did they differ? Why do you think they differed? How did the point method groups' results differ from the ratings developed by the "ranking" groups?

5. The job descriptions for five secretarial jobs begin on page 257. They are *not* necessarily now in order of difficulty. The appropriate order of the jobs from lowest to highest is given below, but please do not read this until *after* you've completed this exercise:

(low) Job "D"; Job "A"; Job "E"; Job "C"; Job "B".

DISCUSSION QUESTIONS

1. What is the difference between exempt and nonexempt jobs?
2. Should the job evaluation depend on an appraisal of the jobholder's performance?
3. What is the relationship between compensable factors and job specifications?
4. What are the pros and cons of the following methods of job evaluation: ranking; classification; factor comparison; point method.
5. In what respect is the factor comparison method similar to the ranking method? How do they differ?
6. You'll find five job descriptions presented next, at the end of this chapter. On the assumption that you will at some time want to evaluate these jobs using the point method, define compensable factors for these jobs, as well as factor degrees.

DISTINGUISHING CHARACTERISTICS OF WORK

This is responsible supervisory and/or technically varied and complex typing and clerical work involving the exercise of independent judgment and initiative in the development of specialized work methods and procedures and their application to the solution of technical problems.

An employee in a position allocated to this class independently performs varied and complex clerical functions that require the use of initiative and judgment in carrying assignments to completion; performs specialized technical clerical work of a complex nature; types a variety of materials and reports which frequently include specialized scientific or legal terminology; supervises a small group of employees performing relatively complex clerical and related assignments; or supervises a larger group in the performance of more routinized or less difficult assignments.

Work is performed under the general supervision of a higher level employee. Assignments are restricted only by their subject content and its relation to the activities or functional unit with which the incumbent is connected. Where the work situation involves the performance of individually difficult and varied clerical duties, the number of subordinate personnel for whom the Clerk Typist III is responsible is ordinarily small.

EXAMPLES OF WORK PERFORMED

(Note: These examples are intended only as illustrations of the various types of work performed in positions allocated to this class. The omission of specific statements of duties does not exclude them from the position if the work is similar, related, or a logical assignment to the position.)

Plans, assigns, corrects, and generally reviews the work of a large group of secretarial and clerical employees performing routine uncomplicated clerical activities or a smaller number of subordinate personnel performing individually difficult and varied tasks.

Performs independent clerical work of a technical nature requiring the exercise of independent and unreviewed judgment in making decisions concerning procedures to be followed in accomplishing the assigned tasks.

Compiles and edits information for special reports concerning the operation of the agency in which the employee gathers various information from the agency and other sources, and separates the data into pre-arranged categories.

Verifies, checks, and examines technical and complex surveys and other types of reports for accuracy, completeness, compliance with agency standards and policies, and adequacy.

Types, with speed and accuracy, involved correspondence, reports, records, orders, and other documents from rough drafts, transcribing machines, notes, and oral instructions in rough and/or finished form.

Composes important correspondence without review and/or specific instructions.

May perform all clerical work related to a particular phase of a program for which the supervisor is responsible.

Performs related work as required.

MINIMUM TRAINING AND EXPERIENCE

Graduation from a standard high school and two years of clerical and/or typing experience.

Successful completion of post-high school training from an accredited college or university, or vocational or technical school may be substituted at the rate of 30 semester hours or 720 classroom hours on a year-for-year basis for the required experience.

An equivalency diploma issued by a state department of education or by the United States Armed Forces Institute, or a qualifying score on the Division of Personnel and Retirement Educational Attainment Comparison Test may be substituted for high school graduation.

NECESSARY SPECIAL REQUIREMENT

Ability to type at the rate of 35 correct words per minute.

EFFECTIVE: 12-4-69
(Revised)

DISTINGUISHING CHARACTERISTICS OF WORK

This is varied and highly responsible secretarial, clerical, and administrative work as the assistant to a high level administrator, an agency head, academic dean, major department head, or senior attorney.

An employee in a position allocated to this class performs a variety of secretarial, clerical and administrative duties requiring an extensive working knowledge of the organization and program under the supervisor's jurisdiction. Work involves performing functions that are varied in subject matter and level of difficulty and range from performance of standardized clerical assignments to performance of administrative duties which would otherwise require the administrator's personal attention. Work also includes relieving the supervisor of administrative detail and office management functions.

Work is performed under general supervision and only assigned projects which are highly technical or confidential are given close attention by the supervisor.

EXAMPLES OF WORK PERFORMED

(Note: These examples are intended only as illustrations of the various types of work performed in positions allocated to this class. The omission of specific statements of duties does not exclude them from the position if the work is similar, related, or a logical assignment to the position.)

Takes and transcribes dictation that may vary from simple correspondence to legal, medical, engineering, or other technical subject matter.

Serves as personal assistant to a high level administrative official by planning, initiating, and carrying to completion clerical, secretarial, and administrative activities.

Develops material for supervisor's use in public speaking engagements.

Attends conferences to take notes, or is briefed on meetings immediately after they take place in order to know what amendments were made and what developments have occurred in matters that concern the supervisor.

Makes arrangements for conferences including space, time, and place; and informs participants of topics to be discussed; and may provide them with background information.

Assists in and coordinates the preparation of operating and legislative budgets; examines budget documents to insure that they comply with state regulations.

Receives and routes telephone calls, answering questions which may involve the interpretation of policies and procedures.

Interviews and makes preliminary selection of clerical, stenographic, and secretarial employees, makes assignments, schedules hours of work, provides for office coverage, and reviews the work of subordinate employees.

Serves as office receptionist; greets, announces, and routes visitors.

Performs related work as required.

MINIMUM TRAINING AND EXPERIENCE

Graduation from a standard high school and four years of secretarial and/or clerical experience, two of which must have been at the Secretary II level or above.

Successfully completed classroom studies in secretarial science or commercial subjects beyond high school level may be substituted for the required non-specific experience at the rate of 710 classroom hours or 30 semester hours per year for up to a maximum of two years.

An equivalency diploma issued by a state department of education or by the United States Armed Forces Institute, or a qualifying score on the State Personnel Board Educational Attainment Comparison Test may be substituted for high school graduation.

NECESSARY SPECIAL REQUIREMENT

Ability to take and transcribe dictation at a rate of 80 words per minute and to type at a rate of 35 correct words per minute.

EFFECTIVE: 7-1-68

DISTINGUISHING CHARACTERISTICS OF WORK

This is secretarial work of considerable variety and complexity.

An employee in a position allocated to this class performs duties which involve taking and transcribing dictation for a supervisor who is carrying out a moderately broad program; composing correspondence; and typing memoranda, reports and correspondence. Duties include making travel arrangements and keeping the supervisor's calendar. Assignments at this level involve relieving the supervisor of minor administrative and/or clerical functions and exercising considerable initiative in carrying out legal dictation of ordinary complexity and preparing and processing legal documents and records.

Work is performed under general or administrative supervision. Only projects which entail technical or confidential matters are given close attention by the immediate supervisor.

EXAMPLES OF WORK PERFORMED

(Note: These examples are intended only as illustrations of the various types of work performed in positions allocated to this class. The omission of specific statements of duties does not exclude them from the position if the work is similar, related, or a logical assignment to the position.)

Takes and transcribes dictation.

Receives and reads incoming mail. Screens items which she can handle herself, forwarding the rest to her supervisors or her subordinates, together with necessary background material.

Maintains alphabetical and chronological files and records of office correspondence, documents, reports, and other materials.

Acts as office receptionist; answers telephone, greets, announces and routes visitors.

Assists in expediting the work of the office including such matters as shifting clerical subordinates to take care of fluctuating work loads.

Assembles and summarizes information from files and documents in the office or other available sources for the supervisor's use on the basis of general instructions as to the nature of the information needed.

Performs all clerical work related to a particular phase of the supervisor's program, maintaining all records and composing correspondence relative to the project.

Composes and signs routine correspondence of a non-technical nature in her supervisor's name.

Keeps supervisor's calendar by scheduling appointments and conferences with or without prior clearance.

Performs related work as required.

MINIMUM TRAINING AND EXPERIENCE

Graduation from a standard high school and three years of secretarial and/or clerical experience.

Successfully completed classroom studies in secretarial science or commercial subjects beyond the high school level may be substituted at the rate of 720 classroom hours or 30 semester hours on a year-for-year basis.

An equivalency diploma issued by a state department of education or by the United States Armed Forces Institute, or a qualifying score on the Division of Personnel and Retirement Educational Attainment Comparison Test may be substituted for high school graduation.

NECESSARY SPECIAL REQUIREMENT

Ability to take and transcribe dictation at a rate of 80 words per minute and type at a rate of 35 correct words per minute.

EFFECTIVE: 7-29-68
(Revised)

DISTINGUISHING CHARACTERISTICS OF WORK

This is varied and moderately complex typing and clerical work requiring the exercise of some independent judgment in the use of relatively involved work methods and procedures.

An employee in a position allocated to this class is required to utilize the touch system in typing, from rough drafts and from transcription machine recordings, a variety of materials which may include specialized reports or tabular arrangements of numerical or statistical data. Work includes performing a variety of clerical duties which are individually of moderate complexity and difficulty, or where work is repetitive, there is some latitude for finality of decision or independence of action.

Work is performed under general supervision with detailed instructions given in cases involving new or unusually difficult problems. Assignments may be made through the operation of established unit procedures, and work is reviewed by a higher level clerical or administrative supervisor while in progress or upon completion.

EXAMPLES OF WORK PERFORMED

(Note: These examples are intended only as illustrations of the various types of work performed in positions allocated to this class. The omission of specific statements of duties does not exclude them from the position if the work is similar, related, or a logical assignment to the position.)

Types correspondence, memoranda, reports, records, orders, stencils, and other office documents from rough drafts, transcribing machines, notes, and oral instructions for rough and finalized copy work which is general, complex, and often technical or scientific in nature.

Verifies, codes, or classifies incoming materials and documents, and may be responsible for returning incorrect material to sender for correction and maintains follow-up procedures to be sure that corrected materials are returned; may make computations for reports and records or reduce information to a simple form for use by the agency.

Gathers a variety of information from various sources for use by others in answering correspondence, preparing reports, conducting interviews, or writing speeches, articles, or news releases; may prepare simple reports or draft routine correspondence.

Establishes and may be responsible for the complete maintenance of small files which would include responsibility for accurate filing and retrieval of materials.

Answers telephone, screens and routes calls, takes messages, and may answer routine questions.

May plan, assign, review, and correct work of lower level employees and train them in the performance of assigned duties.

May operate a variety of general office machines with such accuracy as can be acquired from their use on the job and not from any skills possessed before appointment.

Performs related work as required.

MINIMUM TRAINING AND EXPERIENCE

Graduation from a standard high school and one year of clerical and/or typing experience.

Successful completion of post-high school training from an accredited college or university, or vocational or technical school may be substituted at the rate of 30 semester hours or 720 classroom hours for the required experience.

An equivalency diploma issued by a state department of education or by the United States Armed Forces Institute, or a qualifying score on the Division of Personnel and Retirement Educational Attainment Comparison Test may be substituted for high school graduation.

NECESSARY SPECIAL REQUIREMENT

Ability to type at a rate of 35 correct words per minute.

EFFECTIVE: 12-4-69
(Revised)

DISTINGUISHING CHARACTERISTICS OF WORK

This is secretarial and clerical work of moderate variety and complexity.

An employee in a position allocated to this class performs duties which involve taking and transcribing dictation for a supervisor; composing routine correspondence; typing memoranda, reports, and correspondence; and making travel arrangements and keeping supervisor's calendar. Heavy emphasis is placed on relieving the supervisor of as much clerical detail as possible, and work varies widely both in subject matter and level of difficulty.

Work is performed under general supervision and only projects which entail technical or confidential matters are given close attention by the immediate supervisor.

EXAMPLES OF WORK PERFORMED

(Note: These examples are intended only as illustrations of the various types of work performed in positions allocated to this class. The omission of specific statements of duties does not exclude them from the position if the work is similar, related, or a logical assignment to the position.)

Takes and transcribes dictation.

Types correspondence, articles, reports, manuals, and other materials on general or technical subjects; drafts routine acknowledgements in response to inquiries not requiring a supervisor's attention.

Examines, checks, and verifies complex statistical and other reports for completeness, propriety, adequacy, and accuracy of computations; determines conformity to established requirements; and personally follows up the more complicated discrepancies.

Keeps supervisor's calendar by clearing requests for and reminding him of appointments.

Makes travel arrangements and arranges travel itineraries.

Prepares special reports as required and maintains files and records.

Performs related work as required.

MINIMUM TRAINING AND EXPERIENCE

Graduation from a standard high school and one year of secretarial and/or clerical experience.

Successfully completed course work in secretarial science or commercial subjects beyond the high school level may be substituted at the rate of 720 classroom hours or 30 semester hours per year for one year of the required experience.

An equivalency diploma issued by a state department of education or by the United States Armed Forces Institute, or a qualifying score on the State Personnel Board Educational Attainment Comparison Test may be substituted for high school graduation.

NECESSARY SPECIAL REQUIREMENT

Ability to take and transcribe dictation at a rate of 80 words per minute and type at a rate of 35 correct words per minute.

EFFECTIVE: 7-1-68

1. See for example Edward Lawler III, "Using Pay to Motivate Job Performance," reprinted in W. Clay Hamner and Frank Schmidt, *Contemporary Problems in Personnel* (Chicago: St. Claire Press, 1974), pp. 308–322.

2. Edward Lawler III, *Pay and Organizational Effectiveness* (New York: McGraw-Hill, 1971), pp. 273–274, see also Orlando Behling and Chester Schriesheim, *Organizational Behavior* (Boston: Allyn and Bacon, 1976), p. 233.

3. F. Herzberg, B. Mausner, and B. Snyderman, *The Motivation to Work*, 2nd ed. (New York: John Wiley & Sons, 1959) quoted in Behling and Schriesheim, *Organizational Behavior*, p. 234.

4. For support of this idea see Gregg Oldham, J. Hackman, and J. Pearce, "Conditions under which Employees Respond Positively to Enriched Work," *Journal of Applied Psychology*, Vol. 61 (August 1976), pp. 392–403.

5. See for example J. Stacey Adams and Wm. Rosenbaum, "The Relationship of Worker Productivity to Cognitive Dissonance about Wage and Equity," *Journal of Applied Psychology*, Vol. 46 (1962), pp. 161–164.

6. This section is based on and quoted from Richard Henderson, *Compensation Management* (Reston, Va.: Reston Publishing, 1976), pp. 441–446.

7. Henderson, p. 84.

8. Henderson, p. 70; a complete description of exemption requirements is found in U.S. Department of Labor, Executive, Administration, Professional, and Outside salesmen exemption from the fair labor standards act, W. H. publication 1363 (revised) (Washington, D.C.: U.S. Government Printing Office, 1973).

9. See Robert H. Hulme and Richard Bevan, "The Blue Collar Worker Goes on Salary," *Harvard Business Review* (March–April 1975), pp. 104–112.

10. Henderson, *Compensation Management*, pp. 88–99.

11. David Thomsen, "Eliminating Pay Discrimination Caused by Job Evaluation," *Personnel* (September–October 1978), pp. 11–22.

12. Henderson, *Compensation Management*, pp. 101–127.

13. Henderson, p. 115.

14. Edward Hay, "The attitude of the American Federation of Labor on Job Evaluation," Personnel Journal, November 1947, pp. 163–169; Howard James, "Issues in Job Evaluation: The Union's View," *Personnel Journal* (September 1972), pp. 675–679; Henderson, *Compensation Management*, pp. 117–118; Harold Jones, "Union Views on Job Evaluation: 1971 vs. 1978," *Personnel Journal* (February 1979), pp. 80–85.

15. In practice you'll probably find that a single set of compensable factors isn't adequate for describing all of your jobs. Many managers therefore divide their jobs into "job clusters." For example, you might have separate job clusters for factory workers, clerical workers, and managerial personnel. And you would have a somewhat different set of compensable factors for each job cluster. The following discussion of job evaluation methods is from Belcher, *Compensation Administration*, pp. 146–198; Henderson, *Compensation Management*, pp. 150–189; and J. D. Dunn and Frank Rachel, *Wage and Salary Administration* (New York: McGraw-Hill, 1971), Ch. 10.

16. This is based on A. N. Nash and S. J. Carroll Jr., "Installation of a Job Evaluation Program," from *The Management of Compensation* (Monteray, CA: Brooks/Call Publishing Co., 1975), reprinted in Craig Schneider and Richard Beatty, *Personnel Administration Today: Readings and Commentary*, (Reading, Mass.: Addison-Wesley, 1978), pp. 417–425; and Henderson, *Compensation Management*, pp. 231–239.

17. See for example, Donald Petri, "Talking Pay Policy Pays Off," *Supervisory Management* (May 1979), pp. 2–13.

18. Nash and Carroll; Schneider and Beatty, p. 418.

19. As explained below, the practice of *red circling* is used to delay downward adjustments in pay rates that are too high given the newly evaluated job.

20. Henderson, p. 232.

21. Nash and Carroll, pp. 418–419.

22. Nash and Carroll, p. 419.

23. Nash and Carroll, p. 419.

24. Henderson, pp. 232–234.

25. "Job Evaluation Comes of Age," *Personnel* (November 1960), pp. 4–5, quoted in Belcher, *Compensation Administration*, p. 183.

26. Belcher, *Compensation Administration*, pp. 257–276.

27. This section based on Henderson, *Compensation Management*, pp. 202–221.

28. A full list of compensation survey sources, with addresses, can be found in Henderson, *Compensation Management*, 1979, pp. 256–259.

29. Famularo, Joseph, *Handbook of Modern Personnel Administration*, pp. 27–29.

30. Belcher, *Compensation Administration*, p. 265.

31. *Ibid.*, p. 286.

32. This section is based on Dale Yoder, *Personnel Management and Industrial Relations* (Englewood Cliffs: Prentice Hall, 1970), pp. 643–645; and on Phillip Dutter, "Compensation Plans for Executives," and Robert Pursell, "Job Evaluation and Pay Plans: Engineering, Technical, and Professional Personnel," both in Joseph Famularo, *Handbook of Modern Personnel Administration* (New York: McGraw-Hill, 1972), pp. 32-1–32-6 and 30-1–30-8.

33. Dutter, "Compensation Plans for Executives."

34. Dutter, pp. 32–33.

35. Pursell, "Job Evaluation and Pay Plans . . ." pp. 30-1–30-15.

36. Charles M. Futrell, "Effects of Pay Disclosure on Satisfaction for Sales Managers: A Longitudinal Study," *Academy of Management Journal*, Vol. 21, No. 1 (March 1978), pp. 140–144.

37. Mary G. Miner, "Pay Policies: Secret or Open? and Why?" *Personnel Journal* (February 1974), reprinted in Richard Peterson, Lane Tracy, and Alan Cabelly, *Readings in Systematic Management in Human Resources*, pp. 233–239 (Reading: Addison-Wesley, 1979).

THE FACTOR COMPARISON JOB EVALUATION METHOD

The factor comparison technique is a *quantitative* job evaluation method. It has many variations and appears to be one of the most widely used, the most accurate, and most complex job evaluation method.

It entails deciding which jobs have more of certain compensable factors than others and is actually a refinement of the ranking method. With the ranking method you generally look at each job as an entity and rank the jobs. With the factor comparison method you rank each job *several times—once for each compensable factor you choose.* For example, jobs might be ranked first in terms of the factor "skill." Then they're ranked according to their "mental requirements." Next, they're ranked according to their "responsibility," and so forth. Then these rankings are combined for each job into an overall numerical rating for the job. Here are the required steps:

Step 1: Obtain Job Information. This method requires a careful, complete job analysis. First, job descriptions are written. Then job specifications are developed, preferably in terms of the compensable factors the committee has decided to use. *For the factor comparison method, these compensable factors are usually* (1) *mental requirements,* (2) *physical requirements,* (3) *skill requirements,* (4) *responsibility,* and (5) *working conditions.* (Ideally, the people who wrote the job specifications were provided with a set of definitions of each of these factors so that the job specifications are already written around them. Typical definitions of each of these five factors are presented in Exhibit 9.8.)

Step 2: Select Key "Benchmark" Jobs. Next, 15 to 25 key jobs are selected by the job evaluation committee. These jobs will have to be representative of the range of jobs under study. Thus, they have to select "benchmark jobs" that are acceptable reference points, ones that represent the full range of jobs to be evaluated.

Step 3: Rank Key Jobs by Factors. Here evaluators are asked to rank the key jobs on each of the five factors (mental requirements, physical requirements, skill requirements, responsibility, and working conditions). This ranking procedure is based on job descriptions and job specifications. Each committee member usually makes this ranking individually, and then a meeting is held to develop a consensus (among raters) on each job. The result of this process is a table, as in Exhibit 9.9. This shows how each key job ranks on *each* of the five compensable factors.

Exhibit 9.8 Sample Definitions of Five Factors Typically Used in Factor
Comparison Method

1. Mental Requirements

Either the possession of and/or the active application of the following:

A. (inherent) Mental traits, such an intelligence, memory, reasoning, facility in verbal expression, ability to get along with people and imagination.
B. (acquired) General education, such as grammar and arithmetic; or general information as to sports, world events, etc.
C. (acquired) Specialized knowledge such as chemistry, engineering, accounting, advertising, etc.

2. Skill

A. (acquired) Facility in muscular coordination, as in operating machines, repetitive movements, careful coordinations, dexterity, assembling, sorting, etc.
B. (acquired) Specific job knowledge necessary to the muscular coordination only; acquired by performance of the work and not to be confused with general education or specialized knowledge. It is very largely training in the interpretation of sensory impressions.

Examples

(1) In operating an adding machine, the knowledge of *which key* to depress for a sub-total would be skill.
(2) In automobile repair, the ability to determine the significance of a certain knock in the motor would be skill.
(3) In hand-firing a boiler, the ability to determine from the appearance of the firebed how coal should be shoveled over the surface would be skill.

3. Physical Requirements

A. Physical effort, as sitting, standing, walking, climbing, pulling, lifting, etc.; both the amount exercised and the degree of the continuity should be taken into account.
B. Physical status, as age, height, weight, sex, strength and eyesight.

4. Responsibilities

A. For raw materials, processed materials, tools, equipment and property.
B. For money or negotiable securities.
C. For profits or loss, savings or methods' improvement.
D. For public contact.
E. For records.
F. For supervision.
   (1) Primarily the complexity of supervision *given* to subordinates; the number of subordinates is a secondary feature. Planning, direction, coordination, instruction, control and approval characterize this kind of supervision.
   (2) Also, the degree of supervision *received*. If Jobs A and B gave no supervision to subordinates, but A received much closer immediate supervision than B, then B would be entitled to a higher rating than A in the supervision factor.
   To summarize the four degrees of supervision:
   Highest degree — gives much — gets little
   High degree   — gives much — gets much
   Low degree   — gives none — gets little
   Lowest degree — gives none — gets much

5. Working Conditions

A. Environmental influences such as atmosphere, ventilation, illumination, noise, congestion, fellow workers, etc.
B. Hazards—from the work or its surroundings.
C. Hours.

Source: Jay L. Otis and Richard H. Leukart, *Job Evaluation* (Englewood Cliffs, N.J.: Prentice-Hall, Inc., 1954), pp. 98–99. Reprinted by permission.

Exhibit 9.9 Ranking Key Jobs by Factors *

	Mental Requirements	Physical Requirements	Skill Requirements	Responsibility	Working Conditions
Pattern maker	1	4	1	1	2
Blacksmith	3	1	3	4	4
Millwright	2	3	2	2	3
Watchman	4	2	4	3	1

* 1 is high, 4 is low.

Step 4: Distribute Wage Rates by Factors. This is where the factor comparison method gets a bit more complicated. In this step the committee members have to divide up the present wage now being paid for *each key job,* distributing it among the five compensable factors. They do this in accordance with their judgments about the importance to the job of each factor. For example, if the present wage for the job of common laborer is $3.26, our evaluators might distribute this wage as follows:

Mental requirements	$ .36
Physical requirements	1.20
Skill requirements	.42
Responsibility	.28
Working conditions	1.00
Total	$3.26

You make such a distribution for all key jobs.

Step 5: Rank Key Jobs According to Wages Assigned to Each Factor. Here you again rank each job, factor by factor. But here the ranking is based on the wages assigned to each factor. For example (see Exhibit 9.10), for the "mental requirements" factor the pattern maker job ranks first, while the watchman job ranks last.

Exhibit 9.10 Ranking Key Jobs by Wage Rates *

	Hourly Wage	Mental Requirements	Physical Requirements	Skills Requirements	Responsibility	Working Conditions
Pattern maker	$4.90	2.00(1)	.20(4)	1.50(1)	1.00(1)	.20(2)
Blacksmith	$2.80	.70(3)	1.00(1)	.90(3)	.10(4)	.10(4)
Millwright	$3.00	.80(2)	.65(3)	1.00(2)	.40(2)	.15(3)
Watchman	$2.00	.60(4)	.70(2)	.20(4)	.20(3)	.30(1)

* 1 is high, 4 is low.

Each member of the committee first makes this distribution working independently. Then the committee meets and arrives at a consensus concerning
the money to be assigned to each factor for each key job.

***Step 6: Compare the Two Sets of Rankings to Screen Out Unusable Key
Jobs.*** You now have two sets of rankings for each key job. One was your original ranking (from step 3). This shows how each job ranks on each of the five
compensable factors. The second ranking reflects, for each job, the wages assigned to each factor. You can now draw up a table like the one in Exhibit 9.11.

Exhibit 9.11   Comparison of "Factor" and "Wage" Rankings

	Mental Requirements		Physical Requirements		Skill Requirements		Repsonsibility		Working Conditions	
	A*	$**	A*	$**	A*	$**	A*	$**	A*	$**
Pattern maker	1	1	4	4	1	1	1	1	2	2
Blacksmith	3	3	1	1	3	3	4	4	4	4
Millwright	2	2	3	3	2	2	2	2	3	3
Watchman	4	4	2	2	4	4	3	3	1	1

* Amount of each factor based on step 3.
** Ratings based on distribution of wages to each factor from step 4.

For each factor, this shows *both* rankings for each key job. On the left is the
ranking from step 3. On the right is the ranking based on wages paid. For
each factor, the ranking based on the amount of the factor (from step 3)
should be about the same as the ranking based on the wages assigned to the
job (step 5). If there's much of a discrepancy, it suggests that the key job might
be a "fluke," and from this point on, such jobs are no longer used as key jobs.
(*Many managers don't bother to screen out "unusable" key jobs. To simplify
things, they skip our steps 5 and 6, going instead from step 4 to step 7; this is
an acceptable alternative.*)

Step 7: Construct the Job-Comparison Scale. Once you've identified the
usable, "true" key jobs, the next step is to set up the job-comparison scale
(Exhibit 9.12). (Note that there's a separate column for each of the five compensable factors.) To develop it, you'll need the assigned wage table from step 4.
For each of the factors (for all key jobs), you write the job next to the
appropriate wage rate. Thus in the assigned wage table (Exhibit 9.10) the "pattern maker" job has $2.00 assigned to the factor "mental requirement." There-
fore, on the job comparison scale (Exhibit 9.12) write "pattern maker" in the
"mental requirements" factor column, next to the "$2.00" row. Do the same
for all factors for all key jobs.

Step 8: Use the Job-Comparison Scale. Now, all of the other jobs to be
evaluated can be slotted, factor by factor, into the job-comparison scale. For

	Mental Requirements	Physical Requirements	Skill Requirements	Responsibility	Working Conditions
.10				Blacksmith	Blacksmith
.15					Millwright
.20		Pattern maker	Watchman	Watchman	Pattern maker
.25					
.30					Watchman
.35					
.40				Millwright	
.45					
.50					
.55			(Plater)		
.60	Watchman				
.65		Millwright			
.70	Blacksmith	Watchman	(Welder)	(Plater)	
.75		(Welder)			(Welder)
.80	Millwright				
.85	(Plater)				
.90			Blacksmith	(Welder)	
.95					
1.00		Blacksmith	Millwright	Pattern maker	
.10		(Plater)			
.20	(Welder)				(Plater)
.30					
.40					
.50			Pattern maker		
.60					
.70					
.80					
.90					
2.00	Pattern maker				
.10					
.20					
.30					
.40					

example, suppose you have a job of "plater" that you want to slot in. You decide where the "mental requirements" of the plater job would fit as compared with the mental requirements of all the other jobs listed. It might, for example, fit between "millwright" and "welder." Similarly, you would ask where the "physical requirements" of the "plater's" job fit as compared with the other jobs listed. Here you might find that it fits just below "blacksmith." You would do the same for each of the remaining three factors.

An example. Let's work through an example to clarify the factor comparison method. We'll just use four key jobs to simplify the presentation—you'd usually start with 15–25 key jobs.

Step 1: First, we do a job analysis.

Step 2: Here we select our four key jobs:
Pattern maker, Blacksmith, Millwright, and Watchman.

Step 3:   Here (based on the job descriptions and specifications) we rank key jobs by factor, as in Exhibit 9.9 on page 266.

Step 4:   Here we distribute wage rates by factor, as in Exhibit 9.10 on page 266.

Step 5:   Then we rank our key jobs according to wage rates assigned to each key factor. These rankings are shown in parentheses in Exhibit 9.10.

Step 6:   Next, compare your two sets of rankings. In each left-hand column (marked "A") is the job's ranking from step 3 based on the *amount* of the compensable factor. In each right-hand column (marked "$") is the job's ranking from step 5, based on the wage assigned to that factor, as in Exhibit 9.11.

In this case, there are no differences between any of the pairs of "A" (amount) and "$" (wage) rankings, so *all* our key jobs are usable. If there had been any differences (for example, between the "A" and "$" rankings for the pattern maker job's mental requirement factor) we would have dropped that job as a key job.

Step 7:   Now, we construct our job comparison scale as in Exhibit 9.12: For this, we use the wage distributions from step 4. For example, in step 4 we assigned $2.00 to the mental requirement factor of the pattern maker's job. Therefore, we now write "pattern maker" on the $2.00 row under the "mental requirements" column in the exhibit above.

Step 8:   Now, all our other jobs can be slotted, factor by factor, into our job-comparison scale. We do *not* distribute wages to each of the factors for our other jobs to do this. *We just decide where, factor by factor, each of our other jobs should be slotted.* We've done this for two other jobs in the factor comparison scale above: they're shown in parentheses. Now, we also know what the wages for these two jobs should be, and we can also do the same for *all* our jobs.

A Variation.   There are several variations to this basic factor comparison method. One involves converting the dollar values on the factor comparison chart (Exhibit 9.12) to points. (You can do this by multiplying each of the dollar values by 100, for example.) The main advantage in making this change is that your system would no longer be "locked in" to your present wage rates. Instead, each of your jobs would be compared with one another, factor by factor, in terms of a more "constant" point system.

Pros and Cons.   We've presented the factor comparison method at some length because it is (in one form or another) the most widely used job evaluation method. Its wide use derives from several advantages. First, it is an accurate, systematic, quantifiable method for which detailed step by step instructions are available. Second, jobs are compared to other jobs to determine a *relative*

270value. Thus in the job comparison scale you not only see that the pattern maker requires *more* mental ability than a plater: you can also determine about *how much more* mental ability is required—apparently about twice as much ($2.00 vs. $1.20). (This type of calibration is not possible with the ranking or classification methods.) Third, this is also a fairly easy job evaluation system to explain to employees.

Probably the most serious *disadvantage* of the factor comparison method is its complexity. While it is fairly easy to explain the factor comparison scale and its rationale to employees, it is difficult to show them how to *build* one. In addition, the use of the five factors is an outgrowth of the technique developed by its originators. Yet, using the same five factors for all organizations and for all jobs in an organization may not always be appropriate.

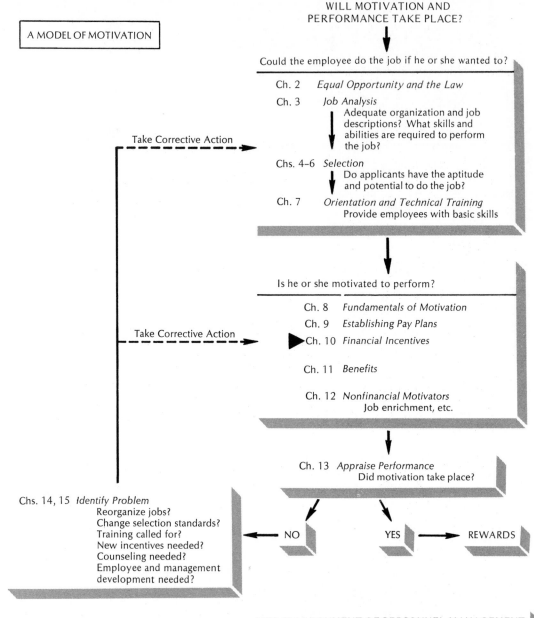

A MODEL OF MOTIVATION

WILL MOTIVATION AND
PERFORMANCE TAKE PLACE?

Could the employee do the job if he or she wanted to?

Ch. 2 *Equal Opportunity and the Law*

Ch. 3 *Job Analysis*
Adequate organization and job descriptions? What skills and abilities are required to perform the job?

Chs. 4–6 *Selection*
Do applicants have the aptitude and potential to do the job?

Ch. 7 *Orientation and Technical Training*
Provide employees with basic skills

Take Corrective Action

Is he or she motivated to perform?

Ch. 8 *Fundamentals of Motivation*

Ch. 9 *Establishing Pay Plans*

Ch. 10 *Financial Incentives*

Ch. 11 *Benefits*

Ch. 12 *Nonfinancial Motivators*
Job enrichment, etc.

Take Corrective Action

Ch. 13 *Appraise Performance*
Did motivation take place?

Chs. 14, 15 *Identify Problem*
Reorganize jobs?
Change selection standards?
Training called for?
New incentives needed?
Counseling needed?
Employee and management development needed?

NO   YES   REWARDS

THE ENVIRONMENT OF PERSONNEL MANAGEMENT

Ch. 16 *Labor Relations and Grievances*

Ch. 17 *Employee Safety and Health*

Ch. 18 *Personnel Management and the Quality of Work Life*

When you finish studying

10 Financial Incentives

You should be able to:

1. *Compare and contrast at least six types of incentive plans.*
2. *Explain at least five reasons why incentive plans fail.*
3. *Discuss when to use—and when not to use—incentive plans.*
4. *Establish and administer an effective incentive plan.*

OVERVIEW

The main purpose of this chapter is to explain how to use financial incentive plans—plans which tie pay to performance—to motivate employees. Several types of incentive plans, including "piecework," "the standard hour plan," "commissions," and "stock options" are explained. Next discussed are why incentive plans fail, and when to use incentive plans.

MONEY AND MOTIVATION: SOME BACKGROUND

The use of financial incentives—financial rewards paid to workers whose production exceeds some predetermined standard—was popularized by Frederick Taylor in the late 1800s. As a supervisory employee of the Midvale Steel Company, he had become increasingly concerned with what he called "systematic soldiering." (This was the tendency of employees to work at the slowest pace possible and produce at the minimum acceptable level.) What especially intrigued him was the fact that some of these same workers still had the energy to run home and work on their cabins, even after a hard twelve-hour day. Taylor knew that if he could find some way to harness this energy during the work day, huge productivity gains would be possible.

At this time, primitive "piecework" systems were already in use. Workers were paid a piecerate (based on informal performance standards) for each piece they produced. However, they knew that if their earnings became excessive, the piecerate would be cut. As a result, most workers produced just enough to earn a decent wage, but little enough so that their rate per piece would not be cut. One of Taylor's great insights was in seeing the need for a standardized, acceptable view of a *fair day's work.* And he saw that this fair day's work should depend not on the vague estimates of foremen but on a careful, formal, scientific process of inspection and observation. It was this need to *scientifically* evaluate each job that led to what became known as the *scientific management* movement.

Scientific management assumed that each worker's main goal was to maximize his or her economic gains. Later, in the 1920s, the human relations movement emerged; this resulted in a new focus on satisfying the workers' social needs. Many of these "human relations" ideas are still with us. Because of this, it is often easy to forget that money—particularly when used as an incentive—has been and is a primary means of motivating employees. [1] As two writers put it:

> Overall, it appears that the charge leveled by the human relationists of 50 years ago—that managers overemphasized the importance of money as a motivator—is incorrect today. It appears that managers fail to recognize the full potential of money, properly used, as a way of improving individual employee performance. [2]

TYPES OF INCENTIVE PLANS

There are many incentive plans in use, and a number of ways to categorize them. It is typical, for example, to distinguish between *individual* and *group* incentive plans, and between plans appropriate for *plant* personnel and *white collar* employees like salesmen and managers. As illustrated in Exhibit 10.1, some incentives, like merit pay, are used primarily as incentives for white collar, office personnel, while "piecerate" is used primarily as an individual or group plan [3] for blue collar, plant personnel.

Exhibit 10.1 Categorizing Incentive Plans

	Personnel:	
	PLANT	*WHITE COLLAR*
Individual	1. Piecework 2. Standard hour plan	1. Commissions 2. Bonuses 3. Merit pay
Group	1. Piecework, and standard hour plans can be adopted to use small groups	
Organizationwide	1. Profit sharing 2. Lincoln incentive system 3. Scanlon plan	

Incentive Plans for Plant Production Personnel

Piecework. This is the oldest type of incentive plan, as well as the most commonly used. Earnings are tied directly to what the worker produces by paying him a "piecerate" for each unit he produces. Thus, if Smith gets 20¢ a piece for stamping out door-jambs, then he would make $20 for stamping out 100 a day, and $40 for stamping out 200.

Developing a workable piecerate plan requires both job evaluation and (usually) industrial engineering. Job evaluation enables the employer to assign an hourly wage rate to the job in question. But the crucial issue in piecerate planning is the production standard, and these standards are usually developed by industrial engineers. The standards are usually stated in terms of a "standard" number of minutes per unit or a "standard" number of units per hour. In Smith's case the job evaluation indicated that his door-jamb stamping job was worth $4 an hour. The industrial engineer determined that 20 jambs per hour was the standard production rate. Therefore, the piecerate (for each door-jamb) was $4.00 ÷ 20 = 20¢ per door-jamb.

With a straight piecework plan Smith would simply be paid on the basis of the number of door-jambs he produced: there would be no guaranteed minimum wage. However, after passage of the Fair Labor Standards Act it became necessary for most employers to guarantee their workers a minimum wage. With a *guaranteed piecerate plan* Smith would be paid $3.10 per hour (the 1980 minimum wage) whether or not he stamped out 15½ door-jambs per hour (at 20¢ each). But *as an incentive* he would also be paid at the piecerate of 20¢ each for each unit (or part) he produced over 15½.

Piecework incentive plans have a number of distinct *advantages*. They are simple to calculate and easily understood by employees. With respect to our discussion of motivation, it is clear that rewards *are* directly tied to performance. Thus, these plans should and do motivate performance.

Piecework also has some *disadvantages*. The production standards become tied (in worker's minds) irrevocably with the amount of money earned. Thus, when industrial engineers attempt to analyze (or re-analyze) production standards they meet considerable worker resistance. In addition, piecerates are stated in monetary terms (like 20¢ per piece) and when a new job evaluation results in a new hourly wage rate the piecerate must similarly be revised: this can be a big clerical chore. Piecerate is also not usually feasible for setting up work *group* incentive plans (unless all the workers' jobs happen to carry the same hourly rate and production standards).

Finally, piecerate plans are still often associated with past shady practices of employers. (It was, for example, common for employers to arbitrarily raise production requirements if they found their workers earning "excessive" wages.) Because of its checkered history (and the other disadvantages), the use of piecerate incentive plans seems to be diminishing, although this is still a very widely used incentive plan. [4]

The Standard Hour Plan. [5] This plan is very similar to the piecerate plan but avoids some of its disadvantages. With the piecerate plan the worker is paid a particular *rate per piece* he or she produces. With the standard hour plan he is rewarded by *a percent premium that equals the percent by which his perform-*

ance is above standard. The plan assumes that the worker has a guaranteed base rate.

As an example, suppose the base rate for Smith's job is $4.00 per hour. (The base rate may, but need not, equal the hourly rate determined by the job evaluation.) And again assume that the production standard for Smith's job is 20 units per hour—or 3 minutes per unit. Suppose that in one day (8 hours) Smith produces 200 door-jambs. According to the production standard, this *should* have taken Smith 10 hours (200 ÷ 20 per hour); instead it took him 8 hours. He produced at a rate that is 25% (40 ÷ 160) higher than the standard rate. The standard rate would be 8 hours × 20 (units per hours) = 160: Smith *actually* produced 40 more, or 200. He will therefore be paid a rate that is 25% above his base rate for the day. His base rate was $4.00 per hour × 8 hours = $32.00. So he'll be paid 1.25 × 32 or $40.00 for the day.

The standard hour plan has most of the advantages of the piecework plan, and is fairly simple to compute and easy to understand. But the incentive is expressed in units of time instead of in monetary terms (as it is with the piece-rate system). Therefore, the clerical job of recomputing piecerates whenever hourly wage rates are re-evaluated is avoided.

Group Incentive Plans. Some organizations use *group* incentive plans. Here, each member of the group receives a bonus based on the output of the group *as a whole.* (This bonus might be based on a piecework or a standard wage plan, for example.)

There are several reasons to use a group plan. Sometimes (as on assembly lines) several jobs are *interrelated.* Here, one worker's performance reflects not only his own effort but that of his co-workers as well: in such cases group incentive plans are advantageous. Group incentive plans also encourage *coopera-tion* among group members. There tends to be *less bickering* among group members as to who has "tight" production standards and who has "loose" ones. We also know that groups can bring *pressure* to bear on their members (through badgering, ostracism, etc.) and help *keep shirkers in line.* This in turn can help eliminate some of the need for close supervision. Group produc-tion levels tend to be more *stable* than individual ones. And group incentive payments *vary less* than individual ones. Group incentive plans also facilitate *on-the-job training,* since each member of the group has a vested interest in getting a new group member trained as well and as quickly as possible. [6]

Group incentive plans are usually applied to small work groups, for ex-ample, 5 or 6 people who must assemble a component together. If the jobs are similar (in terms of hourly wage rates and production standards), either the piecerate or standard hour rate can be adopted for group use. But it is more common to use the standard hour plan, especially when different hourly wage rates make the use of a common piecerate impractical.

The chief *disadvantage* of group plans is that each worker's rewards are no longer based solely or directly on his or her own efforts. To the extent that the person does *not* see his or her effort leading to the desired reward, a group plan is usually not as effective as an individual plan. In one study, however, the researchers arranged to pay the group not based on its overall performance but based on the performance of its best member. This group plan proved as effective as an individual incentive plan in improving performance. [7]

Incentive Plans for White Collar Personnel

Sales Personnel. Compensation plans for salespeople have typically relied heavily on incentives in the form of sales commissions. Although in most cases some minimum salary is also guaranteed. For example, one survey found that about 60% of organizations responding used commissions plus salary to compensate their sales force, while about 20% used straight salary and 20% used straight commission. [8]

The widespread use of incentives for sales staff is due to three things: tradition; the unsupervised nature of most saleswork; and the assumption that incentives are needed to motivate salespeople. And unlike most other employees, sales personnel seem to clearly prefer being paid on an incentive basis: over 95% of the respondents in one study said they preferred to be paid on an incentive basis, for example. [9]

There are numerous sales incentive plans, each geared to different markets, products, and so forth. However, all plans are basically variations of three types of plans: straight salary, straight commission, and combination plans.

At one extreme, straight salary is not, of course, an incentive plan; the salesperson is simply paid on a weekly, monthly, or yearly basis. At the other extreme, straight commission *is* an incentive pay plan; it is analogous to the piecerate system for production. [10]

There are several advantages to paying a salesforce on a straight salary basis. First, the employer has fixed, predictable salesforce expenses. Salespeople know in advance what their income will be. And incentives (like commissions) tend to shift the salesperson's emphasis to just "making the sale" rather than prospecting and cultivating long-term customers: this longer term perspective *is* encouraged by straight salary compensation.

The disadvantage of straight salary is that pay does not depend on results. From our discussion of motivation this should reduce salesmen's performance, and it appears that it does. [11] In fact, *salaries* are often tied to time with the company (rather than to performance) and this can be even more demotivating to potentially "high performing" salespeople, who see "time with company"—not "performance"—being rewarded.

At the other extreme, some companies pay their salesforce on a straight commission basis. Here, salespeople are paid for results and only for results. The employer thus tends to attract high performing salespeople who see that their effort will clearly lead to rewards.

But the straight commission also has some disadvantages. Salespeople naturally focus on making a sale and on high volume items. Cultivating dedicated customers and working to "push" hard-to-sell items are often neglected.

Salespeople tend to be less company oriented and more money oriented, and the firm has less control over them. In addition, each salesperson's income fluctuates.

The vast majority of companies therefore pay their salesforce a *combination* of salary and commissions, and the widespread use of such plans derives from several advantages. Salespeople have a floor to their earnings so they need not worry about their families' security (recall that according to psychologists like Herzberg, it is only when lower-order needs like security are satisfied that workers can truly become "self-starters"). There is therefore a sizable salary component in most combination plans, and the company therefore has more control over its salesforce. Specifically, it can direct salesmen's activities by detailing what services the salary component is being paid for. The commission component provides a built-in incentive for superior performance.

Combination plans provide not only some of the advantages of both straight salary and straight commission plans, but also some of the disadvantages of each. For example, the salary component is not related to performance, and the employer is therefore trading away some of the incentive value of what the person is paid. Combination plans also tend to become very complicated, and misunderstandings often result in frustration.

However, the advantages of combination plans tend to outweigh their disadvantages, so these plans are widely used in several variations. [12] The simplest variation is "salary plus commission," which needs no elaboration. There is also a "commission plus drawing account" plan. Here, the salesperson is paid basically on commissions: however, he or she can *draw* on future earnings to get through low sales periods. In the "commission plus bonus" plan, salespeople are again paid primarily on the basis of commissions. However, they are also given a bonus of some sort for directed activities like selling "slow moving" items. In the "salary plus bonus" plan, salespeople are paid a basic salary. They are then paid a bonus for carrying out specified activities.

Incentives for Management Employees. An increasing number of profit and nonprofit organizations provide bonuses as incentives to its managers; according to one survey, at least half the organizations contacted had such bonus plans. [13] And, the evidence indicates that management bonus plans can pay for themselves by improving management—and company—performance. [14]

Several basic questions enter into the design of such bonus plans: Who should be included in the plan? What proportion of its profits should the company pay out in bonuses? What proportion of those eligible should receive bonuses? What proportion of total compensation should be paid in the form of bonuses? How should results be measured? What impact will the bonus plan have on salary levels? In what form will bonus payments be made?

Since management bonuses are usually tied to company profits, one crucial question concerns what proportion of company profits are to be paid out in management bonuses. Here, there is no hard and fast rule, but one alternative is to reserve a minimum amount of the profits—say 10%—for safeguarding stockholders' investment, and then to establish a fund equal to, say, 20% of the corporate operating profit (before taxes) in excess of this base amount. (Thus, if the operating profits were $100,000, then the management bonus fund might be 20% of $90,000, or $18,000.) [15]

A second question concerns who will participate in the plan and to what extent each person will participate. Here, some firms distinguish between executive (corporate top management), managerial (top divisional management), and supervisory (foremen and functional department head) managers. A decision then has to be made concerning the proportion of total compensation each group of managers can receive in bonuses. The exact proportion varies from firm to firm, but there are some general findings. For example, the size of the bonus is usually much higher for top level executives. Thus, an executive with a $150,000 salary may be able to earn another 80% of his or her salary as a bonus, while a manager in the same firm earning $80,000 can only earn another 30%. Similarly, a supervisor might be able to earn up to 15% of his or her base salary in bonuses. Average bonuses range from a low of 10% to a high of 80% or more: one company recently established a plan whereby executives could earn 45% of base salary, managers 25%, and supervisory personnel 12½%. [16] In general, the trend seems to be towards setting about a 50% limit on bonuses. [17]

The next question concerns how much of a bonus each individual manager should be paid. In most cases, managers' bonuses are tied to performance through the use of a predetermined formula. An important issue, therefore, is "to *what* performance should the bonus be tied?" The important thing to keep in mind here is that there is a difference between a profit sharing plan, and a true, individual incentive bonus. In a profit sharing plan, each person gets a bonus based on the company's results, regardless of the person's actual effort. With a true individual incentive, on the other hand, it is the person's individual effort (and performance) that is rewarded with a bonus. Therefore, to what "performance" should the manager's bonus be tied? To the company's overall profits? To the person's individual performance (as determined by his or her superior)? Or should the bonus be tied to both company and individual performance?

Here, again, there are no hard and fast rules. Top level executive bonuses are generally tied to overall corporate results (or divisional results if the executive is, say, the vice president of a major division). The assumption here is that corporate results reflect the person's individual performance. But as one moves further down the organizational hierarchy, corporate profits become a less accurate gauge of a manager's contribution, and here (say, with supervisory personnel) the person's individual performance as appraised by his or her superior might be a more logical determinant of his or her bonus.

Some experts argue that in most organizations even executive-level bonuses should be tied to *both* organizational and individual performance and there are several ways to do so. [18] For example, the *split award* method breaks the the bonus into two parts, with one part dependent on individual performance and the other on organizational performance. [19] As an example, assume that

280 **Exhibit 10.2** An Example of a Method for Determining Individual Incentive Awards

		Individual Performance				
	Rating:	Poor	Marginal	Good	Superior	Outstanding
	Percent of normal award given this rating:	Below 50%	50 to 80%	90 to 110%	110 to 130%	Over 130%
Organization Performance	Performance percentage, given this performance:					
loss Below 50		0%	0%	0%	0%	100%
marginal 50		0	0	50	65	100
60		0	0	60	80	115
70		0	0	70	90	130
80		0	20	80	100	145
90		0	30	90	110	160
target 100		0	40	100	120	175
110		0	50	110	130	190
120		0	55	120	140	205
130		0	60	130	155	220
140		0	65	140	170	235
outstanding 150		0	70	150	180	250

NOTE: Figures within matrix (0%, 100%, 150%, 250%, etc.) are *examples* only, and are *based on* multiplying organization performance percentage times individual performance percentage. For example, if organization performance is just on "target", and individual performance is "good", then 100% X 100% = 100%, as in matrix. However, the fact that the individual percentages are expressed as ranges means the employer has some leeway in awarding bonuses. For example, look at the last column on the right. Here, if organization performance is "marginal" (50%) then award percentage (100%) might be computed on assumption individual percentage is 200%. (In other words, 50% X 200% = 100%). This ensures "outstanding" person still gets his or her bonus. But if organization performance is "outstanding" (rather than marginal) then award percentage for the same person might be lower—say, 167%. Thus, 150% (for outstanding organization performance) times 167% (for outstanding individual performance) equals about 250% as indicated in last figure on last column. Each employer can thus develop a matrix it believes is most equitable.

Source: Hildebrand, "Individual Expense," *Compensation Review*, 1978, 3rd Qtr. p. 31.

an executive has a salary of $40,000 and a "normal" bonus of 25% of base salary or $10,000. Also assume (as illustrated in Exhibit 10.2) that organization performance can be scored from 50% (if the company has a loss) to 100% (if they obtain target profits) to 150% (for outstanding performance). Further, assume that individual performance (in terms of percent of the person's normal bonus award) can range from poor to outstanding and that individual performance can also be scored from 50% to 150%. Then, if the executive is outstanding and scores 150 and if the organization's performance meets target and scores 100, the award is $10,000 (the "normal" bonus) times the average of 100 and 150 (converted to percentages) or $12,500.

One drawback to the split award approach is that it pays too much to the marginal performer, who might still receive, say, 70% of his bonus if the company does outstanding, and too little to the outstanding performer when the company does not do well. An alternative, therefore, is the *multiplier method.* Here again, as in exhibit 10.2, a numerical score for both individual and organizational performance is determined. However, the manager's bonus is his or her salary times the normal award percent (25% in our example) times the *product* of the two scores for company and individual performance. Thus, the $40,000 executive's bonus would be 10,000 times 100% *times* 150% or $15,000. Using the product rather than an average can help weight individual performance more heavily, and so is superior to the split award method from the point of view of its incentive value. In any case, whether the executive's bonus is tied entirely to company profits, or whether some combination plan is used, the basic point to keep in mind is that:

> truly outstanding performers should never be paid less than their normal award, regardless of organizational performance, and should get substantially larger awards than do other managers. They are people the company cannot afford to lose, and their performance should always be adequately rewarded by the organization's incentive system . . . Marginal or below-average performers should never receive awards that are normal or average, and poor performers should be awarded nothing. The money saved on these people should be given to above-average performers. [20]

Stock options are one of the most popular executive "incentive" plans. These plans usually must be approved (for income tax purposes) within twelve months before or after the corporation adopts the plan and the options (to buy stock at reduced prices) must be exercised within five years after they are granted. The option price itself must usually be at least the fair market price of the stock on the day on which the option is granted. The executive thus hopes to profit by exercising his option (buying the stock) in the future, but at today's price.

The assumption, of course, is that the price of stock will go up, rather than go down or stay the same. Unfortunately this depends partly on considerations quite outside the executive's control. (For example, it is a function of general economic conditions, as well as overall stock market conditions.) Stock price *is* of course also affected by the profitability and growth of the company and, to the extent that the executive can affect these factors, the stock option can be an "incentive." However, in one survey it was found that over half the executives saw little or no relation between their performance and their option rewards. [21] Stock options have thus fallen into some disfavor partly because of their somewhat weak incentive value, and partly because stock market prices had retreated. [22] One alternative, which is becoming increasingly popular is a *book value plan,* under which managers are permitted to purchase stock at current "book value." Executives earn dividends on the stock they own, and as the company grows the book value of their shares may grow too. When these employees leave the company, they can then sell the company back its shares at the new higher book value. [23]

Incentives for Professional Employees. Incentive plans are not widely used for professional employees like engineers and scientists, and there seem to be at least two reasons for this. First, as explained in Chapter 9, these employees' efforts are often related only indirectly to the new products profits: instead, its profitability is more often dependent on sales skills, production skills, and so on. Second, many psychologists believe that instituting incentive plans on jobs that are inherently challenging may actually *detract* from the employee's intrinsic motivation. In any case, incentive plans are not used as widely for these types of employees.

Merit Pay. Generally speaking, *merit pay* (or a merit raise) is any salary increase that is awarded to an employee based on his or her individual performance. It is different from a bonus in that it represents a continuing increment whereas a bonus represents a one-time payment. Although the term *merit pay* can apply to the incentive raises given to any employees—exempt or nonexempt, office or factory, management or nonmanagement, and so on— the term is more often used with respect to office, and especially clerical personnel.

In any case, awarding of merit pay has both its advocates and detractors and is the subject of considerable debate. [24] Basically, advocates of merit pay argue that only pay (or other rewards) that are tied directly to performance can motivate performance. They contend that the effect of awarding pay raises across the board (without regard to individual performance) may actually detract from performance, by showing employees that they will be rewarded the same regardless of how they perform. On the other hand, detractors of merit pay present several cogent arguments for why merit pay plans, as currently administered, can backfire. One is that the usefulness of the merit pay plan is dependent on the validity of the performance appraisal system in use, and that if performance appraisals are viewed as unfair so, too, will the merit pay that's based on them. Similarly, supervisors often tend to minimize differences in employee performance when computing merit pay raises, and to instead give most employees about the same raise (across the board), either because of a reluctance to alienate some employees, or because of a desire to give everyone a raise that will at least help them stay even with the cost of living. A third problem is that almost every employee thinks he or she is an above average performer: being rated below average can therefore be quite demoralizing. However, while problems like these can undoubtedly undermine a merit pay plan, there seems little doubt that merit pay can and does improve performance. The key is to ensure that the performance appraisals are carried out effectively.

Organization-wide Incentive Plans

Many organizations have installed incentive plans in which virtually all employees can participate. We will discuss two of these: profit sharing plans and the Scanlon plan.

Profit-Sharing Plans.   In a profit-sharing plan, most employees receive a share of the company's profits. The number of companies with profit-sharing plans has doubled every five years since 1951, and there are now a multitude of such plans in existence.

Research on the effectiveness of these plans is sketchy. In one survey, about half the companies contacted felt their profit-sharing plans had been beneficial, [25] but these benefits are not necessarily in terms of increased performance and motivation. In terms of our model, profit-sharing plans should have rather little effect on motivation, since company profits depend on many factors over which most individual employees have little or no control. Therefore, with profit-sharing plans the link between effort and rewards is tenuous (at best).

The organizational benefits that derive from profit-sharing plans are probably more subtle. For example, these plans may increase each worker's sense of commitment to the organization, as well as his or her sense of participation and partnership. They may also reduce turnover and encourage employee thrift.

There are several types of profit-sharing plans but the most popular are cash plans. Here a percentage of profits (usually about 15–20%) is distributed as profit shares at regular intervals. One example of this is the *Lincoln Incentive System* which was first instituted at the Lincoln Electric Company of Ohio. In one version of the Lincoln plan most employees work on a guaranteed piecework basis, and total annual profits (less taxes, 6% dividend to stockholders, and a reserve for reinvestment) are distributed each year among employees in accordance with their merit rating. [26] Versions of the Lincoln plan also include a suggestion system which pays individual workers rewards for savings resulting from suggestions. The Lincoln plan has been quite successful, partly because workers are encouraged to learn how effort on their part contributes directly to their rewards.

There are also *deferred profit-sharing* plans. Here a predetermined portion of profits is placed in each employee's account under the supervision of a trustee. There is a tax advantage to such plans, since income (and income taxes) are deferred.

Employee stock ownership plans are also popular. Here employees are allowed to purchase stock below market price, often aided by provisions for payroll deductions and installment payments. One advantage of such a plan is that it may encourage employees to develop a sense of ownership in (and commitment to) company. Another advantage is that the employee retirement income security act (ERISA) allows a firm to borrow against employee stock held in trust, and then repay the loan in pre-tax rather than after tax-dollars: There is thus a tax incentive to establish such plans. [27]

The Scanlon Plan.   Few would argue with the fact that the most powerful way of ensuring high performance is to synchronize the organization's goals with those of its employees; to ensure, in other words, that the two sets of goals are essentially identical, and that by pursuing his or her goals, the person pursues the organization's goals as well. In a very real sense, in other words, each worker becomes a "boss," and it is no longer necessary to cajole or prod workers into working: instead, they each control themselves.

Many techniques have been proposed for obtaining this idealic state of affairs, but few have been implemented as widely or studied so long as the "Scanlon Plan." This plan is a productivity-enhancing technique developed in 1937 by Joseph Scanlon, a former cost accountant, steel worker, United Steel workers union official, and, finally, a lecturer at the Massachusetts Institute of Technology. Scanlon is recognized as having been instrumental in saving Empire Steel and Tinplate Company in the mid-1930s by devising a formula for sharing the profits of the firm with all employees, and by gaining the wholehearted cooperation of all employees in reducing costs and increasing production. [28]

The Scanlon plan has three basic features. The first is the philosophy of cooperation on which it is based. It assumes that managers and workers have to rid themselves of the "us" and "them" attitudes that normally inhibit employees from developing a sense of ownership in the company, substituting instead a climate in which everyone cooperates because he or she understands that economic rewards are contingent on honest cooperation. Managers' attitudes are thus largely the key to success or failure of a Scanlon plan. Where key executives have a genuine respect for each employee, then implementing a Scanlon plan can substantially improve productivity. [29] On the other hand, where such positive attitudes are lacking, it is doubtful that the plan can succeed. First, therefore, for a Scanlon plan to succeed there must be a pervasive philosophy of cooperation throughout the organization and this cooperation, in turn, demands that management have or develop a genuine respect for each person and his or her abilities.

The second feature of the plan is the involvement system. [30] This takes the form of two levels of committees: the departmental level and the executive level. Productivity-improving suggestions are presented by employees to the appropriate departmental level committees, which then selectively transmit viable suggestions to the executive level committee. The latter then decides whether to implement the suggestion. These committees are all superimposed on the regular organizational structure, and thus become a new mechanism for communicating employee productivity-improvement suggestions to management.

The third element of the plan is the sharing of benefits formula. Basically, the Scanlon plan assumes that employees should share directly in any extra profits resulting from their productivity-improving suggestions. As explained below, the formula shows the historical relationship between (1) labor costs and (2) the value of production, and assumes that a reduction of labor costs (assuming production stays the same) or an increase in production (assuming labor costs stay the same) will generate extra profits for the business, part of which should be shared with the workers.

Usually all (or virtually all) employees in the plant participate in the plan. Workers, supervisors, and managers make cost-cutting suggestions that are screened and evaluated by the various screening committees. If a suggestion is implemented and successful, all employees usually share in 75% of the savings. For example, assume that the normal monthly ratio of payroll costs to sales is 50%. (Thus if sales are $600,000, payroll costs should be $300,000.) Assume a suggestion is implemented and results in payroll costs of $250,000, in a month where sales were $550,000, and payroll costs therefore *should have been* $275,000 (50% of sales). The saving attributable to the suggestion is $25,000 ($275,000–$250,000). Personnel would typically share in 75% of this ($18,750) while $6,250 would go to the firm. (In practice a portion—usually one-fourth of the $18,750—is usually set aside for the months in which labor costs exceed the standard.)

The Scanlon plan has been quite successful. Employees make many suggestions, they accept the need for technological changes, and a work climate "hostile to loafing" results. The plan tends to encourage a sense of partnership and sharing among workers, less overtime, and employee insistence on efficient management. [31] In one recent study, labor costs were cut by about 10%, and grievances were cut in half after implementation of the Scanlon plan. [32]

Yet, a number of Scanlon programs have failed, and, we do know that certain conditions seem necessary for Scanlon plans to succeed. They are often more effective where there is a relatively small number of participants (generally less than 1,000). It is more successful where there are stable product lines and costs (it is important that the labor cost/sales ratio remains fairly stable). Good supervision and healthy labor relations seem essential. Finally—but perhaps most importantly—it is crucial that there be strong commitment to the plan on the part of management—particularly during the confusing phase-in period. [33]

Survey: How Incentives are Used. [34]

A survey carried out in conjunction with the American Institute of Industrial Engineers provides a useful perspective on the use of wage incentives in the United States and Canada. In manufacturing industries about 59% of the 275 firms responding indicated that they use some type of wage incentive program. Within this group virtually all respondents in the apparel, lumber, and rubber industries use some type of incentives, while the proportion in other manufacturing industries ranges from about 15% in the printing and publishing industry to 60 or 70% in the fabricated metal products, textile, and instruments industries. Among the 16 non-manufacturing companies responding to this survey only 1 reported using incentives. Among companies using incentives, about 61% reported using the standard hour plan, 36% used straight piecework, about 19% used some type of profit sharing plan, and about 5% use a plant wide bonus plan (some firms use more than one plan, such as piecework plus a plant wide bonus plan). These results indicate that the standard hour plan is by far the most popular type of incentive plan; straight piecework is the second most popular.

What results did companies believe they were getting from their wage incentives? Here the researcher distinguished between incentives for *direct* labor (those who actually assemble the products, for instance) and *indirect* labor (including clerical help). With respect to direct labor, 95% of companies responding felt that their incentives improved productivity, 94% felt that incentives reduced costs, and 60% felt that incentives both improved employee morale and led to better supervisory effectiveness. However, only about 25% of respondents felt that incentives led to improved quality of output. Respondents were not nearly as enthusiastic about the effects of wage incentives for *indirect* labor, however. Here, about 43% said incentives improved productivity and reduced costs, and about 30% said incentives improved employee morale and supervisory effectiveness. Here only about 2½% said that incentives improved quality of output. Overall, the use of incentives seems to have increased slightly—by about 7%—relative to a similar survey made 17 years earlier.

The Responsibility for Developing Incentive Plans

Although it has always been important to develop incentive plans that are workable and objective, it is especially so today. There are two reasons for this. First, managers today are confronted with an increasingly well-educated and assertive work force, one comprised of individuals who may be less likely than their forebears to accept at face value management's explanations for differences in pay between employees. Second, federal legislation concerning equal employment and equal pay demands that managers be able to explain pay differences in terms of measurable performance differences. [35]

Line managers play a pivotal role in the incentive-pay process, particularly in regard to appraising performance. The basic aim of an incentive should be to encourage good performance by linking performance and rewards, and this in turn depends on fair and accurate performance appraisals. When, as is often the case, the supervisor advertently or inadvertently undermines the appraisal system (by indiscriminately scoring everyone "high" so they can all get a raise, or by treating some employees unfairly), the result is to undermine the incentive plan as well.

The personnel department also plays a major role in developing and implementing an incentive plan. First, personnel has to work with the industrial engineering specialist in the area of *work measurement.* Work measurement refers to the techniques used by industrial engineers to scientifically study each job and determine a normal or "base-line" production rate; it is this base rate that the standards for many incentive plans—like the standard hour and piecerate plans—are based on. [36] Personnel is also usually responsible for developing the actual details of the incentive plans, including, for instance who will be eligible for the plan, what percent increases will be awarded for each level of performance, and how large a bonus can be awarded to persons in different grade levels. At Bell and Howell Corporation, for instance the compensation specialist developed a merit pay plan for nonexempt employees that included details like "what criteria will be used to measure performance of employees in each job group (assemblers, machine operators, etc.)," and "how much of a merit increase will employees in each job group be eligible for." [37] The personnel department is also usually responsible for developing and implementing the performance appraisal tool that will be used to appraise performance and on which any merit increases are usually based. Furthermore, personnel is responsible for providing the necessary supervisory training—with regard to how to appraise performance, and how the incentive plan works, for instance. And, they develop the necessary communiques and presentations through which the workers themselves are informed of the mechanics of the new incentive plan. Finally, personnel is responsible for continually reviewing pay differentials between employees, the company's pay relative to other firms, and for monitoring appeals and/or grievances from employees regarding the incentive plan. Personnel's role in incentive pay is therefore an important one.

DEVELOPING EFFECTIVE INCENTIVE PLANS

Problems Undermining Incentive Plans

Why do incentive plans fail? [38] There are a number of reasons, most of which can be explained in terms of our discussion of motivation. For motivation to take place, the worker must (1) believe that effort on his or her part will lead to rewards, and (2) he or she must want that reward. In most cases where incentive plans fail, it is because one (or both) of these conditions are not met. Specific problems, as summarized in Exhibit 10.3, include:

Exhibit 10.3   Why Incentive Plans Fail

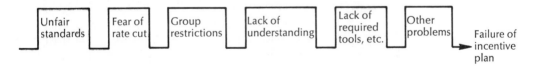

| Unfair standards | Fear of rate cut | Group restrictions | Lack of understanding | Lack of required tools, etc. | Other problems | Failure of incentive plan |

Unfair Standards.   Unfair standards appear to be the single most frequent cause for incentive plan failure. In order to motivate employees *the standard must be viewed as fair and attainable*; to the extent it is not, motivation will not take place.

Fear of Rate Cut or Raising of Standards.   One of the most persistent problems undermining incentive plans is the belief on the part of workers that standards will be raised (or rates cut) if they earn "too much." Years ago sociologist Donald Roy went to work in a machine shop to learn firsthand how such problems manifest themselves. When he was hired he was told by the personnel clerk that as a "radial drill operator" he "should average $1.25

288   per hour on piecework." The drill operator, a man named Starkey, replied that it was *impossible* to average $1.25. Here is the conversation, as reported by Roy:

> "Don't you know," cried Starkey angrily "that $1.25 an hour is the *most* we can make! And more of the time we can't even make that! Have you ever worked on piecerate before?"
>
> "No."
>
> "I can see that! Well, what do you suppose would happen if I turned in (on the average) $1.25 an hour on these pump bodies?"
>
> "Turned in? You mean if you actually did the work?"
>
> "I mean if I actually did the work and turned it in!"
>
> "They'd have to pay you, wouldn't they? Isn't that the agreement?"
>
> "Yes! They'd pay me—once! Don't you know that if I turned in $1.50 an hour on these pump bodies tonight, the whole god damn methods department would be down here tomorrow? And they'd retime this job so quick it would make your head swim! And when they retimed it, they'd cut the price in half! And I'd be working for $.85 per hour instead of $1.25!" **39**

Group Restrictions.   Peer pressure is a double-edge sword when it comes to incentive plans. If the group views the plan as fair, it can keep "loafers" in line and maintain high production. But the opposite is also true. If for any reason the group views the plan as not in its best interest, it will—through education, ostracism, or punishment—see that the production levels of group members is held to a minimum. For example, after Donald Roy had been on the job for some time he was told by a co-worker,

> "Don't let it go over $1.25 an hour or the time study man will be right down here! And they don't waste time either! They watch the records like a hawk! I got ahead so I took it easy for a couple of hours."
>
> "Joe (Roy says) told me that I had made $10.01 yesterday, and warned me not to go over $1.25 an hour. He told me to figure the set-ups and the time on each operation very carefully so that I would not total over $10.25 in any one day."

Employees Don't Understand the Incentive Plan.   Some plans fail because employees do not understand them. In some cases details of the plans are just not communicated to employees. In other cases communications are not understood. For motivation to take place the employee must believe that performance leads to rewards. If employees can not understand how (with the incentive plan) performance will lead to rewards, the plan probably is not going to motivate them.

Other Problems.   There are two other problems to be aware of. First, some incentive plans have failed because they created *inequitable* wage structures within the organization. For example, production workers were placed on an incentive system, under which (it turned out) they earned more than higher skilled workers who were not under the plan. **40**

Other plans result in interworker or intergroup *conflict*. Bickering over who has "tight" standards and who has "loose" ones can lead to conflict and undermine cooperation.

When to Use Incentive Plans [41]

There are two bases on which to compensate employees: time and output. Straight salary or wages involve compensating employees based on increments of time (such as hourly, daily, or weekly). Incentive plans (including piecework or commissions) involve compensating employees based on their output. Under what conditions should employees be paid on a time basis? On an output (incentive) basis? Here some guidelines (as summarized in Exhibit 10.4) are as follows:

Pay on a Time Basis.

1. *When units of output are difficult to distinguish and measure.* One has to be able to clearly distinguish and identify each worker's output to pay them on an incentive basis. Where one cannot, then straight salary or wages (or perhaps a group incentive plan) is more appropriate.
2. *When employees are unable to control quantity of output.* Where employees have little control over the quantity of output (such as on machine-paced assembly lines), pay based on time is more appropriate.
3. *When there is not a clear relationship betwen effort and output.* Similarly, if there is no clear, direct relationship between the worker's effort and his output—as when jobs are highly interrelated—pay based on time is more appropriate.
4. *When delays in the work are frequent and beyond employees' control.* It is impractical to tie workers' pay to their output if production delays are beyond workers' control.
5. *When quality considerations are especially important.* Virtually all incentive plans tie pay to the quantity, rather than the quality of output. When quality is a primary consideration (as with engineering and other professional personnel), pay based on time is more appropriate.
6. *When precise advance knowledge of unit labor costs is not required by competitive conditions.* Installing an incentive plan requires a substantial investment in industrial engineering, methods analysis, and computation of unit labor costs. If this type of precise cost control is not required by competitive conditions, it is probably not worthwhile to develop them just to install an incentive plan.

Payment Should Be Based on Output (Incentive Plans), When:

1. Units of output can be measured.
2. There is a clear relationship between employee effort and quantity of output.

Exhibit 10.4   When to Base Pay on Incentives (Instead of Time)

	Base Pay on Incentives	Base Pay on Time
Units of output	Easy to measure	Hard to measure
Employee's control of output	They can control it	They can't
Effort/Reward relationship	Clear	Not clear
Work delays	Under employee's control	Beyond employee's control
Quality	Not too important	Paramount
Good supervision and agreement on what is a "fair day's work"	No	Yes
Must know precise labor costs to stay competitive	Yes	No

3. The job is standardized, the work flow is regular, and delays are few or consistent.
4. Quality is less important than quantity or, if quality is important, it is easily measured.
5. Competitive conditions require that unit labor costs be definitely known and fixed in advance of production. [42]

Summary: Developing An Effective Incentive Plan

As two experts conclude, incentive plans can motivate employees:

> There is considerable evidence that installation of such plans usually results in greater output per man hour, lower unit cost, and higher wages in comparison with outcomes associated with the straight payment systems. [43]

But incentive plans can also fail. Some additional guidelines for developing effective incentive plans include: [44]

Effort and Rewards Should Be Directly Related.   For an incentive to motivate employees, they must see that effort will lead to obtaining the reward. The incentive plan should therefore reward employees in *direct proportion* to their increased productivity. Employees must also perceive that they can *actually do the tasks* required. Thus, the standard has to be attainable, and they must have the necessary tools, equipment, and training. The employee also has to have *adequate control* over the work process: in other words, increased effort should clearly result in increased performance and therefore rewards. The effort-reward link is usually not as clear under group incentive plans as under individual plans. This is why the latter are generally more effective. [45]

Carefully Study Methods and Procedures.   Effective incentive plans are generally based on a meticulous work methods study. This usually requires the services of an industrial engineer or other methods expert. Through careful

PART TWO: COMPENSATION AND MOTIVATION

observation and measurement they define fair performance standards. The incentive plan is then built on these standards.

291

The Plan Must Be Understandable and Easily Calculable by the Employees. Employees should be able to easily calculate the rewards they will receive for various levels of effort, since it is important for them to see the effort–reward link.

Set Effective Standards. The standards on which the incentive plan is built should be effective, which requires several things. First, of course, the standards should be viewed as *fair and attainable* by employees. The standard should also be *specific*—this is much more effective than telling someone to "do your best." And, the standards should be *guaranteed*. Today, employees remain suspicious that *exceeding* the standard will result in *raising* the standards, and to protect their own long-term interests they do not produce above standard, and the incentive plan fails. Therefore, once the plan is operational, use great caution before decreasing the size of the incentive in any way. [46]

Employee Participation May Be Useful. For example, one case involved a cleaning crew in which absenteeism had become an acute problem. [47] Researchers allowed three (of five) work groups to develop (participatively) their own incentive plans, plans which rewarded high attendance. Management then *imposed* identical incentive plans in two other work groups. During the first 16 weeks following implementation of the plans, the groups that had participatively developed the incentive plans had significant increases in attendance. Attendance in the groups where the plans were imposed did not increase. The researchers report that after the incentive plans had been in existence for some time they were discontinued in two (of the three) "participative" groups. Attendance in these two groups immediately dropped significantly; this tends to support the idea that the participative incentive plans were in fact very effective in improving attendance. When the researchers checked again one year after the plans had been implemented, they found that in the (third) "participative" group (whose participative incentive plan was still in existence), attendance was still very high. Attendance was also somewhat higher in those groups where the incentive plans had been imposed. Attendance had fallen off in the two "participative" groups where the incentive plans had been discontinued.

SUMMARY

1. The "scientific" use of financial incentives can be traced back to Frederick Taylor. While such incentives became somewhat less popular during the "human relations" era, most writers today agree that they can be quite effective.

2. Piecework is the oldest type of incentive plan. Here a worker is paid a "piecerate" for each unit he produces. With a *straight* piecework plan, workers

292

are paid on the basis of the number of units produced. With a *guaranteed* piecework plan each worker receives his or her base rate (such as the minimum wage) regardless of how many units he or she produces.

3. Other useful incentive plans for plant personnel include the standard hour plan and group incentive plans. The former rewards workers by a percent premium that equals the percent by which their performance is above standard. Group incentive plans are useful where the workers' jobs are highly interrelated.

4. Several incentive plans are discussed for white collar personnel. Most sales personnel are paid on some type of salary plus commission (incentive) basis. The trouble with straight commission is that there is a tendency to focus on "big ticket" or "quick sell" items and to disregard long-term customer building. Management employees are often paid according to some bonus formula that ties the bonus to, for example, increased sales. Stock options are one of the most popular executive "incentive" plans.

5. Profit sharing and the Scanlon plan are examples of organization-wide incentive plans. The problem with such plans is that the link between a person's efforts and rewards is sometimes unclear. On the other hand such plans may contribute to developing a sense of commitment among employees.

6. When incentive plans fail it is usually because (1) the worker does not believe that effort on his or her part will lead to obtaining the reward, or (2) the reward is not important to the person. Specific incentive plan problems therefore include: unfair standards, fear of a rate cut, group restrictions, lack of understanding, lack of required tools, training, etc., and other problems (like inequitable wages, or intergroup conflict).

7. We suggested using incentive plans when: units of output are easily measured, employees can control output, the effort/reward relationship is clear, work delays are under employee's control, quality is not paramount, and the organization must know precise labor costs anyway (to stay competitive).

Sales Quotas*

The Superior Floor Covering Company has an incentive program for its salesmen. Incentive earnings are based on the amount of sales in relation to an assigned quota. The quota is computed each year by management, taking into account the number and type of customers in each salesman's territory and the previous year's sales records for the company and for its competitors. In the administration of this incentive program, the following problems have arisen. Suggest the type of analysis you would undertake to provide data that might lead to a solution and the alternative plans you would consider in eliminating these difficulties. Note also the parallels between the problems here and those involving blue collar, manufacturing incentive plans.

1. Some of the best salesmen now have too many accounts in the area assigned to them. From the company's point of view, it would be advantageous to reduce the size of the districts covered by each of these men and to add several new salesmen who could give more thorough coverage. The outstanding salesmen resent this proposal, however, claiming that it would penalize them for their success. Furthermore, they argue that although their sales records are high now, some of their good accounts may go to competitors, and then they will be worse off than other salesmen who have not had their districts "trimmed."
2. The top-earning salesmen also complain that their base quotas increase each year, reflecting their previous success. This, too, they feel is discrimination against success.
3. Management believes that the company is not acquiring as many new accounts as it should. So-called missionary work, trying to induce a store that has not previously purchased Superior products to become a customer, takes more time and energy than selling old customers. Also, the results of this missionary work may not show up for several years. The present incentive plan gives no credit for this type of work.
4. When business is booming within a salesman's territory, he may receive high bonus earnings even without great effort on his part. When there is a great deal of unemployment in his territory or when competition decides to lower prices to penetrate this new market, his bonus earnings may decline even though his sales efforts are at a maximum.

---

* George Strauss and Leonard R. Sayles, *Personnel: The Human Problems of Management*, Third Edition (Englewood Cliffs, NJ: Prentice-Hall, Inc., 1972), p. 635.

Purpose.   The purpose of this exercise is to give you practice in reviewing:

1. The conditions under which time versus performance-based incentives are appropriate.
2. The advantages of company-wide versus individual incentives.
3. The standards (sales, productivity, etc.) to which incentives can be tied.

Required Understanding.   You should be thoroughly familiar with our discussion of financial incentives and come to class prepared to discuss the following case incident: [51]

A *Case of Incentives*: The bonus policy of Ezell Musical Instrument Company. Ezell Musical Instrument Company (EMI) is located in Frederick, Maryland. It is a medium sized operation that has grown out of a family owned company. Like many companies, it has to face tough competition at home and abroad. M. G. Ezell III is now the president of the firm.

Several years ago, when Ezell first took over, he thought about how he might build morale in the company. He felt that the company had good workers and that he would like to reward them for past services to encourage them to be more productive. EMI was not unionized. He hesitated about raising base wages because it might make the firm uncompetitive if foreign competition increased.

EMI was having an exceptionally good year, both for sales and profits. As a result, Ezell thought that the best way to reward the employees was to give them a Christmas-New Year's bonus. As he said to Abe Stick, his personnel manager: "Nothing like the old buck to make a man work harder." His bonus system was as follows:

Wages or Salary	Bonus
<$6,500	$500
$6,501–7,500	$600
$7,501–8,500	$700
$8,501–10,000	$800
>$10,000	8% of salary or wage

The bonuses were well received. Many people thanked the president, and Stick heard lots of good comments from the supervisors in January about how much harder the employees were working.

The next year, more foreign competitors entered the market. Materials were harder to get and more expensive. Sales were down 5 percent, and profits were down 15 percent. Ezell did not feel he could afford the same bonuses as last year. As a result, the bonuses were decreased as follows:

Wages or Salary	Bonus
<$6,500	$250
$6,501–7,500	$300
$7,501–8,500	$350
$8,501–10,000	$400
>$10,000	4% of salary or wage

This time, Stick heard little from the supervisors about increased productivity. He asked Harry Bell, one of the supervisors, what the reaction was to the bonuses.

BELL—To tell you the truth, Abe, I have morale problems. My people worked hard this year. It wasn't their fault sales or profits were down. Many expected last year's bonus or better. So they spent most of the old figure for Christmas gifts. When they got that letter from M. G. telling them they were getting only half of last year's on December 27, there was gloom and doom and some mumblings. Some of my people seem to be working less hard than at any time I can remember.

STICK—But that's not fair, Harry. They never received any bonuses before. Now they should be glad they received anything.

BELL—That's not the way they see it!

Stick decided not to discuss the matter with Ezell. Stick figured the problem would blow over. But, this year was even worse. Sales held but were not up to the prior years' levels. But, profits were almost nonexistent. The board of directors decided to omit the dividend.

Now, Ezell has come to Stick. Ezell says: "Abe, I don't see how we can pay any bonus this year. Do you think we can get by without causing a big drop in morale?"

How to Set Up the Exercise. Divide the class into groups of four or five students. Everyone should briefly review "A Case of Incentives."

Instructions for the Exercise. After discussing the case each group should develop answers to the following questions:

1. What does this case illustrate about the motivational impact of bonuses and incentives?

2. What could Mr. Ezell have done to prevent this problem in the first place?

3. Why should Mr. Bell expect that the employees would react negatively to the reduction in bonuses when they are not guaranteed as part of an employee's compensation?

4. Have rewards been accurately tied to performance by the Ezell compensation policy? If not, how might this failure be the cause of their problems?

5. What alternative formula or policy for discussing extra income to employees would you suggest?

6. What would you do now if you were Ezell? Stick?

If time permits, the class should discuss their recommendations.

DISCUSSION QUESTIONS

1. Compare and contrast six types of incentive plans.
2. Explain five reasons why incentive plans fail.
3. How would you apply the "Expectancy" model of motivation we presented in Chapter 8 to the question of incentives?

NOTES

1. For example, see "Sharing the Wealth: HRO's Role in Making Incentive Plans Work," *Training* (January 1979), pp. 30–31.

2. Orlando Behling and Chester Schriesheim, *Organizational Behavior* (Boston: Allyn and Bacon, 1976), p. 250; J. K. Louden and J. Wayne Deegan, *Wage Incentives* (New York: John Wiley, 1959), p. 4; Robert Opsahl and Marvin Dunnette, "The Role of Financial Compensation in Industrial Motivation," *Psychological Bulletin*, Vol. 66 (1966), pp. 94–118; Gary Yukl, Gary Latham, and Elliott Pursell, "The Effectiveness of Performance Incentives Under Continuous and Variable Ratio Schedules of Reinforcement," *Personnel Psychology*, Vol. 29 (Summer 1976). Gary Latham and Dennis Dassett, "Designing Incentive Plans for Union Employees: A Comparison of Continuous and Variable Ratio Reinforcement Schedules," *Personnel Psychology*, Vol. 31, No 1 (Spring 1978), pp. 47–62.

3. For a discussion, see H. Williams, "A Review of Incentive Schemes," *Work Study and Management Services* (March 1975), pp. 91–95.

4. J. K. Louden and J. Wayne Deegan, *Wage Incentives* (New York: John Wiley, 1959), Ch. 2; David Belcher, *Compensation Administration*, Ch. 13; J. D. Dunn and Frank Rachel, *Wage and Salary Administration* (New York: McGraw-Hill, 1972), Ch. 29; see also Manuel London and Gregg Oldhaus, "Comparison of Group and Individual Incentive Plans," *Psychology of Management Journal*, Vol. 20, No. 1, pp. 34–41.

5. *Measured day work* is a third type of individual incentive plan. See, for example, Mitchell Fein, "Let's Return to NOW for Incentives," *Industrial Engineering* (January 1979), pp. 34–37.

6. See, for example, Peter Daly, "Selecting and Assigning a Group Incentive Plan," *Management Review* (December 1975), pp. 43–45.

7. Manuel Landon and Grey Oldham, "A Comparison of Group and Individual Incentive Plans," *Academy of Management Journal*, Vol. 20, No. 1 (1977), pp. 34–41. Note that the study was carried out under controlled conditions in a "laboratory" setting.

8. John Steinbrink, "How to Pay Your Sales Force," *Harvard Business Review* (July–August 1978), pp. 111–122.

9. Belcher, *Compensation Administration*, pp. 505–507.

10. See Famularo, *Handbook of Modern Personnel Administration*, Ch. 31; Belcher, *Compensation Administration*, Ch. 20; Robert Sibson, *Wages and Salaries: A Handbook for Line Managers* (New York: American Management Association, 1967), Ch. 7; and Jack Douner, "Salesmen's Compensation: Have We Kept Pace?" *Akron Business and Economic Review* (Summer 1972), pp. 33–37.

11. T. H. Patten, "Trends in Pay Practices for Salesmen," *Personnel* (January–February 1968), pp. 54–63; quoted in Belcher, *Compensation Administration*, p. 513.

12. For an interesting explanation of how sales bonuses can be tied to the salesperson's own forecasts see Jacob Gonik, "Tie Salesmen's Bonuses to Their Forecasts," *Harvard Business Review* (May/June 1978), pp. 116–123.

13. Belcher, *Compensation Administration,* p. 545; see also W. E. Reum and Sherry Reum, "Employee Stock Ownership Plans: Pluses and Minuses," *Harvard Business Review* (July–August 1976), pp. 133–143; and Ralph Bavier, "Managerial Bonuses—Multidivision Style," *Industrial Management* (March–April 1978), pp. 1–5.

14. See, for example, S. B. Prasod, "Top Management Compensation and Corporate Performance," *Academy of Management Journal* (September 1974), pp. 554–558. John Bouike, "Performance Bonus Plans; Boon for Managers and Stockholders," *Management Reviews* (November 1975), 13 & 18; "How Pay 'n Save Grows and Grows," *Forbes* (April 16, 1979), p. 113.

15. See, for example, Ralph Bavier, "Managerial Bonuses—Multidivisions Style," *Industrial Management* (March–April 1978), pp. 1–5.

16. Bavier, p. 2.

17. Belcher, *Compensation Administration,* p. 545; Famularo, *Handbook of Modern Personnel Administration,* Ch. 32.

18. F. Dean Hildebrand Jr., "Individual Performance Incentive Compensation," *Compensation Review,* 3rd quarter (1978), pp. 28–33.

19. The following is based on Hildebrand, pp. 31–32.

20. Hildebrand, p. 32.

21. Belcher, *Compensation Administration,* p. 548.

22. Robert Pitts, "Incentive Compensation and Organization Design," *Personnel Journal* (May 1974), p. 338.

23. Basically, book value per share equals the firm's assets minus its liabilities, divided by the number of shares. See, for example, John Annas, "Facing Today's Compensations Uncertainties," *Personnel,* Vol. 53, No. 1 (January–February 1976).

24. See, for example, Herbert Meyer, "The Pay for Performance Dilemma," *Organizational Dynamics,* Vol. 3, No. 3 (Winter 1975), pp. 39–50; Thomas Patten Jr., "Pay for Performance or Placation?" *The Personnel Administrator* (September 1977), pp. 26–29; William Kearney, "Pay for Performance? Not Always," *M.S.U. Business Topics* (Spring 1979), pp. 5–16.

25. Bert Metzger and Jerome Colletti, "Does Profit Sharing Pay?" (Evanstown, Profit Sharing Research Foundation, 1971), quoted in Belcher, *Compensation Administration,* p. 353.

26. Belcher, *Compensation Administration,* p. 351.

27. See, for example, Donald Sullivan, "Esop; Panacea or Placebo," *California Management Review,* Vol. 20, No. 1 (Fall 1977), pp. 55–56.

28. See Brian Moore and Timothy Rosse, *The Scanlon Way to Improve Productivity: A Practical Guide* (New York: Wiley, 1978), p. 2.

29. George Sherman, "The Scanlon Concept: Its Capabilities for Productivity Improvement," p. 19; J. Kenneth White, "The Scanlon Plan: Causes and Correlates of Success," *Academy of Management Journal,* Vol. 22, No. 2 (June 1979), pp. 292–312.

30. This is based on Moore and Ross, pp. 1–2.

31. Belcher, *Compensation Administration,* pp. 329–331.

32. Fred Lesieur and Elbridge Puckett, "The Scanlon Plan Has Proved Itself," *Harvard Business Review,* Vol. 49 (1969), pp. 109–119, reprinted in W. Clay Hamner and Frank Schmidt, *Contemporary Readings in Personnel* (Chicago: St. Clair Press, 1977), pp. 340–351; George Sherman, "The Scanlon Concept: Its Capabilities for Productivity Improvement," *Personnel Administrator* (July 1976); Moore and Ross, *The Scanlon Way . . . ,* 1978.

33. Dunn and Rachel, *Wage and Salary Administration,* p. 253; Behling and Schriesheim, *Organizational Behavior,* pp. 247–248; Belcher, *Compensation Administration,* pp. 330–332. J. Kenneth White, "The Scanlon Plan: Causes and Correlates

298   of Success," *Academy of Management Journal*, Vol. 22, No. 2 (June 1979), pp. 292–312.

34. Robert Rice, "Survey of Work Measurement and Wage Incentives in the U.S.A.," *Management Services* (January 1978), pp. 10–20.

35. See, for example, Don Marshall, "Merit Pay Without Headaches: How to Design a Plan for Nonexempts," *Compensation Review*, Vol. 7, No. 2, second quarter (1975), pp. 32–41.

36. Robert Rice, "Survey of Work Measurement and Wage Incentives in the U.S.A.," *Management Services* (Jan. 1978), p. 10.

37. Don Marshall, "Merit Pay without Headaches. . . ." See also Douglas Fleuter, "A Different Approach to Merit Increases," *Personnel Journal* (April 1979), pp. 225–226.

38. See J. Richard Hackman and J. Lloyd Suttle, *Improving Life at Work: Behavior Science Approaches to Organizational Change* (Santa Monica, Calif.: Goodyear, 1977), pp. 197–289; Robert Pitts and Ken Thompson, "The Supervisors Survival Guide: Alternatives to Monetary Rewards," *Supervisory Management* (1978), pp. 12–17. R. Michael Donovan, "Getting Your Incentive Plan under Control," *Industrial Management* (July–August 1978), pp. 10–11.

39. Donald Roy, "Quota Restriction and Goldbricking in a Machine Shop," *American Journal of Sociology*, Vol. 57 (March 1952), pp. 430–437; reprinted in Joseph Litterer, *Organizations: Structure and Behavior* (New York: Wiley, 1969), p. 201.

40. Leonard Sayles, "The Impact of Incentive on Intergroup Work Relations— A Management and Union Problem," *Personnel* (May 1967), pp. 483–490; quoted in Belcher, *Compensation Administration*, p. 308.

41. Based on Belcher, *Compensation Administration*, pp. 309–311. See also Edward Lawler III, "Reward Systems," in J. R. Hackman and J. L. Suttle, *Improving Life at Work* (Santa Monica, Calif.: Goodyear, 1977), pp. 191–219.

42. Belcher, *Compensation Administration*, pp. 309–310.

43. Robert Opsahl and Marvin Dunnette, "The Role of Financial Compensation in Industrial Motivation," *Psychological Bulletin*, Vol. 66 (1966), pp. 94–118 in Larry Cummings and William Scott, *Readings in Organizational Behavior and Human Performance* (Homewood, Ill.: Irwin/Dorsey, 1969). See also Behling and Schriesheim, *Organizational Behavior*. Both sets of authors point out, though, that the installation of an incentive plan is not (and can't be) an isolated event. Improved work methods, clearer policies, etc., always accompany incentive plans and it's often hard to determine whether it's the incentive plan or these other improvements which led to the improved performance.

44. Based on R. D. Pritchard, C. W. VonBergan, Jr., and P. J. LeDeo, "An Evaluation of Incentive Motivation Techniques in Air Force Technical Training," Air Force Human Resources Laboratory Technical Report (1974); Robert Pritchard, Philip DeLeo, and Clarence W. VonBergan, Jr., "A Field Experiment Test of Expectancy–Valence Incentive Motivation Techniques," *Organizational Behavior and Human Performance*, Vol. 15 (1976), pp. 355–406; J. K. Louden and Jay Wayne Deagan, *Wage Incentives* (New York: John Wiley, 1959), pp. 25–28; Opsahl and Dunnette, *The Role of Financial Compensation in Industrial Motivation*, pp. 350–368.

45. Opsahl and Dunnette, *The Role of Financial Compensation in Industrial Motivation*.

46. Gary Yukl and Gary Latham, "Consequences of Reinforcement Schedules and Incentive Magnitudes for Employee Performance: Problems Encountered in an Industrial Setting," *Journal of Applied Psychology*, Vol. 60 (June 1975).

47. See Kenneth Scheflen, Edward E. Lawler III, and J. Richard Hackman, "Long Term Impact of Employee Participation in the Development of Pay Incentive Plans: A Field Experiment Revisited," *Journal of Applied Psychology*, Vol. 55 (1971), pp. 182–186; Edward F. Lawler III and J. Richard Hackman, "Impact of Employee Participation in the Development of Pay Incentive Plans: A Field Experiment," *Journal of Applied Psychology*, Vol. 53 (1969), pp. 467–471.

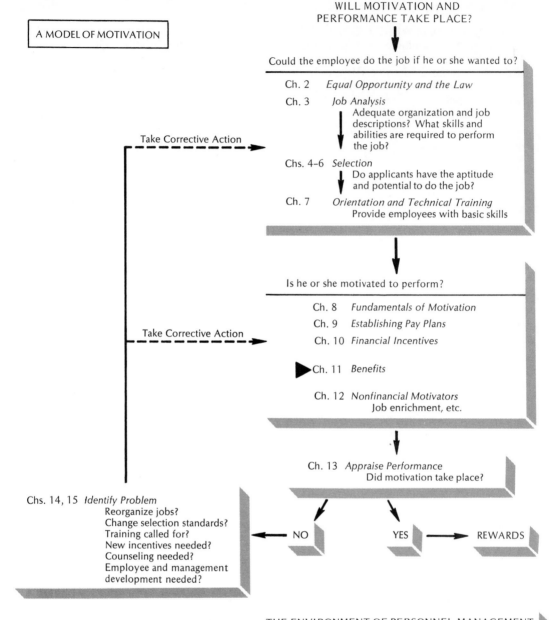

WILL MOTIVATION AND
PERFORMANCE TAKE PLACE?

A MODEL OF MOTIVATION

Could the employee do the job if he or she wanted to?

Ch. 2   *Equal Opportunity and the Law*

Ch. 3   *Job Analysis*
         Adequate organization and job
         descriptions? What skills and
         abilities are required to perform
         the job?

Take Corrective Action

Chs. 4–6 *Selection*
          Do applicants have the aptitude
          and potential to do the job?

Ch. 7   *Orientation and Technical Training*
         Provide employees with basic skills

Is he or she motivated to perform?

Ch. 8   *Fundamentals of Motivation*

Ch. 9   *Establishing Pay Plans*

Ch. 10   *Financial Incentives*

Take Corrective Action

Ch. 11   *Benefits*

Ch. 12   *Nonfinancial Motivators*
         Job enrichment, etc.

Ch. 13   *Appraise Performance*
         Did motivation take place?

Chs. 14, 15 *Identify Problem*
             Reorganize jobs?
             Change selection standards?
             Training called for?
             New incentives needed?
             Counseling needed?
             Employee and management
             development needed?

NO   YES   REWARDS

THE ENVIRONMENT OF PERSONNEL MANAGEMENT

Ch. 16 *Labor Relations and Grievances*

Ch. 17 *Employee Safety and Health*

Ch. 18 *Personnel Management and the
        Quality of Work Life*

When you finish studying

11   Benefits and Services

You should be able to:

1. *Explain the main features of at least ten employee benefit plans.*
2. *Cite the eight policy areas that must be considered in regard to vacations and holidays.*
3. *Cite the four key policy areas involved in pension plans.*
4. *Define vesting.*
5. *Discuss how employees' ages affect their choice of benefits.*
6. *Explain: the cafeteria approach, flextime, the four-day work week.*

OVERVIEW

The main purpose of this chapter is to explain the pros and cons of various employee benefit plans. We discuss four types of plans: supplemental pay benefits (such as unemployment insurance); insurance benefits (such as workmen's compensation); retirement benefits (such as pensions); and employee services (such as dining facilities). We explain that employees' preferences for various benefit plans differ, and that it's therefore useful to individualize an organization's benefit package. We therefore present three techniques for building flexibility into benefit plans (or "customizing them"); the "cafeteria" approach, flextime, and the four-day work week. Benefits and services are important rewards, and therefore influence employees' motivation. And (as we discuss in this chapter) employees' preferences for different benefits vary—with the employee's age, marital status, etc.—and so it's important to "customize" the benefits package to ensure that they contribute to improving performance at work.

INTRODUCTION

Financial incentives are usually paid to *specific* employees whose work is above standard. Employee benefits, on the other hand, are available to *all employees* based on their membership in the organization, (although the amount of the benefit may be in proportion to the importance of the job).

Administering benefits today represents an increasingly specialized and expensive task. It demands increased expertise because workers are becoming more sophisticated in financial matters (and are therefore demanding new types of benefits), and because federal legislation—concerning pregnancy benefits, for instance—requires that benefit plans comply with new laws. Partly as a result of these sorts of changes, partly as a result of increased competition among firms for qualified employees, and partly as a result of inflation (for instance, rising health care costs) benefit plans are also becoming increasingly expensive to administer. For example, benefit costs as a percentage of payroll rose from 22% in 1957 to 37% in 1977, according to a recent U.S. Chamber of Commerce survey, [1] and some predict that this figure could rise to 50% in the 1980s. [2] Benefits therefore represent a major expense for any organization, and an increasingly important area of concern for Personnel Management.

There are many benefit plans and to simplify this discussion, they are classified as: (1) pay supplements (for time not worked); (2) insurance benefits; (3) retirement benefits; and (4) services. Note, however, that embedded in each of these four categories are certain *legally required benefits* including unemployment insurance, social security, and workers' compensation.

SUPPLEMENTAL PAY BENEFITS (PAY FOR TIME NOT WORKED)

All employers provide "supplemental" pay benefits, benefits, in other words, for time not worked: these include unemployment insurance (if the person is laid off), vacation and holiday pay, sick pay, severance pay (if the person is terminated), and supplemental unemployment benefits (which guarantee income if the plant is closed down for a period).

Unemployment Insurance

All states have unemployment "insurance" or compensation acts. These provide for weekly payments if a person is unable to work through some fault other than his or her own. The benefits derive from an "unemployment tax" on employers that can range from 0.1% to 5% of taxable payroll in most states. States (to repeat) each have their own unemployment laws; however, these all follow federal guidelines. The organization's *unemployment tax* reflects its experience with personnel separations.

Reducing the Tax. Unemployment benefits are meant for workers who are terminated through no fault of their own and employers do therefore have the ability to reduce this unemployment tax burden. For example, a worker who is fired for chronic lateness or absenteeism may not have a legitimate claim to benefits. But in practice many managers—supervisors and personnel managers alike—have taken a lackadaisical attitude toward protecting themselves against unwarranted claims. They therefore end up spending thousands of dollars more per year on unemployment taxes than would be necessary if they protected themselves against such claims. One way an employer can protect himself against this is by establishing clearcut personnel policies concerning the disciplinary implications of matters such as lateness, absenteeism, leaves of absence, illness, and violation of company rules. Ideally, the employer protects himself best if he can show that the employee was forewarned and that an employee's termination was a result of his or her inadequate performance rather than lack of work or some other cause beyond the person's control.

Vacations and Holidays

Specific policies concerning holidays and vacations vary from organization to organization. Paid vacations may vary from one week per year to four weeks or more. Paid holidays may range from a minimum of four or five to as many as thirteen or more. But regardless of the organization, there are certain key personnel policy areas that must be addressed: [3]

Eligibility Requirements. The plan should specify the length of service required in order to earn vacations of one or more weeks. Some plans call for the employee to gradually accumulate vacation time: for example, one hour of vacation time for each week of service.

Vacation Pay. Some plans give the employee his or her regular base rate of pay while on vacation; others provide for vacation pay based on average earnings.

Earned Right. Some organizations provide for accrued vacation time which is paid if an employee leaves before taking his vacation.

With respect to *holidays,* key personnel policy areas include:

Number of Paid Holidays. This varies from a minimum of about five to thirteen or more. Some common holidays include:

New Year's Day	Veterans Day
Memorial Day	Thanksgiving Day
Independence Day	Friday after Thanksgiving
Labor Day	Christmas Day

Provision for Holidays on a Saturday or Sunday. Employees are often given the following Monday off when the holiday falls on a Sunday and Friday off when a holiday falls on a Saturday.

Premium Pay for Work on a Regular Holiday. Most organizations provide for some premium—such as time-and-a-half—to employees who work on a holiday.

Sick Leave

Sick leave provides an employee pay when he or she is out of work because of illness. Most sick leave policies grant full pay for a specified number of "permissible" sick days—usually up to about twelve per year. The so-called sick days are usually accumulated at the rate of, say, one day per month of service.

The number of sick days used per year per employee ranges up to 12 or more days in the United States, and organizations have developed some ingenious methods for reducing the costs associated with this much lost time. Most of these methods are based on the assumption that past methods of dealing with sick leave (namely, that if the worker was not "out sick" for the permissible 7 or 8 days per year, the days were forfeited) acted to encourage workers to take their days off. Today, therefore some new approaches are being tried. For example, there is a trend to "buy back" unused sick leave time, often by paying employees a daily equivalent for each sick day not used. [4] As another example, one electronics manufacturer instituted an incentive system in which all employees who had perfect attendance records—including no sick leave—for the month were eligible for a drawing and a cash prize; their names were also listed on the plant bulletin board as having a perfect attendance and punctuality record for that month. [5] Another scheme, this one aimed at reducing sick days taken among public employees in Plainview, Texas, seems to have effectively reduced sick leave per employee per year from about 3.6 to about 1.6 days. The Plainview plan involves paying $10 per day for each unused sick leave day that is not eligible for transfer to accumulated sick leave, not to exceed $60. In this way, some of the sick day payments that would normally be lost (not accumulated year to year) are returned to the employee as a bonus. [6] One drawback to any such approach, however, is that it can encourage honestly sick employees to come to work regardless of their illness. [7] Some employers also object to providing double payment simply to ensure that their employees report to work. [8]

Severance Pay

Some organizations provide a one-time payment when terminating an employee. The payment may range from three or four days' wages to as much as one year's salary. Such payments make sense on several grounds. It is a humanitarian gesture, as well as good public relations. In addition, most managers probably expect employees to give them at least one or two weeks notice if they plan to quit; it therefore seems appropriate to provide at least one or two weeks severance pay if an employee is being terminated.

Supplemental Unemployment Benefits

These benefits provide in effect for a "guaranteed annual income." In some industries (like auto making), shutdowns (to reduce inventories, or change machinery) are common, and in the past, employees here were laid off or "furloughed" and had to depend on unemployment insurance. Supplemental unemployment benefits are paid by the company and *supplement* unemployment benefits, thus enabling the workers to better maintain their standards of living. Supplemental benefits are becoming more prevalent in collective bargaining agreements and provide supplemental unemployment benefits (over and above state employment compensation) for three contingencies: layoffs, reduced work weeks, and relocation. These plans are normally found in heavy manufacturing operations such as in the auto and steel industries. Here, weekly or monthly plant shutdowns are typical, and some plan for guaranteeing minimum annual income is more appropriate.

INSURANCE BENEFITS

Workers' Compensation [9]

Workers' compensation laws are aimed at providing sure, prompt income and medical benefits to work accident victims or their dependents regardless of fault. [10] Every state has its own workers' compensation law. However, there has been continuing congressional interest in the past few years in establishing minimum national standards for state compensation laws, and this has provided an impetus for improving employer's job-related accident and illness benefits. These improvements have included expanded medical coverage, increased weekly benefits, and rehabilitation provisions. [11] Some states have their own insurance programs, but most require all employers to carry workers' compensation insurance with private, state-approved insurance companies.

Workers' compensation benefits can be either monetary or medical. In the event of a worker's death or disablement the person's dependents are paid a cash benefit based on prior earnings—usually one-half to two-thirds of the worker's average weekly wage, per week. In most states there is an established time limit—like 800 weeks—for which benefits can be paid. If the injury causes a specific loss (such as an arm) the employee may receive additional benefits based on a statutory list of losses, even though he may return to work. In addition to these cash benefits, employers must furnish medical, surgical, and hospital services needed by the employee.

For an injury or illness to be covered by workers' compensation, it is *only* necessary to prove that it arose while the employee was on the job. It does not matter that the employee may have been at fault: if he or she was on the job when the injury occurred, he or she is entitled to workers' compensation. For example, suppose all employees are instructed to wear safety goggles when working at their machines. One worker does not wear goggles and is injured while on the job. The company must still provide workers' compensation benefits: the fact that he was at fault in no way waives his claim to such benefits.

Workers' compensation is usually handled by state administrative commissions. However neither the state nor the federal government contributes any funds for workmen's compensation. *Employers* are responsible for insuring themselves or for arranging for the appropriate coverage through an insurance company.

　　　　Life Insurance

Most organizations provide group life insurance plans for their employees. Because it is a group plan it contains several important advantages for employers and employees. As a group, employees can generally obtain lower insurance rates than if they bought such insurance as individuals. And such group plans usually contain a provision for including all employees—including new ones—regardless of health or physical condition.

In most cases the organization pays 100% of the base premium, which usually provides life insurance equal to about 2 years' salary. Additional life insurance coverage is then paid for by the employee. In some cases the cost of even the base premium is split 50/50 or 80/20 between the employer and employee respectively. In general, there are three key personnel policy areas to be addressed: the benefits-paid schedule (benefits are usually tied to the annual earnings of the employee); supplemental benefits (continued life insurance coverage after retirement, double indemnity, etc.); and financing (the amount and percent that the employee contributes). [12]

　　　　Hospitalization, Medical, and Disability Insurance

Most organizations make available to their employees some type of hospitalization, medical, and disability insurance and, in fact, with life insurance, these types of benefits form the cornerstone of almost all benefit programs. [13] Hospitalization, health, and disability insurance is aimed at providing protection against hospitalization costs and loss of income arising from accidents or illness occurring from off-the-job causes. According to one survey, about 80% of all workers are covered by these benefits. [14] Most employers purchase such insurance from life insurance companies, casualty insurance companies, or from Blue Cross (for hospital expenses) and Blue Shield (for physician expenses) organizations.

There is a bewildering array of hospitalization, health, and disability insurance benefit options available to employers. Most health insurance plans provide, at a minimum, *basic hospitalization, surgical, and medical* insurance for all eligible employees as a group. As with life insurance, these group rates tend to be lower than individual rates and are generally available to all employees—including new ones—regardless of health or physical condition. Most basic plans pay for hospital room and board, surgery charges, and medical expenses (such as doctors' visits to the hospital). Some group plans also provide *major medical* coverage to meet high medical expenses that result from long-term or serious illnesses, and with hospitalization costs rapidly rising this is an increasingly popular option. [15] *Accidental death and dismemberment* coverage is another option. It provides a fixed lump sum benefit in addition to life insurance benefits when death is accidental, and also provides a range of benefits in case of accidental loss of limbs or sight. [16] *Other options* provide payments for diagnostic visits to the doctor's office, vision care, hearing aid plans, payment for prescription drugs, and dental care plans. *Disability insurance* is aimed at providing income protection or compensation for loss of salary due to illness or accident. The disability payments usually begin when normal sick leave is used up, and may continue to provide income to age 65 or beyond. [17] The disability benefits usually range from 50 to 75% of the employee's base pay, if he or she is disabled. The *Health Maintenance Organization* (HMO) Act of 1973 was aimed at stimulating a nationwide, prepaid health care system. Many employers now therefore offer membership in an HMO as a new hospital/medical option. The HMO itself is a medical organization consisting of a wide range of specialists (surgeons, psychiatrists, and so on). The HMO generally provides routine round-the-clock medical services at a specific site and usually stresses preventive medicine in a clinic-type arrangement to employees who pay a nominal fee. The HMO also receives a fixed annual fee per employee from the employer (or employer and employee) regardless of whether any service actually has to be provided.

The Pregnancy Discrimination Act. The Pregnancy Discrimination Act (PDA) is technically an amendment to Title VII of the Civil Rights Act, and became law in 1978. It is aimed at prohibiting sex discrimination based on "pregnancy, childbirth, or related medical conditions." [18] Before enactment of this law, temporary disability benefits for pregnancies were generally paid in the form of either sick leave or disability insurance, if at all. However, while most employers provide temporary disability income to their employees for up to 26 weeks for most illnesses, those that provided benefits for pregnancy usually limited the latter to only 6 weeks for normal pregnancies. Many believed that the relatively short duration of pregnancy benefits constituted discrimination based on sex, and it was this issue that the Pregnancy Discrimination Act was aimed at settling.

The act clarifies the fact that prohibitions against sex discrimination specifically include "but are not limited to" discrimination in employment based on "pregnancy, childbirth, or related medical conditions." Specifically, the act requires employers to treat women affected by pregnancy, childbirth, or related medical conditions the same as any employees not able to work, with respect to all benefits, including sick leave and disability benefits, and health and medical insurance. Thus, it is now illegal for most employers to discriminate against women by providing benefits of lower amount or duration for pregnancy, childbirth, or related medical conditions. For example, if an employer had provided up to 26 weeks of temporary disability income to employees for all illnesses, it is now required to also provide up to 26 weeks for pregnancy and childbirth, rather than the more typical 6 weeks that prevailed before the act. The act gave employers a short "grace period" after the enactment of PDA in which to comply: this grace period ended on April 29, 1979.

The act also had several other provisions. It prohibited an employer from reducing its benefits package for about a year after enactment of the act, in other words until the end of 1979. After this date, however, employers could reduce any or all benefits as long as such reductions are not discriminatory as defined by Title VII: in other words, after the "freeze" period an employer can reduce disability payments "across the board" to, say, six weeks, as long as it does so for everyone, men and women alike. Nothing in the act prevents employers from not increasing other benefits (either previously planned or unplanned) nor does the PDA require employers to offer any new benefits if they did not already have them as of the date of the enactment of the law.

RETIREMENT BENEFITS

Social Security

Many people assume that social security is something they only collect when they are old, when in fact it actually provides three types of benefits. First, there are the familiar "retirement" benefits. These provide the employee with an income if he or she retires at age 62 or thereafter *and* is insured under the Social Security Act. Second, there are "survivor's" or "death" benefits. These provide monthly payments to dependents regardless of the persons age at death, again assuming he or she was insured under the Social Security Act. Finally, there are "disability payments." These provide monthly payments to the employee and his or her dependents if the person becomes totally disabled for work and meets certain specified work requirements. [19] The Medicare program (which provides a wide range of health services to people 65 or over) is also administered through the Social Security system.

Social Security (technically "federal old age and survivor's insurance") is paid for by a tax on the employee's wages: employees and their employer share equally in this tax. Those self-employed pay the entire sum.

Pension Plans [20]

There are three basic types of pension plans. In the *group pension* plan, the organization (and possibly the employee) makes a set contribution to a pension fund. A second type of pension plan is actually a *deferred profit-sharing* plan. Here a certain percent of profits is credited to each employee's account. These benefits are then distributed to the employee (or his dependents) upon his retirement or death. Finally, under *savings plans*, employees set aside a fixed percentage of their weekly wages for their retirement; the company usually matches from 50 to 100% of the employees' contribution.

Various types of employee savings plans and "deferred compensation" are, in fact, becoming increasingly popular. An employee savings plan may (but need not) have as its main aim an assured retirement income. In most cases savings plans are actually for shorter range goals like paying college tuition. But whether used for a pension or some other goal, all savings plans encourage systematic savings by employees, with two added incentives: (1) the employer usually matches employees' contributions; and (2) income tax deferral. Contributions to the plan are made by employees from after-tax earnings and these are partially or fully matched by the employer, who typically contributes 50¢ for each $1.00 contributed by the employee. [21] From the point of view of the employer, contributions are immediately tax deductible and in some cases company stock rather than cash can be used as the employer's contribution, thus giving employees stock ownership in the company. From the point of view of the employee, the employer's matching contributions are not taxed as income when made and investment income (such as interest on invested funds) are tax deferred, so that taxes on this income need not be paid until the employee receives his or her cash payment. If the payment occurs after retirement the tax savings to the employee can be substantial, since in most cases the person is then in a much lower tax bracket.

Related to this, the Revenue Act of 1978 makes *voluntary deferred compensation plans* another attractive pension option. [22] Particularly those employees in the highest tax brackets can accumulate income, tax free, during the deferral period and realize a greater return on their money than if the income were paid currently and taxed each year. [23] In the typical deferred compensation plan an irrevocable agreement to defer payment of a set amount of compensation must be made *prior to* the rendering of services by the executive. The compensation to be deferred each year as well as any income earned on the resulting investment are then not taxed until the person finally receives payment.

The entire area of pension planning is an extremely complicated one, partly because of the many federal laws governing pensions. For example, companies want to ensure that their pension contributions are tax deductible and it is therefore necessary to adhere to the pertinent income tax codes. As discussed in Chapter 9 the Employee Retirement Income Security Act of 1974 (ERISA) also restricts what employers can, cannot, and must do in regard to pension plans (more on this in a moment). In unionized companies, the union must be allowed to participate in the administration of the pension plan (under the Taft–Hartley Act).

While an employer usually has to develop a pension plan to meet its own unique needs, there are several key policy issues that must be considered: [24]

Membership Requirements. For example, what is the minimum age or minimum service at which employees become eligible for a pension?

Benefit Formula. This usually ties the pension to the employee's final earnings, or an average of his or her last three or four years' earnings.

Retirement Requirements. Although 65 is often considered a standard retirement age, the mandatory retirement age law of 1978 prohibits forced retirement of any competent employee under 70 years of age. Yet while this seems to suggest that the average age of those employed will be rising, the opposite seems to be the case and the reason is that most people opt for early retirement. [25] In companies like General Motors, IBM, and General Foods, for example, a relatively small proportion of production and office workers retire as late as 65. [26] Partly due to union pressure and partly to the assumption that early retirement may open more jobs for younger employees, many employers now provide for early retirement. For example, some plans call for "30 and out." This permits an employee to retire after 30 years of continuous service, regardless of the person's age. In some cases—such as in the U.S. Army, and among New York city employees—employees can retire with reduced pensions after 20 years of continuous service, regardless of the employee's age. [27]

Funding. The question of how the plan is to be funded is another key issue. One aspect of this is whether the plan will be contributory or non-contributory. In the former, contributions to the pension funds are made by both employees and the employer. In a noncontributory fund—the prevailing type, by the way—only the employer contributes. Another aspect of this is that many pension plans are underfunded. Although under the Employee Retirement Security Act most pension plans are now "guaranteed" (as explained below), the fact of the matter is that in an alarming number of cases many employers' pension funds do not have adequate funds to cover expected pension benefits. [28]

Vesting is another critical issue in pension planning. It refers to the money that the employer and employee have placed in the latter's pension fund *which cannot be forfeited for any reason.* Naturally, the employees' contributions are always theirs, and cannot be forfeited. However, until the passage of ERISA in 1974, the employer's contribution was not necessarily vested. Thus, suppose a person worked for a company for 30 years, and it then went out of business one year before he or she was to retire at age 65. Unless that employee's rights to the company's pension contributions were *vested*—due to a union agreement or company policy, for instance,—he might well find himself with no pension. [29]

ERISA: As a reaction to problems like these, the Employee Retirement Income Security Act (ERISA) was signed into law by President Ford in 1974. [30]

Debate regarding regulation of pension funds had actually began in 1965, at which time private retirement plans covered some 25 million workers. At that time plans were paying nearly $2.75 billion annually in benefits to almost 2½ million beneficiaries, and had accumulated reserves in excess of $75 billion. By the end of 1974 (when ERISA was enacted) the assets of all private pension plans were close to $200 billion, and today over 35 million workers are covered by private retirement ("pension") plans. ERISA was aimed at protecting the interests of these workers and in stimulating the growth of pension plans.

Before enactment of ERISA, pension plans often failed to deliver expected benefits to employees. For example, when the Studebaker Auto Company went out of business in 1964, it terminated its pension plan: this left nearly 8,500 participants with either sharply reduced benefits or none at all. Any number of reasons—business failure, inadequate funding, etc.—could result in employees losing their expected pensions.

Under ERISA pension rights *must* be vested under one of three formulas: [31]

1. 100% vesting after ten years of service.
2. 25% vesting after five years, increasing 5% a year to 50% vesting after ten years, and by 10% a year to 100% vesting after 15 years.

3. 50% vesting after five years of service if the employee's age and years of
   service total 45 (or after ten years of service if less), and increasing by 10%
   a year thereafter.

Among other things, the Pension Benefits Guarantee Corporation (PBGC)
was established under ERISA to assure that pensions meet vesting obligations,
and the PBGC insures pensions should a plan terminate without sufficient
funds to meet its vested obligations. (And, in fact, unfunded pension liabilities
of American firms have continued to grow. For 100 major U.S. companies unfunded vested benefits rose almost 14% in 1979, for instance. In many firms,
in fact, unfunded vested benefits—for which separate funds have not been set
aside—approach the total net worth of the companies. Unfunded vested liabilities
equaled 117% of the net worth of Lockeed in 1979, 87% at LTV, 66% at
Chrysler, and 46% at Bethlehem Steel, for instance.) [32] Furthermore, under
section 404 (A) of ERISA those responsible for administering the pension plan
are obligated to do so "solely in the interests of the participant and beneficiary;
and . . . with the care, skill, prudence, and diligence under the circumstances
that a prudent man . . ." would be expected to use. [33]

Pensions and the Problem of Inflation. [34]   The purchasing power of retirees' pensions has been declining rapidly in recent years as a result of inflation
and lengthened retiree life expectancy. The rate of inflation has risen from
about 1% per year in the first half of the 1960s to about 7% per year in 1970,
and in 1980 approached 18% per year. While economists' opinions vary, it
appears that relatively high rates of inflation will persist well into the 1980s.
For retirees on a fixed income—and most pension plans pay a "defined benefit"
which does fix the amount to be paid—increasing prices result in less purchasing
power and, perhaps, in a lower standard of living. Related to this, the life
expectancy of retirees has been increasing, and as a result retirement benefits
are exposed to inflationary erosion for longer periods of time. This can obviously
be an unfortunate state of affairs for retirees (who see their purchasing power
dwindling), and for employers (who find inflation destroying the effectiveness
of their pension plans). Employers worry, for instance, that as employees become
aware of how inflation is reducing the value of their retirement benefits, those
benefits become less useful for attracting and holding good employees.

Inflation is also undermining the *equitableness* of many pension plans. Most
pension plans are designed to complement social security payments in such a
way that each retiree receives about the same *percentage* of his or her preretirement earnings. (Such plans are referred to as being integrated with social
security.) Therefore, since social security benefits are limited, higher-paid employees are expected to receive a much larger proportion of their pension from
the pension plan than are lower-paid employees. For example, a higher-paid
employee might obtain, at retirement, 75% or his or her (relatively high) pension from the pension plan and 25% from social security, while a lower-paid
employee receives the opposite—25% from the pension, and 75% from social
security. The aim of all this is to provide equitable benefits for all employees,

where "equitable" is defined as each employee receiving, on retirement, about the same percentage of his or her preretirement annual income.

The problem is that while social security payments have been boosted several times over the past few years, pension plan payments (which are "defined" or set ahead of time) usually have not. As a result, a lower-paid employee (who thus received a larger proportion of his or her retirement income from social security) was *not* as adversely affected by inflation (in terms of purchasing power) as was a higher-paid employee, most of whose retirement income consisted of a "frozen" pension component. [35]

As a result of these problems many employers are now providing post retirement increases in benefits payments. They are, in other words, increasing the pension payments made to former, retired employees. For example, a study by the Bankers Trust Company of 190 of the largest employers in the United States showed that 79% of the companies surveyed had granted a post retirement increase since 1969. [36] The study also found that 40% of the firms had granted more than one increase. A similar survey conducted by the Wyatt Company showed that 39% of the companies responding to the pertinent portion of its survey had given a post retirement increase during 1976. [37] On the whole, these surveys ". . . indicate a growing awareness among employers of the need for post retirement increases to preserve the value of their retirement plans. [38]

EMPLOYEE SERVICES BENEFITS

While an employer's insurance and retirement benefits usually account for the major portion of its benefits costs, most employers also provide a range of employee services including:

Stock purchase plans

Credit Unions

Food Services

Educational opportunities and subsidies

Social and recreational activities

Counseling

Legal services

Moving and/or transfer allowance, and

Childcare [39]

First, many companies provide service benefits in the form of *basic* services that most employees need at one time or another: these include credit unions, legal services, counseling, and social and recreational opportunities. *Credit unions* are usually separate businesses that are established with the assistance of the employer. Employees can typically become members of a credit union by purchasing a share of the credit union's stock for $5 or $10. Members can then deposit savings that accrue interest at a rate determined by the credit union's Board of Directors. And, perhaps more important to most employees, loan eligibility and the rate of interest paid on the loan are generally much more favorable than those found in financial institutions like banks and finance companies. Employers are also providing an increasing range of *counseling services* to employees. These include financial counseling (for example, in terms of how to overcome existing indebtedness problems), family counseling (covering marital problems, and so on), career counseling (in terms of analyzing one's aptitudes and deciding on a career), "out-placement" counseling (for helping terminated or disenchanted employees find new jobs), and preretirement counseling (aimed at preparing retiring employees for what many find is the "trauma" of retiring). Many employers also make available to employees a full range of legal counseling through legal insurance plans. In the "open panel" legal plan, employees can choose their own attorney and then be reimbursed according to the fee schedule in the policy. In the "closed panel" legal plan, employees are required to use one of a number of specified attorneys, who are paid directly by the insurance plan. Finally, some employers also provide a wide range of social and *recreational opportunities* for its employees including company-sponsored athletic events, dancing clubs, annual summer picnics, craft activities, and parties.

Job related services (like assistance in moving) that are aimed directly at helping employees perform their jobs constitute a second group of services. For example, *food services* are provided in some form by most employers and enable employees to purchase meals, snacks, or coffee, usually at relatively favorable prices. Most food operations are nonprofit and, in fact some firms provide food services below cost: the advantages to the employee are clear, and for the employer it can mean ensuring that employees do not drift away for long lunch hours. Even employers who do not provide full dining facilities generally make available food services like "coffee wagons" or vending machines. As the number of families in which both parents work has increased, *child care facilities* have become a more popular service. Where successful, the facility itself is usually close to the workplace (often in the same building) and the employer provides 50 to 75% of the operating cost. Finally, while many employers are trying to reduce the number of employee transfers (to provide employees—particularly executives—with a more stable life style in terms of "setting down roots") most are also providing a number of moving/transfer services aimed at minimizing the trauma of the move. For example, employers typically pay the cost of moving the household goods and family, and increasingly provide financial assistance in selling the previous residence and buying the new one. In many cases, companies will actually buy the old residence, if necessary, and provide mortgages at favorable interest rates for new ones.

As mentioned earlier, many employers also establish various types of employee *stock purchase plans*. These plans can both encourage thrift on the part of employees and also stimulate increased employee identification with the company through ownership. In some plans employees are encouraged to purchase

314 shares of company stock at or below market price through weekly or monthly payroll deductions. In other cases employee stock ownership plans—"ESOPs"— are established by the company. Here the company can borrow from a financial institution using the company's stock as collateral and the loan payments then become tax deductible. As the loan is repaid the stock used as collateral is placed into an employee stock ownership trust for distribution at no cost to all employees: the stock in turn becomes part of an employee profit sharing or retirement program.

Educational subsidies like tuition refunds have long been a popular benefit for employees seeking to complete their high school education, for those in college or university programs, or for those interested in some type of vocational-technical program. The educational subsidies may range from total payment of all tuition and expenses to some percentage (50 to 75%), to a flat fee per year of, say $250 to $300. Some companies, like Eastern Airlines have experimented with providing "in-house" college programs like Master of Business Administration programs in which college faculty teach courses on the employers' premises. Other in-house educational programs include remedial work in basic literacy, training for improving leadership skills, and training aimed at improving one's job opportunities.

EMPLOYEES' PREFERENCES FOR VARIOUS BENEFITS

Two researchers carried out a study that provides some useful insights into employees' preferences for various benefits. [40] They mailed questionnaires covering seven possible benefit options to 400 employees of a midwest public utility company. Properly completed questionnaires were received from 149 employees (about 38% of those surveyed). The seven benefit options were as follows:

1. A five-day work week with shorter working days of 7 hours and 35 minutes.
2. A four-day work week consisting of 9 hours and 30 minutes each day.
3. Ten Fridays off each year with full pay. This includes 10 three-day weekends per year, in addition to any three-day weekends previously scheduled.
4. Early retirement through accumulating ten days per year until retirement age. The retirement age will be 65 minus the number of accumulated days. Full pay will continue until age 65 is reached.
5. Additional vacation of two weeks per year with full pay. The additional vacation will be added to the present vacation.
6. A pension increase of $75 per month.
7. Family dental insurance. The company will pay the entire cost of family dental insurance.

Finally, employees were also asked to show their relative preference for a *pay increase of 5%*, in addition to any general wage increase negotiated.

Results

Overall results are presented in Exhibit 11.1. Note that two extra weeks of vacation was clearly the most preferred benefit while the pay increase was second in preference. Overall, the shorter work day was by far the least preferred benefit option.

Exhibit 11.1   Preference for Compensation Options

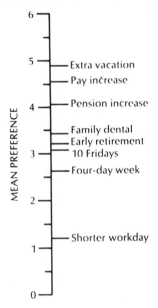

But this is not the full story: as you can see in Exhibit 11.2, the employee's age, marital status, and sex influenced his or her choice of benefits. For example, younger employees were significantly more in favor of the *family dental plan* than were older employees. Younger employees also showed a greater preference for the *four-day work week*. As might be expected, preference for the *pension* option increased significantly with employee age. Married workers showed more preference for the *pension* increase and for the family dental plan than did single workers. The preference for the family dental plan increased sharply as the number of dependents increased.

Implications

The expectancy model of motivation (as explained in Chapter 8) holds that employees will be motivated to obtain rewards only if they view the rewards as attractive. From this study it is apparent that factors like the worker's age, marital status, and sex affect which rewards (in terms of benefits) he or she

Exhibit 11.2 Preferences for Various Benefits, by Type of Employer

PART A

Mean Employee Preference by Age, Marital Status and Sex

Option	Age in Years			Marital Status		Sex	
	18-35 (N=52)	36-49 (N=58)	50-65 (N=39)	Single (N=52)	Married (N=97)	Males (N=114)	Females (N=35)
Extra Vacation	5.00	4.67	5.21	4.86	4.88	4.90	5.07
Pay Increase	4.70	4.71	4.09	4.68	4.34	4.56	4.03
Pension Increase	3.00	4.08	5.59	3.56	4.23	4.08	4.63
Dental Plan	4.35	3.69	1.71	2.78	3.91	3.75	2.30
Early Retirement	2.81	3.48	3.65	3.20	3.32	3.38	3.41
10 Fridays	3.19	2.67	3.48	3.20	3.04	3.02	3.44
Four-Day Week	3.63	2.67	2.26	3.06	2.73	2.92	2.56
Shorter Workday	1.23	1.42	1.47	1.54	1.19	1.28	1.74

1 is low, 5 is high

PART B

Mean Employee Preference by Number of Dependents, Years of Service, and Job Title

Option	Dependents			Years of Service			Job Title	
	0 (N=33)	1-3 (N=60)	4 or more (N=56)	0-10 (N=48)	11-20 (N=63)	21 or more (N=38)	Clerical (N=48)	Operating (N=101)
Extra Vacation	4.72	4.93	4.97	4.77	4.86	4.87	5.00	4.81
Pay Increase	4.79	4.40	4.44	4.56	4.30	4.76	4.70	4.37
Pension Increase	4.67	4.42	3.32	3.41	3.70	5.47	4.15	3.97
Dental Plan	1.79	3.03	4.93	4.47	3.53	2.07	2.70	3.86
Early Retirement	3.64	3.30	3.07	2.52	3.51	3.89	3.09	3.38
10 Fridays	3.48	2.97	3.05	3.37	2.97	3.03	3.48	3.38
Four-Day Week	2.67	2.60	3.30	3.40	3.24	1.63	2.48	2.93
Shorter Workday	1.94	1.28	.96	.97	1.33	1.68	1.63	1.17

1 is low, 5 is high

views as most desirable. One implication is that it seems advisable for organizations to attempt to determine employee's preferences concerning various benefits, and to individualize their benefit plans. Ironically (in most organizations), benefit plans are designed to apply equally to all employees, irrespective of differences in individual preferences. [41] Three methods for building flexibility into benefit plans are discussed next.

FLEXIBLE BENEFITS PLANS

Because employees do have different preferences for benefits, some employers have attempted to individualize their benefit plans. [42]

The "Cafeteria" Approach

One example of this is the *cafeteria benefit plan*. This enables employees to pick and choose from available options and literally develop their own benefit plans. Right now these cafeteria plans are used mostly for management employees, but there seems no doubt their use will spread to nonmanagers as well.

The basic idea of such plans is to allow the employee to put together his or her own benefit plan, subject to two constraints. First, the organization has to carefully set total cost limits. (This limits what it will spend for each total benefit package.) Second, each benefit plan must include certain *non*optional items. These include, for example, social security, workmen's compensation, and, unemployment insurance.

Subject to these two constraints, employees can pick and choose from the available options. Thus, a young married employee might opt for the company's life and dental insurance plans, while an older employee opts for an improved pension plan. The list of possible options can be quite long and would probably include many of the benefits discussed in this chapter: vacations, insurance benefits, pension plans, educational services, etc.

Building this type of individual choice into a benefit plan can obviously be advantageous, but there are also disadvantages. The main problem is that the implementation of a cafeteria plan can involve substantial clerical and administrative costs. Each employee's benefits have to be carefully priced out and updated periodically and even a medium-sized company would undoubtedly have to use a computer to administer such a plan. [43]

Current Use.   While cafeteria plans have received much "press," their use today is limited to only a handful of companies. [44] Several large companies, including the systems group of TRW Corporation, the Educational Testing Service, and American Can Company, have established cafeteria plans.

TRW began by making a survey aimed at estimating how many of its people would choose different benefits. The plan was implemented in late 1974. It covers all 12,000 employees and requires each to take minimum levels of certain benefits: they can then choose which additional benefits they want. (For example, the plan provides 4 separate hospital insurance plans.) The plan appears to have been successful. For example, when the plan was implemented, over 80% of the employees took advantage of the "options" feature and changed their benefits packages. However, it is important to keep in mind that several years of preparation went into gearing up for the cafeteria plan, and it is presently supported by an extensive computer software package.

Flextime

Flextime [45] is another recent approach to individualizing benefits. Here, employees built a flexible work day around a central core of mid-day hours—such as 11 to 2. It is called "flextime" because workers determine their own starting and stopping hours. For example, they may opt to work from 7 to 3, or 11 to 7. As of 1977 about 13% of all U.S. organizations were using this approach. This was roughly 6% of the work force, not counting professionals, managers, salespeople, and self-employed persons, who also customarily set their own hours. [46]

On the whole, flextime programs have been quite successful from the employer's point of view. [47] Because less time is lost due to tardiness, the ratio of manhours worked to manhours paid, a measure of productivity, increases. It has also been shown to reduce absenteeism and to cut down on "sick" leave being used for personal matters. The hours actually worked seem to be more productive, and there is less slowing down toward the end of the work day. Workers tend to leave early when work is slack and work later when it is heavy. Furthermore, surveys covering some 445 organizations including drug companies, banks, electronics firms, and government agencies indicate that the percentage of employees reporting productivity increases as a result of flextime programs ranged from a low of 5 or 10%, to about 95% in one airline. On the whole, about 45% of employees involved in flextime programs report that the program has resulted in improved productivity. [48] The failure rate of flextime is reportedly remarkably low—8% is estimated in one study. [49]

Flextime is also advantageous from the worker's point of view, and this is reflected in both the reported productivity increases as well as in the fact that flextime programs "almost always raised employee morale." [50] It may reduce the tedium associated with the timing of employee's work and democratize their work, by giving them more discretion concerning their comings and goings. Flextime may also bring about better managerial practices, particularly at the supervisory level, by requiring a change from a negative, controlling style to a positive, less restrictive style on the part of supervisors: flextime, in other words, represents a shift toward self-management from the point of view of the employee. [51]

There are also some disadvantages. Flextime is complicated to administer and may be impossible to implement where large groups of workers must work interdependently—in other words, where they must all be present at the same time to complete some tasks. [52] It may also require the use of time clocks or other time records and this can be disadvantageous from the point of view of workers, particularly those not accustomed to using these devices. Another, more technical problem can arise when flextime is extended beyond the employer's normal 5-day, 40-hour (or 37½-hour) work week. [53] Specifically, some flextime programs include an option to debit and credit work hours. For example, an employee might decide to work 45 hours one week and "bank" the extra hours so that he or she need work only 35 hours in some future week. Similarly, an employee might choose to work 6 hours one day and 10 hours some other day. However, the Fair Labor Standards Act, (and the Walsh-Healy Act for government contractors) requires overtime pay for time worked in excess of 8 hours a day or 40 hours a week. Thus, an employee who works 35 hours one week and 45 hours the following week would still have to be compensated *at a time-and-a-half rate* for 5 hours the second week regardless of the fact that only 35 hours was worked the previous week. Some companies have handled this problem by establishing personnel policies that state that work hours may vary from day to day as long as a work day does not exceed 8 hours and a work week more than 40 hours. Others have experimented with letting employees reduce their work week by 1 or 2 hours one week and increase their hours 1 or 2 hours (at overtime rates) the following week. In April 1979, President Carter signed a bill permitting certain federal agencies to relax overtime pay requirements where full-time employees elect to work in excess of 8 hours a day or 40 hours a week, and this may lead to renewed efforts in the private sector to obtain greater flexibility in the use of flextime. [54]

There are several conditions necessary for the successful implementation of a flextime program. [55] The first is that the employer understand that it can not view flextime as a panacea, or pin all its hopes on improving, say, productivity, through one device like flextime. Second, management resistance—particularly at the supervisory level and particularly before the program is actually tried—has torpedoed several programs before they have become operational. Third, the research indicates a tendency for flextime to be more successful with clerical, professional, and managerial jobs, and less so with factory jobs (the nature of which tend to demand interdependence among workers). Fourth, experience indicates that the greater the flexibility of the flextime program, the greater the benefits the program can produce. Finally, how the program is installed is also important. An internal flextime project director to oversee all aspects of the program should be appointed and frequent meetings should take place between supervisors and employees to allay their fears and clear up misunderstandings. A pilot study say, in one department, is advisable.

Four-Day Work Weeks

A number of organizations in North America and Europe have switched to a four-day work week. Here, employees work four ten-hour days instead of the more usual five eight-hour days. [56]

Advantages. Four-day work week plans have been fairly successful since they have several advantages. Productivity appears to increase in response to reduced startup and shutdown times. Workers are often more willing to work some evenings and Saturdays as part of these plans. According to a study by the American Management Association, 80% of the firms on such plans reported that the plan "improves business results"; three-fifths said that production was up and almost two-fifths said that costs were down. Half the firms also reported higher profits. Even the "four-day firms" *not* reporting positive results reported that cost and profit factors at least remained the same. A study by the Bureau of Labor Statistics suggests that the four-day work week *is* generally effective (in terms of reducing paid overtime, reducing absenteeism, and improving efficiency). Furthermore, workers also gain. There is a 20% reduction in commuter trips and an additional "free day" per week. Additional savings (for example in childcare expenses) may also occur.

Keep in mind, though, that there has not been a lot of experience with shortened work weeks, and it is possible that the improvements are short lived. In one study, for example, four-day (40 hour) weeks resulted in greater employee satisfaction and productivity, and less absenteeism when evaluated after 13 months, but these improvements were *not* found after 25 months. [57]

Disadvantages. There are also some disadvantages, some of them potentially quite severe. *Tardiness*, for example, may become a problem. Of more concern is the fact that *fatigue* was cited by a number of firms as a principal disadvantage of the four-day work week (excessive fatigue was the major reason for adopting eight-hour days in the first place). Furthermore, the implications of the extended work day and its impact on family life are at this point is unknown.

SUMMARY

1. The financial *incentives* discussed are paid to specific employees whose work is above standard. Employee *benefits*, on the other hand, are available to *all* employees based on their membership in the organization. We discussed four types of benefit plans: pay supplements, insurance, retirement benefits, and services.

2. Supplemental pay benefits are pay for time not worked. They include unemployment insurance, vacation and holiday pay, severance pay, and supplemental unemployment benefits.

3. Insurance benefits are another type of employee benefit. Workers' compensation, for example, is aimed at ensuring prompt income and medical benefits to work-accident victims or their dependents regardless of fault. Most employers also provide group life insurance and group hospitalization, accident, and disability insurance.

4. Two types of retirement benefits were discussed: social security and pensions. Social security does not just cover "retirement" benefits, but survivors and disability benefits as well. There are three basic types of pension plans: group, deferred profit sharing, and savings plans. One of the critical issues in pension planning involves *vesting*—the money that employer and employee have placed in the latter's pension fund which cannot be forfeited for any reason. ERISA basically ensures that pension rights become vested and protected after a reasonable amount of time.

5. Most employers also provide benefits in the form of employee services. These include food services, recreational opportunities, legal advice, credit unions, and counseling.

6. Surveys suggest two conclusions regarding employee's preferences for benefits. First, *overall*, time off (like two extra weeks vacation) seems to be the most preferred benefit. Second, the employee's age, marital status, and sex clearly influence his or choice of benefits. (For example, younger employees were significantly more in favor of the family dental plan than were older employees.) This suggests the need for individualizing the organization's benefit plans.

7. There are three techniques for building flexibility and individuality into an organization's benefit plans. The *cafeteria approach* allows the employee to put together his or her own benefit plan, subject to total cost limits and the inclusion of certain nonoptional items. Several firms have installed cafeteria plans; they require considerable planning and computer assistance. With *"flextime"* the workers are allowed to determine their own starting and stopping hours (around a central core of midday hours). Flextime has been shown to reduce absenteeism and to cut down on "sick" leave. The *four-day work week* has rather consistently been shown to increase productivity and profits—at least in the short run; however, the long-term effects of fatigue on workers and the effects of the new plan on family life are unknown at this time.

8. Benefits and services are important components in performance. Herzberg, for example, found that if such "extrinsic" rewards were not at least adequate, workers become dissatisfied and difficult to motivate.

Allison Mazy*

Ron Pritchard, a boyish looking thirty-four, had been recently promoted from a district office to an attractive management position in the company's home office. His new job consisted of coordinating the efforts of twenty-five employees who dealt with the acquisition and retention of land for geological purposes. The men in the office were almost all licensed attorneys and ranged in age from about twenty-nine to fifty-five. Primarily their jobs were limited to the confines of the office, but to some extent they went into the field directly to negotiate rights to tracts of land and to enter their bids for government-owned lands.

The oldest employee, in point of tenure within Ron's office, was Allison Mazy. Mazy had been with the firm for thirty-three years, having risen from a filing clerk to his present $15,500-a-year job without the benefit of a college education. Through the years he had become extremely knowledgeable of the company's filing system (having been instrumental in redesigning it four times); he was almost always consulted when there was difficulty in locating an item in the files. In his dealings with subordinates (secretaries, clerks, etc.) Allison was most demanding, in fact to the point of being considered a tyrant by some of his subordinates. Thus, most of the employees who had occasion to serve Allison were quite fearful of him yet seemingly delighted by his keen wit, thorough knowledge, and complete devotion to his wife, children, and grandchildren.

At the end of his first seven weeks in his position, Ron concluded that Allison was definitely a disruptive influence on the office. During this time, Allison had failed to come to work for one seven-day period, four two-day stretches, and had missed five out of the seven Mondays. In each case the reason given was illness. Allison would call one of the women in the office and say he would not be in due to a dental problem, a sprained foot, or a sore back. On the Fridays he did come to work, it had become almost a joke with the other employees about whether he would return the following Monday. Some had even spoken about forming an office pool on the probability of Mazy's coming to work on a given Monday.

After a great internal debate, Ron decided to confront Allison with his apparent abuse of the company sick leave policy and called him to his office the next morning. Allison remained apparently calm and unconcerned as Ron detailed his view of and concern about Allison's absences. But, when Ron asked him to reply, he did, telling Ron bluntly that he had worked long and hard for the company and knew more about it than all the rest of them put together, even if they were "college boys!" Then rising from his chair, he told Ron that, if he wouldn't allow

---

* Arno F. Knapper, *Cases in Personnel Management* (Columbus, Ohio: Grid, Inc., 1977), pp. 30–31.

him time off for his sicknesses after all of his years of devotion to the company, then he could fire him! With this he departed the office leaving Ron in stunned silence. Collecting his wits, Ron pondered whether to approach his superior with the problem, continue to ignore it, or do what Allison had seemingly dared him to do.

1. What are the intent and purpose of sick leave?
2. What might be considered an abuse of sick leave?
3. Evaluate Allison's position of indignation expressed at the end of his conversation with Ron.
4. How should Ron proceed with the problem of Allison's absences?

DISCUSSION QUESTIONS

1. You are applying for a job as a manager, and are at the point of negotiating salary and benefits. What questions would you ask your prospective employer concerning benefits? Describe the benefit package you would try to negotiate for yourself.
2. Explain how you would go about minimizing your organization's unemployment insurance tax.
3. Explain how ERISA protects employees' pension rights.
4. In this chapter we presented findings concerning the preferences by age, marital status, and sex for various benefits. Basically, what were these findings and how would you make use of them if you were a personnel manager?

NOTES

1. William White and James Becker, "Increasing the Motivational Impact of Employee Benefits," *Personnel* (Jan.–Feb. 1980), pp. 32–37.
2. Paul Greenlaw and Diana Foderora, "Some Implications of the Pregnancy Discrimination Act," *Personnel Journal* (October 1979), p. 680.
3. Robert E. Sibson, *Wages and Salaries: A Handbook for Line Managers* (New York: American Management Association, 1967), pp. 236–237.
4. Richard Henderson, *Compensation Management*, (Reston, Va.: Reston Publishing, 1979), p. 328.
5. Jerry Wallin and Ronald Johnson, "The Positive Reinforcement Approach to Controlling Employee Absenteeism," *Personnel Journal* (August 1976), pp. 390–392.
6. Steve Panyan and Michael McGregor, "How to Implement a Proactive Incentive Plan: A Field Study," *Personnel Journal* (Sept. 1976), pp. 460–462.
7. Henderson, p. 328.
8. For a discussion of administering sick leave where many part time employees are involved see Patrick Towle, "Calculating Sick Leave and Vacation with an Hourly Accrual System," *Personnel Journal* (May 1979), pp. 303–305.
9. Famularo, *Handbook*, pp. 51.1–51.12.
10. Henderson, p. 250.
11. Henderson, 1979, p. 90.
12. Sibson, *Wages and Salaries*, p. 235.
13. Henderson, p. 323.

324   14. A. N. Nash and S. J. Carroll, Jr., "Supplemental Compensation," from *The Management of Compensation*, reprinted in Herbert Heneman III and Donald Schwab, *Perspectives on Personnel/Human Resource Management* (Homewood: Irwin, 1978), pp. 219–226.

15. Nash and Carroll, p. 223.

16. Henderson, p. 324.

17. Nash and Carroll, p. 223.

18. This is based on Paul Greenlaw and Diana Foderaro, "Some Practical Implications of the Pregnancy Discrimination Act," *Personnel Journal* (Oct. 1979), pp. 677–681.

19. Jerome B. Cohen and Arthur Hanson, *Personal Finance* (Homewood, Ill.: Richard D. Irwin, 1964), pp. 312–320.

20. See Henderson, *Compensation Management*, pp. 289–290; Famularo, *Handbook*, pp. 37.1–37.9.

21. Edward Katz, "The Unsung Benefits of Employee Savings Plans," *Personnel Journal* (Jan. 1979), pp. 30 & 31.

22. See Edward Redling, "Voluntary Deferred Compensation—Off Again, On Again," *Personnel* (1979), pp. 64–67.

23. Quoted from Edward Redling, "Voluntary Deferred Compensation. . . ."

24. Sibson, *Wages and Salaries*, p. 234.

25. For a discussion of demographic trends with specific reference to average age of employees see, for example, D. Quinn Mills, "Human Resources in the 1980's," *Harvard Business Review* (July–August 1979), pp. 154–163.

26. *The Economist* (August 5, 1978), p. 57; as discussed in George Strauss and Leonard Sayles, *Personnel: The Human Problems of Management* (Englewood Cliffs: Prentice-Hall, 1980), p. 606.

27. For a discussion of the pros and cons of early retirement see, for example, Jeffrey Sonnenfeld, "Dealing with the Aging Workforce" *Harvard Business Review* (Nov.–Dec. 1978), pp. 81–92.

28. A. F. Ehrbar, "Those Pension Plans Are Even Weaker Than You Think," *Fortune*, Vol. 94, No. 5 (Nov. 1977), pp. 104–107; discussed in H. Chruden and A. Sherman Jr., *Personnel Management* (Cincinnati: Southwestern, 1980), pp. 500–501.

29. See also Irwin Tepper, "Risk vs. Return in Pension Fund Investment," *Harvard Business Review* (March–April 1977), pp. 100–107; William Buppert, "Erisa: Compliance May Be Easier Than You Expect and Pay Unexpected Dividends," *Personnel Journal* (April 1976).

30. Robert Paul, "The Impact of Pension Reform on American Business," *Sloan Management Review*, Vol. 18 (Fall 1976), pp. 59–71.

31. Henderson, *Compensation Management*, p. 292.

32. "Pension Survey: Unfunded Liabilities Continue to Grow," *Business Week*: August 25, 1980, pp. 94–97.

33. For an explanation of several "prudent" pension plan alternatives aimed at complying with this situation, see, for example, Paul Greenlaw and Robert Monske, "ERISA and Prudent Pension Plan Investment: A Decision Theory Model," *Personnel Journal* (Sept. 1979), pp. 600–606.

34. Thomas Sassman, "Post Retirement Increase Plans: Why You Need Them and How to Pick the Right One," *Personnel Journal* (1980), pp. 285–291.

35. Of course, the higher paid employee would probably still have the higher pension and might still have a much higher standard of living than the lower paid employee, even though the former's purchasing power has been more seriously eroded.

36. These are all discussed in Sassman, "Post retirement increase plans. . . ."

37. The Bankers Trust Company study was conducted in 1975, and the Wyatt Company Study in 1977.

38. Sassman, p. 289; Sassman also describes several methods that can be used to increase retirees' benefits, pointing out that they can be grouped into two broad categories: those tied directly to inflation and those that attempt to impede inflationary erosion indirectly, for example, by tying benefits to the investment portfolio used for their funding.

39. This section based on Henderson, pp. 336–339.

40. J. Brad Chapman and Robert Ottemann, "Employee Preference for Various Compensation and Fringe Benefit Options" (Berea, Ohio: ASPA Foundation, 1975).

41. *Ibid*; see also William White and James Becker, "Increasing the Motivational Impact of Employee Benefits," *Personnel* (January–February 1980), pp. 32–37.

42. See William White and James Becker, "Increasing the Motivational Import of Employee Benefits," *Personnel* (January–February 1980), pp. 32–37.

43. Henderson, *Compensation Management*, p. 312.

44. Edward Lawler, *Reward Systems*, p. 182.

45. Also called "flexitime."

46. Stanley Nollen, "Does Flexitime Improve Productivity?" *Harvard Business Review* (Sept.–Oct. 1977), pp. 12–22; Donald Petersen, "Flexitime in the United States: The Lessons of Experience," *Personnel* (Jan.–Feb. 1980), pp. 21–31.

47. Janis Hedges, "New Patterns for Working Time," *Monthly Labor Review*, Vol. 96 (February 1973), pp. 3–8; reprinted in Chruden and Sherman, *Readings*.

48. Stanley Nollen, "Does Flexitime Improve Productivity?" *Harvard Business Review* (Sept.–Oct. 1979), pp. 12–22.

49. Stanley Nollen and Virginia Martin, Alternative Work Schedules, Part I: Flexitime (New York: Amacon, 1978), p. 44.

50. Donald Petersen, "Flexitime in the U.S. . . . ," p. 22.

51. Nollen, p. 17.

52. J. H. Foegan, "From Flexitime to Fringe," *Personnel Administrator* (September 1976).

53. This is based on J. Carroll Swart, "Flexitimes Debit and Credit Option," *Personnel Journal* (January–February 1979), pp. 10–12.

54. Swart, p. 12.

55. Donald Petersen, "Flexitime in the United States . . . ," pp. 29–31.

56. Janis Hedges, "New Patterns."

57. John Ivanevich and Herbert Lyon, "The Shortened Work Week: A Field Experiment," *Journal of Applied Psychology*, Vol. 62, No. 1 (1977), pp. 34–37.

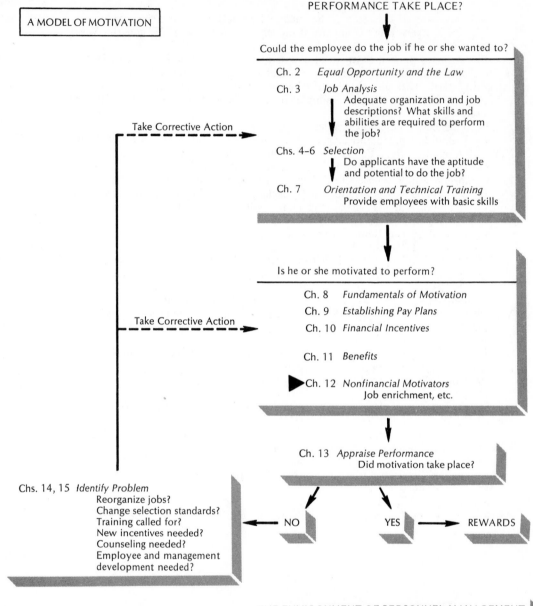

A MODEL OF MOTIVATION

WILL MOTIVATION AND PERFORMANCE TAKE PLACE?

Could the employee do the job if he or she wanted to?

Ch. 2   *Equal Opportunity and the Law*

Ch. 3   *Job Analysis*
Adequate organization and job descriptions? What skills and abilities are required to perform the job?

Chs. 4–6 *Selection*
Do applicants have the aptitude and potential to do the job?

Ch. 7   *Orientation and Technical Training*
Provide employees with basic skills

Is he or she motivated to perform?

Ch. 8   *Fundamentals of Motivation*

Ch. 9   *Establishing Pay Plans*

Ch. 10 *Financial Incentives*

Ch. 11 *Benefits*

Ch. 12 *Nonfinancial Motivators*
Job enrichment, etc.

Ch. 13 *Appraise Performance*
Did motivation take place?

Take Corrective Action

Take Corrective Action

Chs. 14, 15 *Identify Problem*
Reorganize jobs?
Change selection standards?
Training called for?
New incentives needed?
Counseling needed?
Employee and management development needed?

NO   YES ➝ REWARDS

THE ENVIRONMENT OF PERSONNEL MANAGEMENT

Ch. 16 *Labor Relations and Grievances*

Ch. 17 *Employee Safety and Health*

Ch. 18 *Personnel Management and the Quality of Work Life*

When you finish studying

12 Nonfinancial Methods for Improving Performance at Work

You should be able to:

1. *Explain how employee morale affects performance.*
2. *Explain how to implement Management By Objectives, and quality circle programs.*
3. *"Enrich" a subordinate's job.*
4. *Cite the conditions under which job enrichment will more likely result in increased motivation.*
5. *Compare and contrast four types of "reinforcement."*
6. *Develop an example of how to use positive reinforcement.*

OVERVIEW

The main purpose of this chapter is to explain the use of four "nonfinancial" personnel techniques an employer can use to improve employee performance.

Motivation theories like those of Maslow and Herzberg (discussed in Chapter 8) are very useful. They help explain what motivates people, and they help us see what sorts of needs managers can focus on satisfying. But when it comes to managing, employers also need some specific techniques for applying these theories—techniques for motivating employees. In this chapter we explain how to use four such techniques: raising morale; participation; job enrichment; and positive reinforcement.

MORALE AND EMPLOYEE PERFORMANCE

What is Job Satisfaction?

"Job satisfaction" generally refers to how happy a person is with his or her job. "Happiness," however is not an easy thing to measure; so job satisfaction will be defined here as the degree to which one's important needs for health, security, nourishment, affiliation, esteem, and so on are fulfilled on the job or as a result of the job. Thus if we wanted to measure how satisfied an organization's employees are, we would usually start by measuring their satisfaction with important facets of the job such as pay, promotions, and recognition, and then add the results to obtain some measure of the employee's overall job satisfaction. Some of the items for which researchers normally obtain satisfaction measures are presented in Exhibit 12.1 and include the work itself, pay, working conditions, and supervision.

Exhibit 12.1   Measures of Job Satisfaction

Researchers typically measure employees satisfaction with at least the following job dimensions:

Work: including how interesting it is, its variety, opportunity for learning, difficulty, amount, chances for success, and control over pace and methods

Pay: including amount, fairness or equity, and method of payment

Promotions: including opportunities for, fairness of, and basis for

Recognition: including praise for accomplishment, credit for work done, and criticism

Benefits: such as pension, medical, annual leave, paid vacations, and cafeteria

Working conditions: such as hours, rest pauses, equipment, temperature, ventilation, humidity, location, and physical payout

Supervision: including supervisory style, and technical, human relations, and administrative skill

Coworkers: including confidence, helpfulness, and friendliness

Company and management: including concern for employees as well as pay and benefit policies

---

Source: Edwin A. Locke, "Nature and Causes of Job Satisfaction," in Marvin Dunnette, *Handbook of Industrial and Organizational Psychology*, p. 1302.

Relation of Job Satisfaction to Performance

There are two basic theories of how employee satisfaction and performance are related. [1] The first theory is that satisfaction leads to performance; in other words, that the way to improve employees' performance is to "boost their morale." This approach was popularized by the Human Relations movement, the essence of which was that managers could increase productivity by increasing the morale of their employees. [2]

While the idea that "happy workers are better workers" is intuitively appealing, the research findings generally fail to support it. [3,4] In other words, sometimes satisfied workers perform better, and sometimes they do not. And so, taking actions to boost morale will not necessarily lead to better performance.

The second theory is that rewards which are based on performance lead to both satisfaction and subsequent performance. [5] According to this theory it is the reward—either extrinsic or intrinsic—that causes both performance and satisfaction: the expectation of a reward leads to performance, and the reward itself (which results from performance) then results in satisfaction. [6]

As illustrated in Exhibit 12.2, Porter and Lawler, who have studied this theory, thus argue that the relationship between satisfaction and performance is reciprocal: performance leads to rewards and satisfaction, and the expectation of rewards then leads to further performance.

Exhibit 12.2   Lawler-Porter Model of the Relationship of Performance and Satisfaction

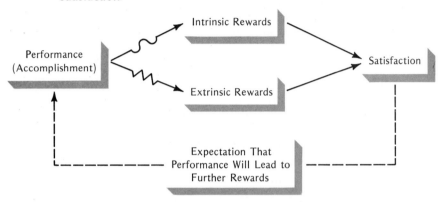

Note: This adaptation of the Porter/Lawler model shows how rewards "lead" to both satisfaction, and future performance.

Source: From Lawler, E. E., and Porter, L. W., "The Effect of Performance on Job Satisfaction." in *Industrial Relations*, 1967, 7, 20–28. Reprinted by permission of the publisher, Industrial Relations.

The research evidence supports this theory. [7] In one study the researchers had two groups of subjects: those whose rewards were based on how well they performed and those whose rewards were not. Subjects who performed well *and were rewarded for doing so* expressed greater satisfaction immediately and subsequently performed better than did subjects whose rewards were not tied to their performance. Similarly, subjects who were paid based on performance and who did *not* perform well (and who were therefore denied rewards), subsequently improved their performance, although they were initially dissatisfied. On the other hand, when a low performer was rewarded anyway (where pay was *not* contingent on performance), the person expressed high satisfaction, but his or her subsequent performance continued at a low level. [8]

In summary, the evidence suggests that "boosting morale" may have some positive effects on the organization but that it will not necessarily lead to better performance. The important thing to remember is that high morale is a result of having one's needs satisfied by some rewards. Thus "rewarding" someone—by providing better pay, a more interesting job, better leadership, or better working conditions, for instance—*will* usually raise morale. But it's only when the reward (and thus the satisfaction) is also seen as a consequence of good performance that satisfaction will seem to "lead" to good performance.

Satisfaction and Its Relation to Attendance and Other Factors

Satisfaction may not "cause" performance, but it's relation to other factors is clear and consistent. For example, employees who are more satisfied generally have better attendance records than those who are not; participate less in unionization activities; and tend to remain with their employers longer.

Satisfaction and its Relation to Attendance and Turnover.   Behavioral scientists have long sought to understand the relationship between satisfaction and attendance, but their efforts have been plagued by several problems. Perhaps the most obvious of these is that attendance depends not just on an employee's satisfaction, but on many other things as well. For example, an employee who fears that staying home may jeopardize her job will probably come to work regardless of whether satisfied with her job or not. Similarly, economic and market conditions, the reward system, work group norms, a person's ability to attend, and whether or not the company penalizes nonattendance also affect the person's attendance. [9]

As a rule, for example, we might expect that where attendance is compulsory, rather than voluntary, and absences are penalized, satisfaction and attendance would not be related. In these situations it is not so much the employee's *satisfaction* that determines whether or not he attends, but instead the fact that attendance is compulsory and he will be penalized if absent. On the other hand, where attendance is more or less voluntary and absences are not penalized, we might expect employee satisfaction to have a considerable effect on whether or not employees come to work.

One recent study provides some fascinating insights into this question. [10] As part of this study, the researcher administered a morale survey to over 3,000 salaried employees in a major retailer's Chicago headquarters. For comparison purposes, satisfaction data were also obtained from 340 salaried employees in the company's New York headquarters office. The survey measured employees' satisfaction with supervision, kind of work, amount of work, career future and security, financial rewards, and company identification.

As it was originally envisioned, the study was simply aimed at determining how (if at all) satisfaction and attendance were related. The satisfaction data were supposed to be related to attendance data that the personnel department collected on April 3, about three months after the satisfaction data had been obtained. However, as it turned out, there was a severe snowstorm in Chicago on April 2, 1975, and this storm greatly hampered the city's transportation system. Now, in this company, occasional absenteeism by managerial people is not subject to financial penalty and is relatively free of social and work group pressure. Furthermore, good attendance following a crippling snowstorm is especially unique because attendance actually requires considerable personal effort. As a result, we would expect to find a rather strong relationship between satisfaction and attendance among the employees in the Chicago office: here, after all, occasional absence was not penalized, and the snowstorm provided a perfect "built-in" excuse for those employees who did not want to come to work. In the New York office, on the other hand, we might expect to find much less of a relationship between satisfaction and attendance: here, employees are also not penalized for an occasional absence, but there was *not* a built-in excuse (the snowstorm) for their staying home.

The results of this study are presented in Exhibit 12.3. As you can see, in Chicago there *was* a significant relationship between all six facets of job satisfaction and attendance. In New York, on the other hand, there was no apparent relationship between satisfaction and attendance. In summary, satisfied employees do have better attendance records—especially when absences are not penalized or are relatively easy to "get away with."

Exhibit 12.3   Correlations Between Job Satisfaction and Attendance in Chicago and New York Groups

Scale	Chicago[a] (n = 27)	New York[b] (n = 1.3)
Supervision	.54*	.12
Amount of Work	.36*	.01
Kind of Work	.37*	.06
Financial Rewards	.46*	.11
Career Future	.60*	.14
Company Identification	.42*	.02

*Statistically significant

[a]Group following storm, April 1975.
[b]Group, April 1975.

Note: that satisfaction and attendance were significantly related in Chicago, where the storm made it "easier" for employees to stay home. In New York there was no such "built in" excuse for staying home, and satisfaction did not seem to matter as much.

Source: Frank Smith, "Work Attitudes as Predictors of Attendance on a Specific Day," Journal of Applied Psychology, 1977, Vol. 62, No. 1, p. 18.

If satisfaction *is* related to attendance, how much money could a company save by increasing the satisfaction of its employees? Mirvis and Lawler used cost accounting techniques to apply costs in dollars to absenteeism and turnover. As you can see in Exhibit 12.4, they first calculated that the total cost of an employee being absent one day was $66.45.

The researchers then correlated employee attitudes with both attendance and turnover. Based on this, they were able to predict what effect improved attitudes would have on attendance and turnover and, therefore, costs. This particular study involved 160 tellers in a Midwestern bank, and the researchers concluded that a slight increase in job satisfaction would result in an expected *direct* cost saving to the bank of over $17,000 per year.

The Relation of Satisfaction and Unionization Activity. There is little doubt that job dissatisfaction is a major reason why workers turn to unions. One study involved almost 88,000 salaried, clerical, sales, and technical em-

Exhibit 12.4 Cost per Incident of Absenteeism and Turnover

Absenteeism		Turnover	
Variable	*Cost (in dollars)*	*Variable*	*Cost (in dollars)*
Absent employee		Replacement acquisition	
Salary	23.04	Direct hiring costs	293.95
Benefits	6.40	Other hiring costs	185.55
Replacement employee:		Replacement training	
Training and staff time	2.31	Preassignment	758.84
Unabsorbed overhead	15.71	Learning curve	212.98
Lost profit contribution	19.17	Unabsorbed burden	682.44
		Lost profit contribution	388.27
Total variable cost	23.04	Total variable cost	293.95
Total cost	66.45	Total cost	2,522.03

Source: Philip Mirvis and Edward Lawler, "Measuring the Financial Impact of Employee Attitudes," *Journal of Applied Psychology*, Vol. 62, no. 1, pp. 1–8. Copyright 1977 by the American Psychological Association. Reprinted with permission.

ployees from 250 units of a large organization. [11] As part of its normal personnel procedures, this company administered an attitude survey to employees in these 250 units. The survey was carried out prior to any history of unionization activity, but, several months later, attempts were made to unionize employees in 125 of these units, and the employees in 31 of them finally opted to "go union." As a result, the researchers could correlate *job satisfaction* (with supervision, kind of work, amount of work, career future, security, financial reward, physical surroundings, and company identification) and whether or not employees in a unit *decided to join the union.* [12]

The results of this study show quite clearly that employees who were more dissatisfied were more prone to engage in unionization activity and to unionize. For example, *in all cases* the units with no unionization activity had employees who were more satisfied than did the units with unionization activity. Furthermore, the company had enough information from the attitude survey to *predict* the degree of future union activity.

Dissatisfaction with *which aspects* of their jobs leads workers to unionize? In one study, a survey of job satisfaction was made just after the union representation election (the election results were kept secret until all questionnaires were completed and returned). [12] The subjects in this study were 59 production employees working for a medium-sized company in the Midwest, and the survey measured three things: (1) eight types of job satisfaction; (2) "union attitudes" (the employees' attitudes toward the local union and toward unions in general); and (3) the question, "How did you vote in the union election which was just conducted?"

The results of this study are presented in Exhibit 12.5. As it illustrates, employee dissatisfaction and pro-union voting seemed to go hand in hand, since (in most cases) there was a significant *inverse* relationship between

Exhibit 12.5   Relationship Between Each Attitude and Pro-union Voting

Attitude	Correlation between this attitude, and pro-union voting
Attitude toward the local union	.57*
Attitude toward unions in general	.51*
Total noneconomic satisfaction	−.38*
Independence satisfaction	−.36*
Variety satisfaction	−.04
Creativity satisfaction	−.17
Achievement satisfaction	−.36*
Total economic satisfaction	−.74*
Security satisfaction	−.41*
Company policy satisfaction	−.55*
Pay satisfaction	−.60*
Working conditions satisfaction	−.76*
Total noneconomic and economic satisfaction	−.64*

*Significant correlations:

Note: That there was a significant *inverse* relationship between most measures of job satisfaction, and pro-union voting.

Source: Chester Schriesheim, "Job Satisfaction, Attitudes toward Unions, and Voting in a Union Representation Election," Journal of Applied Psychology, 1978, Vol. 63, No. 5, p. 550.

satisfaction and pro-union voting. Also notice that it did *not* seem to be *non-economic* factors (like "how much variety the job provided") that were the culprits. Instead, dissatisfaction with "hygienes"—"bread and butter" facets like security and pay—was most associated with pro-union voting.

PARTICIPATION AND PERFORMANCE

Introduction: Why Participation?

There are basically two benefits to be derived from letting subordinates participate in decisions regarding their jobs. First, participation allows one to bring to bear more points of view, and it is therefore a useful approach to obtain advice or to solve a problem where several points of view might be useful. Second, and perhaps most important, participation is generally recognized as an effective way for gaining employees' acceptance of, and commitment to, goals and for motivating them to discipline themselves to accomplish these goals.

Using Management by Objectives

What is Management By Objectives?   Management by Objectives (MBO) is a widely used participation technique in which superior and subordinate jointly set goals for the latter and periodically assess progress toward these goals. While a manager could conceivably engage in a modest MBO program with subordinates by participatively setting goals and periodically providing feedback, the term MBO almost always refers to a comprehensive *organization-wide* program for participatively setting goals.

Management by Objectives has many applications. In one respect it is a *motivation* technique, since its goal-setting, participation, and feedback components can and do enhance motivation. Yet MBO is more than just a motivation device. Especially for professionals and managers, it is also an integral part of the *performance appraisal* system the organization uses: the employees are appraised largely on the basis of how well they accomplish the jointly-set goals. Management by Objectives is also an *organizational change* technique. For example, managers can jointly assess the need for a change, set goals for changing the organization, and then periodically evaluate progress toward the targeted changes. Finally, MBO is in many respects a *planning and control* device since the jointly set goals become "control standards" that can be monitored; deviations from these goals can then be identified and rectified. Management by Objectives, therefore, is a technique that has many applications.

The MBO process itself is actually a fairly simple one and consists of five basic steps:

1. *Set organization's goals.* Organization-wide strategy and goals are established.
2. *Set departmental goals.* Department heads and their superiors jointly set goals for their departments.
3. *Discuss departmental goals.* Department heads discuss department's goals with all subordinates in the department and ask them to develop their own individual goals.
4. *Set individual goals.* Each superior and subordinate jointly set goals for the latter and assign a timetable for accomplishing same.
5. *Feedback.* There are periodic performance review meetings between superior and subordinate to monitor and analyze progress toward latter's goals. [13]

How Effective Is MBO? One would imagine that, with its basis in participation and goal setting, MBO would be a useful management technique, but the findings on its effectiveness are somewhat contradictory. Some programs have been quite successful, some have apparently resulted in little or no performance improvement, and others have actually had to be discontinued because of the confusion they caused. [14]

These findings are especially ironic given that the MBO approach is based on some very firm foundations. For example, MBO involves mutual *goal setting*, and we know that employees who have high, specific goals usually perform better than those who do not. Similarly, letting subordinates *participate* in establishing their goals can increase their commitment to these goals and thereby their performance. Giving employees *feedback* concerning how they are doing is a third basic component of MBO. And, (as with participation and goal setting) the research findings again suggest that providing frequent, timely feedback generally lead to increased performance. [15]

While MBO's components—goal-setting, participation, and feedback—can influence performance, the findings concerning the effectiveness of formal organization-wide MBO programs are very mixed. One major program was implemented at the General Electric Company, where it was called "Work Planning and Review." [16] The program grew out of attempts to improve the firm's performance appraisal system and was quite effective. The employees operating under MBO were much more satisfied and much more likely to have taken specific action to improve performance than those operating within a traditional performance appraisal system. In another study, a researcher analyzed the performance of the subordinates of 181 MBO-involved superiors and found that the subordinates' performance had improved. [17] On the other hand, several recent studies have found that MBO programs often fail and that their apparent success is transitory and disappears within a year after introduction of the program. [18]

Making MBO Successful. While participation, goal-setting, and feedback can lead to higher morale and performance, we also know that formal organization-wide MBO programs also fail, and this anomaly is probably indicative of at least two things. First, implementing an organization-wide MBO program (as we will see below) involves introducing a fairly elaborate new technology into the organization—a technology that includes instruction booklets, training, questionnaires, and so on. This technology is aimed at ensuring that the MBO program is applied consistently throughout the organization, that the program is taken seriously by all concerned, and that the goals that emerge from the MBO process are compatible with each other and with the goals of the organization. An organization-wide MBO program, therefore, introduces a whole new set of complexities and problems that would not exist if we were simply focusing on some joint goal-setting between the manager and his or her subordinates. This is one source of problems.

Second, as with any technique, there is a "right" and a "wrong" way to implement MBO, and we know that there are several conditions for its success. For example, based on their analysis of an extensive MBO program at the Black and Decker Company, two researchers suggest the following conditions for success: [19]

1. *Organizational commitment.* Managers must feel that MBO is important, and that the organization and its top management is serious about it.
2. *Goals must be clear.* Organizational goals—in terms of sales quotas, production increases, and so on—must be clear, since goal-setting at all lower levels is more difficult, if not impossible, without clear goals that can be fashioned into more specific departmental and individual goals.
3. *Time and resources must be adequate.* Implementing an MBO program can be a very time-consuming procedure, and managers must have the time and resources to utilize MBO.
4. *Provide timely feedback.* The subordinate has to receive timely, frequent feedback. While the optimum number of feedback sessions varies from firm to firm, some managers found that four formal feedback sessions annually (between superior and subordinate) instead of just one end-of-the-period evaluation were best. [20] The *content* of the feedback session is also important. We

know, for example, that those receiving more criticism tend to improve less in subsequent periods than those employees who are criticized less. Avoiding the tendency to be overly critical is especially important for those subordinates who are lower in ability, lack confidence, or are operating at lower motivation levels. [21]

When MBO programs do fail, it is often because of several predictable problems. The manager has to meet with subordinates, review their accomplishments, and discuss plans for the ensuing time period: all this can add up to a tremendous commitment of time. The time invested in such a program is probably the most serious problem, but other problems arise as well. For some activities like cutting costs or increasing sales, goals are clear and measuring performance is a straightforward matter. But in many other areas, such as employee training, appraising performance is not so straightforward. Furthermore, there is often a lack of awareness on the part of managers of the rationale and value of MBO, and this can make the time spent on it seem even more exasperating. Finally, a "tug of war" often ensues in which the subordinate tries to set the lowest targets possible and the supervisor the highest.

Some Benefits of MBO.   Many MBO programs are quite successful [22] and numerous benefits have been noted. Employee motivation increases (probably as a result of the participation, goal-setting, and feedback components). MBO also forces and aids in planning, since, to be done properly, top management has to set plans and goals for the entire organization, and the goals of lower levels must then be tied in with these. As a result, work is directed toward organizational goals, since a "chain" of goals and plans develops that link lower and higher level work groups. Another, related benefit is that MBO provides clear standards (goals) for control purposes. Problems can thus be identified better and faster. MBO also results in (or should result in) more concrete, objective, result-oriented performance appraisal criteria, and improved appraisal conferences in which tangible progress can be discussed.

MBO in Practice.   MBO applications range from informal two-person goal-setting and feedback sessions to formal organization-wide programs. With respect to the former, many managers meet periodically with their subordinates to jointly set goals, and subordinate performance is then measured in terms of these goals.

On the other hand, it would seem that to fully take advantage of MBO's benefits a more formal organization-wide program is in order. It is only in this way, for example, that one can ensure that the goals set are compatible with those in other departments. And, it is likely that the effectiveness of the program is enhanced when employees recognize top management's commitment to the program.

One of the most successful company-wide applications to date was implemented at the Black and Decker Company. The Black and Decker program consists of an initial departmental briefing session in which the department's goals are presented by the manager. Then, each employee sets some preliminary targets for himself, with final targets set at a meeting between manager and subordinate. During the year the manager coaches and counsels each subordinate, and each subordinate reviews his or her own progress. Then, at year end, the supervisor completes a special form, thus reviewing each worker's progress, performance, and development needs. Then the manager and subordinate meet to discuss the latter's overall appraisal for the year.

Participation Through "Quality Circles"

Managers today are increasingly recognizing the fact that work groups influence performance, and that this influence can be harnessed through participation to improve performance. The use of "Quality Circles" is one example of this. [23]

A quality circle is a group of about 8-10 employees that meets once a week for the purpose of spotting and solving problems in their work area. The idea of using small groups of workers to solve work-related problems was popularized by U.S. management consultants and then adopted by the Japanese after World War II; U.S. companies, stung by dwindling productivity, in turn borrowed the idea from the Japanese, who believe that such groups are partly responsible for the relatively spectacular productivity gains they have made since the war.

At the present time, quality circles are in use in at least sixty-five U.S. firms, and their number is growing rapidly. Companies using them, for example, include General Motors, Ford Motor, Northrop, Rockwell International, and American Airlines. They were first used in the U.S. in 1974 by Lockheed's space and missile unit and proved so successful they were soon adopted by a growing number of firms.

The basic idea of the quality circle is as follows. A plant steering committee, composed of labor and management, decides which area of a company could benefit from a circle. Then, 8 to 10 workers are asked to serve on a circle and to meet once a week on company time. In addition to the employees, those attending the meeting include the immediate supervisor, and a person trained in personnel or industrial relations; the latter instructs the workers in elementary data gathering and statistics. The circle selects and analyzes a problem, develops a solution, and presents their findings to management which generally accepts the group's recommendations.

Based on the findings to date, quality circles appear to be quite successful, both from the point of management and labor. General Motors has about 100 quality circles operating in various plants of its car divisions, and in at least one case a circle was responsible for saving the company $225,000 annually. A circle at an American Airlines Maintenance Center in Tulsa came up with a savings of $100,000 a year by simply replacing old hand grinders with new more efficient tools. The workers themselves (1) often share in any cost savings (Northrup, for example, pays circle members about 10% for any cost savings), and (2) get a feeling of accomplishment from tackling a challenging task;

they, too, gain from the quality circles, therefore. At present, of course, the evidence is anecdotal, and does not address such questions as whether the cost of the circles warrants the benefits they produce; on the whole, however, the circle idea appears to be an effective one for harnessing, through participation, the performance-stimulating potential in the work group.

Example of an Organization-wide Participation Program. The Advanced Circuitry Division of Litton Industries recently implemented an organization-wide variant of the circle idea that has proved quite successful. [24] When the program was first designed and implemented, employee morale was exceptionally low because of a series of layoffs and a devisive unionization attempt. In addition, the workers were being called upon to assemble new, more complex circuit boards while at the same time the division was having problems with new equipment that had been installed. The net effect of all these problems was that the usually excellent quality levels in this division were at all time lows. As a result, the participation program was aimed at improving quality, as well as at boosting productivity and morale. The program was built around a series of meetings: Level I meetings, Level II meetings, and Level III meetings.

The heart of the program is the Level I meetings, where employees are brought together once every two weeks with their immediate supervisor. The supervisor "guides" the meeting through a series of predetermined "steps," which can be interrupted at any time (and during any step) to conform to the imposed 30-minute time limit for meetings. If all the steps are not completed during one meeting, the next Level I meeting (two weeks later) picks up where the last one left off. The steps that constitute a Level I meeting are as follows:

Step 1. The supervisor introduces a general topic for discussion—such as, "Why do you think our department's product quality is low?"

Step 2. The employees suggest all the problems they can imagine that may be causing the low quality. One such problem might be "the work area is too dirty," for example. One employee records ideas as fast as the others call them out.

Step 3. Here the employees (*not* the supervisor) rank the problems identified in Step 2.

Step 4. Here the employees identify possible solutions to the problems they have ranked as most pressing in Step 3. (An average session often produces 10 or 12 ways to solve the problem.) One solution might be "let's be sure to sweep the floor at least once each shift," for example.

Step 5. This step involves evaluating all the suggested solutions and eliminating the impractical ideas while retaining the workable approaches.

Step 6. Next, the supervisor assigns "action items" to volunteers from the group who must then explore fully the feasibility of the workable solutions identified in Step 5. In addition to encouraging group "ownership" of the final, suggested solution, this step also lets employees gain an opportunity to expand their jobs by performing tasks (like exploring the feasibility of the remaining solutions) that they had not been able to do previously.

Step 7. Finally, the group discusses and evaluates the results of their feasibility studies, and, when possible, the chosen solution is put into effect promptly. If time permits, the group now returns to Step 3 and addresses the next most important problem, again following the step-by-step method. The supervisor directs the group back to Step 1 only after a general subject has been exhausted so that a new general topic can be introduced. This whole process can take many meetings, with, for example, the group taking a full half hour just getting through Step 4 and then picking up Step 5 at the next meeting.

Level II meetings are also held every other week but are arranged so as not to conflict with Level I meetings. Whereas each work group attends its own Level I meeting and tries to solve problems relevant to the group, Level II meetings are aimed at fostering interdepartmental or intergroup coordination at the worker level. Through participation in these meetings, employees come to better appreciate some of the problems their co-workers in other groups face, become more tolerant and understanding of general conditions in the shop, and gain confidence in their co-workers.

Participants at these Level II meetings consist of representatives chosen from preselected work groups, particularly work groups that are closely associated in the production process. Also attending is a supervisor from one of these groups who has been selected from among his peers.

Level II meetings are less structured than the Level I "step" meetings but generally follow a standard format [25] where:

1. Each participant is encouraged to talk about the things that have been accomplished in their respective Level I meetings.
2. Participants then discuss problems common to the groups and are urged to communicate these matters back to their fellow employees at their next Level I meeting.
3. Ideas that cannot be implemented at the first level (because they require the cooperation of other work groups) are brought, in written form, to Level II meetings by the representatives. The supervisor in charge also acts as a "coordinator" to forward good ideas along the Level III group.

The Level III meeting (which is held monthly and attended by the engineering, quality control, production, and industrial relations managers) functions as a review board and serves mostly to sort out deserving ideas from Level I meetings for further study, and to ensure that Level I and II meetings are conducted in a timely manner.

The program has been quite successful. Product quality rose dramatically in those departments where the program was implemented. And, during one early period, a total of 82 quality-related problems were identified, with all but 16 of them ultimately resolved in the Level I meetings. One example of the type of problems employees verbalized and then worked on during the program follows:

In one department, employees said they could get better quality if the work area was cleaner. In discussing possible solutions, it was agreed by the employees that, if the requirement to dust and sweep the floor once per shift was followed religiously, the problem would be resolved. Supervision had experienced difficulty in assigning and following up on this particular task, but once the *employees* had identified it as a problem and voluntarily agreed to take turns, the area became, and remained, clean. The supervisor solved his problem by merely listening! [26]

A successful organization-wide participation program like this cannot be implemented without some problems, but these were kept to a minimum by first carefully designing the program, and then by trying it out with six work groups on an experimental basis. To further facilitate the implementation of the program, supervisors were given six hours of introductory training, designed to acquaint them with the objectives of participative management and to teach them how to conduct the Level I "step" meetings. The most significant problem seemed to be a tendency on the part of supervisors to try to solve too many problems at one time. For example, after ranking the problems in order of their priority, some supervisors would have employees brainstorm solutions to *all* the problems one after another, instead of seeing one solution through to completion. Also, management found that supervisors who strayed too far from the predetermined sequence of seven steps tended to have longer meetings. Problems like these could be solved by training, however, and, on the whole, the program has been a very successful one: it has boosted quality, productivity, and morale by gaining the active participation of employees in solving work-related problems.

JOB ENRICHMENT

Introduction: Intrinsic Rewards and Motivation

Few rewards are as powerful as the sense of accomplishment and achievement that come from doing a job one genuinely wants to do, and doing it well. Thus, the person who collects stamps, builds a radio, or volunteers her time at the hospital generally does not have to be coerced or prodded into doing the job well since the job carries its own intrinsic rewards—in terms of challenge, achievement, and so on. In other words this sort of job—its content, functions, and specific duties—is "designed" in such a way so that performing it contributes to and satisfies people's "higher order" needs for achievement, recognition, and self-actualization. Needless to say, designing jobs at work to provide such intrinsic rewards can substantially increase employee morale and performance since, in the words of Katz and Kahn:

> Motivation is so internalized that performance is autonomous. The supervisor does not have to be present to wave a stick or offer candy. The activities carry their own rewards; they are so much a pattern of motive satisfaction that they need no additional incentives. [27]

Basic Approaches to Job Design

The basic issue in job design is whether jobs should be highly specialized and routine or highly "enriched" and nonroutine. Those who advocate specialized jobs argue for making jobs as simple as possible, so that each worker performs the same highly specialized task over and over again, many times a day, since in this way production efficiencies are obtained. Advocates of job enrichment, on the other hand, claim that such highly specialized jobs lead to unanticipated problems like boredom and animosity and that tasks should actually be recombined into more "enriched" jobs.

The Drawbacks to Specialization.   Scientific managers like Frederick Taylor took a purely "rational" approach to job design, and pursued technical efficiency with a single-minded abandon. They prescribed highly simplified, short-cycle jobs, jobs which consisted of performing the same activity over and over again, hundreds of times a day. The worker in this system was relegated to little more than the proverbial cog in the machine, and the worker was studied, analyzed, and prodded in a manner that many workers found increasingly demeaning and unacceptable. The worker became little more than an adjunct to a machine, and his or her responses were as completely programmed and beyond his or her control as possible.

Almost from the onset of industrialization, however, workers rebelled (and are still rebelling) against being kept in so tight a harness and being dragged so far from the challenge that craft work provides; this rebelliousness has manifested itself in a number of ways. [28] These range from relatively harmless actions like daydreaming [29] to more serious problems like excessive absences [30] and antimanagement activities like wildcat strikes and sabotage. [31] In summary, as Sayles and Strauss point out:

> Management pays a price for the work simplification, routinization, and ease of supervision inherent in mass-production work. The cost is largely in terms of apathy and boredom, as positive satisfactions are engineered out of the jobs. Being confined physically and limited socially to contacting his own immediate supervisor, the factory worker sees very little of the total organization and even less of the total product being manufactured. It is hardly surprising that there is frequently little pride in work or identification with a job. [32]

Toward Less Specialized Jobs

Job Enlargement and Rotation.   Management's initial response to problems like these was often to redesign jobs, either through job enlargement or through job rotation. *Job enlargement* involves assigning workers additional same-level tasks to increase the number of tasks they have to perform. [33] For example, if the work involved assembling chairs, the worker who previously only bolted the seat to the legs might take on the additional tasks of assembling

342   the legs and attaching the back as well. *Job rotation,* involves systematically moving workers from one job to another. Thus, on an assembly line, a worker might spend an hour fitting doors, the next hour installing head lamps, the next hour fitting bumpers, and so on.

Both job enlargement and job rotation are similar in two ways. First, they both represent the antithesis of job specialization. With job specialization the objective is to reduce the job to its most fundamental components and to assign each component to a worker who will then perform it routinely. Job enlargement and rotation involve *recombining* simple jobs, assigning several to a worker to increase the variety of tasks he or she performs. Second, job enlargement and job rotation are not primarily aimed at injecting motivators like "challenge" into jobs. Instead, they are aimed at reducing the monotony and boredom that may be inherent in highly specialized jobs, by increasing the number and variety of simple tasks that are assigned to the worker.

Job Enrichment. *Job enrichment* is an approach to job redesign that *is* aimed at building motivators like opportunities for achievement into the job. It involves redesigning jobs—for example, by telling your secretary she can now research and answer customers' questions, instead of just referring them to you—so as to increase the opportunities for the worker to experience a feeling of responsibility, achievement, growth, and recognition by doing the job well. Job enrichment is always concerned with changing the content—the specific duties and functions—of the job rather than with hygiene factors like salary and working conditions.

An example of what Herzberg recalls "a highly successful job enrichment experiment" is illustrated in Exhibit 12.6. [34] (In this case the jobs were those of people responsible for corresponding with a large corporation's stockholders—answering their questions and so on.) On the left of the exhibit are listed some of the changes that were aimed at enriching the job, such as "removing some controls while retaining accountability." On the right, are listed the motivators—such as recognition—these job changes were aimed at increasing.

While the terms are sometimes used interchangeably, job enlargement and job enrichment are not exactly the same thing. Job enlargement usually involves a *horizontal* expansion of the worker's job, by increasing the number and variety of similar tasks he or she is assigned. Job enrichment, on the other hand, usually involves a *vertical* expansion of the worker's job in that tasks formerly carried out by his or her supervisor are now assigned to the worker. For example, he or she may be given more discretion to *schedule* the day's work, *communicate* directly with clients, and *inspect* the work that is produced.

A Technology for Enriching Jobs

A group of researchers has developed a new technology for implementing job enrichment programs. [35] These researchers say that people "get turned on to"—are motivated to perform—their work if: the activity is *meaningful*

Exhibit 12.6   An Outline of a Successful Job Enrichment Project

Specific changes aimed at enriching jobs	"Motivators" these changes are aimed at increasing
A. Removing some controls while retaining accountability	Responsibility and personal achievement
B. Increasing the accountability of individuals for own work	Responsibility and recognition
C. Giving a person a complete natural unit of work (module, division, area, and so on)	Responsibility, achievement, and recognition
D. Granting additional authority to an employee in his activity; job freedom	Responsibility, achievement, and recognition
E. Making periodic reports directly available to the worker himself rather than to the supervisor	Internal recognition
F. Introducing new and more difficult tasks not previously handled	Growth and learning
G. Assigning individuals specific or specialized tasks, enabling them to become expert	Responsibility, growth, and advancement

Source: Frederick Herzberg, "One More Time: How Do You Motivate Employees?"

to the person, the person knows he or she is solely *responsible* for its completion, and he or she gets *knowledge of results* within a few seconds. [36]

Core Job Dimensions.   The researchers assume that any job has five "core dimensions" that determine whether the person will in fact experience this *meaningfulness, responsibility,* and *knowledge of results:*

Skill variety—the degree to which the job requires the worker to perform activities that challenge his or her skills and abilities.

Task identity—the degree to which the job requires completion of a "whole" identifiable piece of work.

Task significance—the degree to which the job has a substantial and perceivable effect on the lives of other people, in the organization or the world at large.

Autonomy—the degree to which the job gives the worker freedom and independence.

Knowledge of results—the degree to which the worker gets information about the effectiveness of his or her job efforts.

Step 1—Diagnosis.   The first step in developing a job enrichment program, according to these researchers, is to diagnose the problem: here one

344   determines if the job is amenable to job enrichment. This process consists of answering four questions (the researchers have questionnaires to formalize this process):

1. *Are motivation and satisfaction central to the problem?* Or is there some other problem (a poorly designed production system, etc.)?
2. *Is the job low in motivating potential?* Is the *job* the source of the motivation problem identified in Step 1?
3. *What specific aspects of the job are causing the difficulty?* Here examine the job on the five "core dimensions" presented above.
4. *How "ready" are the employees for change?* The researchers found that not everyone is motivated by job enrichment. The extent to which job enrichment is effective depends on the workers' needs—for self-actualization, achievement, and so on.

Step 2—Implementation. After diagnosing the problem, the next step is implementation. Here, enrich the "core dimensions" of the job (skill variety, autonomy, etc.) by taking specific actions to enrich the jobs, for example:

1. *Form natural work groups.* Here we change the job in such a way that each person is responsible for—"owns"—an identifiable body of work. For example, instead of having the typist in a typing pool do work for all departments, we might make the work of one or two departments the continuing responsibility of each typist.
2. *Combine tasks.* For example, let one person assemble a product from start to finish, instead of having it go through several separate operations that are performed by different people.
3. *Establish client relationships.* Let the worker have contact, as often as possible, with the consumer of the product.
4. *Vertical loading.* Let the worker plan and control his or her own job, instead of having it controlled by outsiders. For example, let the worker set his or her own schedule, do his or her trouble shooting, decide when to start and stop working, and so on.
5. *Open feedback channels.* Finally, find more and better ways for the worker to get quick feedback on his or her performance.

Research Results. The researchers tested their job enrichment approach at the Travelers Insurance Company and found it to be effective. The work group chosen was a key punching operation. Here, the employees' function was to transfer the information from printed or written documents onto punched cards for computer input. Prior to enrichment, work output was inadequate, error rates were high, schedules were often missed, and absenteeism and turnover were higher than average. The researchers first carried out a diagnosis, based on the steps we summarized above, and determined that there was a need for job enrichment. As a result, they took the following steps:

Formed natural work groups. Each key punch operator was assigned continuing responsibility for certain accounts—for example, each worked only for particular departments.

Combined tasks. Key punchers began doing more of their own "verifying" or inspecting to see that the cards were punched correctly.

Established client relationships. Each operator was given several channels of direct contact with "clients" from other departments. The operators, not their assignment clerks, now inspect the documents for correctness and legibility. When problems arise, the operators, not the supervisor, take them up with the client.

Provided feedback. In addition to feedback from client contact, other channels of feedback were installed. For example, the computer operators now return incorrect cards to the operators who punched them, and operators correct their own errors.

Vertically loaded jobs. For example, operators may now set their own schedules and plan their daily work as long as they meet the schedules.

According to the researchers, the results of this experiment were dramatic. The number of operators declined from 98 to 60. In the group whose jobs were enriched, quantity of work increased by almost 40 percent, as compared with an increase of only about 8 percent in the control, no change group. Absenteeism in the enrichment group decreased by 24 percent after jobs were enriched, while in the control group absenteeism actually increased by almost 30 percent. Favorable attitudes toward the job increased by over 16 percent in the enrichment group, while they remained about the same in the control group. Actual savings in salary and machine rental charges during the first year totalled $64,305. Thus the application of this particular job enrichment technology apparently resulted in substantial increases in employee morale and productivity. These and other findings indicate, however, that job enrichment is *not* recommended where "hygienes" (like pay, working conditions) are not adequate; the technical and economic feasibility of "despecializing" the jobs must also be considered. [37]

BEHAVIOR MODIFICATION AND POSITIVE REINFORCEMENT AT WORK

The use of behavior modification (a term that is often used synonymously with *operant conditioning*) is a powerful tool for changing employee behavior. It is based on the work of B. F. Skinner and is built on two principles: (1) that behavior which appears to lead to a positive consequence ("reward") tends to be repeated, while behavior that appears to lead to a negative consequence tends not to be repeated; [38] and (2) therefore, by providing the properly scheduled rewards, it is possible to influence people's behavior.

Types of Reinforcement

Let us suppose that you are a manager whose employees are chronically late for work. You want to use operant conditioning to train them to come

346   in on time. There are four types of reinforcement you could use: positive reinforcement, negative reinforcement, extinction, and punishment.

First, you could focus on reinforcing the *desired* behavior (which in this
case is coming to work on time). Here, you could use either positive or negative reinforcement. *Positive* reinforcement would include rewards like praise
or raises. *Negative* reinforcement also focuses on reinforcing the *desired* behavior. But instead of providing a positive reward, the "reward" is that the
employee avoids some negative consequence. For example, the employee is not
harassed or is not reprimanded for coming in late: thus the reward is a "negative" one—employees come in on time to avoid some negative consequences
like harassment, a reprimand, or a pay cut.

Alternatively, you might focus (as many managers seem to) on reducing
the *un*desired behavior (coming in late) rather than on rewarding the desired
behavior. With operant conditioning, there are two types of reinforcement you
can use to reduce *un*desired behavior: extinction and punishment. (These are
all summarized in Exhibit 12.7.) People tend to repeat behavior that they have
learned leads to positive consequences, and with *extinction*, reinforcement is
withheld so that over time the undesired behavior (coming in late) disappears.
For example, suppose an employee learns from experience that coming to work
late invariably leads to a scolding by the foreman, which in turn leads to much

Exhibit 12.7   Types of Reinforcement

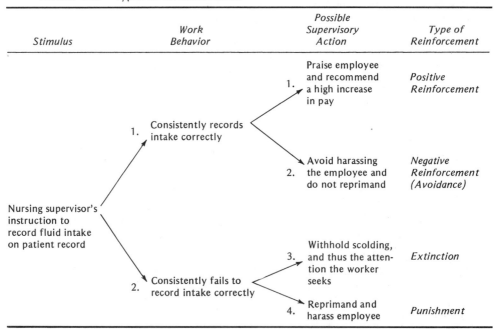

Stimulus	Work Behavior	Possible Supervisory Action	Type of Reinforcement
		1. Praise employee and recommend a high increase in pay	Positive Reinforcement
	1. Consistently records intake correctly	2. Avoid harassing the employee and do not reprimand	Negative Reinforcement (Avoidance)
Nursing supervisor's instruction to record fluid intake on patient record		3. Withhold scolding, and thus the attention the worker seeks	Extinction
	2. Consistently fails to record intake correctly	4. Reprimand and harass employee	Punishment

Source: John Ivancevich, Andrew Szilagyi, Jr., and Marc Wallace, Jr., *Organizational Behavior and Performance* (Santa Monica: Goodyear, 1977), p. 84.

laughter and attention on the part of the worker's peers. Extinction would involve the foreman ignoring the employee, thus removing the attention and laughter—the reinforcement—from the worker's friends as well.

Punishment is a second method of reducing the frequency of undesired behavior. Here, for example, you might reprimand or harass late employees. Punishment is the most controversial method of modifying behavior, and Skinner recommends extinction (rather than punishment) for decreasing the frequency of undesired behaviors at work. [39]

Summary. We have discussed four types of reinforcement: positive reinforcement, negative reinforcement (avoidance), extinction, and punishment. Positive and negative reinforcement are conceptually quite different from extinction and punishment since the first two focus on getting employees to learn the *desired* behavior. Extinction and punishment, on the other hand, focus on unlearning the *un*desired behavior and cannot be of much use in teaching persons the correct, desired behavior. Thus, most industrial applications of behavior modification emphasize positive reinforcement (and, to a lessor extent, negative reinforcement, and extinction).

Schedules of Positive Reinforcement [40]

The schedule with which positive reinforcement is applied is as important as the type of reinforcement used. Basically (as can be seen in Exhibit 12.8), there are two basic schedules one could adhere to. First, there is continuous (or "mass") reinforcement. Here (to use our example) you might praise or otherwise reward an employee *each and every time* that person arrives for work on time. Second, you could follow a "partial" reinforcement schedule and provide positive reinforcement only *part* of the time, according to some schedule. If you opt for such a schedule, there are four specific schedules one could follow: fixed interval, variable interval, fixed ratio, and variable ratio.

Exhibit 12.8   Schedules of Reinforcement

Type of Reinforcement:	*Explanation*
I. Continuous (or "mass")	Reward each and every time desired performance occurs
II. Partial	Reward part of the time
1. Fixed interval	According to fixed *time* periods
2. Variable interval	According to variable *time* periods
3. Fixed ratio	After fixed numbers of desired responses
4. Variable ratio	After varying number of responses

Fixed Interval Schedule. A fixed interval schedule is based on time. Here a reinforcer (reward) is administered only when the desired response occurs *and only after the passage of a specified fixed period of time* (since the previous reinforcement). For example, at the end of each week one might go around and praise each employee who came to work on time every day of that week.

Variable Interval Schedules. Variable interval schedules are also based on time. However, reinforcement is administered at some *variable* interval around some average. For example suppose you want to provide reinforcement on the average of once a day for all employees who come to work on time. You could visit them on an *average* of once a day: once on Tuesday, skip Wednesday, three times on Thursday, etc., in such a way that the praise averages out to about once a day.

Fixed Ratio Schedule. A fixed ratio schedule is based on units of *output* rather than on time. With a fixed ratio schedule, rewards are delivered only when a fixed number of desired responses occurs. Most piecework incentive pay plans are on a fixed ratio schedule. The worker is "rewarded" every time he produces a *fixed number* of pieces.

Variable Ratio Schedule. Variable ratio schedules are also based on units of output, but the number of desired outcomes necessary to elicit a reward changes from time to time, around some average. The Las Vegas-type slot machines are probably the best examples of rewards administered according to variable ratio schedules. The number of times one can expect to "hit a jackpot" with such machines *on the average* over the long term is predictable. Yet the jackpots come randomly, on a variable interval schedule. Thus you might get no jackpots for 5 times and then hit two jackpots in a row; you might go 50 turns without a jackpot and then get one.

Summary. Examples of various schedules of reinforcement are presented below:

Schedules of Reinforcement	Examples of Rewards
Fixed interval	Weekly paycheck
Variable interval	Praising employee once on Monday, twice on Tuesday, skipping Wednesday, etc.
Fixed ratio	Piece-rate pay based on units produced
Variable ratio	Modified piece-rate bonus plan for salesmen, with commission sometimes given after two big sales, sometimes after on big sale, sometimes not at all, etc., averaging out to one bonus per two big sales

Which Ratio Schedule Is Most Effective? Several conclusions can be drawn from research into the effectiveness of different reinforcement schedules:

1. Continuous (or "mass") reinforcement schedules usually result in the *fastest* learning. In other words, the way to get someone to learn quickly is to reinforce desired outcomes continuously, each and every time they occur. The drawback is that the desired behavior also diminishes very rapidly once one stops reinforcing them.

2. Partial reinforcement schedules (any of the four we discussed) lead to slower learning but stronger retention. In other words "learning is more permanent when one rewards correct behavior only part of the time." [41]

3. The two reinforcement schedules based on output (fixed ratio and variable ratio) are both more effective than are those schedules based on time (fixed interval and variable interval). [42]

4. Of the four partial reinforcement schedules discussed (fixed and variable interval, and fixed and variable ratio), variable ratio reinforcement is the most powerful at *sustaining* behavior. [43]

Applications to Personnel Management

Sales Incentives. [44]   Assume an employer wants to increase sales by instituting a reinforcement-based incentive plan. He might start by giving each salesperson a book in which to report—immediately following each sale—the amount of his or her monetary commission. The salesmanager tells each salesperson that the record book will be examined first on a continuous (perhaps daily) basis and later intermittently. The reinforcement that the examination provides will cause each salesperson to make entries immediately after each sale, rather than at a later time. And recording the commission in the book will directly reinforce each sale as it is made, and each sale would in turn serve as a stimulus for each subsequent selling situation. In theory (and probably in practice), the salesperson's recognition that sales are increasing will motivate him to continue making entries and will become a self-generating reward.

Controlling Absenteeism. [45]   Behavioral modification has been used effectively to control employee absenteeism. An electronics manufacturer found that it had an acute absenteeism problem and that tardiness was a problem as well. Management concluded that a program should be initiated to reward the desired behavior (prompt and regular attendance) and a program was initiated. Under this program the employees could qualify for a monthly drawing of a prize only if they had perfect attendance and punctuality records for the month. This eligibility for the monthly drawings was contingent upon the desired behavior—work attendance. All absences of any kind precluded employee eligibility; the program was described in a company bulletin. A drawing was held on the last work day of each month in which a winner was selected *at random* from a basket containing the names of all employees who had maintained perfect attendance and punctuality records for that month. A $10 cash prize was awarded to the winner of each monthly lottery. In addition, the names of all employees who qualified were listed on the plant bulletin board. (Note that this was an example of variable ratio scheduling since the "jack-

350   pot"—the $10 prize—was awarded based on randomly drawing names out of a basket.)

The results of this program are fairly impressive. The average monthly savings amounted to about $282. The total yearly savings was over $3,000.

Cost Savings. [46]   Operant conditioning has been used to cut costs at the Emery Air Freight Company. In the air freight business small shipments intended for the same destinations fly at lower rates when shipped together in containers (rather than separately). Thus by encouraging employees to increase their use of containers, management felt it could obtain better prices from the airlines and thereby incur substantial cost savings.

A "performance audit" aimed at determining how often such containers were actually used was made and showed that workers only used them about 45% of the time. Management felt this could be boosted to 90 or 95%. A reinforcement program was established, complete with elaborate instruction workbooks for managers detailing how to give recognition, rewards, and feedback. These workbooks went so far as to enumerate no less than 150 kinds of rewards ranging from a smile to detailed praise like "you're running pretty consistently at 98% of standard, and after watching you I can understand why." In addition, workers were encouraged to set daily goals for container usage, and were reinforced (with praise) if they attained their goals. This program reportedly saved Emery several million dollars during the first three years.

Reinforcement: Hints and Criticisms

Research on the effectiveness of reinforcement in organizational settings has been very limited, but several conclusions seem warranted. First, it can be effective and *positive* reinforcement in particular has been used successfully. Second, it is important that each employee clearly understands that rewards are contingent on good performance: therefore, emphasizing the relationship between performance and rewards is very important. Third, it is clear that when people are continually *not* rewarded for good performance, decreased motivation and performance may result. Fourth, if you must "punish" an employee for doing something wrong, at least take the opportunity to carefully explain what was done wrong, what the desired results were, and how positive rewards will result from those desired outcomes. Finally, remember that variable ratio schedules of reinforcement are the most powerful for sustaining motivated behavior in people. While this schedule may not be practical for salary, it can certainly be used for praise, financial incentive plans, promotion, and other positive reinforcements (rewards). Most importantly, though, remember that regardless of the schedule, employees should always be rewarded *contingent on their performance*: rewards, where possible, should be performance based. [47]

Criticisms.   Behavior modification (as applied to people) has some powerful detractors who have criticized it on several grounds. It is said that this technique is inhumane and that it restricts freedom of choice. (Visions of a

laboratory pigeon dutifully ringing a bell each time it wants a peanut help lay
the groundwork for such criticisms.) Others say that operant conditioning
ignores the individuality of man, and that it ignores the fact that individuals
can be motivated by the job itself. Its focus on external rewards (like money
and praise) is an attempt by management, some say, to control employees'
behavior so "they'll do what they're told." Yet all of these criticisms have been
themselves criticized and the debate between advocates and detractors of reinforcement is both lively and ongoing. [48]

SUMMARY

1. The evidence concerning how morale and performance are related suggests that boosting morale may have some positive effects but will not necessarily
lead to better performance. On the other hand, high morale does lead to better
attendance, and reduced unionization activities.

2. In simplest terms, management by objectives involves (1) establishing
short-term performance targets between superior and subordinate, and (2) periodically discussing progress toward these targets.

3. MBO should be effective because goal-setting, feedback, and participation
all enhance performance. MBO programs are very often quite successful. They
result in more highly motivated managers, help direct work activity toward
organizational goals, and provide clear standards for control. Excessive paper
work, a lack of awareness concerning the value of MBO, and unclear targets
are some important problems to watch out for.

4. Quality circles are another method for using participation to improve
performance. At Litton, an organization-wide approach to the "circle" idea has
been used successfully.

5. In job enrichment, the worker's job is made interesting and challenging.
A job enrichment program can be implemented by: forming natural work groups;
combining tasks; establishing client relationships; vertically loading jobs; and
opening new feedback channels. It is not as effective where there are severe
difficulties—such as low morale due to low pay levels.

6. Behavior modification is based on two principles: (1) that behavior
which leads to a positive consequence (a "reward") tends to be repeated, while
behavior that leads to a negative consequence tends not to be repeated; and
(2) therefore, by providing the properly scheduled rewards, it is possible to
influence people's behavior.

7. We discussed four types of reinforcement. *Positive* reinforcement includes
rewards like praise. *Negative* reinforcement involves allowing the employee to
avoid some negative consequence: both these types of reinforcement focus on
reinforcing the desired behavior. You might also focus on reducing the *un*desired
behavior. Here, use extinction (by withholding rewards) or punishment.

8. There are basically two schedules of positive reinforcement one can use:
continuous or partial. With the former, you reward an employee each and every
time that person performs the desired behavior. With the latter, you provide
reinforcement only part of the time, following one of four specific schedules:
fixed interval, variable interval, fixed ratio, and variable ratio. Variable ratio is
the most effective at sustaining the desired behavior.

*The Tarnished Company Image**

The Silverstone Corporation was the brainchild of Gordon Silverstone. Gordon persuaded his older brother John, a certified public accountant, and his younger brother Tom, a computer salesman, to join him in this enterprise. Recognizing that their personal resources were insufficient to really get the company going, they managed to secure financial backing from Brainbridge Corporation, which became the fourth principal stockholder of the company.

The organization of the company was built around the background of the three brothers. John, the accountant, was named as president and was responsible for the financial functions. Tom, the salesman, was installed as marketing vice-president, and Gordon, the technician, was also titled vice-president with responsibility for recruiting, staffing individual accounts, and generally managing the day-to-day operations.

Early in the company's history, Tom actively searched for business and managed to line up a few small initial programming contracts. Gordon was busy prospecting for some expert technicians (whom he called "eagles") to form the core of the staff; by use of such phrases as "ground-floor opportunity" and "employee stock option plans" he was successful in attracting three capable individuals.

These "eagles" rapidly performed the work called for by the programming contracts. Estimates were consistently beaten, the company began to develop an excellent reputation, and new business was becoming plentiful. As the amount of work grew, Gordon and the other technicians invested time in recruiting new personnel. The new people brought in more people and within two years the company employed thirty systems engineers (or SE's as the technicians were called) on the payroll. The Silverstone Corporation was a profitable operation from its very first year and the future looked bright.

Underspending estimates became expected, thereby making jobs even more profitable to the company, which usually worked on a fixed-price basis. This resulted in many unpaid overtime hours for the SE's. Sixty-hour work weeks (and more) were common. No one seemed to mind since a true team spirit had developed, and, besides, it would be worth it in the end because, as Gordon would frequently say, "This company will belong to those who build it."

Within four years, the company had grown to 100 people and expanded geographically into five cities. In a number of cases the Silverstone brothers deliberately underestimated contract bids for the purpose of securing a foothold in a new market. They felt this approach was justified by the fact that the Silverstone SE's had traditionally underrun estimates and could be counted on to do so in the future.

---

* Case researched and written by Paul R. Paulson.

The reason for the excellent track record the SE's had established on past con-tracts was primarily because of overtime effort. The effect of low-balling a contract bid, then, was to plan on this overtime effort and thereby remove the profit-loss cushion that it normally provided. Consequently, any error in the estimating pro-cedure would result in an overrun condition even if the normal overtime effort was expanded. This problem was compounded by the fact that many of the SE's were commuting (on a daily or weekly basis depending upon distances involved) from their homes to the client's work site in another city. The travel time involved made it difficult for the SE's to apply even the normal amount of overtime, and almost impossible for them to react to major problems with extended overtime.

The first seeds of discontent among the SE's had taken root in a general pres-sure for improved working conditions: less traveling and less overtime, higher pay (or at least some form of compensation for overtime), and, most importantly, the as yet unseen "piece of the action" (stock options). Gordon Silverstone's reading of this situation was that he was losing control of the SE's. The company, he reasoned, had grown to the point that he could no longer effectively manage all the SE's, spread around as they were. His response was to install Fred Maxwell (an older and well-liked SE) as SE manager. Fred's responsibility was to keep the SE's happy and productive, and lift then from Gordon the burden of dealing with individual SE complaints.

It became apparent to both the SE's and Fred that he was not given the tools to do the job. He had no authority to grant pay increases, modify company policy with respect to overtime pay, or even discuss the stock-option about which he knew nothing. In effect, Fred's real job was to act as a buffer to shield Gordon from the unhappy SE's. A quote attributed to Silverstone in describing Fred's function spread throughout the SE ranks. "He keeps the cattle off my back."

Within three months, five SE's left the company. Four months later a group of six SE's left to work for a client whose Silverstone contract had expired. Three weeks later all SE's were required to sign a document (the legality of which was questioned, but never tested) stating that no Silverstone SE could go to work for a current or previous Silverstone client within two years of the SE's separation from the company. There was a general acceptance of the idea that those who refused to sign (and there were some) might as well start looking for new jobs, since, al-though they might not be fired, they certainly had lost a lot of leverage within the company.

After much informal pressure had been brought to bear on the Silverstone brothers, primarily by the original group of SE's who had been with the company longest, the "key employee stock option plan" was announced. This was greeted with high expectations by the SE's, who assumed that their loyalty, hard work, and their long hours were finally being recognized.

As the details of the plan were made clear, however, the high expectations turned to deep disappointment. The company had, immediately before the an-nouncement of the plan, diluted the stock through a ten for one split. The stock was being made available to certain employees (at the discretion of the Silverstone brothers) in twenty-five share blocks. Each certificate carried on the back an agree-ment which said:

> These shares were purchased for investment purposes only. They cannot be
> sold to anyone without first offering Silverstone Corporation the option to buy

them at the price originally paid by the employee. In the event of termination of employment for any reason, the employee must offer the shares to Silverstone Corporation at the original purchase price. The shares can not be used as collateral for securing any type of debt.

The employee's reaction to this plan was that it was worse than worthless. The number of shares offered was so small as to be insignificant. Even if the stock greatly appreciated in value, the employees could not realize any cash gain if the company elected to exercise its option to buy at the original purchase price. The SE's were close to outrage. They felt cheated and insulted. Distrust of the Silverstone brothers was widespread. This general condition precipitated a new wave of quits, primarily among older, original SE's, which included Fred Maxwell.

This further depressed morale among those left, who, at the same time, were being called upon to put forth greater effort to make up for the diminishing manpower. This extra effort, for the most part, was not forthcoming. Several important accounts were lost, and six years after its birth, the company suffered its first loss. The reputation of the company was severely damaged. It became increasingly difficult to secure new business and more difficult still to attract competent computer professionals to the firm.

1. What accounts for the low morale at Silverstone?
2. What do you think can be done to recapture the trust of the system engineers at Silverstone Corporation?
3. Why do you think the situation at the company was allowed to deteriorate so badly without somebody taking corrective action?
4. How might Gordon Silverstone have prevented the loss of effectiveness in his company?
5. What is the lesson or moral to be learned from this case?
6. Do you think the lack of a stock option plan, by itself, is what's bothering the SE's?
7. Do you think providing a stock incentive was the way to handle the problem? Why? Why not?

EXPERIENTIAL EXERCISE

Purpose. The purpose of this exercise is to give you an opportunity to apply reinforcement to an actual problem.

Required Understanding. You should be thoroughly familiar with our discussion of reinforcement.

How to Set Up the Exercise. Break the class into groups of four or five students. All students should read the following statement:

You are the instructor in this class and, having just attended a seminar on "operant conditioning," you think you'd like to try applying this method in class.

Instructions for the Exercise.

1. Each group should develop at least two good examples of how they would

use behavior modification as instructors in this class. Make sure to indicate the type of reinforcement, and the schedules.

    2. If time permits, a spokesman from each group should provide the class with a synopsis of his or her group's recommendations. Which recommendations seem most likely to get results? What drawbacks do you see to these recommendations? Do you think using operant conditioning would result in a "dehumanizing" experience for students? Can you think of any instructors who seem to use operant conditioning in the classroom?

DISCUSSION QUESTIONS

1. Discuss what is meant by "schedules of positive reinforcement."
2. Develop at least two examples of how you would use positive reinforcement: your answer could include relationships with family, teachers, other students, subordinates at work, etc.
3. Give several concrete examples of how you would "enrich" the following jobs: toll booth attendant; assembly line worker in an auto factory; directory assistance operator; bus driver.
4. Discuss the conditions under which job enrichment will more likely result in increased motivation. Based on this, would you in fact try to enrich all of the jobs listed in discussion question 3?
5. What (if any) is the relationship between management by objectives and operant conditioning—are the two similar in any respect? How?
6. Write an essay entitled "How to motivate employees in one easy lesson."

NOTES

    1. For two reviews in this area see Arthur Brayfield and Walter Crockett, "Employee Attitudes and Employee Performance," *Psychological Bulletin,* 52 (September 1955), pp. 396–424; Donald Schwab and Larry Cummings, "Theories of Performance and Satisfaction: A review," *Industrial Relations,* 9, No. 4 (October 1970), pp. 408–430.

    2. Victor Vroom, *Work and Motivation* (New York: John Wiley & Sons, 1964); L. L. Cummings and W. E. Scott, *Readings in Organizational Behavior and Human Performance* (Homewood, Ill.: Irwin, 1969), ch. 3.

    3. Dennis Organ, "A Reappraisal and Reinterpretation of the Satisfaction Causes Performance Hypothesis," *Academy of Management Review,* 2, No. 1 (1977), pp. 46–53.

    4. John Wanous, "A casual correlational analysis of the job satisfaction and performance relationship," *Journal of Applied Psychology,* 59, No. 2 (1974), pp. 139–144; J. E. Sheridan and J. W. Slocum, Jr., "The direction of the causal relationship between job satisfaction and work performance," *Organizational Behavior and Human Performance,* 14, No. 2 (October 1975), pp. 159–172; Edward Lawler III, and Lyman Porter, "The Effect of Performance on job satisfactions," *Industrial Relations,* 7 (October 1967), pp. 20–28; George Strauss, "Human Relations—1968 style," *Industrial Relations,* 7 (May 1968), p. 264.

356   5. D. Bowen and J. P. Siegel, "The relationship between satisfaction and performance: the question of causality," *Proceedings of the Annual Convention of the American Psychological Association* (1970); C. N. Greene, "A causal interpretation of the relationships among pay, performance, and satisfaction," (paper presented at the annual meeting of the midwest Psychological Association, 1972, Cleveland, Ohio). See also J. P. Siegel, D. Bowen, "Satisfaction and Performance: causal relationships and moderating effects, *Journal of Vocational Behavior,* 7 (1971), pp. 263–269.

6. Some of the recent evidence suggests that other factors like the employee's self-esteem and the leader's behavior influence the degree to which performance leads to satisfaction. See, for example, C. N. Greene, "The reciprocal Nature of Influence between leader and subordinate," *Journal of Applied Psychology,* 60 (1975), pp. 187–193: H. K. Downey, J. E. Sheridan, and J. W. Slocum Jr., "The Path-Goal Theory of Leadership: A longitudinal analysis," *Organizational Behavior and Human Performance* (1976); Jeffrey Greenhaus and Irwin Badin, "Self-esteem, performance, and satisfaction: some tests of the theory," *Journal of Applied Psychology,* 62, No. 4 (1977), pp. 417–421.

7. Charles Greene and Robert Craft, Jr., "The satisfaction-performance controversy revisited," in Kirk Downey, Don Hellreigel, and John Slocum, Jr., *Organizational Behavior: Readings* (St. Paul: West Publishing, 1977), pp. 187–201.

8. D. J. Cherrington, H. J. Reitz, and W. E. Scott, Jr., "Effects of Contingent and Noncontingent reward on the relationship between satisfaction and task performance," *Journal of Applied Psychology,* 55 (1971), pp. 531–536. See also Greene and Craft, "The satisfaction-performance," p. 189; D. A. Kesselman, M. T. Wood, and E. L. Hagen, "Relationship between performance and satisfaction under contingent and noncontingent reward systems," *Journal of Applied Psychology,* 59 (1974), pp. 374–376; these researchers attempted to replicate the findings of Cherrington et al., and their findings were less conclusive. These findings also include the findings on behavior modification discussed in chapter 4; C. N. Greene, "Causal connection between managers' pay, job satisfaction and performance," *Journal of Applied Psychology,* 58 (1973), pp. 95–100; Wanous, "A causal correlational analysis," pp. 139–144; R. A. Sutermeister, "Employee performance and employee need satisfaction—which comes first?" *California Management Review,* 13 (1971), pp. 43–47.

9. For a model describing how these other factors influence attendance, see Richard Steers and Susan Rhodes, "Major influences on employee attendance: a process model," *Journal of Applied Psychology,* 63, No. 4 (1978), pp. 391–407.

10. Frank J. Smith, "Work Attitudes as predictors of attendance on a specific day," *Journal of Applied Psychology,* 62, No. 1 (1977), pp. 16–19.

11. W. Clay Hamner and Frank Smith, "Work Attitudes as predictors of unionization activity," *Journal of Applied Psychology,* 63, No. 4 (1978), pp. 415–421. For some earlier research, see J. G. Getman and S. B. Goldberg, "The Behavioral Assumptions" underlying NLRB regulation of campaign misrepresentations: an empirical evaluation," *Stanford Law Review,* 28 (1976), pp. 263–284; W. J. Bigoness, "Correlates of faculty attitudes toward collective bargaining," *Journal of Applied Psychology,* 63, 228–233.

12. Chester Schriesheim, "Job satisfaction, attitudes toward unions, and voting in a union representation election," *Journal of Applied Psychology,* 63, No. 5 (1978), pp. 548–552.

13. Steven Carroll and Henry Tosi, *Management by Objectives* (New York: Macmillan, 1973).

14. Steven Carroll and Henry Tosi, *Management by Objectives* (New York: Macmillan, 1973), p. 140.

15. Clive Seligman and John Darely, "Feedback as a Means of Decreasing Residential Energy Consumption Level," *Journal of Applied Psychology*, 62, No. 4 (1977), pp. 363–368.

16. J. R. P. French, Jr., E. Kay, and H. H. Meyer, "Participation and the Appraisal System," *Human Relations*, Vol. 19 (1966), pp. 3–19.

17. John Ivancevich, "Changes in Performance in a Management by Objectives Program," *Administrative Science Quarterly* (December 1974).

18. See, for example, Tosi et al., "How Real Are Changes Induced by Management by Objectives?" *Administrative Science Quarterly*, 21, No. 2 (June 1976), pp. 276–306; Bruce Kirchoff, "A Diagnostic Tool for Management by Objectives," *Personnel Psychology*, 28, No. 3 (Autumn 1975), p. 31.

19. Carroll and Tosi, *Management by Objectives*, pp. 45, 105.

20. John Ivancevich, J. H. Donnelly, and H. L. Lyon, "A Study of the Impact of Management by Objectives on Perceived Need Satisfaction," *Personnel Psychology*, 23, No. 2 (Summer 1970), pp. 139–151.

21. Carroll and Tosi, *Management by Objectives*.

22. Henry Tosi, John Hunter, Rob Chesser, Jim Tarter, and Steven Carroll, "How Real are Changes Induced by Management by Objectives?" *Administrative Science Quarterly*, Vol. 2, No. 2 (June 1976).

23. This is based on "U.S. firms worried by productivity lag copy Japan in seeking employees' advice," *Wall Street Journal*, February 21, 1980.

24. H. B. Curtis, "Employee Participation in Solving Production Problems," *Personnel Administration* (June 1977), pp. 33–49.

25. *Ibid.*, p. 35.

26. *Ibid.*, p. 36.

27. Daniel Katz and Robert Kahn, *The Social Psychology of Organizations* (New York: John Wiley & Sons, 1966), p. 345.

28. See Leonard Sayles and George Strauss, *Human Behavior in Organizations* (Englewood Cliffs, N.J.: Prentice-Hall, 1966), pp. 42–50.

29. Daniel Bell, "Work in the Life of an American," in William Haber et al., *Man in Power in the United States* (New York: Harper & Row, 1948), p. 15.

30. Arthur Tomac and Paul Lawrence, *Industrial Jobs and the Worker* (Boston: Harvard Business School, Division of Research, 1965), pp. 35–48; Charles Walker and Robert Guest, *The Man on the Assembly Line* (Cambridge: Harvard University Press, 1952), p. 120.

31. Leonard Sayles, "Wildcat Strikes," *Harvard Business Review*, 32, No. 6 (November 1954), pp. 42–52.

32. Sayles and Strauss, *Human Behavior*, p. 47; see also J. W. Gooding, *The Job Revolution* (New York: Walker, 1972); *Work in America: Report of a Special Task Force to the Secretary of Health, Education, and Welfare* (Cambridge: Massachusetts Institute of Technology Press, 1973).

33. See, for example, Chris Argyris, *Integrating the Individual and the Organization* (New York: John Wiley & Sons, 1964).

34. Frederick Herzberg, "The Wise Old Turk," *Harvard Business Review* (September–October 1974).

35. J. Richard Hackman et al., "A New Strategy for Job Enrichment," *California Management Review*, 17, No. 1, 51–71, reprinted in H. Kirk Downey, Don Hellreigel, and John Slocum, Jr., *Organizational Behavior* (St. Paul: West Publishing, 1977), pp. 304–332. For discussions of some of the work that led up to this development see A. N. Turner and Paul R. Lawrence, *Industrial Jobs and the Worker* (Cambridge: Harvard University Graduate School of Business Administration, 1965); Raymond Aldag and Arthur Brief, *Task Design and Employee Motivation* (Glenview, Ill.: Scott Foresman), pp. 45–48. J. Richard Hackman and Edwin Lawler III,

358   "Employee Reactions to Job Characteristics," *Journal of Applied Psychology*, 55 (1971), pp. 259–296; Wayne Cascio, *Applied Psychology in Personnel Management* (Reston, Va.: Reston Publishing Co., 1978), p. 355. For other studies in this area see, for example, R. J. Aldag and A. P. Brief, "Some Correlates of Work Values," *Journal of Applied Psychology*, 60 (1975), pp. 757–770; A. P. Brief, M. Wallace, and R. J. Aldag, "Linear vs. Nonlinear Models of the Formation of effective responses: The case of Job Enlargement," *Decision Sciences*, 7 (1976), pp. 1–9.

36. J. Richard Hackman and Greg Oldham, "Motivation Through the Design of Work: Test of a Theory," *Organizational Behavior and Human Performance*, 16, No. 2 (August 1976), pp. 250–279.

37. Rollin H. Simmons and John N. Oriff, "Worker Behavior vs. Enrichment Theory," *Administrative Science Quarterly*, Vol. 20 (1975), p. 606; David Whitsett, "Where Are Your Unenriched Jobs?" *Harvard Business Review*, Vol. 53 (January–February 1976); Greg Oldham, J. R. Hackman, and J. Pearce, "Conditions Under Which Employees Respond Positively to Enriched Work," *Journal of Applied Psychology*, Vol. 61 (August 1976), pp. 395–403.

38. W. Clay Hamner, "Reinforcement Theory and Management in Organizational Settings," in Henry Tosi and W. Clay Hamner, *Organizational Behavior and Management: A Contingency Approach* (Chicago: St. Claire, 1974), pp. 86–112. This principle is also known as the *law of effect*.

39. Hamner, *Organizational Behavior*, p. 95.

40. Hamner, *Organizational Behavior*, pp. 99–103.

41. Hamner, *Organizational Behavior*, p. 100.

42. Gary Latham and Gary Yukl, "Assigned Versus Participative Goal Setting with Educated and Uneducated Woodsworkers," *Journal of Applied Psychology*, Vol. 60 (1975), pp. 299–302; also "The Effectiveness of Performance Incentives under Continuous and Variable Ratio Schedules of Reinforcement," *Personnel Psychology*, Vol. 20 (Summer 1976), pp. 233–242. Robert Pritchard, Dale Leonard, Clarence Von Bergen, Jr., and Raymond Kirk, "The Effects of Varying Schedules of Reinforcement on Human Task Performance," *Organizational Behavior and Human Performance*, Vol. 16, No. 2 (August 1976), pp. 205–230.

43. Joblonski and DeVaines, quoted in "Operant Conditioning Principles Extended to the Theory of Management" in Hamner, "Reinforcement Theory," p. 100.

44. This example is from Luthans and White, "Behavior Modification," pp. 41–47, reprinted in J. Richard Hackman, Edward Lawler III, and Lyman Porter, *Perspectives on Behavior and Organization* (New York: McGraw-Hill, 1977), pp. 307–314.

45. This is based on Jerry Wallin and Ronald Johnson, "The Positive Reinforcement Approach to Controlling Employee Absenteeism," *Personnel Journal* (August 1976), pp. 390–392.

46. This is based on "At Emery Air Freight: Positive Reinforcement Boosts," *Organizational Dynamics* (Winter 1973), reprinted in Tosi and Hamner, *Organizational Behavior and Management: A Contingency Approach*, pp. 113–122. For a good discussion of the use of operant conditioning, see W. Clay Hamner and Ellen Hamner, "Behavior Modifications on the Bottom Level," reprinted from *Organizational Dynamics* (New York: Malcolm, 1976) in W. Clay Hamner and Frank Schmidt, *Contemporary Problems in Personnel* (Chicago: St. Clair, 1977), pp. 284–298; also for an excellent review of Behavior Modification Applications, see W. Clay Hamner and Ellen Hamner, "Behavior Modifications on the Bottom Line," *Organizational Dynamics* (Spring 1976); reprinted in Hamner and Schmidt, *Contemporary Problems in Personnel* (rev. ed.).

47. John Ivanevich, Andrew Szilagyi, and Marc Wallace, *Organizational Behavior and Performance* (Santa Monica, Calif.: Goodyear, 1977), p. 124.

48. See also, for example, W. C. Hamner and L. W. Foster, "Are Intrinsic and Extrinsic Rewards Additive: A Test of Deci's Cognitive Evaluation Theory of Task Motivation," *Organizational Behavior and Human Performance*, Vol. 14 (December 1975); W. E. Scott, Jr., "The Effects of Extrinsic Rewards on 'Intrinsic' Motivation," *Organizational Behavior and Human Performance*, Vol. 15 (February 1976); Robert D. Pritchard, Kathleen Campbell, and Donald Campbell, "The Effects of Extrinsic Financial Rewards on Intrinsic Motivation," *Journal of Applied Psychology*, Vol. 62 (1977), pp. 9–15; Craig C. Pinder, "Additivity Versus Nonadditivity of Intrinsic and Extrinsic Incentives: Implications for Work Motivation, Performance and Attitude," *Journal of Applied Psychology*, Vol. 61 (December 1976); William H. Whyte, "Pigeons, Persons, and Piece Rates," *Psychology Today* (April 1972), pp. 67–68, 96, 98, 100, reprinted in Jerry Gray and Frederick Starke, *Readings in Organizational Behavior* (Columbus: Merrill, 1977), pp. 18–56.

Part Three

Appraisal and Development

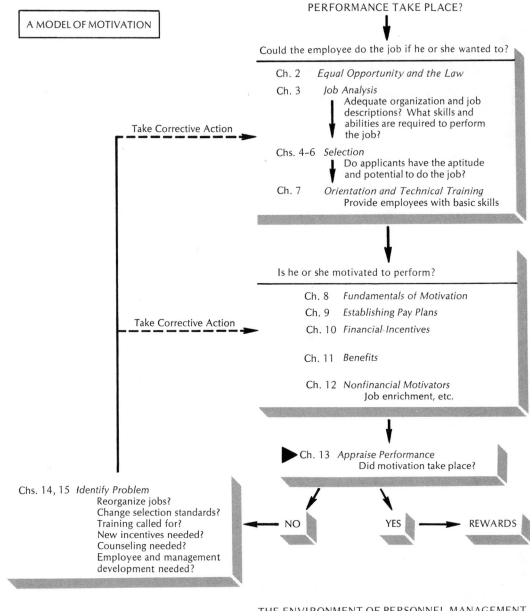

WILL MOTIVATION AND
PERFORMANCE TAKE PLACE?

A MODEL OF MOTIVATION

Could the employee do the job if he or she wanted to?

Ch. 2   *Equal Opportunity and the Law*

Ch. 3   *Job Analysis*
Adequate organization and job
descriptions? What skills and
abilities are required to perform
the job?

Chs. 4–6   *Selection*
Do applicants have the aptitude
and potential to do the job?

Ch. 7   *Orientation and Technical Training*
Provide employees with basic skills

Take Corrective Action

Is he or she motivated to perform?

Ch. 8   *Fundamentals of Motivation*

Ch. 9   *Establishing Pay Plans*

Ch. 10   *Financial Incentives*

Ch. 11   *Benefits*

Ch. 12   *Nonfinancial Motivators*
Job enrichment, etc.

Take Corrective Action

Ch. 13   *Appraise Performance*
Did motivation take place?

Chs. 14, 15   *Identify Problem*
Reorganize jobs?
Change selection standards?
Training called for?
New incentives needed?
Counseling needed?
Employee and management
development needed?

NO   YES   REWARDS

THE ENVIRONMENT OF PERSONNEL MANAGEMENT

Ch. 16   *Labor Relations and Grievances*

Ch. 17   *Employee Safety and Health*

Ch. 18   *Personnel Management and the
Quality of Work Life*

13 Performance Appraisal

You should be able to:

1. *Develop and evaluate at least four performance appraisal tools.*
2. *List and discuss the pros and cons of: graphic rating scales, the alternation ranking method, the paired comparison method, the forced distribution method, the critical incident method, a behaviorally anchored ranking scale.*
3. *Explain the problems to be avoided in appraising performance.*
4. *Discuss the pros and cons of using different potential raters to appraise a person's performance.*

OVERVIEW

This chapter starts a new section of this book. Once workers have been selected, trained, and motivated, the next step is to appraise their perform-ance, and the main purpose of this chapter is to explain several techniques for doing so. We will explain how to use appraisal techniques, and how to avoid common "performance appraisal" problems. Finally, we will discuss the pros and cons of using various appraisers—peers, the boss, etc. Perform-ance appraisal (as shown in our performance motivation model) is the step where the employer finds out how effective it has been at hiring and placing employees, and motivating them. Should any problems be identified, the next steps would involve communicating with the employee and taking remedial action—topics discussed in the following two chapters.

You've probably already had some experience with performance ap-praisal scales. For example, some colleges ask students to rank instructors on scales like the one in Exhibit 13.1. Do you think this is an effective scale? Do you see any ways to improve it? These are two of the questions you should be in a better position to answer by the end of this chapter.

INTRODUCTION

Functions and Nature of Appraisal

Appraising performance serves two main functions.[1] First, performance appraisals are the basis on which various *administrative decisions* are made, decisions that include salary increases, promotions, and transfers. As a result, performance appraisal is the cornerstone of an effective reward system. Ideally, a person's rewards should be tied to his or her performance, and to do this the

---

INSTRUCTOR

DEPARTMENT

COURSE NUMBER OR TITLE

I. The following items reflect some of the ways teachers can be described in and out of the classroom. For the instructor named above, please circle the number which indicates the degree to which you feel each item is descriptive of him or her. In some cases, the statement may not apply to this individual. In these cases, check *Does not apply or don't know* for that item.

	Not at all Descriptive	Very Descriptive	Doesn't apply or don't know
1. Has command of the subject, presents material in an analytic way, contrasts various points of view discusses current developments, and relates topics to other areas of knowledge	1 2 3 4 5 6 7		( )
2. Makes himself clear, states objectives, summarizes major points, presents material in an organized manner, and provides emphasis.			
3. Is sensitive to the response of the class, encourages student participation, and welcomes questions and discussion.			
4. Is available to and friendly towards students, is interested in students as individuals, is himself respected as a person, and is valued for advice not directly related to the course.			
5. Enjoys teaching, is enthusiastic about his subject, makes the course exciting, and has self-confidence			

Note: (Additional items may be presented by instructor and/or department.)

Source: Richard Miller, *Developing Programs for Faculty Evaluation* (San Francisco: Jossey-Bass Publishers, 1974), p. 43.

person's performance should be appraised fairly, and effectively. If, for example employees come to believe that appraisals are biased, unfair, or misleading, the performance-appraisal-reward link will be broken, and performance will deteriorate. Rewards, in other words, will no longer be seen as stemming from performance, and as a result performance will suffer.

In addition to being the basis for various administrative decisions, performance appraisal also serves a *work planning and review* function. The appraisal and subsequent superior/subordinate review provide an opportunity to review the subordinate's progress and to map out a plan for rectifying any performance deficiencies that might be identified. And, the appraisal provides an opportunity to develop a more detailed plan (than exists in the job description) for exactly what sorts of activities the subordinate should engage in during the ensuing period.

The nature of performance appraisal is such that line managers and personnel specialists both play important roles in the process. Line managers play a central role because in almost all cases the supervisor does the actual appraising. As a result, supervisors have a responsibility to see to it that they are completely familiar with the appraisal techniques to be used, that they understand (and can avoid) the problems that can cripple an appraisal system, and that they perform their appraisal function fairly and objectively. The personnel office, on the other hand serves a policy-making and advisory function with respect to performance appraisals. As explained in this chapter, there are many performance appraisal tools in use, and the personnel office should be able to assist line managers in choosing the most appropriate ones. In one recent survey, for example, about 80% of the companies responding said that the personnel office provides advice and assistance regarding appraisal, but leaves final decisions on appraisal procedures to operating division heads; in the rest of the firms the personnel office prepares detailed forms and procedures and insists that they be used by all departments in the organization. [2] The personnel specialist is also responsible for making available "performance appraisal training" for supervisors, training aimed at improving supervisors' appraisal skills. Finally, the personnel office is often responsible for monitoring the use of the appraisal system, particularly in regard to ensuring that the format and criteria being measured do not become outdated. (In fact, organizations rarely install an appraisal system without changing it gradually over the years. In the survey mentioned above, for example one third the organizations surveyed had appraisal systems that had been in use for less than a year, and another third had systems that had been in use for 1 to 5 years. Half the organizations were currently in the process of revising their appraisal programs and several other organizations were conducting reviews to see how well their programs were working.) [3] Related to this, the personnel specialist plays an increasingly important role in ensuring that the employer's appraisal program complies with fair-employment practice, a point to which we now turn.

Performance Appraisal and Fair-Employment Practice [4]

Since the passage of Title VII the courts have addressed various issues (including promotion, layoff, and compensation decisions) in which performance appraisals had played a significant role. And, in their decisions, they have often found that the inadequacies of the employer's appraisal system lay at the root of some discriminatory action concerning promotion, layoff, or compensation. In one case, for example, [5] the court concluded that the failure of blacks to be promoted or transferred resulted from the employer's reliance on all-white supervisory recommendations which were based on subjective and vague standards. Specifically, the court held that, (in violation of Title VII):

1. The foreman's recommendation was the indisputable single most important factor in the promotion process;
2. Foremen were given no written instructions pertaining to the qualifications necessary for promotion;

366

3. The standards that were determined to be important in determining transfer and promotion decisions were vague and subjective;
4. Hourly employees were not notified of promotional opportunities; and
5. No safeguards (like proper supervisory training) had been designed to avert discriminatory practices in the appraisal procedure. The net effect of all this was to "freeze in" past discrimination at General Motors to a significant extent.

Another case involved layoff decisions. Here the court held that the firm had violated Title VII when, on the basis of poor performance ratings, it laid off several Spanish-surnamed employees. [6] The court concluded that the practice was illegal because:

1. The appraisals were based on subjective supervisory observations;
2. The appraisals were not administered and scored in a standardized fashion; and
3. Two of the three supervisory evaluators did not have daily contact with the employees being evaluated. [7]

One of the most important aspects of this case was that the court in effect accepted performance appraisals as tests. In other words, they concluded that the performance appraisal procedure used by the company had to comply with EEOC employee selection guidelines, and that in this case it did not. While the appraisals *were* based on the "best judgments and opinions" of the appraisers, they were *not* based on any objective criteria that were supported by some kind of record of validity.

In summary, the court decided in this case that a performance appraisal procedure constitutes a selection procedure (since it affects selection for promotion, and retention, for example). As a result, performance appraisal has to comply with EEOC guidelines, specifically with respect to being valid. While fair employment law with respect to performance appraisals is relatively new, it seems that a prudent employer should thus take steps like the following to help ensure that its appraisal procedures are defensible: [8]

1. The overall appraisal process should be formalized, standardized, and made as objective as possible. For example, all employees in the same job class should be appraised using the same procedures, and standards should be clear with respect to what is meant by "satisfactory performance," "outstanding performance," and so on.
2. The performance appraisal system should be as job-related as possible. For example, the criteria to be evaluated—such as "quantity of effort," and "punctuality" should make sense in terms of the nature of the job and should (preferably) be shown to be related to actual job performance.
3. A thorough, formal job analysis for all positions being rated should be completed in order to clearly identify the duties of each job, and it's performance standards.
4. While they can be useful, subjective supervisory ratings should be used as only one component of the overall evaluation process.

5. Appraisers should be adequately trained in the use of appraisal techniques.
6. Appraisers should have substantial daily contact with the employee being evaluated.
7. If the appraisal involves several measures of performance (like "attendance," "quality," and "quantity") the weight of each measure in relation to the overall assessment should be fixed ahead of time.
8. Whenever possible, the appraisal should be conducted by more than one appraiser and all such appraisals should be conducted independently. As we explain below, this process can help to "cancel out" individual errors and biases on the part of the individual appraisers.

TOOLS FOR APPRAISING PERFORMANCE

Graphic Rating Scales

Graphic rating scales are probably the most widely used performance appraisal tools since they are relatively easy to develop and use. A typical rating chart is presented in Exhibit 13.2. [9] Notice that the chart lists a number of traits (such as Quality, and Quantity) as well as a range of performance (from Unsatisfactory to Exceptional) for each. Each subordinate is rated by circling or checking the score that best describes his or her level of performance for each trait. The assigned values for each trait are then added up and totaled.

The Alternation Ranking Method

Another popular, simple method for evaluating employees is to rank them from best to worst on some trait. Since it is usually easier to distinguish between the worst and best employees than to simply rank them, an "alternation" ranking method is most popular. First, list all subordinates to be rated and then cross out the names of any not known well enough to rank. Then, on a form such as that in Exhibit 13.3, indicate the employee who is the highest on the characteristic being measured and also the one who is the lowest. Then choose the next highest and the next lowest, *alternating* between highest and lowest until all the employees to be rated have been ranked.

Paired Comparison Method

The paired comparison method helps to make the ranking method more effective. For every trait (quantity of work, quality of work, etc.) every subordinate is compared to every other subordinate in pairs.

Suppose there are five employees to be rated. In the paired comparison method the supervisor makes a chart as in Exhibit 13.4, of all possible pairs of employees *for each trait*. Then for each trait indicate (with a + or −) who is the better employee of the pair. Next, the number of times an employee is rated "better" is added up. In Exhibit 13.4, employee "Bob" was ranked highest for quality of work, while "Art" was ranked highest for creativity.

Exhibit 13.2   Example of a Graphic Rating Scale

Employee: _____   Job title: _____   Date: _____

Department: _____   Job number: _____   Rater: _____

FACTOR	SCORE – RATING				
	UNSATISFACTORY — So definitely inadequate that it justifies release	FAIR — Minimal; barely adequate to justify retention	GOOD — Meets basic requirement for retention	SUPERIOR — Definitely above norm and basic requirements	EXCEPTIONAL — Distinctly and consistently outstanding
QUALITY — Accuracy, thoroughness, appearance and acceptance of output					
QUANTITY — Volume of output and contribution					
REQUIRED SUPERVISION — Need for advice, direction or correction					
ATTENDANCE — Regularity, dependability and promptness					
CONSERVATION — Prevention of waste, spoilage; protection of equipment					

Reviewed by: _____   (Reviewer comments on reverse)

Employee comment: _____

Date: _____   Signature or initial: _____

Note: In this form, the supervisor *checks* the appropriate box.

Source: Dale Yoder, *Personnel Management*, 6th ed. (Englewood Cliffs, N.J.: Prentice-Hall, Inc., 1970), p. 240. Reprinted by permission.

Exhibit 13.3   Rating-Ranking Scale Using Alternation-Ranking Technique   369

RATING-RANKING SCALE

Consider all those on your list in terms of their (quality). Cross out the names of any you cannot rate on this quality. Then select the one you would regard as having most of the quality. Put his name in Column I, below, on the first line, numbered 1. Cross out his name on your list. Consult the list again and pick out the person having least of this quality. Put his name at the bottom of Column II, on the line numbered 20. Cross out his name. Now, from the remaining names on your list, select the one having most of the quality. Put his name in the first column on line 2. Keep up this process until all names have been placed in the scale.

COLUMN I (MOST)

1. ....
2. ....
3. ....
4. ....
5. ....
6. ....
7. ....
8. ....
9. ....
10. ....

COLUMN II (LEAST)

11. ....
12. ....
13. ....
14. ....
15. ....
16. ....
17. ....
18. ....
19. ....
20. ....

Source: Yoder, *Personnel Management*, p. 237. Reprinted by permission.

Forced Distribution Method

The forced distribution method is similar to "grading on a curve." With this method, predetermined percentages of ratees are placed in various performance categories. For example, you may decide to distribute employees as follows:

15% HIGH PERFORMERS

20% HIGH AVERAGE PERFORMERS

30% AVERAGE PERFORMERS

20% LOW AVERAGE PERFORMERS

15% LOW PERFORMERS

(One practical way for doing this is to write each employee's name on a separate

Exhibit 13.4   Ranking Employees by the Paired Comparison Method

FOR THE TRAIT "QUALITY OF WORK"						FOR THE TRAIT "CREATIVITY"					
Men Rated:						Men Rated:					
As Compared to:	A Art	B Bob	C Chuck	D Diane	E Ed	As Compared to:	A Art	B Bob	C Chuck	D Diane	E Ed
A Art		+	+	−	−	A Art		−	−	−	−
B Bob	−		−	−	−	B Bob	+		−	+	+
C Chuck	−	+		+	−	C Chuck	+	+		−	+
D Diane	+	+	−		+	D Diane	+	−	+		−
E Ed	+	+	+	−		E Ed	+	−	−	+	

       ↑   ↑

    Bob Ranks Highest Here   Art Ranks Highest Here

Note: + means "better than"; − means "worse than." For each chart, add up the number of +'s in each column to get the highest ranked employee.

index card. Then, for each trait being appraised (quality of work, creativity, etc.) simply place the employee's card in one of the appropriate categories.

Critical Incident Method

With the "critical incident" appraisal method the supervisor keeps, for each subordinate, a running record of uncommonly good or undesirable examples (or "incidents") of that person's work-related behavior. Then every six months or so, the supervisor and subordinate meet and discuss the latter's performance using the specific incidents as examples. This method, notice, is quite different from the rating and ranking methods we've discussed, in that it relies on a subjective narrative appraisal by the supervisor, rather than the more "objective" and standardized appraisals which, say, a graphic rating scale provides.

There is often no substitute for this sort of narrative appraisal. For one thing (whether or not the employer also uses a rating or ranking tool) the critical incident method provides the supervisor and subordinate with some specific "hard facts" for explaining the latter's appraisal. And, it ensures that the supervisor is forced to think about the subordinate's appraisal all during the year, (since the incidents must be accumulated) and that the rating therefore does not just reflect the employee's most recent performance. Ideally, keeping a running list of critical incidents also provides the supervisor and subordinate with some concrete examples of what specifically the latter can do to eliminate any performance deficiencies. In the example presented in Exhibit 13.5, for example one of the assistant plant manager's continuing duties was to supervise procurement, and a target here was to minimize inventory costs. However, the critical incident shows that he let inventory storage costs rise 15%, and this

Exhibit 13.5   Examples of Critical Incidents for an Assistant Plant Manager   371

Continuing Duties	*Targets*	*Critical Incidents*
Schedule Production for Plant	Full utilization of personnel and machinery in plant; orders delivered on time	Instituted new production scheduling system; he decreased late orders by 10% last month; he increased machine utilization in plant by 20% last month
Supervise procurement of raw materials and inventory control	Minimize inventory costs while keeping adequate supplies on hand	He let inventory storage costs rise 15% last month; over-ordered parts "A" and "B" by 20%, underordered part "C" by 30%
Supervise machinery maintenance	No shutdowns due to faulty machinery	Instituted new preventive maintenance system for plant; he prevented a machine breakdown by discovering faulty part

would provide a specific example of what performance he must improve in the future. In summary, a narrative, nonquantified approach like the critical incident method may not be ideal for comparing employees and making salary or promotion decisions; however, it can be useful for identifying specific examples of good and poor performance and for planning how deficiencies can be corrected.

Behaviorally Anchored Rating Scales (BARS)

A *Behaviorally Anchored Rating Scale* (BARS) aims at combining the benefits of narrative critical incidents and quantified ratings by "anchoring" a quantified performance scale with specific, narrative examples of good or poor performance. Its proponents claim that it provides better, more equitable appraisals than do the other tools we have discussed. [10]

Developing a BARS typically requires five steps: [11]

1. *Generate critical incidents.* Persons with knowledge of the job to be appraised (job holders and/or supervisors) are asked to describe specific illustrations (critical incidents) of effective and ineffective performance behavior.
2. *Develop performance dimensions.* The people developing the BARS then "cluster" these incidents into a smaller set (say five or ten) of performance dimensions. Each cluster (dimension) is then defined.
3. *Reallocate incidents.* Another group of people who also know the job then reallocate the original critical incidents. They are given the clusters' definitions, and the critical incidents, and asked to reassign each incident to the cluster they think fits best. Typically a critical incident is retained if some

percentage (usually 50 to 80%) of this group assigns it to the same cluster as did the group in step 2.

4. *Scale the incidents.* This second group is generally asked to rate (seven- or nine-point scales are typical) the behavior described in the incident as to how effectively or ineffectively it represents performance on the appropriate cluster's dimension.

5. *Develop final instrument.* A subject of the incidents (usually six or seven per cluster) are used as "behavioral anchors" for each dimension.

Example: Three researchers developed a BARS for grocery "checkout" clerks who were working in a large western grocery chain.[12] They collected a number of critical incidents and then clustered them into eight performance criteria or dimensions:

KNOWLEDGE AND JUDGMENT.

CONSCIENTIOUSNESS.

SKILL IN HUMAN RELATIONS.

SKILL IN OPERATION OF REGISTER.

SKILL IN BAGGING.

ORGANIZATIONAL ABILITY OF CHECK-STAND WORK.

SKILL IN MONETARY TRANSACTIONS.

OBSERVATIONAL ABILITY.

Presented in Exhibit 13.6 is the Behaviorally Anchored Rating Scale for one of these dimensions, "Knowledge and Judgment." Notice how there is a scale (ranging from one to seven) for rating performance from "extremely poor" to "extremely good." Notice also how the BARS is "behaviorally anchored" with specific critical incidents. For example, there is a specific critical incident ("by knowing the price of items, this checker would be expected to look for mismarked and unmarked items") that helps "anchor" or specify what is meant by "extremely good" performance. Similarly, there are other critical incident "anchors" all along the scale.

Advantages. Developing a BARS can obviously be more time-consuming and expensive than developing other appraisal tools (such as graphic rating scales). But BARS are also said to have some important advantages:[13,14,15]

1. *A more accurate gauge.* People who know the job and its requirements better than anyone else develop BARS. The resulting BARS should therefore be a very good gauge of performance on that job.
2. *Clearer standards.* The critical incidents along the scale help to clarify what is meant by "extremely good" performance, "average" performance, and so forth.
3. *Feedback.* The use of the critical incidents may be more useful in providing feedback to the people being appraised.
4. *Independent dimensions.* Systematically clustering the critical incidents into

Exhibit 13.6   A Behaviorally Anchored Rating Scale for the Performance Dimension   373
"Knowledge and Judgment" For Grocery Checkout Clerks

Extremely good performance	7	
		By knowing the price of items, this checker would be expected to look for mismarked and unmarked items.
Good performance	6	You can expect this checker to be aware of items that constantly fluctuate in price.
		You can expect this checker to know the various sizes of cans—No. 303, No. 2, No. 2½.
Slightly good performance	5	When in doubt, this checker would ask the other clerk if the item is taxable.
		This checker can be expected to verify with another checker a discrepancy between the shelf and the marked price before ringing up that item.
Neither poor nor good performance	4	
		When operating the quick check, the lights are flashing, this checker can be expected to check out a customer with 15 items.
Slightly poor performance	3	
		You could expect this checker to ask the customer the price of an item that he does not know.
		In the daily course of personal relationships, may be expected to linger in long conversations with a customer or another checker.
Poor performance	2	
		In order to take a break, this checker can be expected to block off the checkstand with people in line.
Extremely poor performance	1	

✦ Notice how the scale (from 1-7) is "Behaviorally anchored" by the "Critical incidents."

Source: Lawrence Fogli, Charles Hulin, and Milton Blood, "Development of First Level Behavioral Job Criteria," *Journal of Applied Psychology*, Vol. 55 (1971), p. 6. Copyright 1971 by the American Psychological Association. Reprinted by permission.

five or six performance dimensions (such as "knowledge and judgment") should help to make the dimensions more independent of one another. For example, a rater should be less likely to rate an employee high on *all* dimensions simply because he or she was rated high in "cooperativeness."
5. *Rater-independent.* [16] BARS evaluations also seem to be relatively unbiased and reliable, in that different raters' appraisals of a person tend to be similar.

Use of Multiple Appraisal Tools

According to one survey the trend is toward using multiple appraisal techniques. [17] In this survey of major companies based in California the researchers found that 14 of the 18 organizations surveyed (78%) used both rating/ranking tools *and* narrative tools, while only 3 (17%) used narrative alone, and only 1 used ratings alone. None of the firms were using the behaviorally anchored rating scales. Of the firms using both rating/ranking tools and narratives, about half used the rating/ranking tool as the primary appraisal technique, 39% used narratives as the primary techniques and 11% (2 of 18) weight the two equally. Most of the firms (15 out of 18) had different appraisal systems for exempt and nonexempt personnel, and 12 of these require more narrative and fewer ratings for exempts. The tendency thus seems to be to emphasize narratives more for exempt positions, and rating/ranking tools for nonexempt employees. The practice of using both narrative and rating/ranking tools to appraise performance probably results from the fact that each serves a somewhat different purpose: quantifiable rating/ranking methods permit comparisons of employees and are therefore useful for making salary, transfer, and promotion decisions. Narratives, on the other hand are especially useful for providing specific examples for use in work planning and review. One alternative is to combine rating and narrative methods on one form, for instance by placing a "comments" section below each trait to be evaluated (like quality, or quantity) on a graphic rating scale.

IMPROVING PERFORMANCE APPRAISALS

Factors Undermining Performance Appraisals

Most people are familiar with the types of inequities that can arise in appraisal systems. For example, some instructors are "easy" graders and tend to give higher grades on the average than others. And some students (or subordinates) become "teacher's pet" and tend to get rated high regardless of their actual performance.

Problems like these can destroy the usefulness of an appraisal system, and thereby undermine the reward system as well. They not only result in inaccurate, invalid appraisals, but in unfair ones. And once employees decide that the appraisals do not fairly reflect performance, it is unlikely that they will view the appraisals or the decisions based on them as equitable or acceptable: animosity, rather than motivation may then arise. Specific problems include unclear standards, halo effect, and central tendency.

Unclear Standards.   Unclear performance standards are one problem. For example, look at the graphic rating chart in Exhibit 13.7. While the chart seems objective enough, actually it might result in unfair ratings. This is because the traits and degrees of merit are open to various interpretations. For example, different supervisors would probably define "good" performance, "fair"

Exhibit 13.7   A Graphic Rating Scale–With Unclear Standards

	EXCELLENT	GOOD	FAIR	POOR
Quality of Work				
Quantity of Work				
Creativity				
Integrity				

For example, What is meant by "good"; quantity of work; and so forth.

performance, and so on, differently. The same is true of traits such as "quality of work" or "creativity." Some traits, such as "integrity," may be almost impossible to rate objectively.

Rectifying this problem involves at least two steps. The first is to develop and include descriptive phrases which define each trait—as was the case in Exhibit 13.2. There, for example, we defined on the chart what was meant by "excellent," "good," "quality of work," and so forth. Second, supervisors have to be trained to apply these standards in a consistent way, so that, say, a "fair" rating by supervisor #1 means about the same as a "fair" from supervisor #2. (This type of training is explained below.)

The Halo Effect Problem.   There is a "halo effect" in the appraisal when the appraiser assigns the same rating to *all* traits regardless of an employee's actual performance on these traits. The problem often occurs with employees who are especially friendly (or unfriendly) toward the supervisor. For example, the "unfriendly" employee will often be rated as unsatisfactory for all traits rather than simply for the trait "gets along well with others." A five- or ten-minute training program, showing supervisors what to avoid, can help alleviate this problem. [18]

The Central Tendency Problem.   Many raters have a "central tendency" when filling in questionnaires or rating scales. For example, if the rating scale ranges from one through seven, many raters will tend to avoid the highs (six and seven) and lows (one and two), and put most of their checkmarks between three and five.

On a graphic rating chart this central tendency could mean that all employees are simply rated "average." Needless to say, this restriction can seriously distort the evaluations, making them almost useless for promotion, salary, or counseling purposes. The *ranking* tools discussed are aimed at avoiding this central tendency problem because all employees here *must* be ranked, and so cannot all be rated "average."

The Leniency or Strictness Problem.   Some supervisors tend to rate all their subordinates consistently high (or low): for example, some instructors are notoriously high graders, and others are not. This strictness/leniency problem is particularly acute with graphic rating scales because the supervisor can conceivably rate *all* subordinates either high or low. When using some form of ranking system, on the other hand, the supervisor is forced to distinguish between high and low performers. Strictness/leniency is thus not as much of a problem with ranking systems.

Individual Differences in Ratees.   Individual differences among ratees in terms of characteristics like age, race, and sex affect the ratings they get, often quite aside from the employee's actual performance. [19] In one study of 9,000 employees, for example researchers found a curvilinear relationship between ratee age and rating: ratings increased as ratees increased in age from 20 to 30–35 and, thereafter, declined with age. [20] Others have also found a systematic tendency to evaluate ratees over 60 years of age lower on "performance capacity" and "potential for development" than younger employees. [21] The ratee's race and sex may also affect the person's rating, although here the bias is not necessarily consistently against the minority or women, as it seems to be in the case of older workers. In one study in which objective performance measures (such as graphic rating scales) were used, high performing females were often rated significantly higher than high performing males. Similarly, low performing blacks were often rated significantly higher than low performing whites. [22]

Lack of Proven Job Relatedness.   As explained above, performance appraisals are often used for screening employees for some future employment opportunity, and are therefore subject to much the same laws and validation procedures as are personnel tests and other "screening" devices. Yet in a survey by the Conference Board only *one* of the 217 firms using performance appraisal said they were validating theirs. About 40% of these firms had not analyzed the jobs being rated, even though job analysis is a logical prerequisite to identifying what specific activities should be appraised. The point here is that (contrary to common practice) employers who seek to avoid charges of unfair discrimination should make an effort to ensure that their appraisal techniques are validly rating job-related performance. [23]

Reducing Rating Errors

There are at least four ways in which an employer can reduce rating errors and improve its appraisal system. First, it can *familiarize all appraisers* with the problems discussed above, on the assumption that a knowledge of the problems will help appraisers avoid them. [24] Second, choose *the right appraisal tool*. Each of the tools, such as the graphic rating scale or forced choice method, has a number of advantages and disadvantages that should be considered before implementation. For example, as summarized in Exhibit 13.8, ranking systems avoid central tendency, but can cause ill-feelings among employees whose performance is in fact very similar—as when all are actually "high." Similarly, rating/ranking methods are good for comparing employees (especially non-exempt ones) for salary and promotion decisions, while narrative methods (like critical incidents) are best for work planning and review. Next, an employer can ensure appraisals are *fair*, and that supervisors are *well-trained* [25] in their use, points to which we now turn.

Exhibit 13.8   Important Advantages and Disadvantages of Appraisal Tools

	Advantages	*Disadvantages*
Graphic Rating Scales	Simple to use: provides a quantitative rating for each employee.	Standards may be unclear; halo effect, central tendency, leniency, bias can also be problems here.
Alteration Ranking	Simple to use (but not as simple as graphic rating scales). Avoids central tendency and other problems of rating scales.	Ranking may still not be precise.
Paired Comparison Method	Results in more precise rankings than does alternation ranking.	More difficult than ranking.
Forced Distribution Method	Here you end up with a pre-determined number of people in each group.	But your appraisal results depend on the adequacy of your original choice of cut-off points.
Critical Incident Method	Helps specify what is "right" and "wrong" about the employee's performance; forces manager to evaluate subordinates on an ongoing basis.	Difficult to rate or rank employees relative to one another.
BARS	Participation of employees in developing the BARS should lead to a more accurate gauge; the critical incidents help "anchor" and clarify the scale.	Very difficult to develop.

Factors that Influence an Appraisal's Perceived Fairness.   What is it about the performance appraisal process that results in some appraisals being perceived as fair, and others unfair? Several studies have addressed this question. [26] One study was based on questionnaire responses from 711 exempt employees in the production division of a large, multidivision manufacturing company. The questionnaire consisted of items aimed at determining what aspects of the appraisal affected its perceived fairness: items dealt with how much criticism and praise occurred during the appraisal, and how often the employee was appraised, for example. The results of this study, (which were supported by a second, follow-up study) indicate that the appraisal *process*—how the supervisor actually goes about administering the appraisal tool and discussing the results—does influence the perceived fairness and accuracy of the appraisal. Specifically, the researchers found that performance appraisals were perceived as fair and accurate: when supervisors evaluated performance frequently; when supervisors were clearly familiar with the performance of the person being evaluated; when there was agreement between subordinates and supervisor concerning the former's job duties; and when the subordinate's help was solicited in formulating plans for eliminating performance weaknesses.

Training of Raters. Training supervisors to eliminate rating errors like halo, leniency, and central tendency can improve their effectiveness as appraisers. In one study of low and middle level insurance company managers, for example, the researcher found that a five-minute training session seemed to result in a significant reduction in the number of halo errors made. [27] In this case the training simply involved defining and presenting some examples of halo effect. Other studies have focussed on determining how intensive (and how comprehensive) the rater training must be to produce good results. Here findings indicate that while relatively short (up to 1 hour) lectures and discussion groups can reduce rater errors, a more intense training module of, say 6 hours is superior in reducing errors like halo and leniency. [28]

In the traditional method, raters are shown a video tape of jobs being performed and are asked to rate the worker. Ratings made by each participant are then placed on a flip chart and the various errors (like leniency, and halo) are explained. For example, if a trainee rated all criteria (like quality, quantity, etc.) about the same, the trainer might explain that halo error had occurred; if a trainee rated all video taped workers very high this might be explained as leniency error. Typically, the trainer gives the correct rating (based on a more "objective" evaluation by, say, experienced raters) and uses the correct ratings to illustrate the rating errors that the participants made. [29]

Rater training is also no panacea for reducing rating errors or improving the accuracy of appraisals. From a practical point of view, several factors including the extent to which pay is tied to performance, union pressure, turnover rates, time constraints, and the need to justify ratings may be more important than training in influencing the motivation of raters. This means that improving an appraisal procedure's accuracy involves not only training but also remedying outside factors like union pressure. And, it means that rater training, to be effective should also address "real life" problems like the fact that union representatives will try to pressure supervisors to rate everyone high. [30]

RESPONSIBILITY FOR APPRAISING

An important question concerns who should actually rate an employee's performance. While ratings by the person's supervisor is still the prevailing approach several options are actually possible. These are illustrated in Exhibit 13.9. In appraising Jones, for example there are at least four potential raters:

1. Smith, Jones' *immediate supervisor.*
2. Brown and Green, Jones' *peers.*
3. A *committee* comprised of the 3 vice presidents and president.
4. Jones himself (self-appraisal).

Exhibit 13.9 Who Are the Potential Raters of Jones?   379

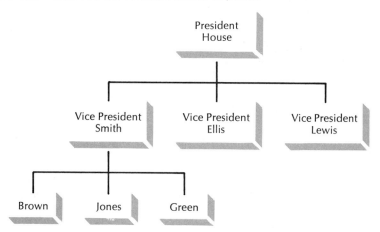

Appraisal by the Immediate Supervisor

Supervisors' ratings are the heart of most appraisal systems. This is because getting a supervisor's appraisal is relatively easy and also makes a great deal of sense. The supervisor should be—and usually is—in the best position to observe and evaluate his or her subordinate's performance. Therefore most appraisal systems rely heavily on the supervisor's evaluation.

Using Peer Appraisals

The appraisal of an individual by his or her peers has proven to be effective in predicting future management success. From a study of military officers, for example, we know that peer ratings were quite accurate in predicting which officers would be promoted and which would not. [31] And in another study that involved over 200 industrial managers, peer ratings were similarly useful in predicting who was promoted. [32] One potential problem here is "logrolling," in which all the peers simply get together to rate each other high.

Using Rating Committees

Many employers use rating committees to evaluate employees. These committees are often composed of the employee's immediate supervisor and 3 or 4 other supervisors; everyone on the committee should be able to intelligently evaluate the employee's performance.

There are several advantages in using multiple raters. First, while there is often a discrepancy in the ratings made by the different supervisors, the composite ratings tend to be more valid then those of individual raters, [33] partly because the combined use of several raters can help "cancel out" problems like

380   bias and halo effect on the part of individual raters. (Fair employment practice thus makes using multiple raters advisable.) Furthermore, where there *are* differences in raters' ratings, they usually stem from the fact that raters at different levels in the organization often observe different facets of an employee's performance; the appraisal ought to reflect these differences. [34] Even where a committee is not used it is common to at least have the appraisal reviewed by the manager immediately above the one who makes the appraisal. This was found to be standard practice in 16 of 18 companies surveyed in one study. [35]

Self-ratings

Some employers have experimented with using employees' self-ratings of performance (usually in conjunction with supervisors' ratings) but this is generally not a recommended option. The basic problem is that the preponderance of studies show that individuals consistently rate themselves higher than they are rated by supervisors or peers. [36] In one study, for example it was found that when asked to rate their own job performances, 40% of the employees in jobs of all types placed themselves in the top 10% ("one of the best"), while virtually all remaining employees rated themselves either in the top 25% ("well above average"), or at least in the top 50% ("above average"). Usually no more than one or two percent will place themselves in a below average category, and then those are almost invariably in the top "below average" category. While these "inflated" self appraisals have been found among employees in all types of jobs, self appraisals tend to be a bit less inflated at lower job levels than at higher levels: In one group of higher level professional and managerial employees, for example, *over 80%* placed themselves in the "top 10%" category. [37] In summary, most studies indicate that self-ratings are consistently higher (more lenient) than are ratings by the person's superior, or peers. [38]

Self appraisals are not completely without merit, however. [39,40] Self appraisals seem to suffer less from halo error, suggesting that an employee may be able to distinguish between his or her strengths or weaknesses more completely than can a supervisor or peers. [41] Yet even here the results suggest that the leniency effect is often so great that the "weaknesses" are not really identified as such, but rather as areas in which the person is "less strong."

Thus, self appraisals should be used quite carefully. Supervisors requesting self appraisals (say, for work planning and review purposes) should be forewarned that their appraisals and the self appraisals of subordinates might be quite discrepant, and that requiring written self appraisals may tend to accentuate differences and rigidify positions. [42] And, of course, even if self appraisals are not formally requested each employee will undoubtedly enter the performance review meeting with his own self appraisal in mind, and this self rating will almost invariably be higher than the supervisor's rating. Handling this discrepancy requires effective interpersonal communication and counseling skills, subjects we address in the following chapter.

SUMMARY

1. Appraising performance is a very important part of the personnel management job. It is the basis on which subordinates' promotion and salary decisions are made. And it provides an opportunity to review with subordinates their work-related behavior.

2. From a legal standpoint, appraisals are considered "tests," and should therefore be job related, standardized, objective, based on a job analysis, and carried out by trained, knowledgeable appraisers.

3. All the performance appraisal tools discussed have their own advantages and disadvantages. Graphic rating scales are simple to use, but are susceptible to problems such as halo effect and central tendency. Ranking methods, such as alternation ranking or the paired comparison method, are still fairly simple to use (though not nearly as easy as the graphic rating scales). They also help you avoid many of the problems to which graphic rating scales are susceptible (such as central tendency). The critical incident method is very useful for coaching subordinates, since it focuses on specific instances of good or bad performance. But it is difficult to rate or rank employees relative to one another with this method, so it is not quite as useful for making salary decisions. BARS appear to have great potential in performance appraisal, but they are relatively difficult to develop and implement.

4. Reducing rating errors and improving an appraisal system involves *informing appraisers* of potential problems, using *the right appraisal tool*, ensuring *fair* appraisals, and *training* raters.

5. One must give some thought as to who actually does the appraising. For example, choose between the person's immediate supervisor, his peers, an appraisal committee, or even allow the person to appraise himself. Most appraisal systems depend on either the supervisor or on a committee for the appraisal.

6. Performance appraisal (as per our model) is the point at which one determines just how effective one has been at eliciting motivation and performance. The next step is to give subordinates feedback on how they are doing, and (if necessary) to identify problems and take corrective actions: We will therefore discuss communicating, and employee and management development in the next two chapters.

Appraising the Secretaries at Sweetwater U

Rob Winchester, newly appointed Vice President for Administrative Affairs at Sweetwater State University, faced a tough problem shortly after his university career began. Three weeks after he came on board in September Sweetwater's president, his boss, told him that one of his first problems would involve ways to improve the appraisal system used to evaluate secretarial and clerical performance at Sweetwater U. Apparently the main difficulty was that the performance appraisal was traditionally tied directly to salary increases given at the end of the year. So most administrators were less than accurate when they used the graphic rating forms that were the basis of the clerical staff evaluation. In fact, what usually happened was that each administrator simply rated his or her clerk or secretary as "excellent." This cleared the way for all support staff to receive a maximum pay increase each year.

But the current university budget simply did not have funds enough to fund another "maximum" annual increase for every staffer. Furthermore, Sweetwater's president felt that the custom of providing invalid feedback to each secretary on his or her year's performance was not a healthy situation so he had asked the new vice president to revise the system. In October the vice president sent a memo to all administrators, telling them that in the future no more than half of the secretaries reporting to any particular administrator could be appraised as "excellent." This move in effect, forced each supervisor to begin ranking his or her secretaries for quality of performance. The vice president's memo met widespread resistance immediately—from administrators who were afraid that many of their secretaries would begin leaving for more lucrative jobs in private industry, and from secretaries who felt that the new system was unfair and reduced each secretary's chance of receiving a maximum salary. A handful of secretaries began quietly picketing outside the president's home, on the University campus. The picketing, caustic remarks by disgruntled administrators, and rumors of an impending "slowdown" by the secretaries (there were about 250 on the campus) made Rob Winchester wonder whether he had made the right decision by setting up forced ranking. He knew, however, that there were a few performance appraisal experts in the University's School of Business so he decided to set up an appointment with them to discuss the matter.

He met with them the next morning. He explained the situation as he had found it: the present appraisal system had been set up when the University first opened ten years earlier, and the appraisal form had been developed primarily by a committee of secretaries. Under that system, Sweetwater's administrators fill out forms similar to the one shown in Exhibit 13.7 (page 375). This once-a-year appraisal (in March) had run into problems almost immediately, since it was apparent from the start that administrators vary widely in their interpretations of job standards, as well as in how conscientiously they filled out the forms and supervised their secretaries. Moreover, the defects of this procedure had become conspicuous at the end of the first year when it became obvious to everyone that each secretary's salary increase was tied directly to the March appraisal. For example, those rated "excellent" received the maximum increases, those rated "good" received smaller increases, and those given neither rating received only the standard across the board cost of living increase. Since universities in general—and Sweetwater U in particular—have generally paid secretaries somewhat lower salaries than those prevailing in private industry, some secretaries left in a huff that first year. From that time on most administrators simply rated all secretaries as excellent in order to save themselves staff turnover, and thus ensuring each a maximum increase. In the process they also avoided the hard feelings aroused by the significant performance differences otherwise highlighted by administrators.

Two of the Sweetwater experts agreed to consider the problem, and in two weeks they came back to the vice president with the following recommendations. First, the form used to rate each secretary was grossly insufficient. As written, it was unclear what "excellent" or "quality of work" meant, for example. As a result most of the administrators they had spoken to were unclear as to the meaning of each item in the rating. They recommended, instead a form like that in Exhibit 13.2 (page 368). In addition, they recommended that the vice president rescind his earlier memo and no longer attempt to force university administrators to arbitrarily rate at least half their secretaries as something less than excellent. The two consultants pointed out that this was, in fact, an unfair procedure since it was quite possible that any particular administrator might have staffers who were all or virtually all excellent—or conceivably, although less likely, all below standard. The experts said that the way to get all the administrators to take the appraisal process more seriously was to stop tying it to salary increases. In other words, they recommended that each administrator fill out a form like that in Exhibit 13.2 for each of his or her secretaries at least once a year and then use this form for the basis of a counseling session. Salary increases, however, would have to be made on some basis other than the performance appraisal so that administrators would no longer hesitate to fill out the rating forms honestly.

The vice president thanked the two experts and went back to his office to ponder their recommendations. Some of the recommendations (such as substituting the new rating form for the old) seemed to make sense. Nevertheless, he still had serious doubts of the efficacy of any graphic rating form, particularly if he were to decide in favor of his original, "forced ranking" approach. The experts' second recommendation—to stop tying the appraisals to automatic salary increases—made a great deal of sense but raised at least one very practical problem. If salary increases were not to be based on performance appraisals, what were they to be based on? He began wondering whether the experts' recommendations weren't simply based on "ivory tower theorizing."

Questions

1. Do you think that the experts' recommendations will be sufficient to get most of the administrators to fill out the rating forms properly? Why? Why not? What additional actions (if any) do you think will be necessary?

2. Do you think that Vice President Winchester would be better off dropping the use of graphic rating forms, substituting instead one of the other techniques we discussed in this chapter, such as a ranking method?

3. What performance appraisal system would you develop for the secretaries if you were Rob Winchester? Defend your answer.

EXPERIENTIAL EXERCISE

Purpose. The purpose of this exercise is to give you practice in developing and using a performance appraisal form.

Required Understanding. You are going to develop a performance appraisal form for an instructor and should therefore be thoroughly familiar with the discussion of performance appraisal in this chapter.

How to Set Up the Exercise. Divide the class into groups of four or five students.

Instructions for the Exercise.

1. First, based upon what you now know about performance appraisal, do you think Exhibit 13.1 is an effective scale for appraising instructors? Why? Why not?

2. Next, your group should develop its own tool for appraising the performance of an instructor. Decide which of the six appraisal tools (graphic rating scales, alternation ranking, etc.) you are going to use, and then design the instrument itself.

3. Next, have a spokesman from each group put his or her group's appraisal tool on the board. How similar are the tools? Do they all measure about the same factors? Which factor appears most often? Which do you think is the most effective tool on the board? Can you think of any way of combining the best points of several of the tools into a resulting performance appraisal tool?

DISCUSSION QUESTIONS

1. Discuss the pros and cons of at least four performance appraisal tools.
2. Develop a graphic rating scale for the following jobs: secretary; engineer; directory assistance operator.
3. Evaluate the rating scale in Exhibit 13.1. Discuss ways to improve it.
4. Explain how you would use: the alternation ranking method; the paired comparison method; and the forced distribution method.
5. Over the period of a week, develop a set of critical incidents covering the classroom performance of one of your instructors.
6. Explain in your own words how you would go about developing a behaviorally anchored rating scale.
7. Explain the problems to be avoided in appraising performance.
8. Discuss the pros and cons of using different potential raters to appraise a person's performance.

NOTES

1. Kenneth Teel, "Performance Appraisal: Current Trends, Persistent Progress," *Personnel Journal* (April 1980), pp. 296–301.

2. Teel, p. 301.

3. Teel, p. 301.

4. This is based primarily on Gary Lubben, Duane Thompson, and Charles Klasson, "Performance Appraisal: The Legal Implications of Title VII," *Personnel*, 1980, pp. 11–21.

5. *Rowe v. General Motors Corporation.*

6. *Brito v. Zia Company.*

7. Lubben et al., p. 17.

8. Lubben et al., p. 19.

9. Dale Yoder, *Personnel Management and Industrial Relations* (Englewood Cliffs, N.J.: Prentice-Hall, 1970).

10. See, for example, Timothy Keaveny and Anthony McGann, "A Comparison of Behavioral Expectation Scales and Graphic Rating Scales," *Journal of Applied Psychology*, Vol. 60 (1975), pp. 695–703. See also, John Ivanovich, "A Longitudinal Study of Behavioral Expectation Scales: Attitudes and Performance," *Journal of Applied Psychology* (April 1980), pp. 139–146.

11. Based on Donald Schwab, Herbert Heneman III, and Thomas DeCotiis, "Behaviorally Anchored Scales: A Review of the Literature," *Personnel Psychology*, Vol. 28 (1975), pp. 549–562.

12. Lawrence Fogli, Charles Hulin, and Milton Blook, "Development of First Level Behavioral Job Criteria," *Journal of Applied Psychology*, Vol. 55 (1971), pp. 3–8. See also Terry Dickenson and Peter Fellinger, "A Comparison of the Behaviorally Anchored Rating and Fixed Standard Scale Formats," *Journal of Applied Psychology* (April 1980), pp. 147–154.

13. Timothy Keaveny and Anthony McGann, "A Comparison of Behavioral Expectation Scales and Graphic Rating Scales," pp. 695–703.

14. Schwab, Heneman, and DeCotiis, "Behaviorally Anchored Rating Scales: A Review of Literature."

15. James Goodale and Ronald Burke, "Behaviorally Based Rating Scales Need Not Be Job Specific," *Journal of Applied Psychology*, Vol. 60 (June 1975).

16. Wayne Cascio and Enzo Valenzi, "Behaviorally Anchored Rating Scales: Effects of Education and Job Experience of Raters and Ratees," *Journal of Applied Psychology*, Vol. 62, No. 3, pp. 278–282; see also Gary P. Latham and Kenneth N. Wexley, "Behavioral Observation Scales for Performance Appraisal Purposes," *Personnel Psychology*, Vol. 30, No. 2 (Summer 1977), pp. 255–268; H. John Bernardin, Kenneth M. Alvares, and C. J. Cranny, "A Recomparison of Behavioral Expectation Scales to Summated Scales," *Journal of Applied Psychology*, Vol. 61, No. 5 (October 1976), p. 564; Frank E. Saal and Frank J. Landy, "The Mixed Standard Rating Scale: An Evaluation," *Organizational Behavior and Human Performance*, Vol. 18, No. 1 (February 1977), pp. 19–35; Frank J. Landy, James L. Farr, Frank E. Saal, and Walter R. Freytag, "Behaviorally Anchored Scales for Rating the Performance of Police Officers," *Journal of Applied Psychology*, Vol. 61, No. 6 (December 1976), pp. 750–758.

17. Teel, pp. 297–298.

18. Gary Latham, Kenneth Wexley, and Elliot Pursell, "Training Managers to Minimize Rating Errors in the Observation of Behavior," *Journal of Applied Psychology*, Vol. 60 (October 1975).

19. For a discussion of this see, for example Wayne Cascio, *Applied Psychology in Personnel Management* (Reston: Reston, 1978), pp. 337–341.

386

20. Cascio, p. 337.

21. B. Rosen and T. H. Gerde, "The Nature of Job Related Age Stereotypes," *Journal of Applied Psychology*, Vol. 61 (1976), pp. 180–183.

22. William J. Bigoness, "Effect of Applicant's Sex, Race and Performance on Employer's Performance Ratings: Some Additional Findings," *Journal of Applied Psychology*, Vol. 61 (February 1976).

23. Allen Patz, "Performance Appraisal: Useful But Still Resisted," *Harvard Business Review* (May–June 1975).

24. Robert Lazer, "The Discrimination Danger in Performance Appraisal," *The Conference Board Record* (March 1976); reprinted in Hamner and Schmidt, *Contemporary Problems in Personnel* (rev. ed.), pp. 239–245.

25. Latham, Wexley, and Pursell, "Training Managers to Minimize Rating Errors in the Observation of Behavior"; Walter Borman, "Effect of Instructions to Avoid Halo Error on Reliability and Validity on Performance Evaluation Ratings," *Journal of Applied Psychology*, Vol. 60 (October 1975).

26. Frank Landy, Janet Barnes, and Kevin Murphy, "Correlates of Perceived Fairness and Accuracy of Performance Evaluation," *Journal of Applied Psychology*, Dec. 1978, Vol. 63, pp. 751–754; Frank Landy, Janet Barnes-Farrell, and Jeanette Cleveland, "Perceived Fairness and Accuracy of Performance Evaluation: A Follow Up," *Journal of Applied Psychology* (June 1980), Vol. 65, pp. 355–356.

27. W. C. Borman, "Effects of Instruction to Avoid Halo Error on Reliability and Validity of Performance Evaluation Ratings," *Journal of Applied Psychology*, 1975, Vol. 65, pp. 556–560: Borman points out that since no control group was available (a group of managers who did not undergo training) it is possible that the observed effects were not due to the short 5-minute training experience.

28. G. P. Latham, K. N. Wexley, and E. D. Pursell, "Training Managers to Minimize Rating Errors in the Observation of Behavior," *Journal of Applied Psychology*, 1975, Vol. 60, pp. 550–555; John Ivanovich, "Longitudinal Study of the Effects of Rater Training on Psychometric Error in Ratings," *Journal of Applied Psychology*, Vol. 64 (1979), pp. 502–508.

29. Walter Borman, "Format and Training Effects on Rating Accuracy and Rater Errors," *Journal of Applied Psychology*, Vol. 64 (August 1979), pp. 410–421.

30. Dennis Warnke and Robert Billings, "Comparison of Training Methods for Improving the Psychometric Quality of Experimental and Administrative Performance Ratings," *Journal of Applied Psychology*, Vol. 64 (April 1979), pp. 124–131.

31. R. G. Downey, F. F. Medland, and L. G. Yates, "Evaluation of a Peer Rating System and for Predicting Subsequent Promotion of Senior Military Officers," *Journal of Applied Psychology*, Vol. 61 (April 1976).

32. Allan Krautt, "Prediction of Managerial Success by Peer and Training Staff Ratings," *Journal of Applied Psychology*, Vol. 60 (February 1975).

33. Robert Libby and Robert Blashfield, "Performance of a Composite as a Function of the Number of Judges," *Organizational Behavior and Human Performance*, Vol. 21 (April 1978), pp. 121–129; Walter Borman, "Exploring Other Limits of Reliability and Validity in Job Performance Ratings," *Journal of Applied Psychology*, Vol. 63 (April 1978), pp. 135–144.

34. Walter C. Borman, "The Rating of Individuals in Organizations: An Alternate Approach," *Organizational Behavior and Human Performance*, Vol. 12 (1974), pp. 105–124.

35. Teel, p. 301.

36. George Thornton III, "Psychometric Properties of Self Appraisals of Job Performance," *Personnel Psychology*, Vol. 33 (Summer 1980), p. 265.

37. Herbert Myer, "Self Appraisal of Job Performance," *Personnel Psychology,* Vol. 33 (Summer 1980), pp. 291–293.

38. Robert Holzbach, "Rater Bias in Performance Ratings: Superior, Self, and Peer Ratings," *Journal of Applied Psychology,* Vol. 63, No. 5 (Oct. 1978), pp. 579–588.

39. Herbert G. Heneman III, "Comparison of Self and Superior Ratings of Managerial Performance," *Journal of Applied Psychology,* Vol. 59 (1974), pp. 638–642; Richard J. Klimoski and Manuel London, "Role of the Rater in Performance Appraisal," *Journal of Applied Psychology,* Vol. 59 (1974), pp. 445–451; Hubert S. Field and William H. Holley, "Subordinates' Characteristics, Supervisors' Ratings, and Decisions to Discuss Appraisal Results," *Academy of Management Journal,* Vol. 20, No. 2 (1977), pp. 215–221.

40. J. W. Parker, et al., "Rating Scale Content: III. Relationships Between Supervisory and Self-Ratings," *Personnel Psychology,* Vol. 12, pp. 49–63, in John B. Miner, "Management Appraisal: A Review of Procedures and Practices," reprinted by W. Clay Hamner and Frank Schmidt, *Contemporary Problems in Personnel* (Chicago: St. Clair, 1974), p. 247.

41. Thornton, p. 268.

42. Myer, pp. 291–293.

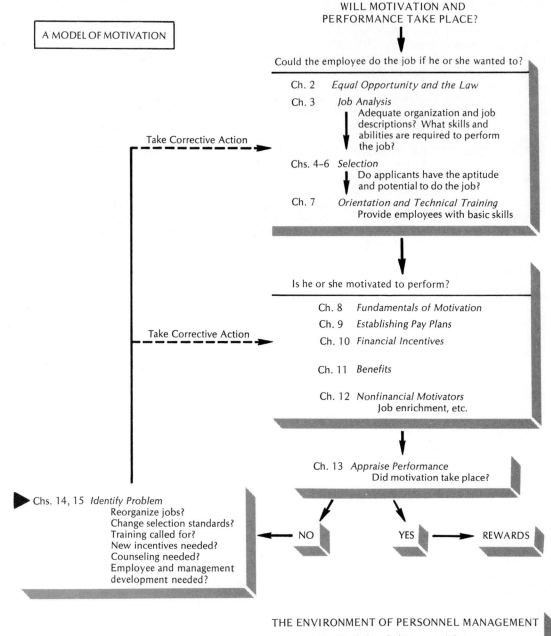

A MODEL OF MOTIVATION

WILL MOTIVATION AND
PERFORMANCE TAKE PLACE?

Could the employee do the job if he or she wanted to?

Ch. 2 *Equal Opportunity and the Law*

Ch. 3 *Job Analysis*
Adequate organization and job descriptions? What skills and abilities are required to perform the job?

Chs. 4–6 *Selection*
Do applicants have the aptitude and potential to do the job?

Ch. 7 *Orientation and Technical Training*
Provide employees with basic skills

Take Corrective Action

Is he or she motivated to perform?

Ch. 8 *Fundamentals of Motivation*

Ch. 9 *Establishing Pay Plans*

Ch. 10 *Financial Incentives*

Ch. 11 *Benefits*

Ch. 12 *Nonfinancial Motivators*
Job enrichment, etc.

Take Corrective Action

Ch. 13 *Appraise Performance*
Did motivation take place?

Chs. 14, 15 *Identify Problem*
Reorganize jobs?
Change selection standards?
Training called for?
New incentives needed?
Counseling needed?
Employee and management development needed?

NO   YES ⟶ REWARDS

THE ENVIRONMENT OF PERSONNEL MANAGEMENT

Ch. 16 *Labor Relations and Grievances*

Ch. 17 *Employee Safety and Health*

Ch. 18 *Personnel Management and the Quality of Work Life*

When you finish studying

14 Face-to-Face Communicating

You should be able to:

1. *Carry out an effective performance appraisal conference.*
2. *Discipline a subordinate effectively.*
3. *"Actively" listen.*
4. *Explain the problems to watch out for when appraisal counseling.*
5. *Explain transactional analysis.*
6. *List the prerequisites to disciplining.*
7. *Cite at least ten guidelines for effective disciplining.*

OVERVIEW

The main purpose of this chapter is to explain how to become more effective at face-to-face communicating—such as when appraising performance, listening to subordinates' problems, or disciplining subordinates. We discuss important problems to watch out for when appraisal counseling (these include defensiveness on the part of your subordinates and criticizing subordinates). We also discuss how to be an "active" listener, and how to use transactional analysis to improve your communicating ability. We review some guidelines for effective appraisal counseling and then discuss disciplining, focusing on how it should be carried out.

INTRODUCTION: WHAT APPRAISAL COUNSELING SHOULD ACCOMPLISH

Once the performance appraisal is completed the supervisor usually meets with each subordinate to feedback the results. In most cases this involves getting together with them once or twice a year to review their performance ratings. Ideally, these meetings should aim to bring about constructive change in the subordinate's behavior, locate the root cause of any performance problem, reduce the subordinate's frustrations by letting the person vent his feelings, and stimulate problem solving so future performance can, if necessary, be improved. Often, instead, these meetings turn out to be frustrating, tense, and useless affairs, since managers tend to make a number of interpersonal communication mistakes, like arguing with the subordinate, or being overly critical. As a result, a good opportunity to improve performance is often lost. Well-developed interpersonal communication and coaching skills, which are discussed in this chapter, are thus essential for these kinds of reviews, as well as for interviewing, disciplining, and, for that matter, virtually all the activities one is involved in as a manager.

BARRIERS TO EFFECTIVE INTERPERSONAL COMMUNICATIONS

Four Main Barriers

There are four main interpersonal communication mistakes that people tend to make. First, while most people hear what the person they are speaking to is saying, much of it doesn't "register," because the listener is busy trying to formulate an answer, or because his mind is wandering, or because he simply is not working hard enough to *actively listen* and thereby figure out the actual meaning and feelings behind the speaker's words. Other people make the mistake of trying to make their point through criticizing, arguing, cajoling and prodding. This kind of behavior is rarely effective at getting another person to change his or her position, and has the added disadvantage of distracting the listener who may become so preoccupied with "making his point" that he misses the meaning behind the speaker's words. Another common mistake is to attack the other person's *defenses,* for example, by saying that "you are just denying fault because you are insecure." While it may be true that the person's denial is just a "defense mechanism" used to protect his or her self image, attacking that defense could well demoralize the person. Others make the mistake of *playing games* with appraisees, for example by maneuvering them into positions where they can say "I told you so." Being able to avoid problems like these can help ensure effective interpersonal communication, and this, in turn, can improve the supervisor's performance and that of his subordinates. The problems of *defensiveness, criticizing, "inactive" listening,* and *playing games* are described below.

Defensiveness

Psychological defenses are important to all people for two reasons. First, they help us maintain our self-image and self-esteem. From childhood on we learn to think of ourselves in certain cherished ways. Based on our experiences with parents, teachers, and peers we each develop a picture of ourselves—a *self-image*. And psychologists know that much of what motivates people derives from their need to be treated in a manner that coincides with this self-image.

Of course, a person's self image does not have to coincide with reality, and, in fact, it often will not; as explained in the last chapter, for instance, self ratings tend to be consistently higher than those assigned by one's peers. But "real" or not, we all have a picture of who we are, and what we deserve. And most people try very hard to screen out experiences that do not fit this ideal self-image: one way to do this is by invoking a *defense mechanism.*

Defenses are also important for a related reason. Psychiatrists know that if

each of us had to absorb the full impact of the problems and tensions of daily   391
living we would probably crack under the strain. [1] Therefore we use defense
mechanisms to help us screen out painful experiences.

So (for both reasons) defense mechanisms are a very important and familiar
aspect of our lives. When a person is accused of poor performance, for example,
his or her immediate reaction will often be *denial*. By denying that he was at
fault he avoids having to question or analyze his own competence. Still others
react to criticism with *anger* and *aggression*. This helps them let off steam and
postpone confronting the immediate problem until they are better able to cope
with it. Still others react to criticism by *retreating* into a "shell."

Criticizing

Since people do have this need to defend themselves against painful experiences, we might assume that criticizing subordinates during appraisal conferences could have disastrous effects and, indeed, this is the case. One of the most
complete studies of this phenomenon was carried out at the General Electric
Company. [2]

The subjects in this study were 92 exempt employees in a company plant.
They included engineers, technicians, foremen, and specialists from the manufacturing, marketing, finance, and purchasing departments. Each of these people
had an appraisal conference with their superior. A research observer was present
at each conference and reported the amount of criticism and praise employed
by the superior, as well as the reactions of the appraisee to the manager's comments. Some of the most important findings concerned the appraisees' reactions
to criticism, as follows.

Criticism and Defensiveness. The first thing the researchers found was
that the more criticism a person received in the appraisal conference, the more
defensively he reacted. In fact, appraisees who received an above average number
of criticisms showed more than five times as much defensive behavior as those
who received a below average number of criticisms. Part of the reason for this
defensiveness seemed to stem from the fact that the employees rated themselves
much higher than did their superiors: almost three-quarters of the employees
saw their manager's rating as being "less favorable" than their own self-estimates.
And, for virtually all the appraisees, the appraisal conference proved a deflating
experience: most of them rated themselves much lower *after* the conference
than they had prior to it.

Criticism and Performance. But even more important is the fact that employees who received an above average number of criticisms generally performed
more poorly ten to twelve weeks later than those who received fewer criticisms.
Similarly, the researchers found that "When we conducted our follow-up investigation ten to twelve weeks later, it revealed that improvement in the *most*
criticized aspects of performance cited was considerably *less* than improvement
realized in other areas." (According to the researchers, subordinates who re-

392   ceived more criticisms were not necessarily poorer performers to begin with.) The reason for both findings seemed to be that ". . . frequent criticism constitutes so strong a threat to self-esteem that it disrupts rather than improves subsequent performance."

These effects were especially pronounced among those appraisees who were already low on self-esteem, while the more confident employees reacted more constructively to criticism.

Arguing has a similar effect on performance. Maier says that most managers use a "tell and sell" approach in the appraisal conference. They try to change their subordinates' behavior and way of looking at things through persuasion, cajoling, scolding, and prodding, and (as often as not) arguments ensue.

Two Other Barriers: Not Listening Actively and "Gaming"

Problems like criticizing, arguing, and evoking defensive behavior sometimes have their origins in either not listening, or in "gaming." The former refers to the fact that while listeners often hear the words being spoken their preoccupation with "making a point," or formulating an answer often leads them to miss or disregard the underlying feelings the speaker is trying to express. "Gaming" refers to people's tendency to try to manipulate others. "Not listening"—or its converse, "active listening," and gaming are important counseling techniques, and are explained in the next two sections.

DEVELOPING ACTIVE LISTENING SKILLS

The distinguishing characteristic of "active listening" is that the listener tries to grasp both the facts *and the feelings* in what he or she hears. The active listener doesn't just passively "hear" what the speaker is saying, in other words, but instead tries to understand and respond to the feelings underlying the words (or content) where "by feelings, we mean emotions such as anger, fear, puzzlement, anxiety, confusion, ambivalence, tension, joy, elation, and so on." The words or content, on the other hand, are often relatively unimportant, and refer "to thoughts, assumptions, philosophies, theories, descriptions of events or places, and the like." [3]

Most experts agree that active listening is an important appraisal skill as well as one that can be used in conjunction with disciplining subordinates, dealing with interpersonal conflicts, or just communicating with subordinates on a day-to-day basis. The ultimate goal of active listening is to bring about some constructive change in the subordinates' behavior.

An Example of Active Listening

Perhaps the best way to explain "active listening" is to begin with two illustrative incidents, as provided by Carl Rogers, a pioneer in this area.

Incident 1

FOREMAN: "Hey, Al, I don't get this rush order. We can't handle any 50,000 run today. What do they think we are?"

SUPERVISOR (AL): "But that's the order. So get it out as soon as you can. We're under terrific pressure this week."

FOREMAN: "Don't they know we're behind schedule already because of that press breakdown?"

SUPERVISOR: "Look, Kelly, I don't decide what goes on upstairs. I just have to see that work gets out and that's what I'm going to do."

FOREMAN: "The guys aren't going to like this."

SUPERVISOR: "That's something you'll have to work out with them, not me."

Incident 2

FOREMAN: "Hey, Ross. I don't get this rush order. We can't handle any run of 50,000 today. What do they think we are?"

SUPERVISOR (Ross): "They're pushing you pretty hard aren't they Kelly?

FOREMAN: "They sure are and I'm getting sore. We were just about back to schedule after the press breakdown. Now this comes along."

SUPERVISOR: "As if you didn't have enough work to do?"

FOREMAN: "Yeah. I don't know how I'm going to tell the pressmen about this."

SUPERVISOR: "Hate to face them now with a rush order, is that it?"

FOREMAN: "I really do. Joe is under a real strain today. Seems like everything we do around here is rush, rush, rush!"

SUPERVISOR: "I guess you feel it's unfair to load anything more on him today."

FOREMAN: Well, Yeah. I know there must be plenty of pressure on everybody to get the work out, but—well, Joe doesn't deserve all the rush orders. But, if that's the way it is—I guess I better get the work to him and see how I can rearrange the work flow."

The main difference between these two incidents is that Ross (the supervisor in the second incident) is using the "active listening" approach. He is "listening and responding in a way that makes it clear that he appreciates both the meaning and the feeling behind what Kelly is saying."

Active listening can be used effectively to change subordinates' behavior. Unlike other approaches (like arguing or criticizing) active listening does not present a threat to subordinates' self-image, and they do not have to defend themselves or deny wrongdoing. Instead, they are able to realistically explore their behavior, analyze it, and draw their own conclusions: and then they are in a position to change themselves.

The Elements of Active Listening

The basic strategy of an active listener is to get "inside" the speaker—to grasp what he (or she) is saying from his point of view—and to *convey* the fact that his point of view is understood. Active listening therefore typically consists of several basic elements.

1. *Listen for total meaning.* Any statement usually has two components: the actual content or words and the feeling or attitude underlying this content. Remember that both the content and the feeling are important: both give the message its meaning and it is this *meaning* that you have to try to understand.

As an illustration, take the foreman's first statement in the example above: "Hey, Al I don't get this rush order. We can't handle any 50,000 run today. What do they think we are?" In this case, the content of the message is clear. And you could respond just to that content as did the supervisor in the first example: "But that's the order. So get it out as soon as you can. We're under terrific pressure this week."

But if you had done that you would not have taken into consideration the feelings or *attitudes* underlying the foreman's statement. Nor would you have seen the problem from his point of view or gotten him to want to get the rush order out. Notice how the supervisor in the second example effectively does this. He gets the foreman to confront his real feelings—about the pressure he's under and his reluctance to put his men under more strain. And in this way he is able to get the foreman to work in the rush order.

2. *Reflect feelings.* "Reflecting feelings" is important because it helps the speaker confront his or her feelings, and to see that you understand those feelings. (In our second incident, for example notice how most of the supervisor's comments are actually reflected feelings: "They're pushing you pretty hard, aren't they Kelly?" and "As if you didn't have enough work to do, huh?")

3. *Note all cues.* Not all communication is verbal. Various other cues—facial expressions, hesitations in speech, the inflection in the voice, etc.—also communicate attitudes. And, as an active listener, it is essential to note all these cues, since it is only by doing this that you can understand the message's complete meaning.

4. *Avoid passing judgment.* Passing judgment and giving advice are almost always seen as efforts to directly change or manipulate a person. They represent exactly those tactics that an active listener should avoid. Remember that the goal is to get the person to confront his or her own attitudes and feelings, and accomplishing this requires that you avoid passing judgment, a tactic that is almost invariably threatening to the speaker's self-image.

AVOIDING GAMES:
USING TRANSACTIONAL ANALYSIS

Transactional analysis (TA) is a relatively new analytical tool that can help a manager analyze the interpersonal "transactions" or communications between the manager and his or her subordinates. It can enable a manager to better analyze any interpersonal situations he or she is in, by helping answer questions like: "why am I saying what I am saying to this subordinate?" and "why is he saying what he is saying to me?" TA began as a form of psychotherapy and was developed primarily by Eric Berne and popularized in his book *Games People Play.* [4]

Games Managers Play

One version of TA has been popularized by Webber as "games managers play." [5] Webber says that people often slip into certain roles or "ego states," and that when in particular roles they behave in characteristic ways. Understanding one's own "role," (and that of the person one is speaking to) can help a manager understand the motives underlying what he (and the person he is speaking with) is saying, contends Webber. Webber's versions of roles managers play include *persecutor, rescuer,* and *victim.*

Persecutor Games. "Persecutors" seem driven to prove that others ought to be perfect or otherwise behave in ways consistent with the persecutor's grandiose expectations; everything the persecutor says or does therefore seems to reflect an underlying feeling of anger or contempt. Persecutors seem driven to manipulate others to feel badly through blame, ridiculing, bullying, criticizing, nitpicking, belittling, threatening, and so on. The person in the role of persecutor uses "gotcha" language laced with phrases like "how could you be so stupid,?" and "you ought to know better!" And these verbal abuses are often accompanied by an accusingly pointed finger, eyes rolled upward, or arms folded across one's chest. Two specific games these people play include *now I've got you,* and *blemish.*

The "now I've got you" manager tries to make others feel bad to cover up his or her own negative feelings. This person criticizes others excessively whenever they violate his or her standards, standards which are often unrealistic or intentionally ambiguous. Persecutors seem to get their kicks out of feeling self righteous and angry and from avoiding intimate or authentic relationships with others. Webber contends that "now I've got you" managers behave this way partly to escape their own underlying feelings of low self-esteem.

As an example, consider this incident:

George Smith, a foreman at Apex Company was teaching a group of subordinates how to set up a new machine. In the middle of a discussion that he felt was not going very well he noticed that Susan Sayles was quietly whispering and smiling to her neighbor. Smith imagined that the workers were laughing about how poorly his class was going and punitively snapped: "Miss Sayles, what are *your* thoughts?" Miss Sayles apologetically admitted that she hadn't followed the prior discussion. Rather than giving her enough information to respond, Smith gave her an icy stare and turned to another employee.

"Now I've got you" can be avoided by providing clear, and achievable standards and by making available the information and resources needed to succeed.

The "blemish" player, on the other hand criticizes insignificant flaws in performance rather than rewarding major successes. He or she persecutes by constantly looking for minor gaps in logic rather than trying to understand the bigger picture. Blemish players seem driven by an uncontrollable need to correct and find fault with others. For example:

> Sydney Rogers asked a young marketing manager to evaluate his company's marketing strategy on their major product lines. When the subordinate submitted his detailed report, Rogers circled a couple of minor typographical errors in red pencil and wrote in red on the cover sheet: "rewrite!". [6]

Victim Games. The person playing victim continually blames, whines, procrastinates, makes mistakes, and apologizes in order to manipulate others to "rescue" or "persecute" him. Unlike a real victim (like someone drowning) the helplessness of the person playing victim is imaginary. In their quest to be rescued or persecuted victims use language like "I've tried everything," "I don't know," and "I can't do it," usually accompanied by dejected postures, pouting, or helpless facial expressions. The things that often keep the victim going are the "negative strokes" they receive when they perform their little acts. For example, an employee who frequently procrastinates or arrives for meetings late may be playing the game of "kick me, kick me." These victims like the attention they get from being scolded by the boss, and the feelings of guilt that these scoldings arouse. Eliminating this game usually requires eliminating the "negative strokes," through what we referred to earlier as extinction: namely, by ignoring the misbehavior, instead of "rewarding" it with the scoldings.

Rescuer Games. Some managers also like to play *rescuer*, which means they like to meddle in other's decisions, give unsolicited advice, or not let subordinates carry their share of the workload. The rescuer's favorite phrases include "if I were you, I'd . . .," "sure, I'd love to do it," and "let me do it for you." People who receive a rescuer's unwanted advice can usually stop this game by telling the person they will ask for help when they need it. Manager/rescuers thus have to guard against alienating competent subordinates with their unwanted advice, or being manipulated into the role of rescuer by a person playing victim.

Using TA. A knowledge of management games is a two-edged sword. Being able to diagnose one's own role and those of others can help you interpret and analyze both your own comments, and those of the person you are talking with. However, gaming also represents a highly simplified picture of "what makes people tick," and you have to guard against arriving at simplistic conclusions: for example, not everyone who procrastinates, or arrives late at meetings is necessarily looking for the negative strokes of a victim.

FUNDAMENTALS OF INTERPERSONAL COMMUNICATION AND COUNSELING

Basic Methods for Improving Interpersonal Communication

Communication Barriers.   There are four barriers to effective interpersonal communication in general, and effective appraisal counseling in particular. Most people hear what the person they are speaking to is saying, but much of it does not register because the listener is busy trying to formulate an answer, or because he or she simply is not working hard enough to figure out the actual meaning and feeling behind the speaker's words: an inability to *actively listen* is one barrier, in other words. Trying to make a point through *criticizing*, arguing, or cajoling is another barrier. Generally speaking, in fact, the more a person is criticized the more defensively that person reacts, in an attempt to protect his or her self image. *Attacking a person's defenses*—for instance, by saying things like "you're just shifting the blame to him because you are so insecure"—can therefore have a very unnerving and detrimental effect on a subordinate, especially one who is insecure to begin with. Finally, *gaming*—whereby someone inadvertently slides into a role like persecutor or victim can undermine communication by literally turning the appraisal conference into a game. Instead of sitting down and intelligently discussing and analyzing a subordinate's performance, for example, a persecutor/manager and victim/subordinate could inadvertently slide into a game of "kick me," and waste their time giving and receiving "negative strokes" instead of developing plans for obtaining more satisfactory performance in the future.

Guidelines for Improving Interpersonal Communication.   Given these four barriers, some general methods for improving interpersonal communication can be summarized with the following guidelines:

1. *Avoid evoking defensive behavior.* Instead, try to concentrate on the act itself (i.e., "sales are down") rather than on the man (i.e., "you aren't selling enough"). Similarly, don't try to psychoanalyze subordinates or explain them to themselves. Sometimes, in fact, it is best just to postpone action, since people often react to sudden threats by instinctively hiding behind their "masks."
2. *Avoid criticizing.* Criticism often just evokes defensive behavior. Where some criticizing is necessary it should be done in a manner that helps the person maintain his or her dignity and sense of worth. Specifically, criticizing should be done in private, and should be done constructively, with you providing

examples of "critical incidents," and specific suggestions of what could be done and why. Avoid once a year "critical broadsides" by appraising subordinates often, on a day-to-day basis, so that at the formal review there are no surprises. Never say the person is "always" wrong (since no one is ever "always" wrong or right) and don't make a joke of the incident (since your joking may just seem sarcastic). Finally, criticism should always be objective, and free of any personal feelings on your part.

3. *Actively listen.* This involves listening for total meaning, noting all (verbal and non-verbal) cues, and reflecting feelings, perhaps by using reflective summaries, or by repeating the person's last comment. For example, if he says, "I don't think we can get that order out." you might restate this as a question: "You don't think you can get that order out?" in order to get the person to explain his or her motives.

4. *Avoid "gaming."* Try not to slip into the role of persecutor, victim or rescuer. Instead, communicate objectively, on an "adult-to-adult" basis.

Specific Methods for Improving Performance-Appraisal Counseling

Like all situations that rely heavily on interpersonal communication, performance reviews can benefit from the guidelines listed above. In addition, however, performance reviews demand some additional skills, since the aim of these reviews is often to achieve actual performance improvements amongst appraisees.

One recent study was aimed at answering the question "What are the characteristics of effective performance review interviews?" [7] The study involved 270 nurses from a large hospital, who anonymously completed a 13-page questionnaire. The questionnaire asked various questions about the respondents most recent appraisal interviews; two categories of information were emphasized. First, information regarding the *nature* of the interview in terms of six characteristics was obtained. These characteristics (and a short example of each) were as follows:

1. *Amount of threat experienced.* "Think about your last performance review session. Did you ever feel threatened during the session?"
2. *Amount of influence.* "In your last performance review session, how much influence did you have in planning self development activities?"
3. *Amount of participation.* "Think of your last performance review session. How well does this statement describe it? 'I had a good opportunity to really present my ideas and feeling's."
4. *Constructive and helpful supervisor.* "Think of your last performance review session. How well does this statement describe it? 'My supervisor was helpful and constructive'."
5. *Solving job problems.* "Think of your last performance review session. How well does this following statement describe it? 'Many job problems were cleared up'."
6. *Goal setting.* "Think of your last performance review session. How well does the following statements describe it? 'Some future job performance objectives or targets were set'."

Second, information regarding seven *outcomes* of this appraisal interview was also obtained:

1. *Would you look forward to future performance reviews?* "Let us suppose you are going to have a performance review session tomorrow. How much would you look forward to it?"
2. *Did greater mutual understanding result?* For example, "to what extent did your last performance review session increase your understanding of what your supervisor expected you to achieve on the job (your job responsibilities)?"
3. *How fair was last performance appraisal?* "How fair did you feel your last performance appraisal session was?"
4. *Were you satisfied with the performance review process?* "Think of your last performance review session. How well does this statement describe it? 'I felt satisfied with the session'."
5. *Were you motivated to improve job performance?* "Think of your last performance review session. How well does this statement describe it? 'I felt I wanted to improve my performance'."
6. *Did your actual performance improve?* "Think of your last performance review session. How well does this statement describe it? 'I actually have improved my performance since then'."
7. *Overall value of performance review interviews.* "In general, how valuable are performance reviews in your opinion?"

The findings of this study indicate that different interview techniques are involved with increasing the appraisee's *satisfaction* with the review than are involved with improving the person's future *performance*. Specifically, all six "interview characteristics" (like "amount of threat," and "amount of influence") contributed to the appraisee's overall satisfaction with the review, as well as to related outcomes like whether or not the person looked forward to other reviews, and thought the review was fair. But for improving subsequent job performance, the interview skills that stood out were the supervisor's ability to use the interview to clear up job problems, and set goals. What these findings seem to show is that interpersonal communication guidelines like "don't evoke defensiveness," "don't criticize," "actively listen," and "avoid games" do apply to performance reviews, but that these reviews also require something more. In particular, managers who want to get the most from the reviews should also emphasize clearing up job-related problems with the appraisee, and setting measurable performance targets and a schedule for achieving them.

FUNDAMENTALS OF DISCIPLINING

There will still undoubtedly be times when a subordinate has to be disciplined. These situations may arise out of the performance appraisal, but, more often, discipline is required because a rule or procedure was violated. The basic purpose of discipline is to encourage employees to behave sensibly at work, where "sensible behavior" is defined in terms of adhering to rules and regulations. In an organization, rules and regulations serve about the same purpose

400   that laws do in society, and discipline is called for when one of these rules or regulations is violated. [8]

Prerequisites to Disciplining

Perhaps the main consideration in disciplining is to ensure that it is fair and just. This in turn begins with three prerequisites: a system of communicated rules and regulations; a system of progressive penalties; and an appeals process.

Communicated Rules and Regulations. The first prerequisite is a set of clear rules and regulations. These generally cover various offenses such as unexcused absences, drinking at work, theft, and insubordination.

The purpose of these rules and regulations is to inform employees *ahead of time* as to what is and is not acceptable behavior. Rules and regulations therefore have to be *communicated*. Employees have to be told (usually in writing) what is not permitted. This is typically done during the employee's orientation, and the rules and regulations are also usually listed in the employee's orientation handbook.

A System of Progressive Penalties. A system of progressive penalties is a second prerequisite to effective disciplining. In most organizations penalties range from simple oral warnings, to written warnings, to suspension from the job, to discharge. [9] The severity of the penalty is usually a function of the type of offense and the number of times the offense has occurred. For example, about 90% of the companies responding to one survey just issue warnings for the first unexcused lateness. However for a fourth offense discharge is the more usual disciplinary action. [10]

An Appeals Process. Finally, it is important to have an appeals process built into the disciplinary procedures: this helps to ensure that discipline is meted out fairly and equitably. Remember that in civil life, if a person appears to have broken a law the policeman only arrests him. The person is then tried before a jury of his or her peers and sentenced by an impartial judge. There is usually not this separation of functions in organizations. Instead, the supervisor is often the policeman, jury, and judge. Most managers are fair, and in most instances this "nonseparation of powers" works fairly well. But there is always the chance of a bad decision on the part of a manager, and so it's important for everyone to know ahead of time that there is a formal appeals process.

Characteristics of Effective Disciplining

The characteristics of effective disciplining can be summarized as follows: [11]

Emphasize Rules, Not Personal Desires. Effective discipline is based on clearly communicated rules, not on the whims or personal desires of managers.

These rules have to be enforced consistently and reasonably. They should be understood. And subordinates should understand why the rule is necessary.

Maintain the Subordinate's Dignity.   Disciplining a subordinate is no easy matter. Unlike the appraisal conference discussed earlier, disciplining usually does not involve a "problem-solving" approach. Instead, the emphasis is usually on "tell and sell": you tell the employee what he or she has done wrong and what the penalty is.

However, this does not mean that the manager has to be overly critical or attack the employee's defenses. Nor does it mean that the person has to be robbed of his or her dignity. Specifically:

1. Discipline the subordinate *in private.*
2. *Avoid "entrapment."* Do not deliberately rig a situation that causes the person to require disciplining.
3. Do not use an otherwise innocent and one-time offender as "an *example."*
4. Do not *suddenly tighten* your enforcement where enforcement has previously been lax.
5. Do not attack the employee's *personal worth. Attack the act, not the man,* and do not base comments about his or her overall worth on one or two specific offenses.

Remember: The Burden of Proof is on the Accuser.   In our society, a person is always considered innocent until proven guilty. This is also the case with disciplinary matters: the burden of proof is always on the supervisor to prove that a rule or regulation was violated and that the penalty was necessary. You therefore have to make sure you have all the facts before disciplining a subordinate. Make sure you can prove there was a clear-cut breach of a rule or regulation and that this can be backed up with positive evidence. Similarly, make sure to keep adequate records of offenses and warnings. This is not only good management practice: it is also crucial when defending the decision to superiors, union arbitrators, and others—like the EEOC.

Make the Offense Clear.   Disciplining is much like training—the main goal is to change behavior. In the case of discipline, you want to bring your subordinate's behavior into line with your organization's rules and regulations, and to do this, it should be made clear exactly what rule or regulation was broken, and how it was broken. Give the specific details—don't just discuss it in generalities.

Provide Adequate Warning.   There are few offenses which require immediate suspension or discharge. In most cases (particularly for a first or second offense) an oral or written warning is adequate. If the decision is appealed—to your own superior, to the union, etc.—you may be asked to show proof that you did in fact warn the subordinate. And when matters like these are brought before union arbitrators or the EEOC there are few more convincing arguments you can make than those provided by your record or prior warnings.

SUMMARY

1. Counseling meetings do not have to be useless affairs, at least not if they are aimed at constructively changing a subordinate's behavior and identifying the root cause of the performance deficiency.

2. Defenses are important for two reasons: they protect our self-image and help us screen out painful experiences.

3. There are four main problems that undermine effective interpersonal communication. These include: defensiveness; criticizing (this just evokes defensiveness and, possibly, diminished performance); not actively listening; and playing games.

4. When counseling, it is important to be an "active" listener—to actively try to grasp both the facts *and* the feelings in what you hear. To do this: listen for total meaning, reflect feelings, note all cues, and do not act as a judge.

5. Based on what has been said to this point, some guidelines for effective communicating include: avoid making your subordinates defensive, be an active listener, don't criticize, and avoid "playing games." In addition, appraisal reviews require solving job-related problems, and setting targets and a schedule for achieving them.

6. You will sometimes have to discipline a subordinate—particularly when rules or regulations are violated. The three prerequisites to disciplining include: make sure you've communicated your rules and regulations beforehand, have a system of progressive penalties, and have an appeals process that everyone is aware of.

7. In addition, the elements of effective disciplining include: emphasize rules, not personal desires; maintain subordinates' dignity; remember that the burden of proof is on you; make the offense clear; provide adequate warning.

CASE INCIDENT

*Get Off My Back**

Joe Toby, director of management services, scheduled a coaching session with Herman Sutherland, a management consultant on his staff:

Joe: As you know, Herman, I've scheduled this meeting with you because I want to talk about certain aspects of your work. And my comments are not all that favorable.

Herman: Since you have formal authority over me, I guess I'll have to go along with the session. Go ahead.

Joe: I'm not a judge reading a verdict to you. This is supposed to be a two-way interchange.

Herman: But you called the meeting, go ahead with your complaints. Particularly any with foundation. I remember once when we were having lunch you told me that you didn't like the fact that I wore a brown knitted suit with a blue shirt. I would put that in the category of unfounded.

Joe: I'm glad you brought appearance up. I think you create a substandard impression to clients because of your appearance. A consultant is supposed to look sharp, particularly at the rates we charge clients. You often create the impression that you cannot afford good clothing. Your pants are baggy. Your ties are unstylish and often food stained.

Herman: The firm may charge those high rates. But as a junior the money I receive does not allow me to purchase fancy clothing. Besides, I have very little interest in trying to dazzle clients with my clothing. I have heard no complaints from them.

Joe: Nevertheless, I think that your appearance should be more business-like. Let's talk about something else I have on my list of things in which I would like to see some improvements. A routine audit of your expense account shows a practice that I think is improper. You charged one client for a Thursday night dinner for three consecutive weeks. Yet your airline ticket receipt shows that you returned home at three in the afternoon. That kind of behavior is unprofessional. How do you explain your charges for these phantom dinners?

Herman: The flight ticket may say three P.M. but with our unpredictable weather, the flight could very well be delayed. If I eat at the airport, then my wife won't have to run the risk of preparing a dinner for me that goes to waste. Food is very expensive.

---

* Andrew J. Dubrin, *Human Relations: A Job Oriented Approach* (Reston, VA: Reston Publishing Company, 1978) pp. 211–212.

Joe: But how can you eat dinner at three P.M. at the airport?

Herman: I consider any meal after one in the afternoon to be dinner.

Joe: Okay for now. I want to comment on your reports to clients. They are much more careless than they should be. I know that you are capable of more meticulous work. I saw an article you prepared for publication that was first rate and professional. Yet on one report you misspelled the name of the client company. That's atrocious.

Herman: A good secretary should have caught that mistake. Besides, I never claimed that I was able to write perfect reports. There are only so many hours in the working day to spend on writing up reports.

Joe: Another thing that requires immediate improvement is the appearance of your office. It's a mess. You have the worst-looking office in our branch. In fact, you have the worst-looking office I have ever seen in a C.P.A. or management-consulting office. Why can't you have a well-organized, cool-looking office?

Herman: What's the difference? Clients never visit me in this office. It's just a work place. Incidentally Joe, could you do me one favor?

Joe: What's that?

Herman: Get off my back.

Question

1. If you were Joe, how would you handle this situation? What mistakes has Joe made so far?

EXPERIENTIAL EXERCISE

Purpose.   The purpose of this exercise is to give you some experience in counseling and active listening.

Required Understanding.   You should be familiar with our discussions of face-to-face communicating.

How to Set Up the Exercise/Instructions.

1. Divide the class into groups of three students. In each group one person will act as observer, a second will play the role of Bob, the interviewee, and the third person will play the role of Mike, the interviewer. (Extra students can join groups as observers.) Their "roles" are presented below, but *please make sure you only read the role of the person whose part you are taking.*

2. ROLES

Role of Bob (the interviewee) (only "Bob" should read this role): Today, as the saying goes, has not been your day. You overslept this morning and in your rush to get to work you got a ticket for not stopping at a stop sign. You got to sleep late because you spent most of the night trying to fix a leaking pipe in the bathroom, which your wife has just informed you will cost $95 to have a plumber fix. You got into work late this morning and in your rush to catch up machined (you're a machinist) about 50 metal parts down to the wrong diameter: you'll now have to remachine all of them, and you know your supervisor, Mike, is probably steaming. He just told you to be in his office at 4:30 P.M. sharp, a fact which upsets you both because you're afraid you're being "called on the carpet," and because you'd wanted to leave work a few minutes early to keep an eye on the plumber.

Role for Mike, the interviewer (only Mike should read this role): The performance report for your department for last month was not as good at it should have been, and your boss has told you to get costs back in line with what they should be. You were therefore startled to be told that Bob has to remachine 50 parts, a process that will probably kill half a day. To make matters worse remachining the parts will probably require overtime (an added expense) since the parts were for a rush job that has to be finished by the end of the week. You're not quite sure what you're going to say to Bob when he comes in, but your first inclination is to "read him the riot act."

Role for the observer (only observers should read this): The observer should not enter into the conversation at all, and should simply take notes of what he or she hears: How well is Mike following the guidelines we set down in this chapter? What could he have improved on? Was he an active listener?

3. Once you have read your respective roles, "Bob" and "Mike" should meet for their "4:30 meeting." Their conversation should last about 15 to 20 minutes.

After the "meeting" the three group members should discuss the following questions (please don't read this until after the "meeting"): Was Mike an active listener? (Be specific.) What could he have done to improve his effectiveness as a communicator? Was Bob an active listener? Why? Why not?

DISCUSSION QUESTIONS

1. What purpose is served by psychological defenses?
2. In terms of what you now know about defensiveness, and operant conditioning, discuss why you think criticizing is not an effective means of changing behavior. Under what conditions might it be effective?
3. Test your ability to distinguish between good and poor reflected responses by taking the short "quiz" presented in Exhibit 14.1 on page 406. Why did you pick the ones you did?
4. Under what conditions is disciplining appropriate? How should such disciplining be handled?

Exhibit 14.1   Examples of Good and Poor Reflected Responses: A Quiz

Remark	*Select Best Response to Reflect*
1. A clerical employee with ten years' experience told his supervisor: "I've been doing this job for years now and nobody had ever complained and now you send my work back and tell me to do it over. It isn't fair and it doesn't make sense. Maybe I do make mistakes now and then, but nobody is perfect and I don't know why I should get all the blame for what goes on around here."	(a) It isn't fair to ask you to correct your own mistakes. (b) Suppose you check your work before you bring it to me. (c) You think you are being blamed for not being perfect. (d) You feel that I am too strict.
2. During an interview with his supervisor, a member of a crew states: "I don't want to work with Jake any more. He's lazy and is always taking a superior attitude and complains about the rest of us not helping him as much as we should. He thinks he is too good for this kind of work and too good to work with the rest of us and I'm sick of being around him."	(a) You feel that Jake ought to be disciplined in some way. (b) Jake doesn't want to cooperate, is that it? (c) Jake's attitude makes the work unpleasant. (d) You think Jake might fit in better somewhere else.
3. A young man whose work showed a sudden drop in quality was sent to the employment manager for an interview. One of the things he said on arriving was: "I don't know why I should be asked to talk to you about my work. I haven't complained and I haven't time for this kind of chit-chat. So give me what help you have in mind and I'll be on my way."	(a) You came to see me because you were sent and not because you feel any need for help. (b) Don't you feel that with my experience in the company I might be of some help? (c) You feel irritated for coming here because you don't think I can help you. (d) You mustn't jump to conclusions. Often people need help when they are unaware of this need.
4. In the middle of a counseling interview with her boss, a fifty-eight-year-old woman said, "You don't want me here, you just want young women. I'm getting old so I guess I should get out."	(a) It's not true that I favor the young women employees. (b) You believe I'd like to have you leave because of your age. (c) You feel you have reason to believe that I prefer young girls. (d) I can see that I must have done something to hurt your feelings.
5. A supervisor was discussing the work of a young man about a year out of high school. The supervisor was trying to determine why important details on procedure were often overlooked or clearly violated. Suddenly the young man shouted "You're the worst supervisor I've ever had. If a person shows initiative you work him over. I refuse to follow silly rules."	(a) Why don't you check with me before you make a change in procedure. (b) You resent me for criticizing your work. (c) Perhaps it's my fault that I didn't train you on the correct procedures. (d) You feel I should have someone else go over your work.

Correct responses: 1-c, 2-c, 3-a, 4-b, 5-b

Adapted from PSYCHOLOGY IN INDUSTRIAL ORGANIZATIONS, 4th edition, by Norman R. F. Maier. Copyright © 1973 by Houghton Mifflin Company. Used by permission.

NOTES

1. Mortimer Feinberg, *Effective Psychology for Managers* (Englewood Cliffs, N.J.: Prentice-Hall, 1967), p. 80.

2. Herbert H. Meyer, Emmanuel Kay, and John R. P. French, Jr., "Split Roles in Performance Appraisal," *Harvard Business Review*, Vol. 43 (January–February 1965), pp. 123–129; reprinted in Dale Beach, *Managing People at Work*, pp. 148–156.

3. Anthony Athos and John Gabarro, *Interpersonal Behavior* (Englewood Cliffs, N.J.: Prentice-Hall, 1978), p. 423.

4. Eric Berne, *Games People Play* (New York: Grove Press, 1964). See also Thomas Harris, *I'm OK You're OK: A Practical Guide to Transactional Analysis* (New York: Harper and Row, 1967); French and Bell, p. 145.

5. This is based on R. Jack Webber, "Games Managers Play," in Anthony Athos and John Gabarro, *Interpersonal Behavior*, pp. 283–289.

6. All examples are from Webber, *Games Managers Play*.

7. Ronald Burke, William Weitzel, and Tamara Weir, "Characteristics of Effective Employee Performance Review and Development Interviews: Replication and Extension," *Personnel Psychology*, Vol. 31 (Winter 1978), pp. 903–919.

8. This and the following section are based on Lester R. Bittel, *What Every Supervisor Should Know* (New York: McGraw-Hill, 1974), pp. 285–298.

9. Dale Beach, *Personnel* (New York: Macmillan, 1970), pp. 608–612.

10. Personnel Policies Forum, *Employee Conduct and Discipline*, survey #102 (Washington, D.C.: The Bureau of National Affairs, 1973), p. 6.

11. These are based on George Odiorne, *How Managers Make Things Happen* (Englewood Cliffs, N.J.: Prentice-Hall, 1961), pp. 132–143; also see Bittel, *What Every Supervisor Should Know*, pp. 285–298; Beach, *Personnel*, pp. 605–610; Robert Mathis and John Jackson, *Personnel* (St. Paul: West, 1976), p. 349.

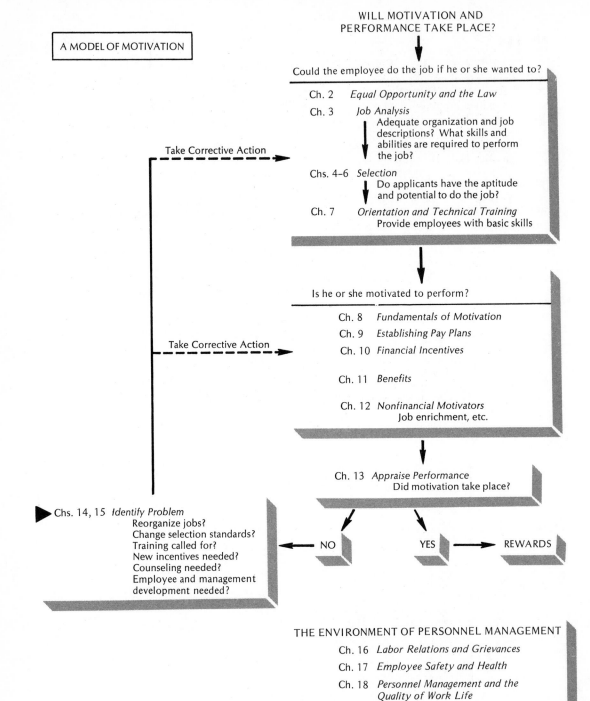

A MODEL OF MOTIVATION

WILL MOTIVATION AND
PERFORMANCE TAKE PLACE?

Could the employee do the job if he or she wanted to?

Ch. 2 *Equal Opportunity and the Law*

Ch. 3 *Job Analysis*
Adequate organization and job
descriptions? What skills and
abilities are required to perform
the job?

Take Corrective Action

Chs. 4–6 *Selection*
Do applicants have the aptitude
and potential to do the job?

Ch. 7 *Orientation and Technical Training*
Provide employees with basic skills

Is he or she motivated to perform?

Ch. 8 *Fundamentals of Motivation*

Ch. 9 *Establishing Pay Plans*

Ch. 10 *Financial Incentives*

Take Corrective Action

Ch. 11 *Benefits*

Ch. 12 *Nonfinancial Motivators*
Job enrichment, etc.

Ch. 13 *Appraise Performance*
Did motivation take place?

Chs. 14, 15 *Identify Problem*
Reorganize jobs?
Change selection standards?
Training called for?
New incentives needed?
Counseling needed?
Employee and management
development needed?

NO   YES ▶ REWARDS

THE ENVIRONMENT OF PERSONNEL MANAGEMENT

Ch. 16 *Labor Relations and Grievances*

Ch. 17 *Employee Safety and Health*

Ch. 18 *Personnel Management and the
Quality of Work Life*

When you finish studying

15   Employee and Management Development

You should be able to:

1. *Explain the role employee and management development plays in improving performance at work.*
2. *Define organizational development.*
3. *Discuss three basic ways to proceed with an organizational change.*
4. *Explain the "action-research" process.*
5. *Compare and contrast "sensitivity training" and "team building."*
6. *Describe one method of administering attitude surveys.*

OVERVIEW

As illustrated in our performance/motivation model, the next step (after performance appraisal and feedback) is to identify performance problems (if any) and take corrective action. In Chapter 7 (technical training) we explained one method for analyzing performance problems, and emphasized the importance of distinguishing between "won't do" and "can't do" problems. Often, for example, you will find that the reason performance is not up to par is because employees "won't" do their jobs, due to inequitable pay, inadequate benefits, unchallenging jobs, or some other "motivational" reason. Solutions here might include reevaluating jobs, performing a wage survey, instituting a new incentive plan, increasing (or personalizing) benefits, and enriching jobs. On the other hand, employees often fail to perform not because they don't want to do their jobs, but they can't do them—perhaps because they shouldn't have been selected for their jobs in the first place, or because their training was inadequate, or because interdepartmental rivalries and frictions prevent them from doing so. Here, solutions include revising selection standards, improving technical training, or, perhaps employee and management development.

The main purpose of this chapter is to explain the nature and procedures of employee and management development. Employee and management development has two basic uses. First, it is used for solving organization-wide problems (concerning, for instance, inadequate interdepartmental communications). Second, it is used for developing employee's and managers' problem solving, leadership, and interpersonal skills for some future jobs with the organization; here it is often used in conjunction with the firm's personnel planning and recruiting process, in that the skills and development needs of high-potential employees are identified and matched

410   *with the organization's future manpower needs. Development methods include classroom development methods (like university programs), simulation-based methods (like "role playing") and "organizational development."*

INTRODUCTION: THE NATURE OF EMPLOYEE AND MANAGEMENT DEVELOPMENT

In Chapter 7 we explained that in this book we distinguish between two types of training: technical training, and employee and management development. Technical training (discussed in Chapter 7) is aimed mostly at providing new employees with the skills they need to perform their current jobs adequately. Employee and management development (discussed in the present chapter) is training of a more long-term nature: its aim is to develop employees for some future jobs with the organization, or to solve organization-wide problems concerning, for instance, inadequate interdepartmental communication.

As with technical training, both line managers and personnel specialists have training responsibilities with regard to employee and management development. The personnel office administers the firm's personnel planning system, through which employees' skills and potential are matched with the firm's needs: in this role, personnel is responsible for identifying employee and management development needs and for ensuring that employees are scheduled for the necessary training. The personnel specialist (and, in larger organizations, the training manager) is also usually responsible for matters like scheduling training programs, ensuring attendance, administering performance tests and questionnaires, obtaining outside instructors and consultants, certifying and qualifying program graduates, and administering payroll and travel expenses. [1] In addition to managing the training function, it is also not unusual to find organizations in which "in house" specialists act as resource persons for actually training employees by holding lectures, seminars, and similar activities. And, of course the personnel or training specialist would also be expected to obtain, design, and make available the pedagogical tools needed for the organization's various training programs, including, for example, workbooks, films, and experiential exercises.

Line managers also play an important role in employee and management development. First, it is often the managers themselves who undergo developmental training such as organizational development, and behavioral modeling. Line managers also play a role by identifying performance problems and candidates for development.

CLASSROOM-TYPE DEVELOPMENT METHODS

Classroom-type methods use traditional educational tools like lectures, conferences, and college courses to develop participants' knowledge and skills.

Lectures

Lectures are one of the most simple ways of imparting knowledge to trainees. Here the instructor presents a series of facts, concepts, or principles, and explains relationships. [2] As most students are painfully aware, lectures are usually a means of "telling" trainees something. The students (or trainees) participate mainly as listeners. In training, the most important uses of lectures include:

1. Reducing anxiety about upcoming training programs or organizational changes by explaining their purposes.
2. Introducing a subject and presenting an overview of its scope.
3. Presenting basic material that will provide a common background for subsequent activities.
4. Illustrating the application of rules, concepts, or principles; reviewing, clarifying, or summarizing. [3]

The main advantage of the lecture method is that it is simple and efficient. The trainer can present more material in a given amount of time than he or she can by almost any other method, [4] and can do so with very large groups.

But as most students know, lectures have some important drawbacks. They usually don't provide for student participation, and unless the material is very interesting, little learning may take place. People learn skills by doing, and therefore lectures are inadequate by themselves for teaching new skills or for changing attitudes. We also know that the necessary stress on verbal communication can prove very frustrating to some students. [5] And while a skillful lecturer can adapt his material to the specific group, usually it is almost impossible to adjust it for individual differences *within* a group.

Programmed Learning

Whether the programmed learning device itself is a textbook or a machine, programmed learning always consists of three functions:

1. Presenting questions, facts, or problems to the learner.
2. Allowing the person to respond.
3. Providing feedback on the accuracy of his or her answers.

The main advantage of programmed learning is that usually it reduces training time by about one-third. [6] And since it lets people learn at their own rate, provides immediate feedback and reduces the risk of error, it should also facilitate learning.

We know, however, that trainees usually do *not* learn much more with programmed learning than they would with a conventional textbook approach. [7] Yet the costs of developing the manuals, books, and machinery for programmed learning can be quite high. Therefore you have to carefully weigh the cost of developing such programs against the accelerated (but not better) learning which should occur.

Conferences

Conferences can be used in various ways. [8] Sometimes the trainer guides the discussion and presents information in such a way that the facts, principles, or concepts are explained. At other times the purpose of a conference is to find an answer to a question or a solution to a problem. Here the group is used to develop the best solution. The instructor's job is to define the problem and encourage full participation in the discussion.

The main advantage of conferences is that they permit your people to actively engage in discussions. This is important because, for most people, the opportunity to express one's own views can be very stimulating.

The main limitation to using conferences is probably the lack of good conference leaders. [9] One expert contends that a good conference leader can:

1. Clearly identify the central problem.
2. See to it that all participants are encouraged to present points of view and develop alternatives.
3. See to it that there is a clear agenda to follow.
4. Minimize debate over unimportant details.
5. Prevent domination by one or two individuals.
6. Provide clear summaries on each point.

University-Related Development Programs [10]

Continued training to upgrade and develop the skills of supervisory, technical, and other employees often involves participation in a college or university-related program, and such programs are of four types. First, as explained in Chapter 11 many employers offer tuition refunds as an incentive for employees to develop job related skills. Thus engineers might be encouraged to enroll in technical courses aimed at keeping them abreast of changes in their field, and supervisors encouraged to enroll in master of business administration programs in order to develop them for higher level management jobs.

Employers are also increasingly granting technical and professional employees extended "sabbaticals"—periods of time off—for purposes of attending a college or university to pursue a higher degree or to upgrade skills. For example, Bell Laboratories has a comprehensive continuing education program which includes a tuition refund, and released time for up to one year on-campus study. In addition, the company has a doctoral support program which permits tuition refund and release time for study one day a week (and, for some, a full year's study on campus to meet residence requirements).

Some companies, like Eastern Airlines have experimented with offering selected employees in-house degree programs in conjunction with colleges and universities. In the case of Eastern, for example faculty members from a university's business school teach master of business administration courses at the company's Miami headquarters and employees who complete their degree requirements can thus earn a full degree "in-house."

Employers also offer a wide range of in-house lectures and seminars by university staff. At Dupont and Allied Chemical, for example university scholars visit corporate research facilities on a regularly scheduled basis. In most cases, the visiting professor presents a lecture on a given subject, usually a new development or technique, and is available for individual discussions with company scientists to exchange views. Various non-profit organizations including the Conference Board, and the American Management Association also offer courses in various phases of business operation.

SIMULATION-BASED DEVELOPMENT METHODS

Simulation-based development methods are distinguished by the fact that their aim to develop participants' problem-solving, leadership, or interpersonal skills by requiring them to perform tasks as similar as possible to those actually used "on the job." (On the other hand, classroom-type methods like those just discussed do not allow for much "practice," and so tend to be best for just imparting new knowledge, rather than for building skills.)

Behavior Modeling

Behavior modeling is a relatively new method that has proved quite successful for both technical training and employee and management development. [11] It has been used, for example, to:

1. Train hard-core employees (and their supervisors) to take and give criticism, ask and give help, and establish mutual trust and respect.
2. Train first line supervisors to better handle "eight common supervisor-employee interactions," including giving recognition, disciplining, introducing changes and improving poor performance.
3. Train middle managers to better handle interpersonal situations involving, for example, giving directions, discussing any performance problems, discussing undesirable work habits, reviewing performance, and discussing salary problems.

To date, behavior modeling has been used primarily to improve and develop employees' and supervisors' interpersonal skills. However, the basic technique, described below, could conceivably be used for other types of skill building, such as teaching employees how to set up a piece of machinery.

The basic behavior modeling procedure can be outlined as follows:

1. *Modeling*. First, trainees watch films or video tapes that show model persons behaving effectively in a problem situation. In other words, trainees are shown the "right" way to behave in a simulated but realistic situation. The film might show, for example, a supervisor disciplining a subordinate, if teaching "how to discipline" is one objective of the training program.
2. *Role playing*. Next, the trainees are given "roles" to play in a simulated situation; here they practice and rehearse the effective behaviors demonstrated by the models.

3. *Social reinforcement.* The trainer provides reinforcement in the form of praise and constructive feedback, based on how the trainee performs in the role playing situation.

4. *Transfer of training.* Finally, trainees are encouraged to apply their new skills when they are back on their jobs.

Behavior modeling has been quite successful as a development method. In the case of hard core employees and their supervisors, for example, three-fourths of the hard core employees trained to handle job related problems stayed on their jobs after 6 months, as compared with only about one-fourth of those not trained. In another case, supervisors who were trained to handle work related problems (like disciplining employees) subsequently performed significantly better than those who were not.

Management Games

People learn best by getting actively involved in the activity itself, and management games can be very useful for gaining such involvement. In the typical game, trainees are divided into five- or six-man "companies." They are given a goal, such as "maximize sales," and are told that they can make several specific decisions. For example, they may be allowed to decide 1) how much to spend on advertising; 2) how much to produce; 3) how much inventory to maintain; 4) and how many of which product to produce. Usually the game itself compresses a two- or three-year period into hours, days, or months.

As in the real world, each company usually doesn't get to see what decisions the other companies have made, although these decisions obviously affect their own sales. For example, if a competitor decides to increase his advertising expenditures, he may end up increasing his sales at the expense of yours.

There is usually a great sense of excitement and enjoyment in playing the game. And in addition to being an enjoyable way to develop problem-solving skills, games also help focus attention on the need for planning rather than on "putting out fires." The companies are apt to elect their own officers and develop their own division of work. They can therefore be useful for developing leadership skills, and for fostering cooperation and teamwork.

A major problem with games is that they can be very expensive to develop and implement, particularly when the game itself is computerized. Also, management games usually force the decision maker to choose alternatives from a "closed" list; in real life managers are more often rewarded for creating new, innovative, alternatives. On the whole, though, trainees almost always react favorably to a well-run game, and it is a good technique for developing problem-solving and leadership skills.

In-House Development Centers

Many employers have established in-house development centers in which prospective managers and executives are exposed to realistic problems and tasks, evaluated on their performance, and encouraged to develop improved management skills. These centers typically combine classroom methods (lectures and seminars, for instance), with other techniques like assessment centers and in-basket exercises (discussed in Chapter 6), and role-playing.

CBS Inc. has used such a center since 1976. [12] The "CBS School for Management," as it is called, is set in country-club surroundings in old Westbury, New York. Its basic aim is to give young managers firsthand experience at decision-making. To accomplish this, both their General Management Program (for upper level managers) and Professional Management Program (for entry level managers) stress the solution of concrete business problems through working with people. The programs use various teaching methods, but particularly special computerized case exercises. In one exercise, for instance, each student acts as a regional sales manager and has to make decisions regarding how to deal with a star saleswoman who wants to leave, and how to choose new salespeople. As participants make decisions (like whether or not to boost the saleswoman's salary to entice her to stay), the computer indicates the implications of the decision; (if she's paid more, for example, others will also want an increase in pay). Then, at the end of each day students get printouts indicating how their decisions reflected their abilities to set goals, and organize work, manage time, and supervise subordinates. The CBS program is in the process of being evaluated, but it appears to have been valuable as a method for developing participants' managerial skills, and for raising their morale, although an original goal—to reduce management turnover at CBS—has yet to materialize.

ORGANIZATIONAL DEVELOPMENT

The Nature of Organizational Development

Organizations and the environments in which they compete are dynamic, and are constantly undergoing change: competitors introduce new products, new production technologies are developed, employees retire or resign, intergroup conflicts arise, or productivity inexplicably drops. These changes and others are the kinds that managers face daily. And very often, an effective response demands modifying some aspect of the organization, perhaps by reorganizing, redesigning jobs, reducing conflict, or installing a new production line or incentive plan.

Once a manager decides that a change is required there are three basic ways to proceed. [13] First, he or she could institute the change *unilaterally*, by analyzing the problem (like poor communication), deciding on the solution (like reorganizing), and unilaterally imposing this solution upon the parties involved via a "one way" decree. Second, the manager could instead take more of a *shared approach* to change, by discussing the problem with the people involved, asking for their advice, and perhaps allowing them to choose from several alternative solutions. On the other hand, the manager could also carry this participation "all the way" by completely *delegating* the problem to subordi-

416   nates. Here employees might be asked to identify the problems themselves, and to formulate, develop, and implement the solutions.

Organizational Development (OD) is such an approach to change, one in which the employees themselves play a major role in the change process. The basic focus in OD is on increasing the level of trust and open communication in the organization, on the assumption that this will make it easier for the organization to react to problems (like the introduction of a new product by a competitor) and to change, by enabling the organization's managers and groups to work together more cooperatively. In other words, the idea is to change the attitudes and values of the parties involved, on the assumption that they will in turn develop and implement the necessary changes. As an example, an OD expert might suggest solving an "intergroup conflict" problem by first making the members of each group more "sensitive" to others. Then, supposedly, the members of each group will be able to work out the problems themselves— by setting common goals that both can shoot for, for instance. The techniques (or, really, set of techniques) used to bring about such changes in attitudes and values are collectively called organizational development or "OD."

OD reverses the normal change process, wherein changes (like reorganizations) are usually mandated at the top of the organization and forced down. Specifically, OD attempts to change skills, structures, and relationships *by changing the values and attitudes of participants.* Hampton and his associates put it this way:

> It is the change in personal values in the system, coupled with the change in ways in which people treat one another, which come first . . . operating procedures, costs, job descriptions, production schedules—the whole rational side of the firm—become dependent on how a group of people feel about themselves as people and about others as people. . . . [14]

Notice that stressing the "people" aspects of the organization does not mean that OD practitioners do not try to bring about changes in the organization's structure, policies, or practices: they often do. But the typical OD program is aimed at changing the attitudes, values, and beliefs of employees and managers so that they themselves can identify and implement these sorts of technical changes.

A Focus on "Action Research." The common denominator underlying most of the different OD techniques (or "interventions") is called *action research.* [15] Action research means that most OD efforts involve (1) gathering data about the organization and its operations and attitudes, with an eye toward solving some particular problem (like conflicts between the sales and production departments), (2) *feeding back* this data to the parties (employees) involved, and then (3) having these parties *team plan solutions* to the problems. OD is thus a research-based effort, and some have even suggested that organization development might be best described as "organization improvement through action research." [16] In any event, the important point is that OD is almost

always research based: the participants (employees) themselves get involved in
gathering data about their organization, analyzing it, and planning solutions
based on it. [17]

For convenience we can categorize OD techniques as either *individual or
interpersonal techniques, team building techniques,* or *organization-wide
techniques.*

Individual and Interpersonal Development Techniques: Sensitivity Training

The OD techniques in this category generally aim at improving the "human
relations" skills of employees and managers by providing them with the insight
and skills needed to more effectively analyze their own and others' behavior.
Then, with these new skills, they should be able to more intelligently solve interpersonal and intergroup problems. One such technique is sensitivity training.

Sensitivity Training Defined.   Sensitivity, laboratory, or T-group training
(the T is for training) was one of the earliest OD techniques, and while its
use has diminished it is still widely used. [18] A "T" group (or sensitivity-training
laboratory) is basically an unstructured, agendaless group session consisting of
about 10 to 12 people and a professional "trainer" who acts as catalyst and
facilitator for the group. [19] The T-group is, according to Argyris,

> ". . . a group experience designed to provide maximum possible opportuni-
> ties for the individuals to expose their behavior, give and receive feedback,
> experiment with new behavior, and develop . . . awareness and acceptance
> of self and others. . . . [20]

The basic aim of sensitivity training is to increase the participant's insight
into and sensitivity for his or her own behavior and the behavior of others *by
encouraging an open expression of feelings* in the trainer-guided T group "laboratory." Sensitivity training seeks to accomplish its aim (of increased interpersonal
sensitivity) by requiring frank, candid discussions in the T group of participants'
personal feelings, attitudes, and behavior; as a result, it is a controversial method,
one surrounded by heated debate. [21]

The T-Group Process.   Although the T-group process varies from trainer
to trainer, a typical meeting has been described as follows: a group of 10 to 15
meets, usually away from the job, and no activities or discussion topics are
planned. The focus is on the "here and now" (including the feelings and
emotions of the members in the group), and the participants are encouraged
to portray themselves *in the group* rather than in terms of past experiences or
future problems. Breaks in the discussions are often filled by feelings of frustration, expressions of hostility, and eventual attempts by some to organize and
impose a hierarchical structure on the rest. Such attempts are usually blocked
spontaneously by the group or through the trainer's intervention. Since the

418 group's behavior is the principle topic of conversation, the success of the training group depends largely on the process of feedback. Specifically, participants must be able to inform each other of how their behavior is being seen, and be able to describe and interpret the kind of feelings that produces. This feedback must be articulate and meaningful, since it is the primary channel through which the trainer must learn. In turn, the success of the feedback process depends upon the members being able to discover how deficient his earlier behavior was, and upon a climate of *psychological safety*. In other words, the person should feel safe to reveal one's self in the group, to expose one's feelings, drop one's defenses, and try out new ways of interacting. [22]

Criticisms. T-group training is very personal in nature, so it is not surprising that it is an extremely controversial subject. Odiorne described a training session in which, during one "horrible weekend," an inadequately trained trainer "broke down the barriers of formal courtesy that had substituted quite successfully for human relations in this successful lab for many years." [23] Everyone spoke frankly of his hostilities, and by the time the participants returned to their job, organized politicking and conflict reigned. Many senior scientists quit, and candid observations helped to sever ties between former colleagues. In general, criticisms of T-groups fall into one of three categories: critics argue that T-groups are either unethical, impractical, or dangerous (or all three):

Unethical. Some argue that T-group training as it is often practiced may be unethical. House, for example points out that when participation in a T-group program is "suggested" by one's superior, attendance cannot be considered strictly voluntary. [24, 25]

Impractical. Others argue that this type of training is impractical insofar as it is not consistent with the "business and economic world we live in." [26] In other words, it is aimed at increasing participants' openness, trust, and sensitivity for others feelings, and yet there is considerable doubt as to whether an alumnus of one of these programs would really be a better manager as a result of it—could the person, for example still make the necessary "hard-nose" decisions and deal with the realities of power, politics, and infighting in organizations once he or she was "sensitized"? [27]

Dangerous. Finally, there are those that argue that T-group training is dangerous in that the anxiety and pressure participants undergo can adversely affect their mental health. Studies indicate, for example that participants almost inevitably experience high levels of anxiety as a result of a T-group during the middle of the process, and become unsettled and uncomfortable about their own opinion and the comments made about them by others. While this anxiety usually receded by the end of the T-group, the anxiety can still have adverse effects on especially unprepared or insecure participants. [28] Similarly, Odiorne points out that sensitivity training is based on creating stress situations for their own sake, and that at present anyone with a registration fee can attend. [29]

Yet T-groups also have their advocates, and the fact that T-groups are still

widely used probably attests to the fact that there are many occasions on which
its advantages outweigh its drawbacks. [30]

French and Bell, for instance, contend that "T-groups are still an excellent
learning and change intervention, particularly for the personal growth and development of the individual." [31]

Findings and Implications for Personnel Management.   When reviewing
the T-group research evidence, three questions are relevant: does participation in
a T-group result in participants subsequently *behaving* differently; are the behavioral changes (if any) *"good" or "bad"* from the point of view of the
participant? And, do T-groups result in improved *organizational performance?*

The answer to the first question is yes: T-groups do change their participants'
behaviors. House, for example, says the studies "lend strong support to the
proposition that T-group training is capable of bringing about changes in job
behavior." [32] Specifically, sensitivity training, done properly, can result in more
supportive behavior, more considerate managers, and more sensitive people. [33]
Campbell and Dunnette note that participants become more open and self
understanding and that improved communications and leadership skills were
reported as well. [34]

There is less agreement as to whether the sorts of behavioral changes are
necessarily "good" or "bad" from the point of view of the participants themselves. The T-group experience itself (being criticized by others, and so on)
can definitely be a source of frustration and anxiety. [35] Furthermore, the participants' increased sensitivity can be a continuing source of frustration and
problems to them if they return to a work place in which the openness, trust,
and sensitivity they were trained to espouse is frowned upon or repulsed. [36]

Does sensitivity training improve *organizational* performance? There seems
little doubt that where handled properly it can improve organizational performance: In a number of instances, for example company performance and profits
improved, apparently as a result of having managers participate in sensitivity
training laboratories. [37] T-groups can thus be a force for either good or ill and
research indicates that there are a number of conditions for its success. These can
be summarized as follows: [38]

> There should be careful selection of participants to ensure that those ad-
> mitted do not have psychiatric case histories, symptoms of emotional insta-
> bility, or low tolerance of anxiety.
>
> Programs should be strictly voluntary.
>
> The training consultant should be a carefully selected, experienced T-group
> professional.
>
> Trainees should know ahead of time what sort of "training" they are getting
> into.
>
> Careful provisions should be given for transferring the learning back to the
> organization. For example provisions should be made to ensure that the
> people with whom participants will have to interact back on the job have

themselves been exposed to (or will shortly be exposed to) sensitivity training.

Team-Building Development Efforts

The Basic Team-Building Process. Most OD efforts focus on improving the effectiveness of teams at work, teams such as: a president and his or her vice presidents; all regional sales managers; all members of the research department; all division directors of a hospital; or the members of any other group in the organization that normally has to work together in order to carry out some tasks.

OD's emphasis on "action research" is perhaps most evident when the development effort is aimed at improving a work team's effectiveness. Data concerning the group's performance is collected, this data is fed back to the members of the group, and these participants then examine, explain, and analyze this data and develop specific "action plans" or solutions for solving the team's problems.

As an example, French and Bell note that the "typical" team-building program often begins with the consultant interviewing each of the team members and the leader, asking them what their problems are, how they think the group functions, and what obstacles are in the way of the group performing better. The consultant usually then categorizes the interview data into themes and presents the themes to the group at the beginning of a special "team building" meeting. (Themes might include, for example "not enough time to get my job done," or "I can't get any cooperation around here.") The themes are then ranked by the group in terms of their importance, and the most important ones form the agenda for the meeting. The group then examines and discusses the issues, examines the underlying causes of the problems, and begins work on some solutions to the problems. During one of these sessions certain "non-agenda" items often emerge as a result of the interactions of the participants. In discussing the theme "I can't get any cooperation around here," for example, the group's discussion in the meeting might uncover the fact that the group's manager is not providing enough direction and is allowing "vacuums" to develop that are leading to conflict, and to a break-down in cooperation. These "new" items (or problems) as well as the agenda items (or themes) are generally pursued under the experienced guidance of the consultant. Next, some action steps are formulated to bring about the changes deemed desirable. Then, a follow up meeting is often scheduled during which it is determined whether the action steps were implemented, and whether or not they were successful. Again, notice how the typical team intervention relies on the basic action-research process, in that the participants themselves become the researchers: information concerning the group's problems are obtained from the group; members of the group then analyze and discuss this data in an atmosphere of cooperativeness; and, finally, the participants then develop solutions or "action steps" for solving the problems that they themselves have identified.

Team interventions like these are useful not only for improving a work team's effectiveness, but as an early stage in a more comprehensive, organization-wide OD effort, to which we now turn.

Intergroup and Organization-Wide Team-Building Efforts

Some team-building efforts are specifically aimed at improving intergroup (rather than just intragroup) effectiveness, or at improving the effectiveness and "health" of the organization as a whole. These efforts often include individual interventions (like T-groups) and team building efforts, but in addition usually include specific, planned activities aimed at ensuring that the benefits of the OD effort permeate the entire organization. [39]

Grid Programs. "Grid" development is one example of this type of program, and is a systematic technology for organization-wide development designed by Blake and Mouton. [40] It is basically a six-phase program lasting from 3 to 5 years for which the necessary lecture material, visual aids, and other pedagogical tools have been developed by (and are made available by) Blake and Mouton.

Grid organization development is based on a device called the managerial grid. As summarized in Exhibit 15.1 the grid represents different possible "leadership styles," and is based on the idea that any manager has two basic matters he or she must attend to, *production,* and *people.* Production means getting results, or accomplishing the mission. The "people" aspect means the manager also has to consider those workers he or she directs since the results the manager gets are obtained through people. According to Blake and Mouton, managers differ in their concern for people, and concern for production, and, they argue that one can "label" managers according to the degree to which they are concerned with people, production, or both. For example, what Blake and Mouton call a "1-9" leader ranks high in his or her concern for people but low in concern for production. This manager's main concern is "keeping everyone happy," and for this person "getting results" is usually secondary to maintaining friendly relations. At the other extreme is a "9-1" leader. This person tends to be preoccupied with getting results, and this concern might manifest itself in continuing efforts to closely plan, direct, and control the work of subordinates, and in a relative absence of any efforts to maintain friendly relationships or high morale. Blake and Mouton contend that the most effective managers are those who score high on both "concern for production" and "concern for people"—they are "9,9" managers. A 9,9 manager is interested in getting results but in doing so through committed, cooperative subordinates. This kind of style would manifest itself in supportive behavior on the part of the manager, attempts by the manager to win the trust and respect of subordinates, and attempts to build a cohesive, problem-solving work group. The assumption is that high production will follow from (or at least be facilitated by having) highly committed subordinates. The grid organization development program

CONCERN   hi
FOR   9 | 1,9 | 9,9 |
PEOPLE   1 | 1,1 | 9,1 |
           lo
               1   9
               lo   hi
        CONCERN FOR PEOPLE

assumes that managers can work toward and develop a 9,9 style. And, it assumes that possessing such a style makes it easier for a manager to work with his or her subordinates, superiors, and peers in analyzing group, intergroup, and organizational problems and developing "action-steps" to solve these problems. That being the case, the first phase of the six phase program is primarily an educational one during which participants learn about the grid concept, and their own managerial styles:

Phase 1: *Study of the managerial grid.* Here managers learn the grid concepts in seminars of a week's length. They learn how to analyze their own and others management styles, to communicate more openly, and to assess work group effectiveness.

Phase 2: *Work team development.* Here the manager and his or her group utilize the concepts and the climate of openness developed in phase 1 to analyze work team problems and generate action plans for their solution. This second phase is basically a "team intervention" of the sort we described in the previous section. Its aim is to develop—in an atmosphere of cooperation—a realistic priority of the work team's problems and specific suggestions for their solutions.

Phase 3: *Intergroup development.* Here the action-research experience of phase 2 is extended to the analysis of intergroup problems, especially intergroup problems between interrelated organizational units. Representatives of interrelated units (like production, and sales) meet in order to achieve "better problem solving between groups through a closer integration of units that have working interrelationships." [41]

Some of these meetings are attended by members of top management: the aim in phase 3 is to improve group cooperation both laterally (say, between the sales, and production managers) as well as vertically (which might therefore entail having the vice president to whom both managers report attend these meetings as well).

Phase 4: *Developing a new "blueprint" for the organization.* In this phase top management works out a new "blueprint" for the organization, a blueprint that basically includes top management's statement concerning where it would like to see the organization move over the next few years in terms of things like new markets, reduced costs, increased profitability, and perhaps a new organization structure. In this phase, in other words, top management clarifies what it believes is the desired direction for the organization, as well as its specific performance goals. This new "blue print" then permeates lower levels (perhaps through an ongoing series of team building meetings) with the outcome, hopefully being an "organization wide understanding of the blue print for the future. [42]

Phase 5: *Blue print implementation.* This phase may last several years and involves an ongoing program during which managers and other "strategic" personnel work together in order to achieve agreement and commitment to the courses of action that are necessary to implement the "blue print for the future" designed in phase 4.

Phase 6: *Stabilization.* This phase is for "reinforcing and making habitual the new patterns of management achieved in phases 1–5. During this phase employees meet in order to determine the extent to which the new communication and problem solving approaches the grid technique is aimed at nuturing are still being used, and to recommend and implement any corrective actions that seem necessary.

Research Findings. Although this is a widely used team-building technique, the research evidence of its effectiveness is sketchy. Few studies have evaluated the effects of an overall managerial grid program, and most of those have been by Blake and Mouton or their associates. One study was carried out in the "sigma plant" of the Piedmont Corporation. [43] Productivity and profits increased during the period in which the grid program was in effect. However, sigma's business involved widely fluctuating market prices, and higher revenues or lower costs might therefore explain the reported doubling of profits. An overall manpower reduction of 600 employees during this period may also have contributed to increased profits. [44] The researchers attempted to measure behavioral changes but apparenlty did not develop adequate measurement scales. However, they did find an increase of 31% in informal meetings and of about 12½% in "team problem solving" meetings. In addition, managers reportedly felt that group and interdepartmental relations had improved.

In another study, researchers tested hypotheses based on Blake and Mouton's grid in a large midwestern manufacturing firm. [45] The results suggested that where a person placed on the grid (in other words, what his or her management style was) was a poor predictor of either the person's managerial effectiveness or the conflict resolution methods he or she used, a finding that has been sharply disputed by Blake and Mouton. [46]

In summary, evaluating the effectiveness of a major, ongoing development program and unscrambling the development effort's effect from other factors (like declines in the economy, or firing 600 employees) is a difficult matter, but one that management should attempt, given the large cost of the development effort itself. At this point, however, there are few reports of such "controlled" evaluations and so the practical effectiveness of a program like the Grid is hard to ascertain. Given the costs of a major OD effort, and given the difficulty of assessing its effectiveness, managers should try to carefully diagnose the problem (like declining sales or intergroup conflict) the proposed OD effort is aimed at solving in order to ensure that there is not some less expensive and more direct way of accomplishing management's aim.

Survey Research. *Attitude surveys* (as in Exhibit 15.2) are often used as a team-building technique. They can be used to dramatically underscore the existence of some problem (like low morale). And they can be used as a basis for discussion among employees and for developing alternative solutions. Finally, they can also be used to "follow-up" on the change to see if it has been successful.

Scott Meyers has proposed what he calls an involvement approach to using attitude surveys. [47] At the Texas Instruments Company where this approach was developed a questionnaire (like that in Exhibit 15.2) is administered to a 10–20% sample of employees throughout the company. Profiles (as in Exhibit 15.3) are prepared from the results and delivered to each of the approximately 160 department managers. The heavy solid line shows the *company* average for this year, and is the same on every department's profile. The thin solid line is this year's *department* results, while the dotted line is last year's results. As you can see, each department manager can therefore compare his or her department's results for each item to both the total company results and to his or her last year's profile.

In order to avoid making department managers defensive, survey results are fed directly back to them (rather than to top management). The department head presents and discusses these results in general terms in a group meeting of his or her department, and then hands them to a committee of employees. These five or six people meet as often as necessary to analyze the results and make recommendations to the department manager. The latter, in turn, analyzes these recommendations with his boss and the final recommendations are transmitted back to departmental employees. "Problems" and "recommendations" might include, for example, "new employees are sometimes hired for good jobs that old employees could fill," so "post job openings on bulletin boards and explain procedure for bidding for these jobs."

SUMMARY

1. Employee and management development is aimed at developing employees for some future jobs with the organization, or at solving organization-wide problems concerning, for instance, inadequate interdepartmental communication.

2. Classroom-type development methods are widely used, and include lectures, conferences, programmed learning, and university courses. These methods are especially useful for imparting knowledge to participants concerning, for instance, new research in their areas.

3. Simulation-based methods like role playing, behavior modeling, games, and in-house development centers focus on giving participants practice on simulated, realistic job-related problems.

4. Organizational development (OD) is an approach to instituting change in which employees themselves play a major role in the change process: by providing data on problems; by obtaining feedback on problems; and by team

Exhibit 15.2 Texas Instruments Incorporated—Attitude Questionnaire

This questionnaire is designed to help you give us your opinions quickly and easily. There are no "right" or "wrong" answers—it is your own, honest opinion that we want. Please do not sign your name.

DIRECTIONS:
Check ( ) one box for each statement to indicate whether you agree or disagree with it. If you cannot decide, mark the middle box.

EXAMPLE:

	Agree	?	Disagree
I would rather work in a large city than in a small town	2☐	1☐	0☐

	Agree	?	Disagree
1. The hours of work here are O.K.	2☐	1☐	0☐
2. I understand how my job relates to other jobs in my group	2☐	1☐	0☐
3. Working conditions in TI are better than in other companies	2☐	1☐	0☐
4. In my opinion, the pay here is lower than in other companies	2☐	1☐	0☐
5. I think TI is spending too much money in providing recreational programs	2☐	1☐	0☐
6. I understand what benefits are provided for TIers	2☐	1☐	0☐
7. The people I work with help each other when someone falls behind, or gets in a tight spot	2☐	1☐	0☐
8. My supervisor is too interested in his own success to care about the needs of other TIers	2☐	1☐	0☐
9. My supervisor is always breathing down our necks; he watches us too closely	2☐	1☐	0☐
10. My supervisor gives us credit and praise for work well done	2☐	1☐	0☐
11. I think badges should reflect rank as well as length of service	2☐	1☐	0☐
12. If I have a complaint to make, I feel free to talk to someone up-the-line	2☐	1☐	0☐
13. My supervisor sees that we are properly trained for our jobs	2☐	1☐	0☐
14. My supervisor sees that we have the things we need to do our jobs	2☐	1☐	0☐
15. Management is really trying to build the organization and make it successful	2☐	1☐	0☐
16. There is cooperation between my department and other departments we work with	2☐	1☐	0☐
17. I usually read most of Texins News	2☐	1☐	0☐
18. They encourage us to make suggestions for improvements here	2☐	1☐	0☐
19. I am often bothered by sudden speed-ups or unexpected slack periods in my work	2☐	1☐	0☐
20. Qualified TIers are usually overlooked when filling job openings	2☐	1☐	0☐
21. Compared with other TIers, we get very little attention from management	2☐	1☐	0☐
22. Sometimes I feel that my job counts for very little in TI	2☐	1☐	0☐
23. The longer you work for TI the more you feel you belong	2☐	1☐	0☐
24. I have a great deal of interest in TI and its future	2☐	1☐	0☐
25. I have little opportunity to use my abilities in TI	2☐	1☐	0☐

	Agree	?	Disagree
26. There are plenty of good jobs in TI for those who want to get ahead	2☐	1☐	0☐
27. I often feel worn out and tired on my job	2☐	1☐	0☐
28. They expect too much work from us around here	2☐	1☐	0☐
29. The company should provide more opportunities for employees to know each other	2☐	1☐	0☐
30. For my kind of job, working conditions are O.K.	2☐	1☐	0☐
31. I'm paid fairly compared with other TIers	2☐	1☐	0☐
32. Compared with other companies, TI benefits are good	2☐	1☐	0☐
33. A few people I work with think they run the place	2☐	1☐	0☐
34. The people I work with get along well together	2☐	1☐	0☐
35. My supervisor has always been fair in his dealings with me	2☐	1☐	0☐
36. My supervisor gets employees to work together as a team	2☐	1☐	0☐
37. I have confidence in the fairness and honesty of management	2☐	1☐	0☐
38. Management here is really interested in the welfare of TIers	2☐	1☐	0☐
39. Most of the higher-ups are friendly toward us	2☐	1☐	0☐
40. I work in a friendly environment	2☐	1☐	0☐
41. My supervisor lets us know what is expected of us	2☐	1☐	0☐
42. We don't receive enough information from top management	2☐	1☐	0☐
43. I know how my job fits in with other work in this organization	2☐	1☐	0☐
44. TI does a poor job of keeping us posted on the things we want to know about TI	2☐	1☐	0☐
45. I think TI informality is carried too far	2☐	1☐	0☐
46. You can get fired around here without much cause	2☐	1☐	0☐
47. I can be sure of my job as long as I do good work	2☐	1☐	0☐
48. I have plenty of freedom on the job to use my own judgment	2☐	1☐	0☐
49. My supervisor allows me reasonable leeway in making mistakes	2☐	1☐	0☐
50. I really feel part of this organization	2☐	1☐	0☐
51. The people who get promotions in TI usually deserve them	2☐	1☐	0☐
52. I can learn a great deal on my present job	2☐	1☐	0☐

(PLEASE CONTINUE ON REVERSE SIDE)

	Agree	?	Disagree
53. My job is often dull and monotonous	2☐	1☐	0☐
54. There is too much pressure on my job	2☐	1☐	0☐
55. I am required to spend too much time on the job	2☐	1☐	0☐
56. I have the right equipment to do my work	2☐	1☐	0☐
57. My pay is enough to live on comfortably	2☐	1☐	0☐
58. I'm satisfied with the way employee benefits are handled here	2☐	1☐	0☐
59. I wish I had more opportunity to socialize with my associates	2☐	1☐	0☐
60. The people I work with are very friendly	2☐	1☐	0☐
61. My supervisor welcomes our ideas even when they differ from his own	2☐	1☐	0☐
62. My supervisor ought to be friendlier toward us	2☐	1☐	0☐
63. My supervisor lives up to his promises	2☐	1☐	0☐
64. We are kept well informed about TI's business prospects and standing with competitors	2☐	1☐	0☐
65. Management ignores our suggestions and complaints	2☐	1☐	0☐
66. My supervisor is not qualified for his job	2☐	1☐	0☐
67. My supervisor has the work well organized	2☐	1☐	0☐
68. I have ample opportunity to see the end results of my work	2☐	1☐	0☐
69. My supervisor has enough authority and backing to perform his job well	2☐	1☐	0☐
70. I do not get enough instruction about how to do a job	2☐	1☐	0☐
71. You can say what you think around here	2☐	1☐	0☐
72. I know where I stand with my supervisor	2☐	1☐	0☐
73. When terminations are necessary, they are handled fairly	2☐	1☐	0☐
74. I am very much underpaid for the work I do	2☐	1☐	0☐

	Agree	?	Disagree
75. I'm really doing something worthwhile in my job	2☐	1☐	0☐
76. I'm proud to work for TI	2☐	1☐	0☐
77. Many TIers I know would like to see the union get in	2☐	1☐	0☐
78. I received fair treatment in my last performance review	2☐	1☐	0☐
79. During the past six months I have seriously considered getting a job elsewhere	2☐	1☐	0☐
80. TI's problem-solving procedure is adequate for handling our problems and complaints	2☐	1☐	0☐
81. I would recommend employment at TI to my friends	2☐	1☐	0☐
82. My supervisor did a good job in discussing my last performance review with me	2☐	1☐	0☐
83. My pay is the most important source of satisfaction from my job	2☐	1☐	0☐
84. Favoritism is a problem in my area	2☐	1☐	0☐
85. I have very few complaints about our lunch facilities	2☐	1☐	0☐
86. Most people I know in this community have a good opinion of TI	2☐	1☐	0☐
87. I usually read most of my division newspaper	2☐	1☐	0☐
88. I can usually get hold of my supervisor when I need him	2☐	1☐	0☐
89. Most TIers are placed in jobs that make good use of their abilities	2☐	1☐	0☐
90. I receive adequate training for my needs	2☐	1☐	0☐
91. I've gone as far as I can in TI			
92. My job seems to be leading to the kind of future I want	2☐	1☐	0☐
93. There is too much personal friction among people at my level in the company	2☐	1☐	0☐
94. The amount of effort a person puts into his job is appreciated at TI	2☐	1☐	0☐
95. Filling in this questionnaire is a good way to let management know what employees think	2☐	1☐	0☐
96. I think some good will come out of filling in a questionnaire like this one	2☐	1☐	0☐

97 Please check on term which most nearly describes the kind of work you do: 1 ☐ Clerical or office   2 ☐ Production

3 ☐ Technical   4 ☐ Maintenance   5 ☐ Manufacturing   6 ☐ R & D   7 ☐ Engineering   8 ☐ Other

98 1 ☐ Hourly   2 ☐ Salaried   **99** 1 ☐ Male   2 ☐ Female   **100** Do you supervise 3 or more TIers?   1 ☐ Yes   2 ☐ No

Name of your department:

Please write any comments or suggestions you care to make in the space below.

Exhibit 15.3 Employee Attitude Profile

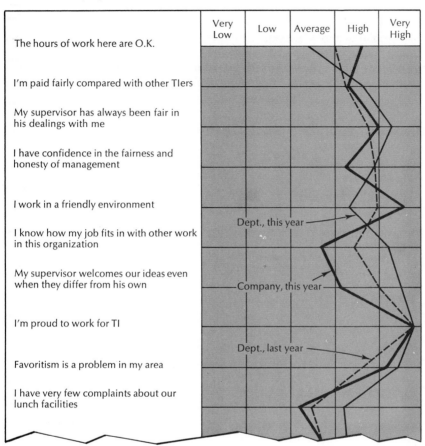

	Very Low	Low	Average	High	Very High
The hours of work here are O.K.					
I'm paid fairly compared with other TIers					
My supervisor has always been fair in his dealings with me					
I have confidence in the fairness and honesty of management					
I work in a friendly environment					
I know how my job fits in with other work in this organization					
My supervisor welcomes our ideas even when they differ from his own					
I'm proud to work for TI					
Favoritism is a problem in my area					
I have very few complaints about our lunch facilities					

Dept., this year

Company, this year

Dept., last year

planning solutions. We describe several OD methods including: sensitivity training; Grid development; and survey feedback.

5. Sensitivity (or "T-group") training can be effective. It can result in managers who are more sensitive to their subordinates and a climate that is more open and less hostile. But it is also widely criticized. So before embarking on such a program an employer should be sure: that the aim is to develop an open, organic organization; that the program is strictly voluntary; that participants are carefully screened; and that the consultant is an experienced professional.

6. "Grid" programs (and other intergroup team building efforts) aim at developing better problem solving and more cooperativeness at work through the "action-research" process. Each work group analyzes work team problems and generates action plans for solving them. Then this same approach is used by special intergroup teams, so that company-wide problems are solved.

7. Survey feedback and particularly the "involvement" approach can be useful at getting employees to recognize the existence of problems, and to team plan solutions and assure they've been carried out.

8. Employee and Management Development is not the only way to react to a present (or projected) performance deficiency. Other ways of attacking "can't do" problems include revising selection standards, improving technical training, or, perhaps, planning to hire more "outside" candidates.

What We Need Around Here is Better Human Relations*

Hank called his three highest-ranking managers together for a surprise luncheon meeting. "Have a drink on United Mutual," said Hank, "you may need it to loosen up your thinking about an important topic I want to bring to your attention."

After Madeline, Raymond, and Allen ordered their drinks, Hank launched into the agenda:

"As office manager, I think we have to move into a rigorous human relations training and development program for our front-line supervisors. It's no longer a question of whether we should have a program, it's now a question of what kind and when."

Allen spoke out, "Okay, Hank, don't keep us in suspense any longer. What makes you think we need a human relations training program?"

"Look at the problems we are facing. Twenty-five percent turnover among the clerical and secretarial staffs; productivity lower than the casualty insurance industry national standards. What better reasons could anybody have for properly training our supervisory staff?"

Madeline commented, "Hold on Hank. Training may not be the answer. I think our high turnover and low productivity are caused by reasons beyond the control of supervision. Our wages are low and we expect our people to work in cramped, rather dismal office space."

Hank retorted, "Nonsense. A good supervisor can get workers to accept almost any working conditions. Training will fix that."

"Hank, I see another problem," said Allen. "Our supervisors are so overworked already that they will balk at training. If you hold the training on company time, they will say that they are falling behind in their work. If the training takes place after hours or on weekends, our supervisors will say that they are being taken advantage of."

"Nonsense," replied Hank. "Every supervisor realizes the importance of good human relations. Besides that, they will see it as a form of job enrichment."

"So long as we're having on open meeting, let me have my input," volunteered Raymond. "We are starting from the wrong end by having our first-line supervisors go through human relations training. It's our top management who needs the training the most. Unless they practice better human relations, you can't expect such behavior from our supervisors. How can you have a top management that is insensi-

* Andrew J. Dubrin, *Human Relations: A Job Oriented Approach* (Reston, VA: Reston Publishing Company, 1978) pp. 242–243.

tive to people and a bottom management that is sensitive. The system just won't work."

"What you say makes some sense," said Hank, "but I wouldn't go so far as to say top management is insensitive to people. Maybe we can talk some more about the human relations program after lunch."

Questions

1. What do you think Hank means by "Human Relations Training?"
2. Should Hank go ahead with his plans for the human relations training and development program? Why or why not?
3. What do you think of Raymond's comment that top management should participate in human relations training first?
4. What is your opinion of Hank's statement that good leadership can compensate for poor working conditions?
5. If you were in Hank's situation, would you try to get top management to participate in a human relations training program?
6. What type of training and development activities would you recommend for first-line supervision at United Mutual? How would you analyze the need for such a program?
7. What other factors could be causing the problems Hank refers to?

EXPERIENTIAL EXERCISE [48]

Purpose. The purpose of this exercise is to give you some experience in dealing with some problems encountered in implementing a change.

Required Understanding. You should be familiar with the contents of Chapter 15, although this exercise can precede reading of the chapter.

How to Set Up the Exercise. Divide the class into groups of four persons. The instructor can assign extra persons to various groups as observers.

Once the class is divided into groups all students should read the "general instructions" and should assign roles to each group member. *Each person should read his or her instructions only.* (Roles are presented at the end of this exercise.)

It would help if role-players Jack, Walt, and Steve wore nametags so that Gus, the foreman, can call them by name. (It also helps to have all Guses stand up when they have finished reading their roles.) They may also continue to refer as needed to the data supplied with their instructions.

Instructions for the Exercise.

1. When all the Guses are standing, the instructor can remind the Jacks, Walts, and Steves that they are waiting for Gus in his office. When he sits down and greets them, this will indicate that he has entered his office, and each person should adopt his role.

2. At the instructor's signal, all Guses are seated. All groups should begin the role-play simultaneously.

3. About 25 minutes should be required for the groups to reach a decision. If certain groups have trouble, the instructor may ask Gus, the foreman, to do the best he can in the next minute or two.

4. While groups are role playing the instructor will write a table on the chalk board with the following column headings: (1) Group Number, (2) Solution, (3) Problem Employees, (4) Expected Production, (5) Method Used by Foreman, and (6) Sharing of Data.

5. Collecting results.

   a. Each group should report in turn, while remaining seated as a group. The instructor will enter in Column 1 the number of the group called on to report.

   b. Each Gus reports the solution he intends to follow. The solutions may be of four types: (*a*) continuation of old method (i.e., rotation through all positions); (*b*) adoption of new method with each person working his best position; (*c*) a compromise (new method in the morning, old in the afternoon); or (*d*) integrative solution containing features of old and new solutions (e.g., each man spends more time on best position; two men exchange positions and third works on his best position; all three exchange but confine changes to work their two best positions). The instructor will enter type of solution in Column 2 and add notes to indicate whether a trial period is involved, a rest pause is added, etc.

   c. Each Gus reports whether he had any special trouble with a particular employee. If so, the initial of the problem individual is entered in Column 3.

   d. Jack, Walt, and Steve report whether production will stay the same, go up, or down, as a result of the conference. The estimates of Jack, Walt, and Steve should be recorded as "0," "+," and "−" signs in Column 4.

   e. Group observers report on the way Gus handled the group and how the group responded. Enter a descriptive term in Column 5 for Gus's method (e.g., tried to sell his plan, used group decision, blamed group, was participative, was arbitrary and somewhat abusive, etc.). If no observers were present in a group, data should be supplied by the group itself. For leading questions about method, see "Instructions for Observer."

6. Class discussion. Discuss differences obtained and see if they can be related to the attitude and the method of Gus. What kinds of resistance were encountered? Classify them into fear, hostility, etc. What are the proper methods of dealing with each of these kinds of resistance? What study that we discussed is this situation similar to?

The instructions and roles follow. Please be sure to read only the general instructions and the roles which you have been assigned.

1. General Instructions

You work in a plant that does a large number of subassembly jobs, such as assembling fuel pumps, carburetors, and starters. Gus Thompson is foreman of several groups, including the one with which we are concerned today. Jack, Walt, and Steve make up your particular group, which assembles fuel pumps. The assembly operation is divided into three positions or jobs. Since the three jobs are rather simple and each of you is familiar with all of the operations, you find it desirable to exchange jobs or positions. You have worked together this way for a long time. Pay is based on a team piece-rate and has been satisfactory to all of you. Presently each of you will be asked to be one of the following: Gus Thompson, Jack, Walt, or Steve. In some instances an observer will be present in your group. Today, Gus, the foreman, has asked Jack, Walt, and Steve to meet with him in his office. He said he wanted to talk about something.

2. Instructions for Observers (May be omitted if desired)

Your job is to observe the method used by Gus in handling a problem with his men. Pay especial attention to the following:

a. Method of presenting problem. Does he criticize, suggest a remedy, request their help on a problem, or use some other approach?

b. Initial reaction of members. Do group members feel criticized or do they try to help Gus?

c. Handling of discussion by Gus. Does he listen or argue? Does he try to persuade? Does he use threats? Or does he let the men decide?

d. Forms of resistance expressed by the group. Did members express fear, hostility, satisfaction with present method, etc.?

e. What does Gus do with the time-study data? (1) Lets men examine the table; (2) mentions some of the results; or (3) makes little or no reference to the data.

Best results are obtained if Gus uses the data to pose the problem of how they might be used to increase production.

3. Roles for Participants

Role for Gus Thompson, foreman.

You are the foreman in a shop and supervise the work of about 20 men. Most of the jobs are piece-rate jobs, and some of the men work in teams and are paid on a team piece-rate basis. In one of the teams, Jack, Walt, and Steve work together. Each one of them does one of the operations for an hour and then they exchange, so that all men perform each of the operations at different times. The men themselves decided to operate that way and you have never given the plan any thought.

Lately, Jim Clark, the methods man, has been around, and studied conditions in your shop. He timed Jack, Walt, and Steve on each of the operations and came up with the following facts:

	Time per operation			
	Position 1	*Position 2*	*Position 3*	*Total*
Jack	3 min.	4 min.	4½ min.	11½ min.
Walt	3½ min.	3½ min.	3 min.	10 min.
Steve	5 min.	3½ min.	4½ min.	13 min.
				34½ min.

He observed that with the men rotating, the average time for all three operations would be one-third of the total time or 11½ minutes per complete unit. If, however, Jack worked in the No. 1 spot, Steve in the No. 2 spot, and Walt in the No. 3 spot, the time would be 9½ minutes, a reduction of over 17 per cent. Such a reduction in time would amount to saving of more than 80 minutes. In other words the lost production would be about the same as that which would occur if the men loafed for 80 minutes in an eight-hour day. If the time were used for productive effort, production would be increased more than 20 per cent.

This made pretty good sense to you so you have decided to take up the problem with the men. You feel that they should go along with any change in operation that is made.

Role for Jack.

You are one of three men on an assembly operation. Walt and Steve are your team mates and you enjoy working with them. You get paid on a team basis and you are making wages that are entirely satisfactory. Steve isn't quite as fast as Walt and you, but when you feel he is holding things up too much each of you can help out.

The work is very monotonous. The saving thing about it is that every hour you all change positions. In this way you get to do all three operations. You are best on the No. 1 position so when you get in that spot you turn out some extra work and so make the job easier for Steve who follows you in that position.

You have been on this job for two years and you have never run out of work. Apparently your group can make pretty good pay without running yourselves out of a job. Lately, however, the company has had some of its experts hanging around. It looks like the company is trying to work out some speedup methods. If they make these jobs any more simple you won't be able to stand the monotony. Gus Thompson, your foreman, is a decent guy and has never criticized your team's work.

Role for Steve.

You work with Jack and Walt on an assembly job and get paid on a team piece-rate. The three of you work very well together and make a pretty good wage. Jack and Walt like to make a little more than you think is necessary, but you go along with them and work as hard as you can so as to keep the production up where they want it. They are good fellows; often help you out if you fall behind; and so you feel it is only fair to try and go along with the pace they set.

The three of you exchange positions every hour. In this way you get to work all positions. You like the No. 2 position the best because it is easiest. When you get in the No. 3 position you can't keep up and then you feel Gus Thompson, the foreman, watching you. Sometimes Walt and Jack slow down when you are on the No. 3 spot and then the foreman seems satisfied.

Lately the methods man has been hanging around watching the job. You wonder what he is up to. Can't they leave guys alone who are doing all right?

Role for Walt.

You work with Jack and Steve on a job that requires three separate operations. Each of you works on each of the three operations by rotating positions once every hour. This makes the work more interesting and you can always help out the other fellow by running the job ahead in case one of you doesn't feel so good. It's all right to help out because you get paid on a team piece-rate basis. You could actually earn more if Steve were a faster worker, but he is a swell guy and you would rather have him in the group than someone else who might do a little bit more.

You find all three positions about equally desirable. They are all simple and purely routine. The monotony doesn't bother you much because you can talk, day-dream, and change your pace. By working slow for a while and then fast you can sort of set your pace to music you hum to yourself. Jack and Steve like the idea of changing jobs, and even though Steve is slow on some positions, the changing around has its good points. You feel you get to a stopping place every time you change positions and this kind of takes the place of a rest pause.

Lately some kind of efficiency expert has been hanging around. He stands some distance away with a stop watch in his hand. The company could get more for its money if it put some of those guys to work. You say to yourself, "I'd like to see one of these guys try and tell me how to do this job. I'd sure give him an earful."

If Gus Thompson, your foreman, doesn't get him out of the shop pretty soon, you're going to tell him what you think of his dragging in company spies.

DISCUSSION QUESTIONS

1. Why do people "resist change"?
2. What are three approaches to organizational change? Give some examples of conditions under which each would probably be more appropriate.
3. How does the "involvement" approach to attitude surveys differ from simply administering surveys and returning the results to top management?
4. Your company's consultants have just suggested to you that you put all your subordinates through sensitivity training. What are some of the questions you would ask of your consultants at this point?
5. Your boss has just suggested that you attend a sensitivity training laboratory. What are some of the questions you would ask of him or her?
6. Compare and contrast several organizational development techniques.

NOTES

1. Joseph Famularo, *Handbook of Modern Personnel Administration* (1972), p. 18-5.
2. William R. Tracey, *Designing Training and Developing Systems* (New York: American Management Association, 1971), p. 192.
3. Tracey, *Designing*, p. 192; G. H. Proctor and W. M. Thornton, *Training: A Handbook for Line Managers* (New York: American Management Association, 1971).
4. Tracey, *Designing*, p. 192.

5. F. Reissman, "The Culturally Deprived Child: A New View," in eds., E. P. Torrence and R. D. Strom, *Mental Health and Achievement* (New York: John Wiley & Sons, 1965), pp. 312–319; McCormick and Tiffin, *Industrial Psychology*.

6. G. N. Nash, J. P. Muczyk, and F. L. Vettori, "The Role and Practical Effectiveness of Programmed Instruction," *Personnel Psychology*, 24 (1971), pp. 397–418; McCormick and Tiffin, *Industrial Psychology*.

7. R. Hedberg, H. Steffen, and D. Baxter, "Insurance Fundamentals—A Programmed Text vs. A Conventional Text," *Personnel Psychology*, 9 (1964), pp. 165–171; McCormick and Tiffin, *Industrial Psychology*, p. 264.

8. Tracey, *Designing*, p. 191.

9. Tracey, *Designing*, p. 191.

10. Famularo, *Handbook of Modern Personnel Administration*, pp. 21-7, 21-8.

11. This section based on: Allen Kraut, "Developing Managerial Skills via Modeling Techniques: Some Positive Research Findings—A Symposium"; Robert Burnaska, "The Effects of Behavior Modeling Training upon Manager's Behavior and Employee's Perceptions"; Joseph Mases and Richard Ritchie, "Supervisory Relationship Training: A Behavioral Evaluation of a Behavior Modeling Program"; Preston Smith, "Management Modeling Training to Improve Morale and Customer Satisfaction"; all in *Personnel Psychology*, Vol. 29, No. 3 (Autumn 1976), pp. 325–361.

12. "A surprise CBS morale booster," *Business Week* (October 20, 1980), pp. 125–126.

13. Larry Greiner and Louis Barnes, "Organizational Change and Development," in Paul Lawrence, Louis Barnes, and Jay Lorsch, *Organizational Behavior and Administration*, pp. 621–633.

14. David R. Hampton, Charles Summer, and Ross Webber, *Organizational Behavior and the Practice of Management* (Glenview: Scott Foresman, 1973), p. 850.

15. Wendel French and Cecil Bell Jr., *Organizational Development* (Englewood Cliffs: Prentice-Hall, 1978), p. 88.

16. French and Bell, p. 17.

17. Mark Frohman, Marshall Sashkin, and Michael Kavanagh, "Action Research as Applied to Organization Development," *Organization and Administrative Sciences*, Vol. 7 (Spring/Summer 1976), pp. 129–142.

18. This classification is adapted from French and Bell, *Organizational Development*, p. 143.

19. Quoted from French and Bell, p. 143.

20. Chris Argyris, "A Brief Description of Laboratory Education," *Training Directors Journal* (October 1963).

21. French and Bell, pp. 143–144; K. D. Benne, L. P. Bradford, and R. Lippitt, "The Laboratory Method," in L. P. Bradford, J. I. Gibb, and K. D. Benne, *T-Group Theory and Laboratory Method* (New York: John Wiley, 1964), pp. 16–17.

22. Based on J. P. Campbell and M. D. Dunnette, "Effectiveness of T-group Experiences in Managerial Training and Development," *Psychological Bulletin*, Vol. 7 (1968), pp. 73–104. Reprinted in W. E. Scott and L. L. Cummings, *Readings in Organizational Behavior and Human Performance* (Homewood: Irwin, 1973), p. 571.

23. George Odiorne, "The Trouble with Sensitivity Training," *Training Directors Journal* (October 1963).

24. House, *Management Development*, p. 71.

25. Martin Lakin, *American Psychologists* (October 1969), pp. 923–928.

26. George Oriorne, "The Trouble with Sensitivity Training."

27. For a good discussion of this see Robert J. House, "T-group Training: Good or Bad?" *Business Horizons* (December 1969), pp. 69–77.

436

28. Robert J. House, "T-group Training Good or Bad?"

29. Odiorne, "The Trouble with Sensitivity Training."

30. Chris Argyris, "In Defense of Laboratory Education," *Training Directors Journal*, October 1963. It should be noted that Argyris' comments were made some time ago and that while they may still be accurate they do not necessarily reflect the current opinions of Professor Argyris.

31. French and Bell, p. 143.

32. House, ibid.

33. House, ibid.

34. Campbell and Dunnette, "Effectiveness of T-group Experiences in Managerial Training and Development," *Psychological Bulletin*, Vol. 70 (1968).

35. House, ibid.

36. See Warren Benis, "Bureaucracy and Social Change: An Anatomy of a Failure," *Human Organization Special Monograph Series* (Fall 1963).

37. John Kimberly and Juan Nielson, "Organization Development and Change in Organizational Performance," *Administrative Science Quarterly*, Vol. 20, No. 2 (June 1975), p. 203; Peter Smith, "Controlled Studies of the Outcome of Sensitivity," *Psychological Bulletin*, Vol. 82 (1976), pp. 597–622.

38. Andre Delbecq, "Sensitivity Training," *Training Development Journal* (January 1970), pp. 32–35.

39. John Kimberly and Warren Nielson, "Organization and Development and Change in Organizational Performance," *Administrative Science Quarterly* (June 1975), pp. 191–206.

40. The following description of the grid approach is based on R. R. Blake and J. S. Mouton, *Building a Dynamic Corporation through Grid Organization of Development* (Reading, Mass.: Addison Wesley, 1969); and Robert Blake and Jane Mouton, "An Overview of the Grid," *Training and Development Journal* (May 1975), pp. 29–37.

41. *Ibid.*

42. *Ibid.*

43. Robert Blake, Jane Mouton, Lewis Bond, and Larry Greiner, "Breakthrough in Organization Development," *Harvard Business Review*, Vol. 42 (November–December 1964). See also Robert Blake, Jane Mouton, Richard Sloma, and Barbara Lofton, "A Second Breakthrough in Organization Development," *California Management Review*, Vol. 11 (Winter 1968), pp. 73–78.

44. The researchers themselves caution against drawing simple cost and effect inclusions about the effectiveness of this grid program.

45. H. John Bernardin and Kenneth Alvarez, "The Managerial Grid as a Predictor of Conflict Resolution Method and Managerial Effectiveness," *Administrative Science Quarterly*, Vol. 21, No. 1 (March 1976).

46. Robert Blake and Jane Mouton, "When Scholarship Fails, Research Falters: A Reply to Bernardin and Alvarez," *Administrative Science Quarterly*, Vol. 21 (March 1976).

47. M. Scott Meyers, "How Attitude Surveys Help You Manage," *Training and Development Journal*, Vol. 21 (October 1967), pp. 34–41; reprinted in Beach, *Personnel*, pp. 311–316; see also Robert Solomon, "An Examination of the Relationship Between a Survey Feedback O.D. Technique and the Work Environment," *Personnel Psychology*, Vol. 29, No. 4 (Winter 1976).

48. Norman R. F. Maier, *Psychology in Industrial Organizations*, 4th ed. (Boston: Houghton Mifflin Co., 1973), pp. 295–299.

Part Four

The Environment of Personnel Management

A MODEL OF MOTIVATION

WILL MOTIVATION AND
PERFORMANCE TAKE PLACE?

Could the employee do the job if he or she wanted to?

Ch. 2   *Equal Opportunity and the Law*

Ch. 3   *Job Analysis*
         Adequate organization and job
         descriptions? What skills and
         abilities are required to perform
         the job?

Chs. 4–6 *Selection*
         Do applicants have the aptitude
         and potential to do the job?

Ch. 7   *Orientation and Technical Training*
         Provide employees with basic skills

Take Corrective Action

Is he or she motivated to perform?

Ch. 8   *Fundamentals of Motivation*

Ch. 9   *Establishing Pay Plans*

Ch. 10   *Financial Incentives*

Ch. 11   *Benefits*

Ch. 12   *Nonfinancial Motivators*
         Job enrichment, etc.

Take Corrective Action

Ch. 13   *Appraise Performance*
         Did motivation take place?

Chs. 14, 15 *Identify Problem*
         Reorganize jobs?
         Change selection standards?
         Training called for?
         New incentives needed?
         Counseling needed?
         Employee and management
         development needed?

← NO   YES →   REWARDS

THE ENVIRONMENT OF PERSONNEL MANAGEMENT

▶ Ch. 16   *Labor Relations and Grievances*

Ch. 17   *Employee Safety and Health*

Ch. 18   *Personnel Management and the
         Quality of Work Life*

When you finish studying

16   Labor Relations and Grievances

You should be able to:

1. *Deal more effectively with a unionization drive and a bargaining session.*
2. *Cite important incidents in the history of the American labor movement.*
3. *Explain the structure and purpose of the "AFL-CIO."*
4. *Discuss "five sure ways" to lose an NLRB election.*
5. *Discuss the main features of at least three major pieces of labor legislation.*
6. *Present examples of what to expect during the union drive and election.*
7. *Give some examples of bargaining that is not "in good faith."*
8. *Develop a grievance procedure.*

OVERVIEW

The main purpose of this chapter is to provide basic information needed to deal effectively with unions and grievances. After briefly discussing the history of the American labor movement we describe some basics of labor legislation, including the subject of "unfair labor practices." We explain labor negotiations, including the union action the employer can expect during the union drive and election. And, we explain what to expect during the actual bargaining sessions.

We also explain how to handle grievances, an activity often called contract administration. We present examples of actual grievances, an actual grievance procedure, and some guidelines for handling grievances.

INTRODUCTION: THE LABOR MOVEMENT

Today over 20 million American workers belong to unions, a number that amounts to around one-fourth of the total number of men and women working in America today. Remove agricultural and management workers, and you would find that about one-third of the available nonagricultural employees belong to unions. In some industries—mining, construction, transportation—it is impossible to get a job without joining a union. And unions do not just appeal to blue-collar workers in the private sector: more and more white-collar workers and public employees are turning to unions as well.

Why have unions become so important today? How did they get that way?

439

440   What do unions want of their members? Why do workers join unions? These are some of the questions addressed in the first section. [1]

A Brief History of the American Union Movement

In order to understand what unions are, and what they want, it is useful to understand "where they've been." In Exhibit 16.1, are summarized important incidents in the American union movement, and the first thing to notice is that unions have been around for quite some time. As early as 1790, for example, skilled craftsmen (shoemakers, tailors, printers, etc.) organized themselves into trade unions. They posted their "minimum wage" demands, and had "tramping committees" go from shop to shop to ensure that no member accepted a lesser wage.

Exhibit 16.1   Some Important Incidents in American Labor Movement

1790	Earliest unions formed	1938	Congress of Industrial Organizations
1850	National Union of Typographers formed		(CIO) formed
1869	Knights of Labor formed	1947	Taft-Hartley Act passed
1886	American Federation of Labor (AFL)	1955	AFL and CIO merge
	formed	1959	Landrum-Griffin Act passed
1893	Knights of Labor dissolved	1963	Executive Order 10988
1929	Start of Great Depression	1964	The Civil Rights Act
1932	Norris LaGuardia Act passed	1969	Executive Order 11491
1935	Wagner Act passed	1975	Executive Order 11838

From these earliest unions to the present time, the history of the union movement has been one of alternate expansions and contractions. Union membership grew until a major depression around 1837 resulted in a decline in membership. Membership then began increasing as America entered its Industrial Revolution. In 1869 a group of tailors met and formed the Knights of Labor: The "Knights" were interested in political reform and agitation, and often sought political changes. By 1885 it had 100,000 members, and (as a result of winning a major strike against a railroad) exploded to 700,000 members the following year. Partially because of their focus on social reform (and partly to a series of unsuccessful strikes) the Knights' membership dwindled rapidly thereafter, and by 1893 (when they were dissolved) they had virtually no members.

In 1886 Samuel Gompers formed the American Federation of Labor. It consisted primarily of skilled workers, and (unlike the Knights) eschewed social reform for practical, "bread and butter" gains for its members. The Knights of Labor had engaged in a "class struggle" to alter the form of society and *thereby* get a bigger chunk of benefits for its members. Gompers, on the other hand, aimed at raising the day-to-day wages and improving the working conditions of his constituents. The "AFL" grew rapidly until after World War I, at which point its membership exceeded 5½ million people.

As can be seen from Exhibit 16.2, the 1920s was a period of stagnation for the American union movement, and by 1923 AFL membership had declined to about 3½ million members. This decline and stagnation was a result of several things including a post-war depression, manufacturers' renewed resistance to unions, the death of Samuel Gompers, and the blossoming (if misleading) prosperity of the 1920s. By 1929 (as a result of the Great Depression) millions of workers lost their jobs, and by 1933 union membership was down to less than 3 million workers.

Exhibit 16.2   Union Membership in United States

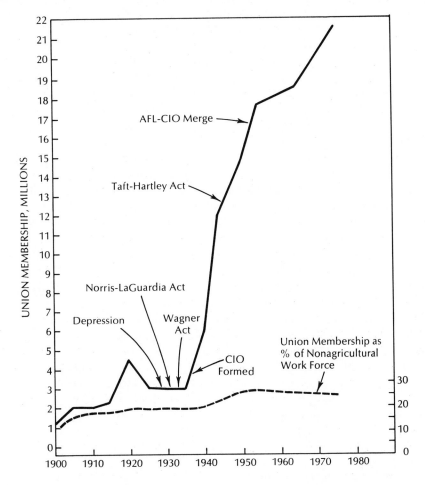

Source: Based on *Statistical Abstract of United States*, U.S. Department of Commerce, 1978, 1979, p. 384.

About midway through the 1930s membership began to increase. As part of his "New Deal" programs, President Roosevelt passed the National Industrial Recovery Act which, among other things, made it easier for labor to organize. Other federal laws (as well as prosperity and World War II) were also contributing factors to the rapid increase in membership from 1935 through the late 1950s. Then membership again began to decline, from about 34% of the labor force in 1955, to about 20% in 1980. [2]

Recent Trends in Unionization

Several things contributed to this recent decline. Unions traditionally had appealed mostly to blue-collar workers, and the proportion of blue-collar jobs was decreasing (as white-collar jobs increased). Furthermore, by 1950 most "easily organized," blue-collar workers in industries like mining, transportation, and in manufacturing had already been unionized. An economic slowdown in the late 1950s further hampered union membership drives. [3]

During the last ten years or so the major union effort has been aimed at organizing white-collar workers (service-oriented industries—insurance, banking, retail trade, government—are now being organized by unions, for example). More than 10% of white-collar workers have already become unionized and the number is increasing rapidly.

Similarly, there has been a trend toward unionization and collective bargaining in the public sector. A major impetus to this was President Kennedy's executive order (E.O.) 10988, issued in 1962. This, according to Davey, "gave positive encouragement to collective bargaining as a process" (for federal employees). Before this there had been no bargaining "in the proper sense" by unionized federal employees, who worked instead through devices like lobbying. E.O. 10988 also stimulated the drive for unionization among employees of state, municipal, and county agencies, and "union growth has been nothing short of spectacular in the period since 1962."

E.O. 10988, however, had some drawbacks. Under it, for example, the decision maker of last resort was the department head. Under the later E.O. 11491 (1969) decision making (over key disputed issues) is centralized in either the newly created Federal Labor Relations Council, or the Assistant Secretary of Labor for Labor-Management Relations. This order also improved on 10988 in other respects, such as by clarifying the rights and responsibilities of the parties to bargaining. The net effect of these two orders has been to encourage the rapid unionization of all public employees (not just those in the Federal Government).

Why Do Workers Organize?

A great deal of time and money has been spent trying to analyze "why workers unionize," and many theories have been proposed. Yet there is no simple answer to the question, partly because each worker probably joins for his or her own unique reasons.

But it does seem clear that workers do not unionize just to get more pay or better working conditions. While these *are* important factors, the urge to unionize seems to boil down to the belief on the part of workers that it is only through unity that they can get their fair share of the "pie," and also protect themselves from the arbitrary whims of management. Here is how one writer describes the reasons behind the early unionization of automobile workers:

> In the years to come, economic issues would make the headlines when union and management met in negotiations. But in the early years the rate of pay was not the major complaint of the autoworker. . . . Specifically, the principal grievances of the autoworkers were the speed-up of production and the lack of any kind of job security. As production tapered off, the order in which workers were laid off was determined largely by the whim of foremen and other supervisors. The system encouraged workers to curry favor by doing personal chores for supervisory employees—by bringing them gifts or outright bribes. The same applied to recalls as production was resumed. The worker had no way of knowing when he would be laid off, and had no assurance when, or whether, he would be recalled. . . . Generally, what the workers revolted against was the lack of human dignity and individuality, and a working relationship that was massively impersonal, cold, and nonhuman. They wanted to be treated like human beings—not like faceless clockcard numbers. [4]

Research Findings.   As explained in Chapter 12, research findings consistently show that job dissatisfaction is a major reason why workers turn to unions. In one study, for example the researcher found that in all cases the departments with no unionization activity had employees who were more satisfied. [5] Similarly, in a study of university professors the researcher found that faculty members attitude's toward collective bargaining were progressively more favorable, the greater their dissatisfaction with their present work, pay, promotions, and supervision. Dissatisfaction with pay was the factor most highly correlated with "attitude toward unionism." [6]

Generally speaking, it seems to be dissatisfaction with economic, "bread and butter" issues that leads to pro union voting, rather than noneconomic issues like opportunities for achievement on the job, and job enrichment. In one study carried out just after a union election, for example the researcher found that satisfaction with economic issues like security, pay, and working conditions seemed to be the best predictors of how employees voted in the election. Employees' satisfaction with the "variety" or "creativity" of their jobs was not related to pro union voting. [7] In another study union members were asked to indicate the percentages of time they thought their union representatives should devote to various negotiation issues like pay, and job enrichment. The employees responded that they felt their representatives should devote 50 to 60% of their time negotiating fringe benefits and pay and should about evenly divide the

444   remainder of their time negotiating working conditions, job security, and "job enrichment." [8]

What Do Unions Want—What Are Their Aims?

We can generalize by saying that unions have two sets of aims, one for *union security* and one for *improved wages*, hours, working conditions, and benefits for their members.

Union Security. First (and probably foremost) unions seek to establish "security" for themselves. They fight hard for the right to represent a firm's workers, and to be the *exclusive* bargaining agent for all employees in the unit. (Here they negotiate contracts for all employees *including* those not members of the union.) In the early days of the union movement getting such "recognition" was a difficult task: employers used lawsuits, blacklists, lockouts, armed guards, and spies to fight unionization. Today federal legislation and a new business environment usually combine to make the union drive less traumatic for all concerned. Five types of "union security" are possible:

1. *The "Closed Shop."* [9] Here the company can hire only union members. This was outlawed in 1947, but still exists in some industries (like printing).
2. *The "Union Shop."* Here the company *can* hire nonunion people but they must join the union after a prescribed period of time, and pay dues. (If not, they can be fired.)
3. *The "Agency Shop."* Here employees who do not belong to the union still must pay union dues (on the assumption that the union's efforts benefit *all* the workers).
4. *The "Open Shop."* Here it is up to the workers whether they join the union or not—those who do not also do not pay dues.
5. *The "Maintenance of Membership" Arrangement.* Here, employees do not have to belong to the union. However *union members* employed by the firm *must* "maintain membership" in the union for the contract period.

Improved Wages, Hours, etc. for Members. Once their security is assured, unions fight to better the lot of their members—to improve their wages, hours, and working conditions, for example. And today, more than ever, the typical labor agreement gives the union an active role in a wide range of personnel management activities including recruiting, selecting, compensating, promoting, training, and discharging employees, on the assumption that this involvement will facilitate the unions' attempts to improve their members' job security, pay, and benefits.

The AFL-CIO [10]

What It Is. The American Federation of Labor and Congress of Industrial Organizations (AFL-CIO) is a voluntary federation of 109 national and international labor unions in the U.S. It was formed by the merger of the AFL and CIO in 1955, with AFL's George Meany as its first president. It has over

14 million members (out of about 20 million union members in the U.S.) and,
for many people, it has become synonymous with the word "unions" in America.

There are about 4½ million workers who belong to unions that are not
affiliated with the AFL-CIO. Of these workers, about three-fourths belong to
the two largest "independent" unions, the Teamsters (almost 2 million members) and the United Auto Workers (almost 1½ million workers). [11]

The Structure of the AFL-CIO.   The organization chart of the AFL-CIO
is shown in Exhibit 16.3. As you can see, it is a federation made up primarily of
national unions and members.

Exhibit 16.3   Organization Chart of AFL-CIO

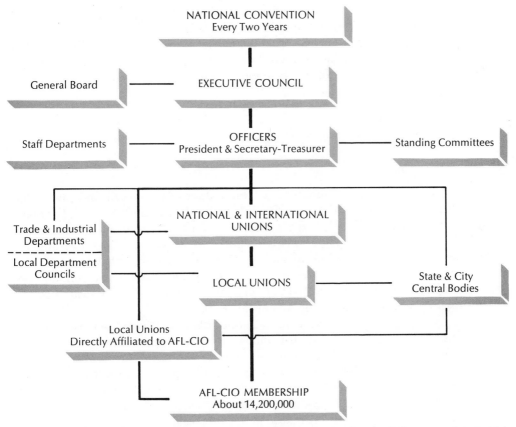

Source: *This is the AFL-CIO;* American Federation of Labor and Congress of Industrial
Organizations, Publication #20, January 1976, p. 15.

As you may also surmise from this exhibit there are three layers in the
structure of the AFL-CIO (and other American unions). First, there is the *local*
union. This is the union the worker joins and pays his or her dues to. And, it

446   is usually the local union that signs the collective bargaining agreement determining his or her wages and working conditions. The local is in turn a single chapter in the *national* union. For example, if you were a typesetter in Detroit you would belong to the local union there; but that local union is one of hundreds of local chapters of the International Typographical Union, whose headquarters is in Colorado Springs.

Now (getting back to Exhibit 16.3), the third layer in the structure of unions is the *national federation*—in this case, the AFL-CIO. This federation is comprised of 109 national (and international) unions, which in turn comprise more than 60,000 local unions.

Once again, most people tend to think of the AFL-CIO as the most important part of the labor movement; but it is not. In fact the AFL-CIO itself really has little power, except what it is allowed to exercise by its constituent national unions: Thus the president of the teachers' union wields more power in that capacity than in his capacity as a vice president of the AFL-CIO. Yet as a practical matter the AFL-CIO does act as a spokesman for labor, and its president, Lane Kirkland, has accumulated a political clout far in excess of some "figurehead" president.

UNIONS AND THE LAW [12]

Background

Today it is almost impossible to read a newspaper and not find some reference to labor law: articles on the "Taft-Hartley" Act, the "NLRB" (National Labor Relations Board), and the "Landrum–Griffin" Act abound, for example. And, as a manager, you are going to find that a working knowledge of these laws may be a prerequisite to success. These laws specify: what you can (and cannot) do when your place of work is being unionized; what "unfair labor practices" are; and a multitude of other important points. We will therefore discuss some important labor laws in this section.

Until about 1930 there were no special labor laws. Employers were not required to engage in collective bargaining with employees, and they were virtually unrestrained in their behavior toward unions: the use of spies, blacklists, and the firing of "agitators" were normally condoned (or at least left undisturbed) by judges. "Yellow dog" contracts (whereby management could require *non*union membership as a condition for employment) were widely enforced. And most union weapons—even strikes—were held illegal.

This one-sided situation lasted in America from the Revolution to the Great Depression (around 1930). Since then (in response to changing public attitudes, values, and economic conditions) labor law has gone through three clear changes: from "strong encouragement" of unions, to "modified encouragement coupled with regulation," and finally to "detailed regulation of internal union affairs." [13]

The Period of Strong Encouragement:
The Norris–LaGuardia Act (1932) and the Wagner Act (1935)

The Norris–LaGuardia and Wagner Acts marked a shift in labor law from repression to strong encouragement of union activity. [14] The first of these acts was passed during the Depression. During this time unemployment was rampant, and many policy-makers—senators, and so on—felt that only through bargaining collectively could employees influence their work situations.

This act set the stage for a new era in which union activity was *encouraged*. It guaranteed to each employee the right to bargain collectively "free from interference, restraint, or coercion." It declared "yellow dog" contracts unenforceable. And it limited the courts' abilities to issue injunctions for activities like peaceful picketing and payment of strike benefits.

Yet as a practical matter this act did little to restrain employers from fighting labor organizations by whatever means they could muster. Therefore in 1935 the National Labor Relations (or Wagner) Act was passed; this added "teeth" to the Norris–LaGuardia Act. It did this by: (1) banning certain types of *"unfair labor practices"*; (2) providing for secret ballot elections and majority rule (for determining whether a firm's employees were to unionize); and (3) creating the National Labor Relations Board (NLRB) for enforcing these two provisions.

Employer Unfair Labor Practices. The Wagner Act deemed "statutory wrongs" (but not crimes) the five following employer "unfair labor practices":

1. It is unfair for managements to "interfere with, restrain, or coerce employees" in exercising their legally sanctioned right of self-organization.
2. It is an unfair practice for company representatives to dominate or interfere with either the formation or the administration of labor unions. Among other management actions found to be unfair under stipulations 1 and 2 are: bribery of employees, company spy systems, moving a business to avoid unionization, and blacklisting union sympathizers.
3. Companies are prohibited from discriminating in any way against employees for their legal union activities.
4. Employers are forbidden from discharging or discriminating against employees simply because the latter had filed "unfair practice" charges against the company.
5. Finally, it made it an unfair labor practice for employers to refuse to bargain collectively with their employees' duly chosen representatives.

From 1935 to 1947. Union membership increased rapidly after passage of the Wagner Act in 1935. Other factors (like an improving economy and aggressive union leadership) contributed to this as well. But by the mid 1940s the tide had begun to turn. Largely because of a series of massive post-war strikes, public policy began to shift against what many viewed as the "union excesses" of the times: the stage was set for passage of the Taft–Hartley Act of 1947.

The Period of Modified Encouragement Coupled with Regulation: The Taft–Hartley Act (1947)

The Taft–Hartley (or "Labor Management Relations") Act reflected the public's less enthusiastic attitudes toward unions. Its provisions were aimed at limiting unions in four ways: (1) by prohibiting *union* unfair labor practices; (2) by enumerating the rights of employees as union members; (3) by enumerating the rights of employers; and (4) by allowing the President of the United States to temporarily bar "national emergency" strikes.

Union Unfair Labor Practices. The Taft–Hartley Act enumerated several labor practices that unions were prohibited from engaging in:

1. First, unions were banned from restraining or coercing employees from exercising their guaranteed bargaining rights. For example, some specific actions on the part of unions that the courts have held illegal under this provision include: stating to an anti-union employee that he will lose his job once the union gains recognition; issuing patently false statements during union organizing campaigns; making threats of reprisal against employees subpoenaed to testify against the union at NLRB hearings.
2. It is also an unfair labor practice for a union to cause an employer to discriminate in any way against an employee in order to encourage or discourage his membership in a union. In other words, the union cannot try to force an employer to fire a worker because he or she doesn't attend union meetings, opposes union policies, or refuses to join a union. There is one exception to this. Where a closed or "union shop" prevails (and union membership is therefore a prerequisite to employment) the union may demand discharge of a worker who fails to pay his initiation fee and dues.
3. It is an unfair labor practice for a union to refuse to bargain "in good faith" with the employer about wages, hours, and other employment conditions. Also, certain types of strikes and boycotts are considered union unfair labor practices; and
4. It is also an unfair labor practice for a union to engage in "feather-bedding." (Here an employer is required to pay an employee for services not performed.)

The Rights of Employees. The Taft–Hartley Act also protected the rights of *employees* against their unions. For example, many people felt that compulsory unionism violated the basic American right of freedom of association. New "right to work" laws sprang up in nineteen states (mainly in the South and Southwest), and outlawed labor contracts that made union membership a condition for retaining employment. In New York, for example, many printing firms have union shops. Here you cannot work as a pressman unless you belong to a printers' union. In Florida such union shops—except those covered by the Railway Labor Act—are illegal. There, printing shops typically employ both union and nonunion pressmen. This provision also allowed an employee to present grievances directly to the employer (without going through the union), and required the employee's authorization before union dues could be subtracted from his paycheck.

The Rights of Employers.   The Taft–Hartley Act also explicitly gave *employers* certain collective bargaining rights. First, it gave them full freedom to express their views concerning union organization. For example, you can as a manager, tell your employees that in your opinion unions are worthless, dangerous to the economy, and immoral. You can even, generally speaking, hint that unionization (and subsequent high wage demands) might result in the permanent closing of the plant (but not its relocation). Employers can set forth the union's record in regard to violence and corruption (if appropriate), and can play upon the racial prejudices of workers (by describing the union's philosophy toward integration). In fact your only major restraint is that you must avoid threats, promises, coercion, and direct interference with workers trying to reach their decision. There can be no threat or reprisal or force or promise of benefit. [15]

In addition, the employer (1) cannot meet with his or her employees on company time within 24 hours of an election; and (2) cannot suggest to employees that they vote against the union *while they are at home or in your office,* although you *can* while they are in their work area or where they normally gather.

National Emergency Strikes.   The Taft–Hartley Act also allows the President of the United States to intervene in the case of "national emergency strikes." These are strikes (for example on the part of steel firm employees) that might "imperil the national health and safety." The president may appoint a board of inquiry and, based on their report, apply for an injunction restraining the strike for 60 days. If no settlement is reached during that time, the injunction can be extended for another 20 days. During this last period employees are polled (in a secret ballot) to ascertain their willingness to accept the employer's last offer.

The Period of Detailed Regulation of Internal Union Affairs: The Landrum–Griffin Act (1959)

In the 1950s, Senate investigations revealed a number of unsavory practices on the part of some unions, and the result was the Landrum–Griffin Act (officially, the "Labor–Management Reporting and Disclosure Act"). An overriding aim of this act was to protect union members from possible wrong doing on the part of their unions.

"Bill of Rights."   First, this law contained a "bill of rights" for union members. Among other things, this provided for certain rights in the nomination of candidates for union office. It also affirms a member's right to sue his or her union and ensures that no member can be fined or suspended without "due process"—which includes a list of specific charges, time to prepare defense, and a fair hearing. It also requires that officers provide copies of the collective bargaining agreement to all union members.

Union Elections.   This act also laid out ground rules covering union elec-

450   tions. For example, national (and international) unions must elect officers at least once every five years, using some type of secret ballot mechanism. Also, local unions must elect officers at least every three years, again by secret ballot. The elections must adhere to the union's constitution and bylaws and every member in good standing is entitled to one vote.

Union Officers.   The act also regulates the kind of person who can serve as a union officer. For example, persons convicted of felonies (bribery, murder, grand larceny, etc.) are barred for a period of five years after conviction from holding a union position as officer.

Employer Wrongdoing.   The senate investigating team also discovered some flagrant examples of employer wrongdoing. Union agents had been bribed, and so-called "labor relations consultants" had been used to buy off union officers, for example.

Such bribery had been a federal crime starting with the passage of the Taft–Hartley Act. But the Landrum–Griffin Act greatly expanded the list of unlawful employer actions. For example, companies can no longer make payments to their own employees for the purpose of enticing them into not joining the union. It also requires an extensive list of reports from both unions and employers, covering things such as use of labor relations consultants.

The Labor Law Reform Bill of 1978.   The Labor Law Reform Bill was debated by the Senate of the United States in June, 1978 and while it did not pass, (and is therefore not law), its proposals help to illustrate some of the ways in which the union movement hopes to bolster its sagging numbers. Basically, the law was aimed at making it more difficult and more costly for employers to stand up to organizing efforts conducted under the NLRB. [16] Specifically, the bill proposed to: expedite representation elections by setting a time limit for the holding of an election; permit unions to address employee meetings on company property if the employer also required employees to attend meetings there in the context of a union organizational campaign; bar from participation in federal contracts for 3 years any person (or corporation) found in willful violation of an order of the NLRB which resulted from a charge involving coercion of employees and which is upheld by a court decision; permit award of double backpay to employees illegally discharged in the context of an organizational campaign; and permit the NLRB to order compensation for employees whose employer is found to have illegally refused to bargain with the union over an initial union contract. [17]

From the lobbying that surrounded the debate it seems apparent that one of organized labor's aims in regard to this bill was to make it more difficult for "anti-union" companies to continue to resist being organized. For example, some companies such as J. P. Stevens, a textile firm headquartered in the Southeast had a long history of engaging in protracted litigation in order to resist union organizing efforts. The purpose of this bill, then, was to close some of the loopholes" of previous labor laws and to make it more difficult for confrontation-oriented employers to maneuver around existing laws—for example, by 451 making it more difficult for employers to fire workers for union activities, and by denying federal contracts to "willful violators of NLRB rulings." After a 19 day filibuster ending June 22, 1978 the Senate failed on its sixth try to get the votes required to shut off debate on the bill, and it was sent back to committee, with the possibility of future action.

THE UNION DRIVE AND ELECTION [18]

It is through the union drive and election that a union tries to be recognized to represent employees. This process involves four basic steps: (1) initial contact, (2) authorization cards, (3) hearing, and (4) the election.

Step 1: Initial Contact

The initiative for the first contact between the employees and the union may come from the employees, from a union already representing other of the firm's employees, or from a union representing workers elsewhere. [19] The law allows union organizers to solicit employees for membership as long as it doesn't endanger the performance or safety of the employees. Therefore much of the contact often takes place off the job—for example at home or at eating places near work. Organizers can also safely contact employees on company grounds during off hours (like lunch or break time). Under some conditions it may be possible for union representatives to solicit employees at their work stations, but this is rare. Yet, in practice, there will be much "informal" organizing going on at the workplace as employees debate the merits of organizing.

In any case, this first stage may be deceptively quiet. In some instances the first inkling management has of a union campaign is a handbill (as in Exhibit 16.4) that is distributed or posted.

Step 2: Obtaining Authorization Cards

In order to petition for an election, the union must show that a sizeable number of employees *may* be interested in being unionized. Therefore the next step is for union organizers to try to get the employees to sign "authorization" cards: 30% must sign before an election is petitioned.

During this stage both union and management typically make use of various forms of propaganda. The union claims it can improve working conditions, raise wages, increase benefits, and generally get the workers better deals. Management need not be silent: it can attack the union on ethical and moral grounds, insist that employees will not be as well off and lose freedom, and could cite the cost of union membership, for example. *But* neither side can threaten, bribe, or coerce employees. And, be careful once the authorization cards are obtained: Some recommend that managers not look through these cards if confronted

Exhibit 16.4   Sample Union Handbill

Now is the time... To join UFF
(United Faculty of Florida)

Join your elected bargaining agent and help finalize the UFF
contract proposals to take to the bargaining table.
UFF Membership Convention
Orlando — March 24-25
Delegates Elected on Each Campus March 11-12

UNITED FACULTY OF FLORIDA — MEMBERSHIP APPLICATION

I hereby apply for membership in the United Faculty of Florida, the elected bargaining agent of faculty
and professional employees in the State University System.

Name _____
Address _____
City _____ Zip _____

(DUES)
(Based on 9-months salary)

	Monthly	Annual
Under $7,000	$ 3.00	$ 35.00
$7,000 $10,000	6.00	70.00
$10,000 $20,000	8.00	90.00
Over $20,000	10.00	110.00

Return to local chapter representative or mail to   United Faculty of Florida
208 West Pensacola Street
Tallahassee, Florida 32304

with them by union representatives. (It could be construed as an unfair labor practice by the NLRB, which could view it as "spying" on those who signed.)

During this period, unions can picket the company, subject to three constraints: (1) they must file a petition for an election within 30 days after the start of picketing; (2) the firm cannot already be lawfully recognizing another union; and (3) there cannot already have been a valid NLRB election during the past 12 months.

Step 3: Hold a Hearing

At this point one of two things can occur. If the employer chooses *not* to contest union recognition, no hearing is needed and a "consent election" is held immediately. Or, the firm could contest the election.

Most companies do contest the election, on the grounds that a significant number of their employees do not really want the union. It is at this point that the National Labor Relations Board (NLRB) gets involved. The NLRB is usually contacted by the union who submits NLRB "form 502." Based on this, the regional director of the NLRB sends a hearing officer to investigate. The examiner sends both management and union a "notice of representation hearing" (NLRB form 852). This states time and place of the hearing.

There are usually two main issues to be investigated. First, Does the record indicate that there is enough evidence to hold an election? For example, did 30% or more of your employees sign the authorization cards?

Second, the examiner also has to decide what the bargaining unit will be. This can be a crucial matter for the union, for employees, and for the employer. The "bargaining unit" is the group of employees which the union will be authorized to represent and bargain collectively for. If the entire organization is viewed as a bargaining unit, then the union will represent all employees. (For example, they might end up representing all professional, white-collar, and blue-collar employees, although the union is oriented mostly toward blue-collar workers.) If the firm disagrees with the examiner's decision regarding the bargaining unit, it can challenge the decision; this will require a separate step and NLRB ruling.

Step 4: The Election

Finally, the actual election can be held. This is contingent on three things: (1) evidence as presented in the hearing that a significant number (30% or more) of the employees are interested in unionizing; (2) agreement concerning the bargaining units; and (3) approval of the examiner's decision by his or her superiors at the NLRB. Given that these conditions are met, employees are notified of the election (and management of its rights) by the NLRB. Then, within 30 to 60 days, an election is held by the NLRB, who also provide secret ballots and ballot boxes, count the votes, and certify the election.

The union becomes the employees' representative if they win the election, and winning means getting a majority of the votes *cast, not* a majority of the workers in the bargaining unit. (It is also important to keep in mind that where an employer commits an unfair labor practice, a "no union" election may be reversed. As representatives of their employer, managers must therefore be very careful not to commit such "unfair" practices.)

How to Lose an NLRB Election [20]

There were 7,345 collective bargaining elections held recently, and of these about 50% were lost by companies: Yet according to a study by the University Research Center about 80% of these elections should probably *not* have been lost. According to expert Matthew Goodfellow, there is no sure way an employer can win an election; however, there are five sure ways an employer could *lose* one.

Reason 1: Asleep at the Switch.   In 68% of the companies studied (of those that lost to the union) executives were caught unawares, having not paid attention to symptoms of low employee morale. In these companies turnover and absenteeism had increased, productivity was erratic, and safety was poor. Grievance procedures were rarely used. When the first reports of authorization cards being distributed began trickling back to top managers they usually responded with a knee-jerk reflex action. A barrage of one-way communications ensued in which top management bombarded workers with letters describing how the company was "one big family" and calling for a "team effort."

It is interesting that, even once union efforts had begun, management often made no serious effort to ascertain *from the employees themselves* what it was that troubled them enough to force them into the arms of the union. As the researcher points out "what must be done—even at the last minute—is to uncover the issues that vex employees." Keep in mind, though, that this can be a ticklish business. Knowing *what* questions to ask, and *how* (without committing unfair labor practices) and knowing how to work within NLRB rules which inhibit "corrective actions" (like giving everyone a raise) in the pre-election period usually requires specialized training. [21]

Yet the best strategy is to not be caught asleep in the first place:

> Overall, prudence dictates that management spend time and effort even when the atmosphere is calm testing the temperature of employee sentiments and finding ways to remove irritants. Doing that cuts down on the possibility that an election will ever take place, while trying to dissipate discontent during a short campaign is difficult.

Reason 2: Appointing a Committee.   Thirty-six percent of the losing companies formed a committee to manage the campaign. According to the expert there are three fallacies in this:

1. *Promptness* is the essence of the election situation and committees are notorious for deliberation.

2. Most of the members of such a committee are *neophytes* so far as an NLRB situation is concerned and their views therefore are mostly reflections of wishful thinking rather than experience.
3. A committee's decision is usually a homogenized decision, with everyone seeking to *compromise* differences. The result is often close to the most conservative opinion—but not necessarily the most knowledgeable or most effective.

This expert suggests, instead, giving full responsibility to a single decisive executive. This person should in turn be assisted by a personnel director and a consultant/adviser with broad experience in labor relations.

Reason 3: Concentrating on Money and Benefits.   In 54% of the elections studied the company lost the election because top management concentrated on the "wrong" issues: money and benefits. As this expert puts it:

> Employees may want more money, but quite often if they feel the company treats them fairly, decently, and honestly, they are satisfied with reasonable, competitive rates and benefits. It is only when they feel ignored, uncared for, and disregarded that money becomes a major issue to express their dissatisfaction.

Reason 4: Industry "Blind Spots."   The researcher found that in some industries employees felt more ignored and disregarded than in others. For example in industries that are highly automated (like paper manufacturing and automotive) there was some tendency for executives to regard hourly employees as "just cogs in the machinery." This also seemed to be the case among white-collar workers in the insurance industry and in most public utilities. Here (as in reason 3 above) a solution is to begin paying more serious attention to the needs and attitudes of employees.

Reason 5: Delegating Too Much to Divisions or Branches.   For companies with plants scattered around the country, unionization of one or more of these plants tends to lead to unionization of others. Organizing several of the plants gives the union a "wedge" in the form of a contract that can be used to tempt workers at other plants.

Part of the solution here is to keep reasons 1–4 in mind, and to thereby keep those first few plants from being organized. Beyond that, employers with "multiplant" operations should not blindly relegate all decisions concerning personnel and industrial relations to the plant managers. Effectively dealing with unionization—taking the "pulse" of the workers' attitudes, knowing what is bothering them, reacting appropriately when the union first appears, etc.— generally requires strong, centralized guidance from the head office and its personnel staff.

The Supervisor's Role

The extent to which supervisors help or hinder their employers' attempts to limit union organizing activity depends largely on the supervisor's knowledge of and training in the rules regarding union organizing. Where supervisors are not thoroughly familiar with what they can and cannot do to legally hamper organizing activities their effect may be to commit an unfair labor practice and thereby (1) cause a new election to be held after the company has won a previous election, or, (2) cause their employer to have to forfeit a second election and go directly to contract negotiation. In one case, for example, a plant superintendent reacted to a union's initial organizing attempt by prohibiting distribution of union literature in the plant's lunchroom. Since solicitation of off-duty workers in non-work areas is generally legal, the company subsequently allowed the union to post union literature on the company's bulletin board and to distribute union literature in non-working areas inside the plant. However the NLRB still ruled that the initial incident of prohibiting distribution of union literature in the lunchroom was an unfair labor practice, one that was not "made right" by the company's subsequent efforts. In this case, the NLRB used the action of the plant superintendent as one reason for invalidating an election that the company had won. [22] In order to avoid such problems, employers should do two things: first, they should develop clear rules governing distribution of literature and solicitation of workers; and, second, they should train supervisors in how to administer these rules. [23]

Rules Regarding Literature and Solicitation.   There are a number of steps an employer can take to validly restrict union organizing activity. [24] *Non*-employees can always be barred from soliciting employees during their work time—that is, when the employee is on duty and not on a break. Thus, if the company cafeteria is open to whomever is on the premises, union organizers *can* solicit off-duty employees who are in the cafeteria, but cannot solicit the cafeteria workers (like cooks) who are not on a break. Employers can usually stop employees from soliciting other employees for any purpose if one or both employees are on paid-duty time and not on a break. Most employers (not including retail stores, shopping centers, and certain other employers) can bar nonemployees from building interiors and work areas as a right of private property owners. In certain cases, nonemployees can also be barred from exterior private property areas such as parking lots—if the rule has a business reason (such as safety) other than interference with union organizers. Employees can be denied access to interior or exterior areas only if the employer can show that the rule is required for reasons of production, safety, or discipline. In general, off-duty employees cannot be considered to have the same status as nonemployees, and therefore cannot be prohibited from remaining on the premises or returning to the premises unless this prohibition is also required for reasons of production, safety, or discipline. In summary, two examples of specific rules aimed at limiting union organizing activity are as follows:

> Solicitation of employees on company property during working time interferes with the efficient operation of our business. Nonemployees are not permitted to solicit employees on company property for any purpose. Except

in break areas where both employees are on break or off the clock, no employee may solicit other employees during working time for any purpose.

Distribution of literature on company property not only creates a litter problem but also distracts us from our work. Nonemployees are not allowed to distribute literature on company property. Except in the performance of his or her job, an employee may not distribute literature unless both the distributor and the recipient are off the clock or on authorized break in a break area or off company premises. Special exceptions to these rules may be made by the company for especially worthwhile causes such as the March of Dimes, but written permission must first be obtained and the solicitation will be permitted only during break periods. [25]

The Need for Training. In addition to instituting rules, supervisors should be trained in their enforcement. As one expert puts it:

Supervisors have a right to prohibit interference with their employer's business activity and to restrict interference with the performance of an employee's job. Employers who have successfully maintained their nonunion status have supervisors who exercise these rights. But to legally dissuade employees from unionizing and to control union activity, supervisors must be trained; they must know the pitfalls and the methods of legitimately implementing their rights. [26]

There are several things to keep in mind when implementing such a training program. First, the overall aim of the program should be to familiarize supervisors with the rules governing organizing activity (as discussed above) and, if at all possible, there should be an emphasis on what the supervisors *can do*, rather than on what they cannot do. (Typically, in these training sessions, the "don'ts" far outnumber the "do's," and the effect is to inhibit supervisory action). Training should also be given in advance of a union organizing attempt: Once the union has begun its efforts, training is often too late in that unsuspecting supervisors have already inadvertently committed unfair labor practices. Training should also provide a practice session in which supervisors can apply the "do's and don'ts." For example, they should be exposed to simulations of the kinds of situations they may encounter and be given an opportunity to apply what they have learned: case studies can be useful here. In summary, first-line supervisors can play an important role in limiting union organizing activities. However, to avoid their creating costly legal headaches they should be properly trained in "preventive labor relations." [27]

COLLECTIVE BARGAINING: WORKING OUT THE LABOR AGREEMENT

What Is Collective Bargaining?

If the union is recognized as the employees' representative, a day is set for meeting at the bargaining table. Here representatives of management and the

458

union meet to negotiate a labor agreement. This will contain agreements on specific provisions covering wages, hours, and working conditions.

What exactly is collective bargaining? According to the National Labor Relations Act:

> For the purposes of (this act) to *bargain collectively* is the performance of the mutual obligation of the employer and the representative of the employees to meet at reasonable times and confer in good faith with respect to wages, hours, and terms and conditions of employment, or the negotiation of an agreement, or any question arising thereunder, and the execution of a written contract incorporating any agreement reached if requested by either party, but such obligation does not compel either party to agree to a proposal or require the making of a concession.

In plain language, this means that both management and labor are required, under law, to negotiate wages, hours, and terms and conditions of employment "in good faith." In a moment we will see that the *specific* items that are negotiable (since "wages," "hours," and "conditions of employment" are too broad to be useful in practice) have been clarified by a series of court decisions.

What Is "Good Faith"?

Bargaining in good faith is the cornerstone of effective labor-management relations. It means that both parties communicate and negotiate. And, it means that proposals are matched with counter-proposals and that both parties make every reasonable effort to arrive at agreement. [28] It does *not* mean that either party is compelled to agree to a proposal. Nor does it *require* that either party make any specific concessions (although as a practical matter some may be necessary).

When Is Bargaining Not "In Good Faith"? As interpreted by the NLRB and the courts a violation of the requirement for good faith bargaining may include the following:

1. *Surface bargaining.* This involves merely going through the motions of bargaining, without any real intention of completing a formal agreement.
2. *Concession.* Although not required to make a concession, the courts' and Board definitions of good faith suggest that a willingness to compromise is an essential ingredient in good-faith bargaining.
3. *Proposals and demands.* The NLRB considers the advancement of proposals as a factor in determining overall good faith.
4. *Dilatory tactics.* The law requires that the parties meet and "confer at reasonable times and intervals." Obviously, refusal to meet at all with the union does not satisfy the positive duty imposed on the employer.
5. *Imposing conditions.* Attempts to impose conditions that are so onerous or unreasonable as to indicate bad faith will be scrutinized by the Board.
6. *Unilateral changes in conditions.* This is viewed as a strong indication that the employer is not bargaining with the required intent of reaching an agreement.

7. *Bypassing the representative.* An employer violates its duty to bargain when it refuses to negotiate with the union representative. The duty of management to bargain in good faith involves, at a minimum, recognition that this *statutory representative* is the one with whom the employer must deal in conducting bargaining negotiations.

8. *Commission of unfair labor practices during negotiations.* Such action may reflect upon the good faith of the guilty party.

9. *Providing information.* Information must be supplied to the union, upon request, to enable it to understand and intelligently discuss the issues raised in bargaining.

10. *Bargaining items.* Refusal to bargain on a "mandatory" item (one *must* bargain over these) or insistence on a "permissive" item (one *may* bargain over these) is usually viewed as bad faith bargaining. [29] (We will present these items below.)

The Negotiating Team

Both union and management send a negotiating team to the bargaining table. The management team is usually smaller, consisting of perhaps three or four persons. If the employer is large enough to have a vice president or director of industrial relations, that person would undoubtedly be on the team. In addition, there might be a line manager and perhaps one or two attorneys from a law firm that specializes in the labor field. On the union side will be the local's business agent, as well as several of its officers. The employer's union steward (local union representative) might attend, as well as a representative of the national union. The latter might be the chief spokesman for the union: more typically, though, he or she provides expert advice and helps maintain consistency among the local agreements that are reached across the country.

Preparations. Both teams usually go into the bargaining sessions having "done their homework." Union representatives have sounded out union members on their desires and conferred with union representatives of related unions. In large industrial unions (like the auto workers) negotiation objectives are usually set by top national officers.

Management also prepares for bargaining. This typically includes: [30]

A thorough study of the current contract with a view to discovering any sections or language which may call for modification at the upcoming negotiations.

A systematic analysis of prior grievances for clues to defective or unworkable contract language or as an indicator of probable union demands.

Frequent conferences with supervisors for the purpose of getting input regarding how the present contract is working out in practice.

Conferences with other employers in the same industry or area who deal with the same union to exchange viewpoints and anticipate the union's demands.

460

Use of attitude surveys to test the reactions of employees to various sections of the contract that management may feel require change or modification.

Informal conferences with local union leaders (stewards, shop committeemen or business agents) to discuss the operational effectiveness of the contract and to send up trial balloons on management ideas for change at the next negotiations, and

Collection and analysis of economic data on matters of importance in the next negotiations.

The Actual Bargaining Sessions

Bargaining items.   Labor law sets out categories of items that are subject to bargaining: these are *mandatory, voluntary,* and *illegal* bargaining items.

Voluntary (or permissible) bargaining items are neither mandatory nor illegal: they become a part of negotiations only through the joint agreement of both management and union. Neither party can be compelled against its wishes to negotiate over voluntary items. And, one party cannot hold up signing the contract because the other refuses to bargain on a voluntary item.

Illegal bargaining items are of course forbidden by law. The clause agreeing to hire "union members exclusively" would be illegal in a right to work state, for example.

There are about 70 basic items over which bargaining is *mandatory* under the law, and these are presented in Exhibit 16.5. They include wages, hours, rest periods, layoffs, transfers, benefits, and severance pay.

Bargaining Stages.   Glueck [31] says that bargaining typically follows several stages of development. [32] *First,* each side presents its demands. (At this stage both parties are usually quite far apart on some issues.) *Second,* there is a reduction of demands. (At this stage each side trades off some of its demands to gain others.) *Third* comes the subcommittee studies: the parties form joint subcommittees to try to work out reasonable alternatives. *Fourth,* an informal settlement is reached and each group goes back to its sponsor: union representatives check informally with their superiors and the union members; management representatives check with top management. *Finally,* once everything is in order, a formal agreement is fine-tuned and signed. According to Richardson, the overall bargaining process can be improved by adhering to some common-sense guidelines, including: [33]

1. Be sure to have set *clear objectives* on every bargaining item. And make sure you understand on what grounds the objectives were established.
2. When in doubt, *caucus* with your associates.
3. Be *well prepared* with firm data supporting your position.
4. Always strive to keep some *flexibility* in your position. Don't get yourself out on a limb.
5. Do not just be concerned with what the other party says and does: *find out*

Exhibit 16.5   Mandatory Bargaining Items

Wages	Severance pay
Hours	Nondiscriminatory hiring hall
Discharge	Plant rules
Arbitration	Safety
Holidays—paid	Prohibition against supervisor's doing unit work
Vacations—paid	Superseniority for union stewards
Duration of agreement	Checkoff
Grievance procedure	Partial plant closing
Layoff plan	Hunting on employer forest reserve where
Reinstatement of economic strikers	previously granted
Change of payment from hourly base to salary base	Plant closedown and relocation
Union security and checkoff	Change in operations resulting in reclassifying
Work rules	workers from incentive to straight time, or cut
Merit wage increase	work force, or installation of cost-saving machine
Work schedule	Plant closing
Lunch periods	Job-posting procedures
Rest periods	Plant reopening
Pension plan	Employee physical examination
Retirement age	Union security
Bonus payments	Bargaining over "Bar List"
Price of meals provided by company	Truck rentals—minimum rental to be paid by
Group insurance—health, accident, life	carriers to employee-owned vehicles
Promotions	Musician price list
Seniority	Arrangement for negotiation
Layoffs	Change in insurance carrier and benefits
Transfers	Profit-sharing plan
Work assignments and transfers	Motor-carrier—union agreement providing that
No-strike clause	carriers use own equipment before leasing out-
Piece rates	side equipment
Stock-purchase plan	Overtime pay
Work loads	Agency shop
Change of employee status to independent	Sick leave
contractors	Employer's insistence on clause giving arbitrator
Management-rights clause	right to enforce award
Cancellation of seniority upon relocation of plant	Company houses
Discounts on company products	Subcontracting
Shift differentials	Discriminatory racial policies
Contract clause providing for supervisors' keeping	Production ceiling imposed by union
seniority in unit	Most-favored-nation clause
Procedures for income tax withholding	

Source: Reed Richardson, *Collective Bargaining by Objectives* (Englewood Cliffs, N.J.: Prentice-Hall, Inc., 1977), pp. 113–15.

why. Remember that economic motivation is not the only explanation for the other party's conduct and actions.

6. Respect the importance of *face-saving* for the other party.

7. Pay close attention to the *wording* of every clause negotiated; words and phrases are often a source of grievances.

8. Remember that collective bargaining negotiations are, by their nature, part of a *compromise* process. There is no such thing as having all the pie. And,

9. Consider the impact of present negotiations on those in *future* years.

The Agreement Itself

The actual agreement may be 20 or 30 pages, or over 100. It may contain just general declarations of policy, or a detailed specification of rules and procedures. The tendency today is toward the longer, more detailed contracts. This is largely a result of the increased number of items the agreements have been covering.

The main sections of a typical contract might cover the following subjects:

1. Management rights.
2. Union security and dues checkoff.
3. Grievance procedures.
4. Arbitration of grievances.
5. Disciplinary procedures.
6. Compensation rates.
7. Hours of work and overtime.
8. Benefits: vacations, holidays, insurance, pensions.
9. Health and safety provisions.
10. Employee security—seniority provisions.
11. Contract expiration date.

(This list just shows the main categories of subjects: The Bureau of National Affairs in Washington has published a "contact clause finder" which can be used as a checklist to guide detailed discussions during bargaining.)

Changes to Expect after Being Unionized

Beach says there are five basic areas in which the union's impact will be felt: [34] it will restrict management's freedom of action; there will be union pressure for uniformity of treatment of all employees; it will require improved personnel policies and practices; it will require one spokesman to be used for the employees; and it will lead to centralization of labor relations decision making.

Perhaps the most obvious impact of the union is that it restricts management's freedom of action. A wide range of personnel decisions that supervisors could previously make unilaterally will, after unionization, have to endure scrutiny and challenge by the union. Decisions such as who gets laid off when business is slow, who gets to work overtime, and who gets a raise are subject to challenge by the union, for example.

Partly because of the prospect of such challenges, (and partly because the union contract contains written provisions regarding pay, benefits, promotion, and the like) unionization also leads to a systematizing, centralizing, and sophistication of the employer's personnel policies, procedures, and rules. Coincident with unionization, for example the employer might take steps to (1) advise all plant managers that union-related questions should be referred to the headquarter's labor relations specialist; (2) formulate a compensation plan and particularly a system of wage classes; and (3) develop an improved, more objective procedure for appraising employee performance, so that union challenges are more easily defended against.

Decertification Elections: When Employees Want to Oust Their Union

Winning an election and signing an agreement does not necessarily mean that the union is in the company "to stay"—quite the opposite. Between 1962 and 1978 the number of decertification elections—elections in which workers vote to disband their union—shot up 400%, and the unions lost most of them. In 1978, for example there were 807 elections and 594 decertifications—a 74% loss rate for the labor movement. [35]

Decertification campaigns themselves do not differ substantially from certification campaigns (those leading up to the initial election). [36] For its part, the union organizes membership meetings, house-to-house visits, and the mailing of literature into the homes, and uses phone calls, NLRB appeals, and, sometimes, threats and harassment to win the election. [37] For its part, managers use meetings—including one-on-one meetings, small-group meetings, and meetings with entire units—as well as legal or expert assistance, letters, and improved working conditions in its attempts to obtain a decertification vote.

Employers are also increasingly turning to what unions refer to as "union-busting" consultants. These consultants (who claim they act as "marriage brokers" between workers and management) [38] provide, among other things, managers and supervisors with detailed advice concerning how to behave during the pre-election period. According to at least one account, some of these consultants may even explain how to pay an illegal pay raise in the middle of a union organizing campaign on the assumption that "the probability is that you will never get caught. If you do get caught the worst that can happen is a second election and the employee loses 96% of these elections." [39] On the whole, however, these consultants' main strategy seems to be to assist management in improving their communications with the shop floor and in identifying and eliminating the basic pressures that led to the pro-union vote in the first place. Ideally, therefore, this is usually not a last minute effort. Instead, a pro-management vote on either a certification, or decertification election tends to be the result of long-term sensible actions on the part of management, actions which have as their goal winning the trust and confidence of employees:

> Decertification cannot be accomplished just at election time. You must earn the confidence of employees over at least a year's period of time, through effective performance evaluation programs, personnel development programs, and overall good communication between employees and management during the contract. Also, through examples at other, nonunion, operations within the company, employees come to realize they would be better off without a union. [40]

464   *HOW TO HANDLE GRIEVANCES*

The Important Role of Contract Administration

Hammering out a labor agreement is not the last step in collective bargaining: in some respects, it is just the beginning. No labor contract can ever be so complete that it covers all contingencies and answers all questions. For example, suppose the contract says an employee can only be discharged for "just cause." You subsequently discharge someone for speaking back to you in harsh terms. Was it within your rights to discharge this person? Was speaking back to you harshly "just cause"?

Problems like this are usually handled and settled through the grievance procedures of the labor contract. This procedure provides an orderly system whereby employer and union determine whether or not the contract has been violated: [41] it is the vehicle for administering the contract on a day-to-day basis. Through this grievance process various clauses are interpreted and given meaning and the contract is transformed into a "living organism." (Remember, though, that this "day-to-day collective bargaining" involves *interpretation* only: it usually does *not* involve negotiating new terms or altering existing ones.) [42]

What Are the Sources of Grievances?

From a practical point of view it is probably easier to list those items that *don't* precipitate grievances than to list the ones that do. Just about any factor involving wages, hours, or conditions of employment has and will be used as the basis of a grievance.

However, some grievances are more serious than others since they are usually more difficult to settle. Discipline cases and seniority problems (including promotions, transfer, and layoffs) would top this list. Others would include grievances growing out of job evaluation and work assignments, overtime, vacations, incentive plans, and holidays. [43] Examples of actual grievances include: [44]

Absenteeism: An employer fired an employee for excessive absences. The employee filed a grievance stating that there had been no previous warnings or discipline related to excessive absences.

Insubordination: An employee on two occasions refused to obey a supervisor's order to meet with him, unless a union representative was present at the meeting. As a result, the employee was discharged and subsequently filed a grievance protesting discharge.

Overtime: Sunday overtime work was discontinued after a department was split. Employees affected filed a grievance protesting loss of the overtime work.

Plant rules: The plant had a posted rule barring employees from eating or drinking during unscheduled breaks. The employees filed a grievance claiming the rule was arbitrary.

Seniority: A junior employee was hired to fill the position of a laid-off senior
employee. The senior employee filed a grievance protesting the action.

Always Ask: What Is the Real Problem?   It is important to remember that
a grievance is often just a symptom of an underlying problem. For example,
an employee's concern for his or her job security may prompt a grievance over
a transfer, work assignment, or promotion. Sometimes bad relations between
supervisors and subordinates are to blame: this is often the cause of grievances
over "fair treatment," for example. Organizational factors like automated jobs
or ambiguous job descriptions that frustrate or aggravate employees are other
potential causes of grievances. Union activism is another cause: for example,
the union may solicit grievances from workers to underscore ineffective supervision. Problem employees are yet another cause of grievances. These are individuals, who, by their nature, are negative, dissatisfied, and grievance-prone. [45]

The Grievance Procedure

Most collective bargaining contracts contain a carefully worded grievance
procedure. This specifies the various steps in the procedure, time limits associated with each step, and specific rules like "all charges of contract violation
must be reduced to writing."

Grievance procedures differ from employer to employer. Some contain simple
two-step procedures. Here the grievant, union representative, and company representative first meet to discus the grievance. If a satisfactory solution is not
found, the grievance is then brought before an independent "third person"
arbitrator, who hears the case, writes it up, and makes a decision.

At the other extreme, the grievance procedure may contain six or more
steps. The first step might be for the grievant and shop steward to meet informally with the grievant's supervisor and try to find a solution. If one is not
found, a formal grievance is filed and a meeting scheduled among the employee,
shop steward, and the supervisor's boss. Each of the next steps involve meetings
between higher and higher echelon managers. Finally, if top management and
the union cannot reach agreement, the grievance may have to go to arbitration.

An Example of What to Expect: Sloane and Witney say that the best
way to demonstrate the working of a grievance procedure is through an example.
They present the following as an actual situation that typifies the grievance
process in industry. [46]

Background: Tom Swift, a rank-and-file member of local 1,000, was employed by the XYZ manufacturing company for a period of five years. His
production record was excellent, he caused management no trouble, and during
his fourth year of employment received a promotion. One day Swift began
preparations to leave the plant 20 minutes before quitting time. He put away
his tools, washed up, got out of his overalls, and put on his street clothes.

Jackson, an assistant foreman in his department, observed Swift's actions. He immediately informed Swift that he was going to the "front office" to recommend his discharge. The next morning Swift reported for work, but Jackson handed Swift a pay envelope. In addition to wages, it included a discharge notice. The notice declared that the company discharged Swift because he had made ready to leave the plant 20 minutes before quitting time. Swift immediately contacted his union steward, Joe Thomas. Swift told Thomas the circumstances, and the steward believed that the discharge constituted a violation of the collective bargaining contract. A clause in the agreement provided that an employee could be discharged only for "just cause." Disagreeing with the assistant foreman and the "front office," shop steward Thomas felt that the discharge was *not* for just cause.

Step 1: The steps in processing the complaint through the grievance procedure were clearly outlined in the collective bargaining agreement. First, it was necessary to present the grievance to the foreman of the department in which Swift worked. Both Thomas and Swift approached the foreman, and the written grievance was presented to him. The foreman was required to give his answer on the grievance within 48 hours after receiving it. He complied with the time requirements, but his answer did not please Swift or Thomas. The foreman supported the action of the assistant foreman and refused to recommend the reinstatement of Swift.

Step 2: Not satisfied with the action of the foreman, the labor union (through Thomas the steward), initiated the second step of the grievance procedure. This step required the appeal of the complaint to the superintendent of the department in which Swift worked. The superintendent supported the decisions of his foreman and assistant foreman. Despite the efforts of the steward (who vigorously argued the merits of Swift's case) the department superintendent refused to reinstate the worker. Hence the second step of the grievance procedure was exhausted, and the union and the employee were still not satisfied with the results. (Keep in mind that the vast majority of grievances *are* usually settled in these first two steps of the grievance procedure.)

Step 3: Accordingly, the union went to the third step of the grievance procedure. Grievance personnel for the third step included, from the company, the general superintendent and his representative. The labor union was represented by the organization's plant-wide grievance committee. The results of the negotiation at this third step proved satisfactory to Swift, the union, and the company. After 45 minutes of spirited discussion, the management group agreed with the union that discharge was not warranted in this particular case. (Management's committee, by the way, was persuaded by the following set of circumstances. Everyone conceded that Swift had an outstanding record before the dismissal occurred. In addition, the discussion revealed that Swift had asked the department foreman whether there was any more work to be done before he left his bench to prepare to leave for home. The foreman had replied in the negative. Finally, it was brought out that Swift had had a pressing problem at home which he claimed was the motivating factor making for his desire to prepare to leave early.) It was concluded that Swift would be reinstated in his job, but would be penalized by a three-day suspension without pay.

Step 4: What would have occurred if the company and the labor union had *not* reached a satisfactory agreement at the third step of the grievance procedure? In this particular contract, the grievance procedure provided for a fourth step. Grievance procedure personnel at the fourth step included (for the company) the vice president in charge of industrial relations or his representative, and (for the union) an officer of the international union or his representative. [47] In most agreements, a final step would require taking the grievance outside the company, to arbitration (the arbitrators' decision generally cannot be appealed to the courts, except in discrimination cases).

Grievance Handling in Nonunion Organizations

Virtually every labor agreement signed today contains a grievance procedure clause, but the fact is that *non*unionized employers need such procedures as well. As illustrated in the "Tom Swift" example above, a grievance procedure helps ensure that every employee is treated fairly and equitably, and employees in unionized firms should not hold a monopoly on fair treatment. [48] The fact is that even where a firm has not been unionized, adhering to a formal grievance procedure can help ensure that morale and productivity remain high, and that labor-management peace prevails. [49]

Many nonunionized companies do offer grievance procedures. [50] In one study 24 out of 41 companies responding (about 58%) reported they have grievance procedures for nonunionized employees. In 10 of these firms the grievance procedures covers all employees (including executives) while in most of the other firms grievance procedures are reserved exclusively for rank-and-file workers and (in some firms) first line supervisors. An example of a typical grievance procedure, one developed for a nonunionized hospital in Maryland can be summarized as follows:

Step 1: Discuss the problem or dissatisfaction with your supervisor who will attempt to resolve it in accordance with established hospital personnel policies within 2 working days, unless there are extenuating circumstances.

Step 2: Should the problem remain unresolved, your supervisor will endeavor to make an appointment for you to discuss the matter with your department head within the next 3 working days.

Step 3: Should the problem continue to remain unresolved, the employee should present the problem or dissatisfaction in writing (a form is available) and forward it to the director, employee relations, who will either schedule a meeting with all interested parties, or will present a recommendation within 5

468   working days for a resolution of the problem based on hospital personnel policies and practices.

Step 4: Most matters of employee concern should be resolved at the conclusion of step 3. However, for that unusual problem which may not have been resolved to the employee's satisfaction, the employee may request that the matter be brought to the attention of administration for consideration and decision. An administrative decision will be rendered and communicated in writing to all interested parties within 10 working days. This decision will be final and binding. [51]

In most nonunion employers' grievance procedures, the employers' top executives were generally the "court of last resort," although occasionally the last person a grievant could appeal to was the personnel, or industrial relations manager. At least one expert has suggested, however, that legislation be passed that gives even nonunionized workers the right to an appeals process and, if necessary to binding arbitration by an outside arbitrator. [52]

Guidelines for Handling Grievances

Developing the Proper Environment. [53] The best way to "handle" a grievance is to develop a work environment in which grievances do not occur in the first place. Because of this, *constructive grievance handling* depends first on the supervisor's ability to recognize, diagnose, and correct the causes of potential employee dissatisfaction *before* they become formal grievances. This in turn involves applying many of the techniques discussed in this book. For example, ask: "Am I an active listener?" "Do I let employees express their points of view without interruption?" "Am I sensitive to the needs of the employees as well as the rules of the organization?" "Do I deal with employees as individuals?" and so forth. [54] Beyond this, there are some specific "Do's and Dont's" to keep in mind when confronted with a grievance. For example: [55]

DO

Investigate and handle each and every case as though it may eventually result in an arbitration hearing.

Talk with the employee about his or her grievance; give the person a good and full hearing.

Require the union to identify specific contractual provisions allegedly violated

Comply with the contractual time limits on the company for handling the grievance

Visit the work area of the grievance

Determine if there were any witnesses

Examine the grievant's personnel record

Fully examine prior grievance records.

Treat the union representative as your equal

Hold your grievance discussions privately

Fully inform your own supervisor of grievance matters

DON'T

Discuss the case with the union steward alone—the grievant should definitely be there

Make agreements with individuals that are inconsistent with the labor agreement

Hold back the remedy if the company is wrong

Admit to the binding effect of a past practice

Relinquish your rights as a manager to the union

Settle grievances on the basis of what is "fair." Instead stick to the labor agreement, which after all should be your standard.

Bargain over items not covered by the contract

Treat as "arbitrable" claims demanding the discipline or discharge of managers

Give long written grievance answers

Trade a grievance settlement for a grievance withdrawal (or try to "make up" for a bad decision in one grievance by "bending over backwards" in another)

Deny grievances on the premise that "your hands have been tied by management"

Agree to informal amendments in the contract

IN CONCLUSION: IS THERE SUCH A THING AS GOOD UNION-MANAGEMENT RELATIONS? [56]

It is often easy to get the impression that labor-management bargaining tends to be violent and abusive. This is because it is the handful of failures—strikes, pickets, etc.—that makes news; not the tens of thousands of amicably hammered out agreements.

But the fact is that collective bargaining *is* quite successful overall. And there are some shining examples of how management and union can work together in their common endeavor. For example the West Coast Pulp and Paper industry has had over 35 years of healthy labor relations. The Nashua Corporation has dealt with seven AFL unions for over 35 years without strikes. And the Hickey-Freeman Company (a men's clothing manufacturer) has dealt with unions for 50 years without a strike.

Success stories like this do not have to mean that managements were "soft" or unions corrupt—just the opposite. Hard bargaining and effective contract administration on both sides is likely to lead to a healthy union agreement while apathy or one-sided dominance leads to agreements that are doomed to failure. As Samuelson says, "in healthy cases, each side has a respect for the rights of the other. The two sides are not in love, but they are compatible."

SUMMARY

1. Union membership has been alternately growing and shrinking since as early as 1790. A major milestone was the creation, in 1886, of the American Federation of Labor, by Samuel Gompers. Most recently the trend in unionization has been toward organizing white-collar workers, particularly since the proportion of blue-collar workers has been declining. In any case we saw that, while wages and benefits are important factors in unionization, workers are also seeking fair, humane, and equitable treatment.

2. In addition to improved wages and working conditions, unions seek "security" when organizing. We discussed five possible arrangements including: the closed shop, the union shop, the agency shop, the open shop, and "maintenance of membership."

3. The "AFL" is a national federation comprised of 109 national (and international) unions. It can exercise only that power it is allowed to exercise by its constituent national unions.

4. During the period of "strong encouragement" of unions, the Norris–LaGuardia and Wagner Acts were passed: these marked a shift in labor law from repression to strong encouragement of union activity. It did this by banning certain types of unfair labor practices, by providing for secret ballot elections, and by creating the National Labor Relations Board.

5. The Taft–Hartley Act reflected the period of "modified encouragement coupled with regulation." It enumerated the rights of employees with respect to their unions, enumerated the rights of employers, and allowed the president to temporarily bar "national emergency" strikes. Among other things, it also enumerated certain union unfair labor practices. For example, it banned unions from restraining or coercing employees from exercising their guaranteed bargaining rights. And employers were explicitly given the right to express their views concerning union organization.

6. The Landrum–Griffin Act reflected the period of "detailed regulation of internal union affairs." It grew out of discoveries of wrongdoing on the part of both management and union leadership and contained a "bill of rights" for union members. (For example it affirms a member's right to sue his or her union.)

7. There are four steps in a union drive and election: the initial contact, obtaining authorization cards, holding a hearing with the NLRB, and the election itself. Remember that the union need only win a majority of the votes *cast*, not a majority of the workers in the bargaining unit.

8. There are five "sure-fire" ways to lose an NLRB election: be caught "sleeping at the switch," form a committee, emphasize money and benefits, have an industry "blind spot," and delegate too much to divisions. Supervisors should be trained regarding how to administer the employer's union literature and solicitation rules.

9. Bargaining collectively "in good faith" is the next step if and when the union wins the election. Good faith means that both parties communicate and negotiate, and that proposals are matched with counter proposals. We discussed the structure of the negotiating teams and their preparation. We also discussed the actual bargaining session and the distinction between mandatory, voluntary, and illegal bargaining items. We also listed some "hints on bargaining," and the changes to expect once you are unionized.

10. Grievance handling has been called "day-to-day collective bargaining." It involves the continuing interpretation of the collective bargaining agreement (but usually not its renegotiation).

11. Just about any management action might lead to a grievance but the most serious actions involve discipline cases, seniority problems, and actions growing out of a job evaluation and work assignments, and overtime and benefits. But remember that a grievance is often just a symptom: always try to find the underlying problem.

12. Most agreements contain a carefully worded grievance procedure. It may be a two-step procedure or (at the other extreme) involve six or more steps. In any case the steps usually involve meetings between higher and higher echelon managers until (if agreement isn't reached) the grievance goes to arbitration. Grievance handling is as important in nonunion organizations as in unionized ones.

France Rivet Company*

The France Rivet Company has no union. Many efforts have been made to organize employees, but no union has asked for recognition as bargaining agent. Whether any or a large proportion of employees may be union members is not known by the employer.

During the past two days, however, pickets representing an international industrial union have appeared before the plant. They carry banners describing the employer as "unfair." The industrial relations director has talked to a half-dozen employees. He asked them if they belonged to a union or if they knew why the plant is being picketed. All answers were negative.

To this time, the pickets have been rather ineffective. Few, if any, employees have been prevented from working. Trucks have continued deliveries. Some feeling of tension, however, is apparent; employees obviously dislike crossing the picket line. Customers may also object, although none is known to have avoided the plant on that account.

The industrial relations director, however, is under pressure to get rid of the pickets. Plant officials and managers are afraid they may shut off customers or interfere with both receiving and shipping of materials. Several managers have suggested that the whole procedure is a "shakedown," that some union official is getting set to ask for a payoff. Other members of the managerial group think legal action should be taken; they want the industrial relations director to get an injunction. The firm's business is nationwide.

Questions

1. What, in your opinion, should the industrial relations director say or do?
2. Has he handled the matter properly to this point?
3. Prepare a memorandum he might hand to his firm's top managers in which he predicts what are likely to be the significant developments and suggests what action, if any, will be appropriate.

---

* Source: Dale Yoder, *Personnel Management and Industrial Relations* (Englewood Cliffs, N.J.: Prentice-Hall, 1970) pp. 480–81.

Wage Rate for a New
Job-job Comparison*

(Where job comparison is used to set a rate for a new job, the judgment of the parties is involved. If the dispute goes to arbitration, of course, the arbitrator's judgment is also called for. In this case, the company originally offered $3.11 and the union demanded $4.50. Later on, in direct negotiations, the spread became smaller, but the parties still could not reach agreement and arbitration was used to settle the dispute.

What complicates this case is that the company at one time offered $3.43 and the union refused the offer—and that later on the union was willing to accept the $3.43 but the company refused and posted and filled the job at $3.29. Note that in this case the arbitrator made a physical inspection of the jobs being compared. Indeed, about four hours were spent in the physical inspection and only about three hours in the hearing room.)

GRIEVANCE

This dispute involves the establishment of the wage rate for the operator of the Travelift, a material handling piece of equipment. In protest against the company's rate for the job, the union filed a grievance, dated December 17, 1968, which states:

The undersigned hereby grieves the rate of pay established by the Company for the Travelift job. The Union feels the rate should be four dollars and fifty cents per hr.

THE BACKGROUND

The Travelift was acquired by the company in late 1968. It is a new piece of equipment, and the rate structure in the labor agreement does not provide a rate of pay for the operator of the Travelift. The Travelift was produced by the D Manufacturing Company, and it is described as a "rubber tired, all hydraulic mobile overhead crane and transporter." Its load capacity is 25 tons, it straddles the material to be lifted, and the products are attached to the crane by means of two chains and hooks which are secured to the products. The Travelift has the capability of operating on two planes. That is, the material can be lifted and lowered, and swung from right to left. Its speed is about 4.2 miles per hour. The operator is located in a cab stationed

---

* Reprinted by permission from Arthur A. Sloane and Fred Witney, *Labor Relations*, 2nd ed. (Englewood Cliffs, N.J.: Prentice-Hall, Inc., 1972), pp. 307–321.

in the left and rear of the equipment. The cab is about 15 feet above the ground. To operate the Travelift, he makes use of levers and pedals located in the cab. A helper or "ground-man" assists the operator. The function of the helper is to affix the chain to the product, and guide the operator as he moves the equipment within the yard.

On December 5, 1968, a meeting was held between representatives of the company and union to deal with the wage rate of the Travelift operator. Before discussions started as to the rate, the parties agreed upon a job description for the Travelift operator. The pertinent features of the job description are as follows:

General Description

Operates Travelift equipment in the yarding and loading of products and in moving forms, materials and equipment.

Duties

The following outlines in general terms the essential duties of this classification, but is not intended to describe these duties in detail.

1. Operate Travelift in proper and efficient manner.
2. Make minor adjustments as needed to Travelift and daily lubrication check.
3. Yard and load products with Travelift.
4. Move forms within storage area, and between plant and storage area.
5. Move raw materials and equipment within storage area and between plant and storage area.
6. Maintain yarding and loading records and submit required (reports) records.
7. Check product for obvious defects such as chips, cracks, etc., and report such defects in accord with standard procedure.
8. Maintain general work area (Travelift Roadways) in a clean, safe manner.
9. Perform other related duties as required within the general framework of this classification.

With regard to the rate, the union first proposed that the operator be paid $4.50 per hour. The basis for this proposal is the fact that the locomotive crane operator receives $4.50 per hour. As C, president of the union, stated:

We proposed $4.50 per hour by comparing [this job with] the Locomotive Crane Operator. As [with] the Locomotive Crane, the Travelift handles enormous products like the Giant T's, which are 80 feet long and weigh up to 22 tons.

The company rejected the $4.50 per hour rate, and asked the union to suggest a figure which would be in the "ballpark." The union then proposed $3.75 as the rate. In turn, the company proposed $3.11 per hour. In part, this company proposal was based upon the area rates for the operators of D Travelift. In this respect, F, industrial relations administrator, testified:

We searched out what other companies were paying. We found out that other employers were paying $3.11 or less for the operator of the Travelift.

To substantiate the area rates for the equipment, the Company presented letters written to it on May 26, 1969, by the M Company, B Company, and SS Corporation. Such letters state as follows:

M *Company*

This is to confirm our telephone conversation of May 26th, during which I stated that prior to February 24, 1969, the rate range for our Yard Crane and Engine Man classification was $2.77 to $3.07 per hour. This classification operates several types of material moving equipment [, one] of which is a D Travel Lift 500 A1. This classification is represented by the International Association of Machinists and Aerospace Workers Local 1281.

B *Company*

We are the owners of 3 500-A D *Travelifts* used in the manufacture and loading of concrete. We are members of . . . Union Local and have been in operation for a period of 5 years. The rate of pay for our Travelift operators is $2.70 per hour as of December 31, 1968 with a 15¢ per hour increase for the year 1969. Our scale for common laborers is $2.40 per hour.

SS *Corporation*

The SS Corporation owns and operates a D Travelift, Model 500-A1. The Travelift is used for the loading and yarding of heavy structural beams, bridge girders, fabricated steel plate, and steel coils. The operator of the D Travelift is classified as a Crane Operator and is paid Three Dollars and Six Cents ($3.06) per hour in accordance with [this] agreement effective as of the 30th day of June, 1968.

The union was not persuaded by the company's effort to establish the wages for the Travelift operator based upon area rates. Consequently, the December 5 meeting ended with the parties poles apart on the wage rate for the job. The union requested $3.75 and the company proposed $3.11 when this meeting was adjourned.

Another session was held on December 6, 1968, attended by representatives of the parties. In this meeting the company originally offered $3.29 for the job in question. F [the industrial relations administrator] testified that

on the basis of the rate structure in the Labor Agreement, and on the basis of what other employers were paying, we offered $3.29.

On its part the union trimmed its request to $3.50 per hour. This meeting was adjourned without an agreement on the wage rate. The parties were twenty-one (21) cents apart.

A third meeting was held on December 9, 1968. When this meeting started, F testified that "our position was still $3.29 per hour."

However, he declared that during this meeting, D a superintendent of the company, stated:

"We would go to $3.43 if this would settle the issue once and for all. It would be out-of-line and be above the maximum rates of my operation."

With regard to what D [the superintendent] stated, C [the union president] testified:

He offered $3.43, and said "this is the maximum that the Company could go. This is as high as we can go."

C also testified that the company

might have said, "look to settle this thing, to get it out of the way, we will offer $3.43."

In any event, the union rejected the offer of $3.43, standing pat on its proposal of $3.50. The meeting ended on this basis. At this time, the parties were seven (7) cents apart.

On December 12, 1968, the company posted the job with a top rate of $3.29 per hour. Apparently the company had difficulty in keeping the job postings on its bulletin board. They were removed by some person or persons. The rationale for posting the job at $3.29 per hour was explained by F as follows:

> We were at an impasse. We had to post the job. We posted it at $3.29 on the grounds that is the rate for the Sewer Pipe Gasoline Crane. We felt it was an equitable rate based upon the rate schedule of the Labor Agreement, and what outside firms were paying.

On January 5, 1969, C [the union president] stated to the company that the union would accept $3.43. This was the rate that the company offered in the December 9, 1968, meeting. In this respect, C testified:

> I told the Company we would accept $3.43 to settle the issue to avoid additional trouble.

The company refused the union proposal to accept $3.43 as the rate for the job. Before the union agreed to accept $3.43 on January 5, 1969, the union filed the instant grievance on December 17, 1969, and F testified that the company received a request from the union for the arbitration of the rate on December 29, 1969.

On January 30, 1969, the company posted the job once again with a top rate of $3.29. However, along with this second posting, the company posted another notice the effect of which was to inform the employees that the rate would be arbitrated and that the company agreed to pay the rate established by the arbitrator. In pertinent part this notice states:

> The Company and the Union have now gone thru all steps, except arbitration, provided for in the contract in an attempt to establish a rate of pay for the Travelift Operator Classification.
>
>   Since no agreement has been reached on a rate of pay, the Union has requested this be settled by arbitration. The Company agrees to abide by the arbitrator's decision as stated in Article 15.4 of the contract.

BASIC QUESTION

The basic question to be determined in this arbitration is framed as follows: What should the rate of pay be for the Travelift operator's job?

Thus, the job was posted with a top rate of $3.29. It was filled by S, the successful bidder, and he has held the job since February 26, 1969. The purpose of this arbitration is to determine the rate of the Travelift operator's job. In this respect, the parties agreed that the arbitrator, if he believes it proper, may establish a rate below $4.50, the rate requested by the union in its grievance, and above $3.29, the rate placed on the job by the company. That is, the rate which he will establish need not be either $4.50 or $3.29 per hour. It may fall between these rates. To put it in other terms, the parties by mutual agreement affirmed that the arbitrator is not restricted to establish either $4.50 or $3.29 as the rate for the job. **

PARTIES' ARGUMENTS

In the first place, the union argues that the company demonstrated bad faith under the circumstances of this case. This charge is based upon the company's rejection of the union's proposal to accept $3.43 per hour for the job, the rate which the company offered in the December 9, 1968, meeting. In this regard, union counsel argues:

> The Company showed bad faith and the facts show it. The Company witness testified that $3.43 would have settled this dispute. This was the highest the Company would go. This was a final offer by the Company. We asked to settle at $3.43 and the Company refused. There is no answer for this Company rejection except that it was stubborn. If it believed that $3.29 was the highest rate, why did the Company offer $3.43? Here is bad faith of the worst kind.

Beyond these observations, the union believes that the rate of $3.29 is not proper in terms of comparable jobs and in the light of the rate structure established in the labor agreement. In this regard, union counsel states:

> We offered a rate of $4.50 per hour to avoid intraplant wage inequities between jobs involving large pieces of equipment and comparable skills.

Also, the union directs attention to the rate paid for the operation of the Ross-Carrier, which is another piece of material handling equipment. The operator of the Ross-Carrier is paid $3.39 per hour. Its argument here is that the operation of the Travelift is much more difficult, responsible, and involves a higher order of skills than the Ross-Carrier. Thus, union counsel argues:

> The Travelift operator must have greater skills and responsibility than the operator of the Ross-Carrier.

Also, the union contends that the company purchased a large piece of equipment, the Travelift, to increase its efficiency, but will not pay a proper rate despite the increase in efficiency.

On its part, the company position is that $3.29 is the proper rate for the job, and requests that this rate not be increased in this arbitration. Relative to the union charge of bad faith, the company argues that it did not display bad faith when it rejected the union offer to accept $3.43 as the rate for the job. In this respect, company counsel states:

> We did not demonstrate bad faith. We bargained with the Union. An impasse was reached. We acted in good faith by establishing a rate for the job, recog-

---

** The arbitrator raised this issue in the arbitration, since at times parties in wage rate cases of the kind involved herein restrict an arbitrator to select either the rate proposed by the employer or the union.

nizing that the rate could be arbitrated. We tried to establish a rate in negotiations which was fair, proper, and one which compares equitably for comparable jobs and what other firms are paying. This does not add up to bad faith.

In addition, the company argues that the arbitrator should consider the area rates for the Travelift job; the Travelift operator has a helper and the Ross-Carrier operator does not; the operation of the Ross-Carrier is more difficult, has a greater speed capability, and there is more danger to people and property in the operation of the Ross-Carrier as compared to the Travelift. Moreover, the company avers that the Ross-Carrier is operated over the road and the Travelift is restricted to the company's yard.

Also the company believes that the locomotive crane operator's job is not comparable to that of the Travelift, and that the arbitrator should give controlling weight to the rate paid to the sewer pipe gasoline crane. It also directs attention to the lift truck operator's Over Ten Ton job which pays $2.96.

ANALYSIS OF THE EVIDENCE

Events in the Negotiation of the Rate

At the outset it is necessary to determine whether or not the arbitrator should establish the rate for the job at $3.43 on the grounds that the company offered this rate in the December 9 meeting. At that time the union rejected the offer, but later on agreed to it. The company refused this offer of the union, and on this basis the union charges that the company displayed bad faith.

In short, it is the union's contention that the arbitrator should establish $3.43 as the rate because the company had offered it during the December 9, 1968, meeting. When it refused the union's subsequent acceptance, the union charges bad faith and on these grounds it avers that the arbitrator should determine the rate at $3.43 per hour.

In evaluating this union position, it is clear that the evidence demonstrates that the company made the offer in an effort to settle the grievance so as to avoid arbitration. Even C [the union president] testified that the company in the December 9 session

> might have said, "look to settle this thing, to get it out of the way, we will offer $3.43."

Such a declaration corroborates the unequivocal testimony of F [the industrial relations administrator] who testified:

> We [the Company] would go to $3.43 if this would settle this issue once and for all.

What the evidence demonstrates is that the company made the offer in the effort to settle and compromise the dispute. It was purely and simply a compromise offer. It was made to get the dispute out of the way and to avoid arbitration with its attendant risks, time, and expense.

In this light, what the substantive issue of this feature of the case amounts to is the weight to be given in arbitration to an offer made in the grievance procedure to compromise or settle a dispute. This is not a novel issue. It has been treated frequently in arbitration by professional and experienced arbitrators, including the instant arbitrator. What has been established as a cardinal and uniform rule is that little or no weight is given in arbitration to offers of settlement made in the grievance procedure. The reason for this principle is easy to understand. If arbitrators regarded as binding offers of settlement and compromise in the grievance procedure, this forum could not operate effectively for the settlement of grievances. If either unions or employers feared that an offer of settlement would be binding in arbitration, they would be reluctant to offer compromises in the grievance procedure. Under these circumstances, the grievance procedure could not perform its fundamental function as a method to settle grievances. The result would be constant arbitration to the detriment of all concerned.

Recently in a discharge case handled by the instant arbitrator, the company involved submitted evidence that the union in the grievance procedure proposed that the employee be reinstated without back pay. The company argued that such an offer on the part of the union established the guilt of the employee. The arbitrator refused to accept as conclusive the offer of the union as proof of guilt, and dealt with the case on its merits. He flatly refused to accept the offer made by the union as proof that the employee was guilty of the charge made by the company.

In the instant case, the company attempted to settle and compromise the wage dispute at $3.43. Unless the instant arbitrator desires to depart from an accepted and sensible rule, and by doing so establish a precedent that would tend to make the grievance procedure a sterile device for the settlement of disputes, he cannot find that the offer made by the company is binding upon it, and is the governing factor in this case. In short, this arbitrator refuses to establish a precedent that could conceivably destroy the grievance procedure as an effective forum for the settlement of grievances.

As stated in a standard volume on arbitration:

> Offers of compromise and admissions made in attempting settlement of "rights" disputes prior to submission to arbitration may be received but probably will be given very little, if any, weight by arbitrators. It is recognized that a party to a dispute may make an offer with the hope that a compromise may be reached and the dispute ended. Even the mere introduction of such evidence may impair future attempts at dispute settlement. *

In short, the company made an effort to compromise the dispute. During grievance procedure negotiations, it offered $3.43. The union originally refused the offer. The effort of the company to compromise the differences between the parties failed. Though the union subsequently agreed to the offer, the fact is that before that time the company, aware that its effort to compromise the dispute failed, posted the job in question at $3.29. Under these circumstances, and in line with a sensible principle of the arbitration process, the arbitrator refuses to regard as controlling for his decision the offer of the company to settle the dispute at $3.43 per hour.

Area Rates

Neither does the arbitrator regard as material and governing the evidence introduced by the company establishing area rates for the operation of the Travelift.

---

* Elkouri and Elkouri, *How Arbitration Works*, rev. ed., 1960, p. 195.

480   Fundamentally, the basic issue in this case is to determine a rate of pay for the job which will establish the job in a proper and equitable manner under the wage structure of the instant labor agreement. The rate should place the job in a wage slot that would be realistic and fair in terms of the rates paid for comparable jobs within the bargaining unit of the instant company.

Surely, reference to area rates is not a proper guide to make such a determination. True, the evidence the company submits in this connection establishes that the rates paid for the job by other companies is substantially lower than the rate proposed by the company. Also, the arbitrator notes that the employers cited in the company's evidence are all organized by strong labor unions. However, to rely on this evidence as a guide would not be proper since the rate to be established must be oriented properly to the wage structure established by the instant labor agreement.

In short, the issue in this case is not a determination of a rate which would be comparable to the rates paid within the area, but to establish a rate which would be equitable in terms of comparable jobs within the bargaining unit of the instant company. It is to this task that we now turn our attention.

Evidence Establishing Rates for Comparable Jobs

Before proceeding with the evaluation of the evidence in this portion of the case, the arbitrator will affirm that the establishment of rates for new jobs in arbitration is a very difficult assignment. Regardless of how conscientious an arbitrator is in the evaluation of the evidence, and regardless of his determination to be fair, the fact is that the parties are better equipped to establish a rate than any arbitrator. The establishment of rates for new jobs is best left to the parties. Still, the parties have not agreed upon a rate, and the task has been turned over to this arbitrator. He recognizes that his responsibility is great, since to establish a rate which is too high or too low would have an adverse effect upon the wage structure, and with implications involving earnings of the employees, worker morale, and company costs. In any event, the arbitrator shall do the best he can to evaluate the evidence, and to determine a wage rate for the job which will be sensible and equitable in terms of comparable jobs.

Locomotive Crane

In the grievance the union has requested that the rate for the job should be $4.50 per hour. The basis for this request is that the locomotive crane operator rate is $4.50. In other words, the union's contention is that the Travelift and the locomotive crane operator jobs are comparable for purposes of this case.

In this respect, the arbitrator rejects this union argument as being without merit. In the first place, the locomotive crane is used essentially as a production piece of equipment. It is an integral part of the productive process. In contrast, the Travelift is used strictly as a material handling piece of equipment. In the second place, the jobs are not comparable in terms of skill, responsibility, and possibility of damage to persons and property. In the third place, the facts demonstrate that an employee can operate the Travelift in a reasonably efficient manner after about a 30 day training period. This was established by both company and union witnesses. On the other hand, the evidence shows that employees assigned to the locomotive crane will be given up to a six month training program. Certainly, jobs are not comparable in terms of skill, responsibility, and complexity if one calls for a training program of about 30 days and the other requires a training program of up to six months. In short, the arbitrator finds that the Travelift and the locomotive crane operator jobs are not comparable for purposes of the establishment of a rate of pay for the Travelift job.

The Sewer Pipe Gasoline Crane

The sewer pipe gasoline crane pays $3.29 per hour, and that is exactly the rate which the company established for the Travelift job. It would appear that the company argues that these two jobs are so comparable in character that they should be paid at the same rate. There is an important defect in the company's argument herein considered. It is that the sewer pipe gasoline crane is not a piece of material handling equipment as compared with the Travelift. As the evidence demonstrates, the crane is used directly in the productive process of sewer pipe. In fact, as one company witness testified, the crane "paces the work" of the production workers involved in the manufacture of sewer pipe. Like the locomotive crane, the sewer pipe gasoline crane, therefore, is an integral part of the productive process. In effect, it is a production piece of equipment, whereas the Travelift is strictly a material handling piece of equipment. The Travelift is not used directly in the manufacture of the products of the company. True, the sewer pipe gasoline crane handles material. It lifts sewer pipe out of the forms, and places the pipe on the ground at designated locations. However, the pipe could not effectively be manufactured without the use of the crane. From this point of view, it is production equipment, and not a piece of material handling equipment like the Travelift.

It is stressed that the task before the arbitrator is to establish a rate for the Travelift in terms of comparable jobs. He believes that the comparison between the Travelift and the sewer pipe gasoline crane or the locomotive crane would not be proper because the essence of these jobs is not the same. The Travelift is used strictly as a piece of material handling equipment. Therefore, the proper comparison should not involve equipment which plays an integral part in the manufacture of products, but with jobs which are exclusively involved in material handling. In all candor, the arbitrator believes that he would undermine the wage structure of the labor agreement if he used as the basis for his decision a comparison of jobs which are unlike in terms of fundamental functional purposes.

Lift Truck, Over Ten Ton

As established in the wage structure, the operator of the lift truck, Over Ten Ton, is paid $2.96. Unlike the sewer pipe gasoline crane, and similar to the Travelift, the lift truck is a piece of material handling equipment. Like the Travelift it is operated in the yard, and performs the same basic function as the Travelift. In fact, it handles some of the same material handled by the Travelift. What is more, the skill and the responsibilities of the Travelift and lift truck operators are somewhat comparable in terms of difficulty and complexity. So here we have a valid basis of comparison for the establishment of the of the rate of the Travelift job.

However, the spread between the company's position of $3.29 for the Travelift and the rate of $2.96 established in the wage structure for the lift truck is so substantial that the comparison of these jobs does not constitute a valid basis for the establishment of the rate for the Travelift job. If the company believed that the two jobs are so comparable in terms of skill, responsibility, and complexity, it surely would not have placed a $3.29 rate on the Travelift job. Company counsel stated that the rate for the Travelift job should be "somewhat higher" than that of the lift truck operator's job. However, since the spread between the rate of the lift truck operator's job at $2.96 and the company's established rate of $3.29 for the Travelift job is so great, a comparison between the jobs for purposes of the case would be far too nebulous in character as a valid basis for wage determination.

Ross-Carrier

If one thing is made clear from the evidence, and as physical inspection by the arbitrator demonstrated, it is that the realistic basis for comparison is between the Ross-Carrier and the Travelift. As *H*, the plant manager, testified:

> The skill levels are somewhat parallel for the Ross-Carrier and the Travelift. The skill levels of the Ross-Carrier would be closer to that of the Travelift.

Here we have two pieces of material handling equipment which perform the same function. Indeed, as company witness *D* declared: "The Travelift will phase out the Ross-Carrier."

In all candor, the arbitrator believes that the rate of the Travelift should be established in and around the rate of the Ross-Carrier which is established at $3.39 per hour. This certainly would be a rate which would be within the "ball park."

In the evaluation of the evidence dealing with the Travelift and the Ross-Carrier, there are some major reasons to establish a rate for the Travelift which would be the same as the Ross-Carrier, or somewhat below this figure. The Ross-Carrier operator works without a helper, and the Travelift operator has a helper. Without a helper, the Ross-Carrier operator must from time to time climb down from his cab to secure and disengage hooks. This task is performed by the helper assigned to the Travelift. The operator does not have the inconvenience and need not engage in the physical discomfort of climbing in and out of his cab to perform this duty. Also the helper is available to guide the operator of the Travelift as he moves his equipment. In contrast, the Ross-Carrier operator is on his own, and must use his judgment and discretion as he moves around the yard to avoid injury to persons and damage to property.

In the second place, the Ross-Carrier can operate at about 12–15 miles per hour (or faster, as the arbitrator and the parties noted during the lunch break!), while the Travelift rate of speed is only about 4 miles per hour. With comparatively greater speed, it follows that the Ross-Carrier operator must be more careful to avoid injury to persons and damage to property. In the third place, the Ross-Carrier may operate over the road. This capability is not within the scope of the Travelift. *M*, vice president of the union, testified that from time to time

> the Ross-Carrier moves material to the dump from the yard. It goes on the street —one long block—a quarter of a mile distance.

In this respect, the Ross-Carrier operator has the responsibility to avoid injury to persons and damage to property when he takes his equipment down the street.

In addition, there is the danger that the Ross-Carrier may topple if loads are not
properly centered on the runners, or if for some reason the operator hauls a load
beyond the weight capability of the equipment. In comparison, the Travelift straddles
the products and it would be impossible to topple the equipment.

As against these considerations, the evidence demonstrates that there are important reasons to establish a rate for the Travelift job which would be equal to that
paid to the Ross-Carrier operator, or a rate which would be somewhat higher. Important in this respect is that the Travelift operates on two planes—it lifts and lowers
material and moves the products suspended on chains from right to left. These
movements may be performed simultaneously by the operator in accordance with
job needs. In contrast, the Ross-Carrier operates on one phase—it only lifts and
lowers.

In addition, the Travelift operator has one important task which is not required
of the Ross-Carrier operator. Note that the two chains of the Travelift which are
separated quite a distance apart are attached to the products being handled. The
operator must make sure that these two chains are kept at the same level or the
material being handled can fracture. As M testified:

> When I assembled the Travelift, I spoke to the factory [D] representative. He
> said that both hooks [one attached to each chain] had to be operated simultane-
> ously or the product can fracture.

No such problem exists for the operator of the Ross-Carrier. He simply places his
runners under the banks upon which the product rests and lifts the banks and the
product. In short, the Travelift operator must perform a task which the Ross-Carrier
operator does not. He must make sure that the chains are in balance to avoid the
fracture of the product being handled. Here is a task which requires judgment, discrimination, and coordination.

Though the arbitrator agrees fully with company counsel that the amount of
weight lifted does not require any additional effort on the part of the operator, it is
material that the Travelift has a load capacity of 25 tons while the Ross-Carrier has
a load capacity of 15 tons. True, as company counsel states, it is the machine that
lifts the weight, and not the operator. In either case, "he just presses a button" to
activate the lifting mechanism. From this point of view, it would not be proper to
base a wage rate on the comparative weight lifting capacity of the Ross-Carrier and
the Travelift.

On the other hand, the fact is that the Travelift operator is responsible for the
handling of heavier and proportionately more expensive loads. The company would
probably suffer a greater loss if the Travelift operator damaged a product weighing
25 tons as compared to damage to a product weighing 15 tons.
[If you are doing the Experiential Exercise for Chapter 16, please do *not* read beyond
this point until after you have finished your group deliberations of the questions
presented in the Experiential Exercise.]

ANSWER

After careful reflection of the evidence dealing with the operation of the Travelift
and the Ross-Carier, the arbitrator is of the judgment that the operation of the
Travelift is somewhat a more responsible job in terms of skill, dexterity, coordination,

judgment, and possible damage to products. In this light, it is the conclusion of the arbitrator that the rate for the Travelift should be established at $3.41 per hour. This, of course, is the arbitrator's judgment, and in cases of this sort everyone concerned with the case could have a different judgment. That is why an arbitrator is placed in a vulnerable and unenviable position in rate setting cases.

In any event, the arbitrator has been faithful to the evidence the best he could, and believes that the rate which he has set places the Travelift job in an equitable, fair, and realistic place in the wage structure of the bargaining unit in terms of comparable jobs.

QUESTIONS

1. Why did the arbitrator refuse to settle this case at the rate of $3.43, the rate which the company at one time offered?
2. Do you believe that the arbitrator was justified in refusing to use area rates as a guide for his decision?
3. Do you think that—following their experience in this arbitration—the parties will be more or less inclined to settle rate cases by themselves without resort to arbitration?
4. Also, see the questions in the Experiential Exercise below.

EXPERIENTIAL EXERCISE

Purpose.   The purposes of this exercise are to:

1. Provide you with some experience in analyzing and handling an actual grievance.
2. Review the impact of collective bargaining on the job evaluation process.

Required Understanding.   Students should be thoroughly familiar with the case at the end of this chapter entitled "Wage Rate for a New Job—Job Comparison." However *do not read the "conclusion" to the case until after the groups have completed their deliberations.*

How to Set Up the Exercise/Instructions.   Divide the class into groups of four or five students. The group should take the arbitrator's point of view and assume that they are to analyze the case and make the arbitrator's decision. Review the case again at this point but please do not read the conclusion.

Each group should answer the following questions:

1. What would your decision be if you were the arbitrator? Why? What did you think of his "job evaluation?"
2. Do you think that—following their experience in this arbitration—the parties will be more or less inclined to settle rate cases by themselves without resorting to arbitration?
3. What does this case tell you about the impact collective bargaining has on personnel management activities like job evaluation?
4. Please do not read the following questions until *after* you have *finished* deliberation on the first three questions:

   a. Why did the arbitrator refuse to settle this case at the rate of $3.43, the rate which the company at one time offered? b. Do you believe that the arbitrator

was justified in refusing to use area rates as a guide for his decision? Why?
Why not?

DISCUSSION QUESTIONS

1. Explain the structure and purpose of the AFL-CIO.
2. Discuss five "sure ways" to lose an NLRB election.
3. Give some examples of what to expect during a union drive and election.
4. Discuss what you as a supervisor should keep in mind about labor relations during the union drive and election.
5. What is meant by "good faith" bargaining? Give some examples of bargaining that is *not* in good faith.
6. You are the president of a small (30 employee) firm and while you are not unionized you would like to have an appeals process that would serve a purpose similar to that of a grievance procedure. Discuss what this appeals process might contain.

NOTES

1. Parts of this section based on: Paul A. Samuelson, *Economics* (New York: McGraw-Hill, 1967), Ch. 7; Yoder, *Personnel Management and Industrial Relations*, Ch. 16; Sloane and Witney, *Labor Relations* (Englewood Cliffs, N.J.: Prentice-Hall, 1977); Leonard Sayles and George Strauss, *Managing Human Resources* (Englewood Cliffs, N.J.: Prentice-Hall, 1977), Ch. 7; Edwin Beal, Edward Wickersham, and Philip Kienast, *The Practice of Collective Bargaining* (Homewood, Ill.: Irwin, 1976), Ch. 2; Gordon Bloom and Herbert Northrup, *Economics of Labor Relations* (Homewood, Ill.: Irwin, 1977), Ch. 2: Dennis Chamot, "Professional Employees Turn to Unions," *Harvard Business Review*, Vol. 54, No. 3 (May–June 1976). Also see Bernard Bass and Charles Mitchell, "Influences on the Felt Need for Collective Bargaining in Business and Science Professionals," *Journal of Applied Psychology*, Vol. 61, No. 6 (December 1976), pp. 770–772; Harold W. Davey, *Contemporary Collective Bargaining* (Englewood Cliffs, N.J.: Prentice-Hall, 1972), pp. 342–360.
2. "American Union Busting," *The Economist* (November 19, 1979), pp. 39–50.
3. See Robert Schrank, "Are Unions An Anachronism?" *Harvard Business Review*, Vol. 57 (September–October 1979), pp. 107–115.
4. Warner Pflug, *The UAW in Pictures* (Detroit: Wayne State University Press, 1971), pp. 11–12.
5. W. Clay Hamner and Frank Smith, "Work Attitudes as Predictors of Unionization Activity," *Journal of Applied Psychology*, Vol. 63, No. 4 (1978), pp. 415–421.
6. William Bigoness, "Correlates of Faculty Attitudes Toward Collective Bargaining," *Journal of Applied Psychology*, Vol. 63, No. 2 (1978), pp. 228–233.
7. Chester Schriesheim, "Job Satisfaction, Attitudes Towards Unions, and Voting in a Union Representation Election," *Journal of Applied Psychology*, Vol. 63, No. 5 (1978), p. 550.
8. William Giles and William Holley, Jr., "Job Enrichment Versus Traditional Issues at the Bargaining Table: What Union Members Want," *Academy of Management Journal*, Vol. 21, No. 4 (Dec. 1978), pp. 725–730.
9. These are based on Richard Hodgetts, *Introduction to Business* (Reading, Mass.: Addison-Wesley, 1977), pp. 213–214.

486

10. Based in part on "This Is the AFL-CIO," a publication of the American Federation of Labor and Congress of Industrial Organizations #20, January 1976.

11. Boardroom Reports, The Conference Board, December 15, 1976, p. 6.

12. Based on Arthur A. Sloane and Fred Witney, *Labor Relations*, Ch. 3; see also Harold W. Davey, *Contemporary Collective Bargaining*, Chs. 2 and 3; Dale Yoder, *Personnel Management*, Ch. 17.

13. The following material is based on Sloane and Witney, *Labor Relations*, p. 137.

14. *Ibid.*, p. 106.

15. *Ibid.*, p. 121.

16. R. Heath Larry, "Labor Power: Myth or Reality?," *MSU Business Topics* (Winter 1978), pp. 20–24.

17. Quoted from D. Quinn Mills, "Flawed Victory in Labor Law Reform," *Harvard Business Review*, Vol. 57 (May–June 1979), pp. 92–102. The law also proposed to increase the size of the NLRB from 5 to 7 members, and to permit the board to speed its processes of review of decisions by administrative law judges.

18. See William F. Glueck, "Labor Relations and the Supervisor," in M. Jean Newport, *Supervisory Management: Tools and Techniques* (St. Paul: West, 1976), pp. 207–234.

19. French, *The Personnel Management Process*, p. 579.

20. Based on Matthew Goodfellow, "How to Lose an NLRB Election," *The Personnel Administrator* (September 1976), pp. 40–44.

21. This is one reason why the use of consultants in this area is increasing. See, for example, "American Union Busting," *The Economist* (November 17, 1979), pp. 39–50.

22. Frederick Sullivan, "Limiting Union Organizing Activity through Supervisors," *Personnel* (July–August 1978), pp. 55–65.

23. *Ibid.*, p. 60.

24. *Ibid.*, pp. 62–65.

25. *Ibid.*, pp. 64–65. The appropriateness of these sample rules may be affected by factors unique to an employer's operation, and they should therefore be reviewed by the employer's attorney before implementation.

26. *Ibid.*, p. 60.

27. For a discussion of this see James Rand, "Preventive-Maintenance Techniques for Staying Union-Free," *Personnel Journal* (June 1980), pp. 497–508.

28. Dale Yoder, *Personnel Management*, p. 486.

29. Quoted in Richardson, *Collective Bargaining by Objectives*; adapted from Charles Morris, ed., *The Developing Labor Law* (Washington, D.C.: Bureau of National Affairs, Inc., 1971), pp. 271–310.

30. Harold Davey, *Contemporary Collective Bargaining* (Englewood Cliffs, N.J.: Prentice-Hall, Inc., 1972), p. 121.

31. Bargaining items based on Richardson, *Collective Bargaining*, pp. 113–115; bargaining stages based on William Glueck, "Labor Relations and the Supervisor."

32. See also Dale Yoder, *Personnel Management*, pp. 517–518.

33. Reed Richardson, *Collective Bargaining by Objectives*, p. 150.

34. Dale Beach, *Personnel* (New York: Macmillan, 1975), pp. 117–119.

35. "American Union Busting," *The Economist* (November 17, 1979), p. 50.

36. William Fulmer, "When Employees Want to Oust Their Union," *Harvard Business Review*, Vol. 56 (March–April 1978), pp. 163–170.

37. *Ibid.*, p. 167.

38. *The Economist* (November 17, 1979), p. 50.

39. *Ibid.*

40. Fulmer, p. 168.

41. Sloane and Witney, *Labor Relations,* pp. 218–219.

42. Richardson, *Collective Bargaining,* p. 184.

43. Bittel, *What Every Supervisor Should Know,* p. 308, based on a study of 1,000 grievances made by the American Arbitration Association.

44. Reed Richardson, *Collective Bargaining by Objectives.*

45. J. Brad Chapman, "Constructive Grievance Handling," in M. Jean Newport, *Supervisory Management* (St. Paul, Minn.: West, 1976), pp. 253–274.

46. Quoted from Sloane and Witney, *Labor Relations,* pp. 219–221.

47. *Ibid.,* p. 221.

48. See, for example Clyde Summers, "Protecting all Employees Against Unjust Dismissal," *Harvard Business Review,* Vol. 58 (January–February 1980), pp. 132–139.

49. Chapman, "Constructive Grievance Handling," p. 253.

50. Thomasine Rendero, "Grievance Procedures for Nonunionized Employees," *Personnel,* (Jan.–Feb. 1980), pp. 4–10.

51. Rendero, p. 7.

52. Summers.

53. *Ibid.,* pp. 264–266.

54. *Ibid.,* p. 273, for an excellent checklist.

55. For a full discussion of these and others see Walter Baer, *Grievance Handling: 101 Guides for Supervisors.* (New York: American Management Association, 1970).

56. See Samuelson, *Economics,* pp. 132–133.

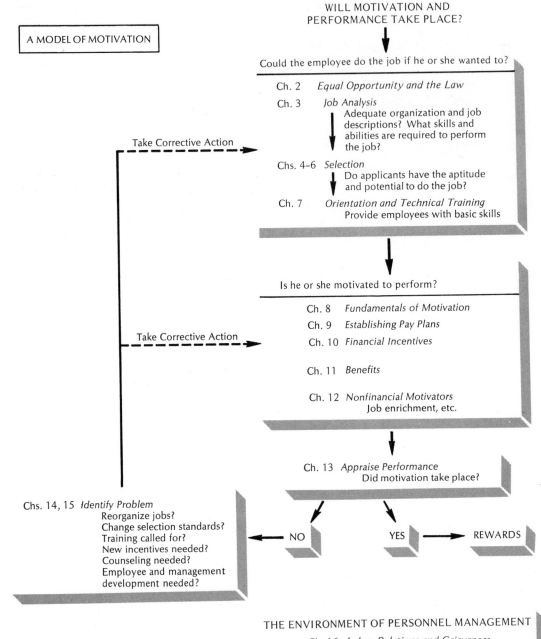

A MODEL OF MOTIVATION

WILL MOTIVATION AND
PERFORMANCE TAKE PLACE?

Could the employee do the job if he or she wanted to?

Ch. 2 *Equal Opportunity and the Law*

Ch. 3 *Job Analysis*
Adequate organization and job descriptions? What skills and abilities are required to perform the job?

Chs. 4–6 *Selection*
Do applicants have the aptitude and potential to do the job?

Ch. 7 *Orientation and Technical Training*
Provide employees with basic skills

Take Corrective Action

Is he or she motivated to perform?

Ch. 8 *Fundamentals of Motivation*

Ch. 9 *Establishing Pay Plans*

Ch. 10 *Financial Incentives*

Ch. 11 *Benefits*

Ch. 12 *Nonfinancial Motivators*
Job enrichment, etc.

Take Corrective Action

Ch. 13 *Appraise Performance*
Did motivation take place?

Chs. 14, 15 *Identify Problem*
Reorganize jobs?
Change selection standards?
Training called for?
New incentives needed?
Counseling needed?
Employee and management development needed?

NO   YES ▶ REWARDS

THE ENVIRONMENT OF PERSONNEL MANAGEMENT

Ch. 16 *Labor Relations and Grievances*

Ch. 17 *Employee Safety and Health*

Ch. 18 *Personnel Management and the Quality of Work Life*

When you finish studying

17 Employee Safety and Health

You should be able to:

1. *Provide a safer environment for employees.*
2. *Minimize the occurrence of unsafe acts on the part of employees.*
3. *Explain the "basic facts" about OSHA—its purpose, standards, inspection, and rights and responsibilities.*
4. *Explain the supervisor's role in safety.*
5. *Compare and contrast unsafe acts and unsafe conditions.*
6. *Explain what causes "unsafe acts."*
7. *Answer the question: "Is there such a thing as 'accident prone' people?"*
8. *Describe at least five techniques for reducing accidents.*
9. *Discuss four important occupational health problems, and how they are dealt with.*

OVERVIEW

The main purpose of this chapter is to present the basic knowledge needed to deal effectively with employee safety and health problems at work. Today every manager needs a working knowledge of OSHA—the Occupational Safety and Health Act,—and so we discuss it at some length. Specifically, we review its purpose, standards, and inspection procedures as well as the rights and responsibilities of employees and employers under OSHA. Early in the chapter we also stress the importance of the supervisor in safety, and stress the importance of obtaining top management's commitment to organization-wide safety.

There are three basic causes of accidents—chance occurrences, unsafe conditions, and unsafe acts,—and we explain the latter two in some detail, as well as how to deal with them. We will see that unsafe acts are caused by people, and that certain personality traits may underlie the "accident prone" employee. We discuss several specific techniques for preventing accidents, and finally discuss four important employee health problems: alcoholism, drug addiction, emotional illness, and stress.

WHY "EMPLOYEE SAFETY AND HEALTH" IS IMPORTANT

The subject of safety and accident prevention is of concern to managers for several reasons. For one thing the figures concerning work-related accidents are staggering. The National Safety Council reports, for example, that for a recent year there were over 14,000 deaths and almost 2½ million injuries resulting from accidents at work. Many safety experts feel that these figures seriously underestimate the actual number of injuries: The U.S. Public Health Service, for the same period, reports almost 8½ million injuries. And even this latter figure does not include injuries that did not restrict the injured person's activities, or for which he received no medical attention. [1]

But these figures hardly tell the full story. They do not reflect the human suffering incurred by the injured workers and their families. They do not reflect the economic costs incurred by these people's employers—costs for things like time off, insurance, and medical payments. Nor do they reflect the legal implications of the problem—like the managers who were sued or imprisoned for failing to ensure safe work places.

Three Reasons for Safety Programs

One safety expert says that safety programs are undertaken for three fundamental reasons: moral, legal, and economic.

Moral.   First, managers undertake accident prevention on purely humane grounds. They do so to minimize the pain and suffering the injured worker and his family are often exposed to as the result of an accident.

Legal.   There are also legal reasons for undertaking a safety program. Today, there are federal, state, and municipal laws covering occupational safety and health, and penalties for noncompliance have become quite severe. Organizations are subject to fines and supervisors can (and have) received jail sentences if found responsible for fatal accidents. In 1971, for example, there was a tunnel disaster outside Los Angeles, California. The company building the tunnel was found guilty of 16 counts of gross negligence and fined $205,000. The project manager on the job was found guilty of 16 counts of gross negligence and was sentenced to five years in jail and ten years probation. [2]

Economic.   Finally, there are economic reasons for being safety-conscious, since the cost to the company for even a small accident can be quite high. Workers' compensation insurance simply compensates the injured worker for his or her injury. It does *not* cover the other direct and indirect costs associated with that injury. For example, Bittell estimates that for an accident that comes to $600 for compensation, a company pays another $2,000 for related expenses. These related expenses cover things like lost time for employees who stop to watch or assist; supervisor's lost time; and changing production schedules. He presents the following example to illustrate his point: [3]

A chemical workman was scalded when a kettle of hot dye slipped from a sling while he was pouring it into a vat: here are what the costs came to:

Compensation paid for burns	$400 491
Medical expense, including first aid	$180
Total "compensation" costs	$580

Time lost away from job:

Injured worker's make-up pay while home 3½ days	$ 90
Follow-up medical visits	$210
Fellow workmen standing by watching at time of accident	$220
Supervisor's time recording, etc.	$120
Total cost of time lost	$640

Production loss:

Downtime on dye operation	$160
Slowed-up production rate of other workers	$ 80
Materials spoiled and labor for cleaning it up	$140
Damage to equipment	$290
Total production and related costs	$670

Total cost of accident (not including overhead which could raise total as much as 50%)	$1,890

BASIC FACTS ABOUT OSHA— THE OCCUPATIONAL SAFETY AND HEALTH ACT[4]

Purpose

The Occupational Safety and Health Act was passed by congress in 1970; its purpose, as stated by congress was ". . . to assure so far as possible every working man and woman in the nation safe and healthful working conditions and to preserve our human resources." In general, the act covers all employers and their employees in the 50 states, the District of Columbia, Puerto Rico, the Canal Zone and all other territories under federal government jurisdiction. The only employers not covered under the act are self-employed persons, farms in which only immediate members of the farm employer's family are employed, and certain work places which are already protected by other federal agencies or under other statutes. Federal agencies are covered by the act, although in most cases provisions of the act do not apply to state and local governments in their role as employers.

Under the provisions of the act, the occupational safety and health administration (OSHA) was created within the department of labor. The basic purpose of OSHA is to set safety and health standards, standards which apply to almost all workers in the United States. The standards are enforced through the department of labor, and to ensure compliance, OSHA has inspectors working out of branch offices throughout the country.

OSHA Standards

The basic "general" standard under which OSHA operates states that each employer:

> . . . shall furnish to each of his employees employment and a place of employment which are free from recognized hazards that are causing or are likely to cause death or serious physical harm to his employees.

In carrying out this basic mission, OSHA is responsible for promulgating legally enforceable standards. The standards themselves are contained in five volumes covering: general industry standards, maritime standards, construction standards, other regulations and procedures, and a field operations manual.

The standards are extremely complete and seem to cover just about any hazard one could think of in great detail. The volume containing general industry standards, for example sets detailed standards for 17 separate areas as follows:

Walking-working surfaces	Compressed gas and compressed air
Means of egress	equipment
Powered platforms, man lifts, and vehicle-mounted work platforms	Materials handling and storage
	Machinery and machine guarding
Occupational health and environmental control (ventilation, etc.)	Hand and portable powered tools and other hand-held equipment
Hazardous materials	Welding, cutting, and braising
Personal protective equipment	Special industries (textiles, etc.)
General environmental controls (sanitation, etc.)	Electrical
	Toxic and hazardous substances
Medical and first aid	
Fire protection	

The standards themselves, as mentioned above are presented in considerable detail. For example, a small part of the standard governing scaffolds is presented in Exhibit 17.1:

Exhibit 17.1 OSHA Standards Example

Guardrails not less than 2" × 4" or the equivalent and not less than 36" or more than 42" high, with a midrail, when required, of a 1" × 4" lumber or equivalent, and tow boards, shall be installed at all open sides on all scaffolds more than 10 feet above the ground floor. Tow boards shall be a minimum of 4" in height. Wire mesh shall be installed in accordance with (a) (17) of this section.

Source: General Industries Standards, U.S. Department of Labor, OSHA (Revised November 7, 1978) p. 36.

OSHA Record-Keeping Procedures

Under OSHA, employers with 11 or more employees must maintain records of occupational injuries and illnesses as they occur. (Employers having 10 or fewer employees are now exempt from record keeping unless they are selected to participate in the annual statistical survey carried out by the Bureau of Labor Statistics, a move aimed at simplifying OSHA compliance for small businesses.)

Both occupational injuries, and occupational illnesses must be reported. An occupational illness is any abnormal condition or disorder caused by exposure to environmental factors associated with employment. Included here are acute and chronic illnesses which may be caused by inhalation, absorption, ingestion or direct contact with toxic substances or harmful agents. *All* occupational illnesses must be reported. [5] Similarly, *most* occupational injuries also must be reported. Specifically, all occupational injuries must be recorded if they result in medical treatment (other than first aid), loss of consciousness, restriction of work (one or more lost work days), restriction of motion, or transfer to another job. [6] If an on-the-job accident occurs which results in the death of an employee or in the hospitalization of 5 or more employees, all employers, regardless of size, are required to report the accident, in detail, to the nearest OSHA office.

Inspections and Citations

OSHA standards are enforced through a series of inspections and citations. Every employer covered by the act is subject to inspection by OSHA compliance officers who are authorized to "enter without delay and at reasonable times any factory, plant, establishment . . . where work is performed . . . ," and to "inspect and investigate during regular working hours, and at other reasonable times, . . . any such place of employment and all pertinent conditions, structures, machines, . . . and to question privately any such employer, owner, operator, agent or employee." [7] However, based on a 1978 Supreme Court ruling (*Marshall* versus *Barlow's, Inc.*), OSHA may no longer conduct warrantless inspections without an employer's consent. It may, however, inspect after acquiring a judicially authorized search warrant or its equivalent. [8]

Inspection Priorities. To determine which employers to visit OSHA has established a list of inspection priorities ranging from "imminent danger," to "random inspections." Imminent danger situations are given top priority. This is a condition where it is likely a danger exists that can cause death or serious physical harm immediately. Second priority is given to investigation of catastrophies, fatalities, and accidents that have already occurred. (Such situations must be reported to OSHA within 48 hours.) Third priority is given to valid employee complaints of alleged violation of standards. Next in priority are periodic "high-hazard" inspections: These are aimed at high-hazard industries, occupations, or health substances. Finally, random inspections (and reinspections) generally have last priority.

Under a new inspection policy instituted September 1, 1979 OSHA no longer follows up on *every* employee complaint with an inspection, as they previously did. The enforcement thrust now is to focus attention on priority problems in order to make the agency's inspection program more productive. [9] Under the new priority system, OSHA will conduct an inspection within 24

494   hours when a complaint indicates an immediate danger, and within 3 working days when a "serious hazard" exists. For a "non-serious" complaint filed in writing by a worker or a union OSHA will respond within 20 working days. Otherwise, "non-serious" complaints are now handled by writing to the companies involved and requesting corrective action. This shift to "high priority" inspections is at least partly a result of restrictions placed on OSHA inspections by Congress and the courts: the need to obtain warrants, and to exempt firms having 10 or fewer employees and good safety records from safety inspections are some examples of these restrictions.

The Inspection Itself.   Before an inspection, the OSHA inspector becomes familiar with as many relevant facts as possible about the workplace. [10] The inspection itself begins when the OSHA officer arrives at the place of work. He or she displays official credentials and asks to meet an appropriate employer representative. (Always insist upon seeing the officer's credentials, which include photograph and serial number.) The officer explains the purpose of the visit, the scope of the inspection, and the standards that apply. An authorized *employee* representative is also given an opportunity to accompany the officer during the inspection. Other employees will also be consulted during the inspection tour, and the inspector can stop and question workers (in private if necessary) about safety and health conditions. Each employee is protected, under the act, from discrimination for exercising his or her disclosure rights.

Finally (after checking the premises and employer's records) a closing conference is held between the inspector and the employer (or his representative). Here the inspector discusses with the employer what has been found in terms of all apparent violations for which a citation may be issued or recommended. Note that the inspector does *not* indicate any proposed penalties: only the OSHA area director has that authority. At this point the employer can produce records to show compliance efforts.

Citations and Penalties.   After the inspection report is submitted to the OSHA office, the area director determines what citations, if any, will be issued. The citations inform the employer and employees of the regulations and standards that have been violated, and of the time set for rectifying the problem: These citations must be posted at or near the place the violation occurred. Under some circumstances the inspector can post a citation immediately. (This is to ensure that employees receive protection in the shortest possible time.)

The area director can also propose penalties. These range up to $1,000 for serious violations, and up to $10,000 and six months in jail for falsifying records or reports. Any employer who willfully or repeatedly violates the act can be fined up to $10,000 for each such violation.

While such penalties may seem substantial many believe the penalty is not effective, for two reasons. First, in large companies penalties of even $10,000 "are a joke" according to one OSHA representative. [11] The second problem is the built-in appeals process. Under the act an employer can appeal the penalty through the independent Occupational Safety and Health Review Commission and thus "buy" an extension. The review process normally lasts about 3 years and during this period the employer is not required to correct a violation, and OSHA cannot enforce the standard unless there is some imminent danger: "As a result, more than 40% of the serious-hazard citations OSHA issues are challenged." [12]

The Responsibilities and Rights of Employers and Employees

Both employers and employees have certain responsibilities and rights under the Occupational Safety and Health Act. Employers, for example are responsible: for meeting their general duty to provide "a work place free from recognized hazards"; for being familiar with mandatory OSHA standards; for informing all employees about OSHA; and for examining work place conditions to make sure they conform to applicable standards. Employers have the right: to seek advice and off-site consultation from OSHA; to request and to receive proper identification of the OSHA compliance officer before inspection; to be advised by the compliance officer of the reason for an inspection; and to file a "notice of contest" with the OSHA area director within 15 working days of receipt of a notice of citation and proposed penalty. Furthermore, employers have the right to apply for a temporary or permanent variance on a standard, and to be assured of the confidentiality of any trade secrets observed by an OSHA compliance officer during an inspection.

Employees also have certain rights and responsibilities, although employees cannot be cited for violations of their responsibilities. They are responsible, for example: for complying with all applicable OSHA standards; for following all employer safety and health rules and regulations; for reporting hazardous conditions to the supervisor; and for reporting job related injury or illness to the employer. Employees have a right to demand safety and health on the job without fear of punishment, and employers are specifically forbidden to punish or discriminate against workers for exercising rights such as complaining to an employer, union, or OSHA about job safety and health hazards.

Dealing with Employee Resistance.   While employees have a responsibility to comply with OSHA standards the fact is they often resist complying, and in most such cases the *employer* remains liable for the penalties. [13] The problem of employee resistance is typified by the general refusal of longshoremen to wear hardhats as mandated by the OSHA requirements. Historically, longshoremen have resisted wearing hardhats and their resistance did not cease with the advent of OSHA. Employers have attempted to defend themselves against penalties for such noncompliance by citing worker intransigence, and employer fear of wildcat strikes and walkouts; yet in most cases courts have held that employers were liable for safety violations at the work place regardless of the fact that the violations were due to employee resistance. [14] The result is that the employer is often in a difficult position: on the one hand, the courts and the occupational safety and health review commission have held that employers must vigorously seek employee compliance; yet on the other hand doing so is often all but impossible.

There are several tactics an employer can use to overcome this problem. [15] First, the courts have held that an employer can bargain in good faith with representatives of its employees for the right to discharge or discipline any employee who disobeys an OSHA standard. Yet from a practical point of view unions have thus far refused to bargain over hardhats (and many other OSHA issues) because they oppose having penalties assessed against their members for noncompliance. As a second alternative, one expert suggests greater use of arbitration in safety disputes. Arbitration is, of course, already widely used to resolve employee grievances, and the use of a formal arbitration process by aggrieved employers could provide a relatively quick and inexpensive method for resolving an OSHA-related complaint. As discussed at a later point in this chapter some employers have also turned to incentive plans and training for the purpose of gaining employee compliance.

The Changing Nature of OSHA

The Occupational Safety and Health Act and administration have both been criticized on many grounds, and at any point in time it is not unusual for the United States Congress to have over 100 OSHA reform bills on its agenda. [16] Critics have argued, for example that too many of OSHA's rules are "nit-picking"; that OSHA has had an overly adverse affect on very small businesses (for whom the penalties are, relatively, more difficult to bear); and that its emphasis on complying with standards has been ineffective, (instead, one critic argues the emphasis should be on performance—on number of accidents and illnesses reduced—rather than on dictating the specific means for doing so). [17]

In response to these sorts of criticisms (and in response to various court decisions) OSHA has made a number of changes in its policies and procedures over the last few years. Small businesses with 10 or less employees no longer have to file accident reports or undergo routine inspections, and the accident report itself has been simplified and condensed. [18] As mentioned above, OSHA inspectors must also now obtain warrants before entering an employer's premises.

Other changes have taken place as well. Although its safety inspectors still number about 1,000, it has increased its health inspectors from about 135 in 1976 to about 600 today, reflecting a shift in the agency's efforts toward emphasizing reduction of occupational illnesses. Training of safety inspectors has also been beefed up. Furthermore, OSHA has eliminated about 1,000 of its more "nit-picking" standards, and has begun to focus its enforcement activities on industries with high injury rates. Generally speaking businessmen seem to feel that OSHA has become less "heavy handed" than it has been in the past, and better trained and more professional. And, its new emphasis on health (on occupation-related illnesses) has done much to raise OSHA's credibility. Yet an attorney with the U.S. Chamber of Commerce still argues that many of OSHA's

changes have been more "public relations than substance," and that nuisance
inspections, inspection of firms with good safety records, and hostility toward
business remain. OSHA, therefore continues to be a controversial approach to
improving occupational safety and health. [19]

THE SUPERVISOR'S ROLE IN SAFETY

As a safety-minded manager or employer, your basic aim must be *to instill
in your workers the desire to work safely*. Minimizing hazards (by ensuring that
spills are wiped up, machine guards are adequate, and so forth) is important,
but no matter how safe the workplace is, there will be accidents unless workers
want to act safely, and do. Of course, you could try closely watching each subordinate, but most managers know this won't work. In the final analysis the
best (and perhaps only) alternative is to instill in workers the desire to work
safely. Then, where needed, enforce the safety rules. [20]

Top Management Commitment

Most safety experts agree that this "worker commitment" to safety has to
begin with top management. And the fact is that companies that do have this
safety-commitment have much better safety records than those who do not.
Historically, for example, DuPont Chemical's accident rate has been much
lower than that of the chemical industry as a whole. (In one recent year, it was
one twentieth of the average, according to one report.) And, it seems likely that
this good safety record is at least partly due to an organizational commitment
to safety, a commitment that is evident in the following description: [21]

> One of the best examples I know of in setting the highest possible priority
> for safety takes place at a DuPont Plant in Germany. Each morning at the
> DuPont Polyester and Nylon Plant the director and his assistants meet at
> 8:45 to review the past 24 hours. The first matter they discuss is not pro-
> duction, but safety. Only after they have examined reports of accidents and
> near misses and satisfied themselves that corrective action had been taken
> do they move on to look at output, quality, and cost matters.

In summary, it is probably safe to say that without the full commitment of
all levels of management, any attempts to reduce unsafe acts on the part of
workers will meet with little success. And, it is the first-line supervisor who is a
critical link in the chain of management. As safety expect Willie Hammer states:

> A prime requisite for any successful accident prevention program is to leave
> no doubt in the mind of any employee that his managers are concerned
> about accident prevention. The most effective means by which this can be
> done is for the manager at the highest level possible to issue a directive
> indicating his accident prevention policies and then to insure that his lower
> level managers, supervisors, and other employees carry them out. . . . For

the workers the foreman represents management. He has to see that the intention and orders of management are carried out by exerting his personal authority and influence. If the foreman does not take safety seriously, those under him will not either. . . .

Safety and the Supervisor

There are basically three areas in which the supervisor influences safety and health on the job. First, as mentioned above, the first line supervisor is management's main link with employees, and as such is responsible for enforcing management's safety and health rules. As Hammer points out, however, the supervisor's role here goes beyond just perfunctory enforcement; instead, the supervisor has to make it clear through word and deed that safety and health is a serious matter, one that deserves a full-fledged commitment. Second, the supervisor is often directly responsible for training and educating employees concerning safe and healthy job practices. This means learning the proper practice—the safe way to feed a machine, using safety goggles, and so on—and then ensuring that each subordinate receives the training needed to understand the "safe" way to work. Finally, the supervisor is responsible for identifying and eliminating (or at least reporting) unsafe conditions or acts at work. This requires understanding the causes of accidents and how to prevent them, topics to which we now turn.

WHAT CAUSES ACCIDENTS?

The Three Basic Causes of Accidents

Safety experts know that there are three basic factors that contribute to accidents in organizations: chance occurrences, unsafe conditions, and unsafe acts on the part of employees. Chance occurrences (like walking past a plate-glass window just as someone hits a ball through it) contribute to accidents but are more or less beyond management's control: we will therefore focus on *unsafe conditions* and *unsafe acts*.

Unsafe Conditions (work-related accident-causing factors)

Unsafe conditions are one main cause of accidents. They include such things as:

Improperly guarded equipment
Defective equipment
Hazardous arrangement or procedure in, on, or around, machines or equipment
Unsafe storage: congestion, overloading
Improper illumination—glare, insufficient light
Improper ventilation—insufficient air change, impure air source [22]

The OSHA standards are aimed at eliminating or minimizing these kinds of unsafe conditions. (On a day-to-day basis many supervisors also find that a checklist of "unsafe conditions" like those summarized in this chapter's exercise can be useful for spotting problems.)

While accidents can happen anywhere, there are some "high danger" zones. About one-third of industrial accidents occur around forklift trucks, wheelbarrows, and other handling and lifting areas, for example. The most serious accidents usually occur near metal and woodworking machines and saws, or around transmission machinery like gears, pulleys, and flywheels. Falls—on stairs, ladders, walkways and scaffolds—are the third most common cause of industrial accidents. Hand tools (like chisels and screwdrivers), and electrical equipment (extension cords, electric drop lights, etc.) are other big accident-causers. [23]

Three Other Work-related Accident Factors. In addition to the unsafe conditions we just discussed, safety experts know that three more *work-related* factors contribute to accidents: *the job itself, the work schedule,* and the *"psychological climate"* of the workplace.

For example, some *jobs* are inherently more dangerous than others. According to one study, for example the job of "craneman" results in about three times more accident-related hospital visits than the job of "foreman." Similarly, the work in some departments in inherently safer than the work in others. For example, the bookkeeping or personnel departments usually have fewer accidents on the whole than do shipping or production departments.

Work schedules also affect accident rates, since accidents increase late in the day. Accident rates usually do not increase too noticeably during the first five or six hours of the workday. But beyond that, the accident rate increases in greater proportion than the increase in the number of hours worked. This is due partly to fatigue and partly to the fact that accidents occur more often during night shifts.

Finally, many experts believe that the *psychological climate* of the workplace also affects the accident rate. For example, accidents occur more frequently in plants with a high seasonal lay-off rate and where there is hostility among employees, many garnisheed wages, and blighted living conditions. Temporary stress factors like high workplace temperature, poor illumination, and a congested workplace are also related to high accident rates. One writer says that these findings mean that "psychological climate" affects accident rates. [24] He says that workers who work under stress, or who feel that their jobs are threatened or insecure, seem to have more accidents than those who do not. [25]

Personal Traits and "Unsafe Acts" (A second basic cause of accidents)

There is little doubt that unsafe acts (not unsafe conditions) are the main cause of accidents, and that *people* cause these unsafe acts.

Most safety experts and managers long ago discovered that it is impossible to eliminate accidents simply by reducing unsafe conditions. This is because *people* cause accidents, and to date no one has found a sure-fire way to make employees work safely. The result is a number of unsafe acts like:

Failing to secure equipment

Failing to use safe attire or personal protective equipment

Throwing materials

Operating or working at unsafe speeds, either too fast or too slow

Making safety devices inoperative by removing, adjusting, disconnecting them

Using unsafe equipment, or using equipment unsafely

Using unsafe procedures in loading, placing, mixing, combining

Taking unsafe positions under suspended loads

Lifting improperly

Distracting, teasing, abusing, startling, quarreling, horseplay

Unsafe acts like these can shortcircuit even the best attempts to minimize unsafe conditions, and we should therefore discuss the causes of such unsafe acts. [26]

Personal Characteristics and Accidents. McCormick and Tiffin have developed a model that summarizes how personal characteristics (like personality) are linked to accidents: it is presented in Exhibit 17.2. They say that personal characteristics (personality, motivation, etc.) serve as the basis for certain "behavior tendencies"—such as the tendency to take risks—and undesirable attitudes. These behavior tendencies in turn result in unsafe acts—such as failure to follow procedures and inattention. In turn, such unsafe acts drastically increase the probability of a person's incurring an accident.

Are There "Accident Prone" People? You have probably come across people whom you would consider "accident prone." (Perhaps it is the person who is always dropping things, or bumping into doors, or falling, for example.) But to a psychologist, the phrase "accident prone" means something quite specific. It implies the possession of those *qualities or traits* that have been found from research to lead to an undue number of accidents. [27] Thus, to most psychologists, accident proneness is a *personality type*, and a person who is accident prone can be identified by a number of specific and measurable personality traits.

What Traits Characterize "Accident Prone" People? For years psychologists have tried to determine what "package" of traits distinguishes those who are accident prone from those who are not. The original interest in this was based on the discovery that a small percentage of workers (say 20%) were responsible for a large percentage (say 70%) of the accidents. Researchers

Exhibit 17.2   Manner in Which Personal Factors May Influence Accident Behaviors   501
of Individuals

Personal Characteristics	→	Predisposing Behavior Tendencies	→	Types of Behaviors in Specific Circumstances	→	Incidence of Specific Accident Behavior
Personality		Undesirable Attitudes and Habits		Inattention		Probability Rate of Individual's Accident Behaviors
Intelligence				Forgetfulness		
Motivation		Lack of Specific Abilities		Misperception		
Sensory Skills				Failure to Follow Procedures		
Motor Skills		Tendency to Assume Risk, Etc.		Inadequate Performance		
Experience, Etc.				Assuming Excessive Risk, Etc.		

Source: Ernest J. McCormick and Joseph Tiffin, *Industrial Psychology* (Englewood Cliffs, N.J.: Prentice-Hall, Inc., 1974), p. 517. Reprinted by permission.

assumed that the workers having more accidents were accident prone, and set about trying to find a bundle of traits that made them so.

Today it is generally recognized that these original findings were probably inaccurate and misleading: They were more a result of the statistical analysis than the "accident proneness" of the workers. (One problem was the small number of accidents per worker the researchers had to deal with. For example, suppose you flip a coin many, many times. Over the long run you would expect to get one-half heads and one-half tails. But suppose you just flipped the coin several times—say three or four. Here, you might well get three tails in a row, or four heads. In that case you obviously would not consider yourself "heads prone," or "tail prone": yet that is about what early researchers concluded from the accident proneness experiments.)

In any case, years of research failed to unearth any set of traits that accident repeaters seemed to have in common. Today we believe that the personal traits that contribute to accidents probably differ from situation to situation. For example *personality traits* (like emotional stability) may distinguish accident prone workers on jobs involving risk; and *motor skills* may distinguish accident prone workers on jobs involving coordination. In fact, many personal traits have been found to be related to accident repetition, *in specific situations:* [28] For example:

Vision.   Vision is related to accident frequency for many jobs. For example, in a study of passenger car drivers, inter-city bus drivers, and machine operators researchers found that those who had high visual skills had fewer injuries than those who did not. [29]

502   *Age and Length of Service.*   We also know that accidents are generally most frequent between the ages of 17 and 28, declining thereafter to reach a low in the late 50s and 60s. [30] This is based on studies of workers in a steel mill, drivers, and workers in the California Civilian Labor Force. [31] (While different patterns might be found with different jobs, this "age" factor seems to be a fairly general one.)

   Perceptual Versus Motor Skills.   One researcher concludes that: "where [a worker's] perceptual [visual inspection] skill is equal to, or higher than, his motor skill, the employee is a relatively safe worker. But where the perception level is *lower* than the motor level, the employee is accident prone and his accident proneness becomes greater as this difference increases. [32] This theory seems to be a twist on the "look before you leap" theme: a worker who reacts quicker than he can perceive is more likely to have accidents.

   Vocational Interests.   In the Strong–Campbell Vocational Interest Test (discussed in Chapter 6) there are scales for, among other things, "aviator" and "banker." One researcher equated "adventuresomeness" with the aviator scale and "cautiousness" with the banker scale. He then developed an "accident proneness" index by subtracting the second from the first. Then, in a study of both hazardous and nonhazardous jobs in a food processing plant he found that employees with high "accident proneness" scores had higher accident rates (see Exhibit 17.3) on *both* the hazardous and nonhazardous jobs.

   These findings are not a complete picture of the personal traits that have been found to be related to higher accident rates. (Some researchers, for example, believe that accident proneness is a type of deviant behavior that is characterized

Exhibit 17.3   "Accident Proneness" Index and Accidents

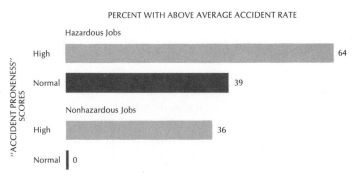

Note: Relationship between an "accident proneness" index (based on the Strong Vocational Interest Blank) and accident rates of 62 male employees on jobs rated hazardous and nonhazardous in a food processing plant.

Source: J. T. Kunce, "Vocational Interest and Accident Proneness," *Journal of Applied Psychology*, Vol. 51 (1967), pp. 223–225. Copyright 1967 by the American Psychological Association. Reprinted with permission.

by impulsiveness and is found in *all* accident prone people.) [33] What they *do*
suggest is that *for specific jobs* it seems to be possible to identify "accident
prone" individuals and to screen them out.

Summary: What Causes Accidents?

Three factors contribute to accidents: chance occurrences, unsafe conditions,
and unsafe acts. Chance occurrences are more or less beyond management's
influence, so we focussed on unsafe conditions and acts.

Unsafe conditions are a major cause of accidents. They include such things
as poorly maintained machines, unguarded moving parts, and sloppy housekeeping. We also discussed three other work-related sources of accidents: the
job itself, the work schedule, and the psychological climate of the workplace.

Unsafe acts are a third major cause of accidents. We said that unsafe acts
(like not wearing protective goggles) often have their origin in the personal
traits of the workers themselves. And we saw that it is possible to identify traits
that are associated with accident proneness *for specific jobs.* (For example, visual
skills are highly related to accident rates for drivers and machinists.)

METHODS OF REDUCING UNSAFE ACTS

Basic Approaches to Preventing Accidents [34]

In practice, accident prevention boils down to two basic activities: reducing
unsafe conditions and reducing unsafe acts. Reducing unsafe *conditions* is primarily in the domain of safety engineers: their task is to remove or reduce
physical hazards. (However, supervisors and managers also play a role in reducing unsafe conditions, particularly with regard to identifying and eliminating
unsafe conditions like unguarded machinery and slippery floors.) Reducing unsafe *acts*, on the other hand, *is* an activity in which supervisors and managers
play a major role. Methods for reducing unsafe acts include selection and placement, persuasion, training, and behavior modification.

Reducing Unsafe Acts Through
Selection and Placement

One way to reduce accidents is to screen out "accident prone" individuals
before they are hired. Accidents are similar to other types of poor performance,
and employers should therefore be interested in screening out these people, just
as they might be interested in screening out applicants who are potentially
"short tenure," "theft-prone," or "low performers." We discussed the techniques
for doing so in Chapters 3–6.

Psychologists have in fact had some success in screening out persons who
might be accident prone for some specific job. The basic technique involves
identifying the personal factor (such as visual skill) that might be related to

504 accidents on the job. Then determine whether scores (on this characteristic) are indeed related to accidents on the job. Biographical (application blank) data, tests, and interview questions are some of the tools that can be used. For example: [35]

> *Emotional stability and personality tests.* Psychological tests—especially tests of emotional stability—have been used to screen out accident prone taxicab drivers. Here (as you might imagine) the test was an especially effective screening device when administered to the applicant under disturbing and distracting conditions (as he might encounter on the road). In this case, researchers found that taxi drivers who made five or more errors on such tests averaged three accidents, while those who made less than five averaged only 1.3 accidents. [36]

> *Measures of muscular coordination.* We also know that *coordination* is a predictor of safety for certain jobs. In one study over 600 employees were divided into two groups according to test scores on coordination tests. Here it was found that the poorest quarter had 51% more accidents than those in the better three-quarters. [37]

> *Tests of visual skills.* We have already seen that good vision plays an important part in preventing accidents in many occupations, including driving and operating machines. In another study (made in a paper mill) 52 accident-free employees were compared with 52 "accident prone" employees. Here the researcher found that 63% of the "no accident" group passed a vision test while only 33% of the accident group passed it. [38]

In summary, Maier concludes that:

> Of great practical importance is the fact that there is a definite relationship between these accident-proneness tests and proficiency on the job. By selecting employees who do well—that is, score low—on accident-proneness tests, managers can reduce accidents and improve the caliber of the employees at the same time. [39]

Persuasion and Propaganda

Many organizations use "propaganda" of one sort or another—such as safety posters—as part (or all) of their safety programs. Such posters and other propaganda can be useful: in one study, for example, their use apparently increased "safe behavior" by more than 20%. [40]

On the other hand, it is also true that an employer cannot substitute posters for a comprehensive safety program: instead, they should be used in conjunction with other attempts to reduce unsafe conditions and acts. For example, it helps to key posters to the employer's own safety program. Thus, if the company is emphasizing "protective gloves" this month, the "poster of the month" should underscore this emphasis. It is also important to change posters frequently. [41]

Reducing Unsafe Acts Through: Behavior Modification and Training

A safety program combining behavior modification and training has been used successfully to improve safety at work. [42,43] One study of such a program was conducted in a wholesale bakery that bakes, wraps, and transports pastry products to retail outlets nationwide. [44] This plant was considered a prime candidate for a safety improvement program since there had been a dramatic increase in the injury rate and a corresponding rise in workers' compensation premiums during the year preceding the study.

An analysis of the safety-related conditions existing in the plant before the study suggested a number of areas that needed improvement. For example, new hires received no formalized safety training, and safety was rarely mentioned on a day-to-day basis. Commercial safety posters were placed at the entrance to the work area and on a bulletin board in the dining room but were often not updated for up to six months. No single person was responsible for safety. Similarly, a "behavioral analysis"—an assessment of the consequences of desired and undesired safety-related behaviors—revealed that safe practices were probably not being maintained by employees because they received little or no positive reinforcement for performing safely. Managers said little or nothing to employees who took the time to act safely. Similarly, employees were rarely notified of or given an opportunity to unlearn unsafe practices. Although the accident rate had been climbing many employees had yet to experience an injury because of performing unsafely, so this "negative consequence" too, was missing.

The behavioral change program stressed behavior modification and training. A reasonable goal for "percent of incidents performed safely" was set and communicated to workers to ensure that they knew what was expected of them in terms of good performance. Next, training was provided to ensure the workers could behave satisfactorily if they wanted to. This involved a training phase in which employees were presented with safety information during a 30-minute training session. Here employees were shown pairs of slides (35-mm transparencies) which depicted scenes which were staged in the plant. In one transparency, for example the wrapping supervisor was shown climbing over a conveyor; the parallel slide illustrated the supervisor walking around the conveyor. After viewing an unsafe act, employees were asked to describe verbally what was wrong ("what's unsafe here?"). Then, once the problem had been aired the same incident was again shown performed in a safe manner and the safe conduct rule was explicitly stated ("go around, not over or under conveyors"). At the conclusion of the training phase the employees were shown a graph with their pretraining safety record (in terms of "percent of incidents performed safely") plotted, and were encouraged to consider increasing their performance to the new safety goal for the following reasons: for their own protection; to decrease costs for the company; and, lastly to help the plant get out of last place in the safety ranking of the parent company. Then the graph and a list of safety rules (do's and don'ts) were posted in a conspicuous place in the employees' work area.

The graph then played an important role in the final "reinforcement" phase of the study during which workers received feedback from supervisors that provided reinforcement for safe performance. First, whenever observers walked through the plant collecting safety data, they posted on the graph the percentage of incidents they had seen performed safely by the group as a whole, thus providing the workers with feedback on their safety performance. Workers could therefore compare their current safety performance with their previous performance, and with their assigned goal. In addition, supervisors recognized workers when they performed selected incidents safely: For example, each supervisor was told to comment specifically when he saw an employee performing safely. Supervisors also got reinforcement for recognizing and reinforcing safe behavior. For one thing, each had to fill out a check list indicating how often ("always, sometimes, never, did not observe") he had commented when he saw a worker engaged in any of five selected safety-related incidents each day. To further ensure the participation of the supervisors, the president and the plant manager were asked to talk with each supervisor about the safety program at least once each week. Both were also asked to fill out a similar check list indicating when they had spoken with the supervisors. These check lists supplied built in reinforcement to supervisors and managers for the safety-related tasks they performed. And, of course, the supervisors' comments to the employees provided much-needed reinforcement to the latter for safe performance at work. Safety in the plant subsequently improved markedly.

In summary, a combined behavior modification/training approach can be useful for improving safety at work. Such a program would typically begin with an analysis in which the cause of the safety problem is identified and a determination is made concerning why safety is lacking. In the study just described, goal setting, a simple training program, and a simple mechanism for providing feedback apparently resulted in a marked improvement in the plant's safety record. Training by itself can and will result in modest safety improvements, [45] but it appears that to fully realize the benefits of the training a more comprehensive program including feedback and goal setting is preferable. [46]

Reducing Unsafe Acts Through: Top Management Commitment

Finally, it is important to repeat that reducing accidents is largely a result of developing a safety conscious attitude on the part of employees, and that without the full commitment of top management these attitudes will probably not materialize. According to one researcher, in fact, "one of the most consistent findings in the literature is that in factories having successful safety programs, there was a strong management commitment to safety." [47] This research showed that this commitment typically manifested itself in: top management being personally involved in safety activities on a routine basis; top management giving safety matters high priority in company meetings and production scheduling; and in top management giving the company safety officer higher rank and status and by building safety training into new workers' training.

EMPLOYEE HEALTH: PROBLEMS AND REMEDIES[48]

Three Important Health Problems

Managers today deal with a complex set of problems, and among the most frustrating are the problems of alcoholism, drug addiction, and emotional illness among workers, all of which seem to be increasing.

It is hard to determine just how many workers suffer from these problems, or what their costs are to the companies involved. According to a study conducted by the American Society for Personnel Administration and the Bureau of National Affairs, from 3 to 6% of employees exhibit these problems. Yet these findings may understate the problem. Other studies estimate that over 5% of employees in this country suffer from alcoholism, for example. But, regardless of the exact numbers, it is apparent that these health problems are serious, and that most managers can expect to be confronted by workers with such problems sooner or later.

Alcoholism. [49] Trice and his associates have made extensive studies of alcoholism on the job, and their findings paint a vivid problem of the alcoholic and the problems he creates (most alcoholics are men—the male/female ratio is about 5 to 1).

The effects of alcoholism on the worker and his work are considerable. Both the quality and quantity of his work decline sharply. A form of "on-the-job absenteeism" occurs as efficiency declines. The alcoholic's on-the-job accidents do *not* appear to increase significantly, apparently because he becomes much more cautious (but his effectiveness suffers as well). However the *off*-the-job accident rate is three to four times higher than for non-alcoholics. Contrary to general opinion turnover among alcoholics is not unusually high. The morale of other workers is affected as they have to do the work of their alcoholic peer.

Recognizing the alcoholics on the job is also a major problem. The early symptoms are often similar to those of other problems and are thus hard to classify. The supervisor is not a professional psychiatrist, and without specialized training, identifying—and dealing with—the alcoholic is a difficult task.

Techniques Used to Deal with These Problems

Four popular techniques for dealing with these problems include disciplining, discharge, in-house counseling, and referral to an outside agency. Discipline short of discharge is used more often with alcoholics; this technique is used infrequently for dealing with drug problems or emotional illness. Discharge is frequently used to deal with alcoholism and drug problems; it is almost never used in the case of serious emotional illness.

In-house counseling is used quite often in dealing with alcoholics, and those with emotional disorders. In most cases the counseling is offered by the personnel department or the company's staff medical personnel. Immediate supervisors who have received special training also provide counseling in many instances.

Many companies use outside agencies like Alcoholics Anonymous, psychiatrists, and clinics to deal with the problems of alcoholism and emotional illness. Outside agencies are used rarely in the case of drug problems.

In summary, discipline (short of discharge), in-house counseling, and referral to an outside agency are the techniques apparently used most often to cope with alcoholism and emotional illness. There seems to be a tendency to discharge employees with drug problems; however, many respondents in this survey "did not indicate how they cope with drug problems." [50]

Trice [51] suggests a number of specific actions managers can take to deal with employee alcoholism, actions which all involve supervisory training or company policy. He says supervisors should be trained to identify the alcoholic and the problem he creates. Employers should also establish a company policy that recognizes alcoholism as a health problem and places it within the firm's health plan.

The Problem of Job Stress

To some extent, problems like alcoholism and drug abuse are often a consequence of stress, and especially *job* stress. Here job-related factors like overwork, required relocation, and problems with customers eventually put the person under so much stress that the result is some pathological reaction like drug abuse.

There are two main sources of job stress: environmental, and personal. [52] First, a variety of external, *environmental* factors can lead to job stress. These include the person's work schedule, pace of work, job security, route to and from work, and the number and nature of customers or clients. Yet no two people will react to the same job in the very same way, since *personal* factors also influence the person's stress. For example, "Type A" personalities—people who are "workaholics" and who feel driven to always be on time and meet deadlines—normally place themselves under greater stress than do others. Similarly, a person's tolerance for ambiguity, impatience, self-esteem, health and exercise, work, and sleep patterns can similarly affect how he or she reacts to stress.

Regardless of its source, however, job stress has serious consequences for both the employee and the organization. For example, the human consequences of job stress include anxiety, depression, anger, and various physical consequences like cardiovascular disease, headaches, and accidents. In some cases it can lead to other human consequences including drug abuse, over and under eating, and poor interpersonal relations. Stress also has serious consequences for the organization, including changes in the quantity and quality of job performance, increased absenteeism and turnover, and increased grievances.

Yet job stress is not necessarily dysfunctional. DuBrin makes the point that some stress can actually have positive consequences for the person and the organization. Some people, for example, only work well under at least modest stress, and find they are more productive as a deadline approaches. Others find that stress may result in a search that leads to a better job or to a career that makes more sense given the person's aptitudes. A modest level of stress may even lead to more creativity if a competitive situation results in new ideas being generated. [53] As a rule, however, employers do not worry about the sorts of modest stress that lead to such positive consequences. Instead, and for obvious reasons, they focus on dysfunctional stress and its negative conequences.

There are a number of thing the individual, and the organization can do to alleviate stress. For the individual, responses range from common-sense remedies like getting more sleep and eating better (so as to build resistance to stress), to more exotic remedies like "biofeedback" and meditation. Finding a more suitable job, getting counseling, and planning and organizing each day's activities are other sensible responses. [54]

The organization and its personnel specialists and supervisors also play an important role in identifying and remedying job stress. For the supervisor this typically involves monitoring each subordinate's performance in order to identify the symptoms of stress, and then informing the person of the organizational remedies that may be available, remedies like job transfers, or counseling. The personnel specialist's role includes using attitude surveys to identify organizational sources of stress (like high pressure jobs), refining selection and placement procedures to ensure the most effective "person-job" match, and making available career planning aimed at ensuring that the employee moves toward a job that makes sense in terms of his or her aptitudes and aspirations.

SUMMARY

1. The area of safety and accident prevention is of concern to managers at least partly because of the staggering number of deaths and accidents occurring at work. We said there are three reasons for safety programs: moral, legal, and economic.

2. The purpose of OSHA is to ensure every working person a safe and healthful workplace. OSHA standards are very complete and detailed, and are enforced through a system of inspections in which inspectors, following a list of inspection priorities, visit workplaces. These inspectors can issue citations and recommend penalties to their area directors.

3. Supervisors play a key role in safety since there will always be accidents unless workers want to act safely and do. A commitment to safety on the part of top management, and a filtering down of this commitment through the management ranks, is an important aspect of any safety program.

4. There are three basic causes of accidents: chance occurrences, unsafe conditions, and unsafe acts on the part of employees. Unsafe *conditions* (like defective equipment) are one big cause of accidents. In addition, three other work-related factors (the job itself, the work schedule, and the psychological climate) also contribute to accidents.

5. Unsafe acts on the part of employers are a second basic cause of accidents. Such acts are to some extent the result of certain behavior tendencies on the part of employees, and these tendencies are possibly the result of certain personal characteristics.

6. Most experts doubt that there are "accident prone" people who have accidents regardless of the job. Instead the consensus seems to be that the person who is accident prone in one job may not be on a different job. For example vision is related to accident frequency for drivers and machine operators but might not be for other jobs, like accountants.

7. There are several approaches you could use to prevent accidents. One is to reduce unsafe *conditions* (although this is somewhat more in the domain of safety engineers). The other approach is to reduce unsafe *acts,* for example through selection and placement, training and behavior modification, persuasion and propaganda, and top management commitment.

8. Alcoholism, drug addiction, stress, and emotional illness are four important and growing health problems among employees. Alcoholism is a particularly serious problem and one that can drastically lower the effectiveness of your organization. Techniques including disciplining, discharge, in-house counseling, and referrals to an outside agency are used to deal with these problems.

CASE INCIDENT

Beamon Plating Company*

The Beamon Plating Company specialized in cleaning and plating all types of small metal objects. Its service was good, prices were reasonable, and its work was guaranteed. As a result, it enjoyed a healthy business—mostly from industrial concerns located within a 500-mile radius. Some of its work, however, consisted of silver-plating and gold-plating objects of art as well as silver services and the like.

Several hazards exist in any plating shop, and due precautions must be taken. Fumes from the plating tanks, for example, are very dangerous and can cause sickness, and even death, from prolonged exposure. To preclude such a mishap, the management of Beamon Plating installed one of the most efficient air exhaust systems obtainable. In fact, air purity tests showed that the air in the plating room contained less toxic gases than air elsewhere in the plant. In addition, three emergency showerheads were installed beside the plating tanks. In case an employee spilled acid on himself, he quickly stepped under the closest shower and pulled a chain. This automatically opened a valve sending a full-force shower over him, thus dissipating the effects of the acid. The company also furnished all its plating room employees with special uniforms, rubber boots, rubber aprons, and rubber gloves. These protected them from the plating fluids and acids.

Chemicals used in the plating tanks were purchased in 50-gallon drums, and acids came in large, glass containers called carboys. Both the acids and the chemicals in drums were stored under a shed, which was 150 feet from the main building. Other less bulky items such as cadmium balls, soda ash, etc., were stored in a small storeroom in the plant. When material from either of these storerooms was needed, any one of the employees who wasn't busy at the time was sent to get the material. If it was not too heavy, the employee could choose one of the several handtrucks that were always available. Occasionally, the material fell off and spilled on the floor. In several instances, an employee dropped material on his feet, causing a lost-time accident. Some of the workers complained of straining their backs from lifting, but this could not be positively linked to lifting the material for the plating shop.

Despite its precautions and the provision of protective equipment, the company had some trouble in the plating room. Several of the employees almost refused to wear the rubber boots and aprons provided by the company. In fact, they removed them quite frequently, claiming they were bulky, hot, and uncomfortable. Management realized that this was a dangerous practice, but if the employees would not wear the safety equipment after management had bought it, they admitted they did not know what to do about the situation.

Several accidents of a minor nature occurred recently. For example, one of the girls who wired parts to racks so they could be individually plated stuck one of the

---

* From Claude S. George, Jr., *Management in Industry*, (Englewood Cliffs, New Jersey: Prentice-Hall, Inc., 1959) pp. 337–8. Reprinted by permission of the publisher.

512   sharp parts in her finger. This would not have happened if she had been wearing the gloves furnished by the company.

While this may be looked upon as a minor item, the Beamon Plating Company does not want its employees to forget that serious injuries can occur. They also want them to realize that the company is trying to provide maximum protection for its workers during their work day.

Questions

1. What do you think of the safety program of the Beamon Plating Company?
2. What changes, if any, would you recommend? Explain why.

EXPERIENTIAL EXERCISE

Purpose. The purpose of this exercise is to give you practice in identifying unsafe conditions.

Required Understanding. You should be familiar with material covered in this chapter, particularly that on unsafe conditions and that in Exhibit 17.4.

How to Set Up the Exercise/Instructions. Divide the class into groups of four or five students.

Assume that you are a safety committee retained by the school to identify and report on any possible unsafe conditions in and around the school building.

Each group will spend about 45 minutes in and around the college building you are now in for the purpose of identifying and listing possible unsafe conditions. (*Hint:* Make use of Exhibit 17.4.)

Return to the class in about 45 minutes and a spokesman from each group should list on the board the unsafe conditions you think you have identified. How many were there? Do you think these also violate OSHA standards? How would you go about checking?

DISCUSSION QUESTIONS

1. How would you go about providing a safer environment for your employees to work in?
2. Discuss how you would go about minimizing the occurrence of unsafe acts on the part of your employees.
3. Discuss the basic facts about OSHA—its purpose, standards, inspection, and rights and responsibilities.
4. Explain the supervisor's role in safety.
5. Explain what causes unsafe acts.
6. Answer the question, "Is there such a thing as an 'accident prone' person?"
7. Describe at least five techniques for reducing accidents.

NOTES

1. Willie Hamner, *Occupational Safety Management and Engineering* (Englewood Cliffs, N.J.: Prentice-Hall, 1976), p. 6.
2. *Ibid.*, p. 7.

Exhibit 17.4   Checklist of Mechanical or Physical Accident-Causing Conditions

I. General Housekeeping

Adequate and wide aisles—no materials protruding into aisles

Parts and tools stored safely after use—not left in hazardous positions that could cause them to fall

Even and solid flooring—no defective floors or ramps that could cause falling or tripping accidents

Waste cans and sand pails—safely located and properly used

Material piled in safe manner—not too high or too close to sprinkler heads

Floors—clean and dry

Fire fighting equipment—unobstructed

Work benches—orderly

Stockcarts and skids—safely located, not left in aisles or passageways

Aisles kept clear and properly marked—no air lines or electric cords across aisles

II. Material Handling Equipment and Conveyances

On all conveyances, electric or hand, check to see that the following items are all in sound working conditions:

Brakes—properly adjusted
Not too much play in steering wheel
Warning device—in place and working
Wheels—securely in place; properly inflated
Fuel and oil—enough and right kind
No loose parts

Cables, hooks or chains—not worn or otherwise defective
Suspended chains or hooks—conspicuous
Safely loaded
Properly stored

III. Ladders, Scaffold, Benches, Stairways, etc.

The following items of major interest to be checked:

Safety feet on straight ladders
Guard rails or hand rails
Treads, not slippery
Not splintered, cracked, or rickety

Properly stored
Extension ladder ropes in good condition
Toe boards

IV. Power Tools (stationary)

Point of operation guarded
Guards in proper adjustment
Gears, belts, shafting, counter weights guarded
Foot pedals guarded
Brushes provided for cleaning machines
Adequate lighting
Properly grounded
Tool or material rests properly adjusted

Adequate work space around machines
Control switch easily accessible
Safety glasses worn
Gloves worn by persons handling rough or sharp materials
No gloves or loose clothing worn by persons operating machines

V. Hand Tools and Miscellaneous

In good condition—not cracked, worn, or otherwise defective
Properly stored

Correct for job
Goggles, respirators, and other personal protective equipment worn where necessary

VI. Welding

Arc shielded
Fire hazards controlled
Operator using suitable protective equipment

Adequate ventilation
Cylinder secured
Valves closed when not in use

VII. Spray Painting

Explosion-proof electrical equipment
Proper storage or paints and thinners in approved metal cabinets

Fire extinguishers adequate and suitable; readily accessible
Minimum storage in work area

VIII. Fire Extinguishers

Properly serviced and tagged
Readily accessible

Adequate and suitable for operations involved

Source: Courtesy of the American Insurance Association. From "A Safety Committee Man's Guide," I-64.

514

3. Bittel, *What Every Supervisor Should Know.*

4. Much of this is based on "All About OSHA" (revised), U.S. Department of Labor, Occupational Safety and Health Administration (1980).

5. "All About OSHA," 1980, p. 13.

6. "What Every Employer Needs to know about OSHA Record Keeping," U.S. Department of Labor Bureau of Labor Statistics, 1978, report 412-3, p. 3.

7. All about OSHA," p. 18.

8. "Supreme Court Says OSHA Inspectors Need Warrants," *Engineering News Record* (June 1, 1978), pp. 9–10.

9. Michael Verespej, "OSHA Revamps Its Inspection Policies," *Industry Week* (September 17, 1979), pp. 19–20.

10. This section is based on "All About OSHA," pp. 23–25.

11. Michael Verespej, "Has OSHA Improved?" *Industry Week* (August 4, 1980), pp. 48–56.

12. *Ibid.*, p. 55.

13. Roger Jacobs, "Employee Resistance to OSHA Standards: Toward a More Reasonable Approach," *Labor of Law Journal* (April 1979), pp. 219–230.

14. Jacobs, p. 220.

15. These are based on Jacobs, pp. 227–230.

16. Verespej, "Has OSHA Improved?" p. 50.

17. Murray Weidenbaum, "Four Questions for OSHA," *Labor Law Journal* (August 1979), pp. 528–531; Barry Crickmer, "Regulation: How Much is Enough?" *Nation's Business* (March 1980), pp. 26–33.

18. "What Every Employer Needs to Know about OSHA Record Keeping," U.S. Department of Labor, Bureau of Labor Statistics, (1978).

19. Verespej, "Has OSHA Improved?", pp. 50–51; "New Ways to Short Cut Costly Rules," *Duns Review* (February 1980), pp. 62–69.

20. Bittel, *What Every Supervisor Should Know*, p. 25.

21. Hammer, *Occupational Safety Management and Engineering.*

22. "A Safety Committee Man's Guide," Aetna Life and Casualty Insurance Company, Catalog 872684.

23. *Ibid.*, pp. 17–21.

24. Willard Kerr, "Complementary Theories of Safety Psychology," in Edwin Fleishman and Alan Bass, *Industrial Psychology* (Homewood, Ill.: Dorsey, 1974), pp. 493–500.

25. See also Dove Zohar, "Safety Climate in Industrial Organization: Theoretical and Applied Implications," *Journal of Applied Psychology*, Vol. 65 (February 1980), pp. 96–102.

26. List of unsafe acts from "A Safety Committee Man's Guide," Aetna Life and Casualty Insurance Company.

27. A. G. Arbous and J. E. Kerrich, "The Phenomenon of Accident Proneness," *Industrial Medicine and Surgery*, Vol. 22 (1953), pp. 141–148, reprinted in Fleishman and Bass, *Industrial Psychology*, p. 485.

28. McCormick and Tiffin, *Industrial Psychology*, pp. 522–523; Maier, *Psychology and Industrial Organization*, pp. 458–462; Milton Blum and James Nayler, *Industrial Psychology* (New York: Harper and Row, 1968), pp. 519–531.

29. McCormick and Tiffin, *Industrial Psychology*, p. 523.

30. John Miner and J. Frank Brewer, "Management of Ineffective Performance," in Dunnette, *Handbook of Industrial and Organizational Psychology*, pp. 995–1031.

31. McCormick and Tiffin, *Industrial Psychology*, pp. 524–525.

32. Blum and Nayler, *Industrial Psychology*, p. 522.

33. Miner and Brewer, "Management of Ineffective Performance," in Dunnette, *Handbook of Industrial and Organizational Psychology*, pp. 1004–1005.

34. Bittel, *What Every Supervisor Should Know*, p. 249.

35. Maier, *Psychology and Industrial Organization*, pp. 463–467; McCormick and Tiffin, *Industrial Psychology*, pp. 533–536; Blum and Nayler, *Industrial Psychology*, pp. 525–527.

36. D. Wechsler, "Test for Taxicab Drivers," *Journal of Personnel Research*, Vol. 5 (1926), pp. 24–30, quoted in Maier, *Psychology and Industrial Organization*, p. 64.

37. Maier, *Psychology and Industrial Organization*, p. 463.

38. S. E. Wirt and H. E. Leedkee, "Skillful Eyes Prevent Accidents," Annual Newsletter, National Safety Counsel, Industrial Nursing Section (November 1945), pp. 10–12, quoted in Maier, *Psychology and Industrial Organization*, p. 466.

39. Maier, *Psychology and Industrial Organization*, p. 464.

40. S. Laner and R. J. Sell, "An Experiment on the Effect of Specially Designed Safety Posters," *Occupational Psychology*, Vol. 34 (1960), pp. 153–169, in McCormick and Tiffin, *Industrial Psychology*, p. 536.

41. McCormick and Tiffin, *Industrial Psychology*, p. 537.

42. OSHA has published two useful training manuals: *Training Requirements of OSHA Standards*, U.S. Department of Labor, Occupational Safety and Health Administration, (February 1976); *Teaching Safety and Health in the Work Place*, U.S. Department of Labor, Occupational Safety and Health Administration (1976).

43. J. Surry, "Industrial Accident Research: Human Engineering Approach" (Toronto: University of Toronto, Department of Industrial Engineering, June 1968), Ch. 4, quoted in McCormick and Tiffin, *Industrial Psychology*, p. 534.

44. Judi Komaki, Kenneth Barwick, and Lawrence Scott, "A Behavioral Approach to Occupational Safety: Pinpointing and Reinforcing Safe Performance in a Food Manufacturing Plant," *Journal of Applied Psychology*, Vol. 63 (August 1978), pp. 434–445.

45. Judi Komaki, Arlene Heinzmann, and Lorealie Lawson, "Effect of Training and Feedback: Component Analysis of a Behavioral Safety Program," *Journal of Applied Psychology*, Vol. 65 (June 1980), pp. 261–270.

46. Komaki, et al., "Effect of Training and Feedback," p. 268.

47. Zohar, "Safety climate . . . ," *Journal of Applied Psychology*, p. 97.

48. This section based largely on John B. Miner and J. Frank Brewer, "The Management of Ineffective Performance," in Marvin D. Dunnette, ed., *Handbook of Industrial and Organizational Psychology* (Chicago: Rand-McNally, 1976), pp. 1005–1023.

49. Harrison Trice, "Alcoholism and the Work World," Sloan Management Review, No. 2 (Fall 1970), pp. 67–75; reprinted in Hammer and Schmidt, *Contemporary Problems in Personnel*, rev. ed., pp. 496–502.

50. Based on John B. Miner and J. Frank Brewer, "Management of Ineffective Performance," in Dunnette, *Handbook of Industrial and Organizational Psychology*; the survey was conducted jointly by the American Society for Personnel Administration and the Bureau of National Affairs, Inc. The results were based on an analysis of the questionnaire data made by Professors Miner and Brewer who acknowledge the assistance of John B. Schappi, Associate Editor of the Bureau of National Affairs, Inc., and Mary Green Miner, Director of BNA Surveys, in making this information available.

51. Trice, "Alcoholism and the Work World."

52. This is based on Terry Beehr and John Newman, "Organizational Stress, Employer Health, and Organizational Effectiveness: A Facet Analysis, Model, and Literature Review," *Personnel Psychology*, Vol. 31 (Winter 1978), pp. 665–699.

53. Andrew DuBrim, Human Relations: A Job Oriented Approach (Reston, Reston Publishing, 1978), pp. 66–67.

54. John Newman and Terry Beehr, "Personal and Organizational Strategies for Handling Job Stress: A Review of Research and Opinion," *Personnel Psychology* (Spring 1979), pp. 1–43.

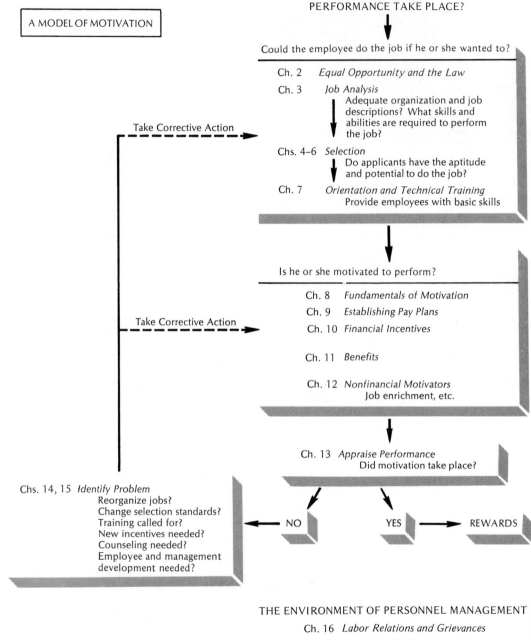

A MODEL OF MOTIVATION

WILL MOTIVATION AND
PERFORMANCE TAKE PLACE?

Could the employee do the job if he or she wanted to?

Ch. 2   *Equal Opportunity and the Law*

Ch. 3   *Job Analysis*
Adequate organization and job
descriptions? What skills and
abilities are required to perform
the job?

Chs. 4–6   *Selection*
Do applicants have the aptitude
and potential to do the job?

Ch. 7   *Orientation and Technical Training*
Provide employees with basic skills

Take Corrective Action

Is he or she motivated to perform?

Ch. 8   *Fundamentals of Motivation*

Ch. 9   *Establishing Pay Plans*

Ch. 10   *Financial Incentives*

Ch. 11   *Benefits*

Ch. 12   *Nonfinancial Motivators*
Job enrichment, etc.

Take Corrective Action

Ch. 13   *Appraise Performance*
Did motivation take place?

Chs. 14, 15   *Identify Problem*
Reorganize jobs?
Change selection standards?
Training called for?
New incentives needed?
Counseling needed?
Employee and management
development needed?

NO   YES → REWARDS

THE ENVIRONMENT OF PERSONNEL MANAGEMENT

Ch. 16   *Labor Relations and Grievances*

Ch. 17   *Employee Safety and Health*

Ch. 18   *Personnel Management and the
Quality of Work Life*

When you finish studying

Conclusion: Personnel Management, Career Planning, and the Quality of Work Life

18

You should be able to:

1. *Better understand what your philosophy of personnel management is and might be.*
2. *Define "quality of work life" and cite some factors that contribute to it.*
3. *Compare and contrast "quality of work life" and "motivation."*
4. *Give some examples of how personnel management activities affect the quality of work.*
5. *Explain "career planning" and its relationship to quality of work life and "human resource planning and development."*

OVERVIEW

The main purpose of this chapter is to explain the nature and functions of "career planning," and to show how it contributes to the quality of work life and human resource development. We discuss the "quality of work life," a concept that can provide you with both a theme around which to form your personnel management philosophy, and one standard against which many personnel-related decisions can be measured. And, we discuss career planning and development, including the stages in one's career, and how an employer can improve it's own career planning system.

TOWARD A PHILOSOPHY OF PERSONNEL MANAGEMENT

The Need for a Philosophy

In Chapter 1 we said that people's actions are always based in part on the assumptions they make, and that this was especially true in regard to personnel management. The basic assumptions you make about people—Can they be trusted? Do they dislike work? Can they be creative? Why do they act as they do? etc.—together comprise your philosophy of personnel management. And every personnel decision you make—the people you hire, the training you

517

provide, your leadership style, etc.—reflects (for better or worse) this basic philosophy.

In Chapter 1 we also discussed some factors that will mold and influence your own philosophy, including the philosophy of your organization's top management, environmental factors (like new laws) and life styles, and your own basic assumptions about people. In addition, we have seen that *motivation* and *performance* is a central issue, one that should be a cornerstone of your personnel management philosophy.

Yet throughout this book we have emphasized the "nuts and bolts" of personnel management by focussing mainly on the concepts and techniques all managers need to carry out their personnel-related tasks. It is therefore easy to lose sight of the fact that these techniques—while important—cannot be administered effectively without some unifying philosophy. For (to repeat) it is this philosophy that helps guide you in deciding *what* people to hire, *what* training to provide, and *how* to motivate employees, etc.

A Performance/Motivation Model

Because performance is so important we have used our model to introduce and tie together the chapters in this book. Performance, we said requires two things:

First, ensure that the subordinate has the ability to do the job. For this, the employer has to provide an adequate organization structure and clear job descriptions. The "human requirements" of the job (in terms of knowledge, skills, etc.) have to be identified, and people who meet these requirements have to be recruited and screened; finally, the employer has to provide the necessary training. We covered these topics in Chapters 2–7: *Recruitment and Selection.*

Second, find out what the person wants, holding it out as a possible reward (make sure the person has the *motivation*—the *desire*—to do the job.) This requires an understanding of what motivates people, and a sound understanding of the financial and nonfinancial rewards that can be used. We covered these topics in Chapters 8–12: *Compensation and Motivation.*

Finally, check on the *results* of the efforts—the performance—and take the necessary corrective action. This involves appraisal, communication, and employee and management and development; we discussed this in Chapters 13–15: *Appraisal and Development.*

A Broader View of the Role of Personnel Management: The Quality of Work Life [1]

What Is "Quality of Work Life"?   The term "quality of work life" means different things to different people. To a worker on an assembly line it may just mean a fair day's pay, safe working conditions, and a supervisor who treats him with dignity. To a young college graduate it may mean opportunities for advancement, creative tasks, and a successful career. To Suttle it means "the degree to which members of a work organization are able to satisfy important personal needs through their experiences in the organization." [2]

As you might expect, there are many factors that can contribute to "quality of work life." Walton, for example, cites the following, among others: [3]

1. Adequate and fair compensation
2. A safe and healthy environment
3. Jobs aimed at developing and using employees' skills and abilities
4. Growth and security: jobs aimed at expanding employees' capabilities, rather than leading to their obsolescence
5. An environment in which employees develop self-esteem and a sense of identity
6. Protection and respect for employees' rights—to privacy, dissent, equity, etc.
7. A sensible integration of job, career, and family life and leisure time.

Quality of Work Life and Employee Performance

"Quality of work life" and employee performance often go hand in hand. For one thing, most conditions that contribute to performance (like equitable salaries, financial incentives, and effective employee selection) will *also* contribute to the quality of work life. Some of these activities (like job enrichment) might contribute indirectly to the quality of work life by tapping workers' "higher-order needs," and motivating them. Still other's activities may contribute directly to the quality of work life—by providing for a safer workplace, less discrimination on the job, and so forth.

In any case, "improving the quality of work life" can help provide a theme around which to form your personnel management philosophy, and a criteria against which many of your personnel decisions are measured. And, in fact, virtually every personnel-related action you take affects the quality of work life in some way. Here are some examples:

Personnel Management Activity	Effect on the Quality of Work Life
Job analysis	Finding out what human requirements are necessary so people with the necessary skills and aptitudes can be placed into jobs where they can perform best and be most satisfied.
Selection	Placing the right person on the right job should provide that person with a more satisfying, rewarding (and motivating) experience.
Job Evaluation	Having adequate, equitable wages is a major consideration of most people in defining the quality of their work life.
Job Enrichment	By tapping "higher-order needs" you encourage the employee to grow and use all his or her abilities.

520 Safety and Health | A safe, healthy work environment is an obvious element contributing to the quality of work life.

A Grievance Procedure | Helps protect employee rights and dignity and therefore contributes to the quality of work life.

Equal Employment Opportunities | Protects rights of minority workers and thereby contributes to their quality of work life.

The Reward System | Lawler says that the following criteria help assure a high quality of work life for your employees: [4] *Adequate* rewards; rewards (wages) that are equitable *externally* (vis-à-vis organizations in the area), and *internally* (vis-à-vis other jobs in the organization); and *individuality*—of incentive systems, and benefits, for instance.

Career Planning and the Quality of Work Life. Activities like screening, training, and appraising serve two basic functions in organizations. First, their traditional function has been to "staff" the organization—in other words, to fill the organization's open positions with employees who have the requisite interests, abilities, and skills. Increasingly, however these activities are taking on a second role, that of ensuring that the long-run interests of the employees are protected by the organization and that, in particular, the employee is encouraged to grow and realize his or her full potential. The trend toward referring to "staffing" or "personnel management" as "human resource planning and development" reflects this second role. The basic, if implicit, assumption underlying the focus on human resource planning aad development is, thus, that the organization has an obligation to utilize its employees' abilities to the fullest, and to give each employee an opportunity to grow and to realize his or her full potential. To some experts, this means that the organization has an obligation to improve the *quality of work life* of its employees: notice, though, that "quality of work life" refers not just to things like working conditions or pay but also to the extent to which each employee is able to fully utilize his or her abilities, engage in jobs that interest him, and obtain the training and guidance that allows the person to engage in jobs that fully utilize their potential. [5]

CAREER PLANNING, PERSONNEL MANAGEMENT, AND HUMAN RESOURCE DEVELOPMENT

One way this trend is manifesting itself is in the increased emphasis many managers are placing on *career planning and development*, an emphasis, in other words, on providing employees with the assistance and opportunities that will enable them to form realistic career goals, and realize them. Enabling employees to pursue expanded, more realistic career goals should be, many experts believe, the major aim of an organization's "personnel" system, partly because they believe (to repeat) that organizations have a duty to help their employees realize their full potential, and partly because they believe that by integrating the "careers" of both the individual and the organization that both will gain. For the employee, his or her satisfaction, personal development, and quality of work life are the clearest benefits. [6] For the organization, increased productivity levels, creativity, and long-range effectiveness may occur, since the organization would be staffed by a cadre of highly committed employees who are carefully trained and developed for their jobs.

Activities like manpower planning, screening, and training play a crucial role in the career development process. Manpower planning, for example, can be used not just to forecast open jobs, but to identify potential internal candidates and the training they would need to fill these jobs. Similarly, an organization can use its periodic employee appraisals not just for salary decisions but for identifying the development needs of individual employees and for ensuring that these needs are met. All the "staffing" activities, in other words, can be used to satisfy the needs of both the organization and the individual in such a way that they both gain: the former from improved performance from a more dedicated work force, and the latter from a richer, more challenging career.

How Careers Evolve

Each person's career goes through several stages, and there are two reasons why it is important that managers understand the nature of this "career cycle." First, it is important because it enables managers to better plan their own careers and to deal with occasional career "crises" if and when they occur. Second, it is important because it improves their performance as managers by giving them better insight into their employees' behavior. (For example, many employees undergo a "mid-life crisis" at the age of 40 or so during which they agonize over the fact that their accomplishments have not kept pace with their expectations; the result of this introspection can be a period of prolonged disappointment for the employee during which his or her performance can be adversely affected). [7]

The Stages in a Person's Career. Each person's career goes through several stages. Many descriptions of these stages have been proposed, [8] but one of the best known descriptions of these stages or "career cycles" was developed by Donald Super and was based on a 20-year study of career patterns. The study began in 1951 and involved 158 eighth-grade and 142 ninth-grade boys. [9] Based on their research these experts concluded that persons go through five basic life stages as follows: [10]

1. *The growth stage*. This period lasts roughly from birth to age 14 and is a period during which the person develops a self concept—a concept of "who I am," and "what I can do"—by identifying with and interacting with other people like family, friends, and teachers. Toward the beginning of this period role playing is important, and children experiment with different ways of acting; this helps them to form impressions of how other people react to different behaviors and contributes to their developing a unique self concept or identity.

522   Toward the end of this stage the adolescent (who by this time has developed some preliminary ideas of what his or her interests and abilities are) begins some realistic thinking about alternative occupations.

2. *The exploration stage.* This is the period, roughly from ages 15 to 24 during which the person seriously explores various occupational alternatives, attempting to match these alternatives with what the person has learned about them (and about his own interests and abilities) from school, leisure activities, and part-time work. Some tentative, broad occupational choices are usually made toward the beginning of this period. This choice is then refined as the person learns more about the choice and about himself until, toward the end of this period a "seemingly appropriate choice" is made and the person tries out for a beginning job. Probably the most important task the person has in this (and the preceding) stage is that of developing a realistic understanding of his or her abilities and talents. Similarly, the person has to discover and develop his or her own values, motives, and ambitions and make sound educational decisions based on reliable sources of information about occupational alternatives. [11]

3. *The establishment stage.* The establishment stage is the period that spans roughly the ages 24–44 and which forms the heart of most peoples' work lives. Sometime during this period (hopefully, toward the beginning) a suitable occupation is found and the person engages in those activities that help him or her to earn a permanent place in it. Often (and particularly in the professions) the person locks onto a chosen occupation early, but in most cases this is a period during which the person is continually testing his or her capabilities and ambitions relative to the initial occupational choice. [12] The establishment stage is itself comprised of three substages. [13] The *trial* substage lasts from about ages 25 to 30: during this period the person determines whether or not the chosen field of work is suitable, and, if not, several changes might be attempted. Jane Smith might have her heart set on a career in retailing, for example, but after several months of constant travel as a newly hired assistant buyer for a department store might decide that a less travel-oriented career like one in market research is more in tune with her needs. Between the ages of roughly 30 and 40 the person goes through a *stabilization* substage during which firm occupational goals are set and during which the person does more explicit career planning to determine the sequence of promotions, job changes, and/or educational activities that seem necessary for accomplishing these goals.

Finally, somewhere between the mid-thirties and mid-forties the person may enter the *mid-career crisis* substage. During this period people often make a major reassessment of their progress relative to original ambitions and goals. Often, during this period people find that they are not going to realize their dreams (such as being a company president) or that, having accomplished what they set out to that their dreams are not all they were cut out to be. Also during this period the person has to decide how important work and career are to be in the persons total life. It is often during this "mid-career crisis" substage that the person is for the first time faced with the difficult decisions of what he or she really wants and can accomplish and how much the person is willing to sacrifice to get what he wants. It is usually during this crisis stage that some people first realize they have what Schein calls *career anchors*—basic concerns—for security, or for independence and freedom, for example, which they will not give up if a choice has to be made.

4. The maintenance substage. Super and his associates found that between the ages of 45 and about 64 many people simply slid from the stabilization sub-stage into a maintenance stage. During this latter period the person typically created for himself or herself a place in the world of work and most efforts were directed to securing that place.

5. The decline stage. As the person approaches retirement age there is often a deceleration period during which many people are faced with the prospect of having to accept reduced levels of power and responsibility and during which they have to learn to accept and develop new roles as mentor and confidant for those who are younger. There is then the more or less inevitable retirement after which the person is faced with the prospect of finding alternative uses for the time and effort formally expended on his or her occupation.

Factors That Affect Career Choices

While some career development theories (like Super's) aim to explain the *process* through which careers evolve, others focus on the *factors* that affect career choices. In other words, these latter theories try to explain *what kinds of people* enter what occupations by explaining the "match" between an occupation and factors like the person's interests, personality, or background. *Interests,* for example, have long been assumed to be a determinant of a person's career choices. Basically, experts assume that as a person matures his or her interests—for the outdoors, to work with people, and so on—results in that person moving toward occupations that match these interests: a person interested in the outdoors, for example might be inclined toward occupations like civil engineer, or forest ranger. [14]

Holland's Theory: Personality as a Factor in Career Choices. Personality, including values, motives, and needs is another important determinant of career choices. [15] For example, Holland assumes that there is an interaction between personality and "environment" such that people are drawn to environments that are congruent with their "personal orientations." Thus a person with a very strong social orientation might be attracted to an "environment" that consists of interpersonal rather than intellectual or physical activities, and so to occupations like social work. Holland proposed six personality types or "personal orientations" and six matching occupational environments as follows:

1. *Realistic orientation.* Involves aggressive behavior, and physical activities requiring skill, strength, and coordination. (Examples: forestry, farming, architecture).
2. *Investigative orientation.* Involves cognitive (thinking, organizing, understanding) rather than effective (feeling, acting, or interpersonal and emotional) activities. (Examples: biology, mathematics, oceanography).
3. *Social orientation.* Involves interpersonal rather than intellectual or physical activities. (Examples: clinical psychology, foreign service, social work).
4. *Conventional orientation.* Involves structural, rule-regulated activities and subordination of personal needs to an organization or person of power and status. (Examples: accounting, finance).

524

5. *Enterprising orientation.* Involves verbal activities to influence others, to obtain power and status. (Examples: management, law, public relations).

6. *Artistic orientation.* Involves self expression, artistic creation, expression of emotions, and individualistic activities. (Examples: art, music, education).

Holland recommends using a version of a special test, the "vocational preference inventory" (VPI) to determine the persons personal orientation—whether it is realistic, investigative, social, conventional, enterprising, or artistic. Occupations have already been matched to each of these orientations, and so a counselor can review the results of the persons VPI and, based on these results, recommend occupational alternatives to the counselee.

Most people turn out to have more than one orientation (they might be both realistic, and investigative, for example) and Holland believes that the more similar or compatible these orientations are the less internal conflict or indecision that person will face in making a career choice. To help illustrate this, Holland has developed the model presented in Exhibit 18.1. As you can see, the model has six corners, each of which represents one personal orientation (like "enterprising"). According to Holland's research, the closer two orientations are in this figure, the more compatible they are. Thus, adjacent categories (realistic-investigative, enterprising-social) are quite similar, while those diagonally opposite (enterprising-investigative, artistc-conventional) are highly dis-

Exhibit 18.1 Holland's Model of Occupational Personality Types

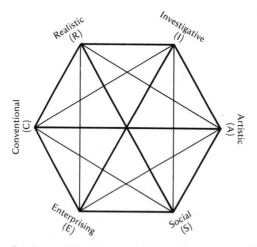

From John L. Holland, *Making Vocational Choices: A Theory of Careers* (Englewood Cliffs, N.J.: Prentice-Hall, 1973), p. 23. Used by permission. (This model originally appeared in J. L. Holland et al., "An Empirical Occupational Classification Derived from a Theory of Personality and intended for Practice and Research." ACT Research Report No. 29, Iowa City: The American College Testing Program, 1969.) Reprinted in Hall, *Careers in Organizations,* p. 14.

NOTE: According to Holland, people with adjacent personality tendencies (like a person who is both social and artistic) would not have much dissonance in making a career choice; someone with non-adjacent and especially opposite tendencies (like realistic and social) *would* experience dissonance in making a career choice.

similar. Holland believes that persons whose orientations scores fall roughly in the order shown in the hexagon are "internally consistent," and should not find themselves torn in divergent directions in making career choices. On the other hand, those with high scores in diagonal categories (such as high on both artistic, and conventional) would likely experience a great deal of dissonance about their choices.

Aptitudes and Special Talents. A persons aptitudes and special talents also play an important role in career decisions and have long been used by career counselors for helping guide their clients. Aptitudes include intelligence, numerical aptitude, mechanical comprehension, and manual dexterity. For career planning purposes, a person's aptitudes are usually measured with a test battery like the general aptitude test battery (GATB), an instrument that measures a variety of aptitudes including intelligence and mathematical ability. Considerable work has been done to relate aptitudes like those measured by the GATB to specific occupations. For example, the U.S. Department of Labor's *Dictionary of Occupational Titles* lists the nature and titles of hundreds of occupations along with the aptitudes required for success in these occupations, as measured by the GATB. [16]

Social Background As a Factor in Career Choices. A person's social background (including his or her parents' socio-economic status, occupation, and education) is also an important factor in career choice. [17] In one study, Goodale and Hall found a high correlation between the occupational level of fathers and the aspired occupational levels of a group of tenth grade high school students. [18] One thing they found was that *parental* background and attitudes seemed to have a stronger influence on career choice then did that of peers, teachers, or other significant people in the persons social environment. [19] (Interestingly though, a person's social background had an effect mostly on the occupational *level* he or she aspired to, rather than on the *occupation* he or she aspired to, although background could affect the latter too). [20]

Career Anchors As Factors in Career Choices. Schein argues that the career development process is a period of discovery during which the person develops a clearer "occupational self concept" in terms of what his or her talents, abilities, motives, needs, and attitudes and values are. He further argues that as a person's occupational self concept crystalizes it becomes apparent to the person that he or she has a dominant "career anchor," a *concern or value which the person will not give up, if a choice has to be made.* These career anchors, as their name implies, are the pivots around which the person's career swings; a person becomes conscious of them as a result of what he or she learns about his or her talents and abilities, motives and needs, and attitudes and values. [21] Based on his research at the Massachusetts Institute of Technology, Schein believes that these career anchors, while crucial in career decisions, cannot be predicted ahead of time because they are evolutionary and a product of a process of discovery. Some people, in fact may never really find out what their career

526   anchors are until they have to make a major choice—such as whether to take
the promotion to the headquarters staff or strike out on ones own by starting
a business—and it is at this point that all the person's past work experiences,
interests, aptitudes and aspirations converge into a meaningful pattern (or career
anchor) that helps show that person what the most important thing is to him.
Based on his study of MIT graduates Schein identified five career anchors:

1. *The technical/functional career anchor.* People that have a strong technical/
   functional career anchor seem to make career choices based on the technical
   or functional content on the work (such as engineering, or financial analysis.)
   In other words, they tend to avoid decisions that would drive them toward
   general management, and instead make decisions that will enable them to
   remain and grow in their chosen technical or functional fields.

2. *Managerial competenance as a career anchor.* Other graduates showed a
   strong motivation to positions of managerial responsibility, "and their career
   experiences enable them to believe that they have the skills and values necessary to rise to such general management positions." A management position
   of high responsibility is the ultimate goal of these people, and when pressed
   to explain why they believed they had the skills necessary to obtain such
   positions these people answered that they were each qualified for these jobs
   as a result of what they saw as their *competances* in a combination of three
   areas: (1) analytical competance (ability to identify, analyze, and solve
   problems under conditions of incomplete information and uncertainty) [22];
   (2) interpersonal competance (ability to influence, supervise, lead, manipulate, and control people at all levels); and (3) emotional competance (the
   capacity to be stimulated by emotional and interpersonal crises rather than exhausted or debilitated by them, and the capacity to bear high levels of responsibility without becoming paralyzed). [23] Therefore, Schein concludes that "the
   person who wants to rise to higher levels of management and be given higher
   levels of responsibility must be *simultaneously* good at analyzing problems,
   handling people, and handling his or her own emotions in order to withstand
   the pressures and tensions of the "executive suite." [24]

3. *Creativity as a career anchor.* Some of the graduates have gone on to become
   successful entrepreneurs, and to Schein these people seem to have an encom-
   passing need "to build or to create something that was entirely their own
   product—a product or process that bears their name, a company of their own,
   or a personal fortune that reflects their accomplishments. [25] For example, one
   man had become a successful purchaser, restorer, and renter of townhouses
   in a large city, while others had built a successful consulting firm, and a new
   computer-based financial service organization.

4. *Autonomy and independence as career anchors.* Some respondents seemed
   driven by the need to be "on their own," free from the kind of dependence
   that can arise when a person elects to work in a large organization where
   promotions, transfers, and salary decisions make them dependent on other
   people. Many of these alumni also had strong technical/functional orientations; but instead of pursuing this orientation in an organization, they had
   decided instead to become consultants, working either alone or as part of a

relatively small firm. Others in this group had become a professor of business, a free lance writer, and a proprietor of a small retail business.

5. *Security as a career anchor.* A few of the MIT alumni seemed to be mostly concerned with long run career stability and job security. They seemed willing to do what was required to maintain job security, a decent income, and a stable future in the form of a good retirement program, benefits, etc. They were therefore much more willing to accept an *organizational* definition of their careers and to trust the organization to do right by them. [26] Maintaining a stable secure career in familiar surroundings was generally more important to these people than was aggressively pursuing alternative, superior career choices, if choosing the latter meant injecting instability or insecurity into their lives—by forcing them to "pull up their roots" and move to a distant city, for example. For some people security meant *organizational* security, and they might join organizations like the Bell System, or IBM where organizational security is high but where the person will likely have to move every few years in response to organizational needs. For others security is more *geographically* based and involves a feeling of settling down, planting roots, and stabilizing the family. For these latter people it is possible that if their organizations tried to move them they might well leave and try to find similar jobs in other organizations so as to remain where they planted their roots. [27]

CAREER DEVELOPMENT AND THE PERSONNEL MANAGEMENT PROCESS

Career planning has an important impact on employees' quality of work life. Employees, we have said, should have a good quality of work life, where quality is defined not just in terms of material things like rewards and working conditions but also in terms of self respect, satisfaction, and an opportunity to use talents, make contributions, and learn and grow. Career planning plays a pivotal role in this, since, ideally, it is through career planning that the needs of the individual and organization are integrated, and the employees are given an opportunity to grow and to satisfy their important needs through their membership in the organization.

What the Organization Can Do

There are many ways in which an organization can improve the quality of work life of its employees: job enrichment, leader training, eliminating discrimination, and improving material rewards and working conditions are some of these. In addition, however, the organization can use its personnel process—its manpower planning, recruiting, screening, placement, training, and appraising activities—not just to satisfy the organizations manpower needs but also to ensure that its employees are given adequate opportunities to develop their potential, and to formulate and accomplish realistic career goals. From this perspective organizational career planning and development involves more than

528   occasional "career planning" seminars and meetings; instead, it entails injecting a "career development perspective" into all the personnel activities, the goal being to meld these activities into what today is often called, for reasons that should now be clearer, a "human resource planning and development system."

What exactly can the organization do, to inject a career planning and development perspective into its personnel process? Some specifics are as follows:

Avoid Reality Shock.   Perhaps at no other stage in the person's career is it more important for the organization to take "career development" issues into account than at the initial, entry stage during which the person is recruited, hired, and given a first assignment, and boss. For the employee this is a critical period, a period during which he or she has to develop a sense of confidence, learn to get along with the first boss and with co-workers, learn how to accept responsibility, and, most importantly, quickly gain an insight into his or her talents, needs, and values as they relate to the persons initial career goals: for the new employee, in other words this is (or should be) a period of "reality testing" during which his or her initial hopes and goals first confront the reality of organizational life and of the person's actual talents and needs.

For many first-time workers, this turns out to be a disastrous period, one in which their often naive expectations first confront the realities of organizational life. The young graduate MBA or CPA, for example might come to his or her first job seeking a challenging, exciting assignment in which to apply the new techniques learned in school and to prove his abilities and gain a promotion. In reality, however the trainee is often turned off—by being relegated to an unimportant, low risk job where he or she "can't cause any trouble while we're trying him out," or by the harsh realities of interdepartmental conflict and politicing, or by a boss who is neither rewarded for nor trained in the unique mentoring tasks needed to properly supervise new employees. [28]

Reality shock can be disasterous for both employee and employer. For the employee it could be perceived as a period of failure, one which causes the person to needlessly question or perhaps change occupational goals. For the organization the result can be low morale, low productivity, and high turnover. According to one report, for example, some companies lose as many as one-third to one-half of their new recruits in their first year or two of employment and the cost of this turnover can be substantial. In 1973 it was estimated that the cost of recruiting, training, and replacing a manager was over $25,000 so that if an organization hires 50 new MBAs and loses 10 of them the first year the cost of "reality shock" could add a quarter of a million dollars to the organization's operating expenses. [29]

Provide Challenging Initial Jobs.   Most experts therefore agree that one of the most important things the organization can do is to provide its new employees with challenging first jobs. In one study of young managers at AT&T, for example the researchers found that the more challenging a person's job was in his or her first year with the company, the more effective and successful the person was even 5 or 6 years later. [30] Based on his own research, Hall contends that challenging initial jobs provide "one of the most powerful yet uncomplicated means of aiding the career development of new employees . . ." [31] In most organizations, however providing such jobs seems more the exception than the rule. In one survey of research and development organizations, for example only 1 out of 22 companies had a formal policy of giving challenging first assignments. [32] And this, as one expert has pointed out, is an example of "glaring mismanagement" when one considers the effort and money invested in recruiting, hiring, and training new employees. [33]

Provide Realistic Job Previews in Recruiting. Providing recruits with realistic previews of what to expect once they begin working in the organization appears to be an effective way of minimizing "reality shock" and improving the long-term performance of the candidates. Schein points out that one of the biggest problems recruits (and management) encounter during the crucial "entry" stage involves obtaining accurate information in a "climate of mutual selling." [34] The recruiter, anxious to "hook" good candidates, and the candidate (anxious to present as favorable an impression as possible) often give and receive unrealistic information during the interview, the result being that the interviewer may not be able to form a realistic picture of the candidates career goals, while at the same time the candidate forms an unrealistically favorable image of the organization.

Research results suggest that giving candidates a realistic preview of the organization and job can reduce turnover of new hires, particularly those who are recruited for relatively complex jobs like those of management trainees. [35] For example, two studies found that there was a significantly higher survival rate among students at West Point who had received realistic information on what to expect, than among those who did not. [36] Similar results were found for life insurance agents. [37] Schein believes that "many career problems stem from false hopes that are built up by both the organization and the individual in the early stages of the career." [38]

Keep in mind, however, that in several studies realistic job previews have not increased survival rates (although they *do* usually result in fewer job acceptances on the part of employees). [39] Realistic job previews do seem to improve survival rates for those (like West Point Cadets and life insurance agents) whose jobs are relatively complex. However such previews do not seem to make much difference in the survival rates of those, (like telephone operators or sewing machine operators) who have less complex jobs.

Improve Manpower Planning and Forecasting. [40] Employers can also improve their manpower planning and forecasting systems, particularly by improving the quality of information on which the manpower plans are built. At a minimum this would involve an improved inventory of current employees'

530   career interests, talents, and performance, which could then be matched with better information about jobs to be filled and the human characteristics needed to fill those jobs.

Improve Selection Methods.   Particularly during the early career stages it is important that both the applicant and the organization accurately assess the former's potential so that job assignments are realistic. Tests can be useful here in that they can help, predict job performance, and identify latent aptitudes. Management assessment centers have also been used to identify high potential candidates. Advocates claim that these assessment centers can identify high-potential management candidates, who can then be directed onto the company's management development track. [41]

Assign the New Recruit to Demanding, Specially Trained First Bosses. Livingston argues that there is a "pygmalion effect" in the relationship between a new employee and his or her boss. [42] In other words, the more the boss expects and the more confident and supportive the boss is of the new employee, the better the recruit will perform. Therefore, as two experts put it, "don't assign a new employee to a 'dead wood,' undemanding, or unsupportative supervisor." [43] Instead, choose specially trained, high performing, supportive supervisors who can set high standards for new employees during their critical, exploratory first year.

Provide Periodic Job Rotation, and Job Pathing.   It is likely that the best way new employees can test themselves and crystalize their "career anchors" is by trying out a variety of challenging jobs. By rotating the person to jobs in various specializations—from financial analysis, to production, to personnel, for example,—the employee gets an opportunity to assess his or her aptitudes and preferences while at the same time the organization obtains a manager with a broader, multifunctional view of the organization. [44] One extension of this is called *job pathing,* [45] which is based on the assumption that carefully sequenced job assignments can have a greater impact on personal development than any other kind of training experience. Some companies, like one large retailer, have therefore laid out a sequence of carefully planned, interdisciplinary job assignments leading to an executive job like that of store manager. The preliminary results here indicate that job pathing can substantially reduce the amount of time and training usually required to bring a novice trainee to the point where he or she is ready for the executive position.

Improved, Career-Oriented Performance Appraisals. [46]   Performance appraisals can play three important roles in career development. First, they can provide the employee with an honest, realistic appraisal of his or her performance on the job, and can thus provide a basis for the person determining to what extent his or her career goals—such as to be a salesmanager, or teacher—are realistic. Second, (and related to the first) the appraisal can help to *predict* the person's future performance by identifying specific aptitudes that have manifested themselves on the jobs (the U.S. Army tries to identify "leadership potential" through its appraisals, for example.) Finally, the appraisal can be the basis for identifying specific development needs the employee has, such as for leadership training, or for additional job rotation.

Schein believes that generating career-oriented appraisal information requires involving supervisors in the career development process. Perhaps most importantly, those responsible for appraising subordinates need to come to understand that valid information is in the long run more important than protecting the short-term interests of one's immediate subordinates. And, supervisors need concrete information regarding the appraisee's potential career path; information, in other words, about the nature of the future work for which he or she is appraising the subordinate. [47]

Career Planning Activities. Organizations also have to take specific steps to increase employees' involvement in their own career planning and development. For example, some organizations are experimenting with activities designed specifically to make employees aware of the need for career planning and of improving career decisions. Here, for example employees might learn about the rudiments of career planning and the stages in ones career, and engage in various activities aimed at crystalizing career anchors and formulating more realistic career goals. [48] Similarly, organizations are increasingly engaging in career counseling meetings (perhaps as part of the performance appraisal meeting) during which the employee and his or her supervisor (or perhaps a personnel director) assesses the employees progress in light of his or her career goals and identifies development needs. [49]

What the Individual Can Do

There are two basic things an individual can and should do to improve the career decisions he or she makes. [50] First, the person has to "take charge" of his or her own career by understanding that there are major decisions to be made and that making them requires considerable personal planning and effort. In other words, a person cannot leave his or her choices in the hands of others but must decide where he wants to go in terms of a career and what job moves and education are required to get there. Related to this, a person has to become an effective *diagnostician*. The person has to determine (through career counseling, testing, self-diagnostic books, and so on) what his or her talents or values are and how these fit with the sorts of careers the person is considering. [51] In summary, therefore, the key to career planning is self insight—into what you want out of a career, into your talents and limitations, and into your values and how they will fit in with the alternatives being considered. As Schein points out: "too many people never ask, much less attempt to answer, these kinds of questions. It was shocking to me when I conducted the interviews for the MIT panel study and discovered how many respondents said that they had never in 10 years of their careers asked themselves the kinds of questions which I was asking just to fill in the details of their job history." [52]

532   *IN CONCLUSION: THE ROLE OF*
PERSONNEL MANAGEMENT

One writer has pointed out that improving the quality of work life really boils down to the development of a role for the personnel function that is both new and at the same time very traditional. It is traditional because it involves all those activities that line managers (in their personnel management roles) and staff personnel managers have traditionally carried out. These activities include recruiting, selecting, training, compensating, motivating, appraising, counseling, and developing.

Yet the growing importance of the quality of work life, of human resource development, and of improving performance at work also means a new orientation—and new challenges—for all personnel managers. For *line* managers, it means the skills and techniques we discussed need to be applied with an eye toward motivating and improving the quality of work life of an increasingly better educated and career-conscious workforce. For *staff* personnel managers it probably means more direct involvement in traditionally "line" activities like performance appraisal; more coordination of the assessment, selection, and development functions; and increased influence with line management (with respect to redesigning jobs, changing reward systems, and dealing with government agencies and social action groups, for instance). In either case, it is apparent that personnel management represents not only a challenging role for line managers but a challenging "staff" job as well. [53]

SUMMARY

1. We said that people's actions are always based in part on the basic assumptions they make, and that this is especially true in regard to personnel management.

2. One important cornerstone of such a philosophy would be the need to improve performance. We have therefore used our model to introduce and tie together the chapters in this book. We said that performance involves: (1) ensuring that the subordinate *could* do the job if he or she wanted to, and (2) finding out what the person wants and holding it out as a possible reward—*motivating* the person.

3. "Quality of work life" means different things to different people but usually reflects such things as adequate and fair compensation, a safe, healthy environment, and opportunities for growth and self-respect on the job.

4. Quality of work life and employee performance go hand in hand. For example, many of the same conditions (job enrichment, equitable salaries, financial incentives, effective employee selection, etc.) that contribute to performance would also contribute to the quality of work life. Other activities contribute directly to the quality of work life—by providing for a safer work place, less discrimination on the job, and so forth. Finally, we saw that all of the personnel management activities we discussed in this book have the potential for adding to or detracting from the quality of your employee's work life.

5. Career planning has an important impact on employees quality of work life. We explained that it is through career planning that the needs of the individual and organization are integrated and the employees are given an opportunity to grow and to satisfy their important needs through their membership in the organization. Minimizing reality shock, realistic job previews, and supervisor training are some of the specific "personnel" techniques that can improve an organization's career development process.

EXPERIENTIAL EXERCISE

CAREER CHOICE: A COUNSELLING INTERVIEW *

Purpose.

1. To help you become more aware of your career orientations and the motivation behind them.

2. To increase your skills in career counselling.

Required Understanding. You should understand the nature of career stages, and the contents of chapter 18.

Introduction. Because you are reading this book, you are probably at a point in your career where you have already made some important choices, such as choice of an occupation or general field of work, or choice of a degree program. However, there are always other issues to be resolved and decisions to be made throughout a career.

It sometimes helps to talk the decision over with someone else. In this exercise, you will be working in groups of three. Each person will have the opportunity to be interviewed about his or her career choices, to be a career interviewer (or counselor), and to be an observer. Try to learn from each role—how to be a better career decision maker, how to be a better career counselor, and how to be a more sensitive observer of interviewing and helping processes.

Instructions for the Exercise. The class should split into groups of three. There will be three rounds to the exercise. In each round, there will be three roles: interviewer, interviewee, and observer. At the end of each round, you will switch roles and assume a role you haven't played yet. Therefore, at the end of the third round, each person in the trio should have had a chance to try every role.

Step 1: Round 1. Pick one person to act as interviewer, one as interviewee, and one as observer. For 15 minutes, the interviewer will conduct a counseling interview with the interviewee on the topic of career choices. The interview questions in Table 1 are provided as a guide; questions may be selected from Table 1, or the interviewer may make up his or her own.

During the interview, the observer should be silent and should take notes on the process of the interview. The observer should also as as *timekeeper,* stopping the interview after 15 minutes.

---

* **Source:** Douglas Hall, *Careers in Organizations* (Pacific Palisades, Goodyear, 1976)

For the next 5 minutes, the observer will feed back his or her observations, and all three members will discuss the interview. Focus on the following two issues:

a. What did the interviewee learn?
b. What did the interviewer or interviewee do that helped or hindered the interview?

Step 2: Round 2. Switch roles, (e.g. interviewer becomes interviewee, interviewee becomes observer, observer becomes interviewer). Follow the same procedure as in Round 1.

Step 3: Round 3. Switch roles again, as in Round 2. Be sure that no one plays the same role twice. Follow the same procedure as in Round 1.

Step 4: Class Discussion. Meet again as a class. Discuss what the interviewees seemed to be learning. What career choice issues were discussed most frequently? What choices or solutions were considered?

Also discuss what people learned about the process of interviewing and counseling. What did the interviewer do that helped or hindered the decision-making process? What did the interviewee do to help or hinder his or her own progress?

Table 1: Questions

1. How would you describe yourself as a person?
2. What are you best at doing? Worst?
3. What do you really enjoy doing most? Least?
4. What have been one or two of your best successes—times when you felt especially productive and proud of your capabilities and potential?
5. What would you stop doing if you could?
6. What would you like to do more?
7. What would you like to learn more about?
8. What aspects of yourself do you like most? Least?
9. Could you describe your ideal self?
10. Who are your heroes? What do you like about them?
11. If you could have any job at all, what would you do? What would be an ideal job for you?
12. What do you plan to do during the next five years? (If you haven't yet decided, pretend you had to decide *right now*. What would you choose to do?)
13. What are the pros and cons of the different career options you are considering right now?
14. Which way are you leaning?
15. Pretend a person amazingly similar to you (background, interests, plans, etc.) came to you for advice on the same issue you're wrestling with now. What advice would you give this person?

DISCUSSION QUESTIONS

1. Define quality of work life and cite some factors that contribute to it.
2. Compare and contrast quality of work life and motivation.
3. Explain how personnel management activities affect the quality of work life.
4. Explain why career development is an important aspect of "human resource planning and development."
5. Explain the factors that influence career choices.

NOTES

1. Except as noted, this section is based on J. Richard Hackman and J. Lloyd Suttle, *Improving Life at Work: Behavioral Science Approaches to Organizational Change* (Santa Monica, Calif.: Goodyear, 1977), see also William Steiges, "Can We Legislate the Humanization of Work?" in W. Clay Hamner and Frank Schmidt, *Contemporary Problems in Personnel*, pp. 503–508.

2. *Ibid.*, p. 4.

3. *Ibid.*, pp. 3–4.

4. Edward Lawler, *Reward Systems*.

5. See, for example J. Richard Hackman and J. Lloyd Suttle, *Improving Life at Work*, p. 4.

6. Schein, *Career Dynamics*, pp. 4–5.

7. See, for example, Schein, *Career Dynamics*, p. 19.

8. See for example Donald Super, "A Theory of Vocational Development," *American Psychologists*, Vol. 8 (1953), pp. 189–190; Eli Ginzberg, "Autobiography," "The Development of a Developmental Theory of Occupational Choice," and "Selected Writings," in *Guidance in the Twentieth Century*, edited by William H. VanHoose and John Tietrofesa (Boston: Houghton Mifflin, 1970), pp. 58–67; and Anne Roe, "Perspectives on Vocational Development," in *Perspectives on Vocational Development*, edited by John Whiteley and Arthur Resnikoff (Washington: American Personnel and Guidance Association, 1972), pp. 62–68.

9. Described in Talbert, pp. 33–34.

10. Donald Super, John Crites, Raymond Hummel, Helen Moser, Phoebe Overstreet, and Charles Warnath, *Vocational Development: A Framework for Research* (New York: Teachers College Press 1957), pp. 40, 41.

11. These tasks are based on Edgar Schein, *Career Dynamics*, p. 40.

12. See Edgar Schein, *Career Dynamics*, pp. 37–39.

13. Super et al. identified only the trial, and stabilization substages. Our discussion of the third, mid career substage is based on the work of other writers, including Schein, *Career Dynamics*, pp. 39–46, and Hall, Chapter 3.

14. Much of the remainder of this section is based on Douglas T. Hall, *Careers in Organizations* (Pacific Palasades: Goodyear, 1976), pp. 10–46. Note above six factors including aptitudes.

15. John Holland, *Making Vocational Choices: A Theory of Careers* (Englewood Cliffs: Prentice-Hall, 1973).

16. See, for example Benjamin Schneider, *Staffing Organizations* (Pacific Palasades: Goodyear, 1976), pp. 83–84.

17. See, for example Peter Blau, and Otis Duncan, *The American Occupational Structure* (New York: Wiley, 1967); W. H. Sewell, A. O. Haller, and G. W. Ohlendorf, "The Early Educational and Early Occupational Attainment Process: Replication and Revisions," *American Sociological Review*, Vol. 35 (1970), pp. 1014–1027; A. O. Haller and A. Portes, "Status Obtainment Processes," *Sociology of Education*, Vol. 46 (1973), pp. 51–91.

536   18. James Goodale and Douglas Hall, "Inheriting A Career: The Effects of Sex, Values, and Parents," *Journal of Vocational Behavior* (1976). Quoted in Hall, Careers in Organizations, p. 22.

19. *Ibid.*, p. 22.

20. *Ibid.*, p. 23.

21. Schein, pp. 128–129. Donald Super developed a somewhat similar concept based on research began in the late 1930s. He says that people develop a self concent or image of themselves—in terms of their abilities, interests, needs and values, aspirations, and so on. Discussed in Hall, p. 12. Donald Super, *The Psychology of Careers* (New York: Harper and Row, 1957).

22. Schein, p. 135

23. Schein, p. 136.

24. Schein, p. 138.

25. Schein, p. 149.

26. Schein, p. 147.

27. Add to Holland study: James Rounds, Jr., Alexander Shubsachs, Rene Dawis, and Lloyd Lofquist, "A Test of Holland's Environment Formulation," *Journal of Applied Psychology*, Vol. 63 (October 1978), pp. 609–616.

28. For discussions of this see, for example Douglas T. Hall, *Careers in Organizations*, p. 66; Schein, Career Dynamics, p. 85; Douglas T. Hall and Francine Hall, "What's New in Career Management?" *Organizational Dynamics*, Vol. 4 (Summer 1976).

29. Explained in Hall and Hall, "What's New in Career Management?"

30. Dave Berlew and Douglas Hall, "The Socialization of Managers: Effects of Expectations on Performance," *Administrative Science Quarterly*, Vol. 11 (1966), pp. 207–223; also see Bruce Buchanan, II, "Building Organizational Commitment: The Socialization of Managers in Work Organizations," *Administrative Science Quarterly*, Vol. 19 (1974), pp. 533–546.

31. Hall, p. 154.

32. Douglas Hall and Edward Lawler, III, "Unused Potential in Research and Development Organizations," *Research Management*, Vol. 12 (1969), pp. 339–354.

33. John Hinrichs, *The Motivation Crisis* (New York: Amacom, 1974), p. 64.

34. See Schein, p. 86.

35. As opposed to more routine jobs, for example as telephone operators, or sewing machine operators.

36. D. W. Ilgen, and W. Seely, "Realistic Expectations as an Aid in Reducing Voluntary Resignations," *Journal of Applied Psychology*, Vol. 59 (1974), pp. 452–455.

37. See F. Youngberg, "An Experimental Study of Job Satisfaction and Turnover in Relation to Job Expectations and Self Expectations," unpublished doctoral dissertation, New York University (1963), quoted in Richard Reilly, Mary Tenopyr, and Steven Sperling, "The Effects of Job Previews on Job Acceptance and Survival Rates of Telephone Operator Candidates," *Journal of Applied Psychology*, Vol. 64 (1979), p. 218; also see Jean Dalton, Paul Thompson, and Raymond Price, "The Four Stages of Professional Careers—A New Look at Performance by Professionals," *Organizational Dynamics* (Summer 1977).

38. Schein, *Career Dynamics*, p. 82.

39. Reilly et al., pp. 218–220.

40. Van Maanen and Schein, pp. 84–85.

41. Douglas Bray, Richard Campbell and Donald Grant, *Formative Years in Business* (New York: Wiley, 1974).

42. J. Sterling Livingston, "Pygmalion in Management," *Harvard Business Review* (July–August 1969), pp. 81–89.

43. Hall and Hall, "What's New in Career Management?" *Organizational Dynamics*, Vol. 4 (Summer 1976).

44. H. G. Kaufman, *Obsolescence and Professional Career Development* (New York: Amacom, 1974).

45. Hall and Hall. p. 350, Schneier.

46. For a discussion of the role played by the supervisor in appraisals, see Donald Hall, "Career Planning for Employee Development: A Primer for Managers," *California Management Review*, Vol. 20 (1977), pp. 23–35.

47. Schein, *Career Dynamics*, p. 19.

48. See, for example D. B. Miller, Personal Vitality (Reading: Addison Wesley, 1977); Personal Vitality Workbook (Reading: Addison-Wesley, 1977).

49. Albert Griffith, "Career Development: What Organizations are Doing About It," *Personnel* (1980), pp. 63–69; see also Richard Vosburgh, "The Annual Human Resource Review (A Career Planning System)," *Personnel Journal* (October 1980), pp. 830–837.

50. Schein, Career Dynamics, pp. 252–253; Bowen and Hall, "Career Planning and Employee Development," p. 279.

51. For self diagnosis books, see, for example Miller, Op.Cit.; G. A. Ford and G. L. Lippitt, A *Life Planning Workbook* (Fairfax Virginia, NTL Learning Resources Corp. 1972).

52. Schein, p. 253.

53. Fred Foulkes, "The Expanding Role of the Personnel Function," *Harvard Business Review*, Vol. 53 (March–April 1975), pp. 71–84.

Glossary

Accident-proneness. To psychologists, "accident-prone" implies the possession of those qualities or traits that have been found from research to lead to an undue number of accidents. There is considerable doubt as to whether such a personality type exists, and most experts believe accident-proneness is "situational."

Achievement need. Those with high needs to achieve derive satisfaction from accomplishing their tasks, and prefer situations which have moderate risks and in which they can see their own contributions. They also prefer receiving quick, concrete feedback concerning their performance.

Active listening. A counseling technique in which the counselor actively tries to grasp both the facts and the feelings in what he or she hears. It involves listening for total meaning, reflecting feelings, noting all cues, not acting as a judge, and showing interest.

Adverse impact. Refers to the total employment process which results in a significantly higher percentage of a protected group in the candidate population being rejected for employment, placement, or promotion. For example, if 80% of white applicants pass the test, but only 20% of black applicants pass, a black applicant has a prima facie case proving adverse impact. Then, once he has proven his point, the burden of proof shifts to the employer.

Affiliation need. People with high needs for affiliation have strong desires to maintain close friendships and to receive affection from others. They are constantly seeking to establish friendly relationships.

Affirmative action. Includes those specific actions (in recruitment, hiring, upgrading jobs, etc.) that are designed and taken for the purpose of eliminating the present effects of past discrimination.

Age Discrimination in Employment Act. Passed in 1967, this act prohibits arbitrary age discrimination and specifically protects individuals 40-65 years old.

Agency shop. A form of union security. Employees who do not belong to the union still must pay union dues (on the assumption that union efforts benefit all workers).

Alternation ranking method. A method used in job evaluation and performance appraisal for ranking jobs from lowest to highest in importance. First the highest is chosen, then the lowest, then the next highest and the next lowest, etc., until all jobs are ranked.

Appraisal problems. These include unclear standards, halo effect, central tendency, leniency or strictness, and bias.

Authorization cards. In order to petition for a union election, the union must show that a sizable number of employees may be interested in being unionized. Therefore, union organizers try to get employees to sign authorization cards: 30% must sign before an election is petitioned.

Bakke reverse discrimination case. This case involved a white male applicant rejected by a California medical school who contended that he was unfairly discriminated against because minority candidates with qualifications lower than his were accepted. Bakke won his case.

BARS. BARS (Behaviorally Anchored Rating Scales) represent a new appraisal technique that requires five steps: generate critical incidents; develop performance dimensions; reallocate incidents; scale incidents; and develop the final instrument.

Behavior modification. Used synonymously with *reinforcement* and *operant conditioning*, this is based on the work of B. F. Skinner and is built on two principles: (1) that behavior which appears to lead to a positive consequence tends to be repeated, while behavior that tends to lead to a negative consequence tends not to be repeated; and (2) therefore, by providing the properly scheduled rewards, it is possible to influence people's behavior.

Behaviorally Anchored Rating Scales. *See* BARS.

Benchmark jobs. Used in the factor comparison job evaluation method, these are 15–25 key jobs that must be representative of the range of jobs under study, and that are evaluated first.

"Bill of rights" for union members. A part of the Landrum-Griffin Act, this provides for certain rights in the nomination of candidates for union office, affirms a member's right to sue his or her union, and ensures that no member can be fined or suspended without "due process."

BFOQ. A "bona fide occupational qualification." According to the Civil Rights Act, it is not an unlawful employment practice to hire an employee on the basis of religion, sex, or national origin in those certain instances where religion, sex, or national origin is a bona fide occupational qualification reasonably necessary to normal operation of that particular business or enterprise. Sex would be a BFOQ for an actress, for example.

Business necessity. Can be used to justify an otherwise discriminatory employment practice. There must be an overriding legitimate business purpose to use such a practice.

Cafeteria benefit plan. Enables employees to pick and choose from available benefit options and literally develop their own benefit plans.

Cash plans. A profit-sharing plan where a percentage of profits (usually about 15-20%) is distributed at regular intervals.

Central tendency. An appraisal problem in which all traits tend to be rated about average.

Civil Rights Act. The 1964 Civil Rights Act (as amended) and 1967 Age Discrimination in Employment Act bar discrimination with respect to race, color, age, religion, sex, and national origin. They were bolstered in 1972 by the Equal Employment Opportunity Act which set up the EEOC.

Class description. In job evaluation the class description is equivalent to an individual job's job description.

Classical conditioning. Similar to *operant conditioning*. In classical conditioning, the sequence of events leading to a reward is independent of the subject's behavior. With operant conditioning, the consequences (rewards or punishments) are made to occur as a consequence of the subject's response or lack of response.

Closed shop. A form of union security in which the company can hire only union members. This was outlawed in 1947, but still exists in some industries (like printing).

Collective bargaining. The process through which representatives of management and the union meet to negotiate a labor agreement.

Compensable factors. In job evaluation, those basic factors which determine your definition of job content and through which jobs are compared to one another. Examples are skill, effort, responsibility, know-how, and problem solving.

Concurrent validation. A validation method in which the predictor (like your test) is compared with employee's current performance.

Continuous (or mass) reinforcement. Here

the subject is rewarded each and every time he or she performs the desired behavior.

Contract administration. Involves a system whereby employer and union determine whether or not the contract has been violated: It is the vehicle for administering the contract on a day-to-day basis and operates through the grievance process.

Correlation analysis. A statistical technique that is used to determine the degree of relationship between two variables.

Critical incident method. An appraisal technique where you keep, for each subordinate, a running record of uncommonly good or undesirable incidents.

Cross validation. The process in test validation through which you again administer the test, measure performance, and relate test scores and criteria to check the original validation; it is the same as *revalidation*.

Davis-Bacon Act. This act provides for the Secretary of Labor to set wage rates for laborers and mechanics employed by contractors working for the federal government. Amendments to the act provide for employee benefits.

Decentralization. A philosophy of organization and management which involves both selective delegation of authority, as well as concentration of authority through the imposition of policies, and selective but adequate control.

Decree approach. In organizational change, a one-way announcement originating with a person with high formal authority and passed on to those in lower positions.

Deferred profit-sharing plan. Here a predetermined portion of profits is placed in each employee's account under the supervision of a trustee. There is a tax advantage to such plans, since income (and income taxes) are deferred.

Delegation. The process through which authority is pushed down from superior to subordinate.

Departmentalization. The process through which the work of the organization is divided into departments such as production, sales, and finance. We distinguished

between divisional and function departmentation and said division-oriented departments could be built around products, customers, marketing channels, or locations.

Discrimination. According to the EEOC, discrimination is defined as follows: The use of any test which adversely affects hiring, promotion, transfer, or any other employment or membership opportunity of classes protected by Title VII constitutes discrimination *unless*: (a) the test has been validated and evidences a high degree of utility as hereinafter described, or (b) is required as a BFOQ.

Disparate treatment. According to the EEOC, disparate treatment occurs where members of a minority or sex group have been denied the same employment, promotion, transfer, or membership opportunities as have been made available to other employees or applicants. Thus, no new test or employee selection standard can be imposed upon a class of individuals protected by Title VII who, but for prior discrimination, would have been granted the opportunity to qualify under less stringent standards previously enforced.

EEOC. The Equal Employment Opportunity Commission created under Title VII.

EEOC Guidelines. Published by the EEOC, providing "highly recommended" selection procedures, records and reports, procedural regulations, preemployment inquiries, and overall affirmative action programs.

Employee Retirement Income Security Act (ERISA). This provides for the creation of government-run, employer-financed corporations that will protect employees against a failing pension plan.

Equal Employment Opportunity Act. Title VII of the 1964 Civil Rights Act (as amended in 1972) is known as the Equal Employment Opportunity Act. It established the Equal Employment Opportunity Commission and specifically bars discrimination with respect to race, color, religion, sex, or national origin.

Equal Pay Act. Requires equal pay for equal work and states that employees of one sex may not be paid wages at a rate lower than that paid to employees of the opposite sex for doing roughly equivalent work.

ERISA. *See* **Employee Retirement Income and Security Act.**

Exempt vs. nonexempt jobs. The Fair Labor Standards Act of 1938 specifically exempts certain employees from its provisions. For example, nonexempt employees must be paid for overtime at least 1½ times their normal 40-hour wage rate; exempt employees do not.

Expectancy chart. An aid to graphically presenting the relationship between a test and job performance. Employees are split into groups by test score and the percentages of high performing employees in each of these test groups are presented on the chart.

Expectancy model of motivation. Based on the work of Victor Vroom, this model describes the process of motivation and takes the person's expectations for success into account. Basically, Vroom says that motivation will take place if the valence or value of the particular outcome is very high for the person, and if the person feels he has a reasonably good chance of accomplishing the tasks and obtaining the outcome.

Extinction. In operant conditioning, the situation in which positive reinforcement is withheld so that over time the undesired behavior disappears.

Factor comparison method. A job evaluation method in which the job is ranked several times; once for each compensable factor you choose.

Fair Labor Standards Act. Passed in 1938, this act contains laws governing minimum wage, overtime pay, and maximum hours for most employees in America.

Federal Old Age and Survivors' Insurance. The technical name for *Social Security* which provides retirement income, survivors' or death benefits, and disability payments.

Fixed interval schedule. In operant conditioning, such a schedule is based on time.

Fixed ratio schedule. A fixed ratio schedule is based on units of output rather than time. Most piecework incentive pay plans are on a fixed ratio schedule.

Flagged rates. The same as *red circle* or *overrates*. In compensation management, these are rates being paid to overpaid employees which fall above the wage curve.

Flextime. Here workers themselves determine their own starting and stopping hours around a central core of midday hours—such as 11:00 a.m.–2:00 p.m.

Forced distribution method. A performance appraisal method similar to grading on a curve. Here predetermined percentages of ratees are placed in various performance categories.

Good faith bargaining. Good faith bargaining means that both parties communicate and negotiate. And, it means that proposals are matched with counterproposals and that both parties make every reasonable effort to arrive at agreements. It does not mean that either party is compelled to agree to a proposal.

Graphic rating scales. A performance appraisal chart that lists a number of traits (like job knowledge) and a range of performance (unsatisfactory to exceptional) for each.

Grid training. A development technique based on the Managerial Grid. It is aimed at developing open confrontation of organizational problems and "9.9" (high people–high production) leaders.

Griggs vs. Duke Power Company case. Plaintiff Willie Griggs claimed that the company's requirement that its coalhandlers be high school graduates was unfairly discriminatory. Duke Power Company lost the case and the Supreme Court laid out three crucial rulings: discrimination need not be overt; the employment practice must be shown to be related to job performance; and the burden of proof is placed on the employer to show that his hiring standard is job related.

Guaranteed annual income. Also known as *supplemental unemployment benefits,* these provide for income in the event the company must shut down for tool changes, etc. (as in the auto industry). The benefits are paid by the company and supplement unemployment benefits.

Guaranteed piecework plan. A piecerate plan in which the worker is paid a guaranteed hourly wage regardless of his or her performance.

Halo effect. In performance appraisal, the problem in which a rater rates an employee high (or low) on all dimensions of his performance based on his performance on one of those dimensions.

Hay System. A job evaluation method that focuses on know-how, problem solving, and accountability as compensable factors.

Illegal bargaining items. In collective bargaining, those items that are forbidden by law. For example, the clause agreeing to hire "union members exclusively" would be illegal in a right-to-work state.

Interest inventory. Interest inventories compare a person's interest with those of people in various occupations. They can be used for career counseling, and to help predict a person's interest in (and success on) the job for which you are recruiting.

Involvement approach. A technique for using attitude surveys that gets the employees and department managers involved in reviewing results of the attitude survey and suggesting changes.

Job classification evaluation method. A job evaluation method in which jobs are classified into classes (or grades) based on decision rules or the job's overall difficulty.

Job compensation scale. In the factor comparison job evaluation method, the scale on which for each of the factors you write the job next to the appropriate wage rate.

Job descriptions. One of the products of job analysis, the job descriptionn shows for each job such things as: duties; responsibilities; reporting relationships; working conditions; and supervisory responsibilities.

Job enrichment. A technique for motivating workers which involves forming natural work groups, combining tasks, establishing client relationships, vertical loading, and opening feedback channels; it is aimed at tapping employees' "higher order" needs.

Job evaluation. Job evaluation is aimed at determining the relative worth of a job and involves a formal and systematic comparison of jobs in order to determine the worth of one job relative to another.

Job instruction training. The training method that involves listing all necessary steps in the job, each in its proper sequence. Alongside each step are also listed the corresponding key points of each step.

Job rotation. A training technique which shifts employees periodically from job to job.

Job specifications. One of the products of job analysis, job specifications present the "human requirements" of the job in terms of education, skill, personality, etc.

Labor Management Relations Act. Also known as the *Taft-Hartley Act,* its provisions were aimed at limiting unions in four ways: by prohibiting union unfair labor practices; by enumerating the rights of employees as union members; by enumerating the rights of employers; and by allowing the president of the United States to temporarily bar "national emergency" strikes.

Labor-Management Reporting and Disclosure Act. Also known as the *Landrum-Griffin Act,* this was aimed at protecting union members from possible wrongdoing on the part of their unions and resulted in a union member's "bill of rights," among other things.

Landrum-Griffin Act. *See* **Labor-Management Reporting and Disclosure Act.**

Leniency problem. In performance appraisal, the problem in which a supervisor is lenient in evaluating all his employees. Conversely, there is also a strictness problem in performance appraisals.

Lincoln Incentive System. With this incentive plan, most employees work on a guaranteed piecework basis, and total annual profits (less taxes, 5% dividend to stockholders, and a reserve for reinvestment) are distributed each year among employees in accordance with their merit rating.

Line managers. Managers who have direct responsibility for carrying out the basic functions of the organization and who also have supervisory responsibility.

McDonnell-Douglas Test. Used to prove adverse impact, this test involves showing that the applicant was qualified, but was rejected by an employer who is still seeking applicants for the position.

Maintenance of membership. A form of union security. Here, employees do not have to belong to the union. However, union members employed by the firm must maintain membership in the union for the contract period.

Managerial Grid. The Managerial Grid shows leadership styles reflecting different combinations of concern for people and concern for production. The aim is to emphasize the superiority of the high people–high production leader.

Mandatory bargaining items. In collective bargaining, these are those items that a party must bargain over if they are introduced by the other party—for example, pay.

Motivator factors. In Herzberg's motivation theory, the job content or motivator factors include such things as achievement and recognition. Herzberg says that it is only by building these motivators into the job that an employee can be motivated.

National Labor Relations Act. Also known as the *Wagner Act*, it bans certain types of unfair labor practices, provides for secret ballot elections and majority rule, and created the National Labor Relations Board (NLRB).

Needs hierarchy. Developed by Abraham Maslow, the hierarchy ranged up from physiological to safety to affiliation to achievement to self-actualization needs, and suggests that higher-order needs do not become activated until lower-level needs are fairly well satisfied.

Negative reinforcement. Like positive reinforcement, negative reinforcement focuses on reinforcing the desired behavior. But instead of providing a positive reward, the reward is that the employee avoids some negative consequence.

NLRB. The National Labor Relations Board, which was created by the Wagner Act for the purpose of enforcing its two provisions: banning certain types of unfair labor practices, and providing for secret ballot elections and majority rule.

Norris-LaGuardia Act. This marked the beginning of the era of strong encouragement of unions, and guaranteed to each employee the right to bargain collectively "free from interference, restraint, or coercion."

Occupational Safety and Health Act. Passed in 1970, its stated purpose was to "assure so far as possible every working man and woman in the nation a safe and healthful working condition, and to preserve our human resources."

O.D. (Organizational Development) is a group of personnel development techniques aimed at increasing the level of support and trust among participants, increasing open confrontation of organizational problems, increasing personal enthusiasm and self control, and increasing the openness and authenticity of organizational communications.

OFCC. The Office of Federal Contract Compliance, which is responsible for implementing Executive Orders 11246 and 11375. These Executive Orders prohibited employment discrimination by employers with federal contracts of more than $10,000 (and their subcontractors).

Office of Federal Contract Compliance. *See* OFCC.

Open shop. Perhaps the least attractive type of "union security" from the union's point of view. Here it is up to the workers whether they join the union or not, and those who do not also do not pay dues.

Operant conditioning. Also known as *behavioral modification* and *reinforcement. See* **behavior modification.**

Organization chart. A chart showing the titles of positions in the organization, and, by means of interconnecting lines, who reports to whom.

OSHA. The Occupational Safety and Health Administration which was established to administer the Occupational Safety and Health Act.

Out of line rates. In job evaluation, once the wage curve is drawn, out of line rates reflecting underpaid or overpaid employees may be identified.

Packaged point plans. A number of groups such as the National Electrical Manufacturers Association and the National Trade Association have developed point plans to facilitate job evaluation.

Partial reinforcement. In operant conditioning, a partial reinforcement schedule provides positive reinforcement only part of the time, according to some schedule.

Pay grades. A pay (or wage) grade is comprised of jobs of approximately equal difficulty or importance as determined by job evaluation.

Peer appraisals. In performance appraisal, a technique in which one's peers appraise his or her performance.

Pension Benefits Guarantee Corporation (PBGC). Established under ERISA to assure that pensions meet vesting obligations.

Personnel director (or manager). Usually a staff position in organizations, the personnel manager usually carries out three distinct functions: a line function within his own personnel department; a coordinative function (coordinating personnel activities throughout the organization); and a staff or service function in which personnel assists in hiring, training, evaluating, rewarding, counseling, promoting, and firing employees.

Personnel management philosophy. The most basic values, beliefs, and assumptions one makes with respect to how the basic personnel management functions like recruiting, interviewing, selecting, compensating, developing, etc., should be carried out.

Physiological needs. The first level of needs on Maslow's needs hierarchy. They refer to people's needs for food, clothing, shelter, etc.

Piecerate. In a piecework incentive plan, the rate per piece that is paid.

Piecework. An incentive plan which pays employees in direct proportion to the number of pieces produced.

Point method of job evaluation. The job evaluation method in which a number of compensable factors are identified and then the degree to which each of these factors is present on the job is determined.

Population comparison. A method for proving adverse impact. Here a comparison is made of the percentage of the minority group employees and the percentage of that minority in the general population in the surrounding community.

Position Analysis Questionnaire. In job analysis, a questionnaire used to collect data concerning the duties and responsibilities of the job.

Positive reinforcement. Like negative reinforcement, positive reinforcement focuses on reinforcing the desired behavior. Positive rewards include praise or raises.

Predictive validation. A validation technique in which tests are administered to applicants before they are hired. You then hire those applicants using only your existing selection techniques. Then, after these people have been on the job for some time, measure their performance and compare it to their earlier test results.

Projective personality tests. Here an ambiguous stimulus such as an ink blot or a clouded picture is presented to the person taking the test, and he or she is asked to interpret or react to it. The person's interpretation must come from "within" himself.

Punishment. In operant conditioning, a method aimed at reducing the frequency of undesired behavior.

Quality of work life. This has been defined as "the degree to which members of a work organization are able to satisfy important personal needs through their experiences in the organization."

Quota systems. Rather than go through the time and cost involved in validating tests separately for minorities and nonminorities, many managers have opted for a quota system for selection. In other words, if they hire 30% of their white applicants, they also hire 30% of their black applicants, etc.

Ranking. Used in both job evaluation and performance appraisal to rank jobs (or persons) from lowest to highest.

Ranking key jobs. In the factor comparison job evaluation method, this involves ranking key jobs factor by factor or according to wage rates.

Rate ranges. Used in job evaluation to provide a range of possible pay rates within each pay grade.

Ratio schedule. In operant conditioning, there are two reinforcement schedules (fixed ratio and variable ratio) that are based on output. With the former, the worker is rewarded after a fixed number of units is produced. With the variable ratio schedule, reward is based on output but after varying amounts of the unit are produced.

Red circle rates. *See* **Flagged rates.**

Reinforcement. *See* **Behavior modification.**

Reliability. Reflects the consistency with which a test or other device measures the attribute it is designed to measure.

Representation hearing. One stage in the union drive and election. After obtaining authorization cards, the union usually contacts the NLRB to request an election, and if the election is contested by the company, the NLRB holds a hearing to determine if 30% or more of the employees signed the authorization cards, and what the bargaining unit will be.

Restricted policy. One method for proving adverse impact. Restricted policy is a demonstration that the employer has been using a hiring practice either intentionally or not to exclude members of a minority group.

Revalidation. *See* **Cross validation.**

Scanlon Plan. An organization-wide incentive plan that has two basic features. First, financial incentives aimed at cutting costs are installed. Second, a network of departmental and plant screening committees is established to evaluate employee and management cost-cutting suggestions.

Schedules of reinforcement. There are two basic schedules of reinforcement: continuous or mass reinforcement and partial reinforcement. Partial reinforcement schedules include the fixed interval schedule, variable interval schedule, fixed ratio schedule, and variable ratio schedule.

Scientific management. Scientific management grew out of the work of Frederick Taylor and his desire to scientifically evaluate each job to determine the "one best way" for doing that job. Taylor felt that financial incentives used in conjunction with an optimally designed job would result in optimal efficiency, company profits, and employee remuneration.

Self-actualization need. The top in Maslow's needs hierarchy, self actualization refers to the need to become all that one has the potential for becoming.

Self appraisal. In performance appraisal, an appraisal carried out by the ratee himself.

Shared power approach to development.

The use of participation and group decision making and problem solving to identify problems and develop suggested alternatives for improving the situation.

Social needs. Also known as *affiliation needs*, these are midway in Maslow's hierarchy.

Staff managers. Staff managers are responsible for advising and assisting line managers.

Staffing. Along with planning, organizing, leading, and controlling, staffing is one of the five basic functions all managers perform. Staffing is used synonymously in this book with *personnel management* to include all personnel management-related activities that managers perform—such as developing job descriptions, recruiting, selecting, compensating, etc.

Standard hour plan. This is similar to the piecework plan, but with the standard hour plan, the employee is rewarded by a percent premium that equals the percent by which his performance is above standard.

Straight piecework plan. An incentive plan in which the employee is simply paid on the basis of the number of units produced; there is no guaranteed minimum wage.

Strictness problem. *See* **Leniency problem.**

Survey feedback. An O.D. technique in which attitude surveys are administered to employees who then receive back the data, analyze it, and with their supervisor jointly develop alternative solutions to any problems that the surveys identified.

Systematic soldiering. What Frederick Taylor saw as the tendency of employees to work at the slowest pace possible and produce at the minimum acceptable level.

Systems I and IV organizations. Based on the work of Rensis Likert. In System I organizations, he says management is seen as having little confidence or trust in subordinates. In System IV organizations, management does have complete confidence and trust in employees, and decision making is widely dispersed and decentralized.

Taft-Hartley Act. Also known as the *Labor Management Relations Act*, this prohibited union unfair labor practices and enumerated the rights of employees as union members. It also enumerated the rights of employers, and allowed the president of the United States to temporarily bar national emergency strikes.

Test. A test is basically a sample of behavior. According to the EEOC, the term "test" is defined as any paper-and-pencil or performance measure used as a basis for any employment decision and can include biographical information blanks, interviewer's rating scales, scored application forms, etc.

Test battery. Several tests which are combined to better predict job success or failure.

Theory X and Theory Y. Developed by Douglas McGregor. He said that some managers have a Theory X set of assumptions that hold that workers dislike work, cannot be trusted, and must therefore be prodded and closely supervised. Theory Y assumptions hold that workers do not dislike work and are capable of self control.

Title VII. Title VII of the 1964 Civil Rights Act says that you cannot discriminate on the basis of race, color, religion, sex, or national origin with respect to employment.

Underutilization. An affirmative action term. Based on the employee survey (as part of the affirmative action program), you may find that certain groups are underutilized in certain areas or jobs in your work force. For example, women and minority groups, according to the EEOC, are often underutilized in managerial and professional jobs.

Unfair discrimination. Robert Guion says that unfair discrimination exists when persons with equal probabilities of job success have unequal probabilities of being hired.

Unfair labor practices. Under the Wagner Act, it is unfair for management to "interfere with, restrain, or coerce employees" in exercising their legally sanctioned right of self organization.

Union security. A primary aim of unions, union security reflects their desire to establish "security" for themselves by gaining the right to represent a firm's workers and, where possible, be the exclusive bargaining agent for all employees in the unit. Five types of union security are possible: closed shop; union shop; agency shop; open shop; maintenance of membership arrangement.

Union shop. A form of union security. Here the company can hire nonunion people, but they must join the union after a prescribed period of time, and pay dues. (If they do not, they can be fired.)

U.S. Civil Service Procedure. In job analysis, a technique that makes use of the job analysis record sheet.

U.S. Department of Labor Procedure. In job analysis, a technique that describes what the worker does in terms of data, people, and things.

Valence. Basically, in Vroom's expectancy theory of motivation, valence represents the value placed on the incentive or reward.

Validity. Represents the accuracy with which a test, interview, etc., measures what it purports to measure or fulfills the function it was designed to fulfill.

Validity coefficient. A correlation coefficient used in the special case of validating a test or other measure.

Variable interval schedule. In reinforcement, a schedule based on varying time intervals.

Variable ratio schedule. In reinforcement, a schedule based on varying numbers of units produced.

Vesting. In compensation, vesting refers to the money that the employer and employee have placed in the latter's pension fund which cannot be forfeited for any reason.

Voluntary bargaining items. In collective bargaining, these are the items over which bargaining is neither illegal nor mandatory. Neither party can be compelled against its wishes to negotiate over voluntary items.

Wage curve. The wage curve relates to pay grades and shows the relationship between (1) the value of the job, and (2) the average wage rate of these grades (or jobs).

Wage structure. The wage curve gives basic information for building a wage structure. However, additional information must be taken into consideration before a wage structure is finalized. This information includes: market wages, compensation policies; and the need for rate ranges. The wage structure reflects the final wages to be paid by the organization categorized by pay grades and showing rate ranges.

Wagner Act. *See* **National Labor Relations Act.**

Walsh-Healy Public Contract Act. This act set basic labor standards for employees working on any government contract which amounts to more than $10,000. It contains minimum wage, maximum hours, and safety and health provisions.

Work sampling. In employee selection, a technique which uses the person's actual performance on the same (or a very similar) job to predict the person's future job performance.

Workmen's compensation. Every state has its own workmen's compensation law, but all these laws are aimed at providing sure, prompt income and medical benefits to work accident victims or their dependents, regardless of fault.

Yellow dog contracts. In labor relations, a contract whereby management could require nonunion membership as a condition for employment. These were declared unenforceable by the Norris-LaGuardia Act.